Practical .NET Chart Development and Applications

Advanced Chart Programming
for Real-World .NET 4.5 Applications
Using C#, WPF, and MVVM

Practical .NET Chart Development and Applications

Advanced Chart Programming
for Real-World .NET 4.5 Applications
Using C#, WPF, and MVVM

Jack Xu, PhD

UniCAD Publishing

Practical .NET Chart Development and Applications

Copyright © 2016 by Jack Xu, PhD
Printed and bound in the United States of America 9 8 7 6 5 4 3 2 1UC

Editor: Anna Hsu

Contact:
jxu@dxudotnet.com
Visit us at our website: www.drxudotnet.com

Published by UniCAD Publishing.
New York, USA
ISBN-13: 978-0-9793725-4-4
ISBN-10: 0-9793725-4-2

Publisher's Cataloging-in-Publication Data

Xu, Jack
Practical .NET Chart Development and Applications – Advanced Chart Programming for Real-World .NET 4.5 Applications Using C#, WPF, and MVVM/ Jack Xu
– 1st ed.
p.cm.
ISBN 978-0-9793725-4-4

1. C# Programming. 2. Charts and Graphics. 3. XAML. 4. Windows Presentation Foundation. 5. Data Binding. 6. .NET Applications. 7. Model-View-ViewModel. 8. MVVM. 9. SQL Database. 10. ADO.NET. 11. Entity Framework. 12. LINQ
I. Title. II. Title. III Title: Practical .NET Chart Development and Applications

For my wonderful family

Contents

Introduction

Overview

Welcome to *Practical .NET Chart Development and Applications*. This book will provide all the tools you need to develop professional chart applications and reusable chart control packages using C#, the Windows Presentation Foundation (WPF), and the Model-View-View Model (MVVM) pattern based on the .NET 4.5 Framework. I hope this book will be useful for .NET programmers of all skill levels.

We have all heard the saying "A picture's worth a thousand words", and charts are some of the most informative pictures there are. Charts play an important role in every Windows application. They make data easier to understand, add interest to reports, and have wide applications in our daily life. The scientific, engineering, mathematics, and financial communities always have a need to present data and results graphically. Microsoft's .NET platform with C# and WPF is one of the few and best development tools available for providing the capability both to generate data as a simulation engine and to display it in a variety of graphical representations based on the .NET graphics capacity.

As a C# programmer, you are probably already familiar with Windows Forms, the mature and full-featured development tool built on top of the .NET Framework that uses the Windows Application Programming Interface (API) to create the visual appearance of standard user interface elements. It provides all kinds of tools for laying out windows, menus, dialogs, and controls. You can also develop graphics applications based on Windows Forms using the Graphics Device Interface (GDI+). However, creating a feature-rich graphics application using Windows Forms can be a difficult and tedious task. For example, Windows Forms provides no tools for creating three-dimensional (3D) graphics applications. Even a 3D point, the simplest of 3D graphics objects, must be defined first in a suitable 3D coordinate system before it can be used as a 3D graphics object.

WPF changes the landscape of graphics programming completely. At first, you might think that WPF simply provides another way to create windows, menus, dialogs, and controls. However, WPF has much more to offer than any other Windows programming framework. It integrates three basic Windows elements – text, controls, and graphics – into a single programming model and puts these three elements into the same element tree in the same manner.

Without WPF, developing a chart and graphics application would involve a number of different technologies, ranging from GDI/GDI+ for 2D graphics to Direct3D or OpenGL for 3D graphics. WPF, on the contrary, is designed as a single model for graphics application development, providing seamless integration between such services within an application. Similar constructs can be used for creating animation, data binding, and 3D models.

To take further advantage of new, powerful graphics hardware technologies, WPF implements a vector-based graphics model. This allows for graphics to be scaled based on screen-specific resolution without the loss of image quality, something impossible with fixed-size raster graphics. In addition, WPF leverages Direct3D for vector-based rendering and makes use of the graphics processing unit (GPU) on any video card that implements DirectX in hardware.

With WPF, graphics elements can easily be integrated into any part of your user interface. For example, WPF provides 2D shape elements that can be involved in the user interface (UI) tree like other elements can. You are free to mix these shapes with any other kind of element, such as a button. The WPF 3D model is based on Direct3D technology and allows you to create a custom 3D shape library that can be reused in your projects. The main benefits that WPF offers in 3D are its ease of use and its ability to integrate 3D content anywhere in a WPF application.

Another powerful feature of WPF is its data binding, which provides a simple and consistent way for applications to present and interact with data. WPF data binding is the process that establishes a connection between the application UI and business logic. If the data has the correct settings and provides the proper notifications, then when the data changes its value, the elements that are bound to the data reflect the changes automatically. WPF also provides two-way data binding: namely, if an outer representation of the data in an element changes, then the underlying data can be automatically updated to reflect the change. The data binding functionality in WPF has several advantages over traditional models, including a broad range of properties that inherently support data binding, flexible UI representation of data, and clean separation of business logic from UI.

The Model-View-View Model (MVVM) pattern is the most used architecture for WPF applications. MVVM introduces three layers of separation of application code: *Model*, *View*, and *ViewModel*. *View* holds the actual UI; *ViewModel* holds the collection of properties, commands, and property changed notifications; while *Model* holds business data, business logic, and business rules. You will gain several advantages using the MVVM pattern, including: 1) proper separation of the view and the data. The data is not stored in the view and the view is just for presenting the data; 2) clean, testable, and manageable code; and 3) no code-behind so that the presentation layer and the logic are loosely coupled.

As you may have already noticed, a plethora of WPF programming books are currently available in bookstores. The vast majority of these books are general-purpose user guides and tutorials that explain the basics of WPF and how to use it to implement simple WPF applications. Users who want to take full advantage of WPF graphics and other advanced features, however, require a book that provides an in-depth introduction specifically to WPF chart development and applications based on WPF's good practice of data binding and MVVM.

This book is written with the intention of providing a complete and comprehensive explanation of .NET chart programming, and it pays special attention to creating various charts and reusable chart control packages that can be used directly in real-world .NET applications. Much of this book contains original work based on my own programming experience when I was developing commercial Computer Aided Design (CAD) packages and chart applications for quantitative analysis in the financial field. Without C#, WPF, and the .NET framework, developing advanced charts is a difficult and time-consuming task. To add even simple charts or graphs to your applications, you often have to waste effort creating a chart program, or buy commercial graphics and chart add-on packages.

Using third-party graphics and chart add-on products in your applications has several drawbacks, however:

- It is not cost effective – it might cost hundreds or thousands of dollars for a sophisticated graphics and chart package.

- Compatibility is an issue – these third-party graphics and chart add-on tools are usually provided as DLL or COM components, which often leads to unexpected interface exceptions and unstable operations.

- There is little flexibility – from users' point of view, these packages appear to be black boxes because the source code is usually not provided, making it hard for users to add or modify any functionalities. You might find that these third-party products lack the special features you want in your applications, even while they often provide an excess of extraneous functionalities you will never use.

- The coding is inefficient – these third-party add-on tools are often very large packages that contain far more functionalities than you will ever need in your applications. Even a simple program can end up with a huge final release due to the use of third party add-ons. This is very inefficient for both coding management and distribution.

- License royalty is another issue – some third-party add-ons require not only the developing license, but also the distributed license royalty, resulting in an unnecessary increase in development cost.

- Finally, maintenance is a problem – in most cases, third-party tools use a different programming language than the one you use in developing your applications, so you have to maintain the codes in an unmanaged manner.

Practical .NET Chart Development and Applications provides everything you need to create your own advanced chart applications and reusable chart control packages using C# and WPF based on the MVVM pattern. It shows you how to use C# and WPF to create a variety of chart applications that range from simple two-dimensional (2D) *X-Y* plots to complicated 3D surfaces and combination charts. I will try my best to introduce you to C# and WPF chart programming in a simple way – simple enough to be easily followed by a .NET developer who has basic prior experience in developing .NET applications. From this book, you can learn how to create a full range of 2D and 3D chart applications and how to use custom chart controls to create impressive charts without having to buy expensive third-party add-on products.

What this Book Includes

This book and its sample code listings, which are available for download at my website at www.drxudotnet.com, provide you with:

- A complete, in-depth instruction on practical .NET chart programming with C#, WPF, and MVVM. After reading this book and running the example programs, you will be able to add various sophisticated charts to your .NET applications.

- Ready-to-run example programs that allow you to explore the charting techniques described in the book. You can use these examples to understand how the chart algorithms work. You can modify the code examples or add new features to them to form the basis of your own projects. Some of the example code listings provided in this book are already sophisticated chart packages that you can use directly in your own real-world .NET applications.

- Many classes in the sample code listings that you will find useful in your .NET chart development. These classes include matrix manipulation, coordinate transformation, color maps, chart controls, and the other useful utility classes. You can extract these classes and plug them into your own applications.

Is This Book for You?

You do not have to be an experienced .NET developer or an expert to use this book. I designed this book to be useful to people of all levels of .NET programming experience. In fact, I believe that if you have some prior experience with the programming language C#, Windows Forms, and the .NET framework, you will be able to sit down in front of your computer, start up Microsoft Visual Studio Community 2013 and .NET 4.5, follow the examples provided in this book, and quickly become proficient in .NET chart programming. For those of you who are already experienced .NET developers, I believe this book has much to offer as well. A great deal of the information about chart programming in this book is not available in other .NET tutorial and reference books. In addition, you can use most of the example programs directly in your own real-world application development. This book will provide you with a level of detail, explanation, instruction, and sample program code that will enable you to do just about anything related to .NET chart development and applications.

Perhaps you are a scientist, an engineer, a mathematician, a quant developer in finance, a student, or a teacher rather than a professional programmer; nevertheless, this book is still a good bet for you. In fact, my own background is in theoretical physics, a field involving extensive numerical calculations as well as graphical representations of calculated data. I devoted my effort to this field for many years, all the way from undergraduate to PhD. My first computer experience was with FORTRAN. Later on, I had programming experience with Basic, C, C++, and MATLAB. I still remember how hard it was in the early days to represent computational results graphically. I often spent hours creating a publication-quality chart by hand, using a ruler, graph paper, and rub-off lettering. A year later, our group bought a graphics and chart package; however, I still needed to prepare my data in a proper format in order to process it with this package. During that time, I started paying attention to various development tools that I could use to create integrated applications. I tried to find an ideal development tool that would allow me not only to generate data easily (computation capability) but also to represent data graphically (graphics and chart power). The C# and Microsoft Visual Studio .NET development environment made it possible to develop such integrated applications. Ever since Microsoft .NET 1.0 came out, I have been in love with the C# language, and I have used it successfully to create powerful graphics and chart applications, including commercial CAD packages and powerful 2D and 3D chart applications for quantitative analysis when I worked on Wall Street.

.NET developers and technical professionals can use the majority of the example programs in this book routinely. Throughout the book, I will emphasize the usefulness of chart programming to real-world applications. If you closely follow the instructions presented in this book, you will easily be able to develop various practical .NET chart applications, from 2D charts to a sophisticated 3D surface chart library. At the same time, I won't spend too much time discussing programming style, execution speed, and code optimization, because a plethora of books out there already deal with these topics. Most of the example programs you will find in this book omit error handlings. This makes the code easier to understand by focusing only on the key concepts and practical applications.

What Do You Need to Use This Book?

You will need no special equipment to make the best use of this book and understand the algorithms. To run and modify the sample programs, you will need a computer capable of running either Windows 7,

8, or 10. The software installed on your computer should include Visual Studio 2013 (Community version is fine), .NET 4.5 standard edition or higher, and SQL Server Express 2012 or higher. If you have Visual Studio 2012, .NET 4.0, and SQL Server Express 2008 or older versions, you can also run most of the sample code with few modifications. Please remember, however, that this book is intended for Visual Studio 2013, .NET 4.5, and SQL Server Express 2014, and that all of the example programs were created and tested on this platform, so it is best to run the sample code on the same platform.

How the Book Is Organized

This book is organized into nine chapters, each of which covers a different topic about .NET chart programming and applications. The following summaries of each chapter should give you an overview of the book's content:

Chapter 1, *Overview of C# and WPF Programming*

This chapter introduces the basics of WPF and reviews some of the general aspects of WPF programming, including XAML files used to define user interfaces.

Chapter 2, *Introduction to MVVM*

This chapter introduces processes for implementing the MVVM pattern in WPF applications, including data binding with property changed notifications, command binding, lambda expressions, and observable collections. It also reviews some free open-source MVVM toolkits, and explains why we will use Caliburn.Micro in this book.

Chapter 3, *Databases and the ADO.NET Entity Framework*

This chapter introduces the SQL Server Data Tool (SSDT) and LocalDB, two built-in features shipped as part of the core product of Visual Studio 2013, and shows how to create simple databases and interact with data. It also reviews the ADO.NET Entity Framework, which allows developers without extensive knowledge of SQL to interrogate the database, create complex queries, and generate classes with the help of a user-friendly interface.

Chapter 4, *2D Line Charts*

This chapter contains instructions on how to create elementary 2D *X-Y* line charts. It introduces basic chart elements, including the chart area, axes, title, labels, ticks, gridlines, symbols and legend. These basic chart elements are common in the other types of charts as well.

Chapter 5, *Specialized 2D Charts*

This chapter covers the specialized 2D charts often found in commercial chart packages and spreadsheet applications. These specialized charts include bar charts, stair-step charts, stem charts, charts with error bars, pie charts, area charts, and polar charts.

Chapter 6, *Stock Charts*

This chapter shows how to create a variety of stock charts in WPF, including the interface that interacts with market data stored in the database, the standard Hi-Lo-Open-Close stock charts, candlestick stock charts, volume charts, moving averages, and linear analysis. In addition, it also discusses how to retrieve data from stock charts.

Chapter 7, *2D Chart Controls*

This chapter shows how to convert 2D chart applications into a custom user control and how to reuse such a control in WPF applications based on data binding and the MVVM pattern

Chapter 8, *3D Charts*

This chapter begins with a description of 3D matrix transformation and the coordinate system used in 3D charts, and shows how to create 3D coordinate axes, tick marks, axis labels, and gridlines using the azimuth-elevation view. It then explains techniques for creating various 3D charts.

Chapter 9, *3D Chart Controls*

This chapter converts the 3D chart application developed in Chapter 8 into a custom user control that includes three modules: 3D line charts, 3D surface-like charts, and 3D specialized charts. It also shows you how to reuse this 3D chart control in your .NET applications based on WPF's advanced features such as data binding and the MVVM pattern.

Changes in this Book

I have received plenty of feedback from readers since I first published my books *Practical C# Charts and Graphics* (2007), *Practical WPF Graphics Programming* (2007), and *Practical WPF Charts and Graphics* (2009). Many of you asked for an updated edition. I realize that .NET technology has advanced and changed a lot in the past few years, and I now need to incorporate these new developments in the .NET Framework into my book. In this new book, I rewrite most of the example programs to reflect both the advancement of .NET and the new programming experience I have gained as a quant developer/analyst in the last few years. The key new features in this book include

- *Data binding*: In Windows Forms applications, data binding is mainly used for populating elements on your application with information. The beauty of data binding is that you can populate the interface while writing little to no code. With data binding in WPF you can take data from almost any property of any object and bind it to almost any other dependency property of another object. In this book, I will try to use data binding whenever possible to implement code examples.

- *Databases and the ADO.NET Entity Framework.* For the past several years, I have worked with a financial firm as a quant analyst/developer on Wall Street. The most important thing I deal with every day is market data. Most .NET applications in different fields also need to interact with data stored in databases. Therefore, this book includes a chapter that deals with databases and the ADO.NET entity Framework. It shows you how to create a simple database and how to use the entity data model to access the database data.

- *The MVVM pattern*: In traditional UI development, you create a view using a window or user control and then write all logical code in the code-behind. This approach creates a strong dependency between UI and data logic, which is hard to maintain and test. In MVVM, however, the glue code is the view model. If property values in the view model change, those new values automatically propagate to the view via data binding and notification. In this book, I will introduce the MVVM pattern and try to use the view model for data binding. In some examples, I may not use the full version of MVVM and instead write some code-behind code for dynamically creating WPF elements for simplicity's sake.

- *Powerful Chart Controls*: In this new book, I convert 2D line charts, stock charts, and 3D charts into powerful chart controls that you can easily reuse in your own .NET applications. In particular, these chart controls are MVVM compatible and allow you to develop .NET applications with 2D and 3D charts based on the MVVM pattern.

- *Financial Market*: This new book incorporates more topics and examples in the financial market, based mainly on my own working experience, including interaction with market data, moving average calculation, linear regression, principal component analysis (PCA) for pair trading, retrieving market data from stock charts, and implementing reusable stock chart controls.

- *Real-time Charts*: Many fields require real-time chart capability. For example, if you design a stock trading system, you need to develop a real-time data feeder and a chart control to display the real-time stock market data on your screen. This new book provides some examples that show how to create such real-time chart applications using our reusable chart controls.

Using Code Examples

You may use the code in this book in your own applications and documentation. You do not need to contact the author or the publisher for permission unless you are reproducing a significant portion of the code. For example, writing a program that uses several chunks of code from this book does not require permission. Selling or distributing the example code listings does require permission. Incorporating a significant amount of example code from this book into your applications and documentation also requires permission. Integrating the example code from this book into commercial products is not allowed without written permission of the author.

Customer Support

I am always interested in hearing from readers, and I would enjoy hearing your thoughts about this book. You can send me comments by e-mail to `jxu@DrXuDotNet.com`. I also provide updates, bug fixes, and ongoing support via my website:

`www.DrXuDotNet.com`

You can also obtain the complete source code for all of the examples in this book from the website.

Chapter 1
Overview of C# and WPF Programming

Windows Presentation Foundation (WPF) is a next generation graphics platform included in the Microsoft .NET Framework. It allows you to build advanced user interfaces (UI) that incorporate documents, media, 2D and 3D graphics, animations, and weblike characteristics. Built on the .NET framework, WPF provides a managed environment for developing applications using the Windows operating system. Like other features of the .NET Framework, WPF is available for Windows XP, Windows 7, Windows 8, and Windows 10.

In a pre-WPF world, developing a Windows application would have required the use of several different technologies. For instance, in order to add forms and user controls to your application, you needed to use Windows Forms, a part of the .NET framework. You had to use GDI+ to create images and 2D graphics. To add 3D graphics, you would have needed to use Direct3D or OpenGL.

WPF is designed to be a unified solution for application development, providing a seamless integration of different technologies. With WPF, you can create vector graphics or complex animations and incorporate media into your applications to address all of the areas just listed.

New Features in WPF

WPF introduces several new features that you can take advantage of when you develop your WPF applications. To utilize powerful new graphics hardware, WPF implements a vector graphics model based on the Direct3D technology. This allows graphics to scale according to screen-specific resolution without losing image quality, something impossible to do with fixed-size raster graphics. WPF leverages Direct3D for vector-based rendering, using the graphics-processing unit on any video card with built-in DirectX implemented. In anticipation of future technology, such as high-resolution displays, WPF uses a floating-point logical pixel system and supports 32-bit ARGB colors.

Furthermore, to easily represent UI and user interaction, WPF introduces a new XML based language, called Extensible Application Markup Language (XAML). XAML allows applications to dynamically parse and manipulate user interface elements at either design time or runtime. It uses the code-behind model, similar to ASP.NET programming, allowing designers and developers to work in parallel and to seamlessly combine their work into a compelling user experience. XAML also opens up world of possibilities for the MVVM pattern, which uses data binding via the view model to eliminate code-behind code. Of course, WPF also allows you to opt out of using XAML files when you develop WPF applications, meaning you can still develop your applications entirely in code such as C#, C++, or Visual Basic.

Another new feature is the resolution-independent layout. All WPF layout dimensions are specified using device-independent pixels. A device-independent pixel is one ninety-sixth of an inch in size and resolution-independent, so your results will be similar regardless of whether you render to a 72-DPI (dots per inch) monitor or a 19,200-DPI printer.

WPF is also based on a dynamic layout. This means that a UI element arranges itself on a window or page according to its content, its parent layout container, and the available screen area. Dynamic layout facilitates localization by automatically adjusting the size and position of UI elements when the strings they contain change length. By contrast, the layout in Windows Forms is device-dependent and more likely to be static. Typically, Windows Forms controls are positioned absolutely on a form using dimensions specified in hardware pixels.

XAML basics

As mentioned previously, using XAML to create UI is a new feature in WPF. In this section, I will present an introduction to XAML and consider its structure and syntax. Once you understand the basics of XAML, you can easily create a UI and layout in your WPF applications.

Why Is XAML Needed?

Since WPF applications can be developed entirely in code, it is perfectly natural to ask, "Why do I even need XAML in the first place?" The reason can be traced back to the issue of efficient implementation of complex, graphically rich applications. A long time ago, developers realized that the most efficient way to develop such applications was to separate the graphics portion from the underlying code. This way, designers could work on the graphics while developers could work on the code behind the graphics. Both parts could be separately designed and refined, without any versioning headaches.

Before WPF, is was impossible to separate the graphics content from the code. For example, when you work with Windows Forms, you define every form entirely in C# code or any other language. As you add controls to the UI and configure them, the program needs to adjust the code in corresponding form classes. If you want to decorate your forms, buttons, and other controls with graphics that designers have developed, you have to extract the graphic content and export it to a bitmap format. This approach works for simple applications, but it is very limited for complex, dynamic applications. In addition, graphics in bitmap format can lose their quality when they are resized.

The XAML technology introduced in WPF resolves these issues. When you develop a WPF application in Visual Studio, the window you create is not translated into code. Instead, it is serialized into a set of XAML tags. When you run the application, these tags are used to generate the objects that compose the UI.

XAML is not necessary in order to develop WPF applications. You can implement your WPF applications entirely in code. However, the windows and controls created in code will be locked into the Visual Studio environment and only available to programmers; there is no way to separate the graphics portion from the code.

In other words, WPF does not require XAML. However, XAML opens up world of possibilities for collaboration, because many design tools understand the XAML format.

Creating XAML Files

There are some standard rules for creating an XAML file. First, every element in an XAML file must relate to an instance of a .NET class. The name of the element must match the name of the class exactly. For example, *<TextBlock>* tells WPF to create a *TextBlock* object.

In an XAML file, you can nest one element inside another. This way, you can place an element as a child of another element. For example, if you have a *Button* inside a *Canvas*, this means that your UI contains a *Canvas* that has a *Button* as its child. You can also set the properties of each element through attributes.

Let's look at a simple XAML structure:

```
<Window x:Class="Chapter01.MainWindow"
    xmlns="http://schemas.microsoft.com/winfx/2006/xaml/presentation"
    xmlns:x="http://schemas.microsoft.com/winfx/2006/xaml"
    Title="Chapter 1" Height="300" Width="300">
    <Grid>
        <TextBlock>Hello, WPF!</TextBlock>
    </Grid>
</Window>
```

This file includes three elements: the top-level Window element, which represents the entire window; the *Grid*; and a *TextBlock* that is placed inside the *Grid* as a child. You can use either a Window or a Page as the top-level element in WPF. A Page is similar to a Window, but it is used for navigable applications. WPF also involves an Application file that defines application resources and startup settings. If you start with a new WPF Window (or Page) project, Visual Studio will automatically generate an Application file called *App.xaml*. In this book, I will use Window as the top-level WPF element, though you can just as easily use Page.

The starting tag for the Window element includes a class name and two XML namespaces. The *xmlns* attribute is a specialized attribute in XML that is reserved for declaring namespaces. The two namespaces in the preceding code snippet will appear in every WPF XAML file. You only need to know that these namespaces simply allow the XAML parser to find the right classes. Also, notice the three properties inside the tag: *Title*, *Height*, and *Width*. Each attribute corresponds to a property of the Window class. These attributes tell WPF to create a fixed 300 x 300 window with the title *Chapter01*.

Inside the Window tag, there is a *Grid* control that contains a *TextBlock* with its *Text* property set to "Hello, WPF!" You can also create the same *TextBlock* using the following snippet:

```
<TextBlock Text="Hello, WPF!"/>
```

Code-Behind Files

XAML is used to create the UI and graphics elements, but in order to make your application function, you need to attach event handlers to the UI. XAML makes this easy using the class attribute:

```
<Window x:Class="Chapter01.MainWindow"... ... >
```

The *x* namespace prefix places the class attribute in the XAML namespace, which means that this is a more general part of the XAML language. This example creates a new class named *Chapter01.MainWindow*, which derives from the base Window class.

When you create a WPF application, Visual Studio will automatically create a partial class where you can place your event-handling code. Previously, we discussed the simple XAML file *Chapter01.xaml*. If you create a WPF Windows application named *MainWindow*, Visual Studio will automatically generate the following code-behind file:

```
using System;
using System.Windows;
using System.Windows.Controls;
Namespace Chapter01
{
    /// <summary>
    /// Interaction logic for MainWindow.xaml
    /// </summary>

    public partial class MainWindow : Window
    {
        public MainWindow()
        {
            InitializeComponent();
        }
    }
}
```

When you compile this application, XAML is translated into a CLR-type declaration that is merged with the logic in the code-behind class file (*Chapter01.xaml.cs* in this example) to form one single unit.

The foregoing code-behind file only contains a default constructor, which calls the *InitializeComponent* method when you create an instance of the class. This is similar to the C# class in Windows Forms.

Your First WPF Program

Let's consider a simple WPF example. Open Visual Studio 2013 and create a new WPF Windows application project called *Chapter01*. Visual Studio will automatically add the default *MainWindow.xaml* and *MainWindow.xaml.cs* files to your project. This default window will be the main menu window with tabs, from which you can access all of the examples in this chapter. You can examine the source code of these two files to see how to implement them. I will use this file structure for accessing code examples in each chapter throughout the book.

Add a new *UserControl* to the project and name it *FirstWPFProgram*. Figure 1-1 shows the results of running this example. It includes several controls: a *Grid*, which is the most common control for arranging layouts in WPF, and a *StackPanel* inside the *Grid* used to hold other controls, including a *TextBlock*, a *TextBox*, and two *Button* controls. The goal of this example is to change the text in the *TextBlock* accordingly when the user enters text in the *TextBox*. At the same time, the program can change the text color or font size of the text in the *TextBlock* control when the user clicks the *Change Text Color* or *Change Text Size* button.

Properties in XAML

First, let's examine the *MainWindow.xaml* file:

```
<Window x:Class="Chapter01.MainWindow"
        xmlns="http://schemas.microsoft.com/winfx/2006/xaml/presentation"
```

```
        xmlns:x="http://schemas.microsoft.com/winfx/2006/xaml"
        xmlns:view="clr-namespace:Chapter01"
        Title="MainWindow" Height="350" Width="525">
    <Grid Margin="10 0 10 0">
        <TabControl Margin="0 5 0 0">
            <TabItem Header="FirstWpfProgram">
                <view:FirstWPFProgram HorizontalAlignment="Center"
                    VerticalAlignment="Center" Height="Auto" Width="Auto"/>
            </TabItem>
        </TabControl>
    </Grid>
</Window>
```

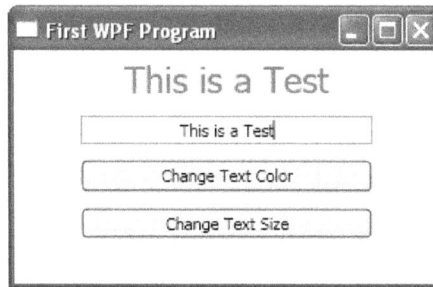

Figure 1-1. Your first WPF program example.

Here, I add a *TabControl* to the *Grid* and add the *FirstWPFProgram* to the *TabControl* as its *TabItem*. This way, the *FirstWPFProgram* will be displayed as the first tab item of the *MainWindow*.

The following is the XAML file for the *UserControl* of the *FirstWPFProgram*:

```
<UserControl x:Class="Chapter01.FirstWPFProgram"
    xmlns="http://schemas.microsoft.com/winfx/2006/xaml/presentation"
    xmlns:x="http://schemas.microsoft.com/winfx/2006/xaml"
    xmlns:mc="http://schemas.openxmlformats.org/markup-compatibility/2006"
    xmlns:d="http://schemas.microsoft.com/expression/blend/2008"
    mc:Ignorable="d"
    d:DesignHeight="300" d:DesignWidth="300">
    <Grid>
        <StackPanel>
            <TextBlock x:Name="txBlock" Margin="5" TextAlignment="Center"
                Text="Hello WPF!"/>
            <TextBox x:Name="txBox" Margin="5" Width="200"
                TextAlignment="Center" TextChanged="txBox_TextChanged"/>
            <Button x:Name="btnChangeColor" Margin="5" Width="200"
                Content="Change Text Color" Click="btnChangeColor_Click"/>
            <Button x:Name="btnChangeSize" Margin="5" Width="200"
                Content="Change Text Size" Click="btnChangeSize_Click"/>
        </StackPanel>
    </Grid>
</UserControl>
```

You can see that the attributes of an element set properties of the corresponding object. For example, the *TextBlock* control in the preceding XAML file configures the name, margin, text alignment, and text:

```
<TextBlock x:Name="txBlock" Margin="5" TextAlignment="Center"
```

```
Text="Hello WPF!"/>
```

In order for this to work, the *TextBlock* class in WPF must provide corresponding properties. You specify various properties for other controls that affect your layout and UI in a similar fashion.

To achieve the goal of this example, you will need to manipulate the *TextBlock*, *TextBox*, and *Button* controls programmatically in the code-behind file. First, you need to name the *TextBlock* and *TextBox* controls in your XAML file. In this example, these controls are named *txBlock* and *txBox*. Although in a traditional Windows Forms application every control must have a name, in a WPF application you only need to name the elements that are manipulated programmatically. Here, for example, you do not need to name the *StackPanel* and *Grid* controls.

Event Handlers in Code-Behind Files

In the previous section, you learned how to map attributes to corresponding properties. However, to make controls function you may sometimes need to attach attributes with event handlers. In the foregoing XAML file, you must attach a *txBox_TextChanged* event handler to the *TextChanged* property of the *TextBox*. You must also define the *Click* property of the two buttons using two click event handlers: *btnChangeColor_Click* and *btnChangeSize_Click*.

This assumes that there should be methods associated with the names *txBox_TextChanged*, *btnChangeColor_Click*, and *btnChangeSize_Click* in the code-behind file. Here is the corresponding code-behind file for this example:

```
using System.Windows;
using System.Windows.Controls;
using System.Windows.Media;

namespace Chapter01
{
    /// <summary>
    /// Interaction logic for FirstWPFProgram.xaml
    /// </summary>
    public partial class FirstWPFProgram : UserControl
    {
        public FirstWPFProgram()
        {
            InitializeComponent();
        }

        private void txBox_TextChanged(object sender, TextChangedEventArgs e)
        {
            txBlock.Text = txBox.Text;
        }

        private void btnChangeColor_Click(object sender, RoutedEventArgs e)
        {
            if (txBlock.Foreground == Brushes.Black)
                txBlock.Foreground = Brushes.Red;
            else
                txBlock.Foreground = Brushes.Black;

        }
```

```
        private void btnChangeSize_Click(object sender, RoutedEventArgs e)
        {
            if (txBlock.FontSize == 11)
                txBlock.FontSize = 24;
            else
                txBlock.FontSize = 11;
        }
    }
}
```

Note that event handlers must have the correct signature. The event model in WPF is slightly different than that in earlier versions of .NET. WPF supports a new model based on event routing. The rest of the preceding code-behind file is very similar to that used in Windows Forms applications with which you are already familiar.

Running this example produces the results shown in Figure 1-1. If you type any text in the text box field, the same text in the text block will appear. In addition, the color or font size will change depending on which button is clicked.

Code-Only Example

As mentioned previously, XAML is not necessary for creating WPF applications. WPF fully supports code-only implementation, although the use of this approach is less common. There are some pros and cons with the code-only approach. An advantage of the code-only method is that it gives you full control over customization. For example, when you want to conditionally add or substitute controls depending on the user's input, you can easily implement a condition logic in code. This is hard to do in XAML because controls in XAML are embedded in your assembly as fixed, unchanging resources. A disadvantage is that since WPF controls do not include constructors with parameters, developing a code-only application in WPF is sometimes tedious. Even adding a simple control like a button to your application takes several lines of code.

In the following example, we will convert the previous example, *FirstWPFProgram*, into a code-only application. Open the *Chapter01* project, add a new *UserControl* to the project, and name it *CodeOnly*. Do not forget to add the *CodeOnly* control to the *MainWindow.xaml* as a *TabItem* of the *TabControl*. Open the *CodeOnly.xaml* file and remove the *Grid* control from the file. The file should look as follows:

```
<UserControl x:Class="Chapter01.CodeOnly"
    xmlns="http://schemas.microsoft.com/winfx/2006/xaml/presentation"
    xmlns:x="http://schemas.microsoft.com/winfx/2006/xaml"
    xmlns:mc="http://schemas.openxmlformats.org/markup-compatibility/2006"
    xmlns:d="http://schemas.microsoft.com/expression/blend/2008">
</UserControl>
```

Open the code-behind file, *CodeOnly.xaml.cs*, and add the following code to the file:

```
using System.Windows;
using System.Windows.Controls;
using System.Windows.Media;

namespace Chapter01
{
    /// <summary>
    /// Interaction logic for CodeOnly.xaml
    /// </summary>
```

```csharp
public partial class CodeOnly : UserControl
{
    private TextBlock txBlock;
    private TextBox txBox;

    public CodeOnly()
    {
        InitializeComponent();
        Initialization();
    }

    private void Initialization()
    {
        // Configure the UserControl:
        this.Height = 300;
        this.Width = 300;

        // Create Grid and StackPanel and add them to UserControl:
        Grid grid = new Grid();
        StackPanel stackPanel = new StackPanel();
        grid.Children.Add(stackPanel);
        this.Content = grid;

        // Add a text block to stackPanel:
        txBlock = new TextBlock();
        txBlock.Margin = new Thickness(5);
        txBlock.Height = 30;
        txBlock.TextAlignment = TextAlignment.Center;
        txBlock.Text = "Hello WPF!";
        stackPanel.Children.Add(txBlock);

        // Add a text box to stackPanel:
        txBox = new TextBox();
        txBox.Margin = new Thickness(5);
        txBox.Width = 200;
        txBox.TextAlignment = TextAlignment.Center;
        txBox.TextChanged += OnTextChanged;
        stackPanel.Children.Add(txBox);

        // Add button to stackPanel used to change text color:
        Button btnColor = new Button();
        btnColor.Margin = new Thickness(5);
        btnColor.Width = 200;
        btnColor.Content = "Change Text Color";
        btnColor.Click += btnChangeColor_Click;
        stackPanel.Children.Add(btnColor);

        // Add button to stackPanel used to change text font size:
        Button btnSize = new Button();
        btnSize.Margin = new Thickness(5);
        btnSize.Width = 200;
        btnSize.Content = "Change Text Color";
        btnSize.Click += btnChangeSize_Click;
        stackPanel.Children.Add(btnSize);
    }
```

```
        private void OnTextChanged(object sender,
            TextChangedEventArgs e)
        {
            txBlock.Text = txBox.Text;
        }

        private void btnChangeColor_Click(object sender,
            RoutedEventArgs e)
        {
            if (txBlock.Foreground == Brushes.Black)
                txBlock.Foreground = Brushes.Red;
            else
                txBlock.Foreground = Brushes.Black;
        }

        private void btnChangeSize_Click(object sender,
            RoutedEventArgs e)
        {
            if (txBlock.FontSize == 11)
                txBlock.FontSize = 24;
            else
                txBlock.FontSize = 11;
        }
    }
}
```

This code listing will reproduce the results shown in Figure 1-1.

You can see that the *CodeOnly* class is similar to a form class in a traditional Windows Forms application. It derives from the base *UserControl* class and adds private member variables for *TextBlock* and *TextBox*. Pay close attention to how controls are added to their parents and how event handlers are attached.

XAML-Only Example

In the previous sections, you learned how to create the same WPF application using the XAML-plus-code and the code-only techniques. The standard approach for developing WPF applications is to use both XAML and a code-behind file. Namely, you first use XAML to lay out your UI, then code to implement event handlers. For applications with a dynamic UI, you may want to go with the code-only method.

However, for simple applications, it is also possible to use an XAML-only file without writing any C# code. This is called a *loose* XAML file. At first glance, a loose XAML file appears useless – after all, what's the point of a UI with no code to drive it? However, XAML provides several features that allow you to perform certain functions without using code-behind files. For example, you can develop an XAML-only application including features such as animation, event triggers, and data binding.

Here we will create a loose XAML application that mimics the *FirstWPFProgram* example. Even though it cannot reproduce exactly the results shown in Figure 1-1, the XAML-only application still generates a much more impressive result than static HTML would.

Add a new *UserControl* to the project *Chapter01* and name it *XamlOnly*. Here is the markup for this example:

```xml
<UserControl x:Class="Chapter01.XamlOnly"
    xmlns="http://schemas.microsoft.com/winfx/2006/xaml/presentation"
    xmlns:x="http://schemas.microsoft.com/winfx/2006/xaml"
    xmlns:mc="http://schemas.openxmlformats.org/markup-compatibility/2006"
    xmlns:d="http://schemas.microsoft.com/expression/blend/2008"
    mc:Ignorable="d"
    d:DesignHeight="300" d:DesignWidth="300">
    <Grid>
        <StackPanel>
            <TextBlock Name="txBlock" Margin="5"
                TextAlignment="Center" Height="30"
          Text="{Binding ElementName=txBox,Path=Text}"/>
            <TextBox Name="txBox" Margin="5" Width="200"
                TextAlignment="Center" Text="Hello, WPF!"/>
            <Button Margin="5" Width="200"
                Content="Change Text Color">
                <Button.Triggers>
                    <EventTrigger RoutedEvent="Button.Click">
                        <BeginStoryboard>
                            <Storyboard>
                                <ColorAnimation
    Storyboard.TargetName="txBlock"
    Storyboard.TargetProperty=
        "(TextBlock.Foreground).(SolidColorBrush.Color)"
    From="Black" To="Red" Duration="0:0:1"/>
                            </Storyboard>
                        </BeginStoryboard>
                    </EventTrigger>
                </Button.Triggers>
            </Button>

            <Button Margin="5" Width="200"
                Content="Change Text Size">
                <Button.Triggers>
                    <EventTrigger RoutedEvent="Button.Click">
                        <BeginStoryboard>
                            <Storyboard>
                                <DoubleAnimation


                    Storyboard.TargetName="txBlock"
                    Storyboard.TargetProperty="FontSize"
                    From="11" To="24" Duration="0:0:0.5"/>
                            </Storyboard>
                        </BeginStoryboard>
                    </EventTrigger>
                </Button.Triggers>
            </Button>
        </StackPanel>
    </Grid>
</UserControl>
```

This XAML file first binds the *Text* property of the *TextBlock* to the *Text* property of the *TextBox*. This data binding allows you to change the text of the *TextBlock* by typing text in the *TextBox* field. Then two buttons are created, which function to change text color and font size. This is done by using the buttons' event triggers, which start the color animation or the double animation, depending on which button is clicked.

Even though this application lacks a code-behind file, the buttons can still function. Of course, this XAML-only example cannot replicate the previous example involving a code-behind file. The reason is that although the event triggers in XAML files can start an animation, they cannot involve if-statements, for-loops, methods, and any other computation algorithm.

Chapter 2
Introduction to MVVM

In this chapter, I will introduce the Model-View-ViewModel (MVVM) pattern in WPF. In the preceding chapter, I outlined the WPF programming style, which involves XAML plus a code-behind file. You might ask "Why is MVVM needed in WPF applications?" In traditional UI development, we create a view using WPF Windows or *UserControls* in XAML and then write event handling and logical code in the code-behind file. Thus, we basically make the code-behind file a part of the view definition class itself. This approach increases the size of the view class and creates a strong coupling between UI and data logic and events. In this situation, it is difficult for two developers to work simultaneously on the same view, because one developer's changes might break the other's code. So putting UI, data logic, event handling, and business operations in one place is not suitable from a maintainability, extendibility, and testability perspective.

The MVVM pattern includes three key parts: *View* (UI defined in XAML), *Model* (business rules, data access, model classes), and *ViewModel* (agent between *View* and *Model*). If property values in the *ViewModel* change, those new values will automatically propagate to the view via data binding via property-changed notifications. When the user performs actions in the *View*, a command in the *ViewModel* will execute to perform the requested action. In the process, it is the *ViewModel* that modifies model data, while the *View* never modifies it. The *ViewModel* acts as an interface between *Model* and *View*. It provides data binding between *View* and model data and handles all UI actions by using commands. It is interesting to note that in MVVM, the *Model* should know nothing about the *ViewModel* or the *View*, the *ViewModel* should only know about the *Model* but not the *View*, and the *View* should only know about the *ViewModel* but not the *Model*.

The *Model* in MVVM can be very simple but can also be very complicated. It includes the interface to database access, computation processes, and business operations. The *ViewModel* should basically delegate everything to the *Model* except for exposing data for the *View*, while the *View* should simply bind to the *ViewModel* and make the UI look nice.

In a well-designed MVVM pattern, the code-behind code should be empty. This way, the *ViewModel* and *Model* are easier to test, and you will have achieved a good level of loose coupling that provides benefits from a maintenance and extensibility perspective. For instance, when you want to change your UI, say from using a *ListView* to a *DataGrid*, you can just replace the *ListView* with the *DataGrid* in XAML and bind the corresponding property in your *ViewModel* to its *ItemsSource*. You do not need to make any changes in your *Model* and *ViewModel*. Otherwise, you would have to make corresponding changes in your code-behind code.

MVVM is a very useful tool in developing WPF applications, but you should not treat it as a rigid set of rules, and do not overdo it. A good example is implementing a close window command in MVVM. In a code-behind implementation, it is a simple single line of code:

```
this.Close();
```

However, a MVVM version of this simple statement would require more effort. You are trying to replace a single *Close* call with a complicated MVVM implementation. You gain nothing out of moving the closing code from the *View* to the *ViewModel*. In fact, in some situations, MVVM allows for a code-behind that manipulates the controls and resources contained within the *View*; i.e., the code must be purely UI-related.

A Simple MVVM Example

The best way to learn MVVM is through an example. In this simple example, I want the view to display stock data information, including the ticker, date, open price, high, low, close price, and volume; and then update the fields by clicking a button.

Why Don't the Fields Update?

Let's start with Visual Studio 2013 and create a new WPF Windows application project called *Chapter02*. I will use the default window, *MainWindow*, as the main menu window with tabs, from which you can access all of the examples in this chapter. Now, add two folders to the project and name them *Models* and *Views* respectively. I will put all model-related files in the *Models* folder and all the view (UI)-related files in the *Views* folder.

Now add a new class to the *Models* folder in the project and name it *DataModel*. Here is the code for this class:

```
using System;
namespace Chapter02.Models
{
    public class DataModel
    {
        private string ticker;
        private DateTime date;
        private double priceOpen;
        private double priceHigh;
        private double priceLow;
        private double priceClose;
        private double volume;

        public string Ticker
        {
            get { return ticker; }
            set { ticker = value; }
        }

        public DateTime Date
        {
            get { return date; }
            set { date = value; }
```

```
    }

    public double PriceOpen
    {
        get { return priceOpen; }
        set { priceOpen = value; }
    }

    public double PriceHigh
    {
        get { return priceHigh; }
        set { priceHigh = value; }
    }

    public double PriceLow
    {
        get { return priceLow; }
        set { priceLow = value; }
    }

    public double PriceClose
    {
        get { return priceClose; }
        set { priceClose = value; }
    }

    public double Volume
    {
        get { return volume; }
        set { volume = value; }
    }
  }
}
```

In MVVM terminology, the *DataModel* class is our *Model*, which just defines properties for a stock. The UI is our *View*. The data binding is through the *ViewModel*, which acts as an adapter that translates our *Model* into something that the *View* can use. We can easily create the *ViewModel* for a stock. Add another class to the *Models* folder and name it *WrongWayViewModel*. How do we implement this *ViewModel* class? The rule of thumb is that the properties exposed in the *ViewModel* are what we want to display in the *View*. Suppose we just care about a stock's prices, not the volume, then we can define the *WrongWayViewModel* as follows:

```
using System;
namespace Chapter02.Models
{
    public class WrongWayViewModel
    {
        DataModel model;

        public WrongWayViewModel()
        {
            model = new DataModel
            {
                Ticker = "IBM",
                Date = Convert.ToDateTime("7/14/2015"),
```

```
                PriceOpen = 169.43,
                PriceHigh = 169.54,
                PriceLow = 168.24,
                PriceClose = 168.61
        };
    }

    public DataModel Model
    {
        get { return model; }
        set { model = value; }
    }

    public string Ticker
    {
        get { return Model.Ticker; }
        set { Model.Ticker = value; }
    }

    public DateTime Date
    {
        get { return Model.Date; }
        set { Model.Date = value; }
    }

    public double PriceOpen
    {
        get { return Model.PriceOpen; }
        set { Model.PriceOpen = value; }
    }

    public double PriceHigh
    {
        get { return Model.PriceHigh; }
        set { Model.PriceHigh = value; }
    }

    public double PriceLow
    {
        get { return Model.PriceLow; }
        set { Model.PriceLow = value; }
    }

    public double PriceClose
    {
        get { return Model.PriceClose; }
        set { Model.PriceClose = value; }
    }
    }
}
```

Note here that in the constructor I create a default stock, *IBM*, using the *DataModel*, which will be initially displayed in the *View*.

Now, add a *UserControl* to the *Views* folder in the project and name it *WrongWayView*. Please note that in MVVM, I use a naming convention of *xxxView* for the *View* and *xxxViewModel* for the *ViewModel* to easily identify their functions. Here is the XAML file for the *WrongWayView*:

```
<UserControl x:Class="Chapter02.Views.WrongWayView"
    xmlns="http://schemas.microsoft.com/winfx/2006/xaml/presentation"
    xmlns:x="http://schemas.microsoft.com/winfx/2006/xaml"
    xmlns:mc="http://schemas.openxmlformats.org/markup-compatibility/2006"
    xmlns:d="http://schemas.microsoft.com/expression/blend/2008"
    xmlns:model="clr-namespace:Chapter02.Models"
    mc:Ignorable="d"
    d:DesignHeight="300" d:DesignWidth="300">

    <UserControl.DataContext>
        <model:WrongWayViewModel/>
    </UserControl.DataContext>

    <Grid>
        <StackPanel>
            <StackPanel Orientation="Horizontal">
                <TextBlock Text="Ticker" Width="80"/>
                <TextBox Text="{Binding Ticker}" Width="80"/>
            </StackPanel>
            <StackPanel Orientation="Horizontal" Margin="0 5 0 0">
                <TextBlock Text="Date" Width="80"/>
                <TextBox Text="{Binding Date, StringFormat=d}" Width="80"/>
            </StackPanel>
            <StackPanel Orientation="Horizontal" Margin="0 5 0 0">
                <TextBlock Text="Open Price" Width="80"/>
                <TextBox Text="{Binding PriceOpen}" Width="80"/>
            </StackPanel>
            <StackPanel Orientation="Horizontal" Margin="0 5 0 0">
                <TextBlock Text="High Price" Width="80"/>
                <TextBox Text="{Binding PriceHigh}" Width="80"/>
            </StackPanel>
            <StackPanel Orientation="Horizontal" Margin="0 5 0 0">
                <TextBlock Text="Low Price" Width="80"/>
                <TextBox Text="{Binding PriceLow}" Width="80"/>
            </StackPanel>
            <StackPanel Orientation="Horizontal" Margin="0 5 0 0">
                <TextBlock Text="Close Price" Width="80"/>
                <TextBox Text="{Binding PriceClose}" Width="80"/>
            </StackPanel>
            <Button x:Name="btnUpdate" Content="Update"
                    Width="100" Height="25" Margin="30 20 0 0"
                    HorizontalAlignment="Left" Click="btnUpdate_Click"/>
        </StackPanel>
    </Grid>
</UserControl>
```

Here, WPF uses the *Binding* key word to bind the *Text* fields of different *TextBox* controls to the stock properties of the object returned by *DataContext*. As you see in the preceding code, I set the *DataContext* to an instance of the *WrongWayViewModel*. Note also that I introduce the *ViewModel* in XAML (the bold part in the preceding code). This is equivalent to doing this in the code-behind *WrongWayView.xaml.cs*:

```
public partial class WrongWayView : UserControl
{
    WrongWayViewModel viewModel = new WrongWayViewModel();
    public WrongWayView()
    {
        InitializeComponent();
        this.DataContext = viewModel;
    }
}
```

and removing the *DataContext* element in the XAML. The purpose of this example is to update the stock field in the *View* by clicking the *Update* button. We expect to achieve this with the following code-behind code:

```
using Chapter02.Models;
using System;
using System.Windows;
using System.Windows.Controls;

namespace Chapter02.Views
{
    /// <summary>
    /// Interaction logic for WrongWay.xaml
    /// </summary>
    public partial class WrongWayView : UserControl
    {
        WrongWayViewModel viewModel;
        public WrongWayView()
        {
            InitializeComponent();
            viewModel = (WrongWayViewModel)base.DataContext;
        }

        private void btnUpdate_Click(object sender, RoutedEventArgs e)
        {
            viewModel.Ticker = "MSFT";
            viewModel.Date = Convert.ToDateTime("7/14/2015");
            viewModel.PriceOpen = 45.45;
            viewModel.PriceHigh = 45.96;
            viewModel.PriceLow = 45.31;
            viewModel.PriceClose = 45.62;
        }
    }
}
```

Inside the button click handler, we change the stock from the default *IBM* to *MSFT*. However, when we run this example, the view never updates the corresponding fields when you click the *Update* button (see Figure 2-1). There must be something wrong with our current *ViewModel* class.

Ticker	IBM
Date	7/14/2015
Open Price	169.43
High Price	169.54
Low Price	168.24
Close Price	168.61

Update

Figure 2-1. The result of the wrong way example.

Right Way for Data Binding

To ensure that the *View* keeps up to date when the data changes in the *ViewModel* class, we need to implement the appropriate change-notification interface. If we are defining properties that can be data bound, we need to implement the *INotifyPropertyChanged* interface. This interface defines an event that is raised whenever the underlying data changes. Any data bound controls in the *View* will then be automatically updated when these events are raised. Therefore, we will have to modify the *ViewModel* class.

Add a new class to the *Models* folder in the project and name it *RightWayViewModel*. The modified class should look like the following:

```
using System;
using System.ComponentModel;

namespace Chapter02.Models
{
    public class RightWayViewModel : INotifyPropertyChanged
    {
        DataModel model;

        public RightWayViewModel()
        {
            model = new DataModel
            {
                Ticker = "IBM",
                Date = Convert.ToDateTime("7/14/2015"),
                PriceOpen = 169.43,
                PriceHigh = 169.54,
                PriceLow = 168.24,
                PriceClose = 168.61
            };
        }

        public DataModel Model
        {
            get { return model; }
            set { model = value; }
        }
```

```csharp
public string Ticker
{
    get { return Model.Ticker; }
    set
    {
        Model.Ticker = value;
        OnPropertyChanged("Ticker");
    }
}

public DateTime Date
{
    get { return Model.Date; }
    set
    {
        Model.Date = value;
        OnPropertyChanged("Date");
    }
}

public double PriceOpen
{
    get { return Model.PriceOpen; }
    set
    {
        Model.PriceOpen = value;
        OnPropertyChanged("PriceOpen");
    }
}

public double PriceHigh
{
    get { return Model.PriceHigh; }
    set
    {
        Model.PriceHigh = value;
        OnPropertyChanged("PriceHigh");
    }
}
public double PriceLow
{
    get { return Model.PriceLow; }
    set
    {
        Model.PriceLow = value;
        OnPropertyChanged("PriceLow");
    }
}
public double PriceClose
{
    get { return Model.PriceClose; }
    set
    {
        Model.PriceClose = value;
        OnPropertyChanged("PriceClose");
```

```
            }
        }

    // Declare the PropertyChanged event
    public event PropertyChangedEventHandler PropertyChanged;

    // OnPropertyChanged will raise the PropertyChanged event passing
    // the source property that is being updated
    private void OnPropertyChanged(string propertyName)
    {
        PropertyChangedEventHandler handler = PropertyChanged;
        if (handler != null)
            handler(this, new PropertyChangedEventArgs(propertyName));
    }
    }
}
```

This class inherits from the *INotifyPropertyChanged* interface. We also define the *INotifyPropertyChanged* event member and implement an interface contract (bolded part in the preceding code). For each property we want to display on the *View*, we add a call to the *OnPropertyChanged* method, which notifies the databinding framework on the *ViewModel* and the *View* of any changes to the property, allowing the *View* to update seamlessly.

Now add a *UserControl* to the *Views* folder and name it *RightWayView*. The XAML and code-behind files of this control are the same as those used in the *WrongWayView* example. By running this project and clicking the *Update* button, you will find that the stock is updated, as shown in Figure 2-2.

Ticker	MSFT
Date	7/14/2015
Open Price	45.45
High Price	45.96
Low Price	45.31
Close Price	45.62

Update

Figure 2-2. The result of the right way example.

Command Binding

In the preceding examples, you may notice that the button-click event was still handled in the code-behind file, which violates the MVVM rule. Indeed, WPF provides a better way to handle it, which is *ICommand* interface. Many controls like buttons have a *Command* attribute that allows binding in the same way as *Text*, *Content*, and *ItemsSource*, except it needs to be bound to a property that returns an *ICommand*. Commands provide a convenient way to represent actions or operations that can be easily bound to controls in the *View*, and to encapsulate the actual code that implements the action or operation.

ICommand requires defining two methods: *CanExecute* and *Execute*. The *CanExecute* method just tells you "can I execute this command?" which is useful for controlling the context in which you can perform UI actions. If the *CanExecute* method returns *true*, it indicates that the application can always call the

Execute method. However, if you want to bind a conditional command to a button control, so that the command can only execute under certain conditions, you then need to implement the corresponding conditional logic in the *CanExecute* method.

Now add a new class to the *Models* folder and name it *CommandModel*. Here is the code for this class:

```
using System;
using System.Diagnostics;
using System.Windows.Input;

namespace Chapter02.Models
{
    public class CommandModel : ICommand
    {
        private Func<Boolean> canExecute;
        private Action execute;

        public CommandModel(Action action)
            : this (action, null)
        {
        }

        public CommandModel(Action action, Func<Boolean> canAction)
        {
            if (action == null)
                throw new ArgumentNullException("action");
            execute = action;
            canExecute = canAction;
        }

        public event EventHandler CanExecuteChanged
        {
            add
            {
                if(canExecute!=null)
                    CommandManager.RequerySuggested += value;
            }
            remove
            {
                if (canExecute != null)
                    CommandManager.RequerySuggested -= value;
            }
        }

        [DebuggerStepThrough]
        public Boolean CanExecute(Object parameter)
        {
            return canExecute == null ? true : canExecute();
        }

        public void Execute(Object parameter)
        {
            execute();
        }
    }
}
```

The preceding code listing shows how to implement the *CanExecute* and *Execute* methods. Add another class to the *Models* folder and name it *OnCommandViewModel*. Here is the code listing for this class:

```csharp
using System;
using System.ComponentModel;
using System.Windows.Input;

namespace Chapter02.Models
{
    public class OnCommandViewModel : INotifyPropertyChanged
    {
        DataModel model;

        public OnCommandViewModel()
        {
            model = new DataModel
            {
                Ticker = "IBM",
                Date = Convert.ToDateTime("7/14/2015"),
                PriceOpen = 169.43,
                PriceHigh = 169.54,
                PriceLow = 168.24,
                PriceClose = 168.61,
                Volume = 2974900
            };
        }

        public DataModel Model
        {
            get { return model; }
            set { model = value; }
        }

        public string Ticker
        {
            get { return Model.Ticker; }
            set
            {
                Model.Ticker = value;
                OnPropertyChanged("Ticker");
            }
        }

        public DateTime Date
        {
            get { return Model.Date; }
            set
            {
                Model.Date = value;
                OnPropertyChanged("Date");
            }
        }

        public double PriceOpen
        {
```

```
        get { return Model.PriceOpen; }
        set
        {
            Model.PriceOpen = value;
            OnPropertyChanged("PriceOpen");
        }
    }

    public double PriceHigh
    {
        get { return Model.PriceHigh; }
        set
        {
            Model.PriceHigh = value;
            OnPropertyChanged("PriceHigh");
        }
    }
    public double PriceLow
    {
        get { return Model.PriceLow; }
        set
        {
            Model.PriceLow = value;
            OnPropertyChanged("PriceLow");
        }
    }
    public double PriceClose
    {
        get { return Model.PriceClose; }
        set
        {
            Model.PriceClose = value;
            OnPropertyChanged("PriceClose");
        }
    }
    public double Volume
    {
        get { return Model.Volume; }
        set
        {
            Model.Volume = value;
            OnPropertyChanged("Volume");
        }
    }


    public event PropertyChangedEventHandler PropertyChanged;

    private void OnPropertyChanged(string propertyName)
    {
        PropertyChangedEventHandler handler = PropertyChanged;
        if (handler != null)
            handler(this, new PropertyChangedEventArgs(propertyName));
    }
```

```
private void UpdateStockExecute()
{
    Ticker = "MSFT";
    Date = Convert.ToDateTime("7/14/2015");
    PriceOpen = 45.45;
    PriceHigh = 45.96;
    PriceLow = 45.31;
    PriceClose = 45.62;
}

private bool CanUpdateStockExecute()
{
    return true;
}

public ICommand UpdateStock
{
    get { return new CommandModel(UpdateStockExecute,
        CanUpdateStockExecute); }
}
    }
}
```

Pay special attention to the bolded part of the preceding code listing, in which I implement two private methods, *CanUpdateStockExecute* and *UpdateStockExecute*, as well as a public property that returns an *ICommand* object from a new instance of the *CommandModel* class we recently discussed. The *UpdateStockExecute* method includes code that is similar to the button-click handler in the code-behind of the *RightWayView* example.

Add a new *UserControl* to the *Views* folder and name it *OnCommandView*. The XAML file is the same as that used in the previous example, except for the *Update* button:

```
<Button x:Name="btnUpdate" Content="Update"
        Width="100" Height="25" Margin="30 20 0 0"
        HorizontalAlignment="Left" Command="{Binding UpdateStock}"/>
```

Here, we bind the *Command* attribute of the button to the *UpdateStock* property, which is an *ICommand* type, and eliminate the click event handler. In this case, the code-behind file of the *OnCommandView* becomes empty:

```
using System.Windows.Controls;

namespace Chapter02.Views
{
    /// <summary>
    /// Interaction logic for OnCommand.xaml
    /// </summary>
    public partial class OnCommandView : UserControl
    {
        public OnCommandView()
        {
            InitializeComponent();
        }
    }
}
```

Running this project, selecting the *OnCommand* tab in the *MainWindow,* and clicking the update button generate the same results as shown in Figure 2-2.

Advanced Topics in MVVM

In the preceding sections, we implemented a simple stock updating example using the MVVM approach. If you followed the example closely, you may have noticed that a lot of repetitive code exists in the *ViewModel* class, such as in the definitions for *INotifyPropertyChanged* and *ICommand*. In addition, the following code for raising the property-changed event uses a string that is nonstandard C# code:

```
public string Ticker
{
    get { return Model.Ticker; }
    set
    {
        Model.Ticker = value;
        OnPropertyChanged("Ticker");
    }
}
```

Here, we deal only with simple property binding, and have not yet considered complicated bindings such as collection. In this section, we will try to improve the basic MVVM model used in WPF applications.

Lambda Expression

In the call for raising the property-changed event, MVVM uses magic strings that lead to several issues. The first issue is that you might type a wrong string or misspell it, and your UI would not complain, making it hard to track errors at either runtime or compile-time. The other issue is that you will not have Visual Studio's Intellisense support when you write the property name. Finally, magic strings are not refactoring friendly when you want to change properties' names. .NET developers have proposed various workarounds that try to get rid of such magic strings. Here I will present two approaches: one is to use Lambda expressions and the other is to use the new feature in C# 5.0: *CallerMemberName*. First, let's consider the Lambda expression method.

Add a new class to the *Models* folder and name it *LambdaViewModel*. Here is code listing for this class:

```
using System;
using System.ComponentModel;
using System.Linq.Expressions;
using System.Windows.Input;

namespace Chapter02.Models
{
    public class LambdaViewModel : INotifyPropertyChanged
    {
        DataModel model;
        public LambdaViewModel()
        {
            model = new DataModel
            {
                Ticker = "IBM",
                Date = Convert.ToDateTime("7/14/2015"),
```

```csharp
            PriceOpen = 169.43,
            PriceHigh = 169.54,
            PriceLow = 168.24,
            PriceClose = 168.61,
        };
    }

    public DataModel Model
    {
        get { return model; }
        set { model = value; }
    }

    public string Ticker
    {
        get { return Model.Ticker; }
        set
        {
            Model.Ticker = value;
            OnPropertyChanged(() => Ticker);
        }
    }

    public DateTime Date
    {
        get { return Model.Date; }
        set
        {
            Model.Date = value;
            OnPropertyChanged(() => Date);
        }
    }

    public double PriceOpen
    {
        get { return Model.PriceOpen; }
        set
        {
            Model.PriceOpen = value;
            OnPropertyChanged(() => PriceOpen);
        }
    }

    public double PriceHigh
    {
        get { return Model.PriceHigh; }
        set
        {
            Model.PriceHigh = value;
            OnPropertyChanged(() => PriceHigh);
        }
    }
    public double PriceLow
    {
        get { return Model.PriceLow; }
```

```csharp
        set
        {
            Model.PriceLow = value;
            OnPropertyChanged(() => PriceLow);
        }
    }
    public double PriceClose
    {
        get { return Model.PriceClose; }
        set
        {
            Model.PriceClose = value;
            OnPropertyChanged(() => PriceClose);
        }
    }

    public event PropertyChangedEventHandler PropertyChanged;
    private void OnPropertyChanged(string property)
    {
        if (PropertyChanged != null)
            PropertyChanged(this, new PropertyChangedEventArgs(property));
    }

    protected void OnPropertyChanged<T>(Expression<Func<T>>
        propertyExpression)
    {
        if (propertyExpression.Body.NodeType == ExpressionType.MemberAccess)
        {
            var memberExpr = propertyExpression.Body as MemberExpression;
            string propertyName = memberExpr.Member.Name;
            this.OnPropertyChanged(propertyName);
        }
    }

    private void UpdateStockExecute()
    {
        Ticker = "MSFT";
        Date = Convert.ToDateTime("7/14/2015");
        PriceOpen = 45.45;
        PriceHigh = 45.96;
        PriceLow = 45.31;
        PriceClose = 45.62;
    }

    private bool CanUpdateStockExecute()
    {
        return true;
    }

    public ICommand UpdateStock
    {
        get { return new CommandModel(UpdateStockExecute,
            CanUpdateStockExecute); }
    }
}
```

```
                PriceOpen = 169.43,
                PriceHigh = 169.54,
                PriceLow = 168.24,
                PriceClose = 168.61,
        };
}

 public DataModel Model
 {
     get { return model; }
     set { model = value; }
 }

public string Ticker
{
    get { return Model.Ticker; }
    set
    {
        Model.Ticker = value;
        OnPropertyChanged(() => Ticker);
    }
}

public DateTime Date
{
    get { return Model.Date; }
    set
    {
        Model.Date = value;
        OnPropertyChanged(() => Date);
    }
}

public double PriceOpen
{
    get { return Model.PriceOpen; }
    set
    {
        Model.PriceOpen = value;
        OnPropertyChanged(() => PriceOpen);
    }
}

public double PriceHigh
{
    get { return Model.PriceHigh; }
    set
    {
        Model.PriceHigh = value;
        OnPropertyChanged(() => PriceHigh);
    }
}
public double PriceLow
{
    get { return Model.PriceLow; }
```

```
        set
        {
            Model.PriceLow = value;
            OnPropertyChanged(() => PriceLow);
        }
    }
    public double PriceClose
    {
        get { return Model.PriceClose; }
        set
        {
            Model.PriceClose = value;
            OnPropertyChanged(() => PriceClose);
        }
    }

    public event PropertyChangedEventHandler PropertyChanged;
    private void OnPropertyChanged(string property)
    {
        if (PropertyChanged != null)
            PropertyChanged(this, new PropertyChangedEventArgs(property));
    }

    protected void OnPropertyChanged<T>(Expression<Func<T>>
        propertyExpression)
    {
        if (propertyExpression.Body.NodeType == ExpressionType.MemberAccess)
        {
            var memberExpr = propertyExpression.Body as MemberExpression;
            string propertyName = memberExpr.Member.Name;
            this.OnPropertyChanged(propertyName);
        }
    }

    private void UpdateStockExecute()
    {
        Ticker = "MSFT";
        Date = Convert.ToDateTime("7/14/2015");
        PriceOpen = 45.45;
        PriceHigh = 45.96;
        PriceLow = 45.31;
        PriceClose = 45.62;
    }

    private bool CanUpdateStockExecute()
    {
        return true;
    }

    public ICommand UpdateStock
    {
        get { return new CommandModel(UpdateStockExecute,
            CanUpdateStockExecute); }
    }
}
```

```
}
```

You may notice that I added an overloaded version of the *OnPropertyChanged* method (see bolded part of the code) that uses a Lambda expression as the input parameter rather than a string of the property name. This way, we can eliminate magic strings by using a lambda expression when raising the property-changed event in the property declaration; for example:

```
public string Ticker
{
    get { return Model.Ticker; }
    set
    {
        Model.Ticker = value;
        OnPropertyChanged(() => Ticker);
    }
}
```

Add a new *UserControl* to the *Views* folder and name it *LambdaView*. The XAML file is similar to that used in the *OnCommandView* example. Running this project will produce the same results shown in Figure 2-2.

The Lambda version of the *OnPropertyChanged* event provides type-safe implementation and compile time checking. It eliminates binding issues of property names due to passing the mistyped strings to the *OnPropertyChanged* method call.

Although the Lambda version of MVVM allows you to write fluent reading code, it has an issue with performance because it comes with heavy resource usage: speed, CPU, and memory. Two main factors cost the performance of the Lambda version. The first factor is the creation of the expression (such as () => Ticker). The string property-changed events in the simple MVVM version have no "expression creation" processing time since it is just a hard coded string, leading to fast execution. The other factor is the actual WPF binding infrastructure that affects all of the property-changed notification implementations. Considering these factors, you should use the simple MVVM version if a large number of the view models need to be created and speed is critical. On the other hand, you should use the Lambda version for type-safe property-changed notification when speed is not an issue.

Caller Info Attributes

The new C# 5.0 release with .NET 4.5 introduced several attributes that are useful for debugging and error reporting: *CallerMemberName*, *CallerFilePath*, and *CallerLineMember*, all collectively referred to as *Caller Information*. You can use one of these attributes, *CallerMemberName*, to eliminate the magic strings used in the *INotifyPropertyChanged* implementation in MVVM.

The *CallerMemberName* attribute, from the *System.Runtime.CompilerService* namespace, provides the name of the function that calls the function with the attribute in its parameter list. The advantage of using this attribute over using the Lambda version in MVVM is the performance, which is almost identical to that of using simple MVVM with magic strings. The reason is because the caller information values are emitted as literals into the *Intermediate Language* (IL) at compile time; namely, both the *CallerMemberName* version and simple magic string version of MVVM are literally the same at the IL level.

Add a class to the *Models* folder and name it *CallerInfoViewModel*. Here is the code listing for this class:

```
using System;
using System.ComponentModel;
```

```
using System.Runtime.CompilerServices;
using System.Windows.Input;

namespace Chapter02.Models
{
    public class CallerInfoViewModel : INotifyPropertyChanged
    {
        DataModel model;
         public CallerInfoViewModel()
        {
            model = new DataModel
            {
                Ticker = "IBM",
                Date = Convert.ToDateTime("7/14/2015"),
                PriceOpen = 169.43,
                PriceHigh = 169.54,
                PriceLow = 168.24,
                PriceClose = 168.61,
            };
        }

        public DataModel Model
        {
            get { return model; }
            set { model = value; }
        }

        public string Ticker
        {
            get { return Model.Ticker; }
            set
            {
                Model.Ticker = value;
                OnPropertyChanged();
            }
        }

        public DateTime Date
        {
            get { return Model.Date; }
            set
            {
                Model.Date = value;
                OnPropertyChanged();
            }
        }

        public double PriceOpen
        {
            get { return Model.PriceOpen; }
            set
            {
                Model.PriceOpen = value;
                OnPropertyChanged();
            }
```

```
}

public double PriceHigh
{
    get { return Model.PriceHigh; }
    set
    {
        Model.PriceHigh = value;
        OnPropertyChanged();
    }
}
public double PriceLow
{
    get { return Model.PriceLow; }
    set
    {
        Model.PriceLow = value;
        OnPropertyChanged();
    }
}
public double PriceClose
{
    get { return Model.PriceClose; }
    set
    {
        Model.PriceClose = value;
        OnPropertyChanged();
    }
}

public event PropertyChangedEventHandler PropertyChanged;

private void OnPropertyChanged([CallerMemberName] string
    propertyName = null)
{
    PropertyChangedEventHandler handler = PropertyChanged;
    if (handler != null)
        handler(this, new PropertyChangedEventArgs(propertyName));
}

private void UpdateStockExecute()
{
    Ticker = "MSFT";
    Date = Convert.ToDateTime("7/14/2015");
    PriceOpen = 45.45;
    PriceHigh = 45.96;
    PriceLow = 45.31;
    PriceClose = 45.62;
}

private bool CanUpdateStockExecute()
{
    return true;
}
```

```
public ICommand UpdateStock
{
    get { return new CommandModel(UpdateStockExecute,
        CanUpdateStockExecute); }
}
    }
}
```

Here, the only difference from the magic string approach in the *OnPropertyChanged* method (bolded part in the preceding code) is that we add a *CallerMemberName* attribute to its input parameter for the property name. In the property declaration, we just call the *OnPropertyChanged* method without an input parameter. The parameter will be filled automatically with the name of the property at compile time, so there is no runtime reflection lookup or performance-hit like that encountered by the Lambda version. Aside from using third-party MVVM tools, I recommend that you consider using the .NET Framework's built-in *CallerMemberName* attribute in your MVVM applications.

Add a new *UserControl* to the *Views* Folder and name it *CallerInfoView*. The XAML file for this view is similar to that used in the *LambdaView* example. Running this project will produce the same results shown in Figure 2-2.

Property Changed Base Class

By now, if you have been following closely, you may have noticed that a lot of repetitive code exists in the view model class, such as raising the *INotifyPropertyChanged* event and creating commands. For the *INotifyPropertyChanged* event, you can put it into a base class, which I call *PropertyChangeBase*, in a .NET class library. For the *CommandModel* class, you can just move it to the class library. This is how most of the MVVM toolkits begin such as Prism, Caliburn.Micro, MvvmLight, etc.

Right-click on the *Chapter02* Solution, select Add...| New Project..., then select Class Library and name it *MvvmBase*. Add two classes to the library and name them *PropertyChangedBase* and *CommandBase* respectively. Here is the code for these two classes:

```
using System;
using System.ComponentModel;
using System.Diagnostics;
using System.Runtime.CompilerServices;

namespace MvvmBase
{
    public abstract class PropertyChangedBase : INotifyPropertyChanged
    {
        public event PropertyChangedEventHandler PropertyChanged;
        protected void OnPropertyChanged([CallerMemberName]
            string propertyName = null)
        {
            PropertyChangedEventHandler handler = PropertyChanged;
            if (handler != null)
                handler(this, new PropertyChangedEventArgs(propertyName));
        }
    }
}
```

```csharp
using System;
using System.Diagnostics;
using System.Windows.Input;

namespace MvvmBase
{
    public class CommandBase : ICommand
    {
        private Func<Boolean> canExecute;
        private Action execute;

        public CommandBase(Action action)
            : this(action, null)
        {
        }

        public CommandBase(Action action, Func<Boolean> canAction)
        {

            if (action == null)
                throw new ArgumentNullException("action");
            execute = action;
            canExecute = canAction;
        }

        public event EventHandler CanExecuteChanged
        {
            add
            {

                if (canExecute != null)
                    CommandManager.RequerySuggested += value;
            }
            remove
            {

                if (canExecute != null)
                    System.Windows.Input.CommandManager.RequerySuggested -=
                        value;
            }
        }

        [DebuggerStepThrough]
        public Boolean CanExecute(Object parameter)
        {
            return canExecute == null ? true : canExecute();
        }

        public void Execute(Object parameter)
        {
            execute();
        }
    }
}
```

Both the *PropertyChangedBase* and *CommandBase* classes are very basic and the natural results of refactoring. By moving these classes into a small class library, you can reuse them easily in your future WPF applications, which I will demonstrate next.

Add the library *MvvmBase.dll* from *~\Chapter02\MvvmBase\bin\Debug* folder to the References in the *Chapter02* project. Add a new class to the *Models* folder and name it *MvvmBaseViewModel*. Here is the code for this class:

```
using System;
using System.Windows.Input;
using MvvmBase;

namespace Chapter02.Models
{
    public class MvvmBaseViewModel : PropertyChangedBase
    {
        DataModel model;
         public MvvmBaseViewModel()
        {
            model = new DataModel
            {
                Ticker = "IBM",
                Date = Convert.ToDateTime("7/14/2015"),
                PriceOpen = 169.43,
                PriceHigh = 169.54,
                PriceLow = 168.24,
                PriceClose = 168.61,
            };
        }

        public DataModel Model
        {
            get { return model; }
            set { model = value; }
        }

        public string Ticker
        {
            get { return Model.Ticker; }
            set
            {
                Model.Ticker = value;
                OnPropertyChanged();
            }
        }

        public DateTime Date
        {
            get { return Model.Date; }
            set
            {
                Model.Date = value;
                OnPropertyChanged();
            }
        }
    }
```

```csharp
public double PriceOpen
{
    get { return Model.PriceOpen; }
    set
    {
        Model.PriceOpen = value;
        OnPropertyChanged();
    }
}

public double PriceHigh
{
    get { return Model.PriceHigh; }
    set
    {
        Model.PriceHigh = value;
        OnPropertyChanged();
    }
}

public double PriceLow
{
    get { return Model.PriceLow; }
    set
    {
        Model.PriceLow = value;
        OnPropertyChanged();
    }
}

public double PriceClose
{
    get { return Model.PriceClose; }
    set
    {
        Model.PriceClose = value;
        OnPropertyChanged();
    }
}

private void UpdateStockExecute()
{
    Ticker = "MSFT";
    Date = Convert.ToDateTime("7/14/2015");
    PriceOpen = 45.45;
    PriceHigh = 45.96;
    PriceLow = 45.31;
    PriceClose = 45.62;
}

private bool CanUpdateStockExecute()
{
    return true;
}
```

```
        public ICommand UpdateStock
        {
            get { return new CommandBase(UpdateStockExecute,
                CanUpdateStockExecute); }
        }
    }
}
```

The preceding code is similar to that used in the *CallerInfoViewModel* class except that the *MvvmBaseViewModel* class inherits from the *PropertyChangedBase* defined in the class library.

Add a new *UserControl* to the *Views* folder and name it *MvvmBaseView*. The XAML file for this view is the same as that used in the *CallerInfoView* example. Running this project produces the same results shown in Figure 2-2.

ObservableCollection

In the preceding examples, we discussed simple property binding. However, you might notice a drawback of this simple binding: the number of properties will be large, especially when you have a rich view. This can quickly make your view model class too long. The solution to this problem is to display collections of items in your *View* (UI) using *ObservableCollection*.

The advantage of *ObservableCollection* over a conventional *List* is that *ObservableCollection* implements the *INotifyCollectionChanged* interface internally. This interface raises an event whenever the collection is modified by insertion, removal, or replacement. A *List*, to the contrary, does not implement this interface, so anything data bound to it will not be updated when it changes.

Notice that not all collections in the view need to change. Some collections are fixed, and others are loaded from a database or server once and then simply displayed. If the collection does not change, you do not need to use an *ObservableCollection*; just use a *List* instead.

ObservableCollection is designed specifically for data binding. In the MVVM pattern, we bind a view to a view model. Therefore, we should use *ObservableCollection* for presenting collections of items in the view model. When an *ObservableCollection* is modified, it raises an event. You should note that events are handled synchronously; namely, event handlers respond on the same thread as the modification. The handler completes before the *Add* or *Remove* method returns, meaning that you cannot modify an *ObservableCollection* in a background thread.

Now I will show you how to use *ObservableCollection* in MVVM. Add a new class to the *Models* folder and name it *CollectionViewModel*. Here is the code for this class:

```
using System;
using System.Collections.ObjectModel;
using System.ComponentModel;
using System.Windows.Input;

namespace Chapter02.Models
{
    public class CollectionViewModel
    {
        private ObservableCollection<DataModel> dataCollection;

        public CollectionViewModel()
        {
```

```csharp
    dataCollection = new ObservableCollection<DataModel>();
    GetInitialData();
}

public ObservableCollection<DataModel> DataCollection
{
    get { return dataCollection; }
    set { dataCollection = value; }
}

private void GetInitialData()
{
    var model = new DataModel
    {
        Ticker = "IBM",
        Date = Convert.ToDateTime("7/14/2015"),
        PriceOpen = 169.43,
        PriceHigh = 169.54,
        PriceLow = 168.24,
        PriceClose = 168.61,
        Volume = 2974900
    };
    dataCollection.Add(model);

    model = new DataModel
    {
        Ticker = "MSFT",
        Date = Convert.ToDateTime("7/14/2015"),
        PriceOpen = 45.45,
        PriceHigh = 45.96,
        PriceLow = 45.31,
        PriceClose = 45.62,
        Volume = 22723700
    };
    dataCollection.Add(model);

    model = new DataModel
    {
        Ticker = "INTC",
        Date = Convert.ToDateTime("7/14/2015"),
        PriceOpen = 29.66,
        PriceHigh = 30.11,
        PriceLow = 29.44,
        PriceClose = 29.65,
        Volume = 39276800
    };
    dataCollection.Add(model);

    model = new DataModel
    {
        Ticker = "IBM",
        Date = Convert.ToDateTime("7/13/2015"),
        PriceOpen = 167.93,
        PriceHigh = 169.89,
        PriceLow = 167.52,
```

```
                PriceClose = 169.38,
                Volume = 4225500
            };
            dataCollection.Add(model);

            model = new DataModel
            {
                Ticker = "MSFT",
                Date = Convert.ToDateTime("7/13/2015"),
                PriceOpen = 44.98,
                PriceHigh = 45.62,
                PriceLow = 44.95,
                PriceClose = 45.54,
                Volume = 24994700
            };
            dataCollection.Add(model);

            model = new DataModel
            {
                Ticker = "INTC",
                Date = Convert.ToDateTime("7/13/2015"),
                PriceOpen = 29.27,
                PriceHigh = 29.82,
                PriceLow = 29.19,
                PriceClose = 29.73,
                Volume = 26335600
            };
            dataCollection.Add(model);
        }

        private void UpdateStockExecute()
        {
            DataCollection.Add(new DataModel
            {
                Ticker = "AAPL",
                Date = Convert.ToDateTime("7/14/2015"),
                PriceOpen = 126.04,
                PriceHigh = 126.37,
                PriceLow = 125.04,
                PriceClose = 125.61,
                Volume = 31535500
            });
        }

        private bool CanUpdateStockExecute()
        {
            return true;
        }

        public ICommand UpdateStock
        {
            get { return new CommandModel(UpdateStockExecute,
                CanUpdateStockExecute); }
        }
    }
```

```
}
```

Note that this class does not inherit from either *INotifyCollectionChanged* or *PropertyChangedBase*. We define the property of the *DataCollection* using the standard declaration without explicitly raising the property-changed notification (see the bolded part of the preceding code). This is because the *DataCollection* property returns an *ObservableCollection* object that already implements the *INotifyCollectionChange* interface internally. Most of the rest of the preceding code is to set the initial (or default) data for the *DataCollection* via the constructor.

Add a new *UserControl* to the *Views* folder and name it *CollectionView*. Here is its XAML code:

```
<UserControl x:Class="Chapter02.Views.CollectionView"
    xmlns="http://schemas.microsoft.com/winfx/2006/xaml/presentation"
    xmlns:x="http://schemas.microsoft.com/winfx/2006/xaml"
    xmlns:mc="http://schemas.openxmlformats.org/markup-compatibility/2006"
    xmlns:d="http://schemas.microsoft.com/expression/blend/2008"
    xmlns:model="clr-namespace:Chapter02.Models"
    mc:Ignorable="d"
    d:DesignHeight="300" d:DesignWidth="450">

    <UserControl.DataContext>
        <model:CollectionViewModel/>
    </UserControl.DataContext>

    <Grid Margin="10">
        <Grid.RowDefinitions>
            <RowDefinition Height="55"/>
            <RowDefinition Height="*"/>
        </Grid.RowDefinitions>
        <DataGrid ItemsSource="{Binding Path=DataCollection}" ColumnWidth="*"
                CanUserAddRows="False" Grid.Row="0" FontSize="10"/>
        <Button x:Name="btnUpdate" Content="Update"
                Width="100" Height="25" Grid.Row="1"
                Command="{Binding UpdateStock}"/>
    </Grid>
</UserControl>
```

In the preceding XAML file, we add a new *DataGrid* control to the *Grid*. The *ItemsSource* attribute of this *DataGrid* is bound to the *DataCollection* defined in the *CollectionViewModel*. The *DataGrid* control is a UI component for displaying tabular data in the view, typically providing sorting and editing functionality, among others. In this example, if you click the *Update* button, you will add one more record of AAPL stock to the *DataCollection*, which should update automatically in the *DataGird*.

Figure 2-3 shows the results of running this example. Here the top six records are the default values for the *DataCollection* while the last three records are added by clicking the *Update* button three times.

Ticker	Date	PriceOpen	PriceHigh	PriceLow	PriceClose	Volume
IBM	7/14/2015 12:0	169.43	169.54	168.24	168.61	2974900
MSFT	7/14/2015 12:0	45.45	45.96	45.31	45.62	22723700
INTC	7/14/2015 12:0	29.66	30.11	29.44	29.65	39276900
IBM	7/13/2015 12:0	167.93	169.89	167.52	169.38	4225500
MSFT	7/13/2015 12:0	44.98	45.62	44.95	45.54	24994700
INTC	7/13/2015 12:0	29.27	29.82	29.19	29.73	26335600
AAPL	7/14/2015 12:0	126.04	126.37	125.04	125.61	31535500
AAPL	7/14/2015 12:0	126.04	126.37	125.04	125.61	31535500
AAPL	7/14/2015 12:0	126.04	126.37	125.04	125.61	31535500

Update

Figure 2-3. The result of the ObservableCollection example.

Open-Source MVVM Toolkits

Up to now in this chapter, I have presented the basic steps for developing MVVM applications. The goal of using the MVVM pattern is to separate the user interface from the application logic. There is always a one-to-one relationship between the view and view model; namely, a view model belongs to exactly one view and a view has exactly one view model. However, these simple MVVM applications do not include all MVVM features. For example, if you want to communicate between view models, you cannot do so using simple data binding. In this case, you have to use the Mediator, Messenger, or Event Aggregator pattern. In theory, implementing a fully featured MVVM tool on your own should not be very hard, but you need to put some real effort into it.

In practice, you do not need to implement all these MVVM features and reinvent the wheel by yourself. In fact, there are many good open source MVVM frameworks out there. Here I list just a few of them:

- *MVVM Foundation* (http://mvvmfoundation.codeplex.com/): This is Josh Smith's version of MVVM. Josh is one of the fathers of MVVM. This framework is small and intended to provide only the basic tools needed by most MVVM application developers.

- *Prism* (http://compositewpf.codeplex.com/): This is the Microsoft Patterns and Practices Team official guidance for building composite applications in WPF and Silverlight. It intended for building large-scale applications that are flexible in terms of development and maintainability. It provides a lot of functionality but has a high learning curve.

- *MVVM Light* (https://mvvmlight.codeplex.com/): This is a lightweight MVVM toolkit and is not intended to cover every aspect of MVVM applications. It only contains the essential components needed in MVVM. Its main purpose is to accelerate the creation and development of MVVM applications.

- *Cinch* (https://cinch.codeplex.com/): This framework covers more ground than most other MVVM toolkits. It provides UI services, threading, and unit test helpers, taking the UI services route to provide a rich MVVM framework that comes with several standard services out of the box.

- *Caliburn.Micro* (https://github.com/Caliburn-Micro/): A small yet powerful MVVM toolkit that implements a variety of UI patterns for solving real-world problems. Patterns in the Caliburn.Micro framework include MVC, MVP, MVVM, and application controller.

You have many choices among open-source MVVM frameworks. In my .NET development, I have tried several of the above, including Prism and Caliburn.Micro. Prism has some advantages: it was developed by Microsoft, it works with various IoC (Inversion of Control) containers, and it is well documented. However, I found it complicated and not easy to use. I then switched to Caliburn.Micro and found it to be a very straightforward and powerful MVVM framework. I like, in particular, its naming conversion mechanism and its use of an *Actions* system to invoke verbs (methods) on view models from the view. In the following sections, I will show you some useful features in Caliburn.Micro via examples.

MVVM with Caliburn.Micro

Caliburn.Micro (CM) depends considerably on its naming convention mechanism, which simplifies the process of data binding. This naming convention is flexible and fully customizable, and can even be turned off completely if not desired. If you have a property in your view model with the same name as a control in your view, CM will attempt to data bind them automatically.

CM's *Action* mechanism allows you to bind UI event handlers, such as a button click, to methods on your view models, which eliminates the code needed to implemente *Execute* and *CanExecute* command methods. You just need to write the action method as usual in your view model. For example, if you have a method called *UpdateStock* in your view model and a button named "*UpdateStock*" in your view, CM will automatically create an event handler for the *Click* event and assign an *ActionMessage* for the *UpdateStock* method.

Another one of CM's powerful features is its *Event Aggregator*, which follows a publish/subscribe model. You register a message handler with the aggregator, and it sends you any messages you are interested in. This feature plays a key role in communicating between different view models.

For every view model in your application, CM has a basic strategy for automatically locating the view that should render it. Again, CM does this based on naming conventions. For example, if you have a view model called *MyApplication.ViewModels.MainViewModel*, CM will look for *MyApplication.Views. MainView*. In the following, I will explain these features with examples.

Simple Data Binding

First, I will show you how to use CM's naming conventions for simple data binding. Right-click the solution *Chapter02*, select Add | New Project…Select WPF Application from the templates and name it *TestCaliburnMicro*. Now you need to add CM to references in the project. Right-click *References* in the project, then select Manage NuGet Packages… to bring up the Manage NuGet Packages window. In the Search Online field, enter Caliburn.Micro and start searching, as shown in Figure 2-4.

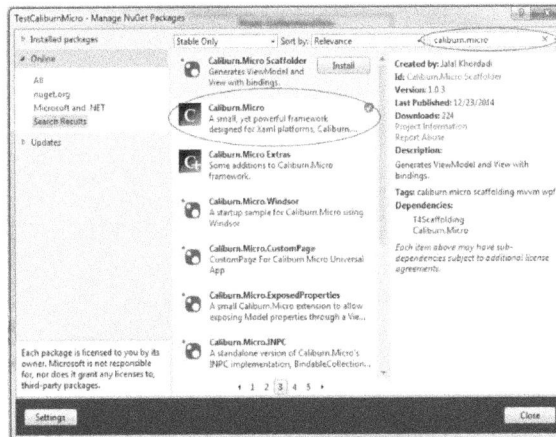

Figure 2-4. Manage NuGet Packages window.

Select Caliburn.Micro and click *Install*. This will add CM to the *References*. Since CM will take care of creating the window for you, you need to delete *MainWindow.xaml* and remove the *StartupUri* attribute from *App.xaml* file. *App.xaml* will now look like this:

```
<Application x:Class="TestCaliburnMicro.App"
             xmlns="http://schemas.microsoft.com/winfx/2006/xaml/presentation"
             xmlns:x="http://schemas.microsoft.com/winfx/2006/xaml">
    <Application.Resources>
    </Application.Resources>
</Application>
```

Here, I want to reproduce the results of the *OnCommandView* example in the *Chapter02* project using CM. Add a *DataModel.cs*, the same as in the *Chapter02* project, to the current project. Add a new class to the project and name it *MainViewModel*. Here is the code for this class:

```csharp
using System;
using Caliburn.Micro;

namespace TestCaliburnMicro
{
    public class MainViewModel : PropertyChangedBase
    {
        DataModel model;
        public MainViewModel()
        {
            model = new DataModel
            {
                Ticker = "IBM",
                Date = Convert.ToDateTime("7/14/2015"),
                PriceOpen = 169.43,
                PriceHigh = 169.54,
                PriceLow = 168.24,
                PriceClose = 168.61,
            };
        }

        public DataModel Model
        {
            get { return model; }
            set { model = value; }
        }

        public string Ticker
        {
            get { return Model.Ticker; }
            set
            {
                Model.Ticker = value;
                NotifyOfPropertyChange(() => Ticker);
            }
        }

        public DateTime Date
        {
            get { return Model.Date; }
            set
            {
                Model.Date = value;
                NotifyOfPropertyChange(() => Date);
            }
        }

        public double PriceOpen
        {
            get { return Model.PriceOpen; }
            set
```

```
            {
                Model.PriceOpen = value;
                NotifyOfPropertyChange(() => PriceOpen);
            }
        }

        public double PriceHigh
        {
            get { return Model.PriceHigh; }
            set
            {
                Model.PriceHigh = value;
                NotifyOfPropertyChange(() => PriceHigh);
            }
        }
        public double PriceLow
        {
            get { return Model.PriceLow; }
            set
            {
                Model.PriceLow = value;
                NotifyOfPropertyChange(() => PriceLow);
            }
        }
        public double PriceClose
        {
            get { return Model.PriceClose; }
            set
            {
                Model.PriceClose = value;
                NotifyOfPropertyChange(() => PriceClose);
            }
        }

        public void UpdateStock()
        {
            Ticker = "MSFT";
            Date = Convert.ToDateTime("7/14/2015");
            PriceOpen = 45.45;
            PriceHigh = 45.96;
            PriceLow = 45.31;
            PriceClose = 45.62;
        }
    }
}
```

Compared to the *OnCommandViewModel*, the code here is much simpler. This class inherits from the *PropertyChangedBase* class included in CM. We set property declarations directly using Lambda expressions to raise the *NotifyOfPropertyChange* event. Essentially, the command looks almost the same as that in a button-click event handler in a code-behind file. Now CM expects a particular naming convention so it can hook up the view model to the appropriate view. The class name of a view model should end with "*ViewModel*". You can put whatever you want to in front of "*ViewModel*".

Now we need to add a view. Add a new Window to the project and name it *MainView*. Following CM's naming convention, the *View*'s names should end with "*View*" and start with the same name you use for the view model. So for this example, *MainView* is the view for rendering the *MainViewModel*. Here is the XAML file for this view:

```xml
<Window x:Class="TestCaliburnMicro.MainView"
        xmlns="http://schemas.microsoft.com/winfx/2006/xaml/presentation"
        xmlns:x="http://schemas.microsoft.com/winfx/2006/xaml"
        Title="Test Caliburn.Micro 1" Height="300" Width="300">
    <Grid Margin="10">

        <StackPanel HorizontalAlignment="Center">
            <StackPanel Orientation="Horizontal">
                <TextBlock Text="Ticker" Width="80"/>
                <TextBox x:Name="Ticker" Width="80"/>
            </StackPanel>
            <StackPanel Orientation="Horizontal" Margin="0 5 0 0">
                <TextBlock Text="Date" Width="80"/>
                <TextBox x:Name="Date" Width="80"/>
            </StackPanel>
            <StackPanel Orientation="Horizontal" Margin="0 5 0 0">
                <TextBlock Text="Open Price" Width="80"/>
                <TextBox x:Name="PriceOpen" Width="80"/>
            </StackPanel>
            <StackPanel Orientation="Horizontal" Margin="0 5 0 0">
                <TextBlock Text="High Price" Width="80"/>
                <TextBox x:Name="PriceHigh" Width="80"/>
            </StackPanel>
            <StackPanel Orientation="Horizontal" Margin="0 5 0 0">
                <TextBlock Text="Low Price" Width="80"/>
                <TextBox x:Name="PriceLow" Width="80"/>
            </StackPanel>
            <StackPanel Orientation="Horizontal" Margin="0 5 0 0">
                <TextBlock Text="Close Price" Width="80"/>
                <TextBox x:Name="PriceClose" Width="80"/>
            </StackPanel>
            <Button x:Name="UpdateStock" Content="Update"
                    Width="100" Height="25" Margin="30 20 0 0"
                    HorizontalAlignment="Left"/>
        </StackPanel>
    </Grid>
</Window>
```

Note that I set the names of the *Text Boxes* to the corresponding names of properties defined in the view model. CM will automatically bind them together, which is a convenient shortcut. For the button-click event, we simply set the name of the control to be the name of the method that we want it to be hooked to. CM will bind the appropriate event of the button to the specified method in the view model.

Now, we have created both the view model and view. However, in order to make CM work, we have to implement a *Bootstrapper* class. The *Bootstrapper* is a mechanism used to incorporate CM into an application. You can also configure CM for the needs of your application in this class. For the purpose of this simple example, we will use a very simple version of Bootstrapper. Add a new class to the project and name it *AppBootstrapper*. Here is the code for this class:

```csharp
using Caliburn.Micro;

namespace TestCaliburnMicro
{
```

```
public class AppBootstrapper : BootstrapperBase
{
    public AppBootstrapper()
    {
        Initialize();
    }

    protected override void OnStartup(object sender,
        System.Windows.StartupEventArgs e)
    {
        base.OnStartup(sender, e);
        DisplayRootViewFor<MainViewModel>();
    }
}
}
```

This simple class just overrides the *OnStartup* method that sets the *MainViewModel* as the startup. Next, we need to tell the application to use the bootstrapper. This can be done by adding our bootstrapper to a resource dictionary in *App.xaml*. After doing this, the XAML should look something like the following:

```
<Application x:Class="TestCaliburnMicro.App"
            xmlns="http://schemas.microsoft.com/winfx/2006/xaml/presentation"
            xmlns:x="http://schemas.microsoft.com/winfx/2006/xaml"
            xmlns:local="clr-namespace:TestCaliburnMicro">
    <Application.Resources>
        <ResourceDictionary>
            <ResourceDictionary.MergedDictionaries>
                <ResourceDictionary>
                    <local:AppBootstrapper x:Key="bootstrapper" />
                </ResourceDictionary>
            </ResourceDictionary.MergedDictionaries>
        </ResourceDictionary>
    </Application.Resources>
</Application>
```

Now we have finished the implementation for this example. Right-click the *TestCaliburnMicro* project and select Set as Startup Project. When you press F5 and click the *Update* button, you will get the same results shown in Figure 2-2. You may notice that we do not need to set *MainView*'s *DataContext* to the *MainViewModel* because CM sets it for us automatically.

Communication between View Models

If you application contains several view models, you may want to communicate between certain view models. You can achieve this using CM's messaging through the *EventAggregator* class. Using this class is a two-step process. First, you subscribe objects, such as view models, to the aggregator and create methods to handle the messages that you want to receive. Second, when another part of your application publishes a message, the aggregator makes sure that the appropriate subscribed objects receive it and perform the appropriate action.

In order to demonstrate CM's communication function using the event aggregator, we need at least two view models in our application. So let us extend the preceding example: add a new project to the *Chapter02* solution and name it *TestCaliburnMicro2*. Following the same steps as in the preceding example, we need to add Caliburn.Micro to the References, remove *MainWindow.xaml*, add a new

Window named *MainView* and the *DataModel.cs* class to the project, and make corresponding changes to the *App.xaml* file.

Now add a new class to the current project and name it *CollectionViewModel*, similar to what we used in the *Chapter02* project. Here is the code for this class:

```
using System;
using Caliburn.Micro;
using System.ComponentModel.Composition;

namespace TestCaliburnMicro2
{
    [Export(typeof(CollectionViewModel))]
    public class CollectionViewModel : PropertyChangedBase
    {
        private BindableCollection<DataModel> dataCollection;
        private readonly IEventAggregator _events;

        [ImportingConstructor]
        public CollectionViewModel(IEventAggregator events)
        {
            _events = events;
            dataCollection = new BindableCollection<DataModel>();
            GetInitialData();
        }

        public BindableCollection<DataModel> DataCollection
        {
            get { return dataCollection; }
            set
            {
                dataCollection = value;
            }
        }

        private void GetInitialData()
        {
            var model = new DataModel
            {
                Ticker = "IBM",
                Date = Convert.ToDateTime("7/14/2015"),
                PriceOpen = 169.43,
                PriceHigh = 169.54,
                PriceLow = 168.24,
                PriceClose = 168.61,
                Volume = 2974900
            };
            dataCollection.Add(model);
            model = new DataModel
            {
                Ticker = "MSFT",
                Date = Convert.ToDateTime("7/14/2015"),
                PriceOpen = 45.45,
                PriceHigh = 45.96,
                PriceLow = 45.31,
                PriceClose = 45.62,
```

```
            Volume = 22723700
        };
        dataCollection.Add(model);
        model = new DataModel
        {
            Ticker = "INTC",
            Date = Convert.ToDateTime("7/14/2015"),
            PriceOpen = 29.66,
            PriceHigh = 30.11,
            PriceLow = 29.44,
            PriceClose = 29.65,
            Volume = 39276800
        };
        dataCollection.Add(model);
        model = new DataModel
        {
            Ticker = "IBM",
            Date = Convert.ToDateTime("7/13/2015"),
            PriceOpen = 167.93,
            PriceHigh = 169.89,
            PriceLow = 167.52,
            PriceClose = 169.38,
            Volume = 4225500
        };
        dataCollection.Add(model);
        model = new DataModel
        {
            Ticker = "MSFT",
            Date = Convert.ToDateTime("7/13/2015"),
            PriceOpen = 44.98,
            PriceHigh = 45.62,
            PriceLow = 44.95,
            PriceClose = 45.54,
            Volume = 24994700
        };
        dataCollection.Add(model);
        model = new DataModel
        {
            Ticker = "INTC",
            Date = Convert.ToDateTime("7/13/2015"),
            PriceOpen = 29.27,
            PriceHigh = 29.82,
            PriceLow = 29.19,
            PriceClose = 29.73,
            Volume = 26335600
        };
        dataCollection.Add(model);
}

int count = 0;
public void UpdateStock()
{
    DataCollection.Add(new DataModel
    {
        Ticker = "AAPL",
```

```
                    Date = Convert.ToDateTime("7/14/2015"),
                    PriceOpen = 126.04,
                    PriceHigh = 126.37,
                    PriceLow = 125.04,
                    PriceClose = 125.61,
                    Volume = 31535500
                });
                count++;
                _events.PublishOnUIThread(new ModelEvent(string.Format("AAPL ({0})
                    just Added to the stock list.", count)));
            }
        }
    }
```

Here, we add the *Export* attribute to this class, which is required by the CM framework. We want this view model to publish a message, so we add a constructor that takes an *IEventAggregator* as an input parameter and stores it in a field. Please do not forget to include the *ImportingConstructor* attribute. We also use *BindableCollection* to replace the *ObservableCollection* used in the *Chapter02* project. *BindableCollection*, included in CM, is a simple collection that inherits from *ObservableCollection*, but it ensures that all its events are raised on the UI thread.

Pay special attention to how we publish the message (see bolded part of code). We publish the message from a new instance of the *ModelEvent* class that returns a string by calling the *PublishOnUIThread* method.

In this example, we want to publish messages from the *CollectionViewModel* to be picked up by the *MainViewModel*. To achieve this we need to implement a class that holds the message information. This class is usually very small and simple: it mainly needs to have properties that hold the information that we want to send. Add a new class to the project and name it *ModelEvent*. Here is the code for this class:

```
using System;
namespace TestCaliburnMicro2
{
    public class ModelEvent
    {
        public ModelEvent(string msg)
        {
            this.Msg = msg;
        }
        public string Msg { get; private set; }
    }
}
```

This class holds a message that is just a simple string type. In order for the *MainViewModel* to handle the appropriate events, we need to implement the *IHandle<TMessage>* interface. In this example, we use *ModelEvent* as the generic type. The *IHandle* interface has a single method called *Handle* that we need to implement. In the *Handle* method, we look at the message string sent in the *ModelEvent* and use it to set the *MSG* property bound to a *TextBlock* control in the *MainView*. Here is the code listing for the *MainViewModel*:

```
using System;
using Caliburn.Micro;
using System.ComponentModel.Composition;

namespace TestCaliburnMicro2
```

```csharp
{
    [Export(typeof(MainViewModel))]
    public class MainViewModel : PropertyChangedBase, IHandle<ModelEvent>
    {
        private DataModel model;
        private readonly IEventAggregator _events;

        [ImportingConstructor]
        public MainViewModel(CollectionViewModel collectionViewModel,
            IEventAggregator events)
        {
            this._events = events;
            _events.Subscribe(this);

            CollectionViewModel = collectionViewModel;

            model = new DataModel
            {
                Ticker = "IBM",
                Date = Convert.ToDateTime("7/14/2015"),
                PriceOpen = 169.43,
                PriceHigh = 169.54,
                PriceLow = 168.24,
                PriceClose = 168.61,
            };
        }

        public CollectionViewModel CollectionViewModel { get; set; }

        public void Handle(ModelEvent msg)
        {
            this.MSG = msg.Msg;
        }

        private string msg;
        public string MSG
        {
            get { return msg; }
            set
            {
                msg = value;
                NotifyOfPropertyChange(() => MSG);
            }
        }


        public DataModel Model
        {
            get { return model; }
            set { model = value; }
        }

        public string Ticker
        {
            get { return Model.Ticker; }
```

```
        set
        {
            Model.Ticker = value;
            NotifyOfPropertyChange(() => Ticker);
        }
    }

    public DateTime Date
    {
        get { return Model.Date; }
        set
        {
            Model.Date = value;
            NotifyOfPropertyChange(() => Date);
        }
    }

    public double PriceOpen
    {
        get { return Model.PriceOpen; }
        set
        {
            Model.PriceOpen = value;
            NotifyOfPropertyChange(() => PriceOpen);
        }
    }

    public double PriceHigh
    {
        get { return Model.PriceHigh; }
        set
        {
            Model.PriceHigh = value;
            NotifyOfPropertyChange(() => PriceHigh);
        }
    }
    public double PriceLow
    {
        get { return Model.PriceLow; }
        set
        {
            Model.PriceLow = value;
            NotifyOfPropertyChange(() => PriceLow);
        }
    }
    public double PriceClose
    {
        get { return Model.PriceClose; }
        set
        {
            Model.PriceClose = value;
            NotifyOfPropertyChange(() => PriceClose);
        }
    }
```

```
        public void UpdateStock()
        {
            Ticker = "MSFT";
            Date = Convert.ToDateTime("7/14/2015");
            PriceOpen = 45.45;
            PriceHigh = 45.96;
            PriceLow = 45.31;
            PriceClose = 45.62;
        }
    }
}
```

For completeness, I will also list the XAML file for *MainView*:

```
<Window x:Class="TestCaliburnMicro2.MainView"
        xmlns="http://schemas.microsoft.com/winfx/2006/xaml/presentation"
        xmlns:x="http://schemas.microsoft.com/winfx/2006/xaml"
        Title="Test Caliburn.Micro 2" Height="400" Width="700">
    <Grid Margin="10">
        <Grid.ColumnDefinitions>
            <ColumnDefinition Width="200"/>
            <ColumnDefinition/>
        </Grid.ColumnDefinitions>

        <StackPanel HorizontalAlignment="Center">
            <TextBlock Text="From MainView" FontSize="14" FontWeight="Bold"
                Margin="0 0 0 20" HorizontalAlignment="Center"/>
            <StackPanel Orientation="Horizontal">
                <TextBlock Text="Ticker" Width="80"/>
                <TextBox x:Name="Ticker" Width="80"/>
            </StackPanel>
            <StackPanel Orientation="Horizontal" Margin="0 5 0 0">
                <TextBlock Text="Date" Width="80"/>
                <TextBox x:Name="Date" Width="80"/>
            </StackPanel>
            <StackPanel Orientation="Horizontal" Margin="0 5 0 0">
                <TextBlock Text="Open Price" Width="80"/>
                <TextBox x:Name="PriceOpen" Width="80"/>
            </StackPanel>
            <StackPanel Orientation="Horizontal" Margin="0 5 0 0">
                <TextBlock Text="High Price" Width="80"/>
                <TextBox x:Name="PriceHigh" Width="80"/>
            </StackPanel>
            <StackPanel Orientation="Horizontal" Margin="0 5 0 0">
                <TextBlock Text="Low Price" Width="80"/>
                <TextBox x:Name="PriceLow" Width="80"/>
            </StackPanel>
            <StackPanel Orientation="Horizontal" Margin="0 5 0 0">
                <TextBlock Text="Close Price" Width="80"/>
                <TextBox x:Name="PriceClose" Width="80"/>
            </StackPanel>
            <Button x:Name="UpdateStock" Content="Update"
                    Width="100" Height="25" Margin="30 20 0 0"
                    HorizontalAlignment="Left"/>
            <GroupBox Header="Message from CollectionView" Width="180"
                    Margin="0 20 0 0">
```

```
                    <TextBlock x:Name="MSG" Margin="5" TextWrapping="Wrap"/>
                </GroupBox>
            </StackPanel>
            <ContentControl x:Name="CollectionViewModel" Grid.Column="1"/>
        </Grid>
</Window>
```

Here, we introduce the *CollectionViewModel* using a *ContentControl* (see the bolded part of the code), which will put the *CollectionView* inside *MainView*. The following is the XAML for *CollectionView*:

```
<UserControl x:Class="TestCaliburnMicro2.CollectionView"
    xmlns="http://schemas.microsoft.com/winfx/2006/xaml/presentation"
    xmlns:x="http://schemas.microsoft.com/winfx/2006/xaml"
    xmlns:mc="http://schemas.openxmlformats.org/markup-compatibility/2006"
    xmlns:d="http://schemas.microsoft.com/expression/blend/2008"
    BorderBrush="Gray" BorderThickness="1"
    mc:Ignorable="d"
    d:DesignHeight="400" d:DesignWidth="300">
    <Grid Margin="10 0 10 10">
        <Grid.RowDefinitions>
            <RowDefinition Height="30"/>
            <RowDefinition Height="*"/>
            <RowDefinition Height="55"/>
        </Grid.RowDefinitions>
        <TextBlock Text="From CollectionView" FontSize="14" FontWeight="Bold"
                   HorizontalAlignment="Center"/>
        <DataGrid x:Name="DataCollection" ColumnWidth="*"
                  CanUserAddRows="False" Grid.Row="1" FontSize="10"/>
        <Button x:Name="UpdateStock" Content="Update"
                Width="100" Height="25" Grid.Row="3"/>
    </Grid>
</UserControl>
```

Note how we data bind the *DataCollection* to the *DataGrid* control using CM's naming convention. You might think that we have already finished the implementation for this example, but if you run the example by pressing F5 now, you will run into an exception saying that the default constructor of *MainViewModel* cannot be found. This is because we have included a constructor in *MainViewModel* that requires two parameters: one is the *CollectionView* object and the other the *IEventAggregator* event. To resolve this issue, we need to update the *AppBootstrapper* class as listed below:

```
using System;
using System.Windows;
using System.ComponentModel;
using System.Collections.Generic;
using System.Linq;
using System.ComponentModel.Composition;
using System.ComponentModel.Composition.Hosting;
using System.ComponentModel.Composition.Primitives;
using Caliburn.Micro;

namespace TestCaliburnMicro2
{
    public class AppBootstrapper : BootstrapperBase
    {
        private CompositionContainer container;
        public AppBootstrapper()
```

```
    {
        Initialize();
    }


    protected override void Configure()
    {
        container = new CompositionContainer(new
            AggregateCatalog(AssemblySource.Instance.Select(x =>
            new AssemblyCatalog(x)).OfType<ComposablePartCatalog>()));
        var batch = new CompositionBatch();
        batch.AddExportedValue<IWindowManager>(new WindowManager());
        batch.AddExportedValue<IEventAggregator>(new EventAggregator());
        batch.AddExportedValue(container);
        container.Compose(batch);
    }

    protected override object GetInstance(Type serviceType, string key)
    {
        string contract = string.IsNullOrEmpty(key) ?
            AttributedModelServices.GetContractName(serviceType) : key;
        var exports = container.GetExportedValues<object>(contract);
        if (exports.Any())
            return exports.First();
        throw new Exception(string.Format("Could not locate any
            instances of contract {0}.", contract));
    }

    protected override IEnumerable<object> GetAllInstances(Type serviceType)
    {
        return container.GetExportedValues<object>(AttributedModelServices.
            GetContractName(serviceType));
    }

    protected override void BuildUp(object instance)
    {
        container.SatisfyImportsOnce(instance);
    }

    protected override void OnStartup(object sender, StartupEventArgs e)
    {
        base.OnStartup(sender, e);
        DisplayRootViewFor<MainViewModel>();
    }

    }
}
```

I will not dive into the details of what this code is doing. If you are interested in learning more, you can get a detailed explanation on this from CM's website, or search for IoC and Managed Extensibility Framework (MEF) on the Internet.

Now you can run the project; Figure 2-5 shows the results. If you click the *Update* button on the *MainView*, the fields in the *TextBoxes* will get updated as expected. However, both the *DataGrid* in the

CollectionView and the *TextBlock* named *MSG* in the *MainView* will also be updated when you click the *Update* button in the *CollectionView*, achieving communication between different view models.

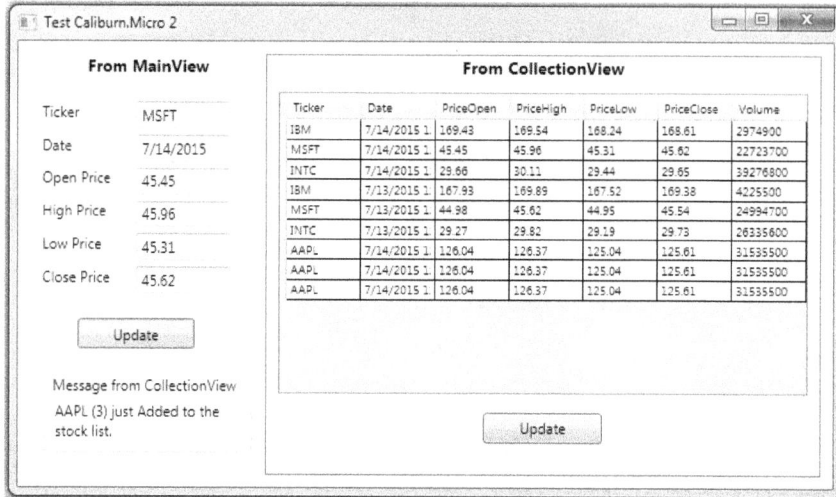

Figure 2-5. Results of the TestCaliburnMicro2 example.

Chapter 3
Databases and the ADO.NET Entity Framework

For the past several years, I have worked with a financial firm as a quant analyst/developer on Wall Street. The most important thing I deal with every day is market data. Most .NET applications in many fields also need to interact with data stored in databases. Therefore, in my opinion, every .NET developer should be familiar with the database and know how to access database data.

In this chapter, I will present you with a brief introduction to the SQL Server Data Tool (SSDT), a built-in feature shipped as part of the core product of Visual Studio 2013. You can also install SSDT as a plugin to Visual Studio 2010 and 2012. The goal of SSDT is to create an integrated development environment (IDE). Traditionally, database development has often been performed outside of Visual Studio; for instance, in the SQL Server Management Studio (SSMS). With SSDT, you have a single IDE for writing not only the application code but also the database code in the same place without switching environments.

If you have used an SQL server before, you should be familiar with SSMS. You can regard SSMS as a database administrative tool whereas SSTD is intended for developers. SSDT does not try to replace SSMS, which is still alive in SQL Server 2014 and will continue to serve as the primary management tool for database administrators. However, as a .NET application developer, you no longer need to have SSMS. Instead, you can use SSDT to perform all database-related functionalities, such as to building, debugging, maintaining, and refactoring database objects, in a simple and interactive manner.

In this chapter, I will show you how to use SSDT and LocalDB to create simple databases and how to interact with stored data. Starting from version 2012, Microsoft SQL Server Express provides a local on-demand server instance called SQL Server Express Local Database Runtime. This local server instance includes a minimum set of files required to start the SQL Server database engine. It allows you to use the SQL Server without complex configuration tasks. LocalDB is specifically designed for developers who have limited or no access to production databases, but would like to test their projects locally before authorized personnel deploy the projects for production.

In addition, I will discuss some important features of the ADO.NET Entity Framework (EF). ADO.NET is a set of libraries that come with the .NET framework. It allows you to interact with different types of data using the same methodology. However, ADO.NET comes with a cost: it does not have any user interface to help you design and access your database; that is, everything you do with .ADO.NET needs to be done manually. Of course, some developers do like this manual approach because it gives you the possibility to design everything from scratch and total control over your database design and access process.

When you develop .NET applications, I suggest that you first consider not using ADO.NET classes directly. If you are still using something like *SqlCommand*, *SqlDataReader*, and *SqlDataAdapter* in your applications, you are writing code you should not be writing. ADO.NET EF will be the better option for what you are trying to do. EF allows developers to focus on data through an object model instead of through the traditional logical/relational data model, by applying layers on top of ADO.NET. With EF, you can write less data access code and access your database via application code.

The purpose of introducing these topics here is to develope better .NET applications that can interact with the data stored in the database. I assume that you have already installed both the SQL Server and SSDT on your machine and you can access these tools. Even though I will use the SQL Server 2014 Express to create the code examples in this book, the version of the SQL Server installed on your machine does not really matter, as long as you can use it to create simple relational databases.

Local Database

A database is just a collection of structured information. It is designed to handle large amounts of information and store data in a special organized way that makes it easy to access. A relational database organizes data into one or more tables (or relations) of rows and columns with a unique key for each row. Tables are the fundamental components of the relational database. In fact, both data and relationships are stored simply as data in tables. Each table is a metaphorical representation of an entity or object in a tabular format consisting of columns and rows. Columns are the fields of a record or the attributes of an entity. The rows contain the values or data instances, which are also called record or tuples.

As I mentioned previously, I will use LocalDB to create databases in this book. If you have installed Microsoft SQL Server 2014 Express on your machine, LocalDB should also be installed. You can quickly check whether LocalDB is installed within Visual Studio 2013. Start Visual Studio 2013, click the View menu, and select SQL Server Object Explorer, as shown in Figure 3-1. This will bring up the SQL Server Object Explorer pane (Figure 3-2). You can see from Figure 3-2 that there are two LocalDB server instances: *(localdb)\MSSQLLocalDB* and *(localdb)\ProjectsV12*. Both instances are a SQL Server 2014-versioned LocalDB instance. In SQL Server 2014, Microsoft moved away from the numbering and versioning for the automatic instance and named it "*MSSQLLocalDB*" instead of "V12.0". You will get these two instances if you upgrade your Visual Studio 2013 to Visual Studio 2013 Update 4.

So which LocalDB instance should you use in your database applications? *(localdb)\ProjectsV12* is the SQL Server Express 2014 LocalDB instance used by SSDT by default to host the sandbox databases created to enable F5 deployment and debugging in your project. Hence, if you create a new database project called *MyDb*, pressing F5 and navigating to the databases in the (local)\ProjectsV12 server should show your database "*MyDb*" there. The *(localdb)\MSSQLLocalDB* instance is the generic SQL Server Express LocalDB instance that is created automatically when LocalDB is installed. This is the default LocalDB server on your machine, which may be used by applications other than SSDT, such as ASP.NET projects. Therefore, in this book, we will use *(localdb)\ProjectsV12*, because we are working on database projects using SSDT.

Figure 3-1. Select SQL Server Object Explorer.

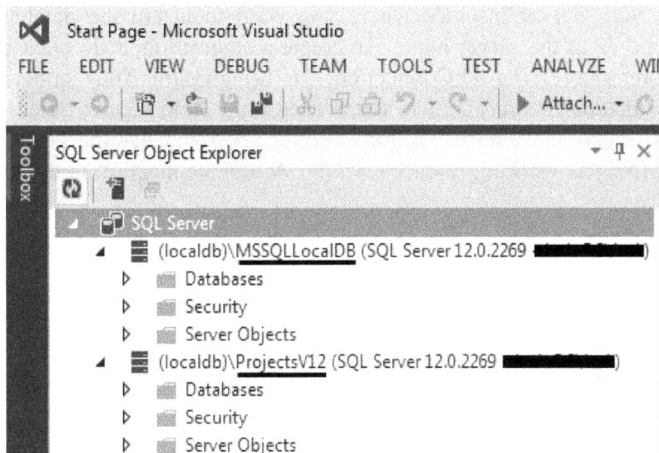

Figure 3-2. The SQL Server Object Explorer pane.

However, if you have SQL Server 2012 Express installed on your machine, you should have the following two instances: *(localdb)\V11.0* and *(localdb)\Projects*. You should use *(localdb)\Projects* for your database projects with SSDT. Since *(localdb)\V11.0* is the generic SQL Server 2012 Express LocalDB, you should use it in your applications other than SSTD, such as ASP.NET applications.

In case you do not find any LocalDB instances inside the SQL Server Object Explorer, you can first examine if you correctly installed the SQL Server Express local database server. Go to the following folder: *C:\Users\User\AppData\Local\Microsoft\Microsoft SQL Server Local DB\Instances* and see if there is any instance there. If you correctly installed SQL Server 2014 LocalDB, you should have the subfolders *MSSQLLocalDB* and *ProjectsV12* (or *V11.0* and *Projects* if SQL Server 2012 was installed). If you do not find any of these instances, you should reinstall the SQL Server Express LocalDB.

If you correctly installed the SQL LocalDB server on your machine and still cannot see the instance in the SQL Server Object Explorer, the problem may come from an out-of-date SSDT which causes a conflict with the built-in tools of Visual Studio 2013. The following step is a quick fix for this problem. Open Visual Studio 2013 and choose the Tools, Extensions and Updates menu. Then, check the Updates section for "Microsoft SQL Server Update for database tooling." If there are any updates there, perform the updating.

Sample Database

In order to examine the database capabilities of SSDT and Visual Studio, we need to install the Northwind sample database, which contains the sales data for a fictitious specialty food import and export company called Northwind Traders.

To install the Northwind sample database for SQL Server Express 2014 LocalDB, follow the steps:

- Go to the Northwind sample database website.

- Download and run the installer, which adds a folder named "SQL Server 2000 Sample Databases" to the root folder on your computer: C:\SQL Server 2000 Sample Databases.

- Locate the SQL script for Northwind and open the *instnwnd.sql* script file.

- Open Visual Studio 2013 and select View | Server Explorer. In the Server Explorer pane, create a connection to a SQL Server instance where you want to install the database. Here I will use *(localdb)\ProjectsV12* as the server name. To create a connection, right click Data Connections in the Server Explorer and select Add Connection... to bring up the Add Connection dialog window. Enter the name *(localdb)\ProjectsV12* in the Server name field. Under Select or enter a database name, choose any database from the list; for example, *tempdb*. Click the Test Connection button to verify that everything is working, then click OK. A new connection node appears in the Server Explorer.

- Right-click the connection node for your server and select New Query to bring up the editor window, which shows an empty *.sql* script file.

- Copy the content of the *instnwnd.sql* file and paste it into the editor window. Now you need to make some modifications to this script in order to make it work in SQL Server 2014, since the Northwind database was originally created for SQL Server 2000. Around line 20 in the script, remove the following two lines:

```
exec sp_dboption 'Northwind','trunc. log on chkpt.','true'
exec sp_dboption 'Northwind','select into/bulkcopy','true'
```

- Replace them with the line shown below:

```
alter database Northwind set recovery simple
```

- Click the Execute Query button (the open green triangle icon at the top left of the query window). If the query succeeds, the message *Command(s) completed successfully* will appear. This means that the Northwind database has been created.

- Now, you still need to add a connection to the Northwind database. In the Server Explorer, right-click the Data Connections node and choose Add Connection... Select the same data server that you chose before, but this time, under Select or enter a database name, choose the Northwind database, and click OK. A new node for the Northwind database appear under Data Connections. Close the edit window, now you can use the sample database.

You can use the same procedure to install other sample databases, such as *Pubs* and *AdventureWorks*, and make them available in your LocalDB projects.

SQL Queries

An SQL query is an approach to extract information from a database. You need a query window into which you type and run your query so that data can be retrieved from the database. Here we will use the SSDT technique in Visual Studio 2013 to open the query window, execute the query, and display the retrieved data.

Open Visual Studio 2013 and choose SQL Server Object Explorer (SSOE) from the View menu. Select the *(localdb)\ProjectsV12* node under SQL Server in SSOE. Expand the Databases node and select Northwind. Click the New Query button in the top-left corner (the third button) of the SSOE pan. A query edit window will appear. Select Northwind from the drop-down list in the query edit window and enter the following query:

```
SELECT * FROM Customers
```

Click the *Execute* button to execute the query; you should see the output shown in the Results window in Figure 3-3.

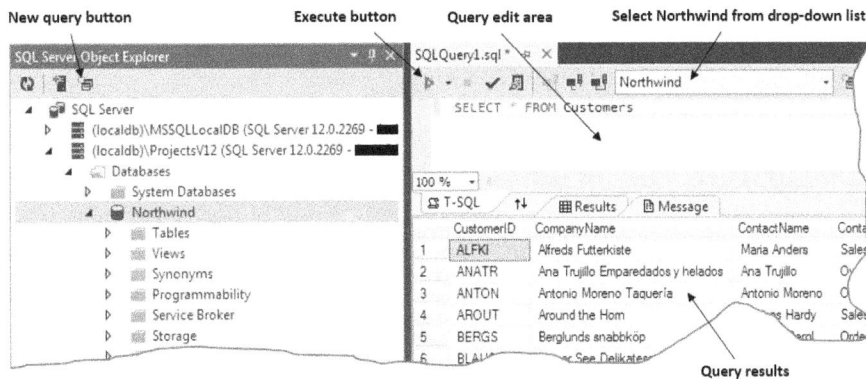

Figure 3-3. SSOE window.

Here we use the asterisk (*) with the *SELECT* statement. The asterisk indicates that all fields from the specified table should be retrieved.

GROUP BY Clause

You can use the *GROUP BY* clause to organize output records into groups. The *SELECT* list can include aggregate functions and produce summary values for each group. You will often want to generate reports from the database with summary values for a particular column or set of columns. For example, the [*Order Details*] table in the *Northwind* database contains detailed information about each order. Say you want to calculate a subtotal for each order identified by *OrderID*. This can be achieved easily using a simple *GROUP BY* clause to aggregate data for each order. Enter the following query in the query edit area and click the *Execute* button. You should see the results shown in Figure 3-4.

```
SELECT OrderID,
    ROUND(SUM(UnitPrice * Quantity * (1 - Discount)),2) as Subtotal
```

```
FROM [Order Details]
GROUP BY OrderID
ORDER BY OrderID;
```

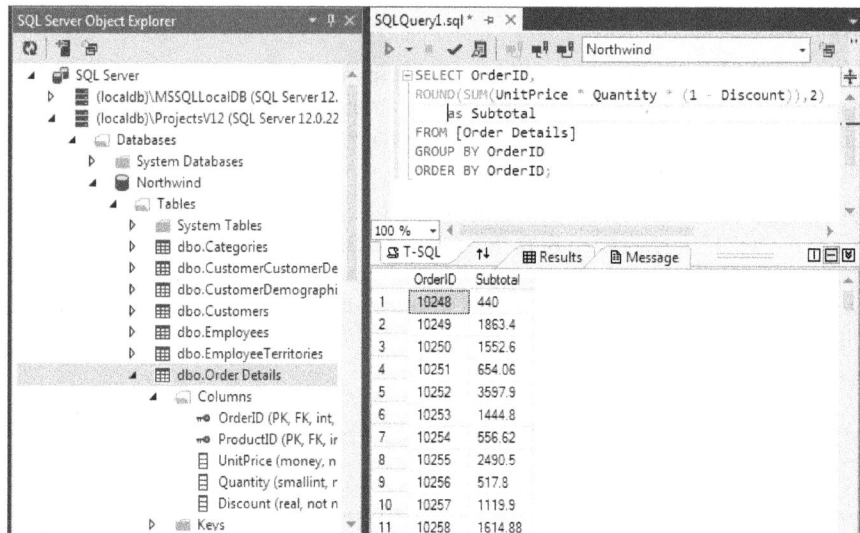

Figure 3-4. Using GROUP BY to aggregate values.

If you want to get the total sales for each region, you can enter the following query in the query edit window and click the *Execute* button. You should see the results shown in Figure 3-5.

```
WITH CTE_EmpRegion AS
(
    SELECT EmployeeID, MAX(RegionID) RegionID
    FROM EmployeeTerritories et
        INNER JOIN territories t ON t.TerritoryID = et.TerritoryID
    GROUP BY EmployeeID
),
CTE_Sales AS
(
    SELECT RegionID, SUM(Quantity * UnitPrice) TotalSales
    FROM Orders o
            INNER JOIN [Order Details] od ON o.OrderID = od.OrderID
            INNER JOIN CTE_EmpRegion er ON o.EmployeeID = er.EmployeeID
    GROUP BY RegionID
)
SELECT s.RegionID, r.RegionDescription, s.TotalSales
FROM CTE_Sales s INNER JOIN Region r on s.RegionID=r.RegionID
ORDER BY s.RegionID
```

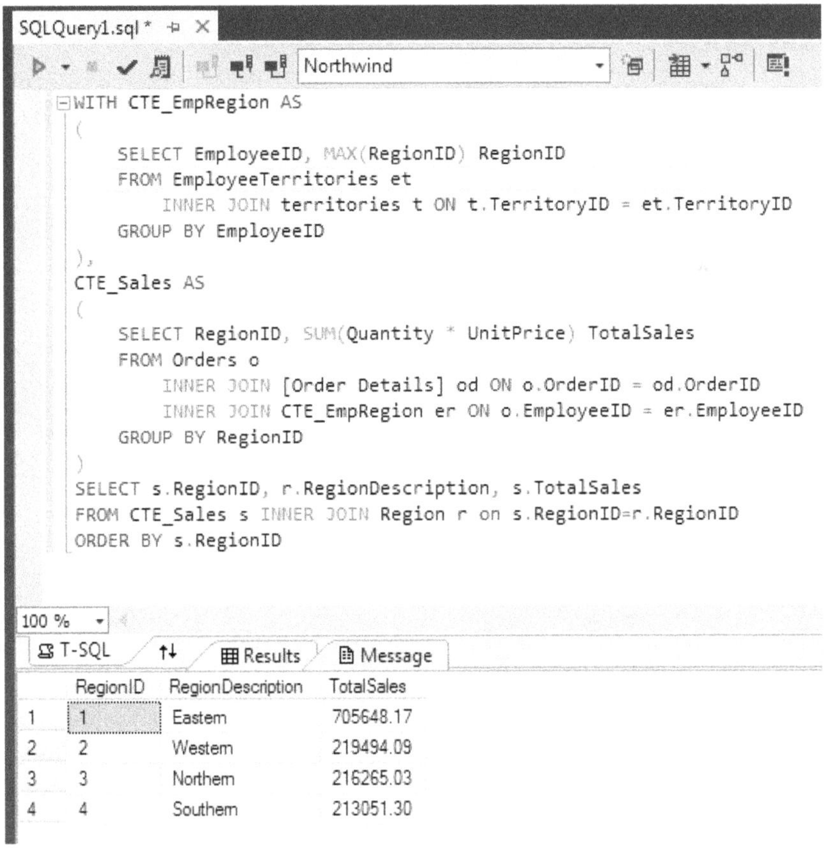

Figure 3-5. Using GROUP BY and Common Table Expressions (CTE)

How does it work here? In the *EmployeeTerritories* table, one employee can have more than one territory, so when you join on it you should multiply all records for each employee. I use the Common Table Expression (CTE) with *GROUP BY* to first find the *RegionID* for each employee and then join on this CTE (CTE_EmpRegion) inside another CTE (CTE_Sales). Finally, I join on CTE_Sales with the *Region* table to find the corresponding *RegionDescription* for each *RegionID*. Note that a CTE is a named temporary result set that can be used by the *FROM* clause of a *SELECT* query.

PIVOT Operation

The *PIVOT* operation, which rotates rows to columns, can be useful when you want to create cross-table queries. Here I will show you how to convert a simple query with *JOIN* and *GROUP BY* into a query using *PIVOT*. The sample code acts on the *Orders* and *Employees* tables in the Northwind database. You need to retrieve information about the total orders of each employee for the years 1996 and 1997. First, let's start with a simple query using *JOIN* and *GOUP BY*. Enter the following query in the query edit window and click the *Execute* button. You should see the results shown in Figure 3-6.

```
SELECT e.LastName, YEAR(o.OrderDate) [Year], COUNT(o.OrderDate) TotalOrders
FROM Employees e
INNER JOIN Orders o on e.EmployeeID = o.EmployeeID
WHERE Year(o.OrderDate) in (1996,1997)
```

```
GROUP BY e.LastName, Year(o.OrderDate)
ORDER BY e.LastName
```

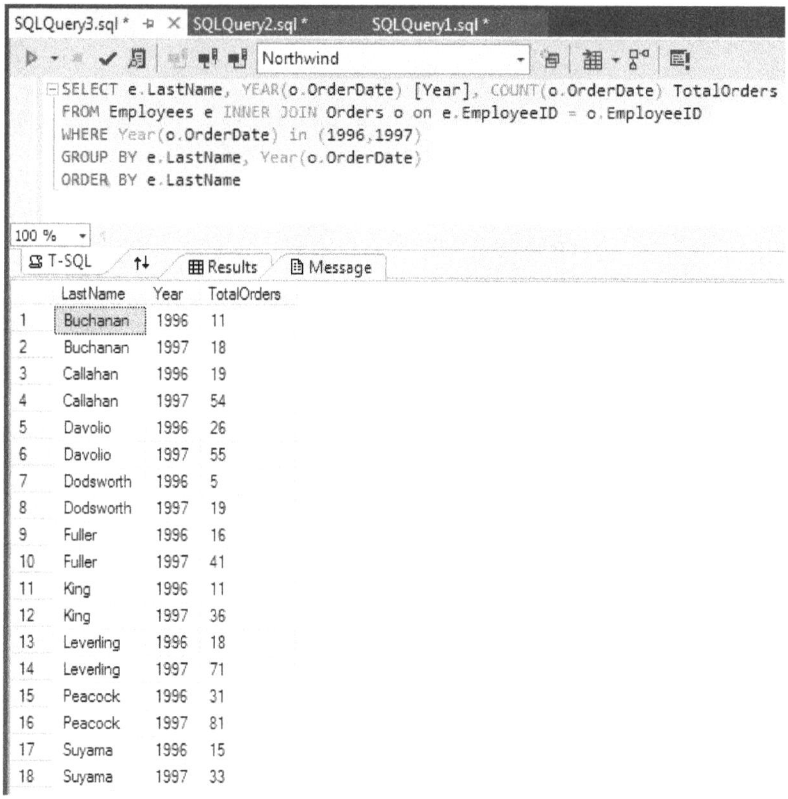

	LastName	Year	TotalOrders
1	Buchanan	1996	11
2	Buchanan	1997	18
3	Callahan	1996	19
4	Callahan	1997	54
5	Davolio	1996	26
6	Davolio	1997	55
7	Dodsworth	1996	5
8	Dodsworth	1997	19
9	Fuller	1996	16
10	Fuller	1997	41
11	King	1996	11
12	King	1997	36
13	Leverling	1996	18
14	Leverling	1997	71
15	Peacock	1996	31
16	Peacock	1997	81
17	Suyama	1996	15
18	Suyama	1997	33

Figure 3-6. Total orders using JOIN and GROUP BY

Here you specify three fields and use the *COUNT* function to count the total number of orders listed in the *OrderDate* column of the *Orders* table. You then *JOIN* the *Employees* table with the *Orders* table on the condition of the same *EmployeeID*.

Next you specify the *WHERE* condition, and the *GROUP BY* and *ORDER BY* clauses. The *WHERE* condition ensures that the year of the *OrderDate* listed will be either 1996 or 1997. The *GROUP BY* clause enforces the grouping on the specified columns: the results should be retrieved in the form of groups for the *LastName* column in the *Employees* table and the year of the *OrderDate* column in the *Orders* table. The *ORDER BY* clause ensures that the result displayed will be organized in a proper sequential order based upon the *LastName* field.

If you look at the preceding query for *GROUP BY* and the results shown in Figure 3-6, the years 1996 and 1997 have also been passed to the *WHERE* clause, but they are displayed only as part of the record and are repeated for each employee separately, which increases the number of rows to eighteen. *PIVOT* achieves the same goal and producesa concise and easy-to-understand report format.

We need to convert the preceding *GROUP BY* query into a simple query with *PIVOT*. Enter the following query in the query edit window and click the *Execute* button. You should see the results shown in Figure 3-7.

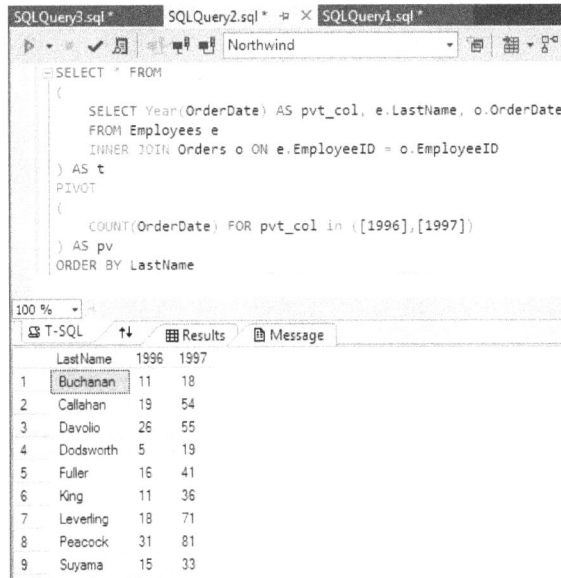

Figure 3-7. Total orders using PIVOT.

```
SELECT * FROM
(
        SELECT Year(OrderDate) AS pvt_col, e.LastName, o.OrderDate
        FROM Employees e
        INNER JOIN Orders o ON e.EmployeeID = o.EmployeeID
) AS t
PIVOT
(
        COUNT(OrderDate) FOR pvt_col in ([1996],[1997])
) AS pv
ORDER BY LastName
```

Here we start with a *SELECT* list and then specify another *SELECT* statement for the joined tables *Employees* and *Orders*, using the column names from which we will be retrieving data. W also assign a *PIVOT* operator to the *SELECT* statement.

Now we count the orders of each employee for the years 1996 and 1997. The *ORDER BY* clause will arrange the employee names under the *LastName* column in ascending order. It appears that the current results have no repeated employee names, and are much more concise and easy to understand.

However, if you look at the syntax of the preceding *PIVOT* example, you will notice that we can only specify the aggregation elements: *COUNT(OrderDate)*. There is no way in *PIVOT* to define the grouping elements explicitly. Some developers try to avoid using the *PIVOT* operator altogether in their database applications. In fact, we can manually get the same results as the preceding example without using *PIVOT*. Enter the following query in the query edit window and click the *Execute* button. You should see the results shown in Figure 3-8.

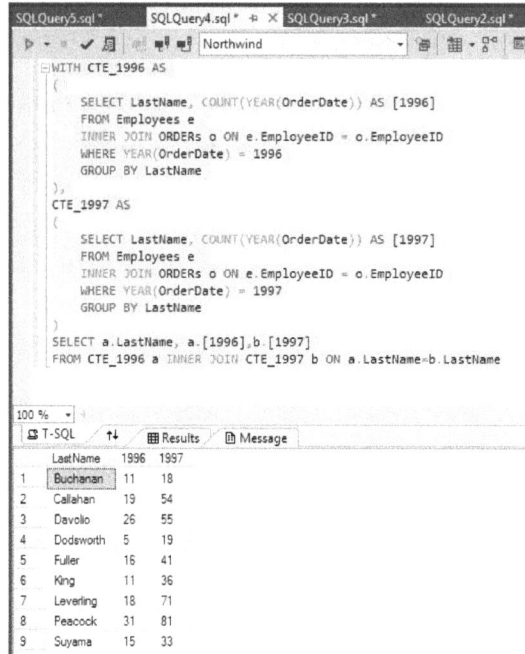

Figure 3-8. Total orders using a manual approach.

```
WITH CTE_1996 AS
(
        SELECT LastName, COUNT(YEAR(OrderDate)) AS [1996]
        FROM Employees e
        INNER JOIN ORDERs o ON e.EmployeeID = o.EmployeeID
        WHERE YEAR(OrderDate) = 1996
        GROUP BY LastName
),
CTE_1997 AS
(
        SELECT LastName, COUNT(YEAR(OrderDate)) AS [1997]
        FROM Employees e
        INNER JOIN ORDERs o ON e.EmployeeID = o.EmployeeID
        WHERE YEAR(OrderDate) = 1997
        GROUP BY LastName
)
SELECT a.LastName, a.[1996], b.[1997]
FROM CTE_1996 a INNER JOIN CTE_1997 b ON a.LastName=b.LastName
```

Here we use two CTE expressions: one is for the total orders for each employee in 1996 and the other for the total orders in 1997. Then we join these two CTEs to get the same results as those obtained using *PIVOT* operator. You might already notice that this manual approach will become unmanageable if you want to get results for many years, for example 10 years.

Aggregate Functions

SQL has several built-in functions that can aggregate the values of a column. I list some of these functions below for your reference:

- *AVG*: Returns the average of the values in a group. Null values are ignored.

- *CHECKSUM_AGG*: Returns the checksum of the values in a group. Null values are ignored. Can be followed by the *OVER* clause. Can be used to detect changes in a table.

- *COUNT*: Returns the number of items in a group. Always returns an *int* data type value.

- *COUNT_BIG*: Returns the number of items in a group. It works like theCOUNT function; the only difference between the two functions is their return values, with *COUNT_BIG* always returning a *bigint* data type value.

- *GROUPING*: Indicates whether a specified column expression in a *GROUP BY* list is aggregated or not. *GROUPING* returns 1 for aggregated or 0 for not aggregated in the result set. It can be used only in the *SELECT* <select> list, *HAVING*, and *GROUP BY* clauses when *GROUP BY* is specified.

- *GROUPING_ID*: Computes the level of grouping. Can be used only in the *SELECT* <select> list, *HAVING*, or *GROUP BY* clauses when *GROUP BY* is specified.

- *MAX*: Returns the maximum value in the expression.

- *MIN*: Returns the minimum value in the expression. May be followed by the *OVER* clause.

- *SUM*: Returns the sum of all the values, or only the *DISTINCT* values, in the expression. Can only be used with numeric columns. Null values are ignored.

- *STDEV*: Returns the statistical standard deviation of all values in the specified expression.

- *STDEVP*: Returns the statistical standard deviation for the population for all values in the specified expression. The difference between *STDEV* and *STDEVP* is that for *STDEV*, the denominator for dividing the sum of squared deviations is $N-1$ (non-biased), where N is the number of observations; for *STDEVP*, the denominator is N (biased).

- *VAR*: Returns the statistical variance of all values in the specified expression. May be followed by the *OVER* clause.

- *VARP*: Returns the statistical variance for the population for all values in the specified expression.

Now I will show you how to use aggregate functions to calculate the average, minimum, and maximum freight of orders placed by each employee. Enter the following query in the query edit window and click the *Execute* button. You should see the results shown in Figure 3-9.

```
SELECT e.EmployeeID,LastName, MIN(Freight) [Min], MAX(Freight) [Max],
    SUM(Freight) [Sum], AVG(Freight) [Avg], STDEV(Freight) [StDev]
FROM Orders o INNER JOIN Employees e ON e.EmployeeID = o.EmployeeID
GROUP BY e.EmployeeID, LastName
ORDER BY LastName
```

Here we use the *MIN* and *MAX* functions to find the minimum and maximum values, the *SUM* function to compute the total value, the *AVG* function to compute the average value, and the *STDEV* function to compute the standard deviation. Since we want the results listed by *EmployeeID* and the employee's last name, we use the *GROUP BY* clause.

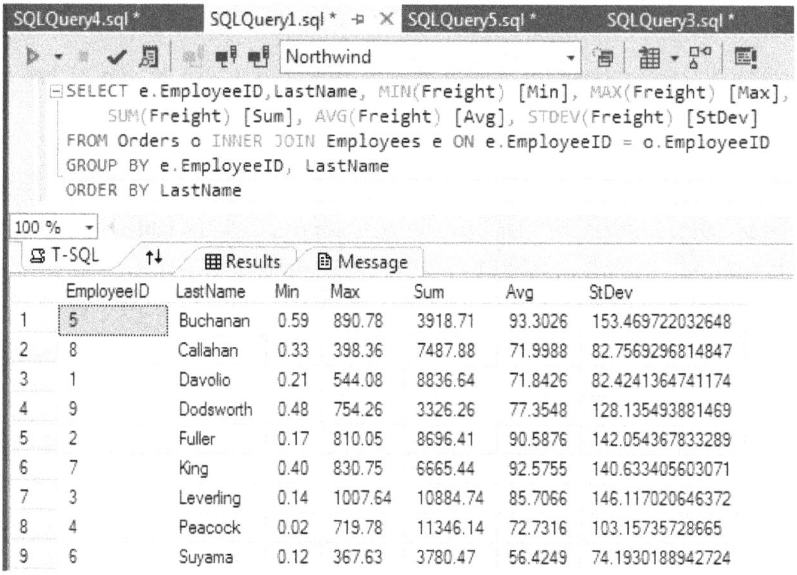
SQLQuery4.sql *
SQLQuery1.sql *
SQLQuery5.sql *
SQLQuery3.sql *
Northwind
SELECT e.EmployeeID,LastName, MIN(Freight) [Min], MAX(Freight) [Max],
SUM(Freight) [Sum], AVG(Freight) [Avg], STDEV(Freight) [StDev]
FROM Orders o INNER JOIN Employees e ON e.EmployeeID = o.EmployeeID
GROUP BY e.EmployeeID, LastName
ORDER BY LastName
100 %
T-SQL
Results
Message
EmployeeID LastName Min Max Sum Avg StDev
1 5 Buchanan 0.59 890.78 3918.71 93.3026 153.469722032648
2 8 Callahan 0.33 398.36 7487.88 71.9988 82.7569296814847
3 1 Davolio 0.21 544.08 8836.64 71.8426 82.4241364741174
4 9 Dodsworth 0.48 754.26 3326.26 77.3548 128.135493881469
5 2 Fuller 0.17 810.05 8696.41 90.5876 142.054367833289
6 7 King 0.40 830.75 6665.44 92.5755 140.633405603071
7 3 Leverling 0.14 1007.64 10884.74 85.7066 146.117020646372
8 4 Peacock 0.02 719.78 11346.14 72.7316 103.15735728665
9 6 Suyama 0.12 367.63 3780.47 56.4249 74.1930188942724

Figure 3-9. Using aggregate functions.

Database Development

In this section, I will describe features provided by SSDT for authoring, building, debugging, and publishing a database project. A local temporary instance of the LocalDB is created on your development computer when you start Visual Studio project. Therefore, for development purposes we do not need to connect to a database server. Using SSDT, we can create an offline database project and implement schema changes by adding, modifying, or deleting the definitions of objects in the project. We can use *Schema Compare* to ensure that our project stays in sync with the production database, and create snapshots for the project at each stage of the development cycle for comparison purposes. When we work on database projects in a team-based environment, we can employ version control for all the files, which is impossible using other tools such as SSMS. After the database project has been developed, tested and debugged, we can hand off the project to authorized personnel to publish it for a production environment.

Here, I will show you how to create an SSDT database project using Visual Studio 2013 and SQL Server Express 2014 LocalDB. Let's start Visual Studio 2013 and create a new WPF Windows application project called *Chapter03.* Right -lick Solution *Chapter03* and choose Add | New Project… to bring up the Add New Project window. Navigate down to Other Languages | SQL Server and select SQL Server Database Project. Name it *MyDb* and click the OK button.

Now that the *MyDb* project has been created, click on Properties under the *MyDb* project to bring up the Project Settings window, as shown in Figure 3-10.

In the Project Settings window, there are several options for controlling build and publish behaviors, which will affect the final output of our database. I want to point out two specific areas under the Project Settings: Target Platform and Database Settings. The Target Platform we choose should be set to SQL Server 2014. Database Settings controls various database-specific options. In this example, we will use the default options for Database Settings.

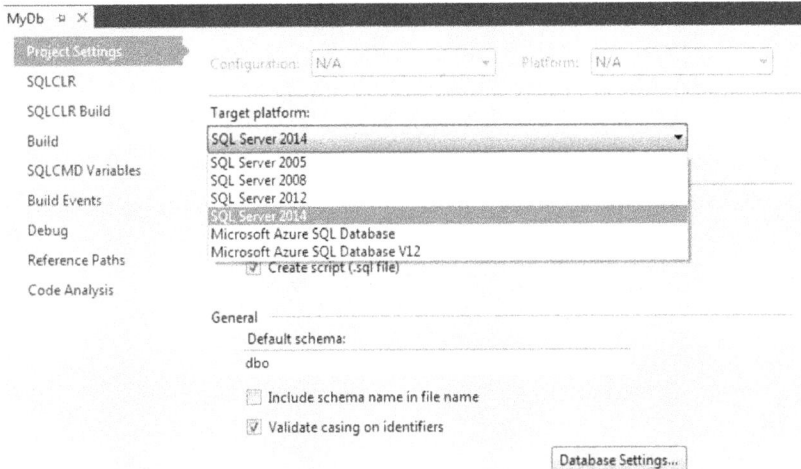

Figure 3-10. Project settings window.

Now we will create two tables, *Symbol* and *Price*, which will be used to store stock data. Right-click the *MyDb* project and choose Add | Table…; name it *Symbol*. The *MyDb* project will show a new script added called *Symbol.sql* and bring up a new dual-pane window: one pane for visual design and the other for T-SQL script editing. We can work in either pane; work we do in one pane will reflect in the other automatically. Enter the following SQL statement in the T-SQL pane. You should get the result shown in Figure 3-11.

```
CREATE TABLE [dbo].[Symbol]
(
    [SymbolID] INT IDENTITY(1,1) NOT NULL PRIMARY KEY,
    [Ticker] NVARCHAR(50) NOT NULL,
    [Region] NVARCHAR(50) NULL,
    [Sector] NVARCHAR(150) NULL,
    CONSTRAINT [UQ_Symbol_Ticker] UNIQUE (Ticker)
)
```

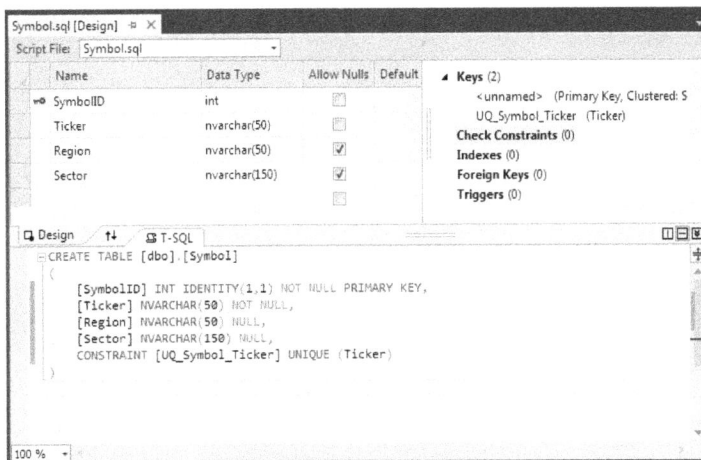

Figure 3-11. Table edit window.

Here we use the key words *CREATE TABLE* followed by the table name to create a new table. We add columns with the column name, data type, and any optional constraints. We set the primary key to the *SymbolID*, which will increment automatically with the property *IDENTITY* setting. We also add a constraint to *Ticker* (the stock's name) so that it should be unique in the table.

Add another table named *Price* to the *MyDb* project. Enter the following SQL statement:

```
CREATE TABLE [dbo].[Price]
(
    [PriceID] INT NOT NULL PRIMARY KEY IDENTITY,
    [SymbolID] INT NOT NULL,
    [Date] DATETIME NULL,
    [PriceOpen] FLOAT NULL,
    [PriceHigh] FLOAT NULL,
    [PriceLow] FLOAT NULL,
    [PriceClose] FLOAT NULL,
    [PriceAdj] FLOAT NULL,
    [Volume] FLOAT NULL,
    CONSTRAINT [FK_Price_Symbol] FOREIGN KEY ([SymbolID]) REFERENCES
        [Symbol]([SymbolID]),
    CONSTRAINT [UQ_Price] UNIQUE ([SymbolID], [Date])
)
```

In the *Price* table, we set *PriceID* as the primary key and add the *SymbolID* from the *Symbol* table as the foreign key. We also add a unique constraint on *SymbolID* and *Date* to ensure no duplicate records in the table.

After creating our database, we need to add data to the tables. Furthermore, we may want to take certain actions on the database before or after the process completes. We can use *Pre* and *Post Deployment* scripts in SSDT to accomplish this goal.

We can insert some initial seed data into the *Symbol* and *Price* tables using a *Post Deploy* script. Right-click the *MyDb* project and choose Add | Script... to bring up the Add New Item dialog, where we can select the type of script we want to create. Choose Post-Deployment Script and use the default name, *Script.PostDeployment1.sql*. A new script template window appears. Here we enter few data entries for both the *Symbol* and *Price* tables, as shown in Figure 3-12.

```
INSERT INTO Symbol (Ticker, Region, Sector)
SELECT 'A','US','Health Care'
WHERE NOT EXISTS (SELECT 1 FROM Symbol WHERE Ticker ='A');
INSERT INTO Symbol (Ticker, Region, Sector)
SELECT 'AA','US','Materials'
WHERE NOT EXISTS (SELECT 1 FROM Symbol WHERE Ticker ='AA');

INSERT INTO Price (SymbolID, [Date], PriceOpen, PriceHigh, PriceLow, PriceClose,
PriceAdj, Volume)
SELECT '1', '1/3/2000', '78.75', '78.937494', '67.375', '72,46.991788',
'46.991788', '4674400'
WHERE NOT EXISTS (SELECT 1 FROM Price WHERE SymbolID = 1 AND Date='1/3/2000');
INSERT INTO Price (SymbolID, [Date], PriceOpen, PriceHigh, PriceLow, PriceClose,
PriceAdj, Volume)
SELECT '1', '1/4/2000', '68.125', '68.875', '64.75', '66.6', '43.40213', '4765100'
WHERE NOT EXISTS (SELECT 1 FROM Price WHERE SymbolID = 1 AND Date='1/4/2000');
INSERT INTO Price (SymbolID, [Date], PriceOpen, PriceHigh, PriceLow, PriceClose,
PriceAdj, Volume)
SELECT '2', '1/3/2000', '83', '83.5625', '80.375', '80.9375', '30.672', '3103200'
```

```
WHERE NOT EXISTS (SELECT 1 FROM Price WHERE SymbolID = 2 AND Date='1/3/2000');
INSERT INTO Price (SymbolID, [Date], PriceOpen, PriceHigh, PriceLow, PriceClose,
PriceAdj, Volume)
SELECT '2', '1/4/2000', '80.9375', '81.8125', '80.3125', '81.3125',
       '30.814179', '4469600'
WHERE NOT EXISTS (SELECT 1 FROM Price WHERE SymbolID = 2 AND Date='1/4/2000');
INSERT INTO Price (SymbolID, [Date], PriceOpen, PriceHigh, PriceLow, PriceClose,
PriceAdj, Volume)
SELECT '2', '1/5/2000', '81.3125', '86.5', '81', '86',    '32.590553', '6243200'
WHERE NOT EXISTS (SELECT 1 FROM Price WHERE SymbolID = 2 AND Date='1/5/2000');
```

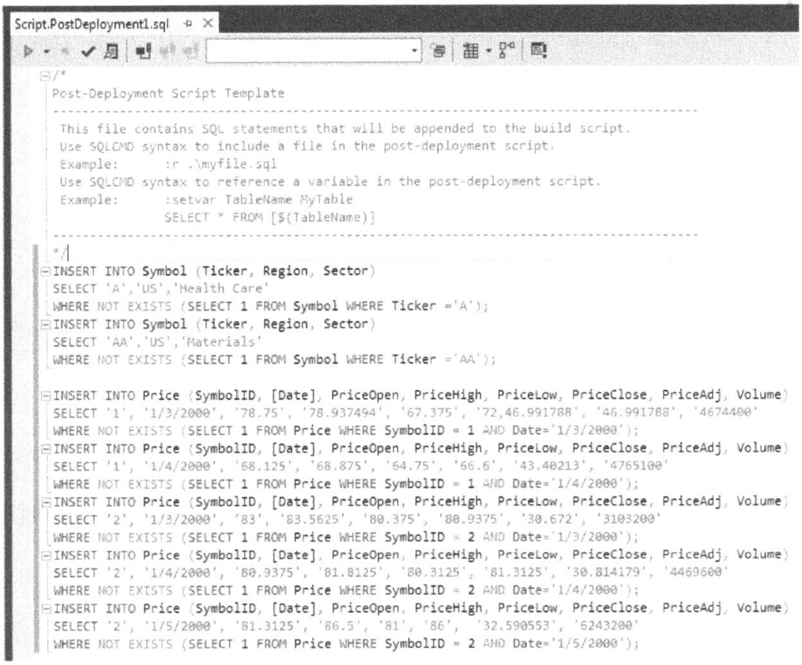

Figure 3-12. SSDT script template window.

Note that in the *INSERT* statement, we use conditional logic. This is because the *Pre* and *Post* deployment scripts always run regardless of whether we are creating or updating. It is critical to make our scripts re-runnable so a refactor of the database does not fail.

Now we are ready to deploy our database to the *LocalDB* server. Right-click the *MyDb* project and choose Set as StartUp Project. Press F5 to run our database project. If no error occurs, we can go to the SQL Server Object Explorer in Visual Studio. The database *MyDb* that we just created in the *MyDb* project should appear, as shown in Figure 3-13.

We can also view the data in the *Symbol* and *Price* tables. Inside the SSOE, right-click the *dbo.Symbol* table and choose View Data. You should see the result shown in Figure 3-14.

Right-click the *dbo.Price* table and choose View Data to check the data in this table. You should see the result shown in Figure 3-15.

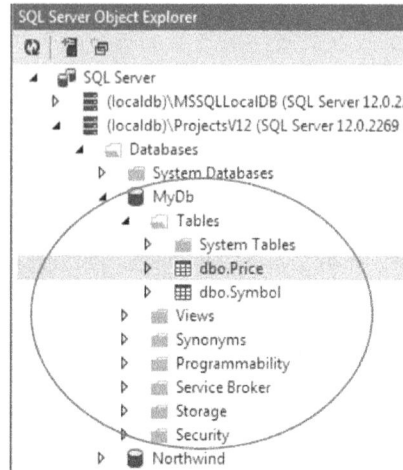

Figure 3-13. MyDb node added to SQL Server Object Explorer.

Figure 3-14. Data in the Symbol table.

Figure 3-15. Data in the Price table.

You can see from the preceding results that the data in both the *Symbol* and *Price* tables are exactly what we have specified in the *Script.PostDeployment1.sql* file of the *MyDb* project. When the project is run, SSDT automatically deploys it to the LocalDB server by default. With SSDT and LocalDB, we can develop and test database projects within Visual Studio's IDE, and then deploy the databases to production servers.

In this section, I gave a brief introduction to SSDT and LocalDB, and showed you how to import existing databases into the LocalDB server and how to manipulate the data using various SQL queries. I then presented a simple database development project using SSDT and LocalDB, which shows how to create a new database from scratch, how to add tables to the database, how to add initial seed data to the tables, and how to deploy the database project to the LocalDB server.

SSDT is a powerful tool that allows you to develop and deploy databases from within the Visual Studio IDE. The simple applications I provided here cannot possibly explain the many features of the tool in detail. In fact, there are even more advantages to creating database projects using SSDT:

- *Source control*: It is easy to keep track of your work changes over time. This is essential in a team environment.

- *Dependencies*: You can detect errors before you even deploy your DB. For example, if one of your views is referencing a non-existent table, the project will not compile and will show you an error, so you can fix it immediately.

- *Testing*: You can debug and unit test your SQL statement easily.

- *Maintainability*: It is easier to maintain your database over time. Normally, in the course of development you will add or drop objects in your database. You will also change some SQL statements in your stored procedures or functions. You can look at the changes you made by comparing different snapshots of your database. You can also test your SQL statement before it is released.

- *Deployment*: You can deploy your database to different servers easily. You can deploy to servers hosting SQL Azure or SQL Server 2005 and above. SSDT can also generate the DDL script, so you can execute it manually if you do not have direct access to your server.

- *Rich environment*: You can take advantage of the tools and features in Visual Studio, such as Intellisense.

ADO.NET Entity Framework

Nowadays Entity Framework (EF) is the most promoted database access technologies in .NET applications. The main reason is that EF allows developers without extensive knowledge about SQL to interrogate the database, create complex queries, and generate classes with the help of a user-friendly interface. The core of ADO.NET EF is in its *Entity Data Model*. EF supports a logical storage model that represents the relational schema from a database. A database often stores data in a different format than what the application can use, which forces you to retrieve data in the same structure as that contained in the database. You then need to feed the data into business entities more suited for handling business rules. EF bridges this gap between data models using mapping layers that allow data to be mapped from a relational database to a more object-oriented business model.

Creating an Entity Data Model

Most applications and databases are highly dependent on each other; namely, they are tightly coupled. It appears that any change made either in the application or in the database will affect the other end. Tight coupling is always two-way, and changing one side will require changes to be synced with the other side. If changes are not responded to properly, the application will not function in the desired manner, and the system will break down.

ADO.NET EF enables applications to access and change data represented as entities and relationships in a conceptual model. It uses information in the model and mapping files to translate object queries against entity types represented in the conceptual model into data source-specific queries. Query results are materialized into objects that EF manages.

In EF, you can define the conceptual model, storage model, and the mapping between the two in the way that best suits your application. The Entity Data Model Tools in Visual Studio allow you to create an *.edmx* file from a database or a graphical user interface and then update that file when either the database or model changes.

I will present an example that shows you how to create an *Entity Data Model* from a database and how to retrieve data from the *Entity Data Model*. Start Visual Studio 2013 and open the project *Chapter03*. Here I want to create an MVVM WPF application using Caliburn.Micro following the same steps used in Chapter 2. Add Caliburn.Micro to the References and delete *MainWindow.xaml* from the project. Add a WPF window to the project and name it *MainView*. Here is the XAML file for this view:

```
<Window x:Class="Chapter03.MainView"
        xmlns="http://schemas.microsoft.com/winfx/2006/xaml/presentation"
        xmlns:x="http://schemas.microsoft.com/winfx/2006/xaml"
        xmlns:mc="http://schemas.openxmlformats.org/markup-compatibility/2006"
        xmlns:d="http://schemas.microsoft.com/expression/blend/2008"
        Title="Chapter 3" Height="700" Width="800"
            WindowStartupLocation="CenterScreen"
        WindowState="Maximized" TextOptions.TextFormattingMode="Display">
    <DockPanel>
        <StatusBar Height="25" DockPanel.Dock="Bottom" Margin="0">
            <StatusBar.ItemsPanel>
                <ItemsPanelTemplate>
                    <Grid>
                        <Grid.RowDefinitions>
                            <RowDefinition Height="*"/>
                        </Grid.RowDefinitions>
                        <Grid.ColumnDefinitions>
                            <ColumnDefinition Width="45"/>
                            <ColumnDefinition Width="110"/>
                            <ColumnDefinition Width="*"/>
                            <ColumnDefinition Width="200"/>
                        </Grid.ColumnDefinitions>
                    </Grid>
                </ItemsPanelTemplate>
            </StatusBar.ItemsPanel>
            <StatusBarItem Grid.Column="0">
                <StackPanel Orientation="Horizontal">
                    <TextBlock Margin="10,0,0,0" Text="Status:" FontSize="10"
                            Foreground="DarkGreen"/>
                </StackPanel>
            </StatusBarItem>
            <StatusBarItem Grid.Column="1">
                <ProgressBar x:Name="ProgressValue" Width="100" Height="16"
                            BorderThickness="0" Minimum="{Binding ProgressMin}"
                            Maximum="{Binding ProgressMax}"/>
            </StatusBarItem>
            <StatusBarItem Grid.Column="2">
                <TextBlock x:Name="StatusText" FontSize="10"
                            Foreground="DarkGreen"/>
            </StatusBarItem>

            <StatusBarItem Grid.Column="3" HorizontalAlignment="Right"
                            Margin="0,0,10,0">
                <StackPanel Orientation="Horizontal">
                    <TextBlock x:Name="reportLabel" Text="{Binding
                            SelectedItem.Header, ElementName=Items}"
                            FontSize="10" Foreground="DarkGreen"
                            VerticalAlignment="Center"/>
                </StackPanel>
```

```
            </StatusBarItem>
        </StatusBar>
        <Grid Margin="10,0,10,0">
            <TabControl x:Name="Items"/>
        </Grid>
    </DockPanel>
</Window>
```

Add a new class to the project and name it *AppBootstrapper*. Here we use the following bootstrapper version:

```
using System;
using System.Collections.Generic;
using System.Linq;
using System.ComponentModel.Composition;
using System.ComponentModel.Composition.Hosting;
using System.ComponentModel.Composition.Primitives;
using Caliburn.Micro;
using System.Windows;
using System.ComponentModel;

namespace Chapter03
{
    public class AppBootstrapper : BootstrapperBase
    {
        private CompositionContainer container;

        public AppBootstrapper()
        {
            Initialize();
        }

        protected override void Configure()
        {
            container = new CompositionContainer(new
                AggregateCatalog(AssemblySource.Instance.Select(x => new
                AssemblyCatalog(x)).OfType<ComposablePartCatalog>())));
            var batch = new CompositionBatch();

            batch.AddExportedValue<IWindowManager>(new WindowManager());
            batch.AddExportedValue<IEventAggregator>(new EventAggregator());
            batch.AddExportedValue(container);

            container.Compose(batch);
        }

        protected override object GetInstance(Type serviceType, string key)
        {
            string contract = string.IsNullOrEmpty(key) ?
                AttributedModelServices.GetContractName(serviceType) : key;
            var exports = container.GetExportedValues<object>(contract);

            if (exports.Any())
                return exports.First();

            throw new Exception(string.Format("Could not locate any
```

```
                            instances of contract {0}.", contract));
            }

        protected override IEnumerable<object> GetAllInstances(Type serviceType)
        {
            return container.GetExportedValues<object>(AttributedModelServices.
                GetContractName(serviceType));
        }

        protected override void BuildUp(object instance)
        {
            container.SatisfyImportsOnce(instance);
        }

        protected override void OnStartup(object sender, StartupEventArgs e)
        {
            DisplayRootViewFor<IMain>();
        }
    }
}
```

Note that I introduce an *IMain* interface as the StartUp window because I want to use Caliburn.Micro's Conductor to automatically manage the *Screen Collection*. The *IMain* interface is very simple:

```
using Caliburn.Micro;

namespace Chapter03
{
    public interface IMain : IConductor, IGuardClose
    {
    }
}
```

You should also modify *App.xaml* according to the following:

```
<Application x:Class="Chapter03.App"
             xmlns="http://schemas.microsoft.com/winfx/2006/xaml/presentation"
             xmlns:x="http://schemas.microsoft.com/winfx/2006/xaml"
             xmlns:local="clr-namespace:Chapter03">
    <Application.Resources>
        <ResourceDictionary>
            <ResourceDictionary.MergedDictionaries>
                <ResourceDictionary>
                    <local:AppBootstrapper x:Key="bootstrapper" />
                </ResourceDictionary>
            </ResourceDictionary.MergedDictionaries>
        </ResourceDictionary>
    </Application.Resources>
</Application>
```

Add a new class to the project and name it *MainViewModel*. Here is the code for this class:

```
using System;
using System.Linq;
using Caliburn.Micro;
using System.ComponentModel.Composition;
using System.Windows;
```

```
using System.Collections.Generic;
using Chapter03.ViewModels;

namespace Chapter03
{
    [Export(typeof(IMain))]
public class MainViewModel : Conductor<IScreen>.Collection.OneActive,
IMain, IHandle<ModelEvents>
    {
        private readonly IEventAggregator _events;

        [ImportingConstructor]
        public MainViewModel([ImportMany]IEnumerable<IScreen> screens,
            IEventAggregator events)
        {
            var sc = screens.OrderBy(item => item.DisplayName);
            Items.AddRange(sc);
            this._events = events;
            _events.Subscribe(this);
            DisplayName = "Chapter 3";
        }

        public void Handle(ModelEvents evnt)
        {
            List<object> lst = evnt.EventList;
            StatusText = lst[0].ToString();
            if (lst.Count > 1)
            {
                ProgressMin = Convert.ToInt32(lst[1]);
                ProgressMax = Convert.ToInt32(lst[2]);
                ProgressValue = Convert.ToInt32(lst[3]);
            }
        }

        private int progressMin = 0;
        public int ProgressMin
        {
            get { return progressMin; }
            set
            {
                progressMin = value;
                NotifyOfPropertyChange(() => ProgressMin);
            }
        }

        private int progressMax = 1;
        public int ProgressMax
        {
            get { return progressMax; }
            set
            {
                progressMax = value;
                NotifyOfPropertyChange(() => ProgressMax);
            }
        }
```

```
        private int progressValue = 0;
        public int ProgressValue
        {
            get { return progressValue; }
            set
            {
                progressValue = value;
                NotifyOfPropertyChange(() => ProgressValue);
            }
        }
        private string statusText;
        public string StatusText
        {
            get { return statusText; }
            set
            {
                statusText = value;
                NotifyOfPropertyChange(() => StatusText);
            }
        }
    }
}
```

Pay special attention to how I use *Conductor* to manage the screen collection that provides the *Items* property. This *Items* property is bound to a *TabControl* defined in *MainView.xaml* using this naming convention:

```
<TabControl x:Name="Items"/>.
```

Now I will create an *Entity Data Model* from our existing database, *Northwind*, created previously in the *LocalDB* server. Right-click the *Chapter03* project and choose Add | New Item… Select Data in the left pane of the Add New Item window and ADO.NET Entity Data Model from the right pane, and name it *NwndModel*. Click Add to bring up the Entity Data Model Wizard, from which we choose EF Designer from database. Click the Next button, as shown in Figure 3-16.

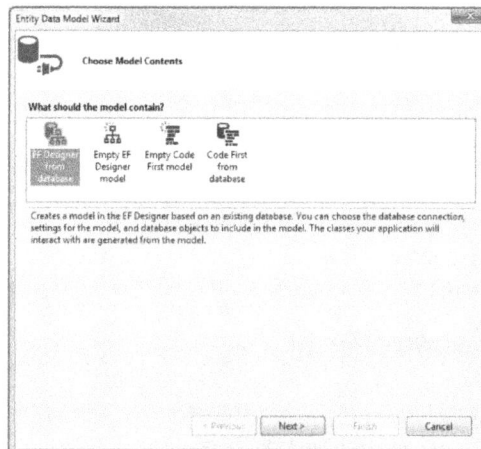

Figure 3-16. Entity Data Model Wizard.

In the next page of the Entity Data Model Wizard, check if your database is in the data connection list. If yes, select it. Otherwise, click New Connection to bring up the Connection Properties dialog. Enter your LocalDB as the Server name: (localdb)\Projects12. Choose *Northwind* in the Select or enter a database name. Click OK to close the Connection Properties dialog. Click Next in the Entity Data Model Wizard. This step will display all the *Tables*, *Views*, and *Stored Procedures* in the *Northwind* database. For this example, choose some the tables shown in Figure 3-17and keep the default checkboxes selected. Click Finish.

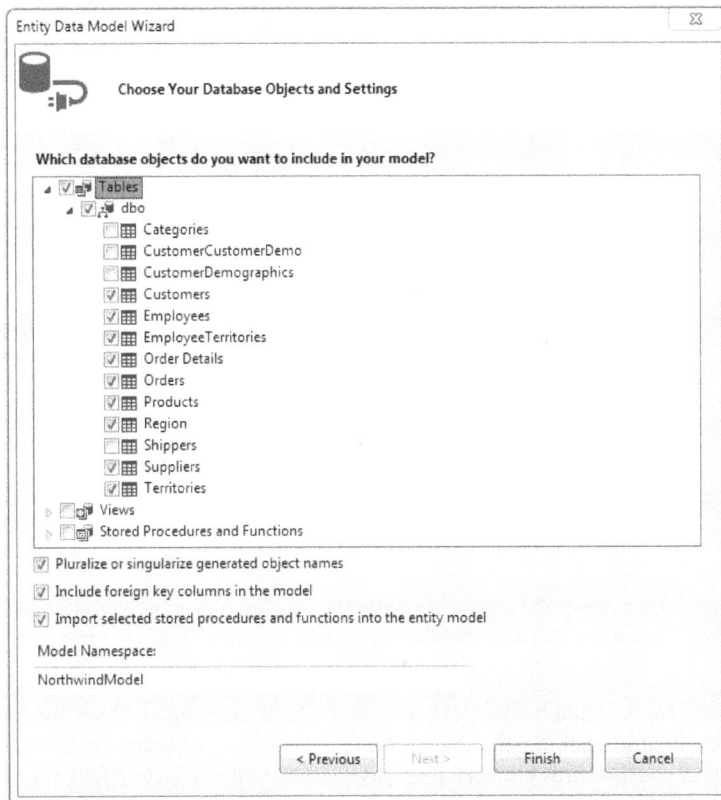

Figure 3-17. Select database objects.

Note that the checkbox *Pluralize or singularize generated object names* singularizes an entity set name if the table name in the database is plural. For example, if *Northwind* has a table names *Orders*, then the entity set would be the singular *Order*. Similarly, relationships between the models will be pluralized if the table has one-to-many or many-to-many relationships with other tables. For example, *Order* has a one-to-many relationship with *Order_Detail* table, so the *Order* entity set will have the plural property name *Order_Details* under Navigation Properties, while the *Order_Detail* entity set will have the singular property name *Order*, as shown in Figure 3-18.

The second checkbox, *Include foreign key columns in the model*, includes a foreign key property explicitly to represent the foreign key. For example, the *Region* table has a one-to-many relationship with the *Territory* table, so every territory is associated with only one region. To represent this in the model, the *Territory* entity set includes a *RegionID* property with a *Region* navigation property. If this checkbox is unchecked, then the *Territory* entity set will include only the *Region* property, but not the *RegionID* (see Figure 3-18).

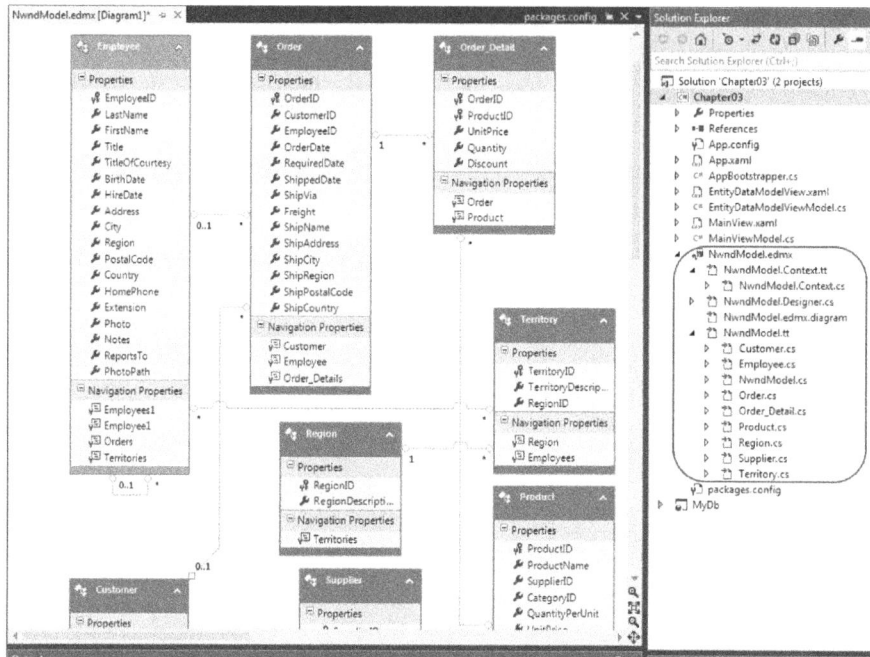

Figure 3-18. Entity Data Model mapping.

The third checkbox, *Import selected stored procedures and functions into entity model*, automatically creates *Function Imports* for the stored procedures and functions. In this example, we will not need this feature.

After clicking Finish, we will add an *NwndModel.edmx* file to the project. Open the *Entity Data Model* (EDM) designer by double-clicking the *NwndModel.edmx*. This will display all the entities for the selected tables and the relationships between them, as shown in Figure 3-18. EDM also adds a connection string in the App.*config* file as shown below:

```
<?xml version="1.0" encoding="utf-8"?>
<configuration>
  <configSections>
<!-- For more information on Entity Framework configuration, visit
       http://go.microsoft.com/fwlink/?LinkID=237468 -->
<section name="entityFramework"
       type="System.Data.Entity.Internal.ConfigFile.EntityFrameworkSection,
       EntityFramework, Version=6.0.0.0, Culture=neutral,
       PublicKeyToken=b77a5c561934e089" requirePermission="false" />
  </configSections>
  <startup>
    <supportedRuntime version="v4.0" sku=".NETFramework,Version=v4.5" />
  </startup>
  <connectionStrings>
<add name="NorthwindEntities"
       connectionString="metadata=res://*/NwndModel.csdl|res://*/NwndModel.ssdl|res:
```

```
//*/NwndModel.msl;provider=System.Data.SqlClient;provider
connection string=&quot;data source=(localdb)\ProjectsV12;
initial catalog=Northwind;integrated
security=True;MultipleActiveResultSets=True;App=EntityFramework&quot;"
providerName="System.Data.EntityClient" />
  </connectionStrings>
  <entityFramework>
<defaultConnectionFactory
      type="System.Data.Entity.Infrastructure.SqlConnectionFactory,
            EntityFramework" />
    <providers>
      <provider invariantName="System.Data.SqlClient"
          type="System.Data.Entity.SqlServer.SqlProviderServices,
          EntityFramework.SqlServer" />
    </providers>
  </entityFramework>
</configuration>
```

This way, you can create a simple EDM from your existing database. Note that every EDM generates one context class (*NwndModel.Context.cs* in this example) and one entity class for each database table included in the EDM.

Working with Entity Data

Now that we have created an entity data model in the preceding section, we will examine the different types of EF-supported queries, which are in turn converted into SQL queries for the underlying database. We can also use LINQ (Language-Integrated Query) to query different data sources. LINQ-to-Entities operates on EF entities to access the data from the underlying database.

Add two new folders to the *Chapter03* project and name them *ViewModels* and *Views*. Add a new *UserControl* to the *Views* folder and name it *CustomersView*. Here is the XAML code for this view:

```
<UserControl x:Class="Chapter03.Views.CustomersView"
            xmlns="http://schemas.microsoft.com/winfx/2006/xaml/presentation"
            xmlns:x="http://schemas.microsoft.com/winfx/2006/xaml"
            xmlns:mc="http://schemas.openxmlformats.org/markup-compatibility/2006"
            xmlns:d="http://schemas.microsoft.com/expression/blend/2008"
            mc:Ignorable="d"
            d:DesignHeight="300" d:DesignWidth="600">
    <Grid>
        <Grid.ColumnDefinitions>
            <ColumnDefinition Width="200"/>
            <ColumnDefinition Width="*"/>
        </Grid.ColumnDefinitions>
        <StackPanel Margin="0 20 0 5">
            <Button x:Name="GetCustomers" Content="Get Customers Data" Width="150"/>
        </StackPanel>
        <DataGrid x:Name="MyCustomers" ColumnWidth="*" CanUserAddRows="False"
                Grid.Column="1" FontSize="10"/>
    </Grid>
</UserControl>
```

Add a new class to the *ViewModels* folder and name it *CustomersViewModel*. Here is the code for this class:

```
using System;
using System.Linq;
using Caliburn.Micro;
using System.Collections.ObjectModel;
using System.ComponentModel.Composition;
using System.Windows.Documents;
using System.Collections.Generic;

namespace Chapter03.ViewModels
{
    [Export(typeof(IScreen)), PartCreationPolicy(CreationPolicy.NonShared)]
    public class CustomersViewModel : Screen
    {
        private readonly IEventAggregator _events;
        private BindableCollection<Customer> myCustomers;

        [ImportingConstructor]
        public CustomersViewModel(IEventAggregator events)
        {
            this._events = events;
            DisplayName = "01. Customers";
            myCustomers = new BindableCollection<Customer>();
        }

        public BindableCollection<Customer> MyCustomers
        {
            get { return myCustomers; }
            set { myCustomers = value; }
        }

        public void GetCustomers()
        {
            using (var db = new NorthwindEntities())
            {
                var query = from d in db.Customers select d;
                MyCustomers.Clear();
                MyCustomers.AddRange(query);
            }
            _events.PublishOnUIThread(new ModelEvents(new List<object>(new
                object[] { "From Customers: Count = " +
                MyCustomers.Count.ToString() })));
        }
    }
}
```

Right-click on the *Chapter03* project and choose Set as StartUp Project. Press F5 to run the application. Click the *Get Customers Data* button; the data will be displayed on your screen as shown in Figure 3-19. Note the message in the status bar area. This message is displayed on *MainView* and is published from *CustomersView*. We achieve this communication between different view models using CM's *IEventAggregator*, as discussed in Chapter 2.

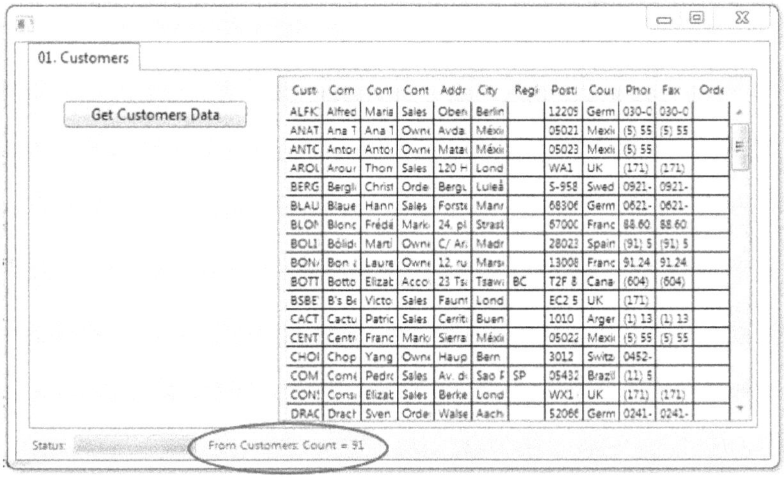

Figure 3-19. Customers' data from Entity Data Model.

Here I use a LINQ query to retrieve the *Customers* data from the EDM entities:

```
using (var db = new NorthwindEntities())
{
    var query = from d in db.Customers select d;
    MyCustomers.Clear();
    MyCustomers.AddRange(query);
}
```

Inside the *using*() statement, I create a new instance of *NorthwindEntities*, *db*, and then query data from the *Customers* entity. The *using* statement ensures that once it goes out of scope it will automatically call the *Dispose* method of the *DbContext*. I also convert the query into a *BindableCollection*, *MyCustomers*. Instead of using LINQ, you can also use a native SQL query to retrieve data from EDM entities. The following SQL query will give you the same result as that shown in Figure 3-19:

```
using (var db = new NorthwindEntities())
{
    var query = db.Customers.SqlQuery("SELECT * FROM Customers");
    MyCustomers.Clear();
    MyCustomers.AddRange(query);
}
```

Previously, we discussed how to use SQL queries for aggregate functions and pivot statement (see Figure 3.7 and 3-8). Now I will show you how to get the same results using LINQ-to-entities. Add a new *UserControl* to the *Views* folder and name it *AggregateView*. Here is the XAML file for this view:

```
<UserControl x:Class="Chapter03.Views.AggregateView"
             xmlns="http://schemas.microsoft.com/winfx/2006/xaml/presentation"
             xmlns:x="http://schemas.microsoft.com/winfx/2006/xaml"
             xmlns:mc="http://schemas.openxmlformats.org/markup-compatibility/2006"
             xmlns:d="http://schemas.microsoft.com/expression/blend/2008"
             mc:Ignorable="d"
             d:DesignHeight="300" d:DesignWidth="600">
    <Grid>
        <Grid.ColumnDefinitions>
            <ColumnDefinition Width="200"/>
```

```xml
            <ColumnDefinition Width="*"/>
        </Grid.ColumnDefinitions>
        <StackPanel Margin="0 20 0 5">
            <Button x:Name="GetAggregate" Content="Start Aggregation" Width="150"/>
            <Button x:Name="GetPivot" Content="Get Pivot Data" Width="150"
                    Margin="0 10 0 0"/>
        </StackPanel>
        <Grid Grid.Column="1">
            <Grid.RowDefinitions>
                <RowDefinition/>
                <RowDefinition/>
            </Grid.RowDefinitions>
            <DataGrid x:Name="MyAggregates" ColumnWidth="*" CanUserAddRows="False"
                    Grid.Row="0" FontSize="10"/>
            <DataGrid x:Name="MyPivots" ColumnWidth="*" CanUserAddRows="False"
                    Grid.Row ="1" FontSize="10"/>
        </Grid>
    </Grid>
</UserControl>
```

Here I add two *DataGrid* controls to the view, which will host the aggregate and pivot results respectively. Add a new class to the *ViewModel* folder and name it *AggregateViewModel*. Here is the code for this class:

```csharp
using System;
using System.Linq;
using Caliburn.Micro;
using System.Collections.ObjectModel;
using System.ComponentModel.Composition;
using System.Windows.Documents;
using System.Collections.Generic;

namespace Chapter03.ViewModels
{
    [Export(typeof(IScreen)), PartCreationPolicy(CreationPolicy.NonShared)]
    public class AggregateViewModel : Screen
    {
        private NorthwindEntities db = new NorthwindEntities();
        private readonly IEventAggregator _events;
        private BindableCollection<AggregateValue> myAggregates;
        private BindableCollection<Pivotdata> myPivots;

        [ImportingConstructor]
        public AggregateViewModel(IEventAggregator events)
        {
            this._events = events;
            DisplayName = "02. Aggregates";
            myAggregates = new BindableCollection<AggregateValue>();
            myPivots = new BindableCollection<Pivotdata>();
        }

        public BindableCollection<AggregateValue> MyAggregates
        {
            get { return myAggregates; }
            set { myAggregates = value; }
        }
```

```
public BindableCollection<Pivotdata> MyPivots
{
    get { return myPivots; }
    set { myPivots = value; }
}

public void GetAggregate()
{
    using (var db = new NorthwindEntities())
    {
        var query = (from o in db.Orders
                    join e in db.Employees on o.EmployeeID equals
                        e.EmployeeID
                    group new { e, o } by new { e.EmployeeID, e.LastName }
                        into g
                    select new
                    {
                        EmployeeID = g.Key.EmployeeID,
                        LastName = g.Key.LastName,
                        Min = g.Min(x => x.o.Freight),
                        Max = g.Max(x => x.o.Freight),
                        Avg = g.Average(x => x.o.Freight),
                        Sum = g.Sum(x => x.o.Freight)
                    }).OrderBy(p => p.LastName);

        foreach (var q in query)
            MyAggregates.Add(new AggregateValue
            {
                EmployeeID = q.EmployeeID,
                LastName = q.LastName,
                Min = (double)q.Min,
                Max = (double)q.Max,
                Sum = (double)q.Sum,
                Avg = (double)q.Avg
            });
    }
    _events.PublishOnUIThread(new ModelEvents(new List<object>(new object[]
        { "From Aggregates: Count = " + MyAggregates.Count.ToString() })));
}

public void GetPivot()
{
    using (var db = new NorthwindEntities())
    {
        var query = (from o in db.Orders
                    join e in db.Employees on o.EmployeeID equals
                        e.EmployeeID
                    select new { e.LastName, o.OrderDate })
                    .GroupBy(x => x.LastName)
                    .Select(y => new
                    {
                        LastName = y.Key,
                        A1996 = (y.Where(z => z.OrderDate.Value.Year ==
                                1996)).Count(),
```

```
                               A1997 = (y.Where(z => z.OrderDate.Value.Year ==
                                      1997)).Count(),
                        }).OrderBy(p => p.LastName);

            foreach (var q in query)
                MyPivots.Add(new Pivotdata
                {
                    LastName = q.LastName,
                    A1996 = q.A1996,
                    A1997 = q.A1997
                });
        }
        _events.PublishOnUIThread(new ModelEvents(new List<object>(new object[]
            { "From Pivots: Count = " + MyPivots.Count.ToString() })));
    }
}

public class AggregateValue
{
    public int EmployeeID { get; set; }
    public string LastName { get; set; }
    public double Min { get; set; }
    public double Max { get; set; }
    public double Sum { get; set; }
    public double Avg { get; set; }
}

public class Pivotdata
{
    public string LastName { get; set; }
    public int A1996 { get; set; }
    public int A1997 { get; set; }
}
}
```

Here, we define two entity classes, *AggregateValue* and *PivotData*, used to represent the aggregate and pivot results. You should pay special attention to the *GetAggregate* and *GetPivot* methods and see how they use the aggregate function, join, group, and Lambda expressions in LINQ- to-Entities. Running the project by pressing F5 produces the results shown in Figure 3-20.

You can compare the results in Figure 3-20 to those shown in Figure 3-7 and 3-8. You may notice that one field, *StDev*, is missing in Figure 3-20 because there is no built-in function for computing standard deviation in LINQ. You can define an extension method in LINQ to perform the calculation for standard deviation, which I will not discuss here.

Yahoo Stock Data Downloader

In the preceding *Database Development* section, we created a database called *MyDb* that contains two tables: *Symbol* and *Price*. The *Symbol* table is used to store the ticker information of the stocks and the *Price* table is used to store the price data for the stocks. These two tables are basically empty except for a few seed records. Here, I will show you how to add more tickers to the *Symbol* table from a CVS file, and then how to create an interface used to insert stock price data into the *Price* table via downloading the market data from the Yahoo Finance website.

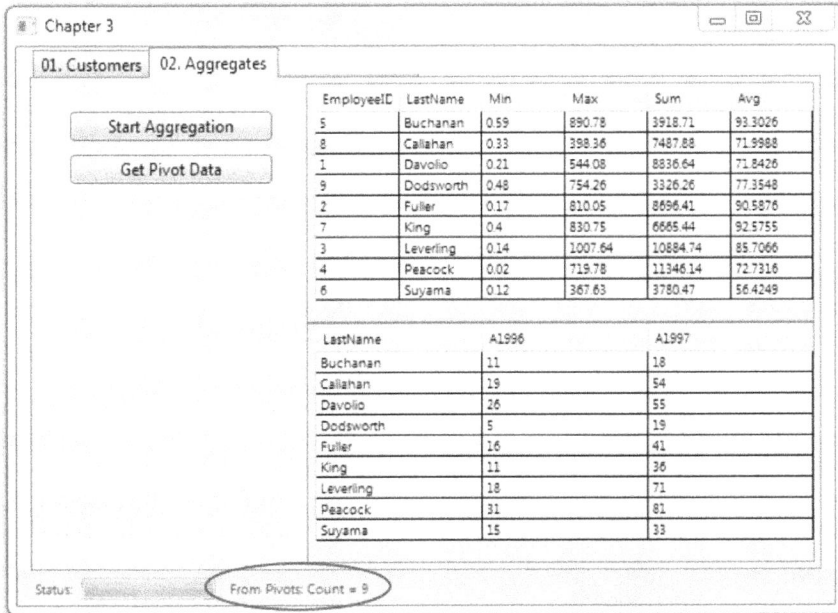

Figure 3-20. Aggregate and pivot results.

CSV Convertor and Yahoo Market Data API

In this section, we will implement an interface for downloading stock market data from Yahoo Finance's website.

First, we need to create an entity data model for our database, *MyDb*. Following the same procedure as we did when we created *Entity Data Model* for the *Northwind* database, we can easily create an *Entity Data Model* for our *MyDb* database, and name it *MyDbModel*. The model should include two tables: *Symbol* and *Price*. Figure 3-21 shows the table diagram in the designer of *MyDbModel.edmx*.

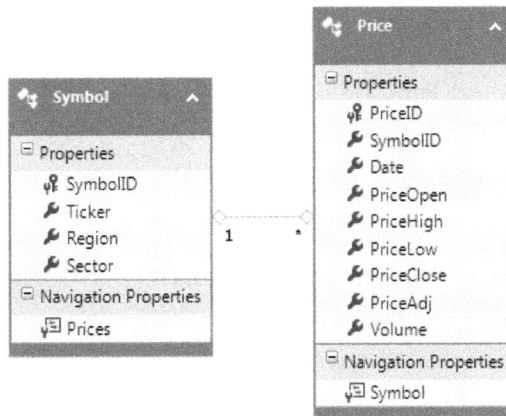

Figure 3-21

I have already created a CSV file called *StockTickers.csv*, which contains the stock tickers to be inserted into the *Symbol* table, and added it to the *ViewModels* folder of the *Chapter03* project. The following shows the format for this CSV file:

```
Ticker,Region,Sector
ABK,US,Financials
ACE,US,Financials
ACGL,US,Financials
ACN,US,Information Technology
ADI,US,Information Technology
ADP,US,Information Technology
AFG,US,Financials
AFL,US,Financials
........
```

The first line in the CSV file is the header, and the comma is used to separate data fields. We need to implement a method to import this file and convert it into a collection that the .NET application can use and display on screen. To that end, add a new class to the *ViewModels* folder and name it *ModelHelper*. I will start by adding some utility functions to this helper class. The first function I will add is the CSV convertor, which converts the CSV file into a *BindableCollection*, as shown in the following code:

```
using System;
using System.Collections.Generic;
using System.Data;
using System.Data.Odbc;
using System.Globalization;
using System.IO;
using System.Linq;
using System.Net;
using Caliburn.Micro;
using System.Data.Entity;
using System.Data.Entity.Core.Objects.DataClasses;

namespace Chapter03.ViewModels
{
    public class ModelHelper
    {
        public static BindableCollection<Symbol> CsvToSymbolCollection(string
            csvFile)
        {
            FileStream fs = new FileStream(csvFile, FileMode.Open, FileAccess.Read,
                FileShare.ReadWrite);
            StreamReader sr = new StreamReader(fs);
            List<String> lst = new List<string>();
            while (!sr.EndOfStream)
                lst.Add(sr.ReadLine());

            string[] fields = lst[0].Split(new char[] { ',' });
            var res = new BindableCollection<Symbol>();

            for (int i = 1; i < lst.Count; i++)
            {
                fields = lst[i].Split(',');
                res.Add(new Symbol
                {
                    Ticker = fields[0],
```

```
                        Region = fields[1],
                        Sector = fields[2]
                });
            }
            return res;
        }
    }
}
```

The *CsvToSymbolCollection* method first reads the CSV file into the application using a stream reader, then splits the fields with comma, and finally puts all the fields into a collection of the *Symbol* type. The *Symbol* type is the *Symbol.cs* entity class generated automatically by *Entity Data Model*.

We will then implement an interface for downloading stock market data from Yahoo Finance's website, which we will convert data into a collection of the *Price* type that can be used in our .NET application. Like the *Symbol* type, the *Price* type is the *Price.cs* entity class that is also generated automatically by *Entity Data Model*. Add the following methods to the *ModelHelper* class:

```
public static BindableCollection<Price> GetYahooStockData(int symbolId,
        string ticker, DateTime? startDate, DateTime? endDate)
    {
        //string ticker = IdToTicker(symbolId);
        string urlTemplate =
            @"http://ichart.finance.yahoo.com/table.csv?s=[symbol]&a=
        [startMonth]&b=[startDay]&c=[startYear]&d=[endMonth]&e=[endDay]&f=
            [endYear]&g=d&ignore=.csv";
        if (!endDate.HasValue) endDate = DateTime.Now;
        if (!startDate.HasValue) startDate = DateTime.Now.AddYears(-5);
        if (ticker == null || ticker.Length < 1)
            throw new ArgumentException("Symbol invalid: " + ticker);

        // NOTE: Yahoo's scheme uses a month number 1 less than actual
        // e.g. Jan. ="0"
        int strtMo = startDate.Value.Month - 1;
        string startMonth = strtMo.ToString();
        string startDay = startDate.Value.Day.ToString();
        string startYear = startDate.Value.Year.ToString();

        int endMo = endDate.Value.Month - 1;
        string endMonth = endMo.ToString();
        string endDay = endDate.Value.Day.ToString();
        string endYear = endDate.Value.Year.ToString();

        urlTemplate = urlTemplate.Replace("[symbol]", ticker);

        urlTemplate = urlTemplate.Replace("[startMonth]", startMonth);
        urlTemplate = urlTemplate.Replace("[startDay]", startDay);
        urlTemplate = urlTemplate.Replace("[startYear]", startYear);
        urlTemplate = urlTemplate.Replace("[endMonth]", endMonth);
        urlTemplate = urlTemplate.Replace("[endDay]", endDay);
        urlTemplate = urlTemplate.Replace("[endYear]", endYear);
        string history = String.Empty;
        WebClient wc = new WebClient();
        try
        {
            history = wc.DownloadString(urlTemplate);
```

```csharp
    }
    catch
    {
        //throw wex;
    }
    finally
    {
        wc.Dispose();
    }
    DataTable dt = new DataTable();
    // trim off unused characters from end of line
    history = history.Replace("\r", "");
    // split to array on end of line
    string[] rows = history.Split('\n');
    // split to colums
    string[] colNames = rows[0].Split(',');
    //add the columns to the DataTable
    foreach (string colName in colNames)
        dt.Columns.Add(colName);

    DataRow row = null;
    string[] rowValues;
    object[] rowItems;
    for (int i = rows.Length - 1; i > 0; i--)
    {
        rowValues = rows[i].Split(',');
        row = dt.NewRow();
        rowItems = StringArrayToObjectArray(rowValues);
        if (rowItems[0] != null && (string)rowItems[0] != "")
        {
            row.ItemArray = rowItems;
            dt.Rows.Add(row);
        }
    }

    var res = new BindableCollection<Price>();
    foreach(DataRow r in dt.Rows)
    {
        DateTime date = (DateTime.ParseExact(r["Date"].ToString(),
            "yyyy-MM-dd", CultureInfo.InvariantCulture).
            ToLocalTime()).AddDays(1);
        date = Convert.ToDateTime(date.ToShortDateString());
        res.Add(new Price
        {
            SymbolID = symbolId,
            Date = date,
            PriceOpen = Convert.ToDouble(r["Open"]),
            PriceHigh = Convert.ToDouble(r["High"]),
            PriceLow = Convert.ToDouble(r["Low"]),
            PriceClose = Convert.ToDouble(r["Close"]),
            PriceAdj = Convert.ToDouble(r["Adj Close"]),
            Volume = Convert.ToDouble(r["Volume"])
        });
    }
    return res;
```

```
    }


    private static object[] StringArrayToObjectArray(string[] input)
    {
        int elements = input.Length;
        object[] objArray = new object[elements];
        input.CopyTo(objArray, 0);
        return objArray;
    }

    public static string IdToTicker(int symbolId)
    {
        string ticker = string.Empty;

        using (var db = new MyDbEntities())
        {
            var query = from s in db.Symbols
                        where (s.SymbolID == symbolId)
                        select s.Ticker;

            foreach (var q in query)
                ticker = q.ToString();
        }
        return ticker;
    }
```

Yahoo Finance has a popular API that allows you to download daily stock data from its library. In the *GetYahooStockData* method, the input parameters include *SymbolID*, *Ticker*, and date range. You do not need *SymbolID* to get stock data from Yahoo, but you will need it to convert Yahoo data into a collection of the *Price* type. With this method, we can download the CSV file with historical prices from Yahoo Finance's website using a special URL template. We construct the URL address from variables inside the method, so that it changes for each value of the stock ticker and the date range required. We convert the Yahoo data into a collection of the *Price* type by a two-step process: first we store the Yahoo data in a *DataTable* format, then we convert the data in the *DataTable* into a *BindableCollection* of the *Price* type. The private method *StringArrayToObjectArray* is used by *GetYahooStockData* when storing data in the *DataTable*. The other method, *IdToTicker*, which allows you to get the *Ticker* from *SymbolID*, will be used later.

Download Data from Yahoo

We have implemented the *CsvToSymbolCollection* method in the *ModelHelper* class. Here we will use it to import the CSV file and add more tickers to the *Symbol* table in the database. Add the following two overloading methods to the *ModelHelper* class:

```
public static void SymbolInsert(Symbol symbol)
{
    using (var db = new MyDbEntities())
    {
        try
        {
            db.Symbols.Add(symbol);
            db.SaveChanges();
        }
```

```
        catch { }
    }
}

public static void SymbolInsert(BindableCollection<Symbol> symbols)
{
    using(var db = new MyDbEntities())
    {
        try
        {
            foreach (var s in symbols)
            {
                var symbol = new Symbol();
                symbol = s;
                db.Symbols.Add(symbol);
            }
            db.SaveChanges();
        }
        catch { }
    }
}
```

The first method takes a single *Symbol* entity as input and saves the information of a single ticker in the *Symbol* table in our *MyDb* database, and the second method takes a collection of *Symbol* entities as input and saves to the database for all the tickers in the collection. The *SaveChanges* method of *ObjectContext* (or *MyDbEntities* here) is a gateway to persist all changes made to entities in the database. When we call the *SaveChanges* method, it performs an insert, update, or delete operation on the database based on the *EntityState* of the entities.

Similarly, we need to add two overloading methods for the *Price* entity to the *ModelHelper* class:

```
public static void PriceInsert(Price price)
{
    using (var db = new MyDbEntities())
    {
        try
        {
            db.Prices.Add(price);
            db.SaveChanges();
        }
        catch { }
    }
}

public static void PriceInsert(BindableCollection<Price> prices)
{
    using (var db = new MyDbEntities())
    {
        try
        {
            foreach (var p in prices)
            {
                var price = new Price();
                price = p;
                db.Prices.Add(price);
            }
```

```
                db.SaveChanges();
            }
            catch { }
        }
    }
}
```

The first method takes a single *Price* entity as input and saves the information of a single ticker into the *Price* table in our *MyDb* database; the second method takes a collection of *Price* entities as input and saves information for all prices in the collection to the database.

Add the following method to the *ModelHelper* class:

```
public static BindableCollection<Symbol> GetTickers()
{
    var res = new BindableCollection<Symbol>();
    using (var db = new MyDbEntities())
    {
        try
        {
            var query = from s in db.Symbols orderby s.Ticker select s;
            res.AddRange(query);
        }
        catch { }
    }
    return res;
}
```

This method will be used to retrieve all tickers from the *Symbol* table in the database.

Add a new *UserControl* to the *Views* folder and name it *YahooLoaderView*. The following is XAML for this view:

```
<UserControl x:Class="Chapter03.Views.YahooLoaderView"
             xmlns="http://schemas.microsoft.com/winfx/2006/xaml/presentation"
             xmlns:x="http://schemas.microsoft.com/winfx/2006/xaml"
             xmlns:mc="http://schemas.openxmlformats.org/markup-compatibility/2006"
             xmlns:d="http://schemas.microsoft.com/expression/blend/2008"
             mc:Ignorable="d"
             d:DesignHeight="600" d:DesignWidth="600">
    <Grid>
        <Grid.ColumnDefinitions>
            <ColumnDefinition Width="200"/>
            <ColumnDefinition Width="*"/>
        </Grid.ColumnDefinitions>
        <StackPanel Margin="0 20 10 5">
            <GroupBox Header="Add Ticker" Margin="0">
                <StackPanel Margin="0 5 0 5">
                    <StackPanel Orientation="Horizontal">
                        <TextBlock Text="Ticker" Width="75"/>
                        <TextBox x:Name="Ticker" Width="100"/>
                    </StackPanel>
                    <StackPanel Orientation="Horizontal" Margin="0 5 0 0">
                        <TextBlock Text="Region" Width="75"/>
                        <TextBox x:Name="Region" Width="100"/>
                    </StackPanel>
                    <StackPanel Orientation="Horizontal" Margin="0 5 0 0">
                        <TextBlock Text="Sector" Width="75"/>
```

```xml
                        <TextBox x:Name="Sector" Width="100"/>
                    </StackPanel>
                    <Button x:Name="AddTicker" Content="Add Ticker" Width="100"
                            Margin="0 10 0 0"/>
                </StackPanel>
            </GroupBox>
            <GroupBox Header="Add Tickers from CSV" Margin="0 10 0 0">
                <StackPanel Margin="0 5 0 5">
                    <TextBlock Text="File Location:"/>
                    <TextBox x:Name="TickerFile" Width="180" Margin="0 5 0 0"/>
                    <Button x:Name="LoadCsv" Content="Load CSV File" Width="100"
                            Margin="0 10 0 0"/>
                    <Button x:Name="AddTickers" Content="Add Tickers" Width="100"
                            Margin="0 10 0 0"/>
                </StackPanel>
            </GroupBox>
            <GroupBox Header="Stock Data from Yahoo" Margin="0 10 0 0">
                <StackPanel Margin="0 5 0 5">
                    <StackPanel Orientation="Horizontal">
                        <TextBlock Text="SymbolID" Width="75"/>
                        <TextBox x:Name="SymbolID" Width="100"/>
                    </StackPanel>
                    <StackPanel Orientation="Horizontal" Margin="0 5 0 0">
                        <TextBlock Text="StartDate" Width="75"/>
                        <TextBox x:Name="StartDate" Width="100"/>
                    </StackPanel>
                    <StackPanel Orientation="Horizontal" Margin="0 5 0 0">
                        <TextBlock Text="EndDate" Width="75"/>
                        <TextBox x:Name="EndDate" Width="100"/>
                    </StackPanel>
                    <Button x:Name="GetPrice" Content="Get Price" Width="100"
                            Margin="0 10 0 0"/>
                    <Button x:Name="SavePrice" Content="Save Price" Width="100"
                            Margin="0 10 0 0"/>
                    <Button x:Name="GetPrices" Content="Get All Prices" Width="100"
                            Margin="0 10 0 0"/>
                </StackPanel>
            </GroupBox>
        </StackPanel>
        <Grid Grid.Column="1">
            <Grid.RowDefinitions>
                <RowDefinition/>
                <RowDefinition/>
            </Grid.RowDefinitions>
            <DataGrid x:Name="TickerCollection" ColumnWidth="*"
                      CanUserAddRows="False" Grid.Row="0" FontSize="10"/>
            <DataGrid x:Name="PriceCollection" ColumnWidth="*"
                      CanUserAddRows="False" Grid.Row ="1" FontSize="10"/>
        </Grid>
    </Grid>
</UserControl>
```

You can see from the designer in Visual Studio that the *Grid* divides the view into two panes. The left pane has three *GroupBox* controls. The first group box, *Add Ticker*, lets you add a single ticker to the database by specifying the ticker name, region, and sector. The second group box, *Add Tickers from*

CSV, lets you add multiple tickers from a CSV file. You can specify the file location and click the *Load CSV File* button to load the file, and the results will be displayed in the *DataGrid* control. After checking the results on the screen, you can click the *Add Tickers* button to insert tickers into the database.

The third group box, *Stock Data from Yahoo*, lets you download stock data from Yahoo Finance's website. You can download data for a single stock by specifying its *SymbolID* and date range; then click the *Save Price* button. Alternatively, clicking on the *Get All Prices* button will download stock data for all tickers stored in the *Symbol* table for the specified date range and save all data to the *Price* table in the database.

Next, we need to implement the corresponding view model for this view. Add a new class to the *ViewModels* folder and name it *YahooLoaderViewModel*. Here is the code for this class:

```
using System;
using System.Collections.Generic;
using System.Linq;
using System.Text;
using System.Threading.Tasks;
using Caliburn.Micro;
using System.ComponentModel.Composition;
using System.Reflection;
using System.IO;

namespace Chapter03.ViewModels
{
    [Export(typeof(IScreen)), PartCreationPolicy(CreationPolicy.NonShared)]
    public class YahooLoaderViewModel : Screen
    {
        private readonly IEventAggregator _events;
        [ImportingConstructor]
        public YahooLoaderViewModel(IEventAggregator events)
        {
            this._events = events;
            DisplayName = "03. Yahoo Loader";
            StartDate = Convert.ToDateTime("1/1/2010");
            EndDate = Convert.ToDateTime("1/1/2015");
            TickerFile = Directory.GetParent(Assembly.GetExecutingAssembly().
                Location).Parent.Parent.FullName + @"\ViewModels\StockTickers.csv";
            TickerCollection = new BindableCollection<Symbol>();
            PriceCollection = new BindableCollection<Price>();
            SymbolID = 1;
        }

        private string ticker;
        public string Ticker
        {
            get { return ticker; }
            set
            {
                ticker = value;
                NotifyOfPropertyChange(() => Ticker);
            }
        }

        private string region;
```

```
public string Region
{
    get { return region; }
    set
    {
        region = value;
        NotifyOfPropertyChange(() => Region);
    }
}

private string sector;
public string Sector
{
    get { return sector; }
    set
    {
        sector = value;
        NotifyOfPropertyChange(() => Sector);
    }
}

private int symbolId;
public int SymbolID
{
    get { return symbolId; }
    set
    {
        symbolId = value;
        NotifyOfPropertyChange(() => SymbolID);
    }
}

private DateTime startDate;
public DateTime StartDate
{
    get { return startDate; }
    set
    {
        startDate = value;
        NotifyOfPropertyChange(() => StartDate);
    }
}

private DateTime endDate;
public DateTime EndDate
{
    get { return endDate; }
    set
    {
        endDate = value;
        NotifyOfPropertyChange(() => EndDate);
    }
}

public string TickerFile { get; set; }
```

```csharp
public BindableCollection<Symbol> TickerCollection { get; set; }
public BindableCollection<Price> PriceCollection { get; set; }


public void AddTicker()
{
    Symbol symbol = new Symbol();
    symbol.Ticker = Ticker;
    symbol.Region = Region;
    symbol.Sector = Sector;

    ModelHelper.SymbolInsert(symbol);
    _events.PublishOnUIThread(new ModelEvents(new List<object>(new
        object[] { "Add single ticker to Symbol: name = " + Ticker })));
}

public void LoadCsv()
{
    var tickers = ModelHelper.CsvToSymbolCollection(TickerFile);
    TickerCollection.Clear();
    TickerCollection.AddRange(tickers);
    _events.PublishOnUIThread(new ModelEvents(new List<object>(new
        object[] { "From CSV file loading: Count = " +
        TickerCollection.Count.ToString() })));
}

public void AddTickers()
{
    ModelHelper.SymbolInsert(TickerCollection);
    _events.PublishOnUIThread(new ModelEvents(new List<object>(new
        object[] { "Add Tickers to Symbol: Count = " +
        TickerCollection.Count.ToString() })));
}

public void GetPrice()
{
    string tk = ModelHelper.IdToTicker(SymbolID);
    var prices = ModelHelper.GetYahooStockData(SymbolID, tk,
        StartDate, EndDate);
    PriceCollection.Clear();
    PriceCollection.AddRange(prices);
    _events.PublishOnUIThread(new ModelEvents(new List<object>(new
        object[] { "Get Price From Yahoo: Count = " +
        PriceCollection.Count.ToString() })));
}

public void SavePrice()
{
    if(PriceCollection.Count>0)
    {
        ModelHelper.PriceInsert(PriceCollection);
        _events.PublishOnUIThread(new ModelEvents(new List<object>(new
            object[] { "Save Price: Count = " +
            PriceCollection.Count.ToString() })));
    }
```

```
        }

    public async void GetPrices()
    {
        await Task.Run(() =>
            {
                TickerCollection.Clear();
                var tks = ModelHelper.GetTickers();
                TickerCollection.AddRange(tks);

                List<object> objs = new List<object>();
                objs.Add("Get  data from Yahoo:");
                objs.Add(0);
                objs.Add(TickerCollection.Count);
                objs.Add(0);

                int count = 0;
                foreach (var tc in TickerCollection)
                {
                    var price = ModelHelper.GetYahooStockData(tc.SymbolID,
                        tc.Ticker, StartDate, EndDate);
                    if (price.Count > 0)
                    {
                        ModelHelper.PriceInsert(price);
                        objs[0] = string.Format("Get data from Yahoo:
                        Ticker = {0}, Count = {1}, Records = {2}", tc.Ticker,
                            count, price.Count);
                        objs[3] = count;
                        _events.PublishOnUIThread(new ModelEvents(objs));
                    }
                    count++;
                }
            });
    }
}
```

Here we first define several properties that will be bound to the controls in the view. Two collections, *TickerCollection* and *PriceCollection*, will be bound to two *DataGrid* controls in the view. Pay attention to the definitions of the methods that call the functions implemented in the *ModelHelper* class. In this example, we place all the database-access related code into the *ModelHelper* class. This class corresponds to the *Data Access Layer* (DAL). The purpose of DAL is to simplify access to the database and isolate data access from applications. This is a good practice in developing .NET applications. Basically, there should be no SQL and *Entity Data Model*-related code anywhere other than DAL, and only DAL should know the structure of your database.

In the past, creating an easy-to-use DAL in your application could be a tedious and long-winded process involving many process steps, such as the connection string, SQL commands, data readers, data adapters, etc. With the *Entity Data Model*, you can easily implement DAL from a database with minimal effort, as we did in the *ModelHelper* class.

You may notice that there is a lot of redundant code in the *ModelHelper*. For example, the structure for the *SymbolInsert* and *PriceInsert* methods is basically the same. In real-world .NET applications, instead of implementing *Create, Read, Update*, and *Delete* (CRUD) methods for each entity, you should use the generic repository pattern. The repository pattern is intended to create an abstraction layer between DAL and the business logic layer of your application. It is a data access pattern that prompts a more loosely coupled approach to data access and eliminates all unnecessary redundant code. To keep the example code simple in this book, I will not go into the details of the generic repository pattern.

The *GetPrices* method uses the new *async* and *await* pattern in .NET Framework 4.5 for doing work in the background. Note that getting five-year historical stock data for over 180 stock tickers from Yahoo and inserting the data into the database will take a lot of time. You need to choose the *async* pattern to ensure that your application is responsive to users. You can see that, inside the *foreach* loop, you publish a list of objects using Caliburn.Micro's *IEventAggregator*. This list will be used to update the status text and the progress bar in *MainView*. *Progress* monitoring is not new with the *async* pattern, but it is an important consideration when you adopt the *async* programming model. To accomplish this progress updating in previous versionsof .NET framework, you would have needed to use threads or a background worker. Fortunately, with the *async* and *await* pattern provided in .NET Framework 4.5, implementing progress updating is relatively easy.

Running the program by pressing F5, choosing the *YahooLoader* tab, and clicking the *Load CSV File* button, should produce the results shown in Fig-3-22.

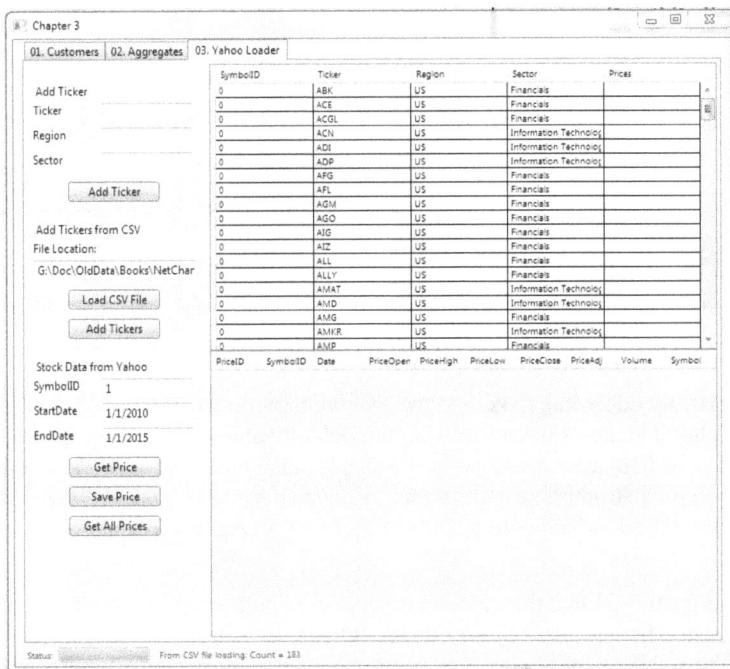

Figure 3-22. Stock tickers from a CSV file.

Here, we call the *CsvToSymbolCollection* method implemented in the *ModelHelper* class and then bind the collection to a *DataGrid* in the view. Note that the *SymbolID* field is assigned a default value of zero and will be reassigned when you insert the collection into the database. There is also a field called *Prices* in the collection, which just indicates there exists a one-to-many relationship between the *Symbol* and *Price* tables through the foreign key *SymbolID* defined in the *Price* table.

Now click the *Add Tickers* button to call the *SymbolInsert* method in the *ModelHelper* class. We will insert all the tickers contained in the *Symbol* collection to the *Symbol* table in database. At this stage, we can double-check whether the tickers were added to the *Symbol* table in SSDT's *SQL Server Object Explorer*. Click the *MyDb* node and the *Tables* node, right-click the *dbo.Symbol* table, and choose View Data. You should see on your screen the results shown in Figure 3-23. There should be more than 180 tickers in the *Symbol* table. If you somehow could not add these tickers to the *Symbol* table, please retry and closely followe the instruction provided in this example. You will need this in the following chapters of this book.

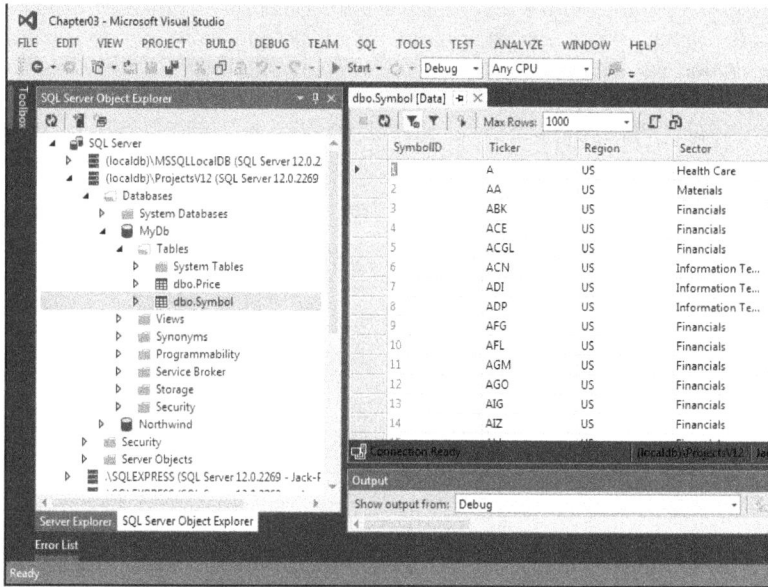

Figure 3-23. Stock tickers in the Symbol table.

If you have successively added the tickers to the *Symbol* table in the database, you can now download stock data from Yahoo Finance's website. Using the default values for the input parameters (*SymbolID* = 1, *StartDate* = 1/1/2010, and *EndDate* = 1/1/2015), and click the *Get Price* button to call the *GetYahooStockData* method implemented in the *ModelHelper* class. You will begin downloading the stock data for *SymbolID* = 1, which corresponds to *Ticker* = A (Agilent Technologies Inc.), as shown in Figure 3-24.

You can see from Figure 3-24 that the *PriceID* is set to zero and will be reset when you insert the price data into the database. There is also a *Symbol* field without any values, which just shows a one-to-many relationship with the *Symbol* table via the foreign key, *SymbolID*, defined during the creation of the *Price* table. Another interesting point is that from the status bar, you can see that there were 1258 stock records (or 1258 workdays) downloaded from Yahoo.

Click the *Save Price* button to save the price data you just downloaded to the database. Again, you can check the data in your database from the SQL Server Object Explorer. Open the SQL query edit window and enter the following SQL query:

```
SELECT * FROM Price WHERE SymbolID=1 ORDER BY Date
```

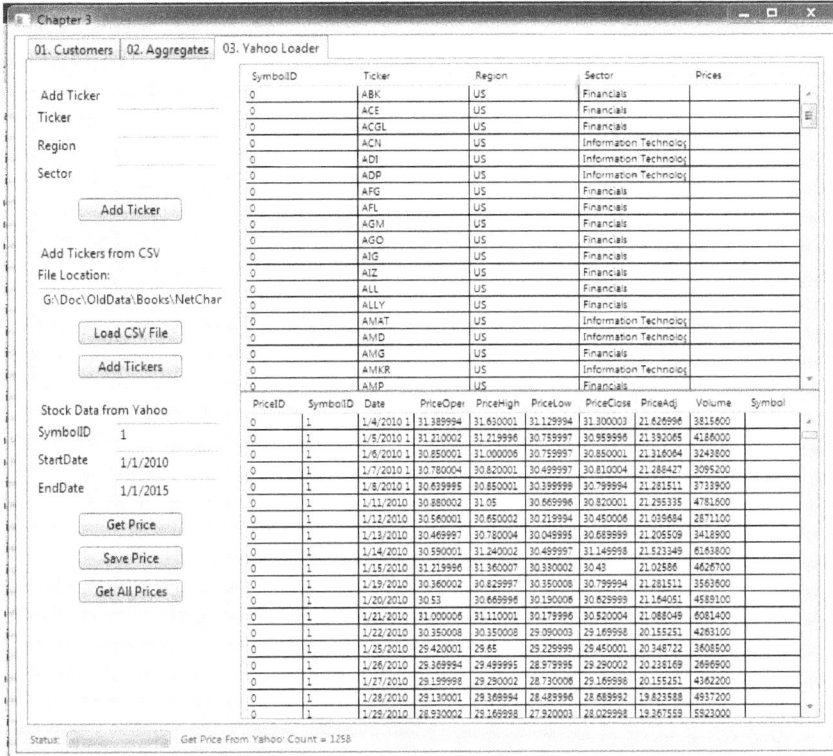

Figure 3-24. Downloading stock data from Yahoo.

By executing the query, you should see the results shown in Figure 3-25.

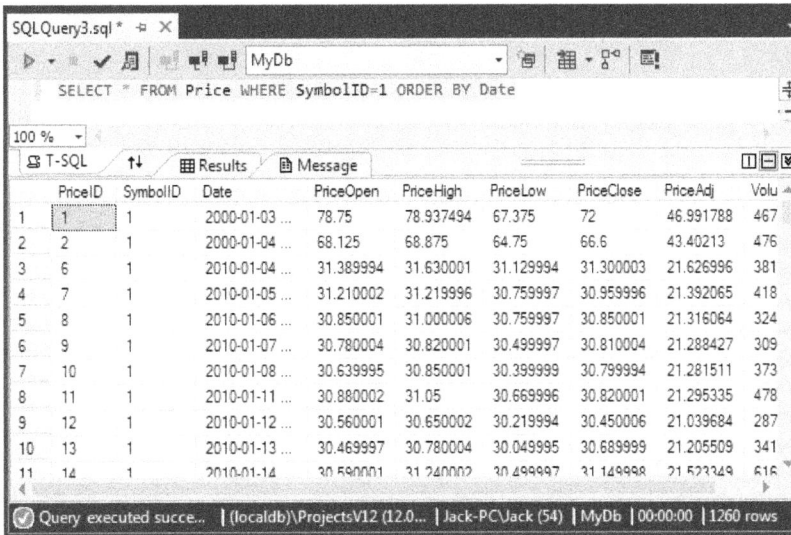

Figure 3-25. Stock data in database.

Note that the first two records are just the seed data you added to the table manually; the rest are stock data downloaded from Yahoo. From the status bar, you can see that there were 1260 rows of data retrieved from the database using the preceding SQL query, 2 rows from seeding data and 1258 rows from Yahoo as expected, meaning you have successfully inserted all the stock data from Yahoo into the *Price* table in the database.

Now we want to download the stock data from Yahoo for all the tickers (>180) stored in the *Symbol* table using the method *GetPrices*, which was implemented in the *YahooLoaderViewModel* class. Click the *GetPrices* button to start downloading the stock data, which will take a while as you are downloading data with over twenty-two thousand records. You can see from the *GetPrices* method that you download data and save data to the database for one ticker at a time; then you go on to the next ticker. Thus, you can monitor the progress either by looking at the status message and progress bar on your screen (see Figure 2-26), or by directly checking the *Price* table in the database from the SQL Server Object Explorer.

The Yahoo downloader shown in the example is a powerful utility for getting free market data. You may notice that there is a *PriceAdj* field, which is the close price adjusted to stock split and dividend distribution events. This adjusted close price may be useful when you back-test your trading strategy.

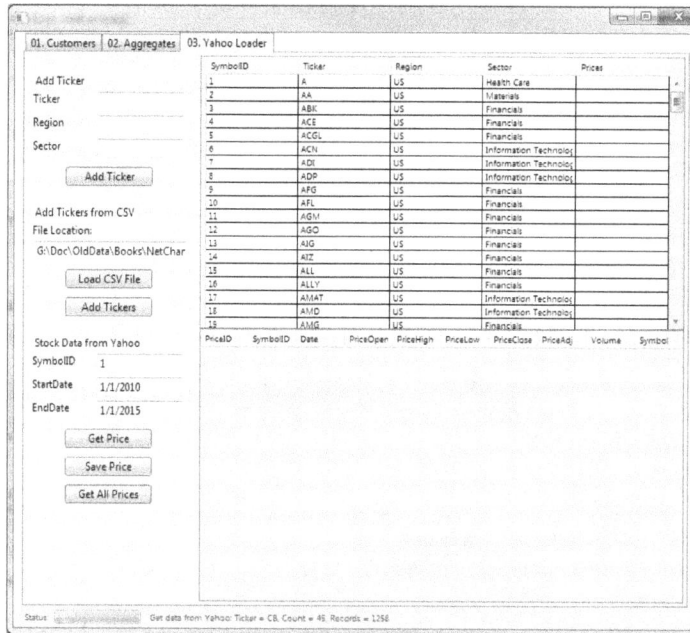

Figure 3-26. Downloading stock data from Yahoo in progress.

Chapter 4
2D Line Charts

WPF provides a unified graphics platform that allows you to easily create a variety of user interfaces and graphics objects in your .NET applications. This chapter begins by describing graphics coordinate systems used in WPF, and shows you several different coordinate systems you can use to make graphics programming easier. Then I will shows you how to create simple two-dimensional (2D) *X-Y* line charts.

In order to create a chart application, you will need to perform various operations in different coordinate systems. Moving from one coordinate space to another requires the use of transformation matrices. At the same time, you will need to create basic shapes, such as gridlines, line symbols, chart legends, etc., using WPF's built-in *Shape* class. In this book, I will skip the tutorial on mathematical transformations and WPF graphics basics. You can find this background information in my previous published books, including *Practical C# Charts and Graphics* and *Practical WPF Charts and Graphics*.

In order to create chart applications, we have two ways to render 2D graphics – by inheriting from *DrawingVisual* and hosting in a *FrameworkElement* or by inheriting from the *Shape* class and instancing your object directly in XAML. For simplicity's sake, in this book, I will use WPF's ready-to-use *Shape* objects, such as *Line*, *Polyline*, *Ellipse*, and *Rectangle*, to create most of the chart applications. Because these shapes derive from *UIElement*, we can use them directly inside panels and most controls. While shapes are very powerful and easy to use, you should be aware that they come with a high memory footprint. The reason is that their base class, *UIElement*, defines various events and properties, which you may not need in creating chart applications.

At the end of this chapter, I will create a line chart application using the *DrawingVisual* objects, which shows the procedure on how to convert chart applications created using *Shape* objects into high-performance chart applications.

2D Coordinate Systems

When you create a graphic object in .NET applications, you must determine where the graphics object or drawing will be displayed. To do this, you need to understand how the .NET Framework measures the coordinates of the graphics object. Each point on a WPF window or page has an *X* and a *Y* coordinate. In the following sections, we will discuss various coordinate systems and their relationships.

Default Coordinate System

For 2D graphics, the WPF coordinate system locates the origin in the upper-left corner of the rendering area. In 2D space, the positive *X*-axis points to the right, and the positive *Y*-axis points to downward, as shown in Figure 4-1.

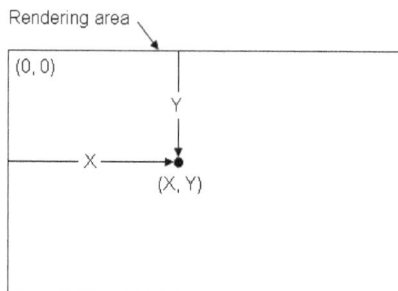

Figure 4-1. Default coordinate system in WPF.

All coordinates and sizes in the default WPF system are measured in units of 96 dots per inch (DPI), called *device-independent pixels*, or denoted by *px*. In this system, you can create adaptive layouts to deal with different resolutions, making sure your controls and graphics objects stretch accordingly when the window is stretched.

You can define the rendering area in WPF using layout elements that derive from the *Panel* class, such as *Canvas*, *DockPanel*, *Grid*, *StackPanel*, *VirtualizingStatckPanel*, and *WrapPanel*. However, it is also possible to use a custom layout component for the rendering area by overriding the default behavior of any of these layout elements.

Let's look at the following XAML example and see how this can be achieved:

```
<Window x:Class="GraphicsBasics.LineInDefaultSystem"
    xmlns="http://schemas.microsoft.com/winfx/2006/xaml/presentation"
    xmlns:x="http://schemas.microsoft.com/winfx/2006/xaml"
    Title="Line in Default System" Height="300" Width="300">
    <Canvas Height="300" Width="300">
        <Line X1="0" Y1="0" X2="100" Y2="100" Stroke="Black" StrokeThickness="2" />
    </Canvas>
</Window>
```

The *Canvas* control, as used in the preceding XAML file, is particularly useful when you need to place graphics and other drawing elements at absolute positions. What's interesting is that *Canvas* elements can be nested. This means you can prepare part of a drawing in a canvas and then insert that entire drawing as a single element into another canvas. You can also apply various transformations, such as scaling and rotation, directly to the canvas. In this example, we draw a line from *Point* (0, 0) to *Point* (100, 100) on the canvas, using the default units of device-independent pixels. Figure 4-2 shows the results of this XAML file.

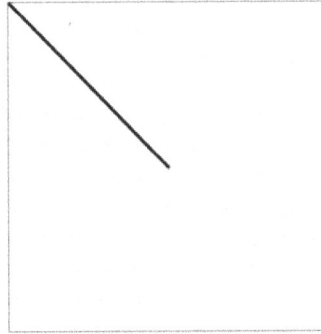

Figure 4-2. Drawing a line from (0, 0) to (100, 100) on a canvas.

Custom Coordinate Systems

In addition to the default WPF coordinate system discussed in the previous section, a WPF application can define its own coordinate system. For example, 2D charting applications usually use a coordinate system in which the *Y*-axis points from bottom to top, as illustrated in Figure 4-3.

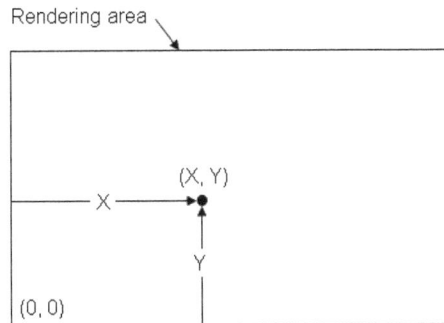

Figure 4-3. A custom coordinate system.

You can easily create this system in WPF by performing the corresponding transformations directly to the canvas. Let's look at the following XAML:

```
<Window x:Class=" GraphicsBasics.LineInCustomSystem"
    xmlns="http://schemas.microsoft.com/winfx/2006/xaml/presentation"
    xmlns:x="http://schemas.microsoft.com/winfx/2006/xaml"
    Title="Line in Custom System" Height="240" Width="220">
    <Border BorderBrush="Black" BorderThickness="1" Height="200" Width="200">
        <Canvas Height="200" Width="200">
            <Canvas.RenderTransform>
                <TransformGroup>
                    <ScaleTransform ScaleY="-1" />
                    <TranslateTransform Y="200" />
                </TransformGroup>
            </Canvas.RenderTransform>
            <Line X1="0" Y1="0" X2="100" Y2="100" Stroke="Black"
                StrokeThickness="2" />
```

```
        </Canvas>
    </Border>
</Window>
```

Here, you perform two successive transforms on the canvas. The scale transform reverses the *Y*-axis, and the translation transform translates 200 *px* (the height of the canvas) in the *Y* direction. These transforms move the origin from the top-left corner to the bottom-left corner.

Figure 4-4 shows the result produced by this XAML. The line from (0, 0) to (100, 100) is now measured relative to the origin of the new custom coordinate system. You can compare this line with that drawn in the default system of Figure 4-2.

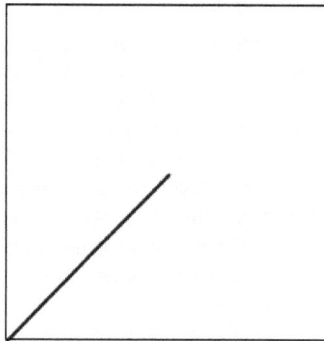

Figure 4-4. Drawing a line from (0, 0) to (100, 100) in a custom coordinate system.

You may have noticed an issue with this custom coordinate system: everything inside the *Canvas* will be transformed the same way the canvas is. For instance, when you add a button control and a text block to the canvas using the following XAML code, the content of the button and the text block will be upside down, as shown in Figure 4-5:

```
<Button Canvas.Top="50" Canvas.Left="80" FontSize="15"
        Foreground="Red" Name="label1" Content="My Button"/>
<TextBlock Canvas.Top="120" Canvas.Left="20" FontSize="12pt"
           Foreground="Blue"> <Bold>My Text Block</Bold>
</TextBlock>
```

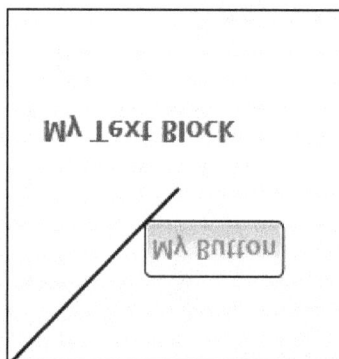

Figure 4-5. The button and text block in the custom coordinate system after reflection.

Another issue is the default unit of measure used in the coordinate system. In real-world applications, real-world units are usually involved. For example, it is impossible to draw a line with a length of 100 miles on the screen in the current coordinate system. In the following section, we will develop a new custom coordinate system that can be used in 2D chart applications.

Custom Coordinate System for 2D Charts

The custom coordinate system used in 2D chart applications must satisfy the following conditions: It must be independent of the units of real-world graphics objects, and its *Y*-axis must point from bottom to top, as it does in most chart applications. This custom coordinate system is illustrated in Figure 4-6.

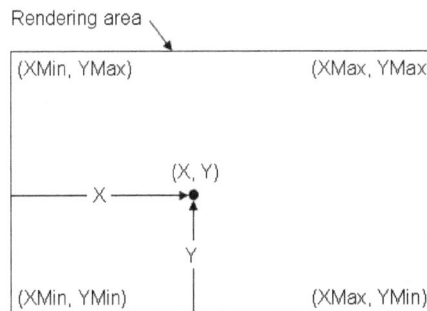

Figure 4-6. Custom coordinate system for 2D chart applications.

You can see that we define the real-world *X-Y* coordinate system within a rendering area. You can create such a coordinate system using a custom panel control by overriding its *MeasureOverride* and *ArrangeOverride* methods. Each method returns the size data needed to position and render child elements. This is a standard method of creating custom coordinate systems. Instead of creating a custom panel control, here we will construct this coordinate system using a different approach, based on direct coding. In next section, I will create a simple line chart that illustrates how to construct our custom 2D chart coordinate system.

Simple Line Charts

The most basic and useful type of chart you can create with WPF is a simple 2D line chart of numerical data. WPF provides a set of commands and methods you can use to create these charts. Even the most elementary 2D chart consists of several basic elements, including lines, symbols, axes, tick marks, labels, a title, and a legend. The following list quickly overviews the most basic chart elements without getting into too much detail. These elements will often be referred to in this chapter.

- *Axes* – a graphics object that defines a region of the chart in which the chart is drawn.
- *Line* – a graphics object that represents the data you have plotted.
- *Text* – a graphics object that is comprised of a string of characters.
- *Title* – the text string object that is located directly above an axis object.
- *Label* – the text string object associated with the axis object (X- or Y- axis).
- *Legend* – the text string array object that represents the color and values of the lines.

The *X-Y* line chart uses two values to represent each data point. This type of chart is very useful for describing relationships between data and is often involved in the statistical analysis of data, with wide applications in the scientific, mathematics, engineering, and finance communities as well as in daily life.

Open Visual Studio 2013, start a new WPF project, and name it *Chapter04*. Following the same procedure that you did in the preceding chapter, add Caliburn.Micro to *References*. Add three new folders named *Models*, *ViewModels*, and *Views* to the project. Add *AppBootstrapper.cs* to the *Models* folder, which is basically identical to that used in the *Chapter03* project, except that the startup becomes the *IMain* interface. Add a new class to the *Models* folder and name it *IMain*:

```
using Caliburn.Micro;
namespace Chapter04.Models
{
    public interface IMain :IConductor, IGuardClose
    {
    }
}
```

Add a WPF *Window* to the *Views* folder and name it *MainView*. Add a class to the *ViewModels* folder and name it *MainViewModel*. We use the main view and the view model to hold the tab items, which are similar to those used in the *Chapter03* project. You can open those files inside Visual Studio and check the code for reference. Also, do not forget to make corresponding changes to *App.xaml*.

After we have finished the preparation for our project, we are ready to start creating a simple line chart. Add a *UserControl* to the *Views* folder and name it *SimpleLineView*. The following is XAML for this view:

```
<UserControl x:Class="Chapter04.Views.SimpleLineView"
             xmlns="http://schemas.microsoft.com/winfx/2006/xaml/presentation"
             xmlns:x="http://schemas.microsoft.com/winfx/2006/xaml"
             xmlns:mc="http://schemas.openxmlformats.org/markup-compatibility/2006"
             xmlns:d="http://schemas.microsoft.com/expression/blend/2008"
             xmlns:cal="http://www.caliburnproject.org"
             mc:Ignorable="d"
             d:DesignHeight="300" d:DesignWidth="300">
    <Border BorderBrush="Gray" BorderThickness="1">
        <Grid ClipToBounds="True" cal:Message.Attach="[Event SizeChanged]=
            [Action AddPoints($this.ActualWidth, $this.ActualHeight)];
            [Event Loaded]=[Action AddPoints($this.ActualWidth,
                            $this.ActualHeight)]">
            <Polyline Points="{Binding SolidLinePoints}" Stroke="Black"
                    StrokeThickness="2"/>
            <Polyline Points="{Binding DashLinePoints}" Stroke="Black"
                    StrokeThickness="2" StrokeDashArray="4,3"/>
        </Grid>
    </Border>
</UserControl>
```

Here we add two *Polylines* to the *Grid*, which are bound to two *PointCollection* objects, *SolidLinePoints* and *DashLinePoints*, respectively. The dash line is specified by a *StrokeDashArray* = "4, 3". These values mean that the line has a value of 4 and a gap of 3, interpreted relative to the *StrokeThickness* of the line. So if your line is 2 units (as it is in this example), the solid portion is 4 × 2 = 8 units, followed by a gap portion of 3 × 2 = 6 units. The line then repeats this pattern for its entire length. You can create a line with a more complex dash pattern by varying the values of the *StrokeDashArray*.

You may also notice that I use Caliburn.Micro's action mechanism to bind UI events in view to methods defined in the view model. Here I use the *Message.Attach* property to bind the *Grid*'s *Loaded* and *SizeChanged* events to the *AddPoints* method in the view model, and pass the *Grid*'s *ActualWidth* and *ActualHeight* properties to the *AddPoints* method. This action will fire whenever the *Grid* is loaded or resized, resulting in a recreation of the point collections and a redrawing of the chart on your screen.

Add a new class to the *ViewModels* folder and name it *SimpleLineViewModel*. Here is the code for this class:

```
using System;
using Caliburn.Micro;
using System.Collections.ObjectModel;
using System.ComponentModel.Composition;
using System.Collections.Generic;
using System.Windows;
using Chapter04.Models;
using System.Windows.Media;
using System.Windows.Controls;

namespace Chapter04.ViewModels
{
    [Export(typeof(IScreen)), PartCreationPolicy(CreationPolicy.NonShared)]
    public class SimpleLineViewModel : Screen
    {
        private readonly IEventAggregator _events;
        [ImportingConstructor]
        public SimpleLineViewModel(IEventAggregator events)
        {
            this._events = events;
            DisplayName = "01. Simple Line";
        }

        private double chartWidth=300;
        private double chartHeight=300;
        private double xmin = 0;
        private double xmax = 6.5;
        private double ymin = -1.1;
        private double ymax = 1.1;

        private PointCollection solidLinePoints;
        public PointCollection SolidLinePoints
        {
            get { return solidLinePoints; }
            set
            {
                solidLinePoints = value;
                NotifyOfPropertyChange(() => SolidLinePoints);
            }
        }

        private PointCollection dashLinePoints;
        public PointCollection DashLinePoints
        {
            get { return dashLinePoints; }
            set
```

```
        {
            dashLinePoints = value;
            NotifyOfPropertyChange(() => DashLinePoints);
        }
    }

    public void AddPoints(double width, double height)
    {
        chartWidth = width;
        chartHeight = height;

        SolidLinePoints = new PointCollection();
        DashLinePoints = new PointCollection();
        double x = 0;
        double y = 0;
        double z = 0;
        for(int i = 0;i<70;i++)
        {
            x = i / 5.0;
            y = Math.Sin(x);
            z = Math.Cos(x);

            DashLinePoints.Add(NormalizePoint(new Point(x, z)));
            SolidLinePoints.Add(NormalizePoint(new Point(x, y)));
        }
    }

    public Point NormalizePoint(Point pt)
    {
        var res = new Point();
        res.X = (pt.X - xmin) * chartWidth / (xmax - xmin);
        res.Y = chartHeight - (pt.Y - ymin) * chartHeight / (ymax - ymin);
        return res;
    }
    }
}
```

Note that the axis limits *xmin*, *xmax*, *ymin*, and *ymax* are defined in the real-world coordinate system. The *Sine* and *Cosine* functions are represented using two point collections, *SolidLinePoints* and *DashLinePoints*, which are bound to *Polyline* objects.

Pay special attention to the *AddPoints* method. We first set the *chartWidth* and *chartHeight* to the *Grid*'s *ActualWidth* and *ActualHeight* properties, ensuring that the chart size will change when the *Gird* is resized. We also recreate the point collections, so the chart will redraw when you resize the screen.

A key step in creating this line chart is transforming the original data points in the world coordinate system into points in the units of device-independent pixels using the *NormalizePoint* method. The *NormalizePoint* method converts points of any unit in the world coordinate system into points with a unit of device-independent pixel in the device coordinate system.

Figure 4-7 shows the results of running this example.

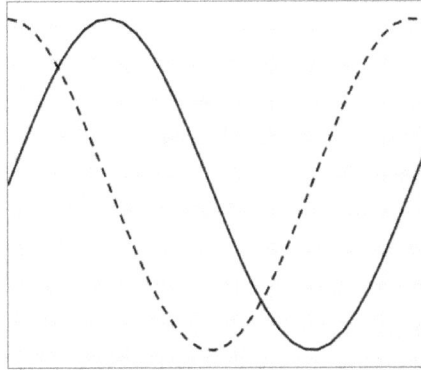

Figure 4-7. A 2D chart for Sine and Cosine functions.

Line Charts with Chart Style

The preceding example demonstrated how easy it is to create a simple 2D line chart in WPF, but did not pay much attention to the program structure. In order for our chart program to be more object-oriented and extensible, we need to define two new classes: *ChartStyle1* and *LineSeries*. The *ChartStyle1* class defines all chart layout–related information and the *LineSeries* class holds the chart data and line styles, including the line color, thickness, dash style, etc.

Chart Style

Now add a new folder to the *Models* folder and name it *ChartModel*, this will hold chart-related utility classes. Add a public class, *ChartStyle1*, to the *ChartModel* folder. The following is the code listing for this class:

```
using System;
using System.Windows;

namespace Chapter04.Models.ChartModel
{
    public class ChartStyle1
    {
        private double chartWidth = 300;
        private double chartHeight = 300;
        private double xmin = 0;
        private double xmax = 6.5;
        private double ymin = -1.1;
        private double ymax = 1.1;

        public double ChartWidth
        {
            get { return chartWidth; }
            set { chartWidth = value; }
        }

        public double ChartHeight
        {
```

```
        get { return chartHeight; }
        set { chartHeight = value; }
    }

    public double Xmin
    {
        get { return xmin; }
        set { xmin = value; }
    }

    public double Xmax
    {
        get { return xmax; }
        set { xmax = value; }
    }

    public double Ymin
    {
        get { return ymin; }
        set { ymin = value; }
    }

    public double Ymax
    {
        get { return ymax; }
        set { ymax = value; }
    }

    public Point NormalizePoint(Point pt)
    {
        if (Double.IsNaN(ChartWidth) || ChartWidth <= 0)
            ChartWidth = 270;
        if (Double.IsNaN(ChartHeight) || ChartHeight <= 0)
            ChartHeight = 250;
        Point result = new Point();
        result.X = (pt.X - Xmin) * ChartWidth / (Xmax - Xmin);
        result.Y = ChartHeight - (pt.Y - Ymin) * ChartHeight / (Ymax - Ymin);
        return result;
    }

    public void SetLines(BindableCollection<LineSeries> dc)
    {
        if (dc.Count <= 0)
            return;
        for (int i = 0; i < dc.Count; i++)
        {
            if (dc[i].SeriesName == "Default")
                dc[i].SeriesName = "DataSeries" + i.ToString();
            dc[i].SetLinePattern();
            for (int j = 0; j < dc[i].LinePoints.Count; j++)
            {
                dc[i].LinePoints[j] = NormalizePoint(dc[i].LinePoints[j]);
            }
        }
    }
}
```

```
        }
    }
```

In this class, we first define two public properties, *ChartWidth* and *ChartHeight*, that are needed to specify the chart area. In addition, the *NormalizePoint* method requires *ChartWidth* and *ChartHeight* in order to obtain the point conversion from the real-world coordinate system to device-independent pixels. We then create member fields and corresponding public properties for the axis limits. You can override the default values of these properties according to your application requirements.

The *SetLines* method applied to the *LineSeries* collection sets up the line dash pattern and converts line points of any unit in the world coordinate system into points with a unit of device-independent pixel in the device coordinate system by calling the *NormalizePoint* method.

Line Series

Now add a new class to the *ChartModel* folder and name it *LineSeries*. The following is the code for this class:

```
using System;
using System.Windows.Media;
using System.Windows.Shapes;
using Caliburn.Micro;
using System.Windows;

namespace Chapter04.Models.ChartModel
{
    public class LineSeries : PropertyChangedBase
    {
        public LineSeries()
        {
            LinePoints = new PointCollection();
        }

        public PointCollection LinePoints { get; set; }
        public Brush LineColor { get; set; }
        public double LineThickness { get; set; }
        public LinePatternEnum LinePattern { get; set; }

        private string seriesName = "Default";
        public string SeriesName
        {
            get { return seriesName; }
            set { seriesName = value; }
        }

        private DoubleCollection lineDashPattern;
        public DoubleCollection LineDashPattern
        {
            get { return lineDashPattern; }
            set
            {
                lineDashPattern = value;
                NotifyOfPropertyChange(() => LineDashPattern);
            }
        }
```

```
        }

        public void SetLinePattern()
        {
            switch (LinePattern)
            {
                case LinePatternEnum.Dash:
                    LineDashPattern = new DoubleCollection() { 4, 3 };
                    break;
                case LinePatternEnum.Dot:
                    LineDashPattern = new DoubleCollection() { 1, 2 };
                    break;
                case LinePatternEnum.DashDot:
                    LineDashPattern = new DoubleCollection() { 4, 2, 1, 2 };
                    break;
            }
        }
    }

    public enum LinePatternEnum
    {
        Solid = 1,
        Dash = 2,
        Dot = 3,
        DashDot = 4,
    }
}
```

This class creates a *PointCollection* object for a given *LineSeries*. It then defines the line style for the line object, including the line color, thickness, line pattern, and series name. The *SeriesName* property will be used later in creating the legend for the chart. The line pattern is defined by a public enumeration called *LinePatternEnum,* in which four line patterns are defined, including *Solid* (default), *Dash*, *Dot*, and *DashDot*.

We create the line pattern via the *SetLinePattern* method. There is no need to create the solid line pattern because it is the default setting of the *Polyline* object. We also create the dashed or dotted line patterns using the *StrokeDashArray* property of the *Polyline*.

Creating Line Charts

Now we can create line charts using the *ChartStyle1* and *LineSeries* classes. Add a new *UserControl* to the *Views* folder and name it *LineStyleView*. Here is XAML for this view:

```xml
<UserControl x:Class="Chapter04.Views.LineStyleView"
        xmlns="http://schemas.microsoft.com/winfx/2006/xaml/presentation"
        xmlns:x="http://schemas.microsoft.com/winfx/2006/xaml"
        xmlns:mc="http://schemas.openxmlformats.org/markup-compatibility/2006"
        xmlns:d="http://schemas.microsoft.com/expression/blend/2008"
        xmlns:cal="http://www.caliburnproject.org"
        mc:Ignorable="d"
        d:DesignHeight="300" d:DesignWidth="300">
    <UserControl.Resources>
        <DataTemplate x:Key="chartTemplate">
            <Polyline Points="{Binding LinePoints}" Stroke="{Binding LineColor}"
```

```
                StrokeThickness="{Binding LineThickness}"
                StrokeDashArray="{Binding LineDashPattern}"/>
        </DataTemplate>
    </UserControl.Resources>


    <Border BorderBrush="Gray" BorderThickness="1">
        <Grid x:Name="ChartGrid" ClipToBounds="True" cal:Message.Attach=
            "[Event SizeChanged]=[Action AddLines($this.ActualWidth,
                $this.ActualHeight)];
            [Event Loaded]=[Action AddLines($this.ActualWidth,
                $this.ActualHeight)]">
        <Canvas Width="{Binding ElementName=ChartGrid, Path=ActualWidth}"
                Height="{Binding ElementName=ChartGrid,Path=ActualHeight}">
            <ItemsControl ItemsSource="{Binding DataCollection}"
                        ItemTemplate="{StaticResource chartTemplate}">
                <ItemsControl.ItemsPanel>
                    <ItemsPanelTemplate>
                        <Grid/>
                    </ItemsPanelTemplate>
                </ItemsControl.ItemsPanel>
            </ItemsControl>
        </Canvas>
        </Grid>
    </Border>
</UserControl>
```

Note that here we use a new MVVM feature, that is, binding a *BindableCollection* of *LineSeries* to a *Grid* control by using an *ItemsControl* and its *ItemsPanelTemplate* property. In order to update the view automatically when the collection changes, we first need to specify how the data items are represented in the view. To do this, we add a *DataTemplate* named *chartTemplate* to *UserControl*'s Resources. The *chartTemplate* defines a *Polyline* object whose properties are bound directly to the corresponding properties of the data item (i.e., *LineSeries* in this example). After defining the polylines using the data item in the *chartTemplate*, we need to place the polylines on a panel (here we use a *Grid*).

Also, note how the *ItemsControl*'s *ItemsSource* property is bound to the *LineSeries* collection. This is where we set up the link between the business logic layer and the UI layer. The items in the *ItemsControl* should be represented using the *chartTemplate* we defined earlier, which can be specified by the *ItemTemplate* property.

This way, regardless of the number of polylines we want to create on the chart, we do not need to change the view. We simply make changes to the *LineSeries* collection in the view model, and our chart will be automatically updated. That is the beauty of the WPF MVVM framework.

Now add a new class to the *ViewModel* class and name it *LineStyleViewModel*. Here is the code for this class:

```
using System;
using System.Linq;
using Caliburn.Micro;
using System.Collections.ObjectModel;
using System.ComponentModel.Composition;
using System.Windows.Documents;
using System.Collections.Generic;
using System.Windows;
```

```
using Chapter04.Models;
using System.Windows.Media;
using System.Windows.Controls;
using Chapter04.Models.ChartModel;

namespace Chapter04.ViewModels
{
    [Export(typeof(IScreen)), PartCreationPolicy(CreationPolicy.NonShared)]
    public class LineStyleViewModel : Screen
    {
        private readonly IEventAggregator _events;
        [ImportingConstructor]
        public LineStyleViewModel(IEventAggregator events)
        {
            this._events = events;
            DisplayName = "02. Chart Style";
            DataCollection = new BindableCollection<LineSeries>();
            cs = new ChartStyle1();
        }

        public BindableCollection<LineSeries> DataCollection { get; set; }
        private ChartStyle1 cs;

        public void AddLines(double width, double height)
        {
            cs.ChartWidth = width;
            cs.ChartHeight = height;

            DataCollection.Clear();
            var ls = new LineSeries();
            ls.LineColor = Brushes.Blue;
            ls.LineThickness = 2;
            ls.LinePattern = LinePatternEnum.Solid;
            for (int i = 0; i < 50; i++)
            {
                double x = i / 5.0;
                double y = Math.Sin(x);
                ls.LinePoints.Add(new Point(x, y));
            }
            DataCollection.Add(ds);

            ls = new LineSeries();
            ls.LineColor = Brushes.Red;
            ls.LineThickness = 2;
            ls.LinePattern = LinePatternEnum.Dash;
            for (int i = 0; i < 50; i++)
            {
                double x = i / 5.0;
                double y = Math.Cos(x);
                ls.LinePoints.Add(new Point(x, y));
            }
            DataCollection.Add(ls);
            cs.SetLines(DataCollection);
        }
    }
}
```

```
}
```

Here we first create a new *BindableCollection* of *LineSeries* called *DataCollection* that holds multiple *LineSeries* objects, and a *ChartStyle1* object called *cs* that sets the chart style. We then create two *LineSeries* objects; define their line style, including the line color, thickness, and dash pattern; and add the data points to their point collection, *LinePoints*. Next, we add multiple line series to the *DataCollection*, and finally we call the *SetLines* method applied to the *LineSeries* collection, which sets up the line dash pattern and converts line points from the world coordinate system into points in the device coordinate system. This way, we complete the creation of the line series collection, which is now ready to be bound to the *ItemControl* in the view.

Running this example produces the result shown in Figure 4-7.

Gridlines and Labels

In the preceding section, we created lines for the *Sine* and *Cosine* functions on the chart using a standard MVVM approach, with perfect separation between the view and the view model. In this section, we will add more features to the 2D line chart, including gridlines, a title, tick marks, and labels for axes. To this end, we need to dynamically create many controls on the view, which will be hard to lay out using XAML. In addition, I want to reuse some code that I already implemented using the code-behind method in my previous books. Therefore, we want the view model to be able to access the view and add controls dynamically to the view. Even though this may violate the MVVM rules, it is the easiest way to reuse the code-behind source code. I will show you later in the book how you can still develop MVVM-compatible chart applications when you convert chart applications implemented using the code-behind approach into a chart user control.

Chart Style with Gridlines

Add a new class to the *ChartModel* folder and name it *ChartStyleBase*. Here is the code for this class:

```
using System;
using System.Windows;
using System.Windows.Controls;
using Caliburn.Micro;

namespace Chapter04.Models.ChartModel
{
    public class ChartStyleBase
    {
        private double xmin = 0;
        private double xmax = 6.5;
        private double ymin = -1.1;
        private double ymax = 1.1;

        public Canvas ChartCanvas { get; set; }

        public double Xmin
        {
            get { return xmin; }
            set { xmin = value; }
        }
    }
}
```

```
public double Xmax
{
    get { return xmax; }
    set { xmax = value; }
}

public double Ymin
{
    get { return ymin; }
    set { ymin = value; }
}

public double Ymax
{
    get { return ymax; }
    set { ymax = value; }
}

public Point NormalizePoint(Point pt)
{
    if (Double.IsNaN(ChartCanvas.Width) || ChartCanvas.Width <= 0)
        ChartCanvas.Width = 270;
    if (Double.IsNaN(ChartCanvas.Height) || ChartCanvas.Height <= 0)
        ChartCanvas.Height = 250;
    Point result = new Point();
    result.X = (pt.X - Xmin) * ChartCanvas.Width / (Xmax - Xmin);
    result.Y = ChartCanvas.Height -
        (pt.Y - Ymin) * ChartCanvas.Height / (Ymax - Ymin);
    return result;
}

public void SetLines(BindableCollection<LineSeries> dc)
{
    if (dc.Count <= 0)
        return;
    for(int i = 0;i<dc.Count;i++)
    {
        if (dc[i].SeriesName == "Default")
            dc[i].SeriesName = "LineSeries" + i.ToString();
        dc[i].SetLinePattern();
        for (int j = 0; j < dc[i].LinePoints.Count; j++)
        {
            dc[i].LinePoints[j] = NormalizePoint(dc[i].LinePoints[j]);
        }
    }
}
}
}
```

This class is very similar to that used in the preceding example, except that you use *ChartCanvas* to replace *ChartWidth* and *ChartHeight*. Usually, the MVVM framework does not allow the *Canvas* control to appear in the model or view model. As I discussed previously, the purpose we do this here is to have the ability to add controls dynamically and reuse existing code-behind code.

Now add a new class to the *ChartModel* folder and name it *ChartStyle*. Here is the code for this class:

```csharp
using System;
using System.Windows;
using System.Windows.Controls;
using System.Windows.Media;
using System.Windows.Shapes;

namespace Chapter04.Models.ChartModel
{
    public class ChartStyle : ChartStyleBase
    {
        private string title = "Title";
        private string xLabel = "X Axis";
        private string yLabel = "Y Axis";
        private bool isXGrid = true;
        private bool isYGrid = true;
        private Brush gridlineColor = Brushes.LightGray;
        private double xTick = 1;
        private double yTick = 0.5;
        private LinePatternEnum gridlinePattern;
        private double leftOffset = 20;
        private double bottomOffset = 15;
        private double rightOffset = 10;
        private Line gridline = new Line();
        public Canvas TextCanvas { get; set; }

        public string Title
        {
            get { return title; }
            set { title = value; }
        }

        public string XLabel
        {
            get { return xLabel; }
            set { xLabel = value; }
        }

        public string YLabel
        {
            get { return yLabel; }
            set { yLabel = value; }
        }

        public LinePatternEnum GridlinePattern
        {
            get { return gridlinePattern; }
            set { gridlinePattern = value; }
        }

        public double XTick
        {
            get { return xTick; }
            set { xTick = value; }
        }
```

```
public double YTick
{
    get { return yTick; }
    set { yTick = value; }
}

public Brush GridlineColor
{
    get { return gridlineColor; }
    set { gridlineColor = value; }
}

public bool IsXGrid
{
    get { return isXGrid; }
    set { isXGrid = value; }
}

public bool IsYGrid
{
    get { return isYGrid; }
    set { isYGrid = value; }
}


public void AddChartStyle(TextBlock tbTitle, TextBlock tbXLabel,
    TextBlock tbYLabel)
{
    Point pt = new Point();
    Line tick = new Line();
    double offset = 0;
    double dx, dy;
    TextBlock tb = new TextBlock();

    //  determine right offset:
    tb.Text = Xmax.ToString();
    tb.Measure(new Size(Double.PositiveInfinity, Double.PositiveInfinity));
    Size size = tb.DesiredSize;
    rightOffset = size.Width / 2 + 2;

    // Determine left offset:
    for (dy = Ymin; dy <= Ymax; dy += YTick)
    {
        pt = NormalizePoint(new Point(Xmin, dy));
        tb = new TextBlock();
        tb.Text = dy.ToString();
        tb.TextAlignment = TextAlignment.Right;
        tb.Measure(new Size(Double.PositiveInfinity,
                            Double.PositiveInfinity));
        size = tb.DesiredSize;
        if (offset < size.Width)
            offset = size.Width;
    }
    leftOffset = offset + 5;
    Canvas.SetLeft(ChartCanvas, leftOffset);
```

```
Canvas.SetBottom(ChartCanvas, bottomOffset);
ChartCanvas.Width = Math.Abs(TextCanvas.Width -
    leftOffset - rightOffset);
ChartCanvas.Height = Math.Abs(TextCanvas.Height -
    bottomOffset - size.Height / 2);

Rectangle chartRect = new Rectangle();
chartRect.Stroke = Brushes.Black;
chartRect.Width = ChartCanvas.Width;
chartRect.Height = ChartCanvas.Height;
ChartCanvas.Children.Add(chartRect);

// Create vertical gridlines:
if (IsYGrid == true)
{
    for (dx = Xmin + XTick; dx < Xmax; dx += XTick)
    {
        gridline = new Line();
        AddLinePattern();
        gridline.X1 = NormalizePoint(new Point(dx, Ymin)).X;
        gridline.Y1 = NormalizePoint(new Point(dx, Ymin)).Y;
        gridline.X2 = NormalizePoint(new Point(dx, Ymax)).X;
        gridline.Y2 = NormalizePoint(new Point(dx, Ymax)).Y;
        ChartCanvas.Children.Add(gridline);
    }
}

// Create horizontal gridlines:
if (IsXGrid == true)
{
    for (dy = Ymin + YTick; dy < Ymax; dy += YTick)
    {
        gridline = new Line();
        AddLinePattern();
        gridline.X1 = NormalizePoint(new Point(Xmin, dy)).X;
        gridline.Y1 = NormalizePoint(new Point(Xmin, dy)).Y;
        gridline.X2 = NormalizePoint(new Point(Xmax, dy)).X;
        gridline.Y2 = NormalizePoint(new Point(Xmax, dy)).Y;
        ChartCanvas.Children.Add(gridline);
    }
}

// Create x-axis tick marks:
for (dx = Xmin; dx <= Xmax; dx += xTick)
{
    pt = NormalizePoint(new Point(dx, Ymin));
    tick = new Line();
    tick.Stroke = Brushes.Black;
    tick.X1 = pt.X;
    tick.Y1 = pt.Y;
    tick.X2 = pt.X;
    tick.Y2 = pt.Y - 5;
    ChartCanvas.Children.Add(tick);

    tb = new TextBlock();
```

```
            tb.Text = dx.ToString();
            tb.Measure(new Size(Double.PositiveInfinity,
                                Double.PositiveInfinity));
            size = tb.DesiredSize;
            TextCanvas.Children.Add(tb);
            Canvas.SetLeft(tb, leftOffset + pt.X - size.Width / 2);
            Canvas.SetTop(tb, pt.Y + 2 + size.Height / 2);

        }

        // Create y-axis tick marks:
        for (dy = Ymin; dy <= Ymax; dy += YTick)
        {
            pt = NormalizePoint(new Point(Xmin, dy));
            tick = new Line();
            tick.Stroke = Brushes.Black;
            tick.X1 = pt.X;
            tick.Y1 = pt.Y;
            tick.X2 = pt.X + 5;
            tick.Y2 = pt.Y;
            ChartCanvas.Children.Add(tick);

            tb = new TextBlock();
            tb.Text = dy.ToString();
            tb.Measure(new Size(Double.PositiveInfinity,
                                Double.PositiveInfinity));
            size = tb.DesiredSize;
            TextCanvas.Children.Add(tb);
            Canvas.SetRight(tb, ChartCanvas.Width + rightOffset + 2);
            Canvas.SetTop(tb, pt.Y);
        }

        // Add title and labels:
        tbTitle.Text = Title;
        tbXLabel.Text = XLabel;
        tbYLabel.Text = YLabel;
        tbXLabel.Margin = new Thickness(leftOffset + 2, 2, 2, 2);
        tbTitle.Margin = new Thickness(leftOffset + 2, 2, 2, 2);
    }

    public void AddLinePattern()
    {
        gridline.Stroke = GridlineColor;
        gridline.StrokeThickness = 1;

        switch (GridlinePattern)
        {
            case LinePatternEnum.Dash:
                gridline.StrokeDashArray = new DoubleCollection() { 4, 3 };
                break;
            case LinePatternEnum.Dot:
                gridline.StrokeDashArray = new DoubleCollection() { 1, 2 };
                break;
            case LinePatternEnum.DashDot:
                gridline.StrokeDashArray = new DoubleCollection()
```

```
                    { 4, 2, 1, 2 };
            break;
        }
    }
}
}
```

This class inherits from the base class, *ChartStyleBase*. Here, I add more member fields and corresponding properties, which we use to manipulate the chart's layout and appearance. You can easily understand the meaning of each field and property from its name. Notice that I add another *Canvas* property, *TextCanvas*, which we use to hold the tick mark labels, while the *ChartCanvas* in the original *ChartStyleBase* class holds the chart itself.

In addition, I add the following member fields to define the gridlines for the chart:

```
private bool isXGrid = true;
private bool isYGrid = true;
private Brush gridlineColor = Brushes.LightGray;
private LinePatternEnum gridlinePattern;
```

These fields and their corresponding properties provide a great deal of flexibility in customizing the appearance of the gridlines. The *GridlinePattern* property allows you to choose various line dash styles, including solid, dash, dot, and dash-dot. You can change the gridlines' color using the *GridlineColor* property. In addition, I define two *bool* properties, *IsXGrid* and *IsYGrid*, which allow you to turn horizontal or vertical gridlines on or off.

I then define member fields and corresponding properties for the *X* and *Y* labels, the title, and the tick marks so that you can change them to your liking. If you like, you can easily add more member fields to control the appearance of your charts; for example, you can change the font and text color of the labels and title.

The *AddChartStyle* method seems quite complicated in this class; however, it is actually reasonably easy to follow. First, I make a lot of effort to define the size of the *ChartCanvas* by considering the suitable offset relative to the *TextCanvas*.

```
ChartCanvas.Width = Math.Abs(TextCanvas.Width - leftOffset - rightOffset);
ChartCanvas.Height = Math.Abs(TextCanvas.Height - bottomOffset - size.Height / 2);
```

Next, I draw gridlines with a specified color and line pattern. Please note that all of the end points of the gridlines have been transformed from the world coordinate system into device-independent pixels using the *NormalizePoint* method.

I then draw the tick marks for the *X* and *Y* axes of the chart. For each tick mark, I find the points in the device coordinate system at which the tick mark joins the axes and draw a black line, 5 pixels long, from this point toward the inside of the *ChartCanvas*.

The title and labels for the *X*- and *Y*-axes are attached to the corresponding *TextBlock* names in code. You can also create data bindings that bind the *Title*, *XLabel*, and *YLabel* properties to the corresponding *TextBlock* directly in the XAML file.

You can clearly see from the preceding code that this class involves dynamically creating and positioning controls, which is hard to achieve using XAML in the view. Here we choose a simple approach where we do all the dynamic creation and placement of the controls in the model or view model classes. In some situations, like the case in this example, you do not need to force yourself to follow the MVVM rules, especially when the rules make a simple problem complicated.

Creating a Chart with Gridlines

Here, you will recreate the chart shown in Figure 4-7, but this time with gridlines, title, and axis labels. Add a new *UserControl* to the *Views* folder and name it *LineGridView*. Here is XAML for this view:

```
<UserControl x:Class="Chapter04.Views.LineGridView"
             xmlns="http://schemas.microsoft.com/winfx/2006/xaml/presentation"
             xmlns:x="http://schemas.microsoft.com/winfx/2006/xaml"
             xmlns:mc="http://schemas.openxmlformats.org/markup-compatibility/2006"
             xmlns:d="http://schemas.microsoft.com/expression/blend/2008"
             xmlns:cal="http://www.caliburnproject.org"
             mc:Ignorable="d"
             d:DesignHeight="400" d:DesignWidth="400">

    <UserControl.Resources>
        <DataTemplate x:Key="chartTemplate">
            <Polyline Points="{Binding LinePoints}" Stroke="{Binding LineColor}"
                      StrokeThickness="{Binding LineThickness}"
                      StrokeDashArray="{Binding LineDashPattern}"/>
        </DataTemplate>
    </UserControl.Resources>

    <Grid Name="grid1" Margin="10">
        <Grid.ColumnDefinitions>
            <ColumnDefinition Width="Auto"/>
            <ColumnDefinition Name="column1" Width="*"/>
        </Grid.ColumnDefinitions>
        <Grid.RowDefinitions>
            <RowDefinition Height="Auto"/>
            <RowDefinition Name="row1" Height="*"/>
            <RowDefinition Height="Auto"/>
        </Grid.RowDefinitions>
        <TextBlock Margin="2" x:Name="tbTitle" Grid.Column="1" Grid.Row="0"
                   RenderTransformOrigin="0.5,0.5" FontSize="14" FontWeight="Bold"
                   HorizontalAlignment="Stretch" VerticalAlignment="Stretch"
                   TextAlignment="Center" Text="Title"/>
        <TextBlock Margin="2" x:Name="tbXLabel" Grid.Column="1" Grid.Row="2"
                   RenderTransformOrigin="0.5,0.5" TextAlignment="Center"
                   Text="X Axis"/>

        <TextBlock Margin="2" Name="tbYLabel" Grid.Column="0" Grid.Row="1"
                   RenderTransformOrigin="0.5,0.5" TextAlignment="Center"
                   Text="Y Axis">
            <TextBlock.LayoutTransform>
                <RotateTransform Angle="-90"/>
            </TextBlock.LayoutTransform>
        </TextBlock>

        <Grid  Margin="0,0,0,0" x:Name ="chartGrid" Grid.Column="1" Grid.Row="1"
               ClipToBounds="False" Background="Transparent"
               cal:Message.Attach="[Event SizeChanged]=[Action
                   AddLines($this.ActualWidth, $this.ActualHeight)];
               [Event Loaded]=[Action AddLines($this.ActualWidth,
                   $this.ActualHeight)]">
```

```
            <Canvas Margin="2" Name="textCanvas" Grid.Column="1"
                Grid.Row="1" ClipToBounds="True"
                Width="{Binding ElementName=chartGrid,Path=ActualWidth}"
                Height="{Binding ElementName=chartGrid,Path=ActualHeight}">
                <Canvas Name="chartCanvas" ClipToBounds="True">
                    <ItemsControl ItemsSource="{Binding DataCollection}"
                                ItemTemplate="{StaticResource chartTemplate}">
                        <ItemsControl.ItemsPanel>
                            <ItemsPanelTemplate>
                                <Grid/>
                            </ItemsPanelTemplate>
                        </ItemsControl.ItemsPanel>
                    </ItemsControl>
                </Canvas>
            </Canvas>
        </Grid>
    </Grid>
</UserControl>
```

Here, we put the title and labels for the *X-* and *Y-*axes into different cells of a *Grid* control, and define two canvas controls: *textCanvas* and *chartCanvas*. The *textCanvas* becomes a resizable *Canvas* control because its *Width* and *Height* properties are bound to *chartGrid*'s *ActualWidth* and *ActualHeight* properties. We use the *textCanvas* control, as a parent of the *chartCanvas*, to hold the tick mark labels; the *chartCanvas* control will hold the chart itself. We can also reuse the *DataCollection* object and *LineSeries* class from the preceding example. Finally, we use the *ChartStyle* class, inheriting from the *ChartStyleBase* class, to create gridlines, labels, and tick marks.

As in the preceding example, we define a *DataTemplate* called *chartTemplate* in *UserControl*'s Resources. The *chartTemplate* defines a *Polyline* object whose properties are bound directly to the corresponding properties of the *LineSeries*. We then bind the *ItemsControl*'s *ItemsSource* property to the *LineSeries* collection called *DataCollection* defined in the view model. The items in the *ItemsControl* should be represented using the *chartTemplate* we defined earlier, which is specified by the *ItemTemplate* property.

Add a new class to the *ViewModels* folder and name it *LineGridViewModel*. Here is the code for this class:

```
using System;
using System.Linq;
using Caliburn.Micro;
using System.Collections.ObjectModel;
using System.ComponentModel.Composition;
using System.Windows.Documents;
using System.Collections.Generic;
using System.Windows;
using Chapter04.Models;
using System.Windows.Media;
using System.Windows.Controls;
using Chapter04.Views;
using Chapter04.Models.ChartModel;

namespace Chapter04.ViewModels
{
    [Export(typeof(IScreen)), PartCreationPolicy(CreationPolicy.NonShared)]
    public class LineGridViewModel : Screen
```

```
{
    private readonly IEventAggregator _events;
    LineGridView view;
    [ImportingConstructor]
     public LineGridViewModel(IEventAggregator events)
    {
        this._events = events;
        DisplayName = "03. Gridlines";
        DataCollection = new BindableCollection<LineSeries>();
    }

    private ChartStyle cs;
    public BindableCollection<LineSeries> DataCollection { get; set; }

    private void SetChartStyle()
    {
        var view = this.GetView() as LineGridView;
        view.chartCanvas.Children.RemoveRange(1,
            view.chartCanvas.Children.Count - 1);
        view.textCanvas.Children.RemoveRange(1,
            view.textCanvas.Children.Count - 1);
        cs = new ChartStyle();
        cs.ChartCanvas = view.chartCanvas;
        cs.TextCanvas = view.textCanvas;
        cs.Title = "Sine and Cosine Chart";
        cs.Xmin = 0;
        cs.Xmax = 7;
        cs.Ymin = -1.5;
        cs.Ymax = 1.5;
        cs.YTick = 0.5;
        cs.GridlinePattern = LinePatternEnum.Dot;
        cs.GridlineColor = Brushes.Black;
        cs.AddChartStyle(view.tbTitle, view.tbXLabel, view.tbYLabel);

    }

    public void AddLines(double width, double height)
    {
        SetChartStyle();

        DataCollection.Clear();
        var ds = new LineSeries();
        ds.LineColor = Brushes.Blue;
        ds.LineThickness = 2;
        ds.LinePattern = LinePatternEnum.Solid;
        for (int i = 0; i < 50; i++)
        {
            double x = i / 5.0;
            double y = Math.Sin(x);
            ds.LinePoints.Add(new Point(x, y));
        }
        DataCollection.Add(ds);

        ds = new LineSeries();
        ds.LineColor = Brushes.Red;
```

```
        ds.LineThickness = 2;
        ds.LinePattern = LinePatternEnum.Dash;
        ds.SetLinePattern();
        for (int i = 0; i < 50; i++)
        {
            double x = i / 5.0;
            double y = Math.Cos(x);
            ds.LinePoints.Add(new Point(x, y));
        }
        DataCollection.Add(ds);
        cs.SetLines(DataCollection);
    }
  }
}
```

Pay special attention to how we access the view from the view model. Caliburn.Micro provides a method called *GetView* that allows you to access the view easily. As discussed in the preceding section, the *ChartStyle* class needs to access the *textCanvas* and *chartCanvas* controls that are created in the view, so within the *SetChartStyle* method we access the view using the following code snippet:

```
var view = this.GetView() as LineGridView;
view.chartCanvas.Children.RemoveRange(1, view.chartCanvas.Children.Count - 1);
view.textCanvas.Children.RemoveRange(1, view.textCanvas.Children.Count - 1);
cs = new ChartStyle();
cs.ChartCanvas = view.chartCanvas;
cs.TextCanvas = view.textCanvas;
```

First we get the view object via the *GetView* method. In order to redraw the chart when the application window is resized, we need to recreate all of the children elements of the *textCanvas* except for the *chartCanvas*, and remove all of the children controls of the *chartCanvas* except for the *ItemControl*, which we achieved with the bolded code statements in the foregoing code snippet. We then create the *ChartStyle* object and set its *ChartCanvas* and *TextCanvas* properties to the view's corresponding controls.

Within the *AddLines* method, we first call the *SetChartStyle* method that sets the gridlines, title, tick marks and axis labels. The rest of the code is similar to that used in the previous example. Figure 4-8 illustrates the results of running this application. You can see that the chart has a title, labels, gridlines, and tick marks. Obviously, there is still no chart legend. I will show you how to add a legend in the next section.

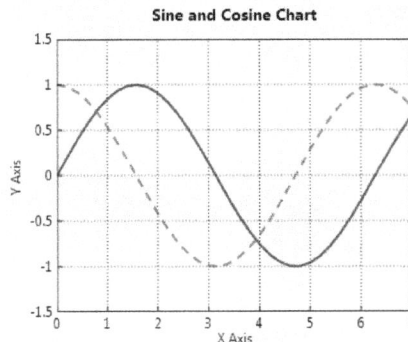

Figure 4-8. A line chart with gridlines and labels.

Legends

For a 2D line chart with multiple curves, you may want to use a legend to identify each curve plotted on your chart. The legend will show a sample of the curve type, marker symbol, color, and text label you specify.

Legend Class

Add a new class to the *ChartModel* folder and name it *Legend*. The following is the code for this class:

```
using System;
using System.Windows.Controls;
using System.Windows;
using System.Windows.Media;
using System.Windows.Shapes;
using Caliburn.Micro;

namespace Chapter04.Models.ChartModel
{
    public class Legend
    {
        private bool isLegend;
        private bool isBorder;
        private Canvas legendCanvas;
        private LegendPositionEnum legendPosition;

        public Legend()
        {
            isLegend = false;
            isBorder = true;
            legendPosition = LegendPositionEnum.NorthEast;
        }

        public LegendPositionEnum LegendPosition
        {
            get { return legendPosition; }
            set { legendPosition = value; }
        }

        public bool IsLegend
        {
            get { return isLegend; }
            set { isLegend = value; }
        }

        public bool IsBorder
        {
            get { return isBorder; }
            set { isBorder = value; }
        }

        public void AddLegend(Canvas chartCanvas, BindableCollection<LineSeries> dc)
        {
            legendCanvas = new Canvas();
```

```
TextBlock tb = new TextBlock();
if (dc.Count < 1 || !IsLegend)
    return;
int n = 0;
string[] legendLabels = new string[dc.Count];
foreach (LineSeries ds in dc)
{
    legendLabels[n] = ds.SeriesName;
    n++;
}

double legendWidth = 0;
Size size = new Size(0, 0);
for (int i = 0; i < legendLabels.Length; i++)
{
    tb = new TextBlock();
    tb.Text = legendLabels[i];
    tb.Measure(new Size(Double.PositiveInfinity,
                        Double.PositiveInfinity));
    size = tb.DesiredSize;
    if (legendWidth < size.Width)
        legendWidth = size.Width;
}

legendWidth += 50;
legendCanvas.Width = legendWidth + 5;
double legendHeight = 17 * dc.Count;
double sx = 6;
double sy = 0;
double textHeight = size.Height;
double lineLength = 34;
Rectangle legendRect = new Rectangle();
legendRect.Stroke = Brushes.Black;
legendRect.Fill = Brushes.White;
legendRect.Width = legendWidth;
legendRect.Height = legendHeight;

if (IsLegend && IsBorder)
    legendCanvas.Children.Add(legendRect);
Canvas.SetZIndex(legendCanvas, 10);

n = 1;
foreach (LineSeries ds in dc)
{
    double xSymbol = sx + lineLength / 2;
    double xText = 2 * sx + lineLength;
    double yText = n * sy + (2 * n - 1) * textHeight / 2;
    Line line = new Line();
    AddLinePattern(line, ds);
    line.X1 = sx;
    line.Y1 = yText;
    line.X2 = sx + lineLength;
    line.Y2 = yText;
    legendCanvas.Children.Add(line);
    ds.Symbols.AddSymbol(legendCanvas,
```

```
                        new Point(0.5 * (line.X2 - line.X1 +
                                  ds.Symbols.SymbolSize) + 1, line.Y1));
            tb = new TextBlock();
            tb.Text = ds.SeriesName;
            legendCanvas.Children.Add(tb);
            Canvas.SetTop(tb, yText - size.Height / 2);
            Canvas.SetLeft(tb, xText);
            n++;
        }
        legendCanvas.Width = legendRect.Width;
        legendCanvas.Height = legendRect.Height;

        double offSet = 7.0;
        switch (LegendPosition)
        {
            case LegendPositionEnum.East:
                Canvas.SetRight(legendCanvas, offSet);
                Canvas.SetTop(legendCanvas,
                        chartCanvas.Height / 2 - legendRect.Height / 2);
                break;
            case LegendPositionEnum.NorthEast:
                Canvas.SetTop(legendCanvas, offSet);
                Canvas.SetRight(legendCanvas, offSet);
                break;
            case LegendPositionEnum.North:
                Canvas.SetTop(legendCanvas, offSet);
                Canvas.SetLeft(legendCanvas,
                        chartCanvas.Width / 2 - legendRect.Width / 2);
                break;
            case LegendPositionEnum.NorthWest:
                Canvas.SetTop(legendCanvas, offSet);
                Canvas.SetLeft(legendCanvas, offSet);
                break;
            case LegendPositionEnum.West:
                Canvas.SetTop(legendCanvas,
                        chartCanvas.Height / 2 - legendRect.Height / 2);
                Canvas.SetLeft(legendCanvas, offSet);
                break;
            case LegendPositionEnum.SouthWest:
                Canvas.SetBottom(legendCanvas, offSet);
                Canvas.SetLeft(legendCanvas, offSet);
                break;
            case LegendPositionEnum.South:
                Canvas.SetBottom(legendCanvas, offSet);
                Canvas.SetLeft(legendCanvas,
                    chartCanvas.Width / 2 - legendRect.Width / 2);
                break;
            case LegendPositionEnum.SouthEast:
                Canvas.SetBottom(legendCanvas, offSet);
                Canvas.SetRight(legendCanvas, offSet);
                break;
        }
        chartCanvas.Children.Add(legendCanvas);
    }
```

```
private void AddLinePattern(Line line, LineSeries ds)
{
    line.Stroke = ds.LineColor;
    line.StrokeThickness = ds.LineThickness;

    switch (ds.LinePattern)
    {
        case LinePatternEnum.Dash:
            line.StrokeDashArray =
                new DoubleCollection(new double[2] { 4, 3 });
            break;
        case LinePatternEnum.Dot:
            line.StrokeDashArray =
                new DoubleCollection(new double[2] { 1, 2 });
            break;
        case LinePatternEnum.DashDot:
            line.StrokeDashArray =
                new DoubleCollection(new double[4] { 4, 2, 1, 2 });
            break;
    }
}
}


public enum LegendPositionEnum
{
    North,
    NorthWest,
    West,
    SouthWest,
    South,
    SouthEast,
    East,
    NorthEast
}
}
```

At first glance, this class looks quite complicated. However, if you read through it carefully, you will actually find it quite easy to follow what is happening. It begins with the following member fields, which describe the legend behavior:

```
private bool isLegend;
private bool isBorder;
private Canvas legendCanvas;
private LegendPositionEnum legendPosition;
```

The *isLegend* allows you to turn the legend on or off. The default setting for this field is false. Therefore, you need to change this default value to true if you want to display the legend on your chart. The *isBorder* field allows you to add a border to the legend. You use the *legendCanvas* to hold the legend and the *legendPosition* to control the location of the legend in the chart. You can add more member fields if you want more control over the legend. For example, you can add corresponding field members and properties for changing the legend's text color, font, background color, etc. Here, I simply want to show you the basic steps of creating a legend, without adding these extra features.

Note that the *Legend* class uses the *LineSeries* class containing the *Symbols*, which we will implement in the next section.

In this class, we use the legend layout shown in Figure 4-9. The placement of the legend in the chart is controlled by the *LegendPosition* property, which we specify in the enumeration *LegendPositionEnum*. We have eight positions from which to choose: *North*, *South*, *West*, *East*, *NorthWest*, *NorthEast*, *SouthWest*, and *SouthEast*. The default setting is *NorthEast*, corresponding to the upper-right corner of the chart.

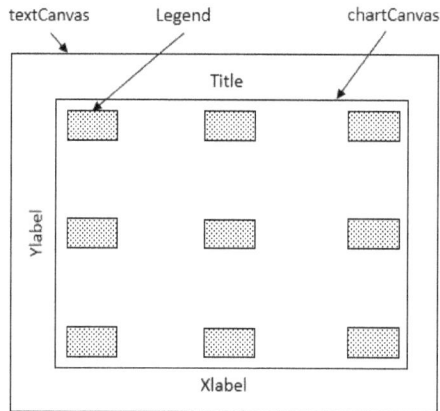

Figure 4-9. Legend layout on the chart.

If you wish, you can also add more positions, such as the right side or the bottom of the chart, to the *LegendPositionEnum*. Next, I implement the properties for all of these member fields using the *get* and *set* statements.

Finally, I use the *AddLegend* method to create the legend. This method defines the contents of a single legend, including the line type, marker symbol, color, and text label. It is also responsible for placing the legend in the suitable position through a *switch* statement by setting the position of the *legendCanvas*.

Creating a Chart with a Legend

Here, I will use an example to demonstrate how to create a line chart with a legend. Add a *UserControl* to the Views folder and name it *LineLegendView*. Here is its XAML:

```
<UserControl x:Class="Chapter04.Views.LineLegendView"
             xmlns="http://schemas.microsoft.com/winfx/2006/xaml/presentation"
             xmlns:x="http://schemas.microsoft.com/winfx/2006/xaml"
             xmlns:mc="http://schemas.openxmlformats.org/markup-compatibility/2006"
             xmlns:d="http://schemas.microsoft.com/expression/blend/2008"
             xmlns:cal="http://www.caliburnproject.org"
             mc:Ignorable="d"
             d:DesignHeight="400" d:DesignWidth="400">

    <UserControl.Resources>
        <DataTemplate x:Key="chartTemplate">
            <Polyline Points="{Binding LinePoints}" Stroke="{Binding LineColor}"
StrokeThickness="{Binding LineThickness}" StrokeDashArray="{Binding
LineDashPattern}"/>
        </DataTemplate>
    </UserControl.Resources>
```

```
    <Grid Name="grid1" Margin="10">
        <Grid.ColumnDefinitions>
            <ColumnDefinition Width="Auto"/>
            <ColumnDefinition Name="column1" Width="*"/>
        </Grid.ColumnDefinitions>
        <Grid.RowDefinitions>
            <RowDefinition Height="Auto"/>
            <RowDefinition Name="row1" Height="*"/>
            <RowDefinition Height="Auto"/>
        </Grid.RowDefinitions>
        <TextBlock Margin="2" x:Name="tbTitle" Grid.Column="1" Grid.Row="0"
                RenderTransformOrigin="0.5,0.5" FontSize="14" FontWeight="Bold"
                HorizontalAlignment="Stretch" VerticalAlignment="Stretch"
                TextAlignment="Center" Text="Title"/>
        <TextBlock Margin="2" x:Name="tbXLabel" Grid.Column="1" Grid.Row="2"
                RenderTransformOrigin="0.5,0.5" TextAlignment="Center"
                Text="X Axis"/>

        <TextBlock Margin="2" Name="tbYLabel" Grid.Column="0" Grid.Row="1"
                RenderTransformOrigin="0.5,0.5" TextAlignment="Center"
                Text="Y Axis">
            <TextBlock.LayoutTransform>
                <RotateTransform Angle="-90"/>
            </TextBlock.LayoutTransform>
        </TextBlock>

        <Grid  Margin="0,0,0,0" x:Name ="chartGrid" Grid.Column="1" Grid.Row="1"
            ClipToBounds="False" Background="Transparent"
            cal:Message.Attach="[Event SizeChanged]=[Action
                AddLines($this.ActualWidth, $this.ActualHeight)];
            [Event Loaded]=[Action AddLines($this.ActualWidth,
                $this.ActualHeight)]">

        <Canvas Margin="2" Name="textCanvas" Grid.Column="1"
                Grid.Row="1" ClipToBounds="True"
                Width="{Binding ElementName=chartGrid,Path=ActualWidth}"
                Height="{Binding ElementName=chartGrid,Path=ActualHeight}">
            <Canvas Name="chartCanvas" ClipToBounds="True">
                <ItemsControl ItemsSource="{Binding DataCollection}"
                            ItemTemplate="{StaticResource chartTemplate}">
                    <ItemsControl.ItemsPanel>
                        <ItemsPanelTemplate>
                            <Grid/>
                        </ItemsPanelTemplate>
                    </ItemsControl.ItemsPanel>
                </ItemsControl>
            </Canvas>
        </Canvas>
        </Grid>
    </Grid>
</UserControl>
```

This markup is basically similar to that used in the previous example. Here you create two canvas controls, *textCanvas* and *chartCanvas*. The *textCanvas* control, as a parent of the *chartCanvas*, will hold the tick mark labels, and the *chartCanvas* control will hold the chart itself and the legend.

Add a new class to the *ViewModels* and name it *LineLegendViewModel*. The following code is for this class:

```
using System;
using System.Linq;
using Caliburn.Micro;
using System.Collections.ObjectModel;
using System.ComponentModel.Composition;
using System.Windows.Documents;
using System.Collections.Generic;
using System.Windows;
using Chapter04.Models;
using System.Windows.Media;
using System.Windows.Controls;
using Chapter04.Views;
using Chapter04.Models.ChartModel;

namespace Chapter04.ViewModels
{
    [Export(typeof(IScreen)), PartCreationPolicy(CreationPolicy.NonShared)]
    public class LineLegendViewModel : Screen
    {
        private readonly IEventAggregator _events;
        [ImportingConstructor]
        public LineLegendViewModel(IEventAggregator events)
        {
            this._events = events;
            DisplayName = "04. Legend";
            DataCollection = new BindableCollection<LineSeries>();
        }

        LineLegendView view;
        private ChartStyle cs;
        private Legend lg;
        public BindableCollection<LineSeries> DataCollection { get; set; }

        private void SetChartStyle()
        {
            cs = new ChartStyle();
            cs.ChartCanvas = view.chartCanvas;
            cs.TextCanvas = view.textCanvas;
            cs.Title = "Chart with Legend";
            cs.Xmin = 0;
            cs.Xmax = 7;
            cs.Ymin = -1.5;
            cs.Ymax = 1.5;
            cs.YTick = 0.5;
            cs.GridlinePattern = LinePatternEnum.Dot;
            cs.GridlineColor = Brushes.Black;
            cs.AddChartStyle(view.tbTitle, view.tbXLabel, view.tbYLabel);
        }
```

```
private void SetLegend()
{
    lg = new Legend();
    lg.IsLegend = true;
    lg.IsBorder = true;
    lg.LegendPosition = LegendPositionEnum.NorthWest;
    lg.AddLegend(view.chartCanvas, DataCollection);
}

public void AddLines(double width, double height)
{
    view = this.GetView() as LineLegendView;
    view.chartCanvas.Children.RemoveRange(1,
        view.chartCanvas.Children.Count - 1);
    view.textCanvas.Children.RemoveRange(1,
        view.textCanvas.Children.Count - 1);
    SetChartStyle();

    DataCollection.Clear();
    var ds = new LineSeries();
    ds.LineColor = Brushes.Blue;
    ds.LineThickness = 2;
    ds.SeriesName = "Sine";
    ds.LinePattern = LinePatternEnum.Solid;
    for (int i = 0; i < 50; i++)
    {
        double x = i / 5.0;
        double y = Math.Sin(x);
        ds.LinePoints.Add(new Point(x, y));
    }
    DataCollection.Add(ds);

    ds = new LineSeries();
    ds.LineColor = Brushes.Red;
    ds.LineThickness = 2;
    ds.SeriesName = "Cosine";
    ds.LinePattern = LinePatternEnum.Dash;
    for (int i = 0; i < 50; i++)
    {
        double x = i / 5.0;
        double y = Math.Cos(x);
        ds.LinePoints.Add(new Point(x, y));
    }
    DataCollection.Add(ds);

    ds = new LineSeries();
    ds.LineColor = Brushes.DarkGreen;
    ds.LineThickness = 2;
    ds.SeriesName = "Sine^2";
    ds.LinePattern = LinePatternEnum.Dash;
    for (int i = 0; i < 50; i++)
    {
        double x = i / 5.0;
        double y = Math.Sin(x) * Math.Sin(x);
```

```
                ds.LinePoints.Add(new Point(x, y));
        }
        DataCollection.Add(ds);
        cs.SetLines(DataCollection);
        SetLegend();
    }
  }
}
```

This class also looks similar to that used in the previous example. The bolded code is specifically required in order to add the legend. Note that you need to specify the *SeriesName* property for each *LineSeries* because the *Legend* uses the *SeriesName* as the legend labels. Otherwise, the legend will use the default *SeriesName* (*LineSeries0, LineSeries1, LineSeries2*, etc.) as its labels. Here, you first create *LineLegendView, ChartStyle*, and *Legend* objects. Both the *ChartStyle* and *Legend* classes need to access the *View*'s controls, which you can clearly see when you look into the *SetChartStyle* and *SetLegend* methods.

In order to have the legend appear on your chart, you need to call the *AddLegend* method. First set the *Legend*'s *IsLegend* property to true. Please note that you must place the *AddLegend* method after the *SetLines* for *DataCollection* object method because the legend needs to know how many curves are on your chart.

Figure 4-10 shows the results of running this example.

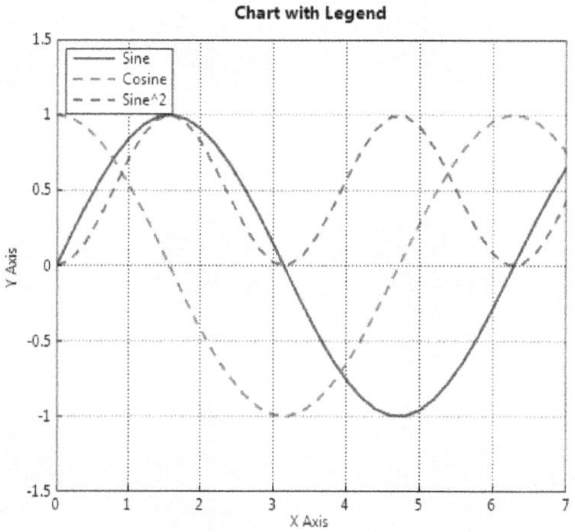

Figure 4-10. Chart with legend.

Symbols

Sometimes, you may want a chart to display not only lines but also symbols as well as the data points. Sometimes you may want to have a chart with only symbols and no lines. In this section, I will show you how to create such charts in WPF.

Defining Symbols

Let's first look at two symbols, the diamond and the triangle, as shown in Figure 4-11. The surrounding dashed-line square outlines the size of the symbol; (x_c, y_c) represent the center coordinates of the symbol in the device coordinate system. Suppose the length of each side of the dotted-line square is *SymbolSize* and that we define *halfsize= SymbolSize/2.* We can then easily determine the coordinates of the points at the vertices of each symbol.

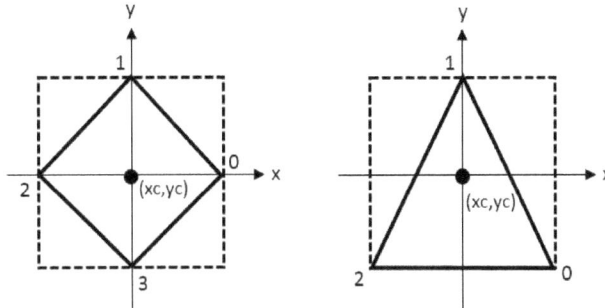

Figure 4-11. Definitions of the diamond symbol (left) and the triangle symbol (right).

For the diamond symbol, we have the following coordinates:

```
Point0: (xc + halfsize, yc)
Point1: (xc, yc + halfsize)
Point2: (xc - halfsize, yc)
Point3: (xc, yc - halfsize)
```

We can then use the *Polygon* object to create either an open or a solid diamond symbol by controlling the *Polygon*'s *Fill* property. For the triangle symbol, the corresponding point coordinates are:

```
Point0: (xc + halfsize, yc - halfsize)
Point1: (xc, yc + halfsize)
Point2: (xc - halfsize, yc - halfsize)
```

Again, we can use the *Polygon* object's *Fill* property to create either an open or a solid triangle symbol. By following the procedure presented here, you can create any symbol you want to use in your chart applications.

Symbol Class

Add a new class to the *ChartModel* folder and name it *Symbols*. The following is the code for this class:

```
using System;
using System.Collections.Generic;
using System.Windows.Controls;
using System.Windows;
using System.Windows.Media;
using System.Windows.Shapes;

namespace Chapter04.Models.ChartModel
{
    public class Symbols
```

```csharp
{
    private SymbolTypeEnum symbolType;
    private double symbolSize;
    private Brush borderColor;
    private Brush fillColor;
    private double borderThickness;

    public Symbols()
    {
        symbolType = SymbolTypeEnum.None;
        symbolSize = 8.0;
        borderColor = Brushes.Black;
        fillColor = Brushes.Black;
        borderThickness = 1.0;
    }

    public double BorderThickness
    {
        get { return borderThickness; }
        set { borderThickness = value; }
    }

    public Brush BorderColor
    {
        get { return borderColor; }
        set { borderColor = value; }
    }

    public Brush FillColor
    {
        get { return fillColor; }
        set { fillColor = value; }
    }

    public double SymbolSize
    {
        get { return symbolSize; }
        set { symbolSize = value; }
    }

    public SymbolTypeEnum SymbolType
    {
        get { return symbolType; }
        set { symbolType = value; }
    }


    public void AddSymbol(Canvas chartCanvas, Point pt)
    {
        Polygon plg = new Polygon();
        plg.Stroke = BorderColor;
        plg.StrokeThickness = BorderThickness;
        Ellipse ellipse = new Ellipse();
        ellipse.Stroke = BorderColor;
        ellipse.StrokeThickness = BorderThickness;
```

```
Line line = new Line();
double halfSize = 0.5 * SymbolSize;

Canvas.SetZIndex(plg, 5);
Canvas.SetZIndex(ellipse, 5);

switch (SymbolType)
{
    case SymbolTypeEnum.None:
        break;
    case SymbolTypeEnum.Square:
        plg.Fill = Brushes.White;
        plg.Points.Add(new Point(pt.X - halfSize, pt.Y - halfSize));
        plg.Points.Add(new Point(pt.X + halfSize, pt.Y - halfSize));
        plg.Points.Add(new Point(pt.X + halfSize, pt.Y + halfSize));
        plg.Points.Add(new Point(pt.X - halfSize, pt.Y + halfSize));
      chartCanvas.Children.Add(plg);
        break;
    case SymbolTypeEnum.OpenDiamond:
        plg.Fill = Brushes.White;
        plg.Points.Add(new Point(pt.X - halfSize, pt.Y));
        plg.Points.Add(new Point(pt.X, pt.Y - halfSize));
        plg.Points.Add(new Point(pt.X + halfSize, pt.Y));
        plg.Points.Add(new Point(pt.X, pt.Y + halfSize));
        chartCanvas.Children.Add(plg);
        break;
    case SymbolTypeEnum.Circle:
        ellipse.Fill = Brushes.White;
        ellipse.Width = SymbolSize;
        ellipse.Height = SymbolSize;
        Canvas.SetLeft(ellipse, pt.X - halfSize);
        Canvas.SetTop(ellipse, pt.Y - halfSize);
        chartCanvas.Children.Add(ellipse);
        break;
    case SymbolTypeEnum.OpenTriangle:
        plg.Fill = Brushes.White;
        plg.Points.Add(new Point(pt.X - halfSize, pt.Y + halfSize));
        plg.Points.Add(new Point(pt.X, pt.Y - halfSize));
        plg.Points.Add(new Point(pt.X + halfSize, pt.Y + halfSize));
        chartCanvas.Children.Add(plg);
        break;
    case SymbolTypeEnum.Cross:
        line = new Line();
        Canvas.SetZIndex(line, 5);
        line.Stroke = BorderColor;
        line.StrokeThickness = BorderThickness;
        line.X1 = pt.X - halfSize;
        line.Y1 = pt.Y + halfSize;
        line.X2 = pt.X + halfSize;
        line.Y2 = pt.Y - halfSize;
        chartCanvas.Children.Add(line);
        line = new Line();
        Canvas.SetZIndex(line, 5);
        line.Stroke = BorderColor;
        line.StrokeThickness = BorderThickness;
```

```
            line.X1 = pt.X - halfSize;
            line.Y1 = pt.Y - halfSize;
            line.X2 = pt.X + halfSize;
            line.Y2 = pt.Y + halfSize;
            chartCanvas.Children.Add(line);
            Canvas.SetZIndex(line, 5);
            break;
        case SymbolTypeEnum.Star:
            line = new Line();
            Canvas.SetZIndex(line, 5);
            line.Stroke = BorderColor;
            line.StrokeThickness = BorderThickness;
            line.X1 = pt.X - halfSize;
            line.Y1 = pt.Y + halfSize;
            line.X2 = pt.X + halfSize;
            line.Y2 = pt.Y - halfSize;
            chartCanvas.Children.Add(line);
            line = new Line();
            Canvas.SetZIndex(line, 5);
            line.Stroke = BorderColor;
            line.StrokeThickness = BorderThickness;
            line.X1 = pt.X - halfSize;
            line.Y1 = pt.Y - halfSize;
            line.X2 = pt.X + halfSize;
            line.Y2 = pt.Y + halfSize;
            chartCanvas.Children.Add(line);
            line = new Line();
            Canvas.SetZIndex(line, 5);
            line.Stroke = BorderColor;
            line.StrokeThickness = BorderThickness;
            line.X1 = pt.X - halfSize;
            line.Y1 = pt.Y;
            line.X2 = pt.X + halfSize;
            line.Y2 = pt.Y;
            chartCanvas.Children.Add(line);
            line = new Line();
            Canvas.SetZIndex(line, 5);
            line.Stroke = BorderColor;
            line.StrokeThickness = BorderThickness;
            line.X1 = pt.X;
            line.Y1 = pt.Y - halfSize;
            line.X2 = pt.X;
            line.Y2 = pt.Y + halfSize;
            chartCanvas.Children.Add(line);
            break;
        case SymbolTypeEnum.OpenInvertedTriangle:
            plg.Fill = Brushes.White;
            plg.Points.Add(new Point(pt.X, pt.Y + halfSize));
            plg.Points.Add(new Point(pt.X - halfSize, pt.Y - halfSize));
            plg.Points.Add(new Point(pt.X + halfSize, pt.Y - halfSize));
            chartCanvas.Children.Add(plg);
            break;
        case SymbolTypeEnum.Plus:
            line = new Line();
            Canvas.SetZIndex(line, 5);
```

```
            line.Stroke = BorderColor;
            line.StrokeThickness = BorderThickness;
            line.X1 = pt.X - halfSize;
            line.Y1 = pt.Y;
            line.X2 = pt.X + halfSize;
            line.Y2 = pt.Y;
            chartCanvas.Children.Add(line);
            line = new Line();
            Canvas.SetZIndex(line, 5);
            line.Stroke = BorderColor;
            line.StrokeThickness = BorderThickness;
            line.X1 = pt.X;
            line.Y1 = pt.Y - halfSize;
            line.X2 = pt.X;
            line.Y2 = pt.Y + halfSize;
            chartCanvas.Children.Add(line);
            break;
    case SymbolTypeEnum.Dot:
            ellipse.Fill = FillColor;
            ellipse.Width = SymbolSize;
            ellipse.Height = SymbolSize;
            Canvas.SetLeft(ellipse, pt.X - halfSize);
            Canvas.SetTop(ellipse, pt.Y - halfSize);
            chartCanvas.Children.Add(ellipse);
            break;
    case SymbolTypeEnum.Box:
            plg.Fill = FillColor;
            plg.Points.Add(new Point(pt.X - halfSize, pt.Y - halfSize));
            plg.Points.Add(new Point(pt.X + halfSize, pt.Y - halfSize));
            plg.Points.Add(new Point(pt.X + halfSize, pt.Y + halfSize));
            plg.Points.Add(new Point(pt.X - halfSize, pt.Y + halfSize));
            chartCanvas.Children.Add(plg);
            break;
    case SymbolTypeEnum.Diamond:
            plg.Fill = FillColor;
            plg.Points.Add(new Point(pt.X - halfSize, pt.Y));
            plg.Points.Add(new Point(pt.X, pt.Y - halfSize));
            plg.Points.Add(new Point(pt.X + halfSize, pt.Y));
            plg.Points.Add(new Point(pt.X, pt.Y + halfSize));
            chartCanvas.Children.Add(plg);
            break;
    case SymbolTypeEnum.InvertedTriangle:
            plg.Fill = FillColor;
            plg.Points.Add(new Point(pt.X, pt.Y + halfSize));
            plg.Points.Add(new Point(pt.X - halfSize, pt.Y - halfSize));
            plg.Points.Add(new Point(pt.X + halfSize, pt.Y - halfSize));
            chartCanvas.Children.Add(plg);
            break;
    case SymbolTypeEnum.Triangle:
            plg.Fill = FillColor;
            plg.Points.Add(new Point(pt.X - halfSize, pt.Y + halfSize));
            plg.Points.Add(new Point(pt.X, pt.Y - halfSize));
            plg.Points.Add(new Point(pt.X + halfSize, pt.Y + halfSize));
            chartCanvas.Children.Add(plg);
            break;
```

```
                }
            }
        }


    public enum SymbolTypeEnum
    {
        Box = 6,
        Circle = 1,
        Cross = 2,
        Diamond = 3,
        Dot = 4,
        InvertedTriangle = 5,
        None = 0,
        OpenDiamond = 7,
        OpenInvertedTriangle = 8,
        OpenTriangle = 9,
        Square = 10,
        Star = 11,
        Triangle = 12,
        Plus = 13
    }
}
```

In this class, we define five private fields and their corresponding public properties. You can select the type of symbol from the *SymbolTypeEnum* enumeration using the *SymbolType* property. The *SymbolTypeEnum* contains 13 different symbols as well as a *None* type, which means that no symbols will be drawn on your chart. This type is the default value, so you must choose a symbol type other than *None* if you want to draw symbols on your chart applications. You can easily add your own symbols to this enumeration as you like.

The *BorderColor* property allows you to specify the border color of a symbol. For the *Star*, *Plus*, and open symbols, the *BorderColor* property is the only property you need to define. The default color for this property is black. The *FillColor* property, with a default color of white, is defined for solid symbols, such as the diamond, triangle, box, and dot. This means that it is possible for a solid symbol to have a border of a different color than its fill by specifying different colors for the *BorderColor* and *FillColor* properties.

The *BorderThickess* property allows you to specify the borderline thickness for a symbol. The default value of this property is 1 pixel. The *SymbolSize* property, which has a default value of 8 pixels, controls the symbol size,

There is a public method in this class called *AddSymbol*, which takes *Canvas* and *Point* objects as input. The *Canvas* object should be the *ChartCanvas* you defined in the *ChartStyle* class, and the *Point* object represents the center location of the symbol. Note that you must define this input *Point* in the device coordinate system. Namely, a *Point* in the world coordinate system must undergo a transformation from the world system into the device system using the *NormalizePoint* method implemented in the *ChartStyle* class.

Notice that the symbols must be associated with a *LineSeries* because each *LineSeries* can have a different symbol. Thus, you need to add the *Symbols* object to the *LineSeries* class. Open the *LineSeries* class and add the following public property to it:

```
using System;
using System.Windows.Media;
```

```
using System.Windows.Shapes;
using Caliburn.Micro;
using System.Windows;

namespace Chapter04.Models.ChartModel
{
    public class LineSeries : PropertyChangedBase
    {
        public LineSeries()
        {
            LinePoints = new PointCollection();
            Symbols = new Symbols();
        }
        public Symbols Symbols { get; set; }


        ......

    }
}
```

In order to add the symbols to your chart, you will also need to add the corresponding code snippet (bolded code) to the *SetLines* method in the *ChartStyleBase* class:

```
using System;
using System.Windows;
using System.Windows.Controls;
using Caliburn.Micro;

namespace Chapter04.Models.ChartModel
{
    public class ChartStyleBase
    {
    ......

        public void SetLines(BindableCollection<LineSeries> dc)
        {
            if (dc.Count <= 0)
                return;
            for(int i = 0;i<dc.Count;i++)
            {
                if (dc[i].SeriesName == "Default")
                    dc[i].SeriesName = "LineSeries" + i.ToString();
                dc[i].SetLinePattern();
                for (int j = 0; j < dc[i].LinePoints.Count; j++)
                {
                    dc[i].LinePoints[j] = NormalizePoint(dc[i].LinePoints[j]);
                    if (dc[i].Symbols.SymbolType != SymbolTypeEnum.None)
                        dc[i].Symbols.AddSymbol(ChartCanvas, dc[i].LinePoints[j]);
                }
            }
        }
    }
}
```

Creating a Chart with Symbols

Now I will demonstrate how to create a line chart with symbols using an example. Add a new *UserControl* to the *Views* folder and name it *LineSymbolView*. The XAML file for this example is the same as that used in the previous example for *LineLegendView*, and I will not list it here.

Add a new class to the *ViewModels* folder and name it *LineSymbolViewModel*. Here is the code for this class:

```
using System;
using System.Linq;
using Caliburn.Micro;
using System.Collections.ObjectModel;
using System.ComponentModel.Composition;
using System.Windows.Documents;
using System.Collections.Generic;
using System.Windows;
using Chapter04.Models;
using System.Windows.Media;
using System.Windows.Controls;
using Chapter04.Views;
using Chapter04.Models.ChartModel;

namespace Chapter04.ViewModels
{
    [Export(typeof(IScreen)), PartCreationPolicy(CreationPolicy.NonShared)]
    public class LineSymbolViewModel : Screen
    {
        private readonly IEventAggregator _events;
        [ImportingConstructor]
        public LineSymbolViewModel(IEventAggregator events)
        {
            this._events = events;
            DisplayName = "04. Symbols";
            DataCollection = new BindableCollection<LineSeries>();
        }

        LineSymbolView view;
        private ChartStyle cs;
        private Legend lg;
        public BindableCollection<LineSeries> DataCollection { get; set; }

        private void SetChartStyle()
        {
            cs = new ChartStyle();
            cs.ChartCanvas = view.chartCanvas;
            cs.TextCanvas = view.textCanvas;
            cs.Title = "Sine and Cosine Chart";
            cs.Xmin = 0;
            cs.Xmax = 7;
            cs.Ymin = -1.5;
            cs.Ymax = 1.5;
            cs.YTick = 0.5;
            cs.GridlinePattern = LinePatternEnum.Dot;
            cs.GridlineColor = Brushes.Black;
```

```
        cs.AddChartStyle(view.tbTitle, view.tbXLabel, view.tbYLabel);
}

private void SetLegend()
{
    lg = new Legend();
    lg.IsLegend = true;
    lg.IsBorder = true;
    lg.LegendPosition = LegendPositionEnum.NorthEast;
    lg.AddLegend(view.chartCanvas, DataCollection);
}

public void AddLines(double width, double height)
{
    view = this.GetView() as LineSymbolView;
    view.chartCanvas.Children.RemoveRange(1,
        view.chartCanvas.Children.Count - 1);
    view.textCanvas.Children.RemoveRange(1,
        view.textCanvas.Children.Count - 1);
    SetChartStyle();

    DataCollection.Clear();
    var ds = new LineSeries();
    ds.Symbols.BorderColor = Brushes.Blue;
    ds.Symbols.SymbolType = SymbolTypeEnum.OpenDiamond;
    ds.LineColor = Brushes.Blue;
    ds.LineThickness = 2;
    ds.SeriesName = "Sine";
    ds.LinePattern = LinePatternEnum.Solid;
    for (int i = 0; i < 50; i++)
    {
        double x = i / 5.0;
        double y = Math.Sin(x);
        ds.LinePoints.Add(new Point(x, y));
    }
    DataCollection.Add(ds);

    ds = new LineSeries();
    ds.Symbols.BorderColor = Brushes.Red;
    ds.Symbols.SymbolType = SymbolTypeEnum.Dot;
    ds.Symbols.FillColor = Brushes.Red;
    ds.LineColor = Brushes.Red;
    ds.LineThickness = 2;
    ds.SeriesName = "Cosine";
    ds.LinePattern = LinePatternEnum.Dash;
    for (int i = 0; i < 50; i++)
    {
        double x = i / 5.0;
        double y = Math.Cos(x);
        ds.LinePoints.Add(new Point(x, y));
    }
    DataCollection.Add(ds);

    ds = new LineSeries();
    ds.Symbols.BorderColor = Brushes.DarkGreen;
```

```
ds.Symbols.SymbolType = SymbolTypeEnum.OpenTriangle;
ds.LineColor = Brushes.DarkGreen;
ds.LineThickness = 2;
ds.SeriesName = "Sine^2";
ds.LinePattern = LinePatternEnum.Dash;
for (int i = 0; i < 50; i++)
{
    double x = i / 5.0;
    double y = Math.Sin(x) * Math.Sin(x);
    ds.LinePoints.Add(new Point(x, y));
}
DataCollection.Add(ds);
cs.SetLines(DataCollection);
SetLegend();
            }
        }
}
```

Here we specify the *Symbol*'s properties for each *LineSeries*, which resembles the way we specify the line styles. Figure 4-12 shows the result of running this example.

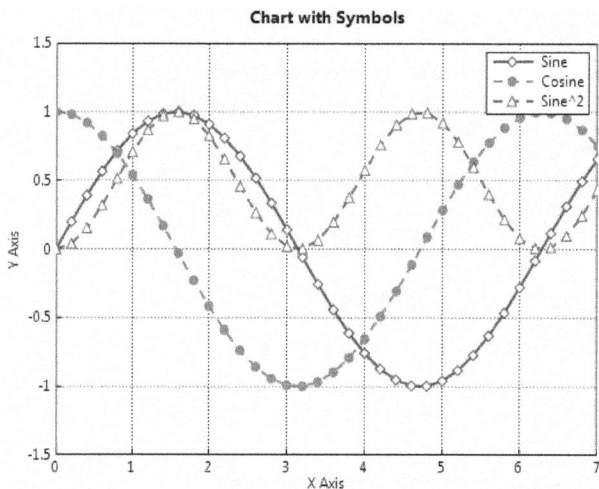

Figure 4-12. A line chart with symbols.

Line Charts with Two Y Axes

In the previous sections, we have implemented a powerful 2D line chart program. There are no restrictions in this program on the number of lines or curves we could add to a single chart. In this section, we will add another feature, an additional *Y*-axis, to the 2D line chart.

Why You Need Two Y Axes

In some instances, you may have multiple data sets you would like to display on the same chart. However, the *Y*-axis data values for each data set are not within the same range. For example, consider the following two functions:

$$y1 = xcos(x)$$

$$y2 = 100 + 20x$$

If you want to display these two functions using the same scale on the Y-axis, you will get the results shown in Figure 4-13.

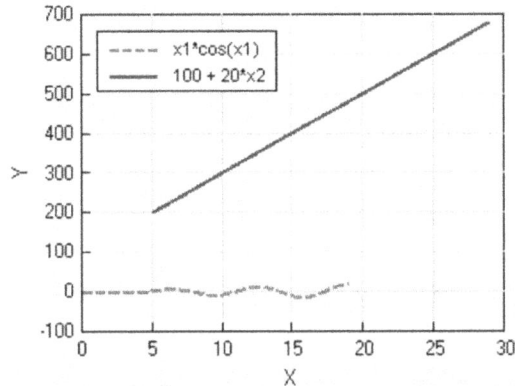

Figure 4-13. A line chart for y1 and y2, whose data values fall in different ranges.

From Figure 4-13, you can see how difficult it is to view the values of the function $xcos(x)$ because the Y-axis limits have been defined to display all of the data points on the same chart; however, the values of the two functions have very different data ranges. This problem can be solved by adding another Y2-axis to the chart program.

Chart Style with Two Y Axes

In order to add another Y-axis to the chart, you first need to have a *LineSeries* that can hold data for both Y-axes. Add a new class to the *ChartModel* folder and name it *LineSeries2Y*. This class inherits from the *LineSeries* class and consists of the following simple code:

```
using System;
namespace Chapter04.Models.ChartModel
{
    public class LineSeries2Y : LineSeries
    {
        private bool is2YData = false;
        public bool Is2YData
        {
            get { return is2YData; }
            set { is2YData = value; }
        }
    }
}
```

The *IsY2Data* property allows you to associate a *DataSeries2Y* object with either the Y-axis or the Y2-axis. If it is false, the *DataSeries2Y* is associated with the original Y-axis. On the other hand, the *DataSeries2Y* is associated with the Y2-axis if this property is set to true.

Now you need to add chart styles to your charts with two *Y*-axes. Add a class to the *ChartModel* class and name it *ChartStyleBase2Y*. Here is the code for this class:

```
using Caliburn.Micro;
using System;
using System.Windows;

namespace Chapter04.Models.ChartModel
{
    public class ChartStyleBase2Y : ChartStyleBase
    {
        private double y2min = 0;
        private double y2max = 10;
        private double y2Tick = 2;

        public double Y2min
        {
            get { return y2min; }
            set { y2min = value; }
        }

        public double Y2max
        {
            get { return y2max; }
            set { y2max = value; }
        }
        public double Y2Tick
        {
            get { return y2Tick; }
            set { y2Tick = value; }
        }

        public Point NormalizePoint2Y(Point pt)
        {
            if (Double.IsNaN(ChartCanvas.Width) || ChartCanvas.Width <= 0)
                ChartCanvas.Width = 270;
            if (Double.IsNaN(ChartCanvas.Height) || ChartCanvas.Height <= 0)
                ChartCanvas.Height = 250;

            Point result = new Point();
            result.X = (pt.X - Xmin) * ChartCanvas.Width / (Xmax - Xmin);
            result.Y = ChartCanvas.Height -
                    (pt.Y - Y2min) * ChartCanvas.Height / (Y2max - Y2min);
            return result;
        }

        public void SetLines2Y(BindableCollection<LineSeries2Y> dc)
        {
            if (dc.Count <= 0)
                return;
            for (int i = 0; i < dc.Count; i++)
            {
                if (dc[i].SeriesName == "Default")
                    dc[i].SeriesName = "DataSeries" + i.ToString();
                dc[i].SetLinePattern();
```

```
            for (int j = 0; j < dc[i].LinePoints.Count; j++)
            {
                if (dc[i].Is2YData)
                    dc[i].LinePoints[j] = NormalizePoint2Y(dc[i].LinePoints[j]);
                else
                    dc[i].LinePoints[j] = NormalizePoint(dc[i].LinePoints[j]);

                if (dc[i].Symbols.SymbolType != SymbolTypeEnum.None)
                    dc[i].Symbols.AddSymbol(ChartCanvas, dc[i].LinePoints[j]);
            }
        }
    }
}
```

This class, inheriting from the *ChartStyleBase* class, allows you to perform normalization and line setting for the *Y2*-axis independently of the original *Y*-axis. This way, you have a separate control over the data ranges for the *Y*-axis and *Y2*-axis respectively.

For a chart that uses the *Y2*-axis, you may also want to add additional gridlines, labels, and tick marks. You can achieve this by adding a new class, named *ChartStyle2Y,* to the current project. This class, inheriting from *ChartStyleBase2Y*, is quite similar to the *ChartStyle* class, except it contains an additional *Y2*-axis. Add a new class to the *ChartModel* folder and name it *ChartStyle2Y*. Here, I will list the code for this new class for your reference:

```
using System;
using System.Collections.Generic;
using System.Linq;
using System.Text;
using System.Threading.Tasks;
using System.Windows;
using System.Windows.Controls;
using System.Windows.Media;
using System.Windows.Shapes;

namespace Chapter04.Models.ChartModel
{
    public class ChartStyle2Y : ChartStyleBase2Y
    {
        private string title = "Title";
        private string xLabel = "X Axis";
        private string yLabel = "Y Axis";
        private string y2Label = "Y2 Axis";
        private bool isXGrid = true;
        private bool isYGrid = true;
        private bool isXGrid2Y = true;
        private Brush gridlineColor = Brushes.LightGray;
        private Brush gridline2YColor = Brushes.LightGreen;
        private double xTick = 1;
        private double yTick = 0.5;
        private LinePatternEnum gridlinePattern;
        private LinePatternEnum gridline2YPattern;
        private double leftOffset = 20;
        private double bottomOffset = 15;
        private double rightOffset = 10;
        private Line gridline = new Line();
```

```
public Canvas TextCanvas { get; set; }

public string Title
{
    get { return title; }
    set { title = value; }
}

public string XLabel
{
    get { return xLabel; }
    set { xLabel = value; }
}

public string YLabel
{
    get { return yLabel; }
    set { yLabel = value; }
}

public string Y2Label
{
    get { return y2Label; }
    set { y2Label = value; }
}

public LinePatternEnum GridlinePattern
{
    get { return gridlinePattern; }
    set { gridlinePattern = value; }
}

public LinePatternEnum Gridline2YPattern
{
    get { return gridline2YPattern; }
    set { gridline2YPattern = value; }
}

public double XTick
{
    get { return xTick; }
    set { xTick = value; }
}

public double YTick
{
    get { return yTick; }
    set { yTick = value; }
}

public Brush GridlineColor
{
    get { return gridlineColor; }
    set { gridlineColor = value; }
}
```

```
public Brush Gridline2YColor
{
    get { return gridline2YColor; }
    set { gridline2YColor = value; }
}

public bool IsXGrid
{
    get { return isXGrid; }
    set { isXGrid = value; }
}

public bool IsXGrid2Y
{
    get { return isXGrid2Y; }
    set { isXGrid2Y = value; }
}

public bool IsYGrid
{
    get { return isYGrid; }
    set { isYGrid = value; }
}


public void AddChartStyle(TextBlock tbTitle, TextBlock tbXLabel,
    TextBlock tbYLabel, TextBlock tbY2Label)
{
    Point pt = new Point();
    Line tick = new Line();
    double offset = 0;
    double dx, dy;
    TextBlock tb = new TextBlock();
    Size size = new Size();

    //  determine right offset:
    for (dy = Y2min; dy <= Y2max; dy += Y2Tick)
    {
        pt = NormalizePoint2Y(new Point(Xmax, dy));
        tb = new TextBlock();
        tb.Text = dy.ToString();
        tb.TextAlignment = TextAlignment.Left;
        tb.Measure(new Size(Double.PositiveInfinity,
                            Double.PositiveInfinity));
        size = tb.DesiredSize;
        if (offset < size.Width)
            offset = size.Width;
    }
    rightOffset = offset + 10;



    // Determine left offset:
    for (dy = Ymin; dy <= Ymax; dy += YTick)
```

```
        {
            pt = NormalizePoint(new Point(Xmin, dy));
            tb = new TextBlock();
            tb.Text = dy.ToString();
            tb.TextAlignment = TextAlignment.Right;
            tb.Measure(new Size(Double.PositiveInfinity,
                                Double.PositiveInfinity));
            size = tb.DesiredSize;
            if (offset < size.Width)
                offset = size.Width;
        }
        leftOffset = offset + 5;
        Canvas.SetLeft(ChartCanvas, leftOffset);
        Canvas.SetBottom(ChartCanvas, bottomOffset);
        ChartCanvas.Width = Math.Abs(TextCanvas.Width -
            leftOffset - rightOffset);
        ChartCanvas.Height = Math.Abs(TextCanvas.Height -
            bottomOffset - size.Height / 2);
        Rectangle chartRect = new Rectangle();
        chartRect.Stroke = Brushes.Black;
        chartRect.Width = ChartCanvas.Width;
        chartRect.Height = ChartCanvas.Height;
        ChartCanvas.Children.Add(chartRect);

        // Create vertical gridlines:
        if (IsYGrid == true)
        {
            for (dx = Xmin + XTick; dx < Xmax; dx += XTick)
            {
                gridline = new Line();
                AddLinePattern();
                gridline.X1 = NormalizePoint(new Point(dx, Ymin)).X;
                gridline.Y1 = NormalizePoint(new Point(dx, Ymin)).Y;
                gridline.X2 = NormalizePoint(new Point(dx, Ymax)).X;
                gridline.Y2 = NormalizePoint(new Point(dx, Ymax)).Y;
                ChartCanvas.Children.Add(gridline);
            }
        }

        // Create horizontal gridlines:
        if (IsXGrid == true)
        {
            for (dy = Ymin + YTick; dy < Ymax; dy += YTick)
            {
                gridline = new Line();
                AddLinePattern();
                gridline.X1 = NormalizePoint(new Point(Xmin, dy)).X;
                gridline.Y1 = NormalizePoint(new Point(Xmin, dy)).Y;
                gridline.X2 = NormalizePoint(new Point(Xmax, dy)).X;
                gridline.Y2 = NormalizePoint(new Point(Xmax, dy)).Y;
                ChartCanvas.Children.Add(gridline);
            }
        }

        // Create horizontal gridlines for Y2:
```

```
if (IsXGrid2Y == true)
{
    for (dy = Y2min + Y2Tick; dy < Y2max; dy += Y2Tick)
    {
        gridline = new Line();
        AddLine2YPattern();
        gridline.X1 = NormalizePoint2Y(new Point(Xmin, dy)).X;
        gridline.Y1 = NormalizePoint2Y(new Point(Xmin, dy)).Y;
        gridline.X2 = NormalizePoint2Y(new Point(Xmax, dy)).X;
        gridline.Y2 = NormalizePoint2Y(new Point(Xmax, dy)).Y;
        ChartCanvas.Children.Add(gridline);
    }
}

// Create x-axis tick marks:
for (dx = Xmin; dx <= Xmax; dx += xTick)
{
    pt = NormalizePoint(new Point(dx, Ymin));
    tick = new Line();
    tick.Stroke = Brushes.Black;
    tick.X1 = pt.X;
    tick.Y1 = pt.Y;
    tick.X2 = pt.X;
    tick.Y2 = pt.Y - 5;
    ChartCanvas.Children.Add(tick);

    tb = new TextBlock();
    tb.Text = dx.ToString();
    tb.Measure(new Size(Double.PositiveInfinity,
                        Double.PositiveInfinity));
    size = tb.DesiredSize;
    TextCanvas.Children.Add(tb);
    Canvas.SetLeft(tb, leftOffset + pt.X - size.Width / 2);
    Canvas.SetTop(tb, pt.Y + 2 + size.Height / 2);

}

// Create y-axis tick marks:
for (dy = Ymin; dy <= Ymax; dy += YTick)
{
    pt = NormalizePoint(new Point(Xmin, dy));
    tick = new Line();
    tick.Stroke = Brushes.Black;
    tick.X1 = pt.X;
    tick.Y1 = pt.Y;
    tick.X2 = pt.X + 5;
    tick.Y2 = pt.Y;
    ChartCanvas.Children.Add(tick);

    tb = new TextBlock();
    tb.Text = dy.ToString();
    tb.Measure(new Size(Double.PositiveInfinity,
                        Double.PositiveInfinity));
    size = tb.DesiredSize;
    TextCanvas.Children.Add(tb);
```

```
            Canvas.SetRight(tb, ChartCanvas.Width + 35);
            Canvas.SetTop(tb, pt.Y - 1);
        }

        // Create y2-axis tick marks:
        for (dy = Y2min; dy <= Y2max; dy += Y2Tick)
        {
            pt = NormalizePoint2Y(new Point(Xmax, dy));
            tick = new Line();
            tick.Stroke = Brushes.Black;
            tick.X1 = pt.X;
            tick.Y1 = pt.Y;
            tick.X2 = pt.X - 5;
            tick.Y2 = pt.Y;
            ChartCanvas.Children.Add(tick);

            tb = new TextBlock();
            tb.Text = dy.ToString();
            tb.Measure(new Size(Double.PositiveInfinity,
                                Double.PositiveInfinity));
            size = tb.DesiredSize;
            TextCanvas.Children.Add(tb);
            Canvas.SetLeft(tb, ChartCanvas.Width + 30);
            Canvas.SetTop(tb, pt.Y - 1);
        }

        // Add title and labels:
        tbTitle.Text = Title;
        tbXLabel.Text = XLabel;
        tbYLabel.Text = YLabel;
        tbY2Label.Text = Y2Label;
        tbXLabel.Margin = new Thickness(leftOffset -rightOffset + 2, 2, 2, 2);
        tbTitle.Margin = new Thickness(leftOffset - rightOffset + 2, 2, 2, 2);
    }

    public void AddLinePattern()
    {
        gridline.Stroke = GridlineColor;
        gridline.StrokeThickness = 1;

        switch (GridlinePattern)
        {
            case LinePatternEnum.Dash:
                gridline.StrokeDashArray = new DoubleCollection() { 4, 3 };
                break;
            case LinePatternEnum.Dot:
                gridline.StrokeDashArray = new DoubleCollection() { 1, 2 };
                break;
            case LinePatternEnum.DashDot:
                gridline.StrokeDashArray =
                        new DoubleCollection() { 4, 2, 1, 2 };
                break;
        }
    }
}
```

```
        public void AddLine2YPattern()
        {
            gridline.Stroke = Gridline2YColor;
            gridline.StrokeThickness = 1;

            switch (Gridline2YPattern)
            {
                case LinePatternEnum.Dash:
                    gridline.StrokeDashArray = new DoubleCollection() { 4, 3 };
                    break;
                case LinePatternEnum.Dot:
                    gridline.StrokeDashArray = new DoubleCollection() { 1, 2 };
                    break;
                case LinePatternEnum.DashDot:
                    gridline.StrokeDashArray =
                            new DoubleCollection() { 4, 2, 1, 2 };
                    break;
            }
        }
    }
}
```

In the foregoing code, the changes made to include the *Y2*-axis have been highlighted using the bolded code.

Creating a Chart with Two Y Axes

Here, I will use an example to illustrate how to create a line chart with two *Y*-axes. Add a new *UserControl* to the *Views* folder and name it *Line2YView*. Here is the XAML file for this view:

```xml
<UserControl x:Class="Chapter04.Views.Line2YView"
             xmlns="http://schemas.microsoft.com/winfx/2006/xaml/presentation"
             xmlns:x="http://schemas.microsoft.com/winfx/2006/xaml"
             xmlns:mc="http://schemas.openxmlformats.org/markup-compatibility/2006"
             xmlns:d="http://schemas.microsoft.com/expression/blend/2008"
             xmlns:cal="http://www.caliburnproject.org"
             mc:Ignorable="d"
             d:DesignHeight="300" d:DesignWidth="300">

    <UserControl.Resources>
        <DataTemplate x:Key="chartTemplate">
            <Polyline Points="{Binding LinePoints}" Stroke="{Binding LineColor}"
                StrokeThickness="{Binding LineThickness}"
                StrokeDashArray="{Binding LineDashPattern}"/>
        </DataTemplate>
    </UserControl.Resources>

    <Grid Margin="10">
        <Grid.ColumnDefinitions>
            <ColumnDefinition Width="auto"/>
            <ColumnDefinition Name="column1" Width="*"/>
            <ColumnDefinition Width="auto"/>
        </Grid.ColumnDefinitions>
        <Grid.RowDefinitions>
            <RowDefinition Height="auto"/>
```

```xml
                <RowDefinition Name="row1" Height="*"/>
                <RowDefinition Height="auto"/>
            </Grid.RowDefinitions>
            <TextBlock Margin="2" x:Name="tbTitle" Grid.Column="1" Grid.Row="0"
                    RenderTransformOrigin="0.5,0.5" FontSize="14" FontWeight="Bold"
                    HorizontalAlignment="Stretch" VerticalAlignment="Stretch"
                    TextAlignment="Center"
                    Text="Title"/>

            <TextBlock Margin="5" x:Name="tbXLabel" Grid.Column="1" Grid.Row="2"
                    RenderTransformOrigin="0.5,0.5" TextAlignment="Center"
                    Text="X Axis"/>

            <TextBlock Margin="5" Name="tbYLabel" Grid.Column="0" Grid.Row="1"
                    RenderTransformOrigin="0.5,0.5" TextAlignment="Center"
                    Text="Y Axis">
                <TextBlock.LayoutTransform>
                    <RotateTransform Angle="-90"/>
                </TextBlock.LayoutTransform>
            </TextBlock>

            <TextBlock Margin="5" Name="tbY2Label" Grid.Column="2" Grid.Row="1"
                    RenderTransformOrigin="0.5,0.5" TextAlignment="Center"
                    Text="Y2 Axis">
                <TextBlock.LayoutTransform>
                    <RotateTransform Angle="-90"/>
                </TextBlock.LayoutTransform>
            </TextBlock>

            <Grid  Margin="0" x:Name ="chartGrid" Grid.Column="1" Grid.Row="1"
                    ClipToBounds="True" Background="Transparent"
                    cal:Message.Attach="[Event SizeChanged]=[Action
                    AddLines($this.ActualWidth, $this.ActualHeight)];
                    [Event Loaded]=[Action AddLines($this.ActualWidth,
                    $this.ActualHeight)]" />
            <Canvas Margin="2" Name="textCanvas" ClipToBounds="True" Grid.Column="1"
                    Grid.Row="1" Width="{Binding
                    ElementName=chartGrid,Path=ActualWidth}"
                    Height="{Binding ElementName=chartGrid,Path=ActualHeight}">
                <Canvas Name="chartCanvas" ClipToBounds="True">
                    <ItemsControl ItemsSource="{Binding DataCollection}"
                                ItemTemplate="{StaticResource chartTemplate}">
                        <ItemsControl.ItemsPanel>
                            <ItemsPanelTemplate>
                                <Grid/>
                            </ItemsPanelTemplate>
                        </ItemsControl.ItemsPanel>
                    </ItemsControl>
                </Canvas>
            </Canvas>
        </Grid>
</UserControl>
```

This XAML code is similar to that used in the previous example, except for the addition of the 2Y label.
Add a new class to the *ViewModels* folder and name it *Line2YViewModel*. Here is the code for this class:

```csharp
using System;
using System.Linq;
using Caliburn.Micro;
using System.Collections.ObjectModel;
using System.ComponentModel.Composition;
using System.Windows.Documents;
using System.Collections.Generic;
using System.Windows;
using Chapter04.Models;
using System.Windows.Media;
using System.Windows.Controls;
using Chapter04.Views;
using Chapter04.Models.ChartModel;

namespace Chapter04.ViewModels
{
    [Export(typeof(IScreen)), PartCreationPolicy(CreationPolicy.NonShared)]
    public class Line2YViewModel : Screen
    {
        private readonly IEventAggregator _events;
        [ImportingConstructor]
        public Line2YViewModel(IEventAggregator events)
        {
            this._events = events;
            DisplayName = "05. 2Y Axes";
            DataCollection = new BindableCollection<LineSeries2Y>();
        }

        Line2YView view;
        private ChartStyle2Y cs;
        private Legend lg;
        public BindableCollection<LineSeries2Y> DataCollection { get; set; }

        private void SetChartStyle()
        {
            cs = new ChartStyle2Y();
            cs.ChartCanvas = view.chartCanvas;
            cs.TextCanvas = view.textCanvas;
            cs.Title = "Chart with 2 Y axes";
            cs.Xmin = 0;
            cs.Xmax = 30;
            cs.Ymin = -20;
            cs.Ymax = 20;
            cs.YTick = 5;
            cs.XTick = 5;
            cs.Y2min = 100;
            cs.Y2max = 700;
            cs.Y2Tick = 100;
            cs.XLabel = "X Axis";
            cs.YLabel = "Y Axis";
            cs.Y2Label = "Y2 Axis";

            cs.GridlinePattern = LinePatternEnum.Dot;
            cs.GridlineColor = Brushes.Black;
            cs.Gridline2YPattern = LinePatternEnum.Dash;
```

```
        cs.Gridline2YColor = Brushes.LightGray;
        cs.AddChartStyle(view.tbTitle, view.tbXLabel,
            view.tbYLabel, view.tbY2Label);
    }

    private void SetLegend()
    {
        lg = new Legend();
        lg.IsLegend = true;
        lg.IsBorder = true;
        lg.LegendPosition = LegendPositionEnum.NorthWest;
        lg.AddLegend(view.chartCanvas, DataCollection);
    }

    public void AddLines(double width, double height)
    {
        view = this.GetView() as Line2YView;
        view.chartCanvas.Children.RemoveRange(1,
            view.chartCanvas.Children.Count - 1);
        view.textCanvas.Children.RemoveRange(1,
            view.textCanvas.Children.Count - 1);
        SetChartStyle();

        DataCollection.Clear();

        //Add Y curve:
        var ds = new LineSeries2Y();
        ds.Symbols.BorderColor = Brushes.Blue;
        ds.Symbols.SymbolType = SymbolTypeEnum.OpenDiamond;
        ds.LineColor = Brushes.Blue;
        ds.LineThickness = 2;
        ds.SeriesName = "x*Cos(x)";
        ds.LinePattern = LinePatternEnum.Solid;
        for (int i = 0; i < 20; i++)
        {
            double x = 1.0 * i;
            double y = x* Math.Cos(x);
            ds.LinePoints.Add(new Point(x, y));
        }
        DataCollection.Add(ds);

        //Add Y2 curve:
        ds = new LineSeries2Y();
        ds.Is2YData = true;
        ds.Symbols.BorderColor = Brushes.Red;
        ds.Symbols.SymbolType = SymbolTypeEnum.Dot;
        ds.LineColor = Brushes.Red;
        ds.LineThickness = 2;
        ds.SeriesName = "100 + 20*x";
        ds.LinePattern = LinePatternEnum.DashDot;
        for (int i = 5; i < 30; i++)
        {
            double x = 1.0 * i;
            double y = 100.0 + 20 * x;
            ds.LinePoints.Add(new Point(x, y));
```

```
        }
        DataCollection.Add(ds);
        cs.SetLines2Y(DataCollection);
        SetLegend();
    }
  }
}
```

Here, we first set different limits and different gridline styles for the *Y*- and *Y2*-axes. Also, note how we associate the *LineSeries2Y* object with the *IsY2Data* property. A *LineSeries2Y* object with an *IsY2Data* = *true* property tells the program that this *LineSeries2Y* object should be drawn using the *Y2*- axis.

By running this example, you should obtain the result shown in Figure 4-14. When you compare this result with the one shown in Figure 4-13, you can see that both sets of data are clearly displayed in Figure 4-14, even though these two sets of data have dramatically different data ranges.

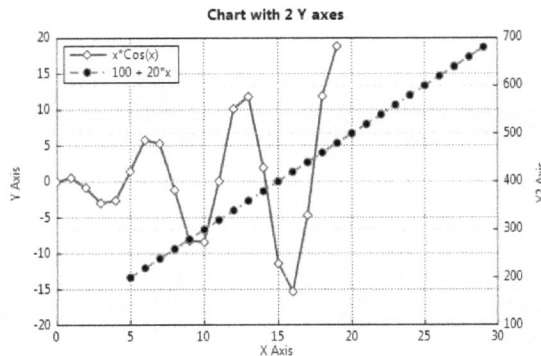

Figure 4-14. A line chart with two Y-axes.

Creating Line Charts using DrawingVisaul

If you need to display large amounts of data or create real-time applications with high performance, you can use the lightweight *Geometry* or *DrawingVisual* objects in WPF to avoid overhead of the *Shape* objects. In my previously published book, *Practical WPF Graphics Programming*, I discusses how to use *Geometry* objects to create various 2D graphics. You can refer to that book for more information. Unlike shapes, *DrawingVisual* objects provide only a means to obtain *DrawingContext* and draw something capable of being displayed in a host *FrameworkElement* container. Of course, the host container will not be lightweight; however, the large numbers of *DrawVisual* objects contained in it will be lightweight.

Even though I use *Shape* objects to create most chart applications, you can still use the chart framework and development process discussed in this book to create high performance charts using the *DrawingVisual* objects. In this section, I will show you how to use the *DrawingVisual* objects to create line charts with gridlines and tick labels, as shown in Figure 4-8. You can follow the same procedure to convert chart applications discussed in this book into high performance charts using the geometry or drawing visual objects.

Line Series

The line series used in the line charts based on *DrawingVisual* objects will be simpler than that used in line charts based on *Shape* objects. Add a new class to the *ChartModel* folder and name it *LineSeriesVisual*. Here is the code for this class:

```
using System;
using Caliburn.Micro;
using System.Windows.Media;

namespace Chapter04.Models.ChartModel
{
    public class LineSeriesVisual  : PropertyChangedBase
    {
        public LineSeriesVisual()
        {
            LinePoints = new PointCollection();
        }

        public Brush LineColor { get; set; }
        public double LineThickness { get; set; }
        public DashStyle LineDashStyle { get; set; }

        private PointCollection linePoints;
        public PointCollection LinePoints
        {
            get { return linePoints; }
            set
            {
                linePoints = value;
                NotifyOfPropertyChange(() => LinePoints);
            }
        }
    }
}
```

Here, we do not need to define the line dash pattern because we can use the built-in *DashStyle* for the *Pen* object, which will be used to draw visuals.

DrawingModel Class

When we created charts using *Shape* objects previously, we implemented the *ChartStyle* class, where we created lines, gridlines, ticks, and label texts using *Shape* objects and *TextBlock* controls. In order to create high performance charts, we need to convert these *Shape* objects and *TextBlock* controls into *DrawingVisual* objects. Add a new class to the *ChartModel* folder, name it *DrawingModel*, and change its namespace to *Chapter04*. Here is the code list for this classs:

```
using Caliburn.Micro;
using Chapter04.Models.ChartModel;
using System;
using System.Collections.Generic;
using System.Globalization;
using System.Windows;
using System.Windows.Controls;
```

```csharp
using System.Windows.Media;

namespace Chapter04
{
    public class DrawingModel : FrameworkElement
    {
        public DrawingModel()
        {
            DataCollection = new BindableCollection<LineSeriesVisual>();
        }

        private double xmin = 0;
        private double xmax = 6.5;
        private double ymin = -1.1;
        private double ymax = 1.1;
        private Brush gridlineColor = Brushes.LightGray;
        private DashStyle gridlineDashStyle = DashStyles.Dash;
        private double xTick = 1;
        private double yTick = 0.5;

        private double leftOffset = 20;
        private double bottomOffset = 15;
        private double rightOffset = 10;
        private double topOffset = 10;
        private double chartWidth = 400;
        private double chartHeight = 300;

        public double Xmin
        {
            get { return xmin; }
            set { xmin = value; }
        }

        public double Xmax
        {
            get { return xmax; }
            set { xmax = value; }
        }

        public double Ymin
        {
            get { return ymin; }
            set { ymin = value; }
        }

        public double Ymax
        {
            get { return ymax; }
            set { ymax = value; }
        }

        public double XTick
        {
            get { return xTick; }
            set { xTick = value; }
```

```
    }

    public double YTick
    {
        get { return yTick; }
        set { yTick = value; }
    }

    public Brush GridlineColor
    {
        get { return gridlineColor; }
        set { gridlineColor = value; }
    }

    public DashStyle GridlineDashStyle
    {
        get { return gridlineDashStyle; }
        set { gridlineDashStyle = value; }
    }


    public BindableCollection<LineSeriesVisual> DataCollection { get; set; }



    public void AddChartStyle(DrawingContext dc)
    {
        Point pt = new Point();
        double offset = 0;
        double dx, dy;


        TextBlock tb = new TextBlock();
        tb.Text = Xmax.ToString();
        tb.Measure(new Size(Double.PositiveInfinity, Double.PositiveInfinity));
        Size size = tb.DesiredSize;
        rightOffset = size.Width / 2 + 2;
        //rightOffset =  5;

        // Determine left offset:
        for (dy = Ymin; dy <= Ymax; dy += YTick)
        {
            pt = NormalizePoint(new Point(Xmin, dy));
            tb = new TextBlock();
            tb.Text = dy.ToString();
            tb.TextAlignment = TextAlignment.Right;
            tb.Measure(new Size(Double.PositiveInfinity,
                                Double.PositiveInfinity));
            size = tb.DesiredSize;
            if (offset < size.Width)
                offset = size.Width;
        }
        leftOffset = offset + 5;
```

```
chartWidth = Math.Abs(this.Width - leftOffset - rightOffset);
chartHeight = Math.Abs(this.Height - bottomOffset -
               topOffset - size.Height / 2);
CreateRect(new Point(leftOffset, topOffset), chartWidth,
           chartHeight, dc);

// Create vertical gridlines:
Pen gridPen = new Pen(GridlineColor, 1);
gridPen.DashStyle = GridlineDashStyle;
gridPen.Freeze();
for (dx = Xmin + XTick; dx < Xmax; dx += XTick)
{
    Point pt1 = NormalizePoint(new Point(dx, Ymin));
    Point pt2 = NormalizePoint(new Point(dx, Ymax));
    CreateLine(pt1, pt2, gridPen, dc);
}

// Create horizontal gridlines:

for (dy = Ymin + YTick; dy < Ymax; dy += YTick)
{
    Point pt1 = NormalizePoint(new Point(Xmin, dy));
    Point pt2 = NormalizePoint(new Point(Xmax, dy));
    CreateLine(pt1, pt2, gridPen, dc);
}

// Create x-axis tick marks:
Pen tickPen = new Pen(Brushes.Black, 1);
tickPen.Freeze();
for (dx = Xmin; dx <= Xmax; dx += XTick)
{
    pt = NormalizePoint(new Point(dx, Ymin));
    CreateLine(pt, new Point(pt.X, pt.Y - 5), tickPen, dc);

    tb = new TextBlock();
    tb.Text = dx.ToString();
    tb.Measure(new Size(Double.PositiveInfinity,
                 Double.PositiveInfinity));
    size = tb.DesiredSize;
    CreateText(dx.ToString(), new Point(pt.X - size.Width / 2,
        pt.Y + 1), 12, dc);
}

// Create y-axis tick marks:
for (dy = Ymin; dy <= Ymax; dy += YTick)
{
    pt = NormalizePoint(new Point(Xmin, dy));
    CreateLine(pt, new Point(pt.X + 5, pt.Y), tickPen, dc);

    tb = new TextBlock();
    tb.Text = dy.ToString();
    tb.Measure(new Size(Double.PositiveInfinity,
        Double.PositiveInfinity));
    size = tb.DesiredSize;
```

```
            CreateText(dy.ToString(), new Point(this.Width - rightOffset -
                chartWidth - size.Width - 3, pt.Y - size.Height / 2), 12, dc);
        }
    }

    private void CreateLine(Point pt1, Point pt2, Pen pen, DrawingContext dc)
    {
        DrawingVisual line = new DrawingVisual();
        dc.DrawLine(pen, pt1, pt2);
    }

    private void CreateRect(Point ptOrig, double width, double height,
        DrawingContext dc)
    {
        DrawingVisual rect = new DrawingVisual();
        Pen pen = new Pen(Brushes.Black, 1);
        pen.Freeze();
        dc.DrawRectangle(Brushes.Transparent, pen,
            new Rect(ptOrig, new Size(width, height)));
    }

    private void CreateText(string text, Point pt, double fontSize,
        DrawingContext dc)
    {
        FormattedText formattedText = new FormattedText(text,
            CultureInfo.GetCultureInfo("en-us"), FlowDirection.LeftToRight,
            new Typeface("Segoe UI"), fontSize, Brushes.Black);

        DrawingVisual drawingText = new DrawingVisual();
        dc.DrawText(formattedText, pt);
    }


    public Point NormalizePoint(Point pt)
    {
        Point result = new Point();
        result.X = leftOffset + (pt.X - Xmin) * chartWidth / (Xmax - Xmin);
        result.Y = topOffset + chartHeight -
            (pt.Y - Ymin) * chartHeight / (Ymax - Ymin);
        return result;
    }

    protected override void OnRender(DrawingContext context)
    {
        AddChartStyle(context);

        if (DataCollection != null)
        {
            if (DataCollection.Count > 0)
            {
                SetLines(DataCollection, context);
            }
        }
    }
```

```
public void SetLines(BindableCollection<LineSeriesVisual> dc,
    DrawingContext context)
{
    if (dc.Count <= 0)
        return;

    DrawingVisual line = new DrawingVisual();

    foreach (LineSeriesVisual ls in dc)
    {
        line = new DrawingVisual();
        ls.LineColor.Freeze();
        Pen pen = new Pen(ls.LineColor, ls.LineThickness);
        pen.DashStyle = ls.LineDashStyle;
        pen.Freeze();
        PointCollection pc = new PointCollection();
        foreach (Point pt in ls.LinePoints)
        {
            if (pt.X <= Xmax && pt.X >= Xmin && pt.Y >= Ymin &&
                pt.Y <= Ymax)
                pc.Add(NormalizePoint(pt));
        }

        for (int i = 0; i < pc.Count - 1; i++)
        {
            context.DrawLine(pen, pc[i], pc[i + 1]);
        }
    }
}


public void SetLines1(BindableCollection<LineSeriesVisual> dc,
    DrawingContext context)
{
    if (dc.Count <= 0)
        return;

    DrawingVisual line = new DrawingVisual();
    StreamGeometry geo = new StreamGeometry();

    foreach (LineSeriesVisual ls in dc)
    {
        line = new DrawingVisual();
        ls.LineColor.Freeze();
        Pen pen = new Pen(ls.LineColor, ls.LineThickness);
        pen.DashStyle = ls.LineDashStyle;
        pen.Freeze();
        PointCollection pc = new PointCollection();

        foreach (Point pt in ls.LinePoints)
        {
            if (pt.X <= Xmax && pt.X >= Xmin && pt.Y >= Ymin &&
                pt.Y <= Ymax)
                pc.Add(NormalizePoint(pt));
```

```
            }

            PointCollection pc1 = new PointCollection();
            for (int i = 1; i < pc.Count; i++)
                pc1.Add(pc[i]);

            using (StreamGeometryContext ctx = geo.Open())
            {
                ctx.BeginFigure(pc[0], false, false);
                ctx.PolyLineTo(pc1, true, false);
            }
            geo.Freeze();
            context.DrawGeometry(null, pen, geo);
        }
    }
}
```

This class is similar to the *ChartStyle* class used previously. It inherits from the *FrameworkElement* class, because DrawingVisual objects need a container to hold them. We render the lines, rectangles, and texts into visual objects using the *DrawLine*, *DrawRectangle*, *DrawGeometry*, and *DrawText* methods of a *DrawingContext*.

The *AddChartStyle* method passes a *DrawingContext* object as its input parameter. First, we define the chart size: *chartWidth* and *chartHeight* by considering the suitable offset relative to the size of our *DrawingModel*. Next, we draw gridlines with a specified color and dash style by calling the *CreateLine* method. Please note that all of the end points of the gridlines have been transformed from the world coordinate system into device-independent pixels using the *NormalizePoint* method.

We then render the tick marks for the *X* and *Y* axes of the chart. For each tick mark, we find the points in the device coordinate system at which the tick mark joins the axes and draw a black line, 5-pixels long, from this point toward the inside of the chart area. We also create the tick mark labels by calling the *CreateText* method.

Next, we implement a *SetLines* method, which draws lines using the *LineSeriesVisual* object contained in the *DataCollection*. For each *LineSeriesVisual*, we add a line to the chart using the specified line style for that line series. Note that we use the *DrawLine* method directly to create line segments that form the curves on the chart. Alternatively, we can also use a *StreamGeometry* to define a geometric shape (a polyline in our case), described using a *StreamGeometryContext*, as implemented in the *SetLines1* method. Generally, you can use a *StreamGeometry* when you need to describe a complex geometry but do not want to the overhead of supporting data binding, animation, event, or modification. For our specific line chart application, we find that the *Setline* method outperforms the *SetLine1* method, so we will use the *SetLine* method to create polylines on the charts.

In order to gain more performance, I freeze the pen used to create gridlines and the curves. For our line chart applications, freezing the pen has a huge impact on performance. Finally, I override the *OnRender* method, in which I call the *AddChartStyle* and *SetLines* methods to render the gridlines and polylines.

Creating Line Charts

Now, we can use the *DrawingModel* class implemented in the previous section to create line charts. Add a *UserControl* to the *Views* folder and name it *LineChartVisualView*. Here is the code for this class:

```xml
<UserControl x:Class="Chapter04.Views.LineChartVisualView"
             xmlns="http://schemas.microsoft.com/winfx/2006/xaml/presentation"
             xmlns:x="http://schemas.microsoft.com/winfx/2006/xaml"
             xmlns:mc="http://schemas.openxmlformats.org/markup-compatibility/2006"
             xmlns:d="http://schemas.microsoft.com/expression/blend/2008"
             xmlns:local="clr-namespace:Chapter04"
             mc:Ignorable="d"
             d:DesignHeight="400" d:DesignWidth="500">
    <Grid Margin="10">
        <Grid.ColumnDefinitions>
            <ColumnDefinition Width="150"/>
            <ColumnDefinition Width="*"/>
        </Grid.ColumnDefinitions>
        <StackPanel>
            <Button x:Name="AddSine" Content="Add Sine/Cosine" Width="120"
                    Height="25" Margin="0 30 0 0" />
            <Button x:Name="AddRandom" Content="Add Random" Width="120"
                    Height="25" Margin="0 30 0 0" />
        </StackPanel>

        <Grid Grid.Column="1" Margin="10">
            <Grid.ColumnDefinitions>
                <ColumnDefinition Width="Auto"/>
                <ColumnDefinition Name="column1" Width="*"/>
            </Grid.ColumnDefinitions>
            <Grid.RowDefinitions>
                <RowDefinition Height="Auto"/>
                <RowDefinition Name="row1" Height="*"/>
                <RowDefinition Height="Auto"/>
            </Grid.RowDefinitions>
            <TextBlock Margin="2" x:Name="Title" Grid.Column="1" Grid.Row="0"
                    Text="Titlte" RenderTransformOrigin="0.5,0.5" FontSize="14"
                    FontWeight="Bold" HorizontalAlignment="Stretch"
                    VerticalAlignment="Stretch" TextAlignment="Center"/>
            <TextBlock Margin="2" x:Name="XLabel" Grid.Column="1" Grid.Row="2"
                    RenderTransformOrigin="0.5,0.5" TextAlignment="Center"
                    Text="X Axis"/>
            <TextBlock Margin="2" Name="YLabel" Grid.Column="0" Grid.Row="1"
                    RenderTransformOrigin="0.5,0.5" TextAlignment="Center"
                    Text="Y Axis">
                <TextBlock.LayoutTransform>
                    <RotateTransform Angle="-90"/>
                </TextBlock.LayoutTransform>
            </TextBlock>

            <Grid x:Name="chartGrid"  Grid.Column="1" Grid.Row="1">
                <local:DrawingModel x:Name="myVisual"
                        Width="{Binding ElementName=chartGrid, Path=ActualWidth}"
                        Height="{Binding ElementName=chartGrid,Path=ActualHeight}"/>
            </Grid>
        </Grid>
    </Grid>
</UserControl>
```

Here, the boded part shows how to create a *DrawingModel* object named *myVisual* in XAML, where we simply treat it as a standard framework element. We place it inside a *Grid* control named *chartGrid* and bind its *Width* and *Height* properties to *chartGrid*'s *ActualWidth* and *ActualHeight*, so that the size of the *myVisual* will change accordingly when *chartGrid* is resized.

Add a new class to the *ViewModels* folder and name it *LineChartVisualViewModel*. Here is the code for this class:

```
using System;
using Caliburn.Micro;
using System.Collections.ObjectModel;
using System.ComponentModel.Composition;
using System.Windows;
using System.Windows.Media;
using System.Windows.Controls;
using Chapter04.Views;
using Chapter04.Models.ChartModel;

namespace Chapter04.ViewModels
{
    [Export(typeof(IScreen)), PartCreationPolicy(CreationPolicy.NonShared)]
    public class LineChartVisualViewModel : Screen
    {
        [ImportingConstructor]
        public LineChartVisualViewModel()
        {
            DisplayName = "06. Drawing Visual";
        }

        public void AddSine()
        {
            var view = this.GetView() as LineChartVisualView;
            view.myVisual.DataCollection.Clear();

            view.myVisual.Xmin = 0;
            view.myVisual.Xmax = 7;
            view.myVisual.XTick = 1;
            view.myVisual.Ymin = -1.5;
            view.myVisual.Ymax = 1.5;
            view.myVisual.YTick = 0.5;
            view.myVisual.GridlineColor = Brushes.LightGray;
            view.myVisual.GridlineDashStyle = DashStyles.Dash;

            var ds = new LineSeriesVisual();
            ds.LineColor = Brushes.Blue;
            ds.LineThickness = 2;
            ds.LineDashStyle = DashStyles.Solid;

            for (int i = 0; i < 50; i++)
            {
                double x = i / 5.0;
                double y = Math.Sin(x);
                ds.LinePoints.Add(new Point(x, y));
            }
            view.myVisual.DataCollection.Add(ds);
```

```
        ds = new LineSeriesVisual();
        ds.LineColor = Brushes.Red;
        ds.LineThickness = 2;
        ds.LineDashStyle = DashStyles.Dash;
        for (int i = 0; i < 50; i++)
        {
            double x = i / 5.0;
            double y = Math.Cos(x);
            ds.LinePoints.Add(new Point(x, y));
        }
        view.myVisual.DataCollection.Add(ds);
        view.myVisual.InvalidateVisual();
    }

    public void AddRandom()
    {
        var view = this.GetView() as LineChartVisualView;
        view.myVisual.DataCollection.Clear();

        view.myVisual.Xmin = 0;
        view.myVisual.Xmax = 100000;
        view.myVisual.XTick = 20000;
        view.myVisual.Ymin = -1.5;
        view.myVisual.Ymax = 1.5;
        view.myVisual.YTick = 0.5;
        view.myVisual.GridlineColor = Brushes.LightGray;
        view.myVisual.GridlineDashStyle = DashStyles.Dash;

        var ds = new LineSeriesVisual();
        ds.LineColor = Brushes.Red;
        ds.LineThickness = 1;
        ds.LineDashStyle = DashStyles.Solid;

        Random random = new Random();
        for (int i = 0; i < 100000; i++)
        {
            double r = random.NextDouble();
            double y = Math.Sin(i / 10000.0) + r / 5.0;
            ds.LinePoints.Add(new Point(1.0 * i, y));
        }
        view.myVisual.DataCollection.Add(ds);
        view.myVisual.InvalidateVisual();
    }
  }
}
```

The code is very similar to that used in the *LineGridViewModel* example. Here, we use the Caliburn.Micro's *GetView* method to get a reference of the *myVisual* object, and then set various parameters for gridlines and tick marks. We implement two methods, *AddSine* and *AddRandom*, where we use *AddSine* to create standard *Sine* and *Cosine* functions, and use *AddRandom* to create a *Sine* modulated random function. The random function with 100K data points will be used to test the performance of our chart application.

Running this example and clicking the *Add Sine/Cosine* button produces the results shown in Figure 4-15.

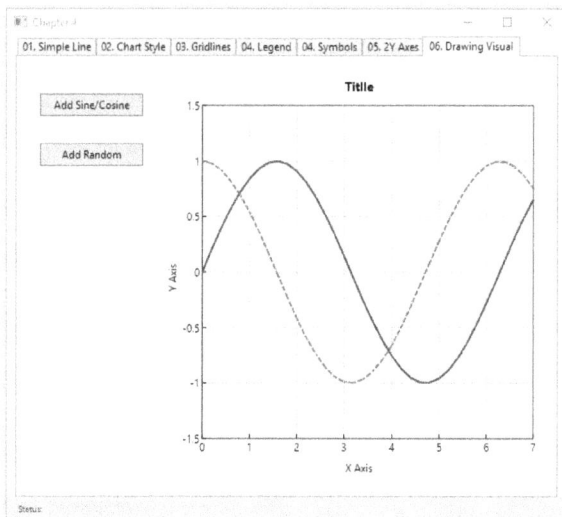

Figure 4-15. A line chart created using DrawingVisual objects.

Now clicking the *Add Random* button generates the result shown in Figure 4-16.

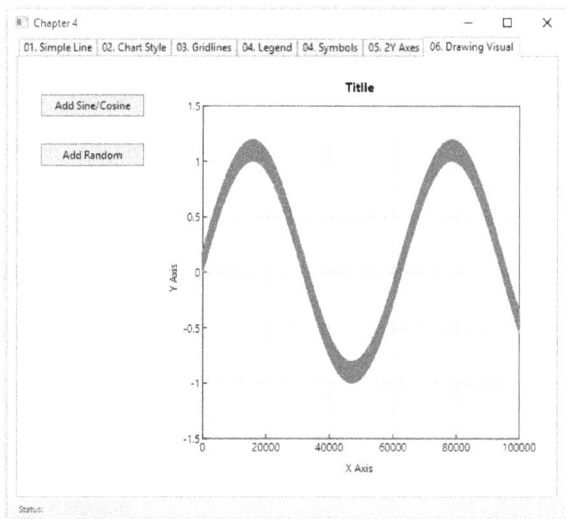

Figure 4-16. A line chart with 100K data points created using DrawingVisual objects.

Our chart application takes about 500 microseconds to create a line chart with 100 K data points on my PC with Intel i7-4790 CPU and 16 GB RAM. If you want to get even better performance, you can try to adjust anti-aliasing parameter, freeze all possible WPF objects, and set the *CacheMode* to *BitmapCache* for rendering a complex element, which are beyond the scope of this book

Chapter 5
Specialized 2D Charts

In the previous chapter, we discussed 2D line charts, which can be used to visualize data in real-world WPF applications. In this chapter, I will show you how to create certain special or application-specific charts in .NET applications. Some of these are charts that are typically found in commercial charting packages or spreadsheet applications. I will discuss a variety of special charts that display statistical distributions of data or discrete data, including bar, stair-step, stem, error bar, and area charts. You will also learn how to create charts in other coordinate systems, such as pie and polar charts.

Bar Charts

The bar chart is useful for comparing classes or groups of data. In a bar chart, a class or group can have a single category of data, or can be broken down further into multiple categories for a greater depth of analysis. A bar chart is often used in exploratory data analysis to illustrate the major features of the data distribution in a convenient form. It displays the data using a number of rectangles of the same width, each of which represents a particular category. The length (and hence area) of each rectangle is proportional to the number of cases in the category it represents, such as, age group, religious affiliation, etc.

BarSeries for Bar Charts

You can use the same *ChartStyle* class implemented in the previous chapter to create bar charts. However, you will need to modify the *LineSeries*.

Open Visual Studio 2013, start a new WPF project, and name it *Chapter05*. Add Caliburn.Micro to *References*. Add three new folders, *Models*, *ViewModels*, and *Views,* to the project. Add *AppBootstrapper.cs*, which is the same as the one we used in the *Chapter04* project, to the *Models* folder.

Add a *Window* to the *Views* folder and name it *MainView*. Add a class to the *ViewModels* folder and name it *MainViewModel*. The main view and view model are used to hold the tab items, which are similar to those used in the *Chapter04* project. You can open the *Chapter04* project files inside Visual Studio and check the code if you need a refresher. Also, do not forget to make corresponding changes to *App.xaml*.

Now, we are ready to start creating bar charts. Add another new folder to the Models folder and name it *ChartModel*. Add all existing classes in the *ChartModel* folder from the *Chapter04* project to the current project's *ChartModel* folder and change their namespaces from *Chapter04* to *Chapter05*. Add a new class to the *ChartModel* class and name it *BarSeries*. Here is the code for this class:

```
using System;
using System.Windows;
using System.Windows.Media;
using System.Windows.Shapes;

namespace Chapter05.Models.ChartModel
{
    public class BarSeries
    {
        private Brush fillColor = Brushes.Black;
        private Brush borderColor = Brushes.Black;
        private double borderThickness = 1.0;
        private double barWidth = 0.8;
        public PointCollection BarPoints { get; set; }

        public BarSeries()
        {
            BarPoints = new PointCollection();
        }

        public Brush FillColor
        {
            get { return fillColor; }
            set { fillColor = value; }
        }

        public Brush BorderColor
        {
            get { return borderColor; }
            set { borderColor = value; }
        }

        public double BorderThickness
        {
            get { return borderThickness; }
            set { borderThickness = value; }
        }

        public double BarWidth
        {
            get { return barWidth; }
            set { barWidth = value; }
        }
    }
}
```

This class is very simple. We just define several member fields and their corresponding properties, which will allow you to specify the bar width, fill color, and border style.

In a line chart, a *LineSeries* contains only one polyline; however, a *BarSeries* usually contains multiple rectangles or polygons. You need a new class to hold these rectangle or polygon objects. Add a new class to the *ChartModel* folder and name it *BarPolygon*. Here is the code for this class:

```
using System;
using System.Windows.Media;

namespace Chapter05.Models.ChartModel
{
    public class BarPolygon
    {
        private Brush fillColor = Brushes.Black;
        private Brush borderColor = Brushes.Black;
        private double borderThickness = 1.0;
        public PointCollection PolygonPoints { get; set; }

        public BarPolygon()
        {
            PolygonPoints = new PointCollection();
        }

        public Brush FillColor
        {
            get { return fillColor; }
            set { fillColor = value; }
        }

        public Brush BorderColor
        {
            get { return borderColor; }
            set { borderColor = value; }
        }

        public double BorderThickness
        {
            get { return borderThickness; }
            set { borderThickness = value; }
        }
    }
}
```

This class is also very simple. Here, we just define properties for polygon objects. Next, we will link the bar border style and fill color properties to those defined in the *BarSeries* class in next section.

BarChartStyle class

The *BarChartStyle* class for bar charts is more complicated than that for line charts, because it is responsible for creating several different types of bar charts. Add a new class to the *ChartModel* folder and name it *BarChartStyle* class. Here is the code for this class:

```
using System;
using System.Collections.Generic;
using System.Linq;
using System.Text;
using System.Threading.Tasks;
```

```csharp
using System.Windows;
using Caliburn.Micro;
using System.Windows.Shapes;

namespace Chapter05.Models.ChartModel
{
    public class BarChartStyle : ChartStyle
    {
        public List<BarPolygon> PolygonCollection { get; set; }

        private BarTypeEnum barType = BarTypeEnum.Vertical;
        public BarTypeEnum BarType
        {
            get { return barType; }
            set { barType = value; }
        }

        public void SetBars(List<BarSeries> BarCollection)
        {
            PolygonCollection = new List<BarPolygon>();
            int nSeries = BarCollection.Count;
            double width;

            switch (BarType)
            {
                case BarTypeEnum.Vertical:
                    if (nSeries == 1)
                    {
                        foreach (var ds in BarCollection)
                        {
                            width = XTick * ds.BarWidth;
                            for (int i = 0; i < ds.BarPoints.Count; i++)
                            {
                                SetVerticalBar(ds.BarPoints[i], ds, width, 0);
                            }
                        }
                    }
                    else
                    {
                        int j = 0;
                        foreach (var ds in BarCollection)
                        {
                            for (int i = 0; i < ds.BarPoints.Count; i++)
                            {
                                SetVerticalBar1(ds.BarPoints[i], ds, nSeries, j);
                            }
                            j++;
                        }
                    }
                    break;

                case BarTypeEnum.VerticalOverlay:
                    if (nSeries > 1)
                    {
                        int j = 0;
```

```
        foreach (var ds in BarCollection)
        {
            width = XTick * ds.BarWidth;
            width = width / Math.Pow(2, j);
            for (int i = 0; i < ds.BarPoints.Count; i++)
            {
                SetVerticalBar(ds.BarPoints[i], ds, width, 0);
            }
            j++;
        }
    }
    break;

case BarTypeEnum.VerticalStack:
    if (nSeries > 1)
    {
        List<Point> temp = new List<Point>();
        double[] tempy =
            new double[BarCollection[0].BarPoints.Count];

        foreach (var ds in BarCollection)
        {
            width = XTick * ds.BarWidth;

            for (int i = 0; i < ds.BarPoints.Count; i++)
            {
                if (temp.Count > 0)
                {
                    tempy[i] += temp[i].Y;
                }
                SetVerticalBar(ds.BarPoints[i], ds,
                               width, tempy[i]);
            }
            temp.Clear();
            temp.AddRange(ds.BarPoints);
        }
    }
    break;

case BarTypeEnum.Horizontal:
    if (nSeries == 1)
    {
        foreach (var ds in BarCollection)
        {
            width = YTick * ds.BarWidth;
            for (int i = 0; i < ds.BarPoints.Count; i++)
            {
                SetHorizontalBar(ds.BarPoints[i], ds, width, 0);
            }
        }
    }
    else
    {
        int j = 0;
        foreach (var ds in BarCollection)
```

```csharp
                    {
                        for (int i = 0; i < ds.BarPoints.Count; i++)
                        {
                            SetHorizontalBar1(ds.BarPoints[i], ds, nSeries, j);
                        }
                        j++;
                    }
                }
                break;

            case BarTypeEnum.HorizontalOverlay:
                if (nSeries > 1)
                {
                    int j = 0;
                    foreach (var ds in BarCollection)
                    {
                        width = YTick * ds.BarWidth;
                        width = width / Math.Pow(2, j);
                        for (int i = 0; i < ds.BarPoints.Count; i++)
                        {
                            SetHorizontalBar(ds.BarPoints[i], ds, width, 0);
                        }
                        j++;
                    }
                }
                break;

            case BarTypeEnum.HorizontalStack:
                if (nSeries > 1)
                {
                    List<Point> temp = new List<Point>();
                    double[] tempy =
                        new double[BarCollection[0].BarPoints.Count];

                    foreach (var ds in BarCollection)
                    {
                        width = YTick * ds.BarWidth;

                        for (int i = 0; i < ds.BarPoints.Count; i++)
                        {
                            if (temp.Count > 0)
                            {
                                tempy[i] += temp[i].X;
                            }
                            SetHorizontalBar(ds.BarPoints[i], ds,
                                        width, tempy[i]);
                        }
                        temp.Clear();
                        temp.AddRange(ds.BarPoints);
                    }
                }
                break;
        }
    }
```

```
private void SetVerticalBar(Point pt, BarSeries ds, double width, double y)
{
    BarPolygon plg = new BarPolygon();
    plg.FillColor = ds.FillColor;
    plg.BorderColor = ds.BorderColor;
    plg.BorderThickness = ds.BorderThickness;

    double x = pt.X - 0.5 * XTick;
    plg.PolygonPoints.Add(NormalizePoint(new Point(x - width / 2, y)));
    plg.PolygonPoints.Add(NormalizePoint(new Point(x + width / 2, y)));
    plg.PolygonPoints.Add(NormalizePoint(new Point(x + width / 2,
        y + pt.Y)));
    plg.PolygonPoints.Add(NormalizePoint(new Point(x - width / 2,
        y + pt.Y)));
    PolygonCollection.Add(plg);
}

private void SetVerticalBar1(Point pt, BarSeries ds, int nSeries, int n)
{
    BarPolygon plg = new BarPolygon();
    plg.FillColor = ds.FillColor;
    plg.BorderColor = ds.BorderColor;
    plg.BorderThickness = ds.BorderThickness;

    double width = 0.7 * XTick;
    double w1 = width / nSeries;
    double w = ds.BarWidth * w1;
    double space = (w1 - w) / 2;
    double x = pt.X - 0.5 * XTick;
    plg.PolygonPoints.Add(NormalizePoint(
                new Point(x - width / 2 + space + n * w1, 0)));
    plg.PolygonPoints.Add(NormalizePoint(
                new Point(x - width / 2 + space + n * w1 + w, 0)));
    plg.PolygonPoints.Add(NormalizePoint(
                new Point(x - width / 2 + space + n * w1 + w, pt.Y)));
    plg.PolygonPoints.Add(NormalizePoint(
                new Point(x - width / 2 + space + n * w1, pt.Y)));
    PolygonCollection.Add(plg);
}

private void SetHorizontalBar(Point pt, BarSeries ds,
    double width, double x)
{
    BarPolygon plg = new BarPolygon();
    plg.FillColor = ds.FillColor;
    plg.BorderColor = ds.BorderColor;
    plg.BorderThickness = ds.BorderThickness;

    double y = pt.Y - 0.5 * YTick;
    plg.PolygonPoints.Add(NormalizePoint(new Point(x, y - width / 2)));
    plg.PolygonPoints.Add(NormalizePoint(new Point(x, y + width / 2)));
    plg.PolygonPoints.Add(NormalizePoint(new Point(x + pt.X,
        y + width / 2)));
    plg.PolygonPoints.Add(NormalizePoint(new Point(x + pt.X,
        y - width / 2)));
```

```
            PolygonCollection.Add(plg);
        }

    private void SetHorizontalBar1(Point pt, BarSeries ds, int nSeries, int n)
    {
        BarPolygon plg = new BarPolygon();
        plg.FillColor = ds.FillColor;
        plg.BorderColor = ds.BorderColor;
        plg.BorderThickness = ds.BorderThickness;

        double width = 0.7 * YTick;
        double w1 = width / nSeries;
        double w = ds.BarWidth * w1;
        double space = (w1 - w) / 2;
        double y = pt.Y - 0.5 * YTick;
        plg.PolygonPoints.Add(NormalizePoint(
                    new Point(0, y - width / 2 + space + n * w1)));
        plg.PolygonPoints.Add(NormalizePoint(
                    new Point(0, y - width / 2 + space + n * w1 + w)));
        plg.PolygonPoints.Add(NormalizePoint(
                    new Point(pt.X, y - width / 2 + space + n * w1 + w)));
        plg.PolygonPoints.Add(NormalizePoint(
                    new Point(pt.X, y - width / 2 + space + n * w1)));
        PolygonCollection.Add(plg);
        }
    }

public enum BarTypeEnum
{
    Vertical = 0,
    Horizontal = 1,
    VerticalStack = 2,
    HorizontalStack = 3,
    VerticalOverlay = 4,
    HorizontalOverlay = 5
}
}
```

This class inherits from the original *ChartStyle* class. Here, we first create a private field member named *barType* and the corresponding public property. There are six types of bar charts defined in the *BarTypeEnum*: vertical, horizontal, vertical stack, horizontal stack, vertical overlay, and horizontal overlay.

The main portion of this class is the *SetBars* method, within which you implement these six types of bar charts. Each bar is defined by the point coordinates of its four corners and created using a *Polygon* object. You can specify the fill color, border color, and border thickness for each bar set through the *BarSeries* object. Notice that the original *ChartStyle* class is used for the bar chart style, such as the title, gridlines, and axis labels.

Creating Simple Bar Charts

In this section, I will show you how to create two simple bar charts: vertical and horizontal. Add a new *UserControl* to the *Views* folder and name it *BarView*. Here is XAML for this view:

```xml
<UserControl x:Class="Chapter05.Views.BarView"
             xmlns="http://schemas.microsoft.com/winfx/2006/xaml/presentation"
             xmlns:x="http://schemas.microsoft.com/winfx/2006/xaml"
             xmlns:mc="http://schemas.openxmlformats.org/markup-compatibility/2006"
             xmlns:d="http://schemas.microsoft.com/expression/blend/2008"
             xmlns:cal="http://www.caliburnproject.org"
             mc:Ignorable="d"
             d:DesignHeight="400" d:DesignWidth="500">

    <UserControl.Resources>
        <DataTemplate x:Key="chartTemplate">
            <Polygon Points="{Binding PolygonPoints}" Stroke="{Binding BorderColor}"
                     StrokeThickness="{Binding BorderThickness}"
                     Fill="{Binding FillColor}"/>
        </DataTemplate>
    </UserControl.Resources>

    <Grid>
        <Grid.ColumnDefinitions>
            <ColumnDefinition Width="170"/>
            <ColumnDefinition Width="*"/>
        </Grid.ColumnDefinitions>
        <StackPanel>
            <Button x:Name="SimpleBar" Content="Simple Bar"
                    Width="150" Margin="0 20 0 0"/>
            <Button x:Name="BarMissingData" Content="Missing Data"
                    Width="150" Margin="0 10 0 0"/>
            <Button x:Name="HorizontalBar" Content="Horizontal Bar"
                    Width="150" Margin="0 10 0 0"/>
            <Button x:Name="GroupBar" Content="Group Bar"
                    Width=" 150" Margin="0 10 0 0"/>
            <Button x:Name="HorizontalGroupBar" Content="Horizontal Group Bar"
                    Width="150" Margin="0 10 0 0"/>
            <Button x:Name="OverlayBar" Content="Overlay Bar"
                    Width="150" Margin="0 10 0 0"/>
            <Button x:Name="HorizontalOverlayBar" Content="Horizontal Overlay Bar"
                    Width="150" Margin="0 10 0 0"/>
            <Button x:Name="StackBar" Content="Stack Bar"
                    Width="150" Margin="0 10 0 0"/>
            <Button x:Name="HorizontalStackBar" Content="Horizontal Stack Bar"
                    Width="150" Margin="0 10 0 0"/>
        </StackPanel>

        <Grid Name="grid1" Grid.Column="1" Margin="10">
            <Grid.ColumnDefinitions>
                <ColumnDefinition Width="Auto"/>
                <ColumnDefinition Name="column1" Width="*"/>
            </Grid.ColumnDefinitions>
            <Grid.RowDefinitions>
                <RowDefinition Height="Auto"/>
                <RowDefinition Name="row1" Height="*"/>
                <RowDefinition Height="Auto"/>
            </Grid.RowDefinitions>
            <TextBlock Margin="2" x:Name="tbTitle" Grid.Column="1" Grid.Row="0"
                    RenderTransformOrigin="0.5,0.5" FontSize="14" FontWeight="Bold"
```

```
                        HorizontalAlignment="Stretch" VerticalAlignment="Stretch"
                        TextAlignment="Center" Text="Title"/>
            <TextBlock Margin="2" x:Name="tbXLabel" Grid.Column="1" Grid.Row="2"
                    RenderTransformOrigin="0.5,0.5" TextAlignment="Center"
                    Text="X Axis"/>

            <TextBlock Margin="2" Name="tbYLabel" Grid.Column="0" Grid.Row="1"
                    RenderTransformOrigin="0.5,0.5" TextAlignment="Center"
                    Text="Y Axis">
                <TextBlock.LayoutTransform>
                    <RotateTransform Angle="-90"/>
                </TextBlock.LayoutTransform>
            </TextBlock>

            <Grid  Margin="0,0,0,0" x:Name ="chartGrid" Grid.Column="1" Grid.Row="1"
                ClipToBounds="False" Background="Transparent"
                cal:Message.Attach="[Event SizeChanged]=[Action AddChart()];
               [Event Loaded]=[Action AddChart()]">

                <Canvas Margin="2" Name="textCanvas" Grid.Column="1"
                        Grid.Row="1" ClipToBounds="True"
                Width="{Binding ElementName=chartGrid,Path=ActualWidth}"
                    Height="{Binding ElementName=chartGrid,Path=ActualHeight}">
                    <Canvas Name="chartCanvas" ClipToBounds="True">
                        <ItemsControl ItemsSource="{Binding PolygonCollection}"
                                    ItemTemplate="{StaticResource chartTemplate}">
                            <ItemsControl.ItemsPanel>
                                <ItemsPanelTemplate>
                                    <Grid/>
                                </ItemsPanelTemplate>
                            </ItemsControl.ItemsPanel>
                        </ItemsControl>
                    </Canvas>
                </Canvas>
            </Grid>
        </Grid>
    </Grid>
</UserControl>
```

Here, I add several buttons that will be used to create different bar charts. Note how I implement the *DataTemplate* inside the view's *Resources*, where I define a polygon whose properties are bound to the *BarPolygon*'s corresponding properties. The rest of this XAML is similar to that used in creating line charts.

Add a new class to the *ViewModels* folder and name it *BarViewModel*. Here is the code for this class:

```
using System;
using System.Linq;
using Caliburn.Micro;
using System.Collections.ObjectModel;
using System.ComponentModel.Composition;
using System.Windows.Documents;
using System.Collections.Generic;
using System.Windows;
using Chapter04.Models;
using System.Windows.Media;
```

```csharp
using System.Windows.Controls;
using Chapter05.Models.ChartModel;
using Chapter05.Views;

namespace Chapter05.ViewModels
{
    [Export(typeof(IScreen)), PartCreationPolicy(CreationPolicy.NonShared)]
    public class BarViewModel : Screen
    {
         private readonly IEventAggregator _events;
        [ImportingConstructor]
        public BarViewModel(IEventAggregator events)
        {
            this._events = events;
            DisplayName = "01. Bar Chart";
            PolygonCollection = new BindableCollection<BarPolygon>();
            BarCollection = new List<BarSeries>();
            cs = new BarChartStyle();
        }

        private BarView view;
        private BarChartStyle cs;
        public BindableCollection<BarPolygon> PolygonCollection { get; set; }
        public List<BarSeries> BarCollection { get; set; }
        private string chartType = "SimpleBar";

        private void SetChartStyle()
        {
            view = this.GetView() as BarView;
            view.chartCanvas.Children.RemoveRange(1,
                view.chartCanvas.Children.Count - 1);
            view.textCanvas.Children.RemoveRange(1,
                view.textCanvas.Children.Count - 1);
            cs.ChartCanvas = view.chartCanvas;
            cs.TextCanvas = view.textCanvas;
        }

        public void AddChart()
        {
            switch (chartType)
            {
                case "SimpleBar":
                    SimpleBar();
                    break;
                case "BarMissingData":
                    BarMissingData();
                    break;
                case "HorizontalBar":
                    HorizontalBar();
                    break;
            }
        }

        public void SimpleBar()
        {
```

```
        chartType = "SimpleBar";
        SetChartStyle();
        cs.BarType = BarTypeEnum.Vertical;
        cs.Xmin = 0;
        cs.Xmax = 5;
        cs.Ymin = 0;
        cs.Ymax = 10;
        cs.XTick = 1;
        cs.YTick = 2;
        cs.GridlinePattern = LinePatternEnum.Dot;
        cs.GridlineColor = Brushes.Black;
        cs.Title = "Simple Bar Chart";
        cs.AddChartStyle(view.tbTitle, view.tbXLabel, view.tbYLabel);

        PolygonCollection.Clear();
        BarCollection.Clear();

        var bar = new BarSeries();
        bar.BorderColor = Brushes.Red;
        bar.FillColor = Brushes.Green;
        bar.BarWidth = 0.6;
        for (int i = 0; i < 5; i++)
        {
            double x = i + 1.0;
            double y = 2.0 * x;
            bar.BarPoints.Add(new Point(x, y));
        }
        BarCollection.Add(bar);
        cs.SetBars(BarCollection);
        foreach (var plg in cs.PolygonCollection)
            PolygonCollection.Add(plg);
    }

    public void BarMissingData()
    {
        chartType = "BarMissingData";
        SetChartStyle();
        cs.BarType = BarTypeEnum.Vertical;
        cs.Xmin = 0;
        cs.Xmax = 5;
        cs.Ymin = 0;
        cs.Ymax = 10;
        cs.XTick = 1;
        cs.YTick = 2;
        cs.GridlinePattern = LinePatternEnum.Dot;
        cs.GridlineColor = Brushes.Black;
        cs.Title = "Bar Chart with Missing Data";
        cs.AddChartStyle(view.tbTitle, view.tbXLabel, view.tbYLabel);

        PolygonCollection.Clear();
        BarCollection.Clear();
        var bar = new BarSeries();
        bar.BorderColor = Brushes.Red;
        bar.FillColor = Brushes.Green;
        bar.BarWidth = 0.6;
```

```
        double[] x = new double[] { 1, 2, 3, 4, 5 };
        double[] y = new double[] { 2, 0, 3, 8, 10 };

        for (int i = 0; i < x.Length; i++)
        {
            bar.BarPoints.Add(new Point(x[i], y[i]));
        }
        BarCollection.Add(bar);
        cs.SetBars(BarCollection);
        foreach (var plg in cs.PolygonCollection)
            PolygonCollection.Add(plg);
    }

    public void HorizontalBar()
    {
        chartType = "HorizontalBar";
        SetChartStyle();
        cs.BarType = BarTypeEnum.Vertical;
        cs.Xmin = 0;
        cs.Xmax = 10;
        cs.Ymin = 0;
        cs.Ymax = 5;
        cs.XTick = 2;
        cs.YTick = 1;
        cs.GridlinePattern = LinePatternEnum.Dot;
        cs.GridlineColor = Brushes.Black;
        cs.Title = "Horizontal Bar Chart";
        cs.AddChartStyle(view.tbTitle, view.tbXLabel, view.tbYLabel);

        PolygonCollection.Clear();
        BarCollection.Clear();
        var bar = new BarSeries();
        cs.BarType = BarTypeEnum.Horizontal;
        bar.BorderColor = Brushes.Red;
        bar.FillColor = Brushes.Green;
        bar.BarWidth = 0.6;
        for (int i = 0; i < 5; i++)
        {
            double x = i + 1.0;
            double y = 2.0 * x;
            bar.BarPoints.Add(new Point(y, x));
        }
        BarCollection.Add(bar);
        cs.SetBars(BarCollection);
        foreach (var plg in cs.PolygonCollection)
            PolygonCollection.Add(plg);
    }
  }
}
```

This view model class is also similar to that used in creating line charts, except that here the *BindableCollection* called *PolygonCollection* is for *BarPolygon*, not *BarSeries*. We also define a *chartType* string field that is used in the *AddChart* method to create different types of bar charts.

Inside the *SimpleBar* method, you set the *BarType* property to *Vertical*, which is also the default value. The other parameters defined in this method are standard properties for all charts. You then associate bar style properties with the *BarSeries*. Here, we have set bar width to 0.6 (the default value is 0.8). This value must be in the range of [0, 1]. Finally, we call the *SetBars* method defined in the *BarChartStyle* class, and convert *cs.PolygonCollection* to the *BindableCollection* object.

Running this example generates the vertical bar chart shown in Figure 5-1.

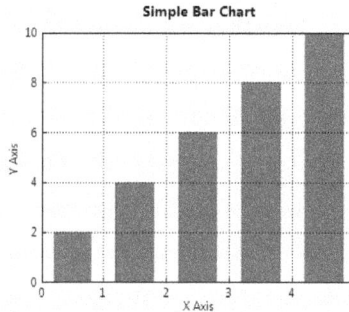

Figure 5-1. A vertical bar chart.

In some cases, some of the data points may be missing data. We can create a bar chart by assigning a zero value for the *Y* value at the missing data point. For example, we have the following set of data: $X = [1, 2, 3, 4, 5]$ and $Y = [2, 0, 3, 8, 10]$, as shown in the *BarMissingData* method. Here, we simply replace this code snippet in the *SimpleBar* method:

```
for (int i = 0; i < 5; i++)
{
    double x = i + 1.0;
    double y = 2.0 * x;
    ds.LineSeries.Points.Add(new Point(x, y));
}
```

with the following code:

```
double[] x = new double[] { 1, 2, 3, 4, 5 };
double[] y = new double[] { 2, 0, 3, 8, 10 };
for (int i = 0; i < x.Length; i++)
{
    ds.LineSeries.Points.Add(new Point(x[i], y[i]));
}
```

Running this example and clicking the *Missing Data* button produces the result shown in Figure 5-2.

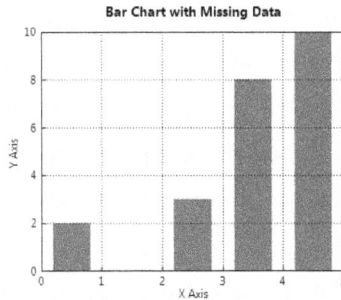

Figure 5-2. A vertical bar chart with a missing data point at x = 2.

We can create a horizontal bar chart just as easily by replacing the *SimpleBar* method with the *HorizonalBar* method, where we need to change the *BarType* to *Horizontal* and switch the *x* and *y* data points. Running this example and clicking the *Horizontal Bar* button generates the result shown in Figure 5-3.

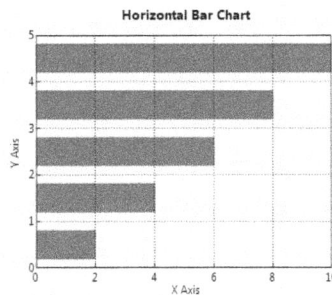

Figure 5-3. A horizontal bar chart.

Creating Group Bar Charts

When we have multiple sets of data with the same *X* values, we can use the current example program to create a group bar chart. The *Y* values are distributed along the *X*-axis, with each *Y* at a different *X* drawn at a different location. All of the *Y* values at the same *X* are clustered around the same location on the *X*-axis. In order to create such a bar chart, you need to add the following *GroupBar* method:

```
public void GroupBar()
{
    chartType = "GroupBar";
    SetChartStyle();
    cs.BarType = BarTypeEnum.Vertical;
    cs.Xmin = 0;
    cs.Xmax = 5;
    cs.Ymin = 0;
    cs.Ymax = 10;
    cs.XTick = 1;
    cs.YTick = 2;
    cs.GridlinePattern = LinePatternEnum.Dot;
    cs.GridlineColor = Brushes.Black;
```

```
cs.Title = "Group Bar Chart";
cs.AddChartStyle(view.tbTitle, view.tbXLabel, view.tbYLabel);

PolygonCollection.Clear();
BarCollection.Clear();

// Add first bar series:
var bar = new BarSeries();
bar.BorderColor = Brushes.Red;
bar.FillColor = Brushes.Green;
bar.BarWidth = 0.9;
for (int i = 0; i < 5; i++)
{
    double x = i + 1.0;
    double y = 2.0 * x;
    bar.BarPoints.Add(new Point(x, y));
}
BarCollection.Add(bar);

// Add second bar series:
bar = new BarSeries();
bar.BorderColor = Brushes.Red;
bar.FillColor = Brushes.Yellow;
bar.BarWidth = 0.9;
for (int i = 0; i < 5; i++)
{
    double x = i + 1.0;
    double y = 1.5 * x;
    bar.BarPoints.Add(new Point(x, y));
}
BarCollection.Add(bar);

// Add third bar series:
bar = new BarSeries();
bar.BorderColor = Brushes.Red;
bar.FillColor = Brushes.Blue;
bar.BarWidth = 0.9;
for (int i = 0; i < 5; i++)
{
    double x = i + 1.0;
    double y = 1.0 * x;
    bar.BarPoints.Add(new Point(x, y));
}
BarCollection.Add(bar);

cs.SetBars(BarCollection);
foreach (var plg in cs.PolygonCollection)
    PolygonCollection.Add(plg);
}
```

Here, we add three sets of data series to the *GroupBar* method, all with the same set of *X* values. The bar width is set to 0.9. The fill colors are green, yellow, and blue respectively, while the border color is red for all of the bars. Note that the bar type is still set to *Vertical*; the program will automatically create a grouped vertical bar chart if more than one set of data is provided. These data sets produce the results shown in Figure 5-4.

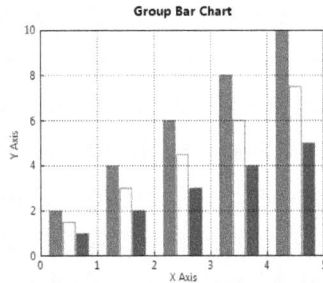

Figure 5-4. A grouped vertical bar chart.

Similarly, we can easily create a grouped horizontal bar chart using the following *HorizontalGroupBar* method:

```
public void HorizontalGroupBar()
{
    chartType = "HorizontalGroupBar";
    SetChartStyle();
    cs.BarType = BarTypeEnum.Vertical;
    cs.Xmin = 0;
    cs.Xmax = 10;
    cs.Ymin = 0;
    cs.Ymax = 5;
    cs.XTick = 2;
    cs.YTick = 1;
    cs.GridlinePattern = LinePatternEnum.Dot;
    cs.GridlineColor = Brushes.Black;
    cs.Title = "Horiozontal Group Bar Chart";
    cs.AddChartStyle(view.tbTitle, view.tbXLabel, view.tbYLabel);

    PolygonCollection.Clear();
    BarCollection.Clear();
    cs.BarType = BarTypeEnum.Horizontal;

    // Add first bar series:
    var bar = new BarSeries();
    bar.BorderColor = Brushes.Red;
    bar.FillColor = Brushes.Green;
    bar.BarWidth = 0.9;
    for (int i = 0; i < 5; i++)
    {
        double x = i + 1.0;
        double y = 2.0 * x;
        bar.BarPoints.Add(new Point(y, x));
    }
    BarCollection.Add(bar);

    // Add second bar series:
    bar = new BarSeries();
    bar.BorderColor = Brushes.Red;
    bar.FillColor = Brushes.Yellow;
    bar.BarWidth = 0.9;
    for (int i = 0; i < 5; i++)
```

```
    {
        double x = i + 1.0;
        double y = 1.5 * x;
        bar.BarPoints.Add(new Point(y, x));
    }
    BarCollection.Add(bar);

    // Add third bar series:
    bar = new BarSeries();
    bar.BorderColor = Brushes.Red;
    bar.FillColor = Brushes.Blue;
    bar.BarWidth = 0.9;
    for (int i = 0; i < 5; i++)
    {
        double x = i + 1.0;
        double y = 1.0 * x;
        bar.BarPoints.Add(new Point(y, x));
    }
    BarCollection.Add(bar);

    cs.SetBars(BarCollection);
    foreach (var plg in cs.PolygonCollection)
        PolygonCollection.Add(plg);
}
```

This method produces the results of Figure 5-5.

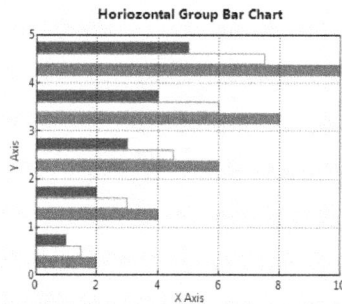

Figure 5-5. A grouped horizontal bar chart.

Creating Overlaid Bar Charts

It is also easy to create an overlaid bar chart using the current example program. Add a new method to the *BarViewModel* class and name it to *OverlayBar*. The code for this method is the same as that used in *GroupBar* method, except we change the *BarType* property to *VerticalOverlay*. This will produce the results shown in Figure 5-6.

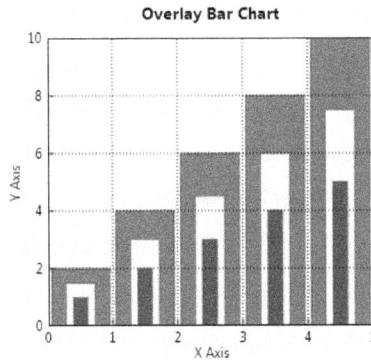

Figure 5-6. An overlaid vertical bar chart.

Similarly, we can create an overlaid horizontal bar chart. Add a new method to the *BarViewModel* class and name it to *HorizontalOverlayBar*. The code for this method is the same as that used in the *HorizontalGroupBar* method, except that we change the *BarType* property to *HorizontalOverlay*. This will produce the results shown in Figure 5-7.

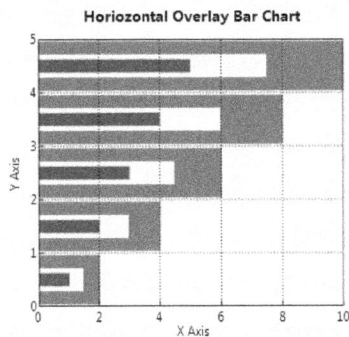

Figure 5-7. An overlaid horizontal bar chart.

Creating Stacked Bar Charts

Bar charts can show how different Y values at the same X point contribute to the sum of all of the Y values at the point. These types of bar charts are referred to as stacked bar charts.

Stacked bar graphs display one bar per X value. The bars are divided into several fragments according to the number of X values. For vertical stacked bar charts, the height of each bar equals the sum of all of the Y values at a given X value. Each fragment is equal to the value of its respective Y value.

We can continue to use the current example program to create stacked bar chart. Add a new method to the *BarViewModel* class and name it *StackBar*. The code for this method is the same as that used in *GroupBar* method, except we change the *BarType* property to *VerticalStack*. This will produce the results shown in Figure 5-8.

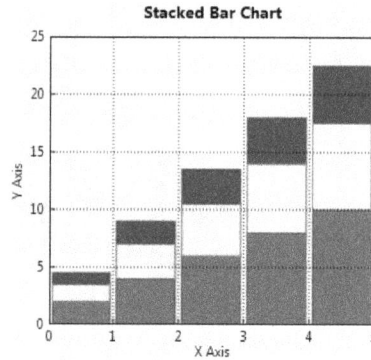

Figure 5-8. A stacked vertical bar chart.

Similarly, we can create a stacked horizontal bar chart. Add a new method to the *BarViewModel* class and name it *HorizontalStackBar*. The code for this method is the same as that used in the *HorizontalGroupBar* method, except we change the *BarType* property to *HorizontalStack*. This will produce the results shown in Figure 5-9.

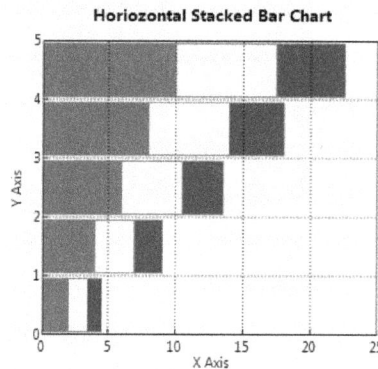

Figure 5-9. A stacked horizontal bar chart.

Stair-Step Charts

In this section, I will show you how to create a stair-step chart. Instead of creating lines that directly connect your data, you can choose to have your data plotted in a way that emphasizes the discrete nature of the data. Namely, stair-step charts draw horizontal lines at the level specified by the *Y* data. This level will be held constant over the period between the values specified by the *X* data values. Stair-step charts are similar to bar charts except that vertical lines are not dropped down all the way to the zero value point on the *Y*-axis. This type of plot is useful for drawing time-history plots of digitally sampled data systems.

Data Series and Chart Style

In this section, I will create common classes for several similar specialized 2D charts, including stair-step, stem, error bar, and area charts. In order to create these specialized 2D charts, we need to add a new collection to hold their points. Add a new class to the *ChartModel* folder and name it *Specialized2DSeries*. Here is the code for this class:

```
using System;
using System.Windows.Media;

namespace Chapter05.Models.ChartModel
{
    public class Specialized2DSeries : LineSeries
    {
        public Specialized2DSeries()
        {
            DataPoints = new PointCollection();
            ErrorPoints = new PointCollection();
        }

        private Brush fillColor = Brushes.White;
        public Brush FillColor
        {
            get { return fillColor; }
            set { fillColor = value; }
        }

        public PointCollection DataPoints { get; set; }
        public PointCollection ErrorPoints { get; set; }
    }
}
```

This class, inheriting from the *LineSeries* class, is very simple. It contains a *DataPoints* property that holds points for creating specialized 2D charts. The *ErrorPoints* property will be used in creating error bar charts and the *FillColor* property will be used in creating area charts.

The chart style for these specialized 2D charts is also very simple and only implements a *SetSpecialized2DLines* method. Add a new class to the *ChartModel* folder and name it *Specialized2DChartStyle*. Here is the code for this class:

```
using System;
using System.Collections.Generic;
using System.Windows;
using Caliburn.Micro;

namespace Chapter05.Models.ChartModel
{
    public class Specialized2DChartStyle : ChartStyle
    {
        public Specialied2DChartTypeEnum Specialized2DChartType { get; set; }

        public Specialized2DChartStyle()
        {
            Specialized2DChartType = Specialied2DChartTypeEnum.Stairstep;
        }
```

```
public void SetSpecialized2DLines(
    BindableCollection<Specialized2DSeries> dc)
{
    if (dc.Count <= 0)
        return;

    for (int i = 0; i < dc.Count; i++)
    {
        dc[i].DataPoints.Clear();
        if (dc[i].SeriesName == "Default")
            dc[i].SeriesName = "LineSeries" + i.ToString();
        dc[i].SetLinePattern();
    }

    switch (Specialized2DChartType)
    {
        case Specialied2DChartTypeEnum.Stairstep:
            foreach (var ds in dc)
            {
                for (int i = 0; i < ds.LinePoints.Count - 1; i++)
                {
                    Point[] pts = new Point[2];
                    pts[0] = ds.LinePoints[i];
                    pts[1] = ds.LinePoints[i + 1];
                    ds.DataPoints.Add(NormalizePoint(pts[0]));
                    ds.DataPoints.Add(
                        NormalizePoint(new Point(pts[1].X, pts[0].Y)));
                }
            }
            break;
    }
}

public enum Specialied2DChartTypeEnum
{
    Stairstep = 1,
    Stem = 2,
    ErrorBar = 3,
    Area = 4,
}
```

Here, the *Specialized2DChartTypeEnum* lets us choose from four different charts (stair-step, stem, error bar, and area). We only need to specify the line style and line point collection in our view model, as what we did in creating a line chart. The *SetSpecialized2DLines* method will generate the corresponding point collection for your stair-step line. Note how you create the stair step data points – for two adjacent points, you recreate two points with the same Y value, which gives the stair-step levels.

Creating Stair-Step Charts

In this section, I will show you how to create stair step charts using the *Specialized2DSeries* and *Specialized2DChartStyle* classes implemented in the previous sections. Add a new *UserControl* to the *Views* folder and name it *StairstepView*. Here is the XAML file for this view:

```
<UserControl x:Class="Chapter05.Views.StemView"
            xmlns="http://schemas.microsoft.com/winfx/2006/xaml/presentation"
            xmlns:x="http://schemas.microsoft.com/winfx/2006/xaml"
            xmlns:mc="http://schemas.openxmlformats.org/markup-compatibility/2006"
            xmlns:d="http://schemas.microsoft.com/expression/blend/2008"
            xmlns:cal="http://www.caliburnproject.org"
            mc:Ignorable="d"
            d:DesignHeight="400" d:DesignWidth="400">

    <UserControl.Resources>
        <DataTemplate x:Key="chartTemplate">
            <Polyline Points="{Binding DataPoints}" Stroke="{Binding LineColor}"
                    StrokeThickness="{Binding LineThickness}"
                    StrokeDashArray="{Binding LineDashPattern}"/>
        </DataTemplate>
    </UserControl.Resources>

    <Grid Name="grid1" Margin="10">
        <Grid.ColumnDefinitions>
            <ColumnDefinition Width="Auto"/>
            <ColumnDefinition Name="column1" Width="*"/>
        </Grid.ColumnDefinitions>
        <Grid.RowDefinitions>
            <RowDefinition Height="Auto"/>
            <RowDefinition Name="row1" Height="*"/>
            <RowDefinition Height="Auto"/>
        </Grid.RowDefinitions>
        <TextBlock Margin="2" x:Name="tbTitle" Grid.Column="1" Grid.Row="0"
                RenderTransformOrigin="0.5,0.5" FontSize="14" FontWeight="Bold"
                HorizontalAlignment="Stretch" VerticalAlignment="Stretch"
                TextAlignment="Center" Text="Title"/>
        <TextBlock Margin="2" x:Name="tbXLabel" Grid.Column="1" Grid.Row="2"
                RenderTransformOrigin="0.5,0.5" TextAlignment="Center"
                Text="X Axis"/>

        <TextBlock Margin="2" Name="tbYLabel" Grid.Column="0" Grid.Row="1"
                RenderTransformOrigin="0.5,0.5" TextAlignment="Center"
                Text="Y Axis">
            <TextBlock.LayoutTransform>
                <RotateTransform Angle="-90"/>
            </TextBlock.LayoutTransform>
        </TextBlock>

        <Grid  Margin="0,0,0,0" x:Name ="chartGrid" Grid.Column="1" Grid.Row="1"
            ClipToBounds="False" Background="Transparent"
            cal:Message.Attach="[Event SizeChanged]=[Action AddChart()];
            [Event Loaded]=[Action AddChart()]">

            <Canvas Margin="2" Name="textCanvas" Grid.Column="1"
```

```
                    Grid.Row="1" ClipToBounds="True"
                    Width="{Binding ElementName=chartGrid,Path=ActualWidth}"
                    Height="{Binding ElementName=chartGrid,Path=ActualHeight}">
                    <Canvas Name="chartCanvas" ClipToBounds="True">
                        <ItemsControl ItemsSource="{Binding DataCollection}"
                                    ItemTemplate="{StaticResource chartTemplate}">
                            <ItemsControl.ItemsPanel>
                                <ItemsPanelTemplate>
                                    <Grid/>
                                </ItemsPanelTemplate>
                            </ItemsControl.ItemsPanel>
                        </ItemsControl>
                    </Canvas>
                </Canvas>
            </Grid>
        </Grid>
</UserControl>
```

This XAML file is basically the same as that used in creating simple line charts, except that here, we replace the *LinePoints* with *DataPoints* in the *DataTemplate*.

Add a new class to the *ViewModels* folder and name it *StairstepViewModel*. Here is the code for this class:

```
using System;
using System.Linq;
using Caliburn.Micro;
using System.Collections.ObjectModel;
using System.ComponentModel.Composition;
using System.Windows.Documents;
using System.Collections.Generic;
using System.Windows;
using Chapter05.Models;
using System.Windows.Media;
using System.Windows.Controls;
using Chapter05.Views;
using Chapter05.Models.ChartModel;

namespace Chapter05.ViewModels
{
    [Export(typeof(IScreen)), PartCreationPolicy(CreationPolicy.NonShared)]
    public class StairstepViewModel : Screen
    {
        private readonly IEventAggregator _events;
        [ImportingConstructor]
         public StairstepViewModel(IEventAggregator events)
        {
            this._events = events;
            DisplayName = "02. Stairstep";
            DataCollection = new BindableCollection<Specialized2DSeries>();
        }

        private Specialized2DChartStyle cs;
        public BindableCollection<Specialized2DSeries> DataCollection { get; set; }

        private void SetChartStyle()
```

```
        {
            var view = this.GetView() as StairstepView;
            view.chartCanvas.Children.RemoveRange(1,
                view.chartCanvas.Children.Count - 1);
            view.textCanvas.Children.RemoveRange(1,
                view.textCanvas.Children.Count - 1);
            cs = new Specialized2DChartStyle();
            cs.Specialized2DChartType = Specialied2DChartTypeEnum.Stairstep;
            cs.ChartCanvas = view.chartCanvas;
            cs.TextCanvas = view.textCanvas;
            cs.Title = "Stairstep Chart";
            cs.Xmin = 0;
            cs.Xmax = 8;
            cs.Ymin = -1.5;
            cs.Ymax = 1.5;
            cs.XTick = 1;
            cs.YTick = 0.5;
            cs.GridlinePattern = LinePatternEnum.Dot;
            cs.GridlineColor = Brushes.Black;
            cs.AddChartStyle(view.tbTitle, view.tbXLabel, view.tbYLabel);
        }

        public void AddChart()
        {
            SetChartStyle();
            DataCollection.Clear();
            var ds = new Specialized2DSeries();
            ds.LineColor = Brushes.Red;
            ds.LineThickness = 2;
            ds.LinePattern = LinePatternEnum.Solid;
            for (int i = 0; i < 50; i++)
            {
                ds.LinePoints.Add(new Point(0.4 * i, Math.Sin(0.4 * i)));
            }
            DataCollection.Add(ds);
            cs.SetSpecialized2DLines(DataCollection);
        }
    }
}
```

Here, we first set the *Specialized2DChartType* property to *Stairstep* and then specify the line style, just as we did for line charts. Finally we call the *SetSpecialized2DLines* method to generate the *DataPoints* object bound to the *Polyline* control's *Points* property in our view. Running this program produces the output of Figure 5-10.

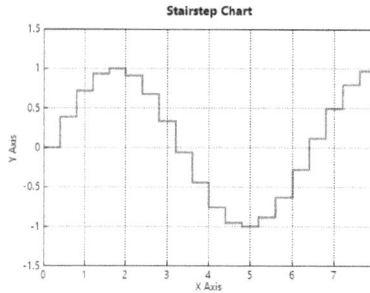

Figure 5-10. A stair step chart of a sine function.

Stem Charts

Stem charts provide another way to visualize discrete data sequences such as digitally sampled time series data. In this type of chart, vertical lines terminate with a marker symbol at each data value. In 2D stem chart, these stem lines extend from the *X* axis.

Creating stem charts is much easier because we can use the *Specialized2DChartStyle* and *Specialized2DSeries* classes implemented in the preceding section. The only code we need to add to the *SetSpecialied2DLines* method in the *Specialized2DChartStyle* class is the detailed procedure for creating the stem charts. Add the following code snippet to the *SetSpecialied2DLines* method:

```
case Specialied2DChartTypeEnum.Stem:
    foreach (var ds in dc)
    {
        for (int i = 0; i < ds.LinePoints.Count; i++)
        {
            Point[] pts = new Point[2];
            pts[0] = NormalizePoint(new Point(ds.LinePoints[i].X, 0));
            pts[1] = NormalizePoint(ds.LinePoints[i]);

            ds.DataPoints.Add(pts[0]);
            ds.DataPoints.Add(pts[1]);
            ds.DataPoints.Add(pts[0]);
            ds.Symbols.AddSymbol(ChartCanvas, pts[1]);
        }
    }
    break;
```

Note that at a given point (x, y), you draw a straight line from $(x, 0)$ to (x, y), which defines the stem line at the point (x, y). The stem line style, such as *LineColor* and *LineThickness*, is specified using the line style defined in the original *LineSeries* class, and the symbols at the data values of the stem line are defined using original *Symbols* class.

Now we are ready to create a stem chart. Add a new *UserControl* to the *Views* folder and name it *StemView*. The XAML file for this example is the same as that used in the preceding example.

Add a new class to the *ViewModels* folder and name it *StemViewModel*. Here is the code for this class:

```
using System;
using System.Linq;
using Caliburn.Micro;
```

```
using System.Collections.ObjectModel;
using System.ComponentModel.Composition;
using System.Windows.Documents;
using System.Collections.Generic;
using System.Windows;
using Chapter05.Models;
using System.Windows.Media;
using System.Windows.Controls;
using Chapter05.Views;
using Chapter05.Models.ChartModel;

namespace Chapter05.ViewModels
{
    [Export(typeof(IScreen)), PartCreationPolicy(CreationPolicy.NonShared)]
    public class StemViewModel : Screen
    {
        private readonly IEventAggregator _events;
        [ImportingConstructor]
        public StemViewModel(IEventAggregator events)
        {
            this._events = events;
            DisplayName = "03. Stem";
            DataCollection = new BindableCollection<Specialized2DSeries>();
        }

        private Specialized2DChartStyle cs;
        public BindableCollection<Specialized2DSeries> DataCollection { get; set; }

        private void SetChartStyle()
        {
            var view = this.GetView() as StemView;
            view.chartCanvas.Children.RemoveRange(1,
                view.chartCanvas.Children.Count - 1);
            view.textCanvas.Children.RemoveRange(1,
                view.textCanvas.Children.Count - 1);
            cs = new Specialized2DChartStyle();
            cs.Specialized2DChartType = Specialied2DChartTypeEnum.Stem;
            cs.ChartCanvas = view.chartCanvas;
            cs.TextCanvas = view.textCanvas;
            cs.Title = "Stem Chart";
            cs.Xmin = 0;
            cs.Xmax = 8;
            cs.Ymin = -1.5;
            cs.Ymax = 1.5;
            cs.XTick = 1;
            cs.YTick = 0.5;
            cs.GridlinePattern = LinePatternEnum.Dot;
            cs.GridlineColor = Brushes.Black;
            cs.AddChartStyle(view.tbTitle, view.tbXLabel, view.tbYLabel);
        }

        public void AddChart()
        {
            SetChartStyle();
            DataCollection.Clear();
```

```
var ds = new Specialized2DSeries();
ds.LineColor = Brushes.Red;
ds.LineThickness = 1;
ds.LinePattern = LinePatternEnum.Solid;
ds.Symbols.SymbolType = SymbolTypeEnum.Diamond;
ds.Symbols.FillColor = Brushes.Yellow;
ds.Symbols.BorderColor = Brushes.DarkGreen;
for (int i = 0; i < 50; i++)
{
    ds.LinePoints.Add(new Point(0.4 * i, Math.Sin(0.4 * i)));
}
DataCollection.Add(ds);
cs.SetSpecialized2DLines(DataCollection);
        }
    }
}
```

This example produces the results shown in Figure 5-11. The current program has the ability to create a stem chart that terminates at any of the symbols defined in the *Symbols* class. In addition, these terminators can be filled or unfilled.

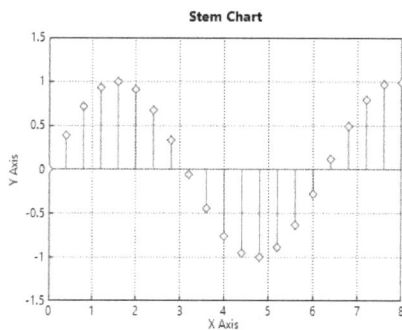

Figure 5-11. A stem chart of a sine function.

Error Bar Charts

Error bars show the confidence level of data or the deviation along a curve. Error bar charts plot the Y data and draw an error bar at each Y data value. The error bar is the distance of the error function above and below the curve so that each bar is symmetric around the curve.

In order to create error bar charts, we need to add the following code snippet to the *SetSpecialized2DLines* method in the *Specialized2DChartStyle* class:

```
case Specialied2DChartTypeEnum.ErrorBar:
    foreach (var ds in dc)
    {
        double barLength = (NormalizePoint(ds.LinePoints[1]).X -
                        NormalizePoint(ds.LinePoints[0]).X) / 3.0;
        for (int i = 0; i < ds.LinePoints.Count; i++)
        {
            Point ep = ds.ErrorPoints[i];
            Point dp = ds.LinePoints[i];
```

```
                Point[] pts = new Point[2];
                pts[0] = NormalizePoint(new Point(dp.X, dp.Y - ep.Y / 2));
                pts[1] = NormalizePoint(new Point(dp.X, dp.Y + ep.Y / 2));
                Line line = new Line();
                line.Stroke = ds.LineColor;
                line.StrokeThickness = ds.LineThickness;
                line.X1 = pts[0].X;
                line.Y1 = pts[0].Y;
                line.X2 = pts[1].X;
                line.Y2 = pts[1].Y;
                ChartCanvas.Children.Add(line);
                line = new Line();
                line.Stroke = ds.LineColor;
                line.StrokeThickness = ds.LineThickness;
                line.X1 = pts[0].X - barLength / 2;
                line.Y1 = pts[0].Y;
                line.X2 = pts[0].X + barLength / 2;
                line.Y2 = pts[0].Y;
                ChartCanvas.Children.Add(line);
                line = new Line();
                line.Stroke = ds.LineColor;
                line.StrokeThickness = ds.LineThickness;
                line.X1 = pts[1].X - barLength / 2;
                line.Y1 = pts[1].Y;
                line.X2 = pts[1].X + barLength / 2;
                line.Y2 = pts[1].Y;
                ChartCanvas.Children.Add(line);
                ds.DataPoints.Add(NormalizePoint(dp));
                ds.Symbols.AddSymbol(ChartCanvas, NormalizePoint(dp));
            }
        }
    break;
```

Here, we need to provide two independent data sets, *LinePoints* and *ErrorPoints* in our view model class. The *LinePoints* object is for the original line curve and the *ErrorPoints* object for the error bars. For error bars, I use the same style as that used in creating the original curve. If we want to have a different style for the error bars, we can add more properties in the *Specialized2DChartStyle* class, such as line color and line thickness for error bars. This way, we can specify the line styles for the original curve and the error bars independently.

Now I will show you how to create error bar charts using the preceding code. Add a new *UserControl* to the *Views* folder and name it *ErrorBarView*. The XAML file for this view is the same as that used in the preceding example and I will not list it here.

Add a new class to the *ViewModels* class and name it *ErrorBarViewModel*. Here is the code for this class:

```
using System;
using System.Linq;
using Caliburn.Micro;
using System.Collections.ObjectModel;
using System.ComponentModel.Composition;
using System.Windows.Documents;
using System.Collections.Generic;
using System.Windows;
using Chapter05.Models;
```

```
using System.Windows.Media;
using System.Windows.Controls;
using Chapter05.Views;
using Chapter05.Models.ChartModel;

namespace Chapter05.ViewModels
{
    [Export(typeof(IScreen)), PartCreationPolicy(CreationPolicy.NonShared)]
    public class ErrorBarViewModel : Screen
    {
        private readonly IEventAggregator _events;
        [ImportingConstructor]
        public ErrorBarViewModel(IEventAggregator events)
        {
            this._events = events;
            DisplayName = "04. Error Bar";
            DataCollection = new BindableCollection<Specialized2DSeries>();
        }

        private Specialized2DChartStyle cs;
        public BindableCollection<Specialized2DSeries> DataCollection { get; set; }

        private void SetChartStyle()
        {
            var view = this.GetView() as ErrorBarView;
            view.chartCanvas.Children.RemoveRange(1,
                view.chartCanvas.Children.Count - 1);
            view.textCanvas.Children.RemoveRange(1,
                view.textCanvas.Children.Count - 1);
            cs = new Specialized2DChartStyle();
            cs.Specialized2DChartType = Specialied2DChartTypeEnum.ErrorBar;
            cs.ChartCanvas = view.chartCanvas;
            cs.TextCanvas = view.textCanvas;
            cs.Title = "Error Bar Chart";
            cs.Xmin = 0;
            cs.Xmax = 12;
            cs.Ymin = -1;
            cs.Ymax = 6;
            cs.XTick = 2;
            cs.YTick = 1;
            cs.GridlinePattern = LinePatternEnum.Dot;
            cs.GridlineColor = Brushes.Black;
            cs.AddChartStyle(view.tbTitle, view.tbXLabel, view.tbYLabel);
        }

        public void AddChart()
        {
            SetChartStyle();
            DataCollection.Clear();
            var ds = new Specialized2DSeries();
            ds.LineColor = Brushes.Blue;
            ds.LineThickness = 1;
            ds.LinePattern = LinePatternEnum.Solid;
            ds.Symbols.SymbolType = SymbolTypeEnum.Diamond;
            ds.Symbols.FillColor = Brushes.Yellow;
```

```
            ds.Symbols.BorderColor = Brushes.DarkGreen;
            for (int i = 2; i < 22; i++)
            {
                ds.LinePoints.Add(new Point(0.5 * i, 10.0 * Math.Exp(-0.5 * i)));
                ds.ErrorPoints.Add(new Point(0.5 * i, 3.0 / (0.5 * i)));
            }
            DataCollection.Add(ds);
            cs.SetSpecialized2DLines(DataCollection);
        }
    }
}
```

Inside the *AddChart* method, I assume that the error function is proportional to 1/*x*. However, you can specify any error function you like, such as the standard deviation. Running this example generates the results shown in Figure 5-12.

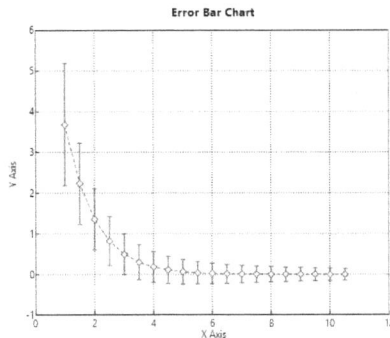

Figure 5-12. An error bar chart.

Area Charts

An area chart displays *Y* data values as one or more curves and fills the area beneath each curve. When the *DataCollection* object has more than one line series, the curves are stacked, showing the relative contribution of each line series to the total height of the curve at each *X* value.

In order to create an area chart, we need to add an *AreaAxis* property to the *Specialized2DChartStyle* class:

```
private double areaAxis = 0;
public double AreaAxis
{
    get { return areaAxis; }
    set { areaAxis = value; }
}
```

This property allows you to offset the *Y* value below which the area is filled. We then need to add the following code snippet to the *SetSpecialized2DLines* method in this class:

```
case Specialied2DChartTypeEnum.Area:
    int nPoints = dc[0].LinePoints.Count;
    double[] ysum = new double[nPoints];
    Point[] ps = new Point[2 * nPoints];
```

```
Point[] p0 = new Point[nPoints];
Point[] p1 = new Point[nPoints];

foreach (var ds in dc)
{
    for (int i = 0; i < nPoints; i++)
    {
        p0[i] = new Point(ds.LinePoints[i].X, ysum[i]);
        ysum[i] += ds.LinePoints[i].Y;
        p1[i] = new Point(ds.LinePoints[i].X, ysum[i]);
        ps[i] = NormalizePoint(p0[i]);
        ps[2 * nPoints - 1 - i] = NormalizePoint(p1[i]);
    }

    for (int i = 0; i < ps.Length; i++)
        ds.DataPoints.Add(ps[i]);
}
break;
```

Here, we stack the *Y* data values from all of the different *Specialized2DSeries* objects to show the relative contribution of each *Specialized2DSeries* to the total height of the curve at each *X* value.

Now we can create an area chart using the preceding code. Add a new *UserControl* to the *Views* folder and name it *AreaView*. The XAML file is basically the same as that used in the previous example, except that we need to replace the polyline inside the *DataTemplate* with a polygon object:

```
<UserControl.Resources>
        <DataTemplate x:Key="chartTemplate">
            <Polygon Points="{Binding DataPoints}" Stroke="{Binding LineColor}"
                StrokeThickness="{Binding LineThickness}" Fill="{Binding FillColor}"
                StrokeDashArray="{Binding LineDashPattern}"/>
        </DataTemplate>
</UserControl.Resources>
```

Add a new class to the *ViewModels* folder and name it *AreaViewModel*. Here is the code for this class:

```
using System;
using System.Linq;
using Caliburn.Micro;
using System.Collections.ObjectModel;
using System.ComponentModel.Composition;
using System.Windows.Documents;
using System.Collections.Generic;
using System.Windows;
using Chapter05.Models;
using System.Windows.Media;
using System.Windows.Controls;
using Chapter05.Views;
using Chapter05.Models.ChartModel;

namespace Chapter05.ViewModels
{
    [Export(typeof(IScreen)), PartCreationPolicy(CreationPolicy.NonShared)]
    public class AreaViewModel : Screen
    {
        private readonly IEventAggregator _events;
        [ImportingConstructor]
```

```
public AreaViewModel(IEventAggregator events)
{
    this._events = events;
    DisplayName = "05. Area";
    DataCollection = new BindableCollection<Specialized2DSeries>();
}

private Specialized2DChartStyle cs;
public BindableCollection<Specialized2DSeries> DataCollection { get; set; }

private void SetChartStyle()
{
    var view = this.GetView() as AreaView;
    view.chartCanvas.Children.RemoveRange(1,
        view.chartCanvas.Children.Count - 1);
    view.textCanvas.Children.RemoveRange(1,
        view.textCanvas.Children.Count - 1);
    cs = new Specialized2DChartStyle();
    cs.Specialized2DChartType = Specialied2DChartTypeEnum.Area;
    cs.ChartCanvas = view.chartCanvas;
    cs.TextCanvas = view.textCanvas;
    cs.Title = "Area Chart";
    cs.Xmin = 0;
    cs.Xmax = 10;
    cs.Ymin = 0;
    cs.Ymax = 10;
    cs.XTick = 2;
    cs.YTick = 2;
    cs.GridlinePattern = LinePatternEnum.Dot;
    cs.GridlineColor = Brushes.Black;
    cs.AddChartStyle(view.tbTitle, view.tbXLabel, view.tbYLabel);
}

public void AddChart()
{
    SetChartStyle();
    DataCollection.Clear();

    // First Area:
    var ds = new Specialized2DSeries();
    ds.LinePattern = LinePatternEnum.Dash;
    ds.LineColor = Brushes.Black;
    ds.LineThickness = 1;
    ds.FillColor = new SolidColorBrush(Color.FromArgb(127,255,182,193));
    for (int i = 0; i < 41; i++)
    {
        ds.LinePoints.Add(new Point(0.25 * i, 2.0 + Math.Sin(0.25 * i)));
    }
    DataCollection.Add(ds);

    // Second Area:
    ds = new Specialized2DSeries();
    ds.LinePattern = LinePatternEnum.Dash;
    ds.LineColor = Brushes.Black;
    ds.LineThickness = 1;
```

```
        ds.FillColor = new SolidColorBrush(Color.FromArgb(127,173,216,230));
        for (int i = 0; i < 41; i++)
        {
            ds.LinePoints.Add(new Point(0.25 * i, 2.0 + Math.Cos(0.25 * i)));
        }
        DataCollection.Add(ds);

        // Third Area:
        ds = new Specialized2DSeries();
        ds.LinePattern = LinePatternEnum.Dash;
        ds.LineColor = Brushes.Black;
        ds.LineThickness = 1;
        ds.FillColor = new SolidColorBrush(Color.FromArgb(127, 144, 238, 144));
        for (int i = 0; i < 41; i++)
        {
            ds.LinePoints.Add(new Point(0.25 * i, 3.0 + Math.Sin(0.25 * i)));
        }
        DataCollection.Add(ds);
        cs.SetSpecialized2DLines(DataCollection);
    }
  }
}
```

Within the *AddChart* method, you add three sets of *Specialized2DSeries* objects. Running this example produces the result shown in Figure 5-13.

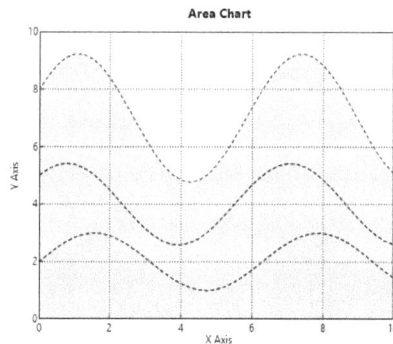

Figure 5-13. An area chart.

Polar Charts

So far, we have discussed various chart applications that make use of the Cartesian coordinate system. Now I want to show you how to plot data in polar coordinates (*r, theta*). Most polar charts, including those in commercial software packages, only plot positive *r*-values; i.e., they plot absolute *r*-values if *r* is both positive and negative. Here I will show you how to create a more generalized polar chart in .NET applications, in which *r* can contain negative values. This new polar chart also allows you to specify the *r* range [*rMin, rMax*] and draw multiple curves on a single polar chart.

Chart Style for Polar Charts

Unlike the charts created previously, where you used the original chart style class for line charts, we need to implement a new chart style class for polar charts. Add a new class to the *ChartModel* folder and name it *PolarChartStyle*. Here is the code for this class:

```
using System;
using System.Windows;
using System.Windows.Controls;
using System.Windows.Media;
using System.Windows.Shapes;
using Caliburn.Micro;

namespace Chapter05.Models.ChartModel
{
    public class PolarChartStyle
    {
        private double angleStep = 30;
        private AngleDirectionEnum angleDirection =
            AngleDirectionEnum.CounterClockWise;
        private double rmin = 0;
        private double rmax = 1;
        private int nTicks = 4;
        private Brush lineColor = Brushes.Black;
        private double lineThickness = 1;
        private LinePatternEnum linePattern = LinePatternEnum.Dash;

        public Canvas ChartCanvas { get; set; }

        public LinePatternEnum LinePattern
        {
            get { return linePattern; }
            set { linePattern = value; }
        }

        public double LineThickness
        {
            get { return lineThickness; }
            set { lineThickness = value; }
        }

        public Brush LineColor
        {
            get { return lineColor; }
            set { lineColor = value; }
        }

        public int NTicks
        {
            get { return nTicks; }
            set { nTicks = value; }
        }

        public double Rmax
        {
```

```csharp
        get { return rmax; }
        set { rmax = value; }
    }

    public double Rmin
    {
        get { return rmin; }
        set { rmin = value; }
    }

    public AngleDirectionEnum AngleDirection
    {
        get { return angleDirection; }
        set { angleDirection = value; }
    }

    public double AngleStep
    {
        get { return angleStep; }
        set { angleStep = value; }
    }

    public DoubleCollection SetLinePattern()
    {
        DoubleCollection collection = new DoubleCollection();
        switch (LinePattern)
        {
            case LinePatternEnum.Dash:
                collection = new DoubleCollection(new double[2] { 4, 3 });
                break;
            case LinePatternEnum.Dot:
                collection = new DoubleCollection(new double[2] { 1, 2 });
                break;
            case LinePatternEnum.DashDot:
                collection = new DoubleCollection(new double[4] { 4, 2, 1, 2 });
                break;
        }
        return collection;
    }

    public double RNormalize(double r)
    {
        double result = new double();
        if (r < Rmin || r > Rmax)
            result = double.NaN;
        double width = Math.Min(ChartCanvas.Width - 40,
            ChartCanvas.Height - 40);
        result = (r - Rmin) * width / 2 / (Rmax - Rmin);
        return result;
    }

    public void SetPolarAxes()
    {
        double xc = ChartCanvas.Width / 2;
        double yc = ChartCanvas.Height / 2;
```

```
// Draw circles:
double dr = (RNormalize(Rmax / NTicks) - RNormalize(Rmin / NTicks));
for (int i = 0; i < NTicks; i++)
{
    Ellipse circle = CircleLine();
    Canvas.SetLeft(circle, xc - (i + 1) * dr);
    Canvas.SetTop(circle, yc - (i + 1) * dr);
    circle.Width = 2.0 * (i + 1) * dr;
    circle.Height = 2.0 * (i + 1) * dr;
    ChartCanvas.Children.Add(circle);
}

//Draw radius lines:
for (int i = 0; i < (int)360 / AngleStep; i++)
{
    Line line = RadiusLine();
    line.X1 = RNormalize(Rmax) *
              Math.Cos(i * AngleStep * Math.PI / 180) + xc;
    line.Y1 = RNormalize(Rmax) *
              Math.Sin(i * AngleStep * Math.PI / 180) + yc;
    line.X2 = xc;
    line.Y2 = yc;
    ChartCanvas.Children.Add(line);
}

// Add radius labels:
for (int i = 1; i <= NTicks; i++)
{
    double rlabel = Rmin + i * (Rmax - Rmin) / NTicks;
    TextBlock tb = new TextBlock();
    tb.Text = rlabel.ToString();
    Canvas.SetLeft(tb, xc + 3);
    Canvas.SetTop(tb, yc - i * dr + 2);
    ChartCanvas.Children.Add(tb);
}

// Add angle Labels:
double anglelabel = 0;
for (int i = 0; i < (int)360 / AngleStep; i++)
{
    if (AngleDirection == AngleDirectionEnum.ClockWise)
        anglelabel = i * AngleStep;
    else if (AngleDirection == AngleDirectionEnum.CounterClockWise)
    {
        anglelabel = 360 - i * AngleStep;
        if (i == 0)
            anglelabel = 0;
    }
    TextBlock tb = new TextBlock();
    tb.Text = anglelabel.ToString();
    tb.TextAlignment = TextAlignment.Center;
    tb.Measure(new Size(Double.PositiveInfinity,
                        Double.PositiveInfinity));
    Size size = tb.DesiredSize;
```

```
            double x = (RNormalize(Rmax) + 1.5 * size.Width / 2) *
                        Math.Cos(i * AngleStep * Math.PI / 180) + xc;
            double y = (RNormalize(Rmax) + 1.5 * size.Height / 2) *
                        Math.Sin(i * AngleStep * Math.PI / 180) + yc;
            Canvas.SetLeft(tb, x - size.Width / 2);
            Canvas.SetTop(tb, y - size.Height / 2);
            ChartCanvas.Children.Add(tb);
        }
    }

    private Ellipse CircleLine()
    {
        Ellipse ellipse = new Ellipse();
        ellipse.Stroke = LineColor;
        ellipse.StrokeThickness = LineThickness;
        ellipse.StrokeDashArray = SetLinePattern();
        ellipse.Fill = Brushes.Transparent;
        return ellipse;
    }

    private Line RadiusLine()
    {
        Line line = new Line();
        line.Stroke = LineColor;
        line.StrokeThickness = LineThickness;
        line.StrokeDashArray = SetLinePattern();
        return line;
    }


    public void SetPolar(BindableCollection<LineSeries> dc)
    {
        double xc = ChartCanvas.Width / 2;
        double yc = ChartCanvas.Height / 2;

        int j = 0;
        foreach (var ds in dc)
        {
            if (ds.SeriesName == "Default Name")
                ds.SeriesName = "DataSeries" + j.ToString();
            ds.SetLinePattern();

            for (int i = 0; i < ds.LinePoints.Count; i++)
            {
                double r = ds.LinePoints[i].Y;
                double theta = ds.LinePoints[i].X * Math.PI / 180;
                if (AngleDirection == AngleDirectionEnum.CounterClockWise)
                    theta = -theta;
                double x = xc + RNormalize(r) * Math.Cos(theta);
                double y = yc + RNormalize(r) * Math.Sin(theta);
                ds.LinePoints[i] = new Point(x, y);
            }
            j++;
```

```
            }
        }
    }

    public enum AngleDirectionEnum
    {
        CounterClockWise = 0,
        ClockWise = 1
    }
}
```

In this class, the *AngleStep* property controls the number of *r* grid lines, and the *AngleDirection* property allows you to draw the polar chart in a counter-clockwise (default) or clockwise manner. The other field members and their corresponding properties allow you to specify the *r* range, the grid line color, dash style, thickness, etc. In particular, you can specify the line styles of the *r* and *theta* gridlines separately to achieve a better visual effect.

The *SetPolarAxes* method in this class draws the *r* and *theta* gridlines, as well as the *r* and *theta* labels. Please pay special attention to the *RNormalize* method, which transforms the *r*-value in the world coordinate system to an *r* in the device coordinates system. A point in polar coordinates is represented by *Point (r, theta)*. The *theta* has the same unit of degree in both the world and device coordinate systems, so you only need to perform the transformation on *r*.

Inside the *SetPolar* method, you transform the polar points *(r, theta)* in the world coordinate system to the points *(x, y)* (the Cartesian coordinates) in the device system using the following relationships:

```
double x = xc + csp.RNormalize(r) * Math.Cos(theta);
double y = yc + csp.RNormalize(r) * Math.Sin(theta);
```

These equations indicate that the origin is located at *(xc, yc)*, and that the *RNormalize* method transforms the polar points *(r, theta)* from the world to the device coordinate system. In this method, the polar chart direction is controlled by setting the angle variable *theta* to be positive (clockwise) or negative (counter clockwise). Note also that you can still use the original *LineSeries* class for polar charts.

Creating Polar Charts

In this section, I will show you how to create polar charts using the *PolarChartStyle* class implemented in the preceding section. Add a new *UserControl* to the Views folder and name it *PolarView*. Here is XAML for this view:

```
<UserControl x:Class="Chapter05.Views.PolarView"
             xmlns="http://schemas.microsoft.com/winfx/2006/xaml/presentation"
             xmlns:x="http://schemas.microsoft.com/winfx/2006/xaml"
             xmlns:mc="http://schemas.openxmlformats.org/markup-compatibility/2006"
             xmlns:d="http://schemas.microsoft.com/expression/blend/2008"
             xmlns:cal="http://www.caliburnproject.org"
             mc:Ignorable="d"
             d:DesignHeight="300" d:DesignWidth="500">

    <UserControl.Resources>
        <DataTemplate x:Key="chartTemplate">
            <Polyline Points="{Binding LinePoints}" Stroke="{Binding LineColor}"
                      StrokeThickness="{Binding LineThickness}"
                      StrokeDashArray="{Binding LineDashPattern}"/>
```

```
            </DataTemplate>
        </UserControl.Resources>

    <Grid Margin="5">
        <Grid.ColumnDefinitions>
            <ColumnDefinition Width="170"/>
            <ColumnDefinition Width="*"/>
        </Grid.ColumnDefinitions>
        <StackPanel Margin="0 20 0 0">
            <Button x:Name="SimplePolar" Content="Simple Polar Chart" Width="150"/>
            <Button x:Name="PolarNegativeR" Content="Polar with Negative r"
                    Width="150" Margin="0 10 0 0"/>
        </StackPanel>

        <Grid Grid.Column="1">
            <Grid.ColumnDefinitions>
                <ColumnDefinition Width="30"/>
                <ColumnDefinition Width="*"/>
                <ColumnDefinition Width="30"/>
            </Grid.ColumnDefinitions>
            <Grid.RowDefinitions>
                <RowDefinition Height="30"/>
                <RowDefinition Height="*"/>
                <RowDefinition Height="30"/>
            </Grid.RowDefinitions>
            <Grid  Margin="0" x:Name ="chartGrid" Grid.Column="1" Grid.Row="1"
                    ClipToBounds="False" Background="Transparent"
                    cal:Message.Attach="[Event SizeChanged]=[Action AddChart()];
                        [Event Loaded]=[Action AddChart()]">
                <Canvas Margin="2" Name="chartCanvas" ClipToBounds="True"
                        Grid.Column="1" Grid.Row="1"
                        Width="{Binding ElementName=chartGrid,Path=ActualWidth}"
                        Height="{Binding ElementName=chartGrid,Path=ActualHeight}">
                    <ItemsControl ItemsSource="{Binding DataCollection}"
                                ItemTemplate="{StaticResource chartTemplate}">
                        <ItemsControl.ItemsPanel>
                            <ItemsPanelTemplate>
                                <Grid/>
                            </ItemsPanelTemplate>
                        </ItemsControl.ItemsPanel>
                    </ItemsControl>
                </Canvas>
            </Grid>
        </Grid>
    </Grid>
</UserControl>
```

Here, we add two buttons, which will be used to create different polar charts. The rest of the code is very similar to that used in creating line charts.

Add a new class to the *ViewModels* folder and name it *PolarViewModel*. Here is the code for this class:

```
using System;
using System.Linq;
using Caliburn.Micro;
using System.Collections.ObjectModel;
```

```
using System.ComponentModel.Composition;
using System.Windows.Documents;
using System.Collections.Generic;
using System.Windows;
using Chapter05.Models;
using System.Windows.Media;
using System.Windows.Controls;
using Chapter05.Views;
using Chapter05.Models.ChartModel;

namespace Chapter05.ViewModels
{
    [Export(typeof(IScreen)), PartCreationPolicy(CreationPolicy.NonShared)]
    public class PolarViewModel : Screen
    {
        private readonly IEventAggregator _events;
        [ImportingConstructor]
         public PolarViewModel(IEventAggregator events)
        {
            this._events = events;
            DisplayName = "06. Polar";
            DataCollection = new BindableCollection<LineSeries>();
        }

        private string chartType = "SimplePolar";
        private PolarChartStyle cs;
        public BindableCollection<LineSeries> DataCollection { get; set; }

        private void SetChartStyle()
        {
            var view = this.GetView() as PolarView;
            view.chartCanvas.Children.RemoveRange(1,
                view.chartCanvas.Children.Count - 1);
            cs = new PolarChartStyle();
            cs.ChartCanvas = view.chartCanvas;
        }

        public void AddChart()
        {
            if (chartType == "SimplePolar")
                SimplePolar();
            else if (chartType == "PolarNegativeR")
                PolarNegativeR();
        }

        public void SimplePolar()
        {
            chartType = "SimplePolar";

            SetChartStyle();
            cs.Rmin = 0;
            cs.Rmax = 0.5;
            cs.NTicks = 4;
            cs.AngleDirection = AngleDirectionEnum.CounterClockWise;
            cs.LinePattern = LinePatternEnum.Dot;
```

```
        cs.LineColor = Brushes.Black;
        cs.SetPolarAxes();

        DataCollection.Clear();

        var ds = new LineSeries();
        ds.LineColor = Brushes.Red;
        for(int i =0;i<360;i++)
        {
            double theta = 1.0 * i;
            double r = Math.Abs(Math.Cos(2.0 * theta * Math.PI / 180) *
                        Math.Sin(2.0 * theta * Math.PI / 180));
            ds.LinePoints.Add(new Point(theta, r));
        }
        DataCollection.Add(ds);
        cs.SetPolar(DataCollection);
    }

    public void PolarNegativeR()
    {
        chartType = "PolarNegativeR";

        SetChartStyle();
        cs.Rmin = -7.0;
        cs.Rmax = 1.0;
        cs.NTicks = 4;
        cs.AngleStep = 30;
        cs.AngleDirection = AngleDirectionEnum.CounterClockWise;
        cs.LinePattern = LinePatternEnum.Dot;
        cs.LineColor = Brushes.Black;
        cs.SetPolarAxes();

        DataCollection.Clear();

        var ds = new LineSeries();
        ds.LineColor = Brushes.Red;
        for (int i = 0; i < 360; i++)
        {
            double theta = 1.0 * i;
            double r = Math.Log(1.001 + Math.Sin(2 * theta * Math.PI / 180));
            ds.LinePoints.Add(new Point(theta, r));
        }
        DataCollection.Add(ds);

        ds = new LineSeries();
        ds.LineColor = Brushes.Blue;
        ds.LineThickness = 3;
        ds.LinePattern = LinePatternEnum.Dash;
        for (int i = 0; i < 360; i++)
        {
            double theta = 1.0 * i;
            double r = Math.Log(1.001 + Math.Cos(2 * theta * Math.PI / 180));
            ds.LinePoints.Add(new Point(theta, r));
        }
        DataCollection.Add(ds);
```

```
            cs.SetPolar(DataCollection);
    }
   }
}
```

Running this example and clicking the *Simple Polar Chart* button generates the result shown in Figure 5-14.

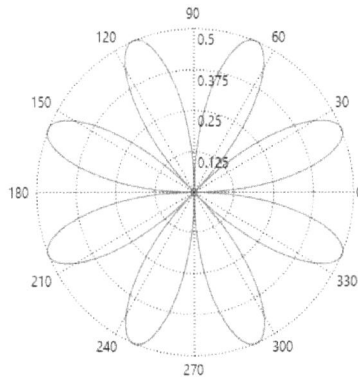

Figure 5-14. A simple polar chart.

We can also create multiple curves on a single polar chart with both positive and negative *r* values. To test these features, I implement the *PolarNegativeR* method where I draw two logarithm functions on the same polar chart. Running this example and clicking the *Polar with Negative r* button will produce results shown in Figure 5-15.

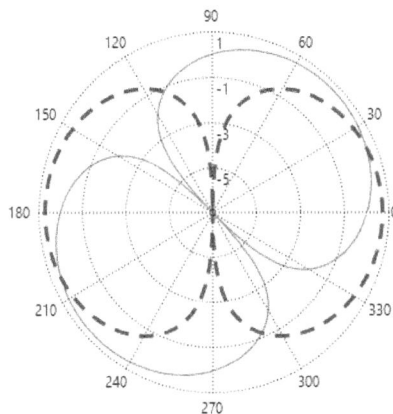

Figure 5-15. A polar chart with negative r value.

Pie Charts

Creating a pie chart in WPF is quite simple, since there is an *ArcSegment* class available. The *ArcSegment* object is defined by its start and end points; its *X* and *Y* radii specified by the *Size* property;

its X-axis rotation factor, a value indicating whether the arc should be greater than 180 degrees; and a value describing the direction in which the arc is drawn. We can use the *ArcSegment* to build the *PathFigure*, which we in turn use to build the *PathGeometry*. Finally, we can create a pie chart using the *Path* object with a specified *Fill* property.

Chart Style for Pie Charts

For a pie chart, we cannot use the original *ChartStyle* class. To create a new pie chart style, add a new class to the ChartModel folder and name it *PieChartStyle*. Here is the code listing of this class:

```
using System;
using System.Windows;
using System.Windows.Controls;
using System.Windows.Media;
using System.Windows.Shapes;
using System.Collections.Generic;

namespace Chapter05.Models.ChartModel
{
    public class PieChartStyle
    {
        private List<double> dataList = new List<double>();
        private List<string> labelList = new List<string>();
        private List<int> explodeList = new List<int>();
        private ColormapBrush colormapBrushes = new ColormapBrush();
        private Brush borderColor = Brushes.Black;
        private double borderThickness = 1.0;

        public Canvas ChartCanvas { get; set; }

        public List<double> DataList
        {
            get { return dataList; }
            set { dataList = value; }
        }

        public List<string> LabelList
        {
            get { return labelList; }
            set { labelList = value; }
        }

        public List<int> ExplodeList
        {
            get { return explodeList; }
            set { explodeList = value; }
        }

        public ColormapBrush ColormapBrushes
        {
            get { return colormapBrushes; }
            set { colormapBrushes = value; }
        }
```

```
public Brush BorderColor
{
    get { return borderColor; }
    set { borderColor = value; }
}

public double BorderThickness
{
    get { return borderThickness; }
    set { borderThickness = value; }
}

public void AddPie(Canvas canvas)
{
    int nData = DataList.Count;
    colormapBrushes.Ydivisions = nData;
    if (ExplodeList.Count == 0)
    {
        for (int i = 0; i < nData; i++)
            ExplodeList.Add(0);
    }

    double sum = 0.0;
    for (int i = 0; i < nData; i++)
    {
        sum += DataList[i];
    }
    double startAngle = 0;
    double sweepAngle = 0;

    for (int i = 0; i < nData; i++)
    {
        Brush brush = ColormapBrushes.ColormapBrushes()[i];
        int explode = ExplodeList[i];

        if (sum < 1)
        {
            startAngle += sweepAngle;
            sweepAngle = 2 * Math.PI * DataList[i];
        }

        else if (sum >= 1)
        {
            startAngle += sweepAngle;
            sweepAngle = 2 * Math.PI * DataList[i] / sum;
        }
        double dx = explode * Math.Cos(startAngle + sweepAngle / 2);
        double dy = explode * Math.Sin(startAngle + sweepAngle / 2);
        DrawArc(brush, startAngle, startAngle + sweepAngle, dx, dy);
    }
}

private void DrawArc(Brush fillColor, double startAngle,
    double endAngle, double dx, double dy)
{
```

```
Path path = new Path();
path.Stroke = BorderColor;
path.StrokeThickness = BorderThickness;
path.Fill = fillColor;
PathGeometry pg = new PathGeometry();
PathFigure pf = new PathFigure();
LineSegment ls1 = new LineSegment();
LineSegment ls2 = new LineSegment();
ArcSegment arc = new ArcSegment();
double xc = ChartCanvas.Width / 2 + dx;
double yc = ChartCanvas.Height / 2 + dy;
double r = 0.8 * xc;

pf.IsClosed = true;
pf.StartPoint = new Point(xc, yc);
pf.Segments.Add(ls1);
pf.Segments.Add(arc);
pf.Segments.Add(ls2);
pg.Figures.Add(pf);
path.Data = pg;

ls1.Point = new Point(xc + r * Math.Cos(startAngle),
            yc + r * Math.Sin(startAngle));
arc.SweepDirection = SweepDirection.Clockwise;
arc.Point = new Point(xc + r * Math.Cos(endAngle),
            yc + r * Math.Sin(endAngle));
arc.Size = new Size(r, r);
ls2.Point = new Point(xc + r * Math.Cos(endAngle),
            yc + r * Math.Sin(endAngle));
ChartCanvas.Children.Add(path);
        }
    }
}
```

In this class, I first define three generic collection list properties: *DataList*, *LabelList*, and *ExplodeList*. These lists hold the data used to create the pie chart, the labels for the data values used in the legend, and the exploding data needed to highlight a particular pie slice by exploding the piece out from the rest of the pie, respectively. I also use the *ColormapBrush* object to fill the pie slices of the pie chart. The *ColormapBrush* class was originally implemented in my previous book, *Practical WPF Graphics Programming*. For more information on how to implement this class, please refer to that book.

Inside the *AddPie* method, I first calculate the summation of the data values. Each value in the *DataList* is normalized via 1/*sum* to determine the area of each slice of the pie. If *sum* $\geq$ 1, the values in the *DataList* directly specify the area of the pie slices. However, if *sum* < 1, the current program draws only a partial pie and the data values are not normalized by 1/*sum*.

Note that the pie chart does not need the *LineSeries* class because this class is already incorporated into the *PieChartStyle* class.

Legend for Pie Charts

The legend class used in pie charts is slightly different than that used in line charts. For completeness, here I will present the code listing of the modified *Legend* class. Add a new class to the ChartModel folder and name it *PieLegend*. Here is the code for this class:

```
using System;
using System.Windows;
using System.Windows.Controls;
using System.Windows.Media;
using System.Windows.Shapes;
using System.Collections.Generic;

namespace Chapter05.Models.ChartModel
{
    public class PieLegend
    {
        private bool isLegendVisible = false;
        public bool IsLegendVisible
        {
            get { return isLegendVisible; }
            set { isLegendVisible = value; }
        }

        public Canvas LegendCanvas { get; set; }

        public void AddLegend(PieChartStyle ps)
        {
            TextBlock tb = new TextBlock();
            if (ps.DataList.Count < 1 || !IsLegendVisible)
                return;

            double legendWidth = 0;
            Size size = new Size(0, 0);
            for (int i = 0; i < ps.LabelList.Count; i++)
            {
                tb = new TextBlock();
                tb.Text = ps.LabelList[i];
                tb.Measure(new Size(Double.PositiveInfinity,
                                    Double.PositiveInfinity));
                size = tb.DesiredSize;
                if (legendWidth < size.Width)
                    legendWidth = size.Width;
            }

            legendWidth += 20;
            LegendCanvas.Width = legendWidth + 5;
            double legendHeight = 17 * ps.DataList.Count;
            double sx = 6;
            double sy = 0;
            double textHeight = size.Height;
            double lineLength = 34;
            Rectangle legendRect = new Rectangle();
            legendRect.Stroke = Brushes.Black;
            legendRect.Fill = Brushes.White;
            legendRect.Width = legendWidth + 18;
            legendRect.Height = legendHeight;

            if (IsLegendVisible)
                LegendCanvas.Children.Add(legendRect);
```

```
            Rectangle rect;
            int n = 1;
            foreach (double data in ps.DataList)
            {
                double xText = 2 * sx + lineLength;
                double yText = n * sy + (2 * n - 1) * textHeight / 2;

                rect = new Rectangle();
                rect.Stroke = ps.BorderColor;
                rect.StrokeThickness = ps.BorderThickness;
                rect.Fill = ps.ColormapBrushes.ColormapBrushes()[n - 1];
                rect.Width = 10;
                rect.Height = 10;
                Canvas.SetLeft(rect, sx + lineLength / 2 - 15);
                Canvas.SetTop(rect, yText - 2);
                LegendCanvas.Children.Add(rect);

                tb = new TextBlock();
                tb.Text = ps.LabelList[n - 1];
                LegendCanvas.Children.Add(tb);
                Canvas.SetTop(tb, yText - size.Height / 2 + 2);
                Canvas.SetLeft(tb, xText - 15);
                n++;
            }
        LegendCanvas.Width = legendRect.Width;
        LegendCanvas.Height = legendRect.Height;
    }
  }
}
```

Here the legend is always located on the right side of the pie chart.

Creating Pie Charts

In this section, I will show you how to create pie charts using the *PieChartStyle* and *PieLegend* classes implemented in the previous sections. Add a new *UserControl* to the *Views* folder and name it *PieView*. Here is the XAML file of this view:

```
<UserControl x:Class="Chapter05.Views.PieView"
             xmlns="http://schemas.microsoft.com/winfx/2006/xaml/presentation"
             xmlns:x="http://schemas.microsoft.com/winfx/2006/xaml"
             xmlns:mc="http://schemas.openxmlformats.org/markup-compatibility/2006"
             xmlns:d="http://schemas.microsoft.com/expression/blend/2008"
             xmlns:cal="http://www.caliburnproject.org"
             mc:Ignorable="d"
             d:DesignHeight="400" d:DesignWidth="670">
    <Grid>
        <Grid.ColumnDefinitions>
            <ColumnDefinition Width="170"/>
            <ColumnDefinition Width="*"/>
        </Grid.ColumnDefinitions>
        <StackPanel Margin="0 20 0 0">
            <Button x:Name="PieChart" Content="Pie Chart" Width="150"/>
            <Button x:Name="PieExplode" Content="Exploding Pie Chart"
                    Width="150" Margin="0 10 0 0"/>
```

```xml
                <Button x:Name="PiePartial" Content="Partial Pie Chart"
                        Width="150" Margin="0 10 0 0"/>
        </StackPanel>

        <Grid Name="grid1" Margin="10" Grid.Column="1">
            <Grid.ColumnDefinitions>
                <ColumnDefinition Width="30"/>
                <ColumnDefinition Width="*"/>
                <ColumnDefinition Width="auto"/>
                <ColumnDefinition Width="30"/>
            </Grid.ColumnDefinitions>
            <Grid.RowDefinitions>
                <RowDefinition Height="30"/>
                <RowDefinition Height="*"/>
                <RowDefinition Height="30"/>
            </Grid.RowDefinitions>

            <Grid  Margin="0" x:Name ="chartGrid" Grid.Column="1"
                   Grid.Row="1" ClipToBounds="False" Background="Transparent"
                   cal:Message.Attach="[Event SizeChanged]=[Action AddChart];
                   [Event Loaded]=[Action AddChart]">
                <Canvas Margin="2" Name="chartCanvas" ClipToBounds="False"/>
            </Grid>
            <Canvas Margin="2" Name="legendCanvas" Grid.Column="2" Grid.Row="1"/>
        </Grid>
    </Grid>
</UserControl>
```

Here I add three buttons that are used to create different pie charts. I also create two Canvas objects, the *chartCanvas* and *legendCanvas*, which are used to host the pie chart and the legend, respectively.

Add a new class to the *ViewModels* folder and name it *PieViewModel*. Here is the code for this class:

```csharp
using System;
using System.Linq;
using Caliburn.Micro;
using System.Collections.ObjectModel;
using System.ComponentModel.Composition;
using System.Windows.Documents;
using System.Collections.Generic;
using System.Windows;
using Chapter04.Models;
using System.Windows.Media;
using System.Windows.Controls;
using Chapter05.Views;
using Chapter05.Models.ChartModel;

namespace Chapter05.ViewModels
{
    [Export(typeof(IScreen)), PartCreationPolicy(CreationPolicy.NonShared)]
    public class PieViewModel : Screen
    {
        private readonly IEventAggregator _events;
        [ImportingConstructor]
        public PieViewModel(IEventAggregator events)
        {
```

```
        this._events = events;
        DisplayName = "07. Pie Chart";
    }

    private string chartType = "PieChart";
    private PieChartStyle cs;
    private PieLegend pl;
    private PieView view;

    private void SetChartStyle()
    {
        view = this.GetView() as PieView;
        view.chartCanvas.Children.Clear();
        view.legendCanvas.Children.Clear();
        double width = view.chartGrid.ActualWidth;
        double height = view.chartGrid.ActualHeight;
        double side = width;
        if (width > height)
            side = height;
        view.chartCanvas.Width = side;
        view.chartCanvas.Height = side;

        cs = new PieChartStyle();
        pl = new PieLegend();
        cs.ChartCanvas = view.chartCanvas;
        pl.LegendCanvas = view.legendCanvas;
    }

    public void AddChart()
    {
        if (chartType == "PieChart")
            PieChart();
        else if (chartType == "PieExplode")
            PieExplode();
        else if (chartType == "PiePartial")
            PiePartial();
    }

    public void PieChart()
    {
        chartType = "PieChart";
        SetChartStyle();

        cs.DataList = new List<double> { 30, 35, 15, 10, 8 };
        cs.LabelList = new List<string> { "Soc. Sec. Tax", "Income Tax",
            "Borrowing", "Corp. Tax", "Misc." };
        cs.ColormapBrushes.ColormapBrushType =
            ColormapBrush.ColormapBrushEnum.Summer;
        cs.AddPie(view.chartCanvas);
        pl.IsLegendVisible = true;
        pl.AddLegend(cs);
    }

    public void PieExplode()
    {
```

```
        chartType = "PieExplode";
        SetChartStyle();

        cs.DataList = new List<double> { 30, 35, 15, 10, 8 };
        cs.LabelList = new List<string> { "Soc. Sec. Tax", "Income Tax",
            "Borrowing", "Corp. Tax", "Misc." };
        cs.ExplodeList = new List<int> { 20, 0, 0, 20, 0 };
        cs.ColormapBrushes.ColormapBrushType =
            ColormapBrush.ColormapBrushEnum.Summer;
        cs.AddPie(view.chartCanvas);
        pl.IsLegendVisible = true;
        pl.AddLegend(cs);
    }

    public void PiePartial()
    {
        chartType = "PiePartial";
        SetChartStyle();

        cs.DataList = new List<double> { 0.3, 0.1, 0.25};
        cs.LabelList = new List<string> { "0.3 - 30%", "0.1 - 10%",
                "0.25 - 25%"};
        cs.ColormapBrushes.ColormapBrushType =
            ColormapBrush.ColormapBrushEnum.Cool;
        cs.AddPie(view.chartCanvas);
        pl.IsLegendVisible = true;
        pl.AddLegend(cs);
    }
}
}
```

Please pay attention to the *PieChart* method, which shows you how to add data values to the *DataList*, how to create labels for each data value, and how to specify the color map for each pie slice. Running this example and clickinf the *Pie Chart* button produces the result shown in Figure 5-16.

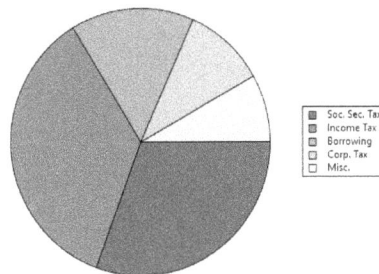

Figure 5-16. A pie chart of revenue data.

The *PieExplode* method gives you the option of highlighting particular pie slices by exploding the pieces out from the rest of the pie. To do this we simply need to specify the *ExplodeList* property. For example, if we want to highlight the pie slices for the Social Security Tax and Corp. Tax data, we need to explode the first and fourth elements in the *ExplodeList* out 20 pixels (the default value is always zero) from the center of the pie chart, since the Social Security Tax and Corp. Tax are the first and fourth elements in the *DataList*. Clicking the *Exploding Pie Chart* button generates the output shown in Figure 5-17.

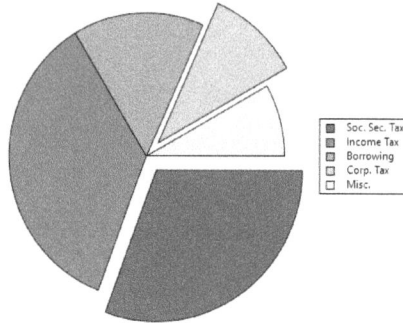

Figure 5-17. A pie chart with exploded slices.

The *PiePartial* method allows you to draw a partial pie chart when the summation of the data values is less than 1. You can see in the example that the summation of the data values is 0.65, which is less than 1. Clicking the *Partial Pie Chart* button will generate a partial pie chart, as shown in Figure 5-18.

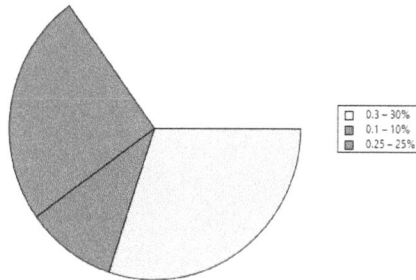

Figure 5-18. A partial pie chart.

Chapter 6
Stock Charts

Stock charts and technical analysis play an important role in stock market research and analysis. Technical analysis, different from fundamental analysis, usually ignores the actual nature of the company, market, currency, or commodity. It is based solely on the stock charts; namely, the price and volume information. Stock charts usually show the high, low, open, close, and volume data of a security. These charts allow you to plot the change of a stock price over time, analyze the history of stock price changes, and predict the future price of a stock based on prior price history.

In this chapter, I will show you how to create a variety of stock charts in WPF, including the standard Hi-Lo-Open-Close and Candlestick stock charts. I will also present some quantitative analysis techniques that are commonly used in the stock market.

Get Stock Data

In order to create stock charts, we need to import stock data into our .NET applications. In Chapter 3, I demonstrated how to download historical stock data from Yahoo Finance and how to store this data in the database. In this chapter, I will show you how to use this stored stock data to create various stock charts.

Here, we can reuse much of the code implemented in Chapter 4. Open Visual Studio 2013, start a new WPF project, and name it *Chapter06*. Add Caliburn.Micro to *References*. Add three new folders, *Models*, *ViewModels*, and *Views,* to the project. Add *AppBootstrapper.cs*, which is the same as that used in the Chapter04 project, to the *Models* folder.

Add a *Window* to the *Views* folder and name it *MainView*. Add a class to the *ViewModels* folder and name it *MainViewModel*. The main view and view model will be used to hold the tab items, which are similar to those used in the *Chapter04* project. You can open those files inside Visual Studio and check the code if you need a refresher. Also, do not forget to make corresponding changes to *App.xaml*.

After the preceding preparation for the project, we need to add another new folder to the *Models* folder and name it *ChartModel*. Add all existing classes in the *ChartModel* folder from the *Chapter04* project to the current project's *ChartModel* folder and change their namespaces from *Chapter04* to *Chapter06*.

Entity Data Model and Data Access Layer

Following the same procedure used in Chapter 3, we can create an Entity Data Model from the existing *MyDb* database that we created previously in the *LocalDB* server. If we create the data model successfully, we should have the file structure shown in Figure 6-1.

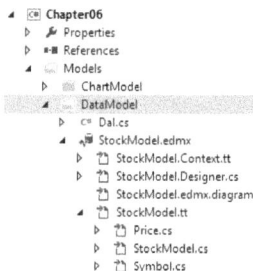

Figure 6-1. File structure for an Entity Data model named StockModel.

You can see that we put the entity data model named *StockModel* in a new folder, *DataModel*. In addition, I have added a new class, *Dal.cs*, to the folder. This class is a data access layer that is used to interact with the entity data model. Here is the code for this class:

```
using System;
using System.Collections.Generic;
using System.Linq;
using Caliburn.Micro;
using System.Data;

namespace Chapter06.Models.DataModel
{
    public class Dal
    {
        public string Ticker { get; set; }
        public string Ticker1 { get; set; }
        public string Ticker2 { get; set; }
        public DateTime DateStart { get; set; }
        public DateTime DateEnd { get; set; }
        public BindableCollection<StockPrice> StockPrices =
            new BindableCollection<StockPrice>();
        public BindableCollection<PairStockPrice> PairStockPrices =
            new BindableCollection<PairStockPrice>();

        public void GetStockPrices()
        {
            StockPrices.Clear();
            using (var db = new MyDbEntities())
            {
                var query = (from s in db.Symbols
                            join p in db.Prices on s.SymbolID equals p.SymbolID
                            where s.Ticker == Ticker && p.Date >= DateStart &&
                                p.Date <= DateEnd
                            select new
                            {
                                s.Ticker,
```

```
                        p.Date,
                        p.PriceOpen,
                        p.PriceHigh,
                        p.PriceLow,
                        p.PriceClose,
                        p.PriceAdj,
                        p.Volume
                    }).OrderBy(x=>x.Date);

        foreach(var p in query)
        {
            StockPrices.Add(new StockPrice
            {
                Ticker = p.Ticker,
                Date = (DateTime)p.Date,
                PriceOpen =(double)p.PriceOpen,
                PriceHigh = (double)p.PriceHigh,
                PriceLow = (double)p.PriceLow,
                PriceClose = (double)p.PriceClose,
                PriceAdj = (double)p.PriceAdj,
                Volume = (double)p.Volume
            });
        }
    }
}

public void GetPairStockPrices()
{
    PairStockPrices.Clear();
    using (var db = new MyDbEntities())
    {
        var query = (from s in db.Symbols
                    join p in db.Prices on s.SymbolID equals p.SymbolID
                    where (s.Ticker.Contains(Ticker1) ||
                        s.Ticker.Contains(Ticker2))
                      && p.Date >= DateStart && p.Date <= DateEnd
                    select new { s.Ticker, p.Date, p.PriceAdj }).GroupBy(
                            x => x.Date).Select(y =>
                        new
                        {
                            Date = y.Key,
                            Price1 = (y.Where(z => z.Ticker ==
                                Ticker1).Select(z => z.PriceAdj)),
                            Price2 = (y.Where(z => z.Ticker ==
                                Ticker2).Select(z => z.PriceAdj))
                        }).OrderBy(xx => xx.Date);

        foreach (var p in query)
        {
            PairStockPrices.Add(new PairStockPrice
            {
                Date = (DateTime)p.Date,
                Price1 = (double)p.Price1.First(),
                Price2 = (double)p.Price2.First()
            });
```

```
                    }
                }
            }
        }

    public class StockPrice
    {
        public string Ticker { get; set; }
        public DateTime Date { get; set; }
        public double PriceOpen { get; set; }
        public double PriceHigh { get; set; }
        public double PriceLow { get; set; }
        public double PriceClose { get; set; }
        public double PriceAdj { get; set; }
        public double Volume { get; set; }
    }

    public class PairStockPrice
    {
        public DateTime Date { get; set; }
        public double Price1 { get; set; }
        public double Price2 { get; set; }
    }
}
```

Here, we first define two entity classes, *StockPrice* and *PairStockPrice*. The *StockPrice* entity is used to hold stock data for a single stock ticker, while the *PairStockPrice* is used to hold the *PriceAdj* field for a pair of tickers. In the data access layer class named *Dal*.cs, we define two collections for the *StockPrice* and *PairStockPrice* entities that hold the stock data for a specified period defined using *DateStart* and *DateEnd*. We then implement two methods, *GetStockPrices* and *GetPairStockPrices*, which are used to retrieve the stock data from the entity data model for a single ticker and a pair of tickers, respectively. You should be familiar with these two methods because we have already implemented a variety of queries using the LINQ-to-Entity Framework technique in Chapter 3.

Retrieve Stock Data

In this section, I will show you how to retrieve stock using the *Dal* class implemented in the preceding section. Add a new *UserControl* to the *Views* folder and name it *StockDataView*. Here is the XAML file for this view:

```
<UserControl x:Class="Chapter06.Views.StockDataView"
             xmlns="http://schemas.microsoft.com/winfx/2006/xaml/presentation"
             xmlns:x="http://schemas.microsoft.com/winfx/2006/xaml"
             xmlns:mc="http://schemas.openxmlformats.org/markup-compatibility/2006"
             xmlns:d="http://schemas.microsoft.com/expression/blend/2008"
             mc:Ignorable="d"
             d:DesignHeight="400" d:DesignWidth="600">
    <Grid>
        <Grid.ColumnDefinitions>
            <ColumnDefinition Width="200"/>
            <ColumnDefinition Width="*"/>
        </Grid.ColumnDefinitions>
        <StackPanel Margin="0 5 10 5">
            <StackPanel Orientation="Horizontal" Margin="0 5 0 0">
```

```
                <TextBlock Text="Start Date" Width="80"/>
                <TextBox x:Name="StartDate" Width="90"/>
            </StackPanel>
            <StackPanel Orientation="Horizontal" Margin="0 5 0 0">
                <TextBlock Text="End Date" Width="80"/>
                <TextBox x:Name="EndDate" Width="90"/>
            </StackPanel>
            <GroupBox Header="Single Stock Data" Margin="0 10 0 0">
                <StackPanel Margin="0 5 0 5">
                    <StackPanel Orientation="Horizontal">
                        <TextBlock Text="Ticker" Width="80"/>
                        <TextBox x:Name="Ticker" Width="90"/>
                    </StackPanel>
                    <Button x:Name="GetStockData" Content="Get Stock Data"
                            Width="120" Margin="0 10 0 0"/>
                </StackPanel>
            </GroupBox>
            <GroupBox Header="Pair Stock Data" Margin="0 10 0 0">
                <StackPanel Margin="0 5 0 5">
                    <StackPanel Orientation="Horizontal">
                        <TextBlock Text="Ticker1" Width="80"/>
                        <TextBox x:Name="Ticker1" Width="90"/>
                    </StackPanel>
                    <StackPanel Orientation="Horizontal" Margin="0 5 0 0">
                        <TextBlock Text="Ticker2" Width="80"/>
                        <TextBox x:Name="Ticker2" Width="90"/>
                    </StackPanel>
                    <Button x:Name="GetPairStockData" Content="Get Pair Stock Data"
                            Width="120" Margin="0 10 0 0"/>
                </StackPanel>
            </GroupBox>

        </StackPanel>
        <Grid Grid.Column="1">
            <Grid.ColumnDefinitions>
                <ColumnDefinition/>
                <ColumnDefinition/>
            </Grid.ColumnDefinitions>
            <DataGrid x:Name="StockPrices" ColumnWidth="*" CanUserAddRows="False"
                      Grid.Column="0" FontSize="10"/>
            <DataGrid x:Name="PairStockPrices" ColumnWidth="*"
                      CanUserAddRows="False" Grid.Column="1" FontSize="10"/>
        </Grid>
    </Grid>
</UserControl>
```

Here, we add two button controls, which we will use to retrieve the stock data for a single stock ticker and for a pair of tickers from the database. We also add two *DataGrid* objects to display the stock data.

Add a new class to the *ViewModels* folder and name it *StockDataViewModel*. Here is the code for this class:

```
using System;
using System.Collections.Generic;
using System.Linq;
using System.Text;
```

```csharp
using System.Threading.Tasks;
using Caliburn.Micro;
using System.ComponentModel.Composition;
using Chapter06.Models.DataModel;
using System.Data;

namespace Chapter06.ViewModels
{
    [Export(typeof(IScreen)), PartCreationPolicy(CreationPolicy.NonShared)]
    public class StockDataViewModel : Screen
    {
        private readonly IEventAggregator _events;
        [ImportingConstructor]
        public StockDataViewModel(IEventAggregator events)
        {
            this._events = events;
            DisplayName = "01. Stock Data";
            StartDate = Convert.ToDateTime("1/1/2010");
            EndDate = Convert.ToDateTime("1/1/2015");
            Ticker = "IBM";
            Ticker1 = "IBM";
            Ticker2 = "MSFT";
            model = new Dal();
            StockPrices = new BindableCollection<StockPrice>();
            PairStockPrices = new BindableCollection<PairStockPrice>();
        }

        private Dal model;
        public BindableCollection<StockPrice> StockPrices { get; set; }
        public BindableCollection<PairStockPrice> PairStockPrices { get; set; }
        private DataTable pairTable = new DataTable();
        public DataTable PairTable
        {
            get { return pairTable; }
            set
            {
                pairTable = value;
                NotifyOfPropertyChange(() => PairTable);
            }
        }

        private string ticker;
        public string Ticker
        {
            get { return ticker; }
            set
            {
                ticker = value;
                NotifyOfPropertyChange(() => Ticker);
            }
        }

        private string ticker1;
        public string Ticker1
        {
```

```
    get { return ticker1; }
    set
    {
        ticker1 = value;
        NotifyOfPropertyChange(() => Ticker1);
    }
}

private string ticker2;
public string Ticker2
{
    get { return ticker2; }
    set
    {
        ticker2 = value;
        NotifyOfPropertyChange(() => Ticker2);
    }
}

private DateTime startDate;
public DateTime StartDate
{
    get { return startDate; }
    set
    {
        startDate = value;
        NotifyOfPropertyChange(() => StartDate);
    }
}

private DateTime endDate;
public DateTime EndDate
{
    get { return endDate; }
    set
    {
        endDate = value;
        NotifyOfPropertyChange(() => EndDate);
    }
}

public void GetStockData()
{
    model.DateStart = StartDate;
    model.DateEnd = EndDate;
    model.Ticker = Ticker;
    model.GetStockPrices();

    StockPrices.Clear();
    StockPrices.AddRange(model.StockPrices);
}

public void GetPairStockData()
{
    model.DateStart = StartDate;
```

```
                model.DateEnd = EndDate;
                model.Ticker1 = Ticker1;
                model.Ticker2 = Ticker2;
                model.GetPairStockPrices();
                PairStockPrices.Clear();
                PairStockPrices.AddRange(model.PairStockPrices);
            }
        }
    }
```

Here, we first define several properties and two collections, *StockPrices* and *PairStockPrices*. We can then get the stock data by calling the *GetStockPrices* method for a single ticker or calling the *GetPairStockPrices* method for a pair of tickers, whcih we implemented in the *Dal* class.

Running this example, clicking the *Get Stock Data* button, then clicking the *Get Pair Stock Data* button, produces the result shown in Figure 6-2.

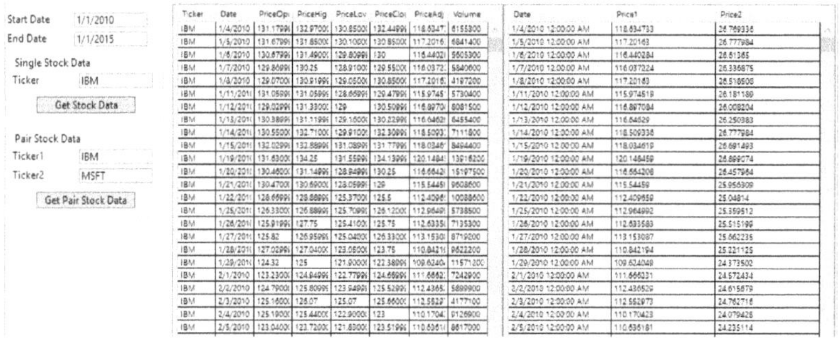

Figure 6-2. Stock data for IBM and the PriceAdj for IBM and MSFT.

Creating Stock Charts

The procedure for creating stock charts is very similar to that used in creating line charts, except that the data type for the X-axis is the *DateTime* instead of *double* or *int*. Also, note that if the X-axis type is *DateTime*, there will exist data gaps for weekends and holidays.

Chart Style for Time Series

Add a new class to the *ChartModel* folder and name it *TimeSeriesChartStyle*. Here is the code for this class:

```
using System;
using System.Collections.Generic;
using System.Linq;
using Caliburn.Micro;
using Chapter06.Models.DataModel;
using System.Windows.Controls;
using System.Windows;
using System.Windows.Shapes;
using System.Windows.Media;

namespace Chapter06.Models.ChartModel
```

```
{
    public class TimeSeriesChartStyle : ChartStyle
    {
        private double leftOffset = 20;
        private double bottomOffset = 15;
        private double rightOffset = 10;

        public List<DateTime> DateList { get; set; }

        public void AddTimeSeriesChartStyle(TextBlock tbTitle,
            TextBlock tbXLabel, TextBlock tbYLabel)
        {
            Point pt = new Point();
            Line tick = new Line();
            double offset = 0;
            double dx, dy;
            TextBlock tb = new TextBlock();

            //  determine right offset:
            tb.Text = Xmax.ToString();
            tb.Measure(new Size(Double.PositiveInfinity, Double.PositiveInfinity));
            Size size = tb.DesiredSize;
            rightOffset = size.Width / 2 + 10;

            // Determine left offset:
            for (dy = Ymin; dy <= Ymax; dy += YTick)
            {
                pt = NormalizePoint(new Point(Xmin, dy));
                tb = new TextBlock();
                tb.Text = Math.Round(dy, 2).ToString();
                tb.TextAlignment = TextAlignment.Right;
                tb.Measure(new Size(Double.PositiveInfinity,
                            Double.PositiveInfinity));
                size = tb.DesiredSize;
                if (offset < size.Width)
                    offset = size.Width;
            }
            leftOffset = offset + 10;
            Canvas.SetLeft(ChartCanvas, leftOffset);
            Canvas.SetBottom(ChartCanvas, bottomOffset);
            ChartCanvas.Width = Math.Abs(TextCanvas.Width - leftOffset -
                            rightOffset);
            ChartCanvas.Height = Math.Abs(TextCanvas.Height - bottomOffset -
                            size.Height / 2);

            Rectangle chartRect = new Rectangle();
            chartRect.Stroke = Brushes.Black;
            chartRect.Width = ChartCanvas.Width;
            chartRect.Height = ChartCanvas.Height;
            Canvas.SetZIndex(chartRect, 10);
            ChartCanvas.Children.Add(chartRect);

            // Create vertical gridlines:
            if (IsYGrid == true)
            {
```

```
        for (dx = Xmin + XTick; dx < Xmax; dx += XTick)
        {
            Gridline = new Line();
            AddLinePattern();
            Gridline.X1 = NormalizePoint(new Point(dx, Ymin)).X;
            Gridline.Y1 = NormalizePoint(new Point(dx, Ymin)).Y;
            Gridline.X2 = NormalizePoint(new Point(dx, Ymax)).X;
            Gridline.Y2 = NormalizePoint(new Point(dx, Ymax)).Y;
            ChartCanvas.Children.Add(Gridline);
        }
    }

    // Create horizontal gridlines:
    if (IsXGrid == true)
    {
        for (dy = Ymin + YTick; dy < Ymax; dy += YTick)
        {
            Gridline = new Line();
            AddLinePattern();
            Gridline.X1 = NormalizePoint(new Point(Xmin, dy)).X;
            Gridline.Y1 = NormalizePoint(new Point(Xmin, dy)).Y;
            Gridline.X2 = NormalizePoint(new Point(Xmax, dy)).X;
            Gridline.Y2 = NormalizePoint(new Point(Xmax, dy)).Y;
            ChartCanvas.Children.Add(Gridline);
        }
    }

    // Create x-axis tick marks:
    for (dx = Xmin; dx <= Xmax; dx += XTick)
    {
        pt = NormalizePoint(new Point(dx, Ymin));
        tick = new Line();

        tick.Stroke = Brushes.Black;
        tick.X1 = pt.X;
        tick.Y1 = pt.Y;
        tick.X2 = pt.X;
        tick.Y2 = pt.Y - 5;
        Canvas.SetZIndex(tick, 10);
        ChartCanvas.Children.Add(tick);

        if (dx >= 0 && dx < DateList.Count)
        {
            tb = new TextBlock();
            tb.FontSize = 10;
            tb.Text = DateList[(int)dx].ToShortDateString();
            tb.Measure(new Size(Double.PositiveInfinity,
                                Double.PositiveInfinity));
            size = tb.DesiredSize;
            TextCanvas.Children.Add(tb);
            Canvas.SetLeft(tb, leftOffset + pt.X - size.Width / 2);
            Canvas.SetTop(tb, pt.Y + 2 + size.Height / 2);
        }
    }
```

```
        // Create y-axis tick marks:
        for (dy = Ymin; dy <= Ymax; dy += YTick)
        {
            pt = NormalizePoint(new Point(Xmin, dy));
            tick = new Line();
            tick.Stroke = Brushes.Black;
            tick.X1 = pt.X;
            tick.Y1 = pt.Y;
            tick.X2 = pt.X + 5;
            tick.Y2 = pt.Y;
            Canvas.SetZIndex(tick, 10);
            ChartCanvas.Children.Add(tick);

            tb = new TextBlock();
            tb.FontSize = 10;
            tb.Text = Math.Round(dy, 2).ToString();
            TextCanvas.Children.Add(tb);
            Canvas.SetRight(tb, ChartCanvas.Width + rightOffset + 2);
            Canvas.SetTop(tb, pt.Y);
        }

        // Add title and labels:
        tbTitle.Text = Title;
        tbXLabel.Text = XLabel;
        tbYLabel.Text = YLabel;
        tbXLabel.Margin = new Thickness(leftOffset + 2, 2, 2, 2);
        tbTitle.Margin = new Thickness(leftOffset + 2, 2, 2, 2);
    }

    public double DateToDouble(DateTime date)
    {
        return BitConverter.ToDouble(BitConverter.GetBytes(date.Ticks), 0);
    }

    public DateTime DoubleToDate(double d)
    {
        return new DateTime(BitConverter.ToInt64(BitConverter.GetBytes(d), 0));
    }
  }
}
```

The method, A*ddTimeSeriesChartStyle*, is very similar to the *AddChartStyle* method in the *ChartStyle* class, except for the bolded code. Here, I make a little modification to the original *AddChartStyle* method in order to correctly display the date ticks along the *X*-axis for time series data. You can see that I specify the tick spacing using the indices for the *X* data and the tick labels using the *DateTime* from the *DataList* object. This way, we not only have the correct *DateTime* tick labels for the *X*-axis but also remove the data gaps for weekends and holidays. The methods *DateToDouble* and *DoubleToDate* are used to convert between the *DateTime* and double types.

Data Series and Chart Style for Stock Charts

Add a new class to the *ChartModel* folder and name it *StockSeries*. Here is the code for this class:

```
using Chapter06.Models.DataModel;
```

```
using System;
using System.Windows.Media;
using Caliburn.Micro;

namespace Chapter06.Models.ChartModel
{
    public class StockSeries : LineSeries
    {
        public BindableCollection<StockPrice> StockPrices { get; set; }

        private Brush fillColor1 = Brushes.Black;
        public Brush FillColor1
        {
            get { return fillColor1; }
            set { fillColor1 = value; }
        }

        private Brush fillColor2 = Brushes.White;
        public Brush FillColor2
        {
            get { return fillColor2; }
            set { fillColor2 = value; }
        }
    }
}
```

This simple class, which inherits from the *LineSeries* class, contains a *StockPrices* collection for the *StockPrice* entity that stores the stock data for a single stock ticker, and two *FillColor* objects that will be used in creating candlestick charts.

Add a new class to the *ChartModel* folder and name it *StockChartStyle*. Here is the code for this class:

```
using System;
using System.Collections.Generic;
using System.Linq;
using Caliburn.Micro;
using Chapter06.Models.DataModel;
using System.Windows.Controls;
using System.Windows;
using System.Windows.Shapes;
using System.Windows.Media;

namespace Chapter06.Models.ChartModel
{
    public class StockChartStyle : TimeSeriesChartStyle
    {
        private StockChartTypeEnum stockChartType = StockChartTypeEnum.LineAdj;
        public StockChartTypeEnum StockChartType
        {
            get { return stockChartType; }
            set { stockChartType = value; }
        }

        public void SetStockChart(BindableCollection<StockSeries> dc)
        {
            switch (stockChartType)
```

```
            {
                case StockChartTypeEnum.LineAdj:
                    AddPolyline(dc, "PriceAdj");
                    break;
                case StockChartTypeEnum.LineOpen:
                    AddPolyline(dc, "PriceOpen");
                    break;
                case StockChartTypeEnum.LineHigh:
                    AddPolyline(dc, "PriceHigh");
                    break;
                case StockChartTypeEnum.LineLow:
                    AddPolyline(dc, "PriceLow");
                    break;
                case StockChartTypeEnum.LineClose:
                    AddPolyline(dc, "PriceClose");
                    break;
                case StockChartTypeEnum.Volume:
                    AddVolume(dc);
                    break;
                case StockChartTypeEnum.HL:
                    AddHL(dc);
                    break;
                case StockChartTypeEnum.HLOC:
                    AddHLOC(dc);
                    break;
                case StockChartTypeEnum.Candlestick:
                    AddCandlestick(dc);
                    break;
            }
            ......
        }
    }

    public enum StockChartTypeEnum
    {
        HL = 0,
        HLOC = 1,
        Candlestick = 2,
        LineOpen = 3,
        LineHigh = 4,
        LineLow = 5,
        LineClose = 6,
        LineAdj = 7,
        Volume = 8,
    }
}
```

Here, we first define the *StockChartType* property using the *StockChartTypeEnum*, which we can use to select from nine predefined types of stock charts; then we implement the *SetStockChart* method to create various stock charts including line charts for stock prices and volume, and high low (HL), high low open close (HLOC), and candlestick charts. In the following sections, we will add detailed implementation for each of the various types of stock charts.

Line Charts for Stock Prices

The simplest stock chart is the line chart. Here, I will show you how to create line stock charts that will display *PriceAdj*, *PriceOpen*, *PriceHigh*, *PriceLow*, or *PriceClose*. Add a new private method, *AddPolyline*, to the *StockChartStyle* class. Here is the code snippet for this method:

```
private void AddPolyline(BindableCollection<StockSeries> dc, string priceType)
{
    Polyline line = new Polyline();
    int j = 0;
    foreach (var ss in dc)
    {
        if (ss.SeriesName == "Default")
            ss.SeriesName = "LineSeries" + j.ToString();
        ss.SetLinePattern();
        line = new Polyline();
        line.Stroke = ss.LineColor;
        line.StrokeThickness = ss.LineThickness;
        line.StrokeDashArray = ss.LineDashPattern;

        for (int i = 0; i < ss.StockPrices.Count; i++)
        {
            line.Points.Add(NormalizePoint(new Point(1.0 * i,
                (double)ss.StockPrices[i].GetType().GetProperty(priceType).
                GetValue(ss.StockPrices[i], null))));
        }
        ChartCanvas.Children.Add(line);
        j++;
    }
}
```

You should already be familiar with this method because it is very similar to the one we used to create ordinary line charts, except that the point collection of the line is directly linked to the *StockPrices* collection. We also use the property name and the *GetType().GetProperty(priceType)* method to get corresponding stock price data, which is a very powerful technique for getting a property's value using its name.

Add a new *UserControl* to the *Views* folder and name it *StockChartView*. Here is the XAML file for this view:

```
<UserControl x:Class="Chapter06.Views.StockChartView"
             xmlns="http://schemas.microsoft.com/winfx/2006/xaml/presentation"
             xmlns:x="http://schemas.microsoft.com/winfx/2006/xaml"
             xmlns:mc="http://schemas.openxmlformats.org/markup-compatibility/2006"
             xmlns:d="http://schemas.microsoft.com/expression/blend/2008"
             xmlns:cal="http://www.caliburnproject.org"
             mc:Ignorable="d"
             d:DesignHeight="400" d:DesignWidth="800">
    <Grid>
        <Grid.ColumnDefinitions>
            <ColumnDefinition Width="170"/>
            <ColumnDefinition Width="1*"/>
            <ColumnDefinition Width="2*"/>
        </Grid.ColumnDefinitions>
        <StackPanel Margin="5">
```

```
<GroupBox Header="Get Stock Data" Margin="0 0 0 0">
    <StackPanel Margin="0 5 0 5">
        <StackPanel Orientation="Horizontal">
            <TextBlock Text="Ticker" Width="60"/>
            <TextBox x:Name="Ticker" Width="80"/>
        </StackPanel>
        <StackPanel Orientation="Horizontal" Margin="0 5 0 0">
            <TextBlock Text="Start Date" Width="60"/>
            <TextBox x:Name="StartDate" Width="80"/>
        </StackPanel>
        <StackPanel Orientation="Horizontal" Margin="0 5 0 0">
            <TextBlock Text="End Date" Width="60"/>
            <TextBox x:Name="EndDate" Width="80"/>
        </StackPanel>
        <Button x:Name="GetStockData" Content="Get Stock Data"
                Width="120" Margin="0 10 0 0"/>
    </StackPanel>
</GroupBox>
<TextBlock Text="Choose Stock Chart Type:" Margin="0 20 0 0"/>
<ComboBox x:Name="StockChartType" Width="150" Margin="0 5 0 0"
          HorizontalAlignment="Left" cal:Message.Attach="[Event
          SelectionChanged]=[Action AddChart]"/>
</StackPanel>

<DataGrid x:Name="StockPrices" ColumnWidth="Auto" CanUserAddRows="False"
          Grid.Column="1" FontSize="10"/>
<Grid Name="grid1" Margin="10" Grid.Column="2">
    <Grid.ColumnDefinitions>
        <ColumnDefinition Width="Auto"/>
        <ColumnDefinition Name="column1" Width="*"/>
    </Grid.ColumnDefinitions>
    <Grid.RowDefinitions>
        <RowDefinition Height="Auto"/>
        <RowDefinition Name="row1" Height="*"/>
        <RowDefinition Height="Auto"/>
    </Grid.RowDefinitions>
    <TextBlock Margin="2" x:Name="tbTitle" Grid.Column="1" Grid.Row="0"
               RenderTransformOrigin="0.5,0.5" FontSize="14" FontWeight="Bold"
               HorizontalAlignment="Stretch" VerticalAlignment="Stretch"
               TextAlignment="Center" Text="Title"/>
    <TextBlock Margin="2" x:Name="tbXLabel" Grid.Column="1" Grid.Row="2"
               RenderTransformOrigin="0.5,0.5" TextAlignment="Center"
               Text="X Axis" FontWeight="Bold"/>

    <TextBlock Margin="2" Name="tbYLabel" Grid.Column="0" Grid.Row="1"
                  FontWeight="Bold"
               RenderTransformOrigin="0.5,0.5" TextAlignment="Center"
               Text="Y Axis">
        <TextBlock.LayoutTransform>
            <RotateTransform Angle="-90"/>
        </TextBlock.LayoutTransform>
    </TextBlock>

    <Grid  Margin="0,0,0,0" x:Name ="chartGrid" Grid.Column="1" Grid.Row="1"
       ClipToBounds="False" Background="Transparent"
```

```
            cal:Message.Attach="[Event SizeChanged]=[Action AddChart];
                           [Event Loaded]=[Action AddChart]">

    <Canvas Margin="2" Name="textCanvas" Grid.Column="1" Grid.Row="1"
            ClipToBounds="True"
            Width="{Binding ElementName=chartGrid,Path=ActualWidth}"
            Height="{Binding ElementName=chartGrid,Path=ActualHeight}">
        <Canvas Name="chartCanvas" ClipToBounds="True"/>
    </Canvas>
        </Grid>
    </Grid>
</Grid>
</UserControl>
```

In this XAML file, we first get the stock data for the specified ticker and period from the database, then choose the chart type from the *ComboBox* control. Note that I also attach this *ComboBox*'s *SelectionChanged* event to the *AddChart* method in the view model, so the program will update the chart whenever we select a different chart type.

Add a new class to the *ViewModels* folder and name it *StockChartViewModel*. Here is the code for this class:

```
using System;
using System.Linq;
using Caliburn.Micro;
using System.Collections.ObjectModel;
using System.ComponentModel.Composition;
using System.Windows.Documents;
using System.Collections.Generic;
using System.Windows;
using Chapter06.Models;
using System.Windows.Media;
using System.Windows.Controls;
using Chapter06.Views;
using Chapter06.Models.ChartModel;
using Chapter06.Models.DataModel;

namespace Chapter06.ViewModels
{
    [Export(typeof(IScreen)), PartCreationPolicy(CreationPolicy.NonShared)]
    public class StockChartViewModel : Screen
    {
        private readonly IEventAggregator _events;
        [ImportingConstructor]
         public StockChartViewModel(IEventAggregator events)
        {
            this._events = events;
            DisplayName = "02. Stock Charts";
            StockPrices = new BindableCollection<StockPrice>();
            StartDate = Convert.ToDateTime("10/1/2014");
            EndDate = Convert.ToDateTime("1/1/2015");
            Ticker = "GS";
            model = new Dal();
            dc = new BindableCollection<StockSeries>();
        }
```

```csharp
private Dal model;
private StockChartStyle cs;
private StockChartView view;
private BindableCollection<StockSeries> dc;

public BindableCollection<StockPrice> StockPrices { get; set; }
private string ticker;
public string Ticker
{
    get { return ticker; }
    set
    {
        ticker = value;
        NotifyOfPropertyChange(() => Ticker);
    }
}

private DateTime startDate;
public DateTime StartDate
{
    get { return startDate; }
    set
    {
        startDate = value;
        NotifyOfPropertyChange(() => StartDate);
    }
}

private DateTime endDate;
public DateTime EndDate
{
    get { return endDate; }
    set
    {
        endDate = value;
        NotifyOfPropertyChange(() => EndDate);
    }
}


private IEnumerable<StockChartTypeEnum> stockChartType;
public IEnumerable<StockChartTypeEnum> StockChartType
{
    get { return Enum.GetValues(typeof(StockChartTypeEnum)).
                Cast<StockChartTypeEnum>(); }
    set
    {
        stockChartType = value;
        NotifyOfPropertyChange(() => StockChartType);
    }
}

private StockChartTypeEnum selectedStockChartType =
        StockChartTypeEnum.LineAdj;
public StockChartTypeEnum SelectedStockChartType
```

```
    {
        get { return selectedStockChartType; }
        set
        {
            selectedStockChartType = value;
            NotifyOfPropertyChange(() => SelectedStockChartType);
        }
    }
}

public void GetStockData()
{
    model.DateStart = StartDate;
    model.DateEnd = EndDate;
    model.Ticker = Ticker;
    model.GetStockPrices();
    StockPrices.Clear();
    StockPrices.AddRange(model.StockPrices);
    AddChart();
}

private void SetChartStyle()
{
    view = this.GetView() as StockChartView;
    view.chartCanvas.Children.Clear();
    view.textCanvas.Children.RemoveRange(1,
        view.textCanvas.Children.Count - 1);
    cs = new StockChartStyle();
    cs.ChartCanvas = view.chartCanvas;
    cs.TextCanvas = view.textCanvas;
    cs.Title = string.Format("{0}: Stock Chart (Chart Type: {1})",
        Ticker, SelectedStockChartType);
    SetAxes();
    cs.DateList = new List<DateTime>();
    foreach (var p in StockPrices)
        cs.DateList.Add(p.Date);
    cs.GridlinePattern = LinePatternEnum.Dot;
    cs.GridlineColor = Brushes.Black;
    cs.AddTimeSeriesChartStyle(view.tbTitle, view.tbXLabel, view.tbYLabel);
}

private void SetAxes()
{
    cs.XLabel = "Date";
    cs.YLabel = "Stock Price";

    cs.Xmin = -1;
    cs.Xmax = StockPrices.Count;
    cs.XTick = (int)((cs.Xmax - cs.Xmin) / 5.01);

    double min = StockPrices.Min(x => x.PriceLow);
    double max = StockPrices.Max(x => x.PriceHigh);
    if (SelectedStockChartType == StockChartTypeEnum.LineAdj)
    {
        min = StockPrices.Min(x => x.PriceAdj);
        max = StockPrices.Max(x => x.PriceAdj);
```

```
        }
        if (SelectedStockChartType == StockChartTypeEnum.Volume)
        {
            min = StockPrices.Min(x => x.Volume);
            max = StockPrices.Max(x => x.Volume);
            cs.YLabel = "Volume";
        }
        double delta = (max - min) / 20.0;
        cs.Ymin = (int)(min - delta);
        cs.Ymax = (int)(max + delta);
        cs.YTick = (int)((max - min) / 5.01);
    }

    public void AddChart()
    {
        if (StockPrices.Count <= 0)
            return;
        SetChartStyle();
        cs.StockChartType = SelectedStockChartType;

        dc.Clear();
        var ss = new StockSeries();
        ss.StockPrices = StockPrices;
        ss.LineColor = Brushes.DarkBlue;
        if (SelectedStockChartType == StockChartTypeEnum.Candlestick)
        {
            ss.FillColor1 = Brushes.DarkBlue;
            ss.FillColor2 = Brushes.White;
        }
        dc.Add(ss);
        cs.SetStockChart(dc);
    }
  }
}
```

Note how I bind the *StockChartTypeEnum* object to the *ComboBox* control. Usually, you can bind the *SelectedItem* of the *ComboBox* to a property of the view model. However, because the *ComboBox* has the name *StockChartType*, the Caliburn.Micro's naming conventions will look for a property called *SelectedStockChartType* (or *ActiveStockChartType*) and automatically bind the *ComboBox*'s *SelectedItem* to it, so we do not need to explicitly specify the binding to the *SelectedItem* in XAML.

We then need to get stock data from the entity data model using the *GetStockPrices* method implemented in the *Dal* class. Setting the chart style for stock charts is little more complicated than it is for ordinary line charts. In particular, we need to specify the *DataList* using the *StockPrices* collection, which will be used for the *X*-axis tick labels. Note how I use the data range of the *StockPrices* collection to set the axis limits and tick spacing for the *X*- and *Y*-axes. This way, the axis limits and tick spacing will be automatically adjusted for different stocks.

Running this example and clicking the *Get Stock Data* button produces the result shown in Figure 6-3. This result is for the default chart type, *LineAdj*. You can choose different line charts from the *ComboBox*, and the application will automatically update the chart. You can play with the stock chart by changing the ticker (as long as it is in the database) and the period.

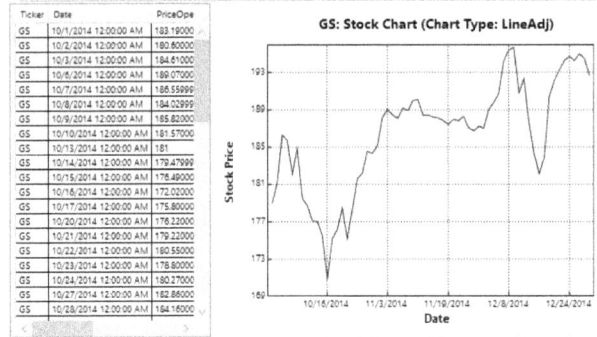

Figure 6-3. A line plot for PriceAdj for Goldman Sachs.

Volume Charts

Usually, we plot volume charts for stocks using a bar chart type, instead of a line chart. Add a new private method, *AddVolume*, to the *StockChartStyle* class. Here is the code snippet for this method:

```
private void AddVolume(BindableCollection<StockSeries> dc)
{
    int j = 0;
    foreach (var ss in dc)
    {
        double barWidth = ChartCanvas.Width / (4.0 * ss.StockPrices.Count);
        if (ss.SeriesName == "Default")
            ss.SeriesName = "LineSeries" + j.ToString();
        ss.SetLinePattern();

        for (int i = 0; i < ss.StockPrices.Count; i++)
        {
            Point py1= NormalizePoint(new Point(1.0 * i, ss.StockPrices[i].Volume));
            Point py0 = NormalizePoint(new Point(1.0 * i, 0));
            Point p0 = new Point(py1.X - barWidth, py1.Y);
            Point p1 = new Point(py1.X + barWidth, py1.Y);
            Point p2 = new Point(py0.X + barWidth, py0.Y);
            Point p3 = new Point(py0.X - barWidth, py0.Y);
            Polygon plg = new Polygon();
            plg.Stroke = ss.LineColor;
            plg.StrokeThickness = ss.LineThickness;
            plg.Fill = ss.LineColor;
            plg.Points.Add(p0);
            plg.Points.Add(p1);
            plg.Points.Add(p2);
            plg.Points.Add(p3);
            ChartCanvas.Children.Add(plg);
        }
        j++;
    }
}
```

Here, we first define the *barWidth* parameter using the *chartCanvas*'s width and the stock's data points, and then use the volume data from the *StockPrices* collection to draw the polygon and create the volume bar. The *Stroke* and *Fill* properties of the polygon are specified using the *StockSeries' LineColor* property. Finally, we add the polygon to the *chartCanvas*. Running the project, clicking the *Get Stock Data* button, and choosing *Volume* from the *ComboBox* generates the result shown in Figure 6-4.

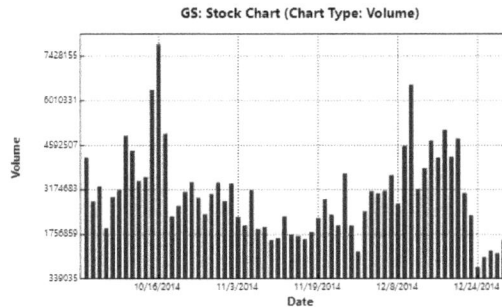

Figure 6-4. A volume chart for Goldman Sachs.

HL and HLOC Stock Charts

The standard high-low and the high-low-open-close stock charts are vertical lines. The top of the line is the high, the bottom is the low, the open is a short horizontal tick to the left, and the close is a short horizontal tick to the right.

Add the following methods to the *StockChartStyle* class:

```
private void AddHL(BindableCollection<StockSeries> dc)
{
    int j = 0;
    foreach (var ss in dc)
    {
        if (ss.SeriesName == "Default")
            ss.SeriesName = "LineSeries" + j.ToString();
        ss.SetLinePattern();

        for(int i =0;i<ss.StockPrices.Count;i++)
        {
            Point ph = NormalizePoint(new Point(1.0 * i,
                ss.StockPrices[i].PriceHigh));
            Point pl = NormalizePoint(new Point(1.0 * i,
                ss.StockPrices[i].PriceLow));
            DrawLine(pl, ph, ss.LineColor, ss.LineThickness);
        }
        j++;
    }
}

private void AddHLOC(BindableCollection<StockSeries> dc)
{
    int j = 0;
    foreach (var ss in dc)
    {
        double barWidth = ChartCanvas.Width / (3.0 * ss.StockPrices.Count);
        if (ss.SeriesName == "Default")
```

```
            ss.SeriesName = "LineSeries" + j.ToString();
        ss.SetLinePattern();

        for (int i = 0; i < ss.StockPrices.Count; i++)
        {
            Point ph = NormalizePoint(new Point(1.0 * i,
                ss.StockPrices[i].PriceHigh));
            Point pl = NormalizePoint(new Point(1.0 * i,
                ss.StockPrices[i].PriceLow));
            Point po = NormalizePoint(new Point(1.0 * i,
                ss.StockPrices[i].PriceOpen));
            Point po1 = new Point(po.X - barWidth, po.Y);
            Point pc = NormalizePoint(new Point(1.0 * i,
                ss.StockPrices[i].PriceClose));
            Point pc1 = new Point(pc.X + barWidth, pc.Y);
            DrawLine(pl, ph, ss.LineColor, ss.LineThickness);
            DrawLine(po, po1, ss.LineColor, ss.LineThickness);
            DrawLine(pc, pc1, ss.LineColor, ss.LineThickness);
        }
        j++;
    }
}
private  void DrawLine(Point pt1, Point pt2, Brush lineColor, double lineThickness)
{
    Line line = new Line();
    line.Stroke = lineColor;
    line.StrokeThickness = lineThickness;
    line.X1 = pt1.X;
    line.Y1 = pt1.Y;
    line.X2 = pt2.X;
    line.Y2 = pt2.Y;
    ChartCanvas.Children.Add(line);
}
```

Here, we simply draw vertical lines for the range of the price change and horizontal ticks for the open and close prices.

Running this example, clicking the *Get Stock Data* button, and selecting *HL* from the *ComboBox* will produce the result shown in Figure 6-5.

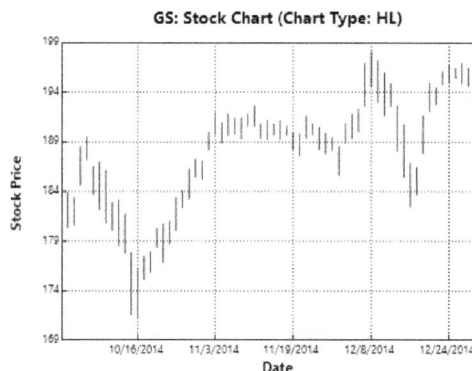

Figure 6-5. A HL chart for Goldman Sachs.

Choosing the *HLOC* chart type from the *ComboBox* generates the result shown in Figure 6-6.

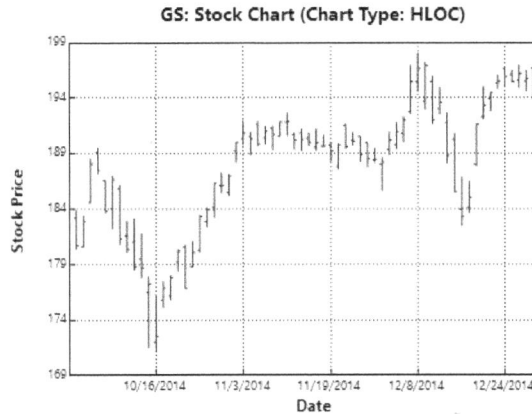

Figure 6-6. A HLOC chart for Goldman Sachs.

Candlestick Stock Charts

In order to create a candlestick chart, you must have a stock data set that contains open, high, low, and close prices for each time period you want to display. The hollow or filled portion of the candlestick is called the body (also called the real body). The long thin lines above and below the body represent the high-low range and are called shadows. The high is marked by the top of the upper shadow and the low by the bottom of the lower shadow. If the stock closes higher than its opening price, a hollow candlestick is drawn with the bottom of the body representing the opening price and the top of the body representing the closing price. If the stock closes lower than its opening price, a filled candlestick is drawn with the top of the body representing the opening price and the bottom of the body representing the closing price, as shown in Figure 6-7.

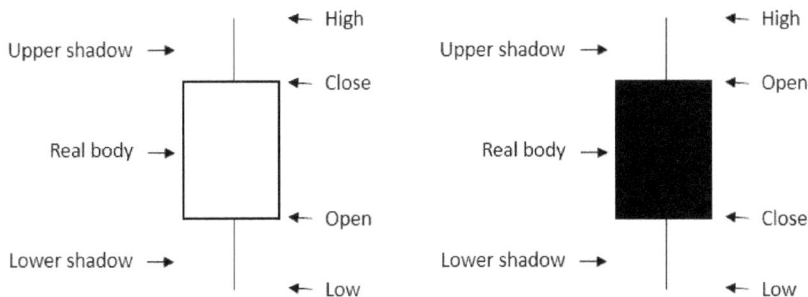

Figure 6-7. The structure of candlesticks.

Add a new private method named *AddCandlestick* to the *StockChartStype* class. Here is the code snippet for this method:

```
private void AddCandlestick(BindableCollection<StockSeries> dc)
{
```

```
int j = 0;
foreach (var ss in dc)
{
    double barWidth = ChartCanvas.Width / (4.0 * ss.StockPrices.Count);
    if (ss.SeriesName == "Default")
        ss.SeriesName = "LineSeries" + j.ToString();
    ss.SetLinePattern();

    for (int i = 0; i < ss.StockPrices.Count; i++)
    {
        Point ph = NormalizePoint(new Point(1.0 * i,
            ss.StockPrices[i].PriceHigh));
        Point pl = NormalizePoint(new Point(1.0 * i,
            ss.StockPrices[i].PriceLow));
        Point po = NormalizePoint(new Point(1.0 * i,
            ss.StockPrices[i].PriceOpen));
        Point po1 = new Point(po.X - barWidth, po.Y);
        Point po2 = new Point(po.X + barWidth, po.Y);
        Point pc = NormalizePoint(new Point(1.0 * i,
            ss.StockPrices[i].PriceClose));
        Point pc1 = new Point(pc.X + barWidth, pc.Y);
        Point pc2 = new Point(pc.X - barWidth, pc.Y);
        DrawLine(pl, ph, ss.LineColor, ss.LineThickness);
        Polygon plg = new Polygon();
        plg.Stroke = ss.LineColor;
        plg.StrokeThickness = ss.LineThickness;
        Brush fillColor = ss.FillColor1;
        if (ss.StockPrices[i].PriceClose > ss.StockPrices[i].PriceOpen)
            fillColor = ss.FillColor2;
        plg.Fill = fillColor;
        plg.Points.Add(po1);
        plg.Points.Add(po2);
        plg.Points.Add(pc1);
        plg.Points.Add(pc2);
        ChartCanvas.Children.Add(plg);
    }
    j++;
}
}
```

Within this method, we draw a line from *PriceLow* to *PriceHigh*, and then create a polygon for the body of the candlestick. There are two fill color properties for the *Fill* property of the polygon, *FillColor1* and *FillColor2*. We will use *FillColor1* when *PriceOpen >PriceClose* and *FillColor2* when *PriceOpen <PriceClose*.

Running this example, clicking the *Get Stock Data* button, and selecting the *Candlestick* chart type from the *ComboBox* produces the result shown in Figure 6-8.

Figure 6-8. A candlestick chart for Goldman Sachs.

Moving Averages

Moving averages are often used in analyzing time series data. They are widely applied in finance, especially in technical analysis. They can be also used as a generic smoothing operation, in which case the data need not be a time series.

A moving average series can be calculated for any time series. In finance, it is most often applied to stock prices, returns, or trading volumes. Moving averages are used to smoothe out short-term fluctuations, thus highlighting longer-term trends or cycles. The threshold between short-term and long-term depends on the application, and the parameters of the moving average will be set accordingly.

A moving average smoothes data by replacing each data point with the average of the neighboring data points defined within the time span. This process is equivalent to low pass filters used in digital signal processing.

Simple Moving Averages

In this section, I will first discuss the simple moving average. A simple moving average (SMA) is the mean value of the previous n data points. For example, a 5-day simple moving average of opening price is the mean of the previous 5 days' opening prices. If those prices are $p_0, p_{-1}, p_{-2}, p_{-3}, p_{-4}$ then the moving average is described by

$$SMA = \frac{p_0 + p_{-1} + p_{-2} + p_{-3} + p_{-4}}{5}$$

In general, for an n-day moving average, you have

$$SMA = \frac{p_0 + p_{-1} + \cdots}{n} \quad \cdots = \frac{1}{n}\sum_{i=0}^{n-1} p_{-i}$$

When calculating successive values, a new value comes into the sum and an old value drops out, meaning a full summation each time is unnecessary

$$SMA_{today} = MSA_{yesterday} - \frac{P_{-n+1}}{n} + \frac{P_1}{n}$$

In technical analysis, there are various popular values for n, like 10 days, 40 days, or 100 days. The period selected depends on the kind of movement you are concentrating on, such as short, intermediate, or long term. In any case, moving average levels are interpreted as support in a rising market, or resistance in a falling market.

In all cases a moving average lags behind the latest data point, simply from the nature of its smoothing. An SMA can lag to an undesirable extent and can be disproportionately influenced by old data points' dropping out of the average. You can address this issue by giving extra weight to more recent data points, as is done in the weighted and exponential moving averages discussed in following sections.

One characteristic of the SMA is that if the data have a periodic fluctuation, then applying an SMA of that period will eliminate that variation.

Add a new class to the *ChartModel* folder and name it *StockAverages*. Here is the code for this class:

```
using Caliburn.Micro;
using Chapter06.Models.DataModel;
using System;
using System.Linq;
using System.Collections.Generic;
using System.Threading.Tasks;

namespace Chapter06.Models.ChartModel
{
    public class StockAverage
    {
        private int nDays = 15;
        public int NDays
        {
            get { return nDays; }
            set { nDays = value; }
        }

        public BindableCollection<StockPrice> StockPrices { get; set; }
        public BindableCollection<StockAverageData> StockAvgs { get; set; }

        public StockAverage()
        {
            StockPrices = new BindableCollection<StockPrice>();
            StockAvgs = new BindableCollection<StockAverageData>();
        }

        public void GetStockAverage()
        {
            StockAvgs.Clear();
            var tmp = new List<StockPrice>();
            for (int i = NDays; i < StockPrices.Count; i++)
            {
                tmp.Clear();
                for (int j = i - NDays; j <= i; j++)
                {
                    tmp.Add(StockPrices[j]);
```

```
            }
            double avg = tmp.Average(x => x.PriceAdj);
            double stdev = tmp.StdDev(x => x.PriceAdj);
            double zscore = (tmp[tmp.Count - 1].PriceAdj - avg) / stdev;
            StockAvgs.Add(new StockAverageData
            {
                Ticker = StockPrices[i].Ticker,
                Date = StockPrices[i].Date,
                PriceAdj = StockPrices[i].PriceAdj,
                Sma = avg,
                Wma = GetWma(tmp),
                Ema = GetEma(tmp),
                Zscore = zscore
            });
        }
    }


    private double GetWma(List<StockPrice> tmp)
    {
        int n = tmp.Count;
        double sum = 0.0;
        for (int i = 0; i < n; i++)
            sum += (i + 1) * tmp[i].PriceAdj;
        return 2.0 * sum / n / (n + 1);
    }

    private double GetEma(List<StockPrice> tmp)
    {
        int n = tmp.Count;
        double alpha = 2.0 / (n + 1);
        double sum = 0.0;
        double sum1 = 0.0;
        for (int i = 0; i < n; i++)
        {
            sum += Math.Pow(1.0 - alpha, n - i) * tmp[i].PriceAdj;
            sum1 += Math.Pow(1.0 - alpha, n - i);
        }
        return sum /sum1;
    }
}

public class StockAverageData
{
    public string Ticker { get; set; }
    public DateTime Date { get; set; }
    public double PriceAdj { get; set; }
    public double Sma { get; set; }
    public double Wma { get; set; }
    public double Ema { get; set; }
    public double Zscore { get; set; }
}

public enum StockAvgTypeEnum
{
```

```
        Sma = 0,
        Wma = 1,
        Ema = 2,
        AllAvgs = 3,
        Zscore = 4,
    }
}
```

Here, we define a *StockAverageData* class entity that we use to represent the stock average data and a public *enum* object, *StockAvgTypeEnum*, which we use to select different types of stock averages. Inside the *StockAverages* class, we use the *NDays* property to specify the size of the moving window for calculating stock averages. This class contains the calculation for several different averages, including the simple moving average (SMA), weighted moving average (WMA), exponential moving average (EMA), and *Z* score.

We can now test the stock average calculation. Add a new *UserControl* to the *Views* folder and name it *StockAvgView*. Here is the XAML file for this view:

```xml
<UserControl x:Class="Chapter06.Views.StockAvgView"
             xmlns="http://schemas.microsoft.com/winfx/2006/xaml/presentation"
             xmlns:x="http://schemas.microsoft.com/winfx/2006/xaml"
             xmlns:mc="http://schemas.openxmlformats.org/markup-compatibility/2006"
             xmlns:d="http://schemas.microsoft.com/expression/blend/2008"
             xmlns:cal="http://www.caliburnproject.org"
             mc:Ignorable="d"
             d:DesignHeight="400" d:DesignWidth="800">

    <Grid>
        <Grid.ColumnDefinitions>
            <ColumnDefinition Width="170"/>
            <ColumnDefinition Width="1*"/>
            <ColumnDefinition Width="2*"/>
        </Grid.ColumnDefinitions>
        <StackPanel Margin="5">
            <GroupBox Header="Get Stock Avg" Margin="0 0 0 0">
                <StackPanel Margin="0 5 0 5">
                    <StackPanel Orientation="Horizontal">
                        <TextBlock Text="Ticker" Width="60"/>
                        <TextBox x:Name="Ticker" Width="80"/>
                    </StackPanel>
                    <StackPanel Orientation="Horizontal" Margin="0 5 0 0">
                        <TextBlock Text="Start Date" Width="60"/>
                        <TextBox x:Name="StartDate" Width="80"/>
                    </StackPanel>
                    <StackPanel Orientation="Horizontal" Margin="0 5 0 0">
                        <TextBlock Text="End Date" Width="60"/>
                        <TextBox x:Name="EndDate" Width="80"/>
                    </StackPanel>
                    <StackPanel Orientation="Horizontal" Margin="0 5 0 0">
                        <TextBlock Text="NDays" Width="60"/>
                        <TextBox x:Name="NDays" Width="80"/>
                    </StackPanel>
                    <Button x:Name="GetStockAvg" Content="Get Stock Avg" Width="120"
                            Margin="0 10 0 0"/>
                </StackPanel>
            </GroupBox>
```

```
            <TextBlock Text="Choose Stock Avg Type:" Margin="0 20 0 0"/>
            <ComboBox x:Name="StockAvgType" Width="150" Margin="0 5 0 0"
                    HorizontalAlignment="Left" cal:Message.Attach="[Event
                    SelectionChanged]=[Action GetStockAvg]"/>
        </StackPanel>

        <DataGrid x:Name="StockAvgs" ColumnWidth="Auto" CanUserAddRows="False"
                Grid.Column="1" FontSize="10"/>
        <Grid Name="grid1" Margin="10" Grid.Column="2">
            <Grid.ColumnDefinitions>
                <ColumnDefinition Width="Auto"/>
                <ColumnDefinition Name="column1" Width="*"/>
            </Grid.ColumnDefinitions>
            <Grid.RowDefinitions>
                <RowDefinition Height="Auto"/>
                <RowDefinition Name="row1" Height="*"/>
                <RowDefinition Height="Auto"/>
            </Grid.RowDefinitions>
            <TextBlock Margin="2" x:Name="tbTitle" Grid.Column="1" Grid.Row="0"
                    RenderTransformOrigin="0.5,0.5" FontSize="14" FontWeight="Bold"
                    HorizontalAlignment="Stretch" VerticalAlignment="Stretch"
                    TextAlignment="Center" Text="Title"/>
            <TextBlock Margin="2" x:Name="tbXLabel" Grid.Column="1" Grid.Row="2"
                    RenderTransformOrigin="0.5,0.5" TextAlignment="Center"
                    Text="X Axis" FontWeight="Bold"/>

            <TextBlock Margin="2" Name="tbYLabel" Grid.Column="0" Grid.Row="1"
                    FontWeight="Bold" RenderTransformOrigin="0.5,0.5"
                    TextAlignment="Center" Text="Y Axis">
                <TextBlock.LayoutTransform>
                    <RotateTransform Angle="-90"/>
                </TextBlock.LayoutTransform>
            </TextBlock>

            <Grid  Margin="0,0,0,0" x:Name ="chartGrid" Grid.Column="1" Grid.Row="1"
                ClipToBounds="False" Background="Transparent"
                cal:Message.Attach="[Event SizeChanged]=[Action AddChart];
                    [Event Loaded]=[Action AddChart]">

                <Canvas Margin="2" Name="textCanvas" Grid.Column="1" Grid.Row="1"
                        ClipToBounds="True" Width="{Binding ElementName=chartGrid,
                        Path=ActualWidth}" Height="{Binding
                        ElementName=chartGrid,Path=ActualHeight}">
                    <Canvas Name="chartCanvas" ClipToBounds="True">
                    </Canvas>
                </Canvas>
            </Grid>
        </Grid>
    </Grid>
</UserControl>
```

Here, we first retrieve stock data from the database by specifying the ticker name and period, and then calculate the stock averages by specifying the *NDays* property. Finally, we can select the stock average type from the *ComboBox* to plot the stock average data on the chart.

Add a new class to the *ViewModels* folder and name it *StockAvgViewModel*. Here is the code for this class:

```
using System;
using System.Linq;
using Caliburn.Micro;
using System.Collections.ObjectModel;
using System.ComponentModel.Composition;
using System.Windows.Documents;
using System.Collections.Generic;
using System.Windows;
using Chapter06.Models;
using System.Windows.Media;
using System.Windows.Controls;
using Chapter06.Views;
using Chapter06.Models.ChartModel;
using Chapter06.Models.DataModel;

namespace Chapter06.ViewModels
{
    [Export(typeof(IScreen)), PartCreationPolicy(CreationPolicy.NonShared)]
    public class StockAvgViewModel : Screen
    {
        private readonly IEventAggregator _events;
        [ImportingConstructor]
        public StockAvgViewModel(IEventAggregator events)
        {
            this._events = events;
            DisplayName = "03. Stock Averages";
            StockAvgs = new BindableCollection<StockAverageData>();
            StartDate = Convert.ToDateTime("1/1/2013");
            EndDate = Convert.ToDateTime("1/1/2015");
            Ticker = "GS";
            NDays = 15;
            model = new Dal();
            sa = new StockAverage();
            dc = new BindableCollection<LineSeries>();
        }

        private StockChartStyle cs;
        private BindableCollection<LineSeries> dc;
        private Dal model;
        private StockAvgView view;
        private Legend lg;
        private StockAverage sa;

        public BindableCollection<StockAverageData> StockAvgs { get; set; }

        private string ticker;
        public string Ticker
        {
            get { return ticker; }
            set
            {
                ticker = value;
```

```
                    NotifyOfPropertyChange(() => Ticker);
            }
    }

    private DateTime startDate;
    public DateTime StartDate
    {
        get { return startDate; }
        set
        {
            startDate = value;
            NotifyOfPropertyChange(() => StartDate);
        }
    }

    private DateTime endDate;
    public DateTime EndDate
    {
        get { return endDate; }
        set
        {
            endDate = value;
            NotifyOfPropertyChange(() => EndDate);
        }
    }

    private int nDays;
    public int NDays
    {
        get { return nDays; }
        set
        {
            nDays = value;
            NotifyOfPropertyChange(() => NDays);
        }
    }

    private IEnumerable<StockAvgTypeEnum> stockAvgType;
    public IEnumerable<StockAvgTypeEnum> StockAvgType
    {
        get { return Enum.GetValues(typeof(StockAvgTypeEnum)).
            Cast<StockAvgTypeEnum>(); }
        set
        {
            stockAvgType = value;
            NotifyOfPropertyChange(() => StockAvgType);
        }
    }

    private StockAvgTypeEnum selectedStockAvgType = StockAvgTypeEnum.Sma;
    public StockAvgTypeEnum SelectedStockAvgType
    {
        get { return selectedStockAvgType; }
        set
        {
```

```
            selectedStockAvgType = value;
            NotifyOfPropertyChange(() => SelectedStockAvgType);
        }
    }


    public void GetStockAvg()
    {
        model.DateStart = StartDate;
        model.DateEnd = EndDate;
        model.Ticker = Ticker;
        model.GetStockPrices();
        sa.StockPrices = model.StockPrices;
        sa.NDays = NDays;
        //sa.StockAvgType = SelectedStockAvgType;
        sa.GetStockAverage();
        StockAvgs.Clear();
        StockAvgs.AddRange(sa.StockAvgs);
        AddChart();

    }

    private void SetChartStyle()
    {
        cs = new StockChartStyle();
        cs.ChartCanvas = view.chartCanvas;
        cs.TextCanvas = view.textCanvas;
        cs.Title = string.Format("{0}: Stock Chart (Chart Type: {1})",
            Ticker, SelectedStockAvgType);
        SetAxes();
        cs.DateList = new List<DateTime>();
        foreach (var p in StockAvgs)
            cs.DateList.Add(p.Date);
        cs.GridlinePattern = LinePatternEnum.Dot;
        cs.GridlineColor = Brushes.Black;
        cs.AddTimeSeriesChartStyle(view.tbTitle, view.tbXLabel, view.tbYLabel);
    }

    private void SetAxes()
    {
        cs.XLabel = "Date";
        cs.YLabel = "Stock Price";

        cs.Xmin = -1;
        cs.Xmax = StockAvgs.Count;
        cs.XTick = (int)((cs.Xmax - cs.Xmin) / 5.01);

        double min = StockAvgs.Min(x => x.PriceAdj);
        double max = StockAvgs.Max(x => x.PriceAdj);
        if (SelectedStockAvgType == StockAvgTypeEnum.Zscore)
        {
            min = StockAvgs.Min(x => x.Zscore);
            max = StockAvgs.Max(x => x.Zscore);
            cs.YLabel = "Zscore";
        }
```

```
        double delta = (max - min) / 20.0;
        if (selectedStockAvgType != StockAvgTypeEnum.Zscore || max > 10.0)
        {
            cs.Ymin = (int)(min - delta);
            cs.Ymax = (int)(max + delta);
            cs.YTick = (int)((max - min) / 5.01);
        }
        else
        {
            cs.Ymin = Math.Round(min - delta, 2);
            cs.Ymax = Math.Round(max + delta, 2);
            cs.YTick = Math.Round((max - min) / 5.01, 2);
        }
    }

    private void SetLegend()
    {
        lg = new Legend();
        lg.IsLegend = true;
        lg.IsBorder = true;
        lg.LegendPosition = LegendPositionEnum.NorthWest;
        lg.AddLegend(view.chartCanvas, dc);
    }

    public void AddChart()
    {
        if (StockAvgs.Count <= 0)
            return;

        view = this.GetView() as StockAvgView;
        view.chartCanvas.Children.Clear();
        view.textCanvas.Children.RemoveRange(1,
            view.textCanvas.Children.Count - 1);
        SetChartStyle();
        dc.Clear();

        var ds = new LineSeries();
        ds.Symbols.BorderColor = Brushes.Blue;
        ds.Symbols.SymbolType = SymbolTypeEnum.OpenDiamond;
        ds.Symbols.SymbolSize = 4;
        ds.LineColor = Brushes.Blue;
        ds.LineThickness = 0;
        ds.SeriesName = "Price";
        for (int i = 0; i < StockAvgs.Count; i++)
            ds.LinePoints.Add(new Point(1.0 * i, StockAvgs[i].PriceAdj));
        dc.Add(ds);

        if (SelectedStockAvgType != StockAvgTypeEnum.AllAvgs)
        {
            ds = new LineSeries();
            ds.LineColor = Brushes.Red;
            ds.LineThickness = 1;
            ds.SeriesName = "Avg: " + SelectedStockAvgType.ToString().ToUpper();
            ds.LinePattern = LinePatternEnum.Solid;
            for (int i = 0; i < StockAvgs.Count; i++)
```

```
                    ds.LinePoints.Add(new Point(1.0 * i,
                    (double)StockAvgs[i].GetType().GetProperty(
                    SelectedStockAvgType.ToString()).GetValue(StockAvgs[i], null)));
                dc.Add(ds);

                // add zero line for zscore:
                if(SelectedStockAvgType == StockAvgTypeEnum.Zscore)
                {
                    ds = new LineSeries();
                    ds.LineColor = Brushes.Black;
                    ds.LineThickness = 1;
                    ds.SeriesName = "Zero line";
                    ds.LinePattern = LinePatternEnum.DashDot;
                    for (int i = 0; i < StockAvgs.Count; i++)
                        ds.LinePoints.Add(new Point(1.0 * i, 0));
                    dc.Add(ds);
                }
            }

            if(selectedStockAvgType == StockAvgTypeEnum.AllAvgs)
            {
                ds = new LineSeries();
                ds.LineColor = Brushes.Red;
                ds.LineThickness = 1;
                ds.SeriesName = "Avg: SMA";
                ds.LinePattern = LinePatternEnum.Solid;
                for (int i = 0; i < StockAvgs.Count; i++)
                    ds.LinePoints.Add(new Point(1.0 * i, StockAvgs[i].Sma));
                dc.Add(ds);

                ds = new LineSeries();
                ds.LineColor = Brushes.Green;
                ds.LineThickness = 1;
                ds.SeriesName = "Avg: WMA";
                ds.LinePattern = LinePatternEnum.Solid;
                for (int i = 0; i < StockAvgs.Count; i++)
                    ds.LinePoints.Add(new Point(1.0 * i, StockAvgs[i].Wma));
                dc.Add(ds);

                ds = new LineSeries();
                ds.LineColor = Brushes.Blue;
                ds.LineThickness = 1;
                ds.SeriesName = "Avg: EMA";
                ds.LinePattern = LinePatternEnum.Solid;
                for (int i = 0; i < StockAvgs.Count; i++)
                    ds.LinePoints.Add(new Point(1.0 * i, StockAvgs[i].Ema));
                dc.Add(ds);
            }

            cs.AddOriginalLines(dc);
            if (SelectedStockAvgType != StockAvgTypeEnum.Zscore)
                SetLegend();
        }
    }
}
```

Most of the code in this class is similar to that used in the preceding example. Here, we use the *LineSeries* to represent the stock average data. Running this example and selecting *Sma* from the *ComboBox* produce the results shown in Figure 6-9.

For comparison, I plotted both the stock's adjusted close price and its 15-day simple moving average in Figure 6-9.

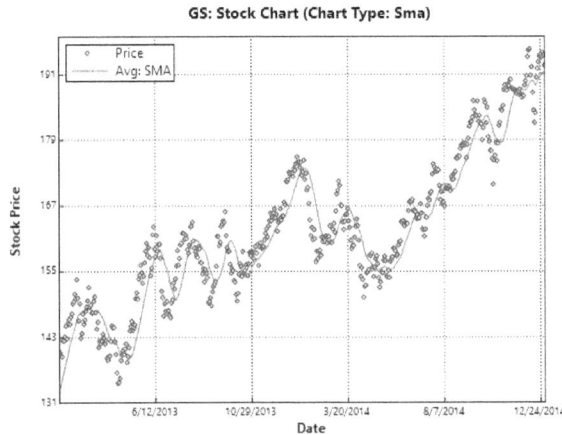

Figure 6-9. A SMA chart for Goldman Sachs.

Weighted Moving Averages

A weighted average is any average that has multiplying factors to give different weights to different data points. In technical analysis a weighted moving average (WMA) specifically means weights that decrease arithmetically. In an *n*-day WMA the latest day has weight *n*, the second latest *n* − 1, etc., down to zero:

$$WMA = \frac{np_0 + (n-1)p_{n-1} + \cdots \, 2 + p_{-n+1}}{n + (n-1) + \cdots} = \frac{2}{n(n+1)} \sum_{i=0}^{n-1} (n-i)p_{-i}$$

Note that when we calculate the WMA across successive values, the difference between the numerators of the WMA$_{+1}$ and WMA is $np_{+1} - p_0 - \cdots$. If we denote $p_0^{sum} = p_0 + p_{-1} + \cdots$, then we have

$$p_{+1}^{sum} = p_0^{sum} + p_{+1} - p_{-n+1}$$

$$Numerator_{+1} = Numerator_0 + np_{+1} - p_0^{sum}$$

$$WMA_{+1} = \frac{2}{n(n+1)} Numerator_{+1}$$

I have already presented the code implementation for WMA in the preceding section. Running the example, clicking the *Get Stock Avg* button, and selecting *Wma* from the *ComboBox* generates the output shown in Figure 6-10.

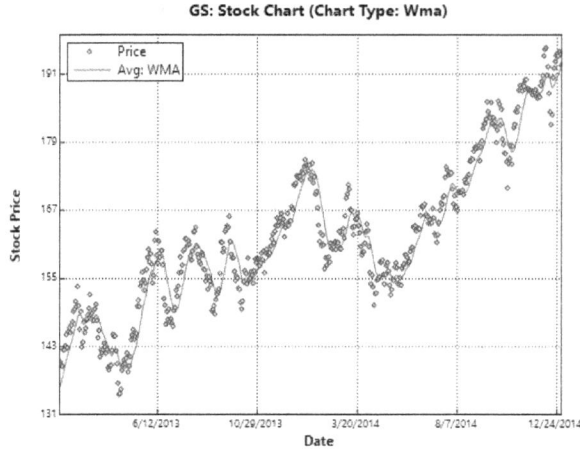

Figure 6-10. WMA chart for Goldman Sachs.

Exponential Moving Averages

One drawback of both simple and weighted moving averages is that they include data only for the number of periods the moving average covers. For example, a five-day simple or weighted moving average only uses five days' worth of data. Data prior to those five days are not included in the calculation of the moving average.

In some situations, however, the prior data is an important reflection of prices and should be included in a moving average calculation. You can achieve this by using an exponential moving average (EMA).

An EMA uses weight factors that decrease exponentially. The weight for each older data point decreases exponentially, giving much more importance to recent observations while not discarding older observations entirely.

The degree of weigh decrease is expressed as a constant smoothing factor α, which is a number between 0 and 1. α may be expressed as a percentage, so a smoothing factor of 10% is equivalent to $\alpha = 0.1$. Alternatively, α may be expressed in terms of n time periods, where $\alpha = 2/(n+1)$. For example, $n = 19$ is equivalent to $\alpha = 0.1$.

The observation at a time period t is designated Y_t, and the value of the EMA at any time period t is designated S_t. S_1 is undefined. S_2 may be initialized in a number of different ways, most commonly by setting S_2 to Y_1, though other techniques exist, such as setting S_2 to an average of the first 4 or 5 observations. The prominence of the S_2 initialization's effect on the resultant moving average depends on α; smaller α values make the choice of S_2 relatively more important than larger α values, since a higher α discounts older observations faster.

The formula for calculating the EMA at time periods $t \geq 2$ is

$$S_t = \alpha Y_{t-1} + (1-\alpha)S_{t-1}$$

This formula can also be expressed in technical analysis terms as follows, showing how the EMA steps towards the latest data point:

$$EMA_{today} = EMA_{yesterday} + \alpha(p_0 - EMA_{yesterday})$$

Where p_0 is the current price. Expanding out $EMA_{yesterday}$ each time results in the following power series, showing how the weighting factor on each data point p_1, p_2, etc., decreases exponentially:

$$EMA = \frac{p_{-1} + (1-\alpha)p_{-2} + (1-\alpha)^2 p_{-3} + \cdots}{1 + (1-\alpha) + (1-\alpha)^2 + \cdots} = \frac{\sum_{j}^{\infty} (1-\alpha)^j p_{-i-1}}{\sum_{i=0}^{\infty} (1-\alpha)^j} = \alpha \sum_{i=0}^{\infty} (1-\alpha)^j p_{-i-1}$$

Theoretically, this is an infinite sum, but because $1-\alpha$ is less than one, the terms become smaller and smaller, and can be ignored once they are small enough.

The n periods in an n-day EMA only specify the α factor. n is not a stopping point for the calculation in the way that it is in an SMA or WMA. The first n data points in an EMA represent about 86% of the total weight in the calculation. As an approximation, we set $\alpha \approx 2/(n+1)$.

I already presented the code implementation for EMA in the SMA section. Running the example, clicking the *Get Stock Avg* button, and selecting *Ema* from the *ComboBox* generates the output shown in Figure 6-11.

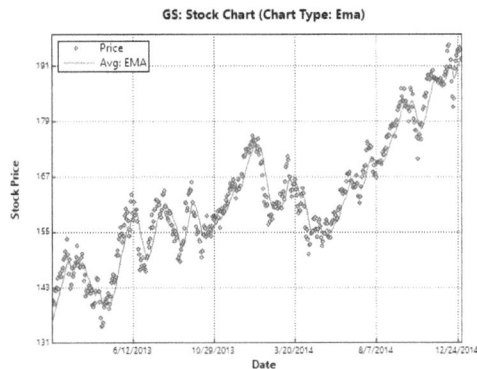

Figure 6-11. EMA chart for Goldman Sachs.

You can compare SMA, WMA, and EMA by plotting them on the same chart. Running the example, clicking the *Get Stock Avg* button, and selecting *AllAvgs* from the *ComboBox* generates the results shown in Figure 6-12.

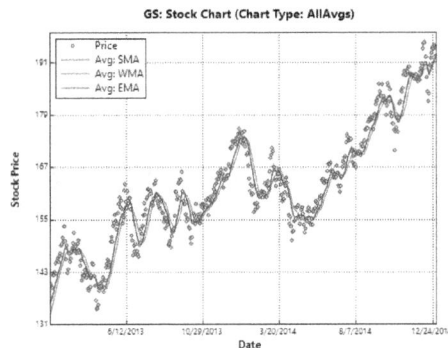

Figure 6-12. Comparing various stock averages for Goldman Sachs.

You can see from the figure that the WMA result almost overlaps with the EMA result. However, you can still tell the difference if you look at them closely. Figure 6-13 shows the results for a short period starting from 10/1/2014 to 12/31/2014.

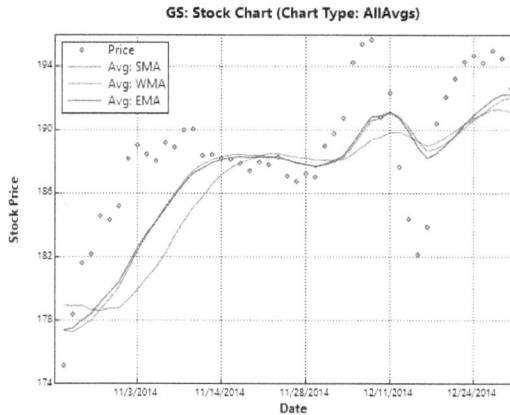

Figure 6-13. Stock averages for a short period.

Z Scores

In stock trading, if you want to compare a certain value of a time series for a particular stock to the value of other stocks for the same date, you can use a *z*-score that represents the distance between the score and the average normalized by the standard deviation. This is called a cross asset *z*-score. In this case, for each date, you will need to get the time series value for every security you are interested in, and then calculate the mean and the standard deviation of these values. You can then calculate the z-score using the following formula:

$$Z = (x - mean)/(standard\ deviation)$$

Here Z is the *z*-score for a stock price (or return), and x for a specific security at a particular day. The *mean* and *standard deviation* parameters are calculated using all of the securities you are interested in.

You can also calculate the *z*-score for a single security, which I call the time-series *z*-score. In this case, the mean and standard deviation parameters are calculated for that single security's price (or return) for a specified period. A negative *z*-score means that the price (or return) at that particular date is lower than its mean value over a prior period. A *z*-score value higher than 2 means that the price (or return) is 2 standard deviations above its average value over a prior period.

In order to calculate the *z*-score, you need to know the mean and standard deviation of the time series. The LINQ-to-Entity Framework has a built-in function for calculating the mean of an entity collection, but not one for standard deviation. Here, I will show you how to create a function for calculating the standard deviation using an extension method. Add a static class to the *Models* folder and name it *ModelHelper*. Add the following code snippet to this class:

```
using System;
using System.Collections.Generic;
using System.Linq;
using System.Text;
using System.Threading.Tasks;
```

```
using System.Windows;

namespace Chapter06.Models
{
    public static class ModelHelper
    {
        public static double StdDev<T>(this IEnumerable<T> list,
            Func<T, double> values)
        {
            var mean = 0.0;
            var stdDev = 0.0;
            var n = 0;

            n = 0;
            foreach (var value in list.Select(values))
            {
                n++;
                mean += value;
            }
            mean /= n;

            foreach (var value in list.Select(values))
            {
                stdDev += (value - mean) * (value - mean);
            }
            stdDev = Math.Sqrt(stdDev / (n - 1));
            return stdDev;
        }
    }
}
```

Here, I implement a generic *StdDev* extension method. This extension method has simplified calling syntax, and uses the *this* key word in its parameter list. Note that this extension method must be located in a static class. Now, you can use this method just like a built-in function.

I already presented the code implementation for the time series *z*-score in the SMA section. Here I will reproduce a code snippet from the implementation that shows how to use this extension method to calculate the standard deviation:

```
public void GetStockAverage()
{
    StockAvgs.Clear();
    var tmp = new List<StockPrice>();
    for (int i = NDays; i < StockPrices.Count; i++)
    {
        tmp.Clear();
        for (int j = i - NDays; j <= i; j++)
        {
            tmp.Add(StockPrices[j]);
        }
        double avg = tmp.Average(x => x.PriceAdj);
        double stdev = tmp.StdDev(x => x.PriceAdj);
        double zscore = (tmp[tmp.Count - 1].PriceAdj - avg) / stdev;
        StockAvgs.Add(new StockAverageData
        {
            Ticker = StockPrices[i].Ticker,
```

```
            Date = StockPrices[i].Date,
            PriceAdj = StockPrices[i].PriceAdj,
            Sma = avg,
            Wma = GetWma(tmp),
            Ema = GetEma(tmp),
            Zscore = zscore
        });
    }
}
```

The bolded code shows how the *StdDev* extension method is used in exactly the same way as the built-in *Average* method.

Now run the example, click the *Get Stock Avg* button, and select *Zscore* from the *ComboBox* to get the results of the time series *z-score*, as shown in Figure 6-14.

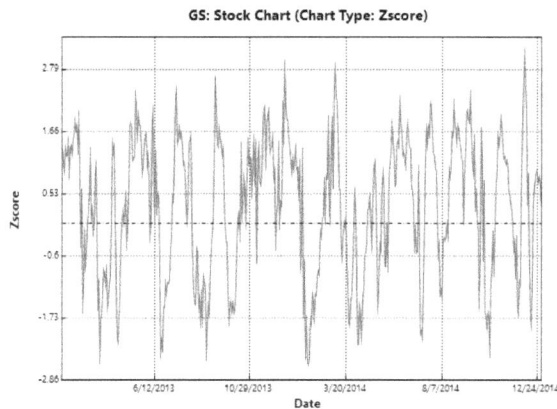

Figure 6-14. The time-series z-score for Goldman Sachs.

Note that I add a zero *z*-score line (the dash-dot line) for clarity. You can see from the figure that the *z*-score always oscillates around zero, and you can use this feature of the *z*-score to implement a trading strategy like the following:

$$Long\ Stock: Entry: when\ Zscore < -2$$
$$Exit: \quad when\ Zscore > 0$$
$$Short\ Stock: Entry: when\ Zscore > 2$$
$$Exit: \quad when\ Zscore < 0$$

You can optimize this strategy by changing entry (for example, one standard deviation) and exit points, as well as the period used to calculate the mean and standard deviation.

Linear Analysis

Linear analysis is a widely used statistical tool in finance and trading. In this section, I will discuss two linear analysis techniques: simple linear regression and principal component analysis (PCA). In statistics, simple linear regression is a least-squares estimator of a linear regression model with a single explanatory variable. In other words, simple linear regression fits a straight line through the set of n data points in a way that minimizes the sum of squared residuals of the model.

PCA is a statistical procedure that uses an orthogonal transformation to convert a set of observations of possibly correlated variables into a set of values of linear uncorrelated variables, called principal components. The first principal component has the largest possible variance. The principal components are orthogonal because they are the eigenvectors of the covariance matrix. I will discuss the simplest case, two-dimensional PCA.

Simple Linear Regression

Simple linear regression refers to the fact that the resultant variable is related to a single predictor variable. The slope of the fitted line is equal to the correlation between these two variables corrected by the ratio of the standard deviations of these variables.

You can construct a simple linear regression by fitting a line through a scatter plot of the prices for a pair of stocks. Suppose you have two stocks, x and y, which have n-day prices (x_0, y_0), (x_1, y_1),...(x_n, y_n). The linear function that describes x and y is:

$$y_i = a + bx_i + \varepsilon_i$$

The goal is to find the equation of the straight line

$$y = a + bx$$

which should provide a best fit for the data points. You can use the least-squares approach to achieve this goal. The least-squares technique minimizes the sum of squared residual of the linear regression model. You can get the parameters a (the intercept) and b (the slope) in the preceding equation from solving the following minimization problem:

$$\min_{a,b} \sum_{i=1}^{n} \epsilon_i^2 = \min_{a,b} \sum_{i=1}^{n} (y_i - a - bx_i)^2$$

Taking the derivative of the above equation relative to a and b and setting them to zero generates the following equations:

$$\sum_{i=1}^{n} (y_i - a - bx_i) = 0$$

$$\sum_{i=1}^{n} x_i(y_i - a - bx_i) = 0$$

Solving these equation gives

$$b = \frac{\overline{xy} - \bar{x}\bar{y}}{\overline{x^2} - \bar{x}^2}, \qquad a = \bar{y} - b\bar{x}$$

where $\bar{u}$ is the average value of the time series u_0, u_1,...u_n. We can now implement simple linear regression by adding a new static method to the *ModelHelper* class and naming it *GetLinearRegression*. Here is the code snippet for this method:

```
public static double[] GetLinearRegression(double[] xa, double[] ya)
{
```

```
double xm = xa.Average();
double ym = ya.Average();
double a1 = 0.0;
double a2 = 0.0;
for (int i = 0; i < xa.Length; i++)
{
    a1 += ya[i] * (xa[i] - xm);
    a2 += xa[i] * (xa[i] - xm);
}

//get coefficients a, b in y = a + b *x:
double a = 0.0;
double b = 0.0;
if (Math.Abs(a2) > 0)
    b = a1 / a2;
a = ym - b * xm;
return new double[] { a, b };
}
```

2D Principal Component Analysis

Principal component analysis, or PCA, is a mathematical procedure that intends to replace a number of correlated variables with a new set of linearly uncorrelated variables. It is a way of identifying patterns in data, and expressing the data in such a way as to highlight their similarities and differences. Since patterns in data are hard to find in data of high dimensions, PCA is a powerful tool for analyzing data.

The other main advantage of PCA is that once you have found these patterns in the data, you can compress the data by reducing the number of dimensions, without much loss of information.

In 2D, PCA is very simple to analyze. Suppose you have a collection of data points $(x_0, y_0), (x_1, y_1),...(x_n, y_n)$. In order for the PCA to work properly, you first need to subtract the mean from each data series. So, all the x values have $\bar{x}$ (the mean of the x values of all the data points) subtracted, and all the y values have $\bar{y}$ subtracted. The new data points correspond to a translation: $(x, y) \rightarrow (x - \bar{x}, y - \bar{y})$. In the new data space with the mean subtracted, the covariance matrix can be simply expressed in the form:

$$\sigma = \begin{pmatrix} \overline{x^2} & \overline{xy} \\ \overline{xy} & \overline{y^2} \end{pmatrix}, \quad \text{where: } \overline{x^2} = \frac{1}{n-1}\sum_{i=1}^{n} x_i x_i, \quad \overline{xy} = \frac{1}{n-1}\sum_{i=1}^{n} x_i y_i$$

The PCA components are just the eigenvectors of the covariance matrix. For a 2D covariance matrix, we can easily find the analytic solution for the eigenvalues and eigenvectors. The eigenvalues can be found by finding the roots of

$$\det \begin{pmatrix} a - \lambda & b \\ b & c - \lambda \end{pmatrix} = 0, \quad \text{with } a = \overline{x^2}, b = \overline{xy}, c = \overline{y^2}$$

This equation has two roots, which are:

$$\lambda_{\pm} = \frac{(a + c) \pm d}{2}, \quad d = \sqrt{(a - c)^2 + 4b^2}$$

Corresponding to each eigenvalue, λ_i, will be an eigenvector e_i that can be obtained by solving a set of linear equations. For the 2D case, we need to solve

$$\begin{pmatrix} a - \lambda & b \\ b & c - \lambda \end{pmatrix} \begin{pmatrix} x \\ y \end{pmatrix} = \begin{pmatrix} 0 \\ 0 \end{pmatrix}$$

The normalized eigenvectors can be written in the form:

$$\frac{1}{\sqrt{2d[d \pm (c - a)]}} \begin{pmatrix} \pm 2b \\ d \pm (c - a) \end{pmatrix}$$

Any non-zero multiple of these vectors is, of course, also an eigenvector. Please note that these eigenvectors are unit eigenvectors; i.e., their lengths are 1. This is very important for PCA. Usually, the eigenvector with the highest eigenvalue is the principal component of the data set. In the 2D PCA case, you always pick the eigenvector with the higher eigenvalue and neglect the eigenvector with the lower eigenvalue.

Now, we can implement 2D PCA. Add a new static method to the *ModelHelper* class and name it *GetPca*. Here is the code snippet for this method:

```
public static double[] GetPca(double[] xa, double[] ya)
{
    double sumx = 0.0;
    double sumy = 0.0;
    double sumxx = 0.0;
    double sumyy = 0.0;
    double sumxy = 0.0;
    int n = xa.Length;

    //substrate mean first:
    double ax = xa.Average();
    double ay = ya.Average();
    for (int i = 0; i < n; i++)
    {
        xa[i] = xa[i] - ax;
        ya[i] = ya[i] - ay;
    }

    for (int i = 0; i < n; i++)
    {
        sumx += xa[i];
        sumy += ya[i];
        sumxx += xa[i] * xa[i];
        sumyy += ya[i] * ya[i];
        sumxy += xa[i] * ya[i];
    }

    //variance and covariance
    double a1 = sumxx / (n - 1);
    double c1 = sumyy / (n - 1);
    double b1 = sumxy / (n - 1);

    //eigen values:
    double d = Math.Sqrt((a1 - c1) * (a1 - c1) + 4.0 * b1 * b1);
    double lp = 0.5 * (a1 + c1 + d);
    double lm = 0.5 * (a1 + c1 - d);

    //eigen vectors:
    double d1 = Math.Sqrt(2.0*d);
```

```
            double dp = Math.Sqrt(d+(c1-a1));
            double dm = Math.Sqrt(d-(c1-a1));
            double ap = 2.0 * b1 / d1 / dp;
            double bp = (d + (c1 - a1)) / d1 / dp;
            double am = -2.0 * b1 / d1 / dm;
            double bm = (d - (c1 - a1)) / d1 / dm;

            //choose pca vector:
            double lMax = Math.Max(lp, lm);
            double[] ab = new double[] { ap, bp };
            if (lMax == lm)
                ab = new double[] { am, bm };

            //get coefficients a, b in y = a + b *x:
            double a = 0.0;
            double b = 0.0;
            if (Math.Abs(ab[0]) > 0)
                b = ab[1] / ab[0];
            a = ay - b * ax;

            return new double[] { a, b };
        }
```

The detailed implementation in the above method is very clear: we first subtract the mean from the data set, then construct the covariance matrix. Next, we find the eigenvalues and eigenvectors of the covariance matrix, and choose the eigenvector with the higher eigenvalue. Finally, we relate the linear coefficients to the principal component of the eigenvectors.

Test Linear Regression and PCA

In the preceding sections, you learned how to implement simple linear regression and 2D PCA. Here, we can apply these linear analysis approaches to a pair of stocks. These analysis methods play an important role in pair-trading strategies.

Add a new class to the *ChartModel* folder and name it *StockAnalysis*. Here is the code of this class:

```
using System;
using System.Collections.Generic;
using System.Linq;
using Caliburn.Micro;
using Chapter06.Models.DataModel;

namespace Chapter06.Models.ChartModel
{
    public class StockAnalysis
    {
        public BindableCollection<PairStockPrice> PairStockPrices { get; set; }
        public BindableCollection<AnalysisData> StockAnalysisData { get; set; }

        public StockAnalysis()
        {
            PairStockPrices = new BindableCollection<PairStockPrice>();
            StockAnalysisData = new BindableCollection<AnalysisData>();
        }
```

```
public void GetLinearAnalysis()
{
    StockAnalysisData.Clear();
    int n = PairStockPrices.Count;
    double[] xa = new double[n];
    double[] ya = new double[n];
    for (int i = 0; i < n; i++)
    {
        xa[i] = PairStockPrices[i].Price1;
        ya[i] = PairStockPrices[i].Price2;
    }
    double[] abLr = ModelHelper.GetLinearRegression(xa, ya);
    double[] abPca = ModelHelper.GetPca(xa, ya);
    for (int i = 0; i < n; i++)
    {
        StockAnalysisData.Add(new AnalysisData
        {
            Date = PairStockPrices[i].Date,
            Price1 = PairStockPrices[i].Price1,
            Price2 = PairStockPrices[i].Price2,
            PriceLR = abLr[0] + abLr[1] * PairStockPrices[i].Price1,
            PricePCA = abPca[0] + abPca[1] * PairStockPrices[i].Price1
        });
    }
}


public class AnalysisData
{
    public DateTime Date { get; set; }
    public double Price1 { get; set; }
    public double Price2 { get; set; }
    public double PriceLR { get; set; }
    public double PricePCA { get; set; }
}
}
```

Here, we first define an *AnalysisData* entity class that represents the prices predicted by linear regression (*PriceLR*) and by PCA (*PricePCA*). Inside the *StockAnalysis* class, we create two collections: the *PairStockPrices* collection, which holds the stock data for a pair of stocks from the database, and the *StockAnalysisData* collection, which stores the analysis data from performing linear regression and PCA computations. Within the *GetLinearAnalysis* method, we first prepare input arrays from the stock data collection and then call the *GetLinearRegression* and *GetPca* methods implemented in the *ModelHelper* class to perform the linear analysis. Finally, we store the analysis results in the *StockAnalysisData* collection, which is ready to be used in our chart application.

Add a new *UserControl* to the *Views* folder and name it *LinearView*. Here is the XAML file for this view:

```
<UserControl x:Class="Chapter06.Views.LinearView"
        xmlns="http://schemas.microsoft.com/winfx/2006/xaml/presentation"
        xmlns:x="http://schemas.microsoft.com/winfx/2006/xaml"
        xmlns:mc="http://schemas.openxmlformats.org/markup-compatibility/2006"
        xmlns:d="http://schemas.microsoft.com/expression/blend/2008"
```

```
                    xmlns:cal="http://www.caliburnproject.org"
                    mc:Ignorable="d"
                    d:DesignHeight="400" d:DesignWidth="800">

    <Grid>
        <Grid.ColumnDefinitions>
            <ColumnDefinition Width="170"/>
            <ColumnDefinition Width="1*"/>
            <ColumnDefinition Width="2*"/>
        </Grid.ColumnDefinitions>
        <StackPanel Margin="5">
            <GroupBox Header="Linear Analysis" Margin="0 0 0 0">
                <StackPanel Margin="0 5 0 5">
                    <StackPanel Orientation="Horizontal">
                        <TextBlock Text="Ticker1" Width="60"/>
                        <TextBox x:Name="Ticker1" Width="80"/>
                    </StackPanel>
                    <StackPanel Orientation="Horizontal" Margin="0 5 0 0">
                        <TextBlock Text="Ticker2" Width="60"/>
                        <TextBox x:Name="Ticker2" Width="80"/>
                    </StackPanel>
                    <StackPanel Orientation="Horizontal" Margin="0 5 0 0">
                        <TextBlock Text="Start Date" Width="60"/>
                        <TextBox x:Name="StartDate" Width="80"/>
                    </StackPanel>
                    <StackPanel Orientation="Horizontal" Margin="0 5 0 0">
                        <TextBlock Text="End Date" Width="60"/>
                        <TextBox x:Name="EndDate" Width="80"/>
                    </StackPanel>
                    <Button x:Name="StartAnalysis" Content="Start Analysis"
                            Width="120" Margin="0 10 0 0"/>
                </StackPanel>
            </GroupBox>
            <Button x:Name="PlotRegression" Content="Plot Regression" Width="120"
                    Margin="0 30 0 0"/>
            <Button x:Name="PlotPca" Content="Plot PCA" Width="120"
                    Margin="0 10 0 0"/>
            <Button x:Name="PlotBoth" Content="Plot Both" Width="120"
                    Margin="0 10 0 0"/>
        </StackPanel>

        <DataGrid x:Name="StockAnalysisData" ColumnWidth="*" CanUserAddRows="False"
                  Grid.Column="1" FontSize="10"/>
        <Grid Name="grid1" Margin="10" Grid.Column="2">
            <Grid.ColumnDefinitions>
                <ColumnDefinition Width="Auto"/>
                <ColumnDefinition Name="column1" Width="*"/>
            </Grid.ColumnDefinitions>
            <Grid.RowDefinitions>
                <RowDefinition Height="Auto"/>
                <RowDefinition Name="row1" Height="*"/>
                <RowDefinition Height="Auto"/>
            </Grid.RowDefinitions>
            <TextBlock Margin="2" x:Name="tbTitle" Grid.Column="1" Grid.Row="0"
                       RenderTransformOrigin="0.5,0.5" FontSize="14" FontWeight="Bold"
```

```
                    HorizontalAlignment="Stretch" VerticalAlignment="Stretch"
                    TextAlignment="Center" Text="Title"/>
            <TextBlock Margin="2" x:Name="tbXLabel" Grid.Column="1" Grid.Row="2"
                    RenderTransformOrigin="0.5,0.5" TextAlignment="Center"
                    Text="X Axis" FontWeight="Bold"/>

            <TextBlock Margin="2" Name="tbYLabel" Grid.Column="0"
                    Grid.Row="1" FontWeight="Bold"
                    RenderTransformOrigin="0.5,0.5" TextAlignment="Center"
                    Text="Y Axis">
                <TextBlock.LayoutTransform>
                    <RotateTransform Angle="-90"/>
                </TextBlock.LayoutTransform>
            </TextBlock>

            <Grid  Margin="0,0,0,0" x:Name ="chartGrid" Grid.Column="1" Grid.Row="1"
                ClipToBounds="False" Background="Transparent"
                cal:Message.Attach="[Event SizeChanged]=[Action AddChart];
                [Event Loaded]=[Action AddChart]">

                <Canvas Margin="2" Name="textCanvas" Grid.Column="1"
                        Grid.Row="1" ClipToBounds="True"
                        Width="{Binding ElementName=chartGrid,Path=ActualWidth}"
                        Height="{Binding ElementName=chartGrid,Path=ActualHeight}">
                    <Canvas Name="chartCanvas" ClipToBounds="True">
                    </Canvas>
                </Canvas>
            </Grid>
        </Grid>
    </Grid>
</UserControl>
```

Here, we first set the parameters for a pair of stocks and then perform linear analysis. Finally, we plot the analysis results on a chart.

Add a new class to the *ViewModels* class and name it *LinearViewModel*. Here is the code for this class:

```
using System;
using System.Linq;
using Caliburn.Micro;
using System.Collections.ObjectModel;
using System.ComponentModel.Composition;
using System.Windows.Documents;
using System.Collections.Generic;
using System.Windows;
using Chapter06.Models;
using System.Windows.Media;
using System.Windows.Controls;
using Chapter06.Views;
using Chapter06.Models.ChartModel;
using Chapter06.Models.DataModel;

namespace Chapter06.ViewModels
{
    [Export(typeof(IScreen)), PartCreationPolicy(CreationPolicy.NonShared)]
    public class LinearViewModel : Screen
```

```
{
    private readonly IEventAggregator _events;
    [ImportingConstructor]
    public LinearViewModel(IEventAggregator events)
    {
        this._events = events;
        DisplayName = "04. Stock Analysis";
        StartDate = Convert.ToDateTime("1/1/2010");
        EndDate = Convert.ToDateTime("1/1/2015");
        Ticker1 = "GS";
        Ticker2 = "JPM";
        model = new Dal();
        sa = new StockAnalysis();
        dc = new BindableCollection<LineSeries>();
        StockAnalysisData = new BindableCollection<AnalysisData>();
    }

    private StockChartStyle cs;
    private BindableCollection<LineSeries> dc;
    private Dal model;
    private LinearView view;
    private Legend lg;
    private StockAnalysis sa;
    public BindableCollection<AnalysisData> StockAnalysisData { get; set; }

    private string plotType = "LinearRegression";

    private string ticker1;
    public string Ticker1
    {
        get { return ticker1; }
        set
        {
            ticker1 = value;
            NotifyOfPropertyChange(() => Ticker1);
        }
    }

    private string ticker2;
    public string Ticker2
    {
        get { return ticker2; }
        set
        {
            ticker2 = value;
            NotifyOfPropertyChange(() => Ticker2);
        }
    }

    private DateTime startDate;
    public DateTime StartDate
    {
        get { return startDate; }
        set
        {
```

```
            startDate = value;
            NotifyOfPropertyChange(() => StartDate);
        }
    }

    private DateTime endDate;
    public DateTime EndDate
    {
        get { return endDate; }
        set
        {
            endDate = value;
            NotifyOfPropertyChange(() => EndDate);
        }
    }

    public void StartAnalysis()
    {
        model.DateStart = StartDate;
        model.DateEnd = EndDate;
        model.Ticker1 = Ticker1;
        model.Ticker2 = Ticker2;
        model.GetPairStockPrices();
        sa.PairStockPrices = model.PairStockPrices;
        sa.GetLinearAnalysis();
        StockAnalysisData.Clear();
        StockAnalysisData.AddRange(sa.StockAnalysisData);
        AddChart();
    }

    public void PlotRegression()
    {
        if (StockAnalysisData.Count <= 0)
            return;

        plotType = "LinearRegression";
        SetChartStyle();

        dc.Clear();
        var ds = new LineSeries();
        ds.Symbols.BorderColor = Brushes.Blue;
        ds.Symbols.SymbolType = SymbolTypeEnum.OpenDiamond;
        ds.Symbols.SymbolSize = 4;
        ds.LineThickness = 0;
        ds.SeriesName = "Orig Data";
        foreach (var p in StockAnalysisData)
            ds.LinePoints.Add(new Point(p.Price1, p.Price2));
        dc.Add(ds);

        ds = new LineSeries();
        ds.LineThickness = 1;
        ds.LineColor = Brushes.Red;
        ds.SeriesName = "LinearRegr";
        foreach (var p in StockAnalysisData)
            ds.LinePoints.Add(new Point(p.Price1, p.PriceLR));
```

```
        dc.Add(ds);
        cs.AddOriginalLines(dc);
        SetLegend();
    }

    public void PlotPca()
    {
        if (StockAnalysisData.Count <= 0)
            return;

        plotType = "PCA";
        SetChartStyle();

        dc.Clear();
        var ds = new LineSeries();
        ds.Symbols.BorderColor = Brushes.Blue;
        ds.Symbols.SymbolType = SymbolTypeEnum.OpenDiamond;
        ds.Symbols.SymbolSize = 4;
        ds.LineThickness = 0;
        ds.SeriesName = "Orig Data";
        foreach (var p in StockAnalysisData)
            ds.LinePoints.Add(new Point(p.Price1, p.Price2));
        dc.Add(ds);

        ds = new LineSeries();
        ds.LineThickness = 1;
        ds.LineColor = Brushes.Red;
        ds.SeriesName = "LinearPca";
        foreach (var p in StockAnalysisData)
            ds.LinePoints.Add(new Point(p.Price1, p.PricePCA));
        dc.Add(ds);
        cs.AddOriginalLines(dc);
        SetLegend();
    }

    public void PlotBoth()
    {
        if (StockAnalysisData.Count <= 0)
            return;

        plotType = "Both";
        SetChartStyle();

        dc.Clear();
        var ds = new LineSeries();
        ds.Symbols.BorderColor = Brushes.Blue;
        ds.Symbols.SymbolType = SymbolTypeEnum.OpenDiamond;
        ds.Symbols.SymbolSize = 4;
        ds.LineThickness = 0;
        ds.SeriesName = "Orig Data";
        foreach (var p in StockAnalysisData)
            ds.LinePoints.Add(new Point(p.Price1, p.Price2));
        dc.Add(ds);

        ds = new LineSeries();
```

```
    ds.LineThickness = 1;
    ds.LineColor = Brushes.Red;
    ds.SeriesName = "LinearRegr";
    foreach (var p in StockAnalysisData)
        ds.LinePoints.Add(new Point(p.Price1, p.PriceLR));
    dc.Add(ds);

    ds = new LineSeries();
    ds.LineThickness = 1;
    ds.LineColor = Brushes.DarkGreen;
    ds.SeriesName = "LinearPca";
    foreach (var p in StockAnalysisData)
        ds.LinePoints.Add(new Point(p.Price1, p.PricePCA));
    dc.Add(ds);
    cs.AddOriginalLines(dc);
    SetLegend();
}

public void AddChart()
{
    if (StockAnalysisData.Count <= 0)
        return;

    if (plotType == "LinearRegression")
        PlotRegression();
    else if (plotType == "PCA")
        PlotPca();
    else if (plotType == "Both")
        PlotBoth();
}

private void SetChartStyle()
{
    view = this.GetView() as LinearView;
    view.chartCanvas.Children.Clear();
    view.textCanvas.Children.RemoveRange(1,
        view.textCanvas.Children.Count - 1);

    cs = new StockChartStyle();
    cs.ChartCanvas = view.chartCanvas;
    cs.TextCanvas = view.textCanvas;
    SetAxes();
    cs.GridlinePattern = LinePatternEnum.Dot;
    cs.GridlineColor = Brushes.Black;
    cs.AddChartStyle(view.tbTitle, view.tbXLabel, view.tbYLabel);
}

private void SetAxes()
{
    if(plotType == "LinearRegression")
        cs.Title = string.Format("Linear Regr: ({0} ~ {1})",
                    Ticker2, Ticker1);
    else if(plotType == "PCA")
        cs.Title = string.Format("PCA: ({0} ~ {1})", Ticker2, Ticker1);
    else if(plotType == "Both")
```

```
            cs.Title = string.Format("Linear Regr and PCA: ({0} ~ {1})",
                        Ticker2, Ticker1);

        cs.XLabel = Ticker1 + ": Price";
        cs.YLabel = Ticker2 + ": Price";

        double min = StockAnalysisData.Min(x => x.Price1);
        double max = StockAnalysisData.Max(x => x.Price1);
        double delta = (max - min) / 20.0;
        cs.Xmin = (int)(min - delta);
        cs.Xmax = (int)(max + delta);
        cs.XTick = (int)((max - min) / 5.01);

        min = StockAnalysisData.Min(x => x.Price2);
        max = StockAnalysisData.Max(x => x.Price2);
        delta = (max - min) / 20.0;
        cs.Ymin = (int)(min - delta);
        cs.Ymax = (int)(max + delta);
        cs.YTick = (int)((max - min) / 5.01);
    }

    private void SetLegend()
    {
        lg = new Legend();
        lg.IsLegend = true;
        lg.IsBorder = true;
        lg.LegendPosition = LegendPositionEnum.NorthWest;
        lg.AddLegend(view.chartCanvas, dc);
    }
  }
}
```

The code for this class is very similar to that used in the previous example. Running this example and clicking the *Start Analysis* button gets the default linear regression results for the stock pair JPM and GS, as shown in Figure 6-15.

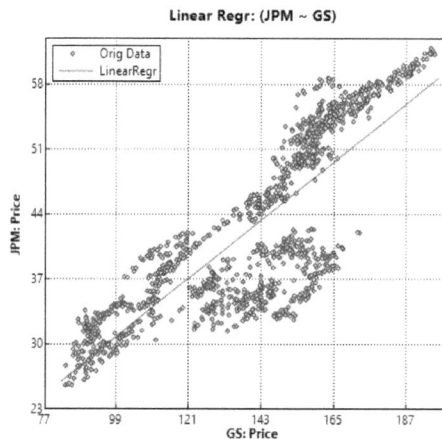

Figure 6-15. A linear regression for JPM and GS.

Unlike a moving average, the linear regression does not exhibit as much delay. Since linear regression fits a straight line to the data points rather than simply averaging the data, the linear regression line becomes more responsive to the changes in prices. When prices are persistently higher or lower than the forecasted price, you can typically expect them to return to a more realistic level. The indicator based on linear regression shows where prices should be trading on a statistical basis and any excessive deviation from the regression line is likely to be short-lived. In practice, you should construct an effective z-score based on the linear regression, and this z-score should provide you the trading signals.

Now click the *Plot PCA* button. You will get the PCA results shown in Figure 6-16.

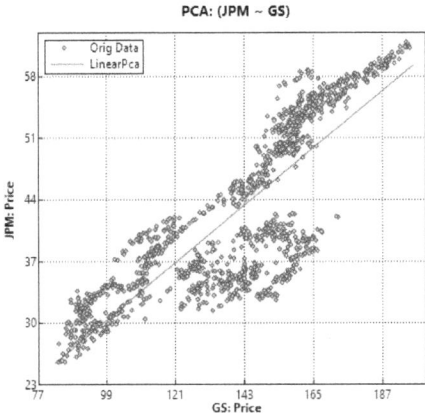

Figure 6-16. PCA results for JPM and GS.

When you compare the PCA results of this figure with the linear regression results in Figure 6-15, you will find that they are very similar. You can plot both results on the same chart by clicking the *Plot Both* button, as shown in Figure 6-17. You can see from Figure 6-17 that the results from linear regression are indeed very similar to those from PCA, which is due to the high correlation between these two stocks.

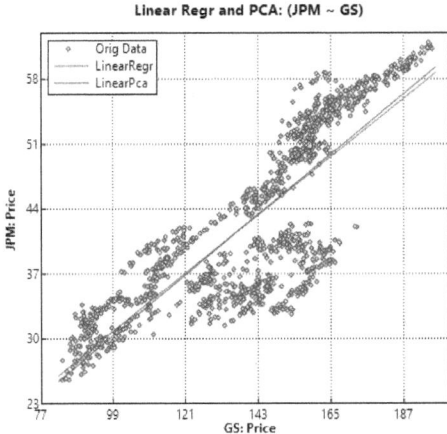

Figure 6-17. Linear regression and PCA results for JPM and GS.

If two stocks have low correlation, the difference between the linear regression and PCA will become significant. Consider two new stocks, INTC and IBM. Clicking the *Plot Both* button for this pair of stocks will get the results shown in Figure 6-18.

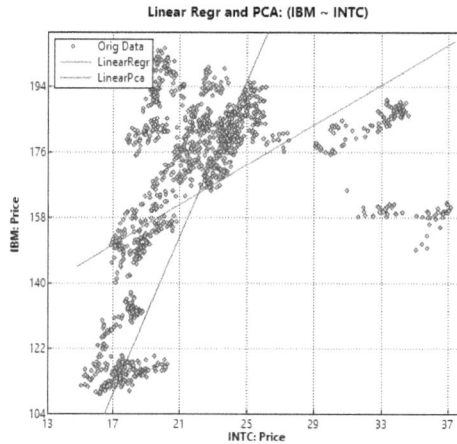

Figure 6-18. Linear regression and PCA results for IBM and INTC.

As you compare the results from linear regression and PCA, you may still wonder what exactly the fundamental difference is between the two. First, I should point out that the linear regression is not symmetric between $y \sim x$ and $x \sim y$. You can see clearly from Figure 6-19 that the linear regression of JPM ~ GS (or $y \sim x$) is not the same as that of GS ~ JPM (or $x \sim y$). The reason for this asymmetry is that the linear regression of $y \sim x$ minimizes error perpendicular to the independent axis (vertical green lines in Figure 6-19). If you want to regress $x \sim y$, it would minimize error perpendicular to the Y-axis (horizontal green lines in Figure 6-19). In general, these two regressions gives different results.

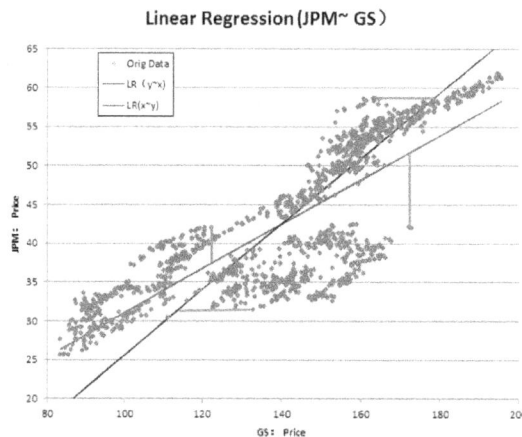

Figure 6-19. Linear regression (y ~ x) vs (x ~ y) for JPM and GS.

On the other hand, PCA effectively minimizes error orthogonal to the principal component axis, as shown in Figure 6-20 (green lines). So PCA results are always symmetric between $(y \sim x)$ and $(x \sim y)$.

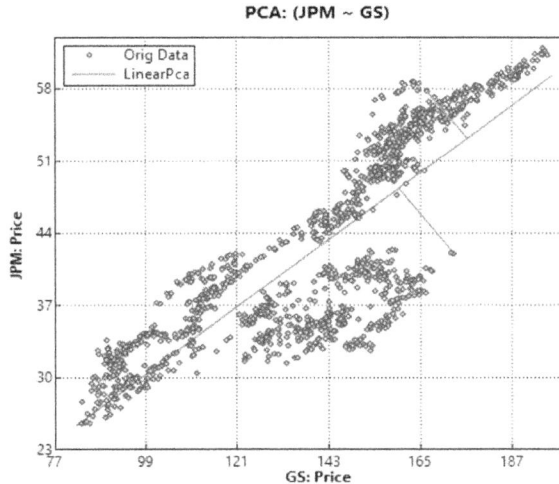

Figure 6-20. PCA for JPM and GS.

Retrieving Chart Data

In some situations, you may want to retrieve data values directly from a chart. You can achieve this interactively using mouse events. Here, I will show you how to retrieve data from a 2D chart and display the result directly on the screen.

Add a new *UserControl* to the *Views* folder and name it *RetrieveDataView*. Here is the XAML file for this view:

```
<UserControl x:Class="Chapter06.Views.RetrieveDataView"
            xmlns="http://schemas.microsoft.com/winfx/2006/xaml/presentation"
            xmlns:x="http://schemas.microsoft.com/winfx/2006/xaml"
            xmlns:mc="http://schemas.openxmlformats.org/markup-compatibility/2006"
            xmlns:d="http://schemas.microsoft.com/expression/blend/2008"
            xmlns:cal="http://www.caliburnproject.org"
            mc:Ignorable="d"
            d:DesignHeight="400" d:DesignWidth="800">

    <Grid>
        <Grid.ColumnDefinitions>
            <ColumnDefinition Width="170"/>
            <ColumnDefinition Width="1*"/>
            <ColumnDefinition Width="2*"/>
        </Grid.ColumnDefinitions>
        <StackPanel Margin="5">
            <GroupBox Header="Get Stock Avg" Margin="0 0 0 0">
                <StackPanel Margin="0 5 0 5">
                    <StackPanel Orientation="Horizontal">
                        <TextBlock Text="Ticker" Width="60"/>
                        <TextBox x:Name="Ticker" Width="80"/>
                    </StackPanel>
                    <StackPanel Orientation="Horizontal" Margin="0 5 0 0">
                        <TextBlock Text="Start Date" Width="60"/>
```

```
                        <TextBox x:Name="StartDate" Width="80"/>
                    </StackPanel>
                    <StackPanel Orientation="Horizontal" Margin="0 5 0 0">
                        <TextBlock Text="End Date" Width="60"/>
                        <TextBox x:Name="EndDate" Width="80"/>
                    </StackPanel>
                    <StackPanel Orientation="Horizontal" Margin="0 5 0 0">
                        <TextBlock Text="NDays" Width="60"/>
                        <TextBox x:Name="NDays" Width="80"/>
                    </StackPanel>
                    <Button x:Name="GetStockAvg" Content="Get Stock Avg"
                            Width="120" Margin="0 10 0 0"/>
                </StackPanel>
            </GroupBox>
            <TextBlock Text="Choose Stock Avg Type:" Margin="0 20 0 0"/>
            <ComboBox x:Name="StockAvgType" Width="150" Margin="0 5 0 0"
                    HorizontalAlignment="Left" cal:Message.Attach=
                    "[Event SelectionChanged]=[Action GetStockAvg]"/>
        </StackPanel>

    <DataGrid x:Name="StockAvgs" ColumnWidth="Auto" CanUserAddRows="False"
            Grid.Column="1" FontSize="10" Background="Transparent"/>
    <Grid Name="grid1" Margin="10" Grid.Column="2">
        <Grid.ColumnDefinitions>
            <ColumnDefinition Width="Auto"/>
            <ColumnDefinition Name="column1" Width="*"/>
        </Grid.ColumnDefinitions>
        <Grid.RowDefinitions>
            <RowDefinition Height="Auto"/>
            <RowDefinition Name="row1" Height="*"/>
            <RowDefinition Height="Auto"/>
            <RowDefinition Height="Auto"/>
        </Grid.RowDefinitions>
        <TextBlock Margin="2" x:Name="tbTitle" Grid.Column="1" Grid.Row="0"
                RenderTransformOrigin="0.5,0.5" FontSize="14" FontWeight="Bold"
                HorizontalAlignment="Stretch" VerticalAlignment="Stretch"
                TextAlignment="Center" Text="Title"/>
        <TextBlock Margin="2" x:Name="tbXLabel" Grid.Column="1" Grid.Row="2"
                RenderTransformOrigin="0.5,0.5" TextAlignment="Center"
                Text="X Axis" FontWeight="Bold"/>
        <StackPanel x:Name="resultPanel" Orientation="Horizontal"
                Grid.Column="1" Grid.Row="3" HorizontalAlignment="Right"/>

        <TextBlock Margin="2" Name="tbYLabel" Grid.Column="0" Grid.Row="1"
                FontWeight="Bold" RenderTransformOrigin="0.5,0.5"
                TextAlignment="Center" Text="Y Axis">
            <TextBlock.LayoutTransform>
                <RotateTransform Angle="-90"/>
            </TextBlock.LayoutTransform>
        </TextBlock>

        <Grid  Margin="0,0,0,0" x:Name ="chartGrid" Grid.Column="1" Grid.Row="1"
            ClipToBounds="False" Background="Transparent"
            cal:Message.Attach="[Event SizeChanged]=[Action AddChart];
          [Event Loaded]=[Action AddChart]">
```

```xml
            <Canvas Margin="2" Name="textCanvas" Grid.Column="1" Grid.Row="1"
                    ClipToBounds="True" Width="{Binding ElementName=chartGrid,
                    Path=ActualWidth}" Height="{Binding
                    ElementName=chartGrid,Path=ActualHeight}">
                <Canvas Name="chartCanvas" ClipToBounds="True"
                        Background="Transparent"
                        cal:Message.Attach="[Event MouseEnter]=
                        [Action MouseEnterEvent($source, $eventArgs)];
                        [Event MouseLeave]=[Action MouseLeaveEvent($source,
                        $eventArgs)];
                        [Event MouseMove]=[Action MouseMoveEvent($source,
                        $eventArgs)]">
                </Canvas>
            </Canvas>
        </Grid>
      </Grid>
    </Grid>
</UserControl>
```

This XAML file is similar to that used in the preceding example, except for the bolded code, in which I add a *StackPanel* control called *resultPanel* to display results from the mouse movement. I also attach three mouse events to the *chartCanvas*: *MouseEnter*, *MouseMove*, and *MouseLeave*, which will setup mouse interaction with the chart.

Add a new class to the *ViewModels* folder and name it *RetrieveDataViewModel*. Here is the code for this class:

```csharp
using System;
using System.Linq;
using Caliburn.Micro;
using System.Collections.ObjectModel;
using System.ComponentModel.Composition;
using System.Windows.Documents;
using System.Collections.Generic;
using System.Windows;
using Chapter06.Models;
using System.Windows.Media;
using System.Windows.Controls;
using Chapter06.Views;
using Chapter06.Models.ChartModel;
using Chapter06.Models.DataModel;
using System.Windows.Shapes;
using System.Windows.Input;

namespace Chapter06.ViewModels
{
    [Export(typeof(IScreen)), PartCreationPolicy(CreationPolicy.NonShared)]
    public class RetrieveDataViewModel : Screen
    {
        private readonly IEventAggregator _events;
        [ImportingConstructor]
        public RetrieveDataViewModel(IEventAggregator events)
        {
            this._events = events;
            DisplayName = "05. Retrieve Data";
            StockAvgs = new BindableCollection<StockAverageData>();
```

```
        StartDate = Convert.ToDateTime("1/1/2013");
        EndDate = Convert.ToDateTime("1/1/2015");
        Ticker = "GS";
        NDays = 15;
        model = new Dal();
        sa = new StockAverage();
        dc = new BindableCollection<LineSeries>();
    }
    private StockChartStyle cs;
    private BindableCollection<LineSeries> dc;
    private Dal model;
    private RetrieveDataView view;
    private Legend lg;
    private StockAverage sa;

    public BindableCollection<StockAverageData> StockAvgs { get; set; }

    private string ticker;
    public string Ticker
    {
        get { return ticker; }
        set
        {
            ticker = value;
            NotifyOfPropertyChange(() => Ticker);
        }
    }

    private DateTime startDate;
    public DateTime StartDate
    {
        get { return startDate; }
        set
        {
            startDate = value;
            NotifyOfPropertyChange(() => StartDate);
        }
    }

    private DateTime endDate;
    public DateTime EndDate
    {
        get { return endDate; }
        set
        {
            endDate = value;
            NotifyOfPropertyChange(() => EndDate);
        }
    }

    private int nDays;
    public int NDays
    {
        get { return nDays; }
        set
```

```
    {
        nDays = value;
        NotifyOfPropertyChange(() => NDays);
    }
}

private IEnumerable<StockAvgTypeEnum> stockAvgType;
public IEnumerable<StockAvgTypeEnum> StockAvgType
{
    get { return Enum.GetValues(typeof(StockAvgTypeEnum)).
        Cast<StockAvgTypeEnum>(); }
    set
    {
        stockAvgType = value;
        NotifyOfPropertyChange(() => StockAvgType);
    }
}

private StockAvgTypeEnum selectedStockAvgType = StockAvgTypeEnum.Sma;
public StockAvgTypeEnum SelectedStockAvgType
{
    get { return selectedStockAvgType; }
    set
    {
        selectedStockAvgType = value;
        NotifyOfPropertyChange(() => SelectedStockAvgType);
    }
}


public void GetStockAvg()
{
    model.DateStart = StartDate;
    model.DateEnd = EndDate;
    model.Ticker = Ticker;
    model.GetStockPrices();
    sa.StockPrices = model.StockPrices;
    sa.NDays = NDays;
    sa.GetStockAverage();
    StockAvgs.Clear();
    StockAvgs.AddRange(sa.StockAvgs);
    AddChart();
}

private void SetChartStyle()
{
    cs = new StockChartStyle();
    cs.ChartCanvas = view.chartCanvas;
    cs.TextCanvas = view.textCanvas;
    cs.Title = string.Format("{0}: Stock Chart (Chart Type: {1})",
        Ticker, SelectedStockAvgType);
    SetAxes();
    cs.DateList = new List<DateTime>();
    foreach (var p in StockAvgs)
        cs.DateList.Add(p.Date);
```

```
        cs.GridlinePattern = LinePatternEnum.Dot;
        cs.GridlineColor = Brushes.Black;
        cs.AddTimeSeriesChartStyle(view.tbTitle, view.tbXLabel, view.tbYLabel);
        isXDateTimeAxis = true;
    }

    private void SetAxes()
    {
        cs.XLabel = "Date";
        cs.YLabel = "Stock Price";

        cs.Xmin = -1;
        cs.Xmax = StockAvgs.Count;
        cs.XTick = (int)((cs.Xmax - cs.Xmin) / 5.01);

        double min = StockAvgs.Min(x => x.PriceAdj);
        double max = StockAvgs.Max(x => x.PriceAdj);
        if (SelectedStockAvgType == StockAvgTypeEnum.Zscore)
        {
            min = StockAvgs.Min(x => x.Zscore);
            max = StockAvgs.Max(x => x.Zscore);
            cs.YLabel = "Zscore";
        }
        double delta = (max - min) / 20.0;
        if (selectedStockAvgType != StockAvgTypeEnum.Zscore || max > 10.0)
        {
            cs.Ymin = (int)(min - delta);
            cs.Ymax = (int)(max + delta);
            cs.YTick = (int)((max - min) / 5.01);
        }
        else
        {
            cs.Ymin = Math.Round(min - delta, 2);
            cs.Ymax = Math.Round(max + delta, 2);
            cs.YTick = Math.Round((max - min) / 5.01, 2);
        }
    }

    private void SetLegend()
    {
        lg = new Legend();
        lg.IsLegend = true;
        lg.IsBorder = true;
        lg.LegendPosition = LegendPositionEnum.NorthWest;
        lg.AddLegend(view.chartCanvas, dc);
    }

    public void AddChart()
    {
        if (StockAvgs.Count <= 0)
            return;

        view = this.GetView() as RetrieveDataView;
        view.chartCanvas.Children.Clear();
        view.textCanvas.Children.RemoveRange(1,
```

```
    view.textCanvas.Children.Count - 1);
SetChartStyle();
dc.Clear();

var ds = new LineSeries();
ds.Symbols.BorderColor = Brushes.Blue;
ds.Symbols.SymbolType = SymbolTypeEnum.OpenDiamond;
ds.Symbols.SymbolSize = 4;
ds.LineColor = Brushes.Blue;
ds.LineThickness = 0;
ds.SeriesName = "Price";
for (int i = 0; i < StockAvgs.Count; i++)
    ds.LinePoints.Add(new Point(1.0 * i, StockAvgs[i].PriceAdj));
dc.Add(ds);

if (SelectedStockAvgType != StockAvgTypeEnum.AllAvgs)
{
    ds = new LineSeries();
    ds.LineColor = Brushes.Red;
    ds.LineThickness = 1;
    ds.SeriesName = "Avg: " + SelectedStockAvgType.ToString().ToUpper();
    ds.LinePattern = LinePatternEnum.Solid;
    for (int i = 0; i < StockAvgs.Count; i++)
        ds.LinePoints.Add(new Point(1.0 * i,
        (double)StockAvgs[i].GetType().GetProperty(
        SelectedStockAvgType.ToString()).GetValue(StockAvgs[i], null)));
    dc.Add(ds);

    // add zero line for zscore:
    if (SelectedStockAvgType == StockAvgTypeEnum.Zscore)
    {
        ds = new LineSeries();
        ds.LineColor = Brushes.Black;
        ds.LineThickness = 1;
        ds.SeriesName = "Zero line";
        ds.LinePattern = LinePatternEnum.DashDot;
        for (int i = 0; i < StockAvgs.Count; i++)
            ds.LinePoints.Add(new Point(1.0 * i, 0));
        dc.Add(ds);
    }
}

if (selectedStockAvgType == StockAvgTypeEnum.AllAvgs)
{
    ds = new LineSeries();
    ds.LineColor = Brushes.Red;
    ds.LineThickness = 1;
    ds.SeriesName = "Avg: SMA";
    ds.LinePattern = LinePatternEnum.Solid;
    for (int i = 0; i < StockAvgs.Count; i++)
        ds.LinePoints.Add(new Point(1.0 * i, StockAvgs[i].Sma));
    dc.Add(ds);

    ds = new LineSeries();
    ds.LineColor = Brushes.Green;
```

```
                    ds.LineThickness = 1;
                    ds.SeriesName = "Avg: WMA";
                    ds.LinePattern = LinePatternEnum.Solid;
                    for (int i = 0; i < StockAvgs.Count; i++)
                        ds.LinePoints.Add(new Point(1.0 * i, StockAvgs[i].Wma));
                    dc.Add(ds);

                    ds = new LineSeries();
                    ds.LineColor = Brushes.Black;
                    ds.LineThickness = 1;
                    ds.SeriesName = "Avg: EMA";
                    ds.LinePattern = LinePatternEnum.Solid;
                    for (int i = 0; i < StockAvgs.Count; i++)
                        ds.LinePoints.Add(new Point(1.0 * i, StockAvgs[i].Ema));
                    dc.Add(ds);
                }

                cs.AddOriginalLines(dc);
                if (SelectedStockAvgType != StockAvgTypeEnum.Zscore)
                    SetLegend();
                AddInteractive();
            }

        private Point startPoint = new Point();
        private Point endPoint = new Point();
        private List<Ellipse> circles = new List<Ellipse>();
        private List<Ellipse> labelCircles = new List<Ellipse>();
        private List<TextBlock> labelResults = new List<TextBlock>();
        private TextBlock xCoordinate = new TextBlock();
        private bool isXDateTimeAxis = false;
        private Line mouseLine = new Line();

        private void AddInteractive()
        {
            circles.Clear();
            labelCircles.Clear();
            labelResults.Clear();
            view.resultPanel.Children.Clear();

            xCoordinate.Text = "X Value";
            xCoordinate.FontSize = 10;
            xCoordinate.Margin = new Thickness(2);
            view.resultPanel.Children.Add(xCoordinate);

            mouseLine.Stroke = Brushes.LightGreen;
            mouseLine.StrokeThickness = 1;
            mouseLine.Visibility = Visibility.Hidden;
            view.chartCanvas.Children.Add(mouseLine);

            foreach (var ds in dc)
                AddMarks(ds);

            for (int i = 0; i < dc.Count; i++)
            {
                view.chartCanvas.Children.Add(circles[i]);
```

```
            Canvas.SetTop(circles[i], 0);
            Canvas.SetLeft(circles[i], 0);
            labelResults[i].Text = string.Format("Y{0} Value", i);
            view.resultPanel.Children.Add(labelCircles[i]);
            view.resultPanel.Children.Add(labelResults[i]);
        }
}

private void AddMarks(LineSeries ds)
{
    Ellipse circle = new Ellipse();
    circle.Width = 8;
    circle.Height = 8;
    circle.Margin = new Thickness(2);
    circle.Fill = ds.LineColor;
    labelCircles.Add(circle);

    TextBlock tb = new TextBlock();
    tb.Text = "Y Value";
    tb.FontSize = 10;
    tb.Margin = new Thickness(2);
    labelResults.Add(tb);

    circle = new Ellipse();
    circle.Width = 8;
    circle.Height = 8;
    circle.Fill = ds.LineColor;
    circle.Visibility = Visibility.Hidden;
    circles.Add(circle);
}



private double GetInterpolatedYValue(LineSeries data, double x)
{
    double result = double.NaN;
    for (int i = 1; i < data.LinePoints.Count; i++)
    {
        double x1 = data.LinePoints[i - 1].X;
        double x2 = data.LinePoints[i].X;
        if (x >= x1 && x < x2)
        {
            double y1 = data.LinePoints[i - 1].Y;
            double y2 = data.LinePoints[i].Y;
            result = y1 + (y2 - y1) * (x - x1) / (x2 - x1);
        }
    }
    return result;
}


public void MouseEnterEvent(object sender, MouseEventArgs e)
{
    if (!view.chartCanvas.IsMouseCaptured)
    {
```

```
        startPoint = e.GetPosition(view.chartCanvas);
        view.chartCanvas.Cursor = Cursors.Cross;
        view.chartCanvas.CaptureMouse();
        for (int i = 0; i < dc.Count; i++)
        {
            double x = startPoint.X;
            double y = GetInterpolatedYValue(dc[i], x);
            Canvas.SetLeft(circles[i], x - circles[i].Width / 2);
            Canvas.SetTop(circles[i], y - circles[i].Height / 2);
            mouseLine.X1 = x;
            mouseLine.Y1 = 0;
            mouseLine.X2 = x;
            mouseLine.Y2 = view.chartCanvas.Height;
        }
    }
}

public void MouseMoveEvent(object sender, MouseEventArgs e)
{
    if (view.chartCanvas.IsMouseCaptured)
    {
        bool isInside = false;
        VisualTreeHelper.HitTest(view.chartCanvas,
            h =>
            {
                if (h == view.chartCanvas)
                {
                    isInside = true;
                }

                return HitTestFilterBehavior.Stop;
            },
            ht => HitTestResultBehavior.Stop, new
                PointHitTestParameters(e.GetPosition(view.chartCanvas)));

        if (isInside)
        {
            endPoint = e.GetPosition(view.chartCanvas);
            if (Math.Abs(endPoint.X - startPoint.X) >
                    SystemParameters.MinimumHorizontalDragDistance &&
                    Math.Abs(endPoint.Y - startPoint.Y) >
                    SystemParameters.MinimumVerticalDragDistance)
            {
                double x, y;
                TranslateTransform tt = new TranslateTransform();
                tt.X = endPoint.X - startPoint.X;
                tt.Y = 0;
                mouseLine.RenderTransform = tt;
                mouseLine.Visibility = Visibility.Visible;

                for (int i = 0; i < dc.Count; i++)
                {
                    try
                    {
                        var tt1 = new TranslateTransform();
```

```
                            tt1.X = endPoint.X - startPoint.X;
                            tt1.Y = GetInterpolatedYValue(dc[i], endPoint.X)
                                - GetInterpolatedYValue(dc[i], startPoint.X);
                            circles[i].RenderTransform = tt1;
                            circles[i].Visibility = Visibility.Visible;

                            x = endPoint.X;
                            x = cs.Xmin + x * (cs.Xmax - cs.Xmin) /
                                view.chartCanvas.Width;
                            y = GetInterpolatedYValue(dc[i], endPoint.X);
                            y = cs.Ymin + (view.chartCanvas.Height - y) *
                                (cs.Ymax - cs.Ymin) / view.chartCanvas.Height;
                            if (!isXDateTimeAxis)
                                xCoordinate.Text = Math.Round(x, 4).ToString();
                            else
                                xCoordinate.Text =
                                    cs.DateList[(int)x].ToShortDateString();
                            labelResults[i].Text = Math.Round(y, 4).ToString();
                        }
                        catch { }
                    }
                }
            }
            else
                view.chartCanvas.ReleaseMouseCapture();
        }
    }

    public void MouseLeaveEvent(object sender, MouseEventArgs e)
    {
        view.chartCanvas.ReleaseMouseCapture();
        view.chartCanvas.Cursor = Cursors.Arrow;
        mouseLine.Visibility = Visibility.Hidden;

        xCoordinate.Text = "X Value";
        for (int i = 0; i < dc.Count; i++)
        {
            circles[i].Visibility = Visibility.Hidden;
            labelResults[i].Text = "Y" + i.ToString() + " Value";
        }
    }
    }
}
```

The bolded code relates to the mouse interaction with the chart. Here, we define two sets of ellipse lists: *circles* and *labelCircles*. The former is used for marking the data points associated with the mouse movement, and the latter for the legend for the results displayed on the screen. We specify the fill color for each of these ellipses using the line color of the corresponding line series. I also add a vertical line called *mouseLine* to highlight the mouse movement. Note also that we initially set the visibility property for the *mouseline* and all of the ellipses in the *circles* list to *Hidden*, meaning that by default the *mousseLine* and these ellipses are invisible on the screen. This property can be toggled between *Visible* and *Hidden* using different mouse events.

When the mouse enters the chart area on your screen, you obtain a position (*startPoint*), set the mouse's *Capture* state, and change *chartCanvas' Cursor* property to *Cross*. You then try to retrieve the *Y* data values for each curve on the chart from the *startPoint*'s *X* coordinate. Notice that you cannot obtain the *Y* data from the curve directly because there may be no *Y* data available in the original data sets used to create the curves at the *startPoint* where you initially placed your mouse. In order to retrieve the *Y* data in this situation, you must generate corresponding *Y* data values at the position of your mouse pointer using interpolation. In this example, we implement a linear interpolation algorithm inside the *GetInterpolatedYValue* method, which allows you to extract *Y* data values from each curve series at any *X* coordinate where your mouse pointer may be placed.

The *MouseMove* event performs the task of data retrieving. When you start to move your mouse, the event fires. First, for each curve series, you create a translation transform using the mouse movement, and then you attach the transform to the corresponding ellipse and *mouseLine*'s *RenderTransform* property. At the same time, you change the *mouseLine* and ellipse's *Visibility* property to *Visible*. This way, the *mouseLine* will move following your mouse pointer and the ellipse objects will move following the curve series corresponding with your mouse. Next, the retrieved data points will be displayed on the *resultPanel* on your screen. Also note how I use WPF's hit-testing feature to determine whether the mouse movement is within the *chartCanvas*. If the mouse pointer is outside of the *chartCanvas*, you need to release the mouse's *Capture* state by calling the *ReleaseMouseCapture* method. Otherwise, your *MouseLeave* event would not fire if the mouse is still in the capture state.

Finally, the *MouseLeave* event finishes the data retrieving process and restores the program to its original state, which includes releasing the mouse's *Capture* state, changing the mouse's cursor to Arrow, and setting the *mouseLine* and ellipses' *Visibility* to *Hidden*.

Running this example, clicking the *Get Stock Avg* button, choosing *AllAvgs* from the *ComboBox*, and moving your mouse inside the chart produce the results shown in Figure 6-21.

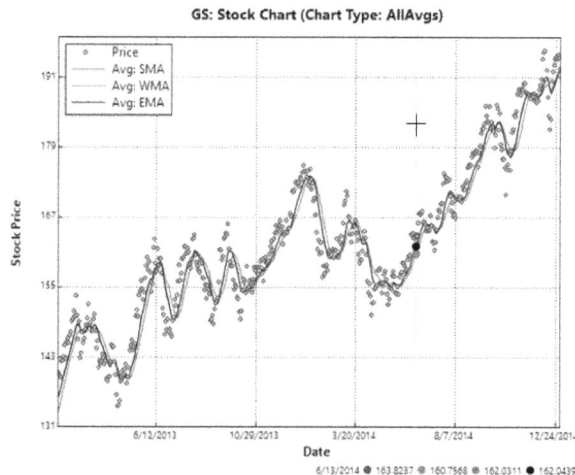

Figure 6-21. Retrieving data from a 2D chart using mouse events.

Chapter 7
2D Chart Controls

In the previous chapters, we implemented the source code for all of the classes in our chart programs directly. This approach works well for simple applications. However, if you want to reuse the same code in multiple .NET applications, this method becomes ineffective. The .NET framework and WPF provide a powerful means, the user control, to solve this problem.

Custom user controls in WPF are just like the simple buttons or text boxes already provided with .NET and WPF. Typically, the controls you design are to be used in multiple windows or to modularize your code. These custom controls can reduce the amount of code you have to type as well as make it easier for you to change the implementation of your program. There is no reason to duplicate code in your applications as this can leave a lot of room for bugs. Therefore, it is good programming practice to create functionalities specific to the user control in the control's source code, which can reduce code duplication and modularize your code.

Custom user controls are a key theme in WPF and .NET development. They can greatly enhance your programming style by improving encapsulation, simplifying a programming model, and making the user interface more pluggable. Of course, custom controls can also have other benefits, such as giving you the ability to transform a generic window into a state-of-the-art modern interface.

In this chapter, you will learn how to put the line charts and stock charts we previously developed in Chapters 4 and 6 into custom user controls, and how to use such controls in your WPF applications using the MVVM style. You will also learn how to make your chart controls into first-class WPF citizens and make them available in XAML. This means that you will need to define dependency properties and routed events for your chart controls in order to get support for essential WPF services, such as data binding, styles, and animation.

Line Chart Control

A *UserControl* in WPF is a content control that can be configured using a design-time surface. Although a user control is basically similar to an ordinary content control, it is typically used when you want to quickly reuse an unchanging block of user interface in more than one application.

Creating a basic chart control based on the line charts developed in Chapter 4 is easy. The layout of the control is the same as that shown in Figure 4-12. The development model for chart user controls is very similar to the model used for application development in WPF.

Here, we can reuse a lot of the code implemented in Chapter 4. Open Visual Studio 2013, start a new WPF project, and name it *Chapter07*. Add Caliburn.Micro to *References*. Add three new folders, *Models*, *ViewModels*, and *Views,* to the project. Add *AppBootstrapper.cs*, which is the same as that used in the *Chapter04* project, to the *Models* folder.

Add a *Window* to the *Views* folder and name it *MainView*. Add a class to the *ViewModels* folder and name it *MainViewModel*. The main view and view model are used to hold tab items, similar to those used in the *Chapter04* project. You can open the files inside Visual Studio to take another look at the code. Also, do not forget to make corresponding changes to *App.xaml*.

Now, it is time to create a chart user control. Right-click the *Chapter07* solution and choose Add | New Project...to bring up the Add New Project dialog. You need to select a new WPF User Control Library from the templates and name it *ChartControl*. When you do this, Visual Studio 2013 creates an XAML markup file and a corresponding custom class to hold your initialization and event-handling code. This will generate a default user control named *UserControl1*. Rename it *LineChart* by right-clicking *UserControl1*.xaml in the solution explorer and selecting Rename. You also need to change the name *UserControl1* to *LineChart* in both the XAML file and the code-behind file for the control. Add a new folder to the control and name it *ChartModel*. Add all of the existing classes from the *ChartModel* folder of the *Chapter04* project to the *ChartModel* folder of the current project, and change their namespaces to *ChartControl*. In addition, you need to add Caliburn.Micro to the References of this project.

Here is the XAML file for the control:

```xml
<UserControl x:Class="ChartControl.LineChart"
             xmlns="http://schemas.microsoft.com/winfx/2006/xaml/presentation"
             xmlns:x="http://schemas.microsoft.com/winfx/2006/xaml"
             xmlns:mc="http://schemas.openxmlformats.org/markup-compatibility/2006"
             xmlns:d="http://schemas.microsoft.com/expression/blend/2008"
             mc:Ignorable="d"
             d:DesignHeight="400" d:DesignWidth="400">

    <Grid Name="grid1" Margin="10">
        <Grid.ColumnDefinitions>
            <ColumnDefinition Width="Auto"/>
            <ColumnDefinition Name="column1" Width="*"/>
        </Grid.ColumnDefinitions>
        <Grid.RowDefinitions>
            <RowDefinition Height="Auto"/>
            <RowDefinition Name="row1" Height="*"/>
            <RowDefinition Height="Auto"/>
        </Grid.RowDefinitions>
        <TextBlock Margin="2" x:Name="tbTitle" Grid.Column="1" Grid.Row="0"
                   RenderTransformOrigin="0.5,0.5" FontSize="14" FontWeight="Bold"
                   HorizontalAlignment="Stretch" VerticalAlignment="Stretch"
                   TextAlignment="Center" Text="Title"/>
        <TextBlock Margin="2" x:Name="tbXLabel" Grid.Column="1" Grid.Row="2"
                   RenderTransformOrigin="0.5,0.5" TextAlignment="Center"
                   Text="X Axis"/>
        <TextBlock Margin="2" Name="tbYLabel" Grid.Column="0" Grid.Row="1"
                   RenderTransformOrigin="0.5,0.5" TextAlignment="Center"
                   Text="Y Axis">
            <TextBlock.LayoutTransform>
                <RotateTransform Angle="-90"/>
            </TextBlock.LayoutTransform>
        </TextBlock>
```

```
<Grid  Margin="0,0,0,0" x:Name ="chartGrid" Grid.Column="1" Grid.Row="1"
        ClipToBounds="False" Background="Transparent"
        SizeChanged="chartGrid_SizeChanged">
    <Canvas Margin="2" Name="textCanvas" Grid.Column="1" Grid.Row="1"
            ClipToBounds="True" Width="{Binding
            ElementName=chartGrid,Path=ActualWidth}" Height="{Binding
            ElementName=chartGrid,Path=ActualHeight}">
        <Canvas Name="chartCanvas" ClipToBounds="True"/>
    </Canvas>
</Grid>
    </Grid>
</UserControl>
```

This markup is simpler compared to that used in creating line charts in Chapter 4. You may note that we are using the code-behind code to implement the chart control because we are not using Caliburn.Micro's *Message.Attach* method for event handlers, such as the *SizeChanged* event. In fact, we have two options in creating a user control library. If the user control we design is consumed only in the current application, we can create the user control using the MVVM approach. In that case, we need to create a separate view model for the control and an instance of it in our parent application that will consume the control. So, the parent view will have the control in it and will bind the control's view model to the control via *ParentVM.UserControlVM*, and our user control will take care of other bindings.

On the other hand, if our control will be used by other applications or by other developers, we will need to create our user control by following a dependency property-based control template implementation. Here, I should point out an important point: whether we decide to use MVVM or code-behind dependency properties to develop our user control, we will not break the MVVM rules for the consumers of our user control.

Here, I will show you how to create a chart control based on dependency properties implemented in the code-behind code, because we want our chart control to be used by other applications and other developers. Dependency properties provide a simple method of data binding when the source object is a WPF element and the source property is a dependency property. This is because dependency properties have built-in support for property-changed notifications. As a result, changing the value of the dependency property in the source object updates the bound property in the target object immediately. This is exactly what we want – and it happens without requiring us to build any additional infrastructure, such as an *INotifyPropertyChanged* interface.

Defining Dependency Properties

Next, we design the public interface that the line chart control exposes to the outside world. In other words, it is time to create the properties, methods, and events that the control consumer (the application that uses the control) will rely on to interact with our chart control.

In order to convert our line chart example into a line chart control, we need to make few changes to the original *LineSeries* and *ChartStyleBase* classes. For the *LineSeries* class, we only need to change the *LinePoints* property from the *PointCollection* type to the *BindableCollection* (or *ObservableCollection*) type, which ensures that we can use the chart control to easily develop real time applications. We also need to add a new public method, *SetLinesControl*, to the *ChartStyleBase* class:

```
public void SetLinesControl(BindableCollection<LineSeries> dc)
{
    if (dc.Count <= 0)
```

```
                        return;

                int i = 0;
                foreach (var ds in dc)
                {
                    PointCollection pts = new PointCollection();

                    if (ds.SeriesName == "Default")
                        ds.SeriesName = "LineSeries" + i.ToString();
                    ds.SetLinePattern();
                    for (int j = 0; j < ds.LinePoints.Count; j++)
                    {
                        var pt = NormalizePoint(ds.LinePoints[j]);
                        pts.Add(pt);
                        if (ds.Symbols.SymbolType != SymbolTypeEnum.None)
                            ds.Symbols.AddSymbol(ChartCanvas, pt);
                    }

                    Polyline line = new Polyline();
                    line.Points = pts;
                    line.Stroke = ds.LineColor;
                    line.StrokeThickness = ds.LineThickness;
                    line.StrokeDashArray = ds.LineDashPattern;
                    ChartCanvas.Children.Add(line);
                    i++;
                }
            }
```

Here, we add the polyline object to the *ChartCanvas* directly because we are creating the line chart using the code-behind approach.

We may want to expose to the outside world most of the properties in the *ChartStyle* class, such as the axis limits, title, and labels; at the same time, we will try to make as few changes as possible to the original line chart example project. In order to support WPF features such as data binding, styles, and animation, the control properties are almost always dependency properties.

The first step in creating a dependency property is to define a static field for it, with the word *Property* added to the end of the property name. Add the following code to the code-behind file:

```
using System;
using System.Windows;
using System.Windows.Controls;
using System.Windows.Media;
using System.Windows.Shapes;
using System.Collections.Specialized;
using Caliburn.Micro;

namespace ChartControl
{
    /// <summary>
    /// Interaction logic for UserControl1.xaml
    /// </summary>
    public partial class LineChart : UserControl
    {
        private ChartStyle cs;
        private Legend lg;
```

```
public LineChart()
{
    InitializeComponent();
    this.cs = new ChartStyle();
    this.lg = new Legend();
    cs.TextCanvas = textCanvas;
    cs.ChartCanvas = chartCanvas;
}

protected override void OnRender(DrawingContext drawingContext)
{
    SetLineChart();
}

private void chartGrid_SizeChanged(object sender, SizeChangedEventArgs e)
{
    ResizeChart();
}

private void SetChart()
{
    cs.Xmin = this.Xmin;
    cs.Xmax = this.Xmax;
    cs.Ymin = this.Ymin;
    cs.Ymax = this.Ymax;
    cs.XTick = this.XTick;
    cs.YTick = this.YTick;
    cs.XLabel = this.XLabel;
    cs.YLabel = this.YLabel;
    cs.Title = this.Title;
    cs.IsXGrid = this.IsXGrid;
    cs.IsYGrid = this.IsYGrid;
    cs.GridlineColor = this.GridlineColor;
    cs.GridlinePattern = this.GridlinePattern;
    lg.IsLegend = this.IsLegend;
    lg.LegendPosition = this.LegendPosition;

    ResizeChart();
}

private void ResizeChart()
{
    chartCanvas.Children.Clear();
    textCanvas.Children.RemoveRange(1, textCanvas.Children.Count - 1);
    cs.AddChartStyle(tbTitle, tbXLabel, tbYLabel);

    if (DataCollection != null)
    {
        if (DataCollection.Count > 0)
        {
            cs.SetLinesControl(DataCollection);
            lg.AddLegend(chartCanvas, DataCollection);
        }
    }
```

```
    }

    public static DependencyProperty XminProperty =
        DependencyProperty.Register("Xmin", typeof(double),
        typeof(LineChart), new FrameworkPropertyMetadata(0.0,
        FrameworkPropertyMetadataOptions.BindsTwoWayByDefault));

    public double Xmin
    {
        get { return (double)GetValue(XminProperty); }
        set { SetValue(XminProperty, value); }
    }

    public static DependencyProperty XmaxProperty =
        DependencyProperty.Register("Xmax", typeof(double),
        typeof(LineChart), new FrameworkPropertyMetadata(10.0,
        FrameworkPropertyMetadataOptions.BindsTwoWayByDefault));

    public double Xmax
    {
        get { return (double)GetValue(XmaxProperty); }
        set { SetValue(XmaxProperty, value); }
    }

    public static DependencyProperty YminProperty =
        DependencyProperty.Register("Ymin", typeof(double),
        typeof(LineChart), new FrameworkPropertyMetadata(0.0,
        FrameworkPropertyMetadataOptions.BindsTwoWayByDefault));

    public double Ymin
    {
        get { return (double)GetValue(YminProperty); }
        set { SetValue(YminProperty, value); }
    }

    public static DependencyProperty YmaxProperty =
        DependencyProperty.Register("Ymax", typeof(double),
        typeof(LineChart), new FrameworkPropertyMetadata(10.0,
        FrameworkPropertyMetadataOptions.BindsTwoWayByDefault));

    public double Ymax
    {
        get { return (double)GetValue(YmaxProperty); }
        set { SetValue(YmaxProperty, value); }
    }

    public static DependencyProperty XTickProperty =
        DependencyProperty.Register("XTick", typeof(double),
        typeof(LineChart), new FrameworkPropertyMetadata(2.0,
        FrameworkPropertyMetadataOptions.BindsTwoWayByDefault));

    public double XTick
    {
        get { return (double)GetValue(XTickProperty); }
        set { SetValue(XTickProperty, value); }
```

```
}

public static DependencyProperty YTickProperty =
    DependencyProperty.Register("YTick", typeof(double),
    typeof(LineChart), new FrameworkPropertyMetadata(2.0,
    FrameworkPropertyMetadataOptions.BindsTwoWayByDefault));

public double YTick
{
    get { return (double)GetValue(YTickProperty); }
    set { SetValue(YTickProperty, value); }
}

public static DependencyProperty XLabelProperty =
    DependencyProperty.Register("XLabel", typeof(string),
    typeof(LineChart), new FrameworkPropertyMetadata("X Axis",
    FrameworkPropertyMetadataOptions.BindsTwoWayByDefault));

public string XLabel
{
    get { return (string)GetValue(XLabelProperty); }
    set { SetValue(XLabelProperty, value); }
}

public static DependencyProperty YLabelProperty =
    DependencyProperty.Register("YLabel", typeof(string),
    typeof(LineChart), new FrameworkPropertyMetadata("Y Axis",
    FrameworkPropertyMetadataOptions.BindsTwoWayByDefault));

public string YLabel
{
    get { return (string)GetValue(YLabelProperty); }
    set { SetValue(YLabelProperty, value); }
}

public static DependencyProperty TitleProperty =
    DependencyProperty.Register("Title", typeof(string),
    typeof(LineChart), new FrameworkPropertyMetadata("My Title",
    FrameworkPropertyMetadataOptions.BindsTwoWayByDefault));

public string Title
{
    get { return (string)GetValue(TitleProperty); }
    set { SetValue(TitleProperty, value); }
}

public static DependencyProperty IsXGridProperty =
    DependencyProperty.Register("IsXGrid", typeof(bool),
    typeof(LineChart), new FrameworkPropertyMetadata(true,
    FrameworkPropertyMetadataOptions.BindsTwoWayByDefault));

public bool IsXGrid
{
    get { return (bool)GetValue(IsXGridProperty); }
    set { SetValue(IsXGridProperty, value); }
```

```
    }

    public static DependencyProperty IsYGridProperty =
        DependencyProperty.Register("IsYGrid", typeof(bool),
        typeof(LineChart), new FrameworkPropertyMetadata(true,
        FrameworkPropertyMetadataOptions.BindsTwoWayByDefault));

    public bool IsYGrid
    {
        get { return (bool)GetValue(IsYGridProperty); }
        set { SetValue(IsYGridProperty, value); }
    }

    public static DependencyProperty GridlineColorProperty =
        DependencyProperty.Register("GridlineColor", typeof(Brush),
        typeof(LineChart), new FrameworkPropertyMetadata(Brushes.Gray,
        FrameworkPropertyMetadataOptions.BindsTwoWayByDefault));

    public Brush GridlineColor
    {
        get { return (Brush)GetValue(GridlineColorProperty); }
        set { SetValue(GridlineColorProperty, value); }
    }

    public static DependencyProperty GridlinePatternProperty =
        DependencyProperty.Register("GridlinePattern",
        typeof(LinePatternEnum), typeof(LineChart),
        new FrameworkPropertyMetadata(LinePatternEnum.Solid,
        FrameworkPropertyMetadataOptions.BindsTwoWayByDefault));

    public LinePatternEnum GridlinePattern
    {
        get { return (LinePatternEnum)GetValue(GridlinePatternProperty); }
        set { SetValue(GridlinePatternProperty, value); }
    }

    public static DependencyProperty IsLegendProperty =
        DependencyProperty.Register("IsLegend", typeof(bool),
        typeof(LineChart), new FrameworkPropertyMetadata(false,
        FrameworkPropertyMetadataOptions.BindsTwoWayByDefault));

    public bool IsLegend
    {
        get { return (bool)GetValue(IsLegendProperty); }
        set { SetValue(IsLegendProperty, value); }
    }

    public static DependencyProperty LegendPositionProperty =
        DependencyProperty.Register("LegendPosition",
        typeof(LegendPositionEnum), typeof(LineChart),
        New FrameworkPropertyMetadata(LegendPositionEnum.NorthEast,
        FrameworkPropertyMetadataOptions.BindsTwoWayByDefault));

    public LegendPositionEnum LegendPosition
    {
```

```
            get { return (LegendPositionEnum)GetValue(LegendPositionProperty); }
            set { SetValue(LegendPositionProperty, value); }
        }

        public static readonly DependencyProperty DataCollectionProperty =
            DependencyProperty.Register("DataCollection",
            typeof(BindableCollection<LineSeries>), typeof(LineChart),
            new FrameworkPropertyMetadata(null,
            FrameworkPropertyMetadataOptions.BindsTwoWayByDefault, OnDataChanged));

        public BindableCollection<LineSeries> DataCollection
        {
            get { return
                (BindableCollection<LineSeries>)GetValue(DataCollectionProperty); }
            set { SetValue(DataCollectionProperty, value); }
        }

        private static void OnDataChanged(object sender,
            DependencyPropertyChangedEventArgs e)
        {
            var lc = sender as LineChart;
            var dc = e.NewValue as BindableCollection<LineSeries>;
            if (dc != null)
                dc.CollectionChanged += lc.dc_CollectionChanged;
        }

        private void dc_CollectionChanged(object sender,
            NotifyCollectionChangedEventArgs e)
        {
            if (DataCollection != null)
            {
                CheckCount = 0;
                if (DataCollection.Count > 0) CheckCount = DataCollection.Count;
            }
        }


        private static DependencyProperty CheckCountProperty =
            DependencyProperty.Register("CheckCount", typeof(int),
            typeof(LineChart), new FrameworkPropertyMetadata(0,
            FrameworkPropertyMetadataOptions.AffectsRender));

        private int CheckCount
        {
            get { return (int)GetValue(CheckCountProperty); }
            set { SetValue(CheckCountProperty, value); }
        }
    }
}
```

You can see that we convert most of the public properties of the *ChartStyle* and *Legend* classes into dependency properties. For example, we use the following code snippet to define the dependency property for the *Xmin* property of the *ChartStyle* class:

```
public static DependencyProperty XminProperty =
    DependencyProperty.Register("Xmin", typeof(double),
```

```
        typeof(LineChart), new FrameworkPropertyMetadata(0.0,
        FrameworkPropertyMetadataOptions.BindsTwoWayByDefault));

public double Xmin
{
    get { return (double)GetValue(XminProperty); }
    set { SetValue(XminProperty, value); }
}
```

Note that WPF comes with a completely new technique for defining the properties of a control. The core of the new property system is the dependency property and the wrapper class called *DepedencyObject*. Here, we use the wrapper class to register the *Xmin* dependency property into a property system to ensure that the object contains the property in it, and we can easily get or set the value of the property. The property wrapper should not contain any logic, because properties may be set and retrieved directly using the *SetValue* and *GetValue* methods of the base *DependencyObject* class.

In some situations, however, we may want to execute some logic and computation methods after setting the value of a dependency property. We can perform these tasks by implementing a callback method that fires when the property changes through the property wrapper or a direct *SetValue* call. For example, after creating the *DataCollection* that contains *LineSeries* objects, we want the chart control to automatically create a corresponding line chart for these *LineSeries* objects. The bolded code in the preceding code-behind file shows how to implement such a callback method. The *DataCollectionProperty* includes a callback method named *OnDataChanged*. Inside this callback method, we add an event handler to the *CollectionChanged* property, which will fire when the *DataCollection* changes. Within the *CollectionChanged* handler, we set another private dependency property called *CheckCount* to the *DataCollection.Count*. If *CheckCount* > 0, we know that the *DataCollection* does contain *LineSeries* objects, and we then set *FrameworkPropertyOptions* to *AffectsRender* for the *CheckCount* property, and WPF will re-render the chart control by calling the *OnRender* method when this property is changed.

Note that inside the *SetChart* method, we set the public properties of the *ChartStyle* and *Legend* classes to the corresponding dependency properties of the chart control. This way, whenever the dependency properties in the *LineChart* class change, the properties of the *ChartStyle* and *Legend* classes will change accorddingly.

Here, we also add a *chartGrid_SizeChanged* event handler to the line chart control. This handler ensures that the chart gets updated whenever the chart control is resized. Now we can build the control library by right clicking the *ChartControl* project and selecting Build.

Using the Line Chart Control

Now that we have created our 2D line chart control, we can easily use it in our *Chapter07* project. To use the control in a WPF application, we need to map the .NET namespace and assembly to an XML namespace, as shown here:

```
xmlns:local="clr-namespace:ChartControl;assembly=ChartControl"
```

If the chart control is located in the same assembly as our application, we only need to map the namespace:

```
xmlns:local="clr-namespace:ChartControl"
```

Using the XML namespace and the user control class name, you can add the user control to the XAML file exactly as you would add any other type of object. You can also set its properties, make data bindings, and attach event handlers directly in the control tag, as shown here:

```
<local:LineChart DataCollection="{Binding DataCollection}" x:Name="myChart"
                 Xmin="0" Xmax="7" XTick="1" Ymin="-1.5" Ymax="1.5" YTick="0.5"
                 XLabel="X" YLabel="Y" Title="My Line Chart" GridlinePattern="Dot"
                 GridlineColor="Green" IsLegend="True"/>
```

Notice how you specify the *GridlinePattern* property – simply choose from the *Solid*, *Dash*, *Dot*, or *DashDot* properties defined in the *LinePatternEnum*. This is much simpler than using code-behind, where you need to type the full path in order to define the gridlines' line pattern. You can also specify other properties standard to WPF elements for the chart control, such as *Width*, *Height*, *CanvasLeft*, *CanvasTop*, and *BackGround*. These standard properties allow you to position the control, set the size of the control, or set the background color of the control.

Creating a Simple Line Chart

Here, you will learn how to use the chart control to create simple sine and cosine functions. Open the *Chapter07* project in Visual Studio 2013. Add a new *UserControl* to the *Views* folder of the *Chapter07* project and name it *LineChartControlView*. Now right-click References and select Add References…in the new project to bring up the "Add References" window. Click the Solution and then Projects in the left pane of this window and highlight the *ChartControl*. Click *OK* to add the *ChartControl* to the current project. By doing this, you can use the control in your WPF application just like a built-in element. Now, in the Solution Explorer, right click the *Chapter07* project and select Set as StartUp Project.

Here is the XAML file for the *LineChartControlView*:

```
<UserControl x:Class="Chapter07.Views.LineChartControlView"
             xmlns="http://schemas.microsoft.com/winfx/2006/xaml/presentation"
             xmlns:x="http://schemas.microsoft.com/winfx/2006/xaml"
             xmlns:mc="http://schemas.openxmlformats.org/markup-compatibility/2006"
             xmlns:d="http://schemas.microsoft.com/expression/blend/2008"
             xmlns:local="clr-namespace:ChartControl;assembly=ChartControl"
             mc:Ignorable="d"
             d:DesignHeight="300" d:DesignWidth="400">
    <Grid>
        <Grid.ColumnDefinitions>
            <ColumnDefinition Width="*"/>
            <ColumnDefinition Width="150"/>
        </Grid.ColumnDefinitions>
    <Button x:Name="AddChart" Content="Add Chart" Width="100"
            Height="25" Grid.Column="1"/>
        <local:LineChart DataCollection="{Binding DataCollection}" x:Name="myChart"
            Xmin="0" Xmax="7" XTick="1" Ymin="-1.5" Ymax="1.5" YTick="0.5"
            XLabel="X" YLabel="Y" Title="My Line Chart" GridlinePattern="Dot"
            GridlineColor="Green" IsLegend="True"/>
    </Grid>
</UserControl>
```

Here, you simply create a line chart control exactly as you would create any other type of WPF element. Now, add a new class to the *ViewModels* folder and name it *LineChartControlViewModel*. Here is the code for this class:

```csharp
using System;
using Caliburn.Micro;
using System.Collections.ObjectModel;
using System.ComponentModel.Composition;
using System.Windows;
using System.Windows.Media;
using ChartControl;

namespace Chapter07.ViewModels
{
    [Export(typeof(IScreen)), PartCreationPolicy(CreationPolicy.NonShared)]
    public class LineChartControlViewModel : Screen
    {
        private readonly IEventAggregator _events;
        [ImportingConstructor]
        public LineChartControlViewModel(IEventAggregator events)
        {
            this._events = events;
            DisplayName = "01. Line Chart";
            DataCollection = new BindableCollection<LineSeries>();
        }

        public BindableCollection<LineSeries> DataCollection{get;set;}

        public void AddData()
        {
            DataCollection.Clear();
            LineSeries ds = new LineSeries();
            ds.LineColor = Brushes.Blue;
            ds.LineThickness = 2;
            ds.SeriesName = "Sine";
            ds.LinePattern = LinePatternEnum.Solid;
            for (int i = 0; i < 50; i++)
            {
                double x = i / 5.0;
                double y = Math.Sin(x);
                ds.LinePoints.Add(new Point(x, y));
            }
            DataCollection.Add(ds);

            ds = new LineSeries();
            ds.LineColor = Brushes.Red;
            ds.LineThickness = 2;
            ds.SeriesName = "Cosine";
            ds.LinePattern = LinePatternEnum.Dash;
            for (int i = 0; i < 50; i++)
            {
                double x = i / 5.0;
                double y = Math.Cos(x);
                ds.LinePoints.Add(new Point(x, y));
            }
            DataCollection.Add(ds);

            ds = new LineSeries();
            ds.LineColor = Brushes.DarkGreen;
```

```
            ds.LineThickness = 2;
            ds.SeriesName = "Sine^2";
            ds.LinePattern = LinePatternEnum.Dash;
            for (int i = 0; i < 50; i++)
            {
                double x = i / 5.0;
                double y = Math.Sin(x) * Math.Sin(x);
                ds.LinePoints.Add(new Point(x, y));
            }
            DataCollection.Add(ds);
        }
    }
}
```

Just like you did when you created line charts in Chapter 4, you first need to create the line series, and then add them to the chart control's *DataCollection*. The beauty of using the chart control is that you can use the standard MVVM pattern in the application, even though you created the chart control using dependency properties and the code-behind approach. Here, you just define the *DataCollection* property in the view model (you do not need to implement the *INotifyCollectionChanged* interface for this collection because it has a built-in implementation of this interface), and bind it to the chart control. The *AddChart* method in the view model is also bound to the *Button* in the view by Caliburn.Micro's naming convention. This way, you have a perfect separation between the view and the view model, which meets the requirements of the MVVM pattern.

Running this example and clicking the *Add Chart* button generates the result shown in Figure 7-1. You can resize the chart to see how the chart gets updated automatically.

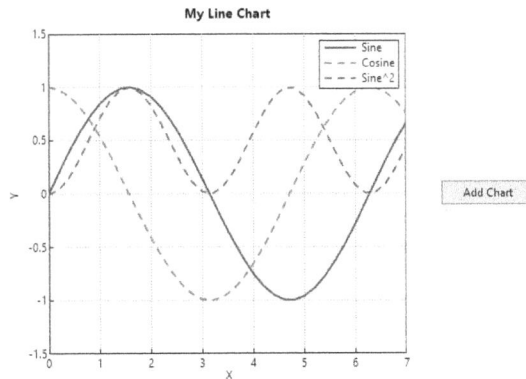

Figure 7-1. A line chart created using the chart control.

Creating Multiple Line Charts

Using the line chart control, you can easily create multiple charts in a single WPF window. Let's add a new *UserControl* to the *Views* folder and name it *MultiChartView*. Create a 2-by-2 *Grid* control and add a chart control to each of the four cells of the *Grid*, using the following XAML file:

```
<UserControl x:Class="Chapter07.Views.MultiChartView"
        xmlns="http://schemas.microsoft.com/winfx/2006/xaml/presentation"
        xmlns:x="http://schemas.microsoft.com/winfx/2006/xaml"
        xmlns:mc="http://schemas.openxmlformats.org/markup-compatibility/2006"
```

```
                  xmlns:d="http://schemas.microsoft.com/expression/blend/2008"
                  xmlns:cal="http://www.caliburnproject.org"
                  xmlns:local="clr-namespace:ChartControl;assembly=ChartControl"
                  mc:Ignorable="d"
                  d:DesignHeight="600" d:DesignWidth="600">
    <Grid cal:Message.Attach="[Event Loaded]=[Action AddChart]">
        <Grid.ColumnDefinitions>
            <ColumnDefinition/>
            <ColumnDefinition/>
        </Grid.ColumnDefinitions>
        <Grid.RowDefinitions>
            <RowDefinition/>
            <RowDefinition/>
        </Grid.RowDefinitions>
        <local:LineChart Width="{Binding ElementName=chartGrid,Path=ActualWidth}"
                         Height="{Binding ElementName=chartGrid,Path=ActualHeight}"
                         DataCollection="{Binding DataCollection}"
                         Xmin="0" Xmax="7" XTick="1" Ymin="-1.5" Ymax="1.5"
                         YTick="0.5" XLabel="X" YLabel="Y"
                         Title="Chart1" GridlinePattern="Dot" GridlineColor="Black"
                         IsLegend="False" Grid.Column="0" Grid.Row="0"/>
        <local:LineChart Width="{Binding ElementName=chartGrid,Path=ActualWidth}"
                         Height="{Binding ElementName=chartGrid,Path=ActualHeight}"
                         DataCollection="{Binding DataCollection}"
                         Xmin="0" Xmax="7" XTick="1" Ymin="-1.5" Ymax="1.5"
                         YTick="0.5" XLabel="X" YLabel="Y"
                         Title="Chart2" GridlinePattern="Dot" GridlineColor="Red"
                         IsLegend="False" Grid.Column="1" Grid.Row="0"/>
        <local:LineChart Width="{Binding ElementName=chartGrid,Path=ActualWidth}"
                         Height="{Binding ElementName=chartGrid,Path=ActualHeight}"
                         DataCollection="{Binding DataCollection}"
                         Xmin="0" Xmax="7" XTick="1" Ymin="-1.5" Ymax="1.5"
                         YTick="0.5" XLabel="X" YLabel="Y"
                         Title="Chart3" GridlinePattern="Dot" GridlineColor="Green"
                         IsLegend="False" Grid.Column="0" Grid.Row="1"/>
        <local:LineChart Width="{Binding ElementName=chartGrid,Path=ActualWidth}"
                         Height="{Binding ElementName=chartGrid,Path=ActualHeight}"
                         DataCollection="{Binding DataCollection}"
                         Xmin="0" Xmax="7" XTick="1" Ymin="-1.5" Ymax="1.5"
                         YTick="0.5" XLabel="X" YLabel="Y"
                         Title="Chart4" GridlinePattern="Dot" GridlineColor="Blue"
                         IsLegend="False" Grid.Column="1" Grid.Row="1"/>
    </Grid>
</UserControl>
```

Here, you create four line chart controls, *Chart1*, *Chart2*, *Chart3*, and *Chart4*. For simplicity's sake, in this example, you will plot the same data functions on each chart, but, with different *GridlineColor* properties for each chart. In practice, you can plot different math functions on each chart according to your application's requirements.

Add a new class to the *ViewModels* folder and name it *MultiChartViewModel*. Here is the code for this class:

```
using System;
using Caliburn.Micro;
using System.Collections.ObjectModel;
```

```
using System.ComponentModel.Composition;
using System.Windows;
using System.Windows.Media;
using System.Windows.Controls;
using Chapter04.Models.ChartModel;

namespace Chapter07.ViewModels
{
    [Export(typeof(IScreen)), PartCreationPolicy(CreationPolicy.NonShared)]
    public class MultiChartViewModel : Screen
    {
        private readonly IEventAggregator _events;
        [ImportingConstructor]
        public MultiChartViewModel(IEventAggregator events)
        {
            this._events = events;
            DisplayName = "02. Multiple Charts";
            DataCollection = new BindableCollection<LineSeries>();
        }

        public BindableCollection<LineSeries> DataCollection { get; set; }

        public void AddChart()
        {
            DataCollection.Clear();

            LineSeries ds = new LineSeries();
            ds.LineColor = Brushes.Blue;
            ds.LineThickness = 2;
            ds.SeriesName = "Sine";
            ds.LinePattern = LinePatternEnum.Solid;
            for (int i = 0; i < 50; i++)
            {
                double x = i / 5.0;
                double y = Math.Sin(x);
                ds.LinePoints.Add(new Point(x, y));
            }
            DataCollection.Add(ds);

            ds = new LineSeries();
            ds.LineColor = Brushes.Red;
            ds.LineThickness = 2;
            ds.SeriesName = "Cosine";
            ds.LinePattern = LinePatternEnum.Dash;
            for (int i = 0; i < 50; i++)
            {
                double x = i / 5.0;
                double y = Math.Cos(x);
                ds.LinePoints.Add(new Point(x, y));
            }
            DataCollection.Add(ds);

            ds = new LineSeries();
            ds.LineColor = Brushes.DarkGreen;
            ds.LineThickness = 2;
```

```
            ds.SeriesName = "Sine^2";
            ds.LinePattern = LinePatternEnum.Dash;
            for (int i = 0; i < 50; i++)
            {
                double x = i / 5.0;
                double y = Math.Sin(x) * Math.Sin(x);
                ds.LinePoints.Add(new Point(x, y));
            }

            DataCollection.Add(ds);
        }
    }
}
```

This class is almost identical to the view model used in the preceding example where you created a single line chart. Here, the four chart controls bind to the same *DataCollection* object. As with any other WPF built-in element, you can place as many line chart controls as you need in a single WPF application.

Figure 7-2 shows the results of running this example.

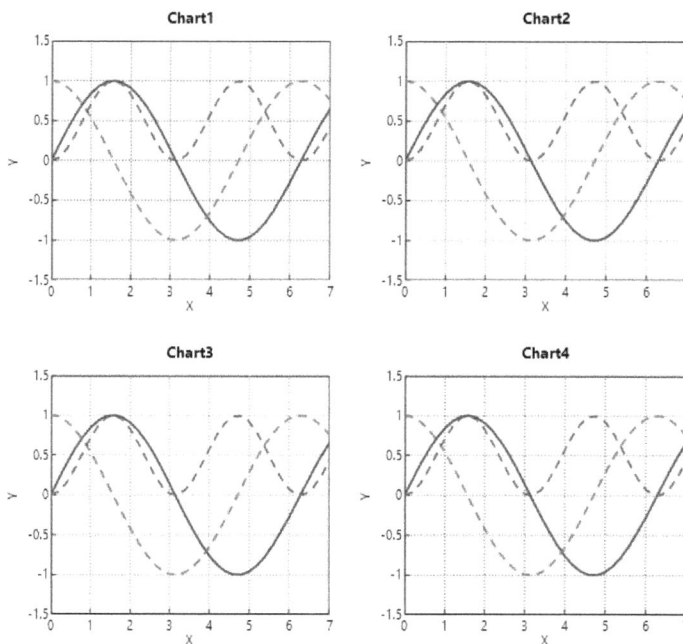

Figure 7-2. Multiple charts created using the chart control.

Line 2Y Chart Control

Following the same procedure as we did for the basic line chart control in the preceding sections, we can easily create a chart control with two *Y* axes. Go back to the *ChartControl* project. Add a new *UserControl* to the *ChartControl* project and name it *Line2YChart*. Here is the XAML file for this view:

```
<UserControl x:Class="ChartControl.Line2YChart"
```

```
        xmlns="http://schemas.microsoft.com/winfx/2006/xaml/presentation"
        xmlns:x="http://schemas.microsoft.com/winfx/2006/xaml"
        xmlns:mc="http://schemas.openxmlformats.org/markup-compatibility/2006"
        xmlns:d="http://schemas.microsoft.com/expression/blend/2008"
        mc:Ignorable="d"
        d:DesignHeight="300" d:DesignWidth="300">

<Grid Margin="10">
    <Grid.ColumnDefinitions>
        <ColumnDefinition Width="auto"/>
        <ColumnDefinition Name="column1" Width="*"/>
        <ColumnDefinition Width="auto"/>
    </Grid.ColumnDefinitions>
    <Grid.RowDefinitions>
        <RowDefinition Height="auto"/>
        <RowDefinition Name="row1" Height="*"/>
        <RowDefinition Height="auto"/>
    </Grid.RowDefinitions>
    <TextBlock Margin="2" x:Name="tbTitle" Grid.Column="1" Grid.Row="0"
            RenderTransformOrigin="0.5,0.5" FontSize="14" FontWeight="Bold"
            HorizontalAlignment="Stretch" VerticalAlignment="Stretch"
            TextAlignment="Center"
            Text="Title"/>

    <TextBlock Margin="5" x:Name="tbXLabel" Grid.Column="1" Grid.Row="2"
            RenderTransformOrigin="0.5,0.5" TextAlignment="Center"
            Text="X Axis"/>

    <TextBlock Margin="5" Name="tbYLabel" Grid.Column="0" Grid.Row="1"
            RenderTransformOrigin="0.5,0.5" TextAlignment="Center"
            Text="Y Axis">
        <TextBlock.LayoutTransform>
            <RotateTransform Angle="-90"/>
        </TextBlock.LayoutTransform>
    </TextBlock>

    <TextBlock Margin="5" Name="tbY2Label" Grid.Column="2" Grid.Row="1"
            RenderTransformOrigin="0.5,0.5" TextAlignment="Center"
            Text="Y2 Axis">
        <TextBlock.LayoutTransform>
            <RotateTransform Angle="-90"/>
        </TextBlock.LayoutTransform>
    </TextBlock>

    <Grid Margin="0" x:Name ="chartGrid" Grid.Column="1" Grid.Row="1"
        SizeChanged="chartGrid_SizeChanged"
        ClipToBounds="True" Background="Transparent"/>
    <Canvas Margin="2" Name="textCanvas" ClipToBounds="True"
            Grid.Column="1" Grid.Row="1"
            Width="{Binding ElementName=chartGrid,Path=ActualWidth}"
            Height="{Binding ElementName=chartGrid,Path=ActualHeight}">
        <Canvas Name="chartCanvas" ClipToBounds="True">
        </Canvas>
    </Canvas>
</Grid>
```

```
</UserControl>
```

This XAML file is simpler than the one we used to create line 2Y charts in Chapter 4. Here, I will show you how to create a chart control based on dependency properties implemented in the code-behind code. The dependency properties provide a simple way to data bind when the source object is a WPF element and the source property is a dependency property, because dependency properties have built-in support for change notification. As a result, changing the value of the dependency property in the source object updates the bound property in the target object immediately. This is exactly what you want – and it happens without requiring you to build any additional infrastructure, like an *INotifyPropertyChanged* interface.

Defining Dependency Properties

Next, we will design the public interface that allows the line chart control to be exposed to the outside world. In other words, it is time to create the properties, methods, and events that the control consumer (the application that uses the control) will rely on to interact with your chart control.

In order to convert the line chart example into a line chart control, we need to add a new public method, *SetLines2YControl*, to the *ChartStyle2YBase* class:

```
public void SetLines2YControl(BindableCollection<LineSeries2Y> dc)
{
    if (dc.Count <= 0)
        return;
    for (int i = 0; i < dc.Count; i++)
    {
        PointCollection pts = new PointCollection();
        if (dc[i].SeriesName == "Default")
            dc[i].SeriesName = "DataSeries" + i.ToString();
        dc[i].SetLinePattern();
        for (int j = 0; j < dc[i].LinePoints.Count; j++)
        {
            Point pt = new Point();
            if (dc[i].Is2YData)
                pt = NormalizePoint2Y(dc[i].LinePoints[j]);
            else
                pt = NormalizePoint(dc[i].LinePoints[j]);
            pts.Add(pt);

            if (dc[i].Symbols.SymbolType != SymbolTypeEnum.None)
                dc[i].Symbols.AddSymbol(ChartCanvas, pt);
        }

        Polyline line = new Polyline();
        line.Points = pts;
        line.Stroke = dc[i].LineColor;
        line.StrokeThickness = dc[i].LineThickness;
        line.StrokeDashArray = dc[i].LineDashPattern;
        ChartCanvas.Children.Add(line);
    }
}
```

Here, we add the polyline object to the *ChartCanvas* directly because we are creating the line chart using the code-behind approach.

You may want to expose to the outside world most of the properties in the *ChartStyle2Y* class of the line 2*Y* chart example from Chapter 4, such as axis limits, title, and labels. The first step in creating a dependency property is to define a static field for it, with the word *Property* added to the end of the property name. Add the following code to the code-behind file:

```
using System;
using System.Windows;
using System.Windows.Controls;
using System.Windows.Media;
using System.Windows.Shapes;
using Caliburn.Micro;
using System.Collections.Specialized;

namespace ChartControl
{
    /// <summary>
    /// Interaction logic for Line2YChart.xaml
    /// </summary>
    public partial class Line2YChart : UserControl
    {
        private ChartStyle2Y cs;
        private Legend lg;

        public Line2YChart()
        {
            InitializeComponent();
            this.cs = new ChartStyle2Y();
            this.lg = new Legend();
            cs.TextCanvas = textCanvas;
            cs.ChartCanvas = chartCanvas;
        }

        Protected override void OnRender(DrawingContext drawingContext)
        {
            SetChart();
        }

        private void chartGrid_SizeChanged(object sender, SizeChangedEventArgs e)
        {
            ResizeChart();
        }

        private void SetChart()
        {
            cs.Xmin = this.Xmin;
            cs.Xmax = this.Xmax;
            cs.Ymin = this.Ymin;
            cs.Ymax = this.Ymax;
            cs.Y2min = this.Y2min;
            cs.Y2max = this.Y2max;
            cs.XTick = this.XTick;
            cs.YTick = this.YTick;
            cs.Y2Tick = this.Y2Tick;
            cs.XLabel = this.XLabel;
            cs.YLabel = this.YLabel;
```

```
        cs.Y2Label = this.Y2Label;
        cs.Title = this.Title;
        cs.IsXGrid = this.IsXGrid;
        cs.IsYGrid = this.IsYGrid;
        cs.Is2YGrid = this.Is2YGrid;
        cs.GridlineColor = this.GridlineColor;
        cs.GridlinePattern = this.GridlinePattern;
        cs.Gridline2YColor = this.Gridline2YColor;
        cs.Gridline2YPattern = this.Gridline2YPattern;
        lg.IsLegend = this.IsLegend;
        lg.LegendPosition = this.LegendPosition;

        ResizeChart();
    }

    private void ResizeChart()
    {
        chartCanvas.Children.Clear();
        textCanvas.Children.RemoveRange(1, textCanvas.Children.Count - 1);
        cs.AddChartStyle(tbTitle, tbXLabel, tbYLabel, tbY2Label);

        if (DataCollection != null)
        {
            if (DataCollection.Count > 0)
            {
                cs.SetLines2YControl(DataCollection);
                lg.AddLegend(chartCanvas, DataCollection);
            }
        }
    }

    public static DependencyProperty XminProperty =
        DependencyProperty.Register("Xmin", typeof(double),
        typeof(Line2YChart), new FrameworkPropertyMetadata(0.0,
        FrameworkPropertyMetadataOptions.BindsTwoWayByDefault));

    public double Xmin
    {
        get { return (double)GetValue(XminProperty); }
        set { SetValue(XminProperty, value); }
    }

    public static DependencyProperty XmaxProperty =
        DependencyProperty.Register("Xmax", typeof(double),
        typeof(Line2YChart), new FrameworkPropertyMetadata(10.0,
        FrameworkPropertyMetadataOptions.BindsTwoWayByDefault));

    public double Xmax
    {
        get { return (double)GetValue(XmaxProperty); }
        set { SetValue(XmaxProperty, value); }
    }

    public static DependencyProperty YminProperty =
        DependencyProperty.Register("Ymin", typeof(double),
```

```
    typeof(Line2YChart), new FrameworkPropertyMetadata(0.0,
    FrameworkPropertyMetadataOptions.BindsTwoWayByDefault));

public double Ymin
{
    get { return (double)GetValue(YminProperty); }
    set { SetValue(YminProperty, value); }
}

public static DependencyProperty YmaxProperty =
    DependencyProperty.Register("Ymax", typeof(double),
    typeof(Line2YChart), new FrameworkPropertyMetadata(10.0,
    FrameworkPropertyMetadataOptions.BindsTwoWayByDefault));

public double Ymax
{
    get { return (double)GetValue(YmaxProperty); }
    set { SetValue(YmaxProperty, value); }
}

public static DependencyProperty Y2minProperty =
    DependencyProperty.Register("Y2min", typeof(double),
    typeof(Line2YChart), new FrameworkPropertyMetadata(0.0,
    FrameworkPropertyMetadataOptions.BindsTwoWayByDefault));

public double Y2min
{
    get { return (double)GetValue(Y2minProperty); }
    set { SetValue(Y2minProperty, value); }
}

public static DependencyProperty Y2maxProperty =
    DependencyProperty.Register("Y2max", typeof(double),
    typeof(Line2YChart), new FrameworkPropertyMetadata(10.0,
    FrameworkPropertyMetadataOptions.BindsTwoWayByDefault));

public double Y2max
{
    get { return (double)GetValue(Y2maxProperty); }
    set { SetValue(Y2maxProperty, value); }
}

public static DependencyProperty XTickProperty =
    DependencyProperty.Register("XTick", typeof(double),
    typeof(Line2YChart), new FrameworkPropertyMetadata(2.0,
    FrameworkPropertyMetadataOptions.BindsTwoWayByDefault));

public double XTick
{
    get { return (double)GetValue(XTickProperty); }
    set { SetValue(XTickProperty, value); }
}

public static DependencyProperty YTickProperty =
    DependencyProperty.Register("YTick", typeof(double),
```

```
        typeof(Line2YChart), new FrameworkPropertyMetadata(2.0,
        FrameworkPropertyMetadataOptions.BindsTwoWayByDefault));

public double YTick
{
    get { return (double)GetValue(YTickProperty); }
    set { SetValue(YTickProperty, value); }
}

public static DependencyProperty Y2TickProperty =
    DependencyProperty.Register("Y2Tick", typeof(double),
    typeof(Line2YChart), new FrameworkPropertyMetadata(2.0,
    FrameworkPropertyMetadataOptions.BindsTwoWayByDefault));

public double Y2Tick
{
    get { return (double)GetValue(Y2TickProperty); }
    set { SetValue(Y2TickProperty, value); }
}

public static DependencyProperty XLabelProperty =
    DependencyProperty.Register("XLabel", typeof(string),
    typeof(Line2YChart), new FrameworkPropertyMetadata("X Axis",
    FrameworkPropertyMetadataOptions.BindsTwoWayByDefault));

public string XLabel
{
    get { return (string)GetValue(XLabelProperty); }
    set { SetValue(XLabelProperty, value); }
}

public static DependencyProperty YLabelProperty =
    DependencyProperty.Register("YLabel", typeof(string),
    typeof(Line2YChart), new FrameworkPropertyMetadata("Y Axis",
    FrameworkPropertyMetadataOptions.BindsTwoWayByDefault));

public string YLabel
{
    get { return (string)GetValue(YLabelProperty); }
    set { SetValue(YLabelProperty, value); }
}

public static DependencyProperty Y2LabelProperty =
    DependencyProperty.Register("Y2Label", typeof(string),
    typeof(Line2YChart), new FrameworkPropertyMetadata("Y2 Axis",
    FrameworkPropertyMetadataOptions.BindsTwoWayByDefault));

public string Y2Label
{
    get { return (string)GetValue(Y2LabelProperty); }
    set { SetValue(Y2LabelProperty, value); }
}

public static DependencyProperty TitleProperty =
    DependencyProperty.Register("Title", typeof(string),
```

```
        typeof(Line2YChart), new FrameworkPropertyMetadata("My Title",
        FrameworkPropertyMetadataOptions.BindsTwoWayByDefault));

public string Title
{
    get { return (string)GetValue(TitleProperty); }
    set { SetValue(TitleProperty, value); }
}

public static DependencyProperty IsXGridProperty =
    DependencyProperty.Register("IsXGrid", typeof(bool),
    typeof(Line2YChart), new FrameworkPropertyMetadata(true,
    FrameworkPropertyMetadataOptions.BindsTwoWayByDefault));

public bool IsXGrid
{
    get { return (bool)GetValue(IsXGridProperty); }
    set { SetValue(IsXGridProperty, value); }
}

public static DependencyProperty IsYGridProperty =
    DependencyProperty.Register("IsYGrid", typeof(bool),
    typeof(Line2YChart), new FrameworkPropertyMetadata(true,
    FrameworkPropertyMetadataOptions.BindsTwoWayByDefault));

public bool IsYGrid
{
    get { return (bool)GetValue(IsYGridProperty); }
    set { SetValue(IsYGridProperty, value); }
}

public static DependencyProperty Is2YGridProperty =
    DependencyProperty.Register("Is2YGrid", typeof(bool),
    typeof(Line2YChart), new FrameworkPropertyMetadata(true,
    FrameworkPropertyMetadataOptions.BindsTwoWayByDefault));

public bool Is2YGrid
{
    get { return (bool)GetValue(Is2YGridProperty); }
    set { SetValue(Is2YGridProperty, value); }
}

public static DependencyProperty GridlineColorProperty =
    DependencyProperty.Register("GridlineColor", typeof(Brush),
    typeof(Line2YChart), new FrameworkPropertyMetadata(Brushes.Gray,
    FrameworkPropertyMetadataOptions.BindsTwoWayByDefault));

public Brush GridlineColor
{
    get { return (Brush)GetValue(GridlineColorProperty); }
    set { SetValue(GridlineColorProperty, value); }
}

public static DependencyProperty GridlinePatternProperty =
    DependencyProperty.Register("GridlinePattern",
```

```
    typeof(LinePatternEnum), typeof(Line2YChart),
    new FrameworkPropertyMetadata(LinePatternEnum.Solid,
    FrameworkPropertyMetadataOptions.BindsTwoWayByDefault));

public LinePatternEnum GridlinePattern
{
    get { return (LinePatternEnum)GetValue(GridlinePatternProperty); }
    set { SetValue(GridlinePatternProperty, value); }
}

public static DependencyProperty Gridline2YColorProperty =
    DependencyProperty.Register("Gridline2YColor", typeof(Brush),
    typeof(Line2YChart), new FrameworkPropertyMetadata(Brushes.Gray,
    FrameworkPropertyMetadataOptions.BindsTwoWayByDefault));

public Brush Gridline2YColor
{
    get { return (Brush)GetValue(Gridline2YColorProperty); }
    set { SetValue(Gridline2YColorProperty, value); }
}

public static DependencyProperty Gridline2YPatternProperty =
    DependencyProperty.Register("Gridline2YPattern",
    typeof(LinePatternEnum), typeof(Line2YChart),
    new FrameworkPropertyMetadata(LinePatternEnum.Solid,
    FrameworkPropertyMetadataOptions.BindsTwoWayByDefault));

public LinePatternEnum Gridline2YPattern
{
    get { return (LinePatternEnum)GetValue(Gridline2YPatternProperty); }
    set { SetValue(Gridline2YPatternProperty, value); }
}


public static DependencyProperty IsLegendProperty =
    DependencyProperty.Register("IsLegend", typeof(bool),
    typeof(Line2YChart), new FrameworkPropertyMetadata(false,
    FrameworkPropertyMetadataOptions.BindsTwoWayByDefault));

public bool IsLegend
{
    get { return (bool)GetValue(IsLegendProperty); }
    set { SetValue(IsLegendProperty, value); }
}

public static DependencyProperty LegendPositionProperty =
    DependencyProperty.Register("LegendPosition",
    typeof(LegendPositionEnum), typeof(Line2YChart),
    new FrameworkPropertyMetadata(LegendPositionEnum.NorthEast,
    FrameworkPropertyMetadataOptions.BindsTwoWayByDefault));

public LegendPositionEnum LegendPosition
{
    get { return (LegendPositionEnum)GetValue(LegendPositionProperty); }
    set { SetValue(LegendPositionProperty, value); }
```

```
        }

        public static readonly DependencyProperty DataCollectionProperty =
        DependencyProperty.Register("DataCollection",
        typeof(BindableCollection<LineSeries2Y>), typeof(Line2YChart),
        new FrameworkPropertyMetadata(null,
        FrameworkPropertyMetadataOptions.BindsTwoWayByDefault, OnDataChanged));

        public BindableCollection<LineSeries2Y> DataCollection
        {
            get { return (BindableCollection<LineSeries2Y>)
                GetValue(DataCollectionProperty); }
            set { SetValue(DataCollectionProperty, value); }
        }

        private static void OnDataChanged(object sender,
            DependencyPropertyChangedEventArgs e)
        {
            var lc = sender as Line2YChart;
            var dc = e.NewValue as BindableCollection<LineSeries2Y>;
            if (dc != null)
                dc.CollectionChanged += lc.dc_CollectionChanged;
        }

        private void dc_CollectionChanged(object sender,
            NotifyCollectionChangedEventArgs e)
        {
            if (DataCollection != null)
            {
                CheckCount = 0;
                if (DataCollection.Count > 0) CheckCount = DataCollection.Count;
            }
        }

        public static DependencyProperty CheckCountProperty =
            DependencyProperty.Register("CheckCount", typeof(int),
            typeof(Line2YChart), new FrameworkPropertyMetadata(0,
            FrameworkPropertyMetadataOptions.AffectsRender));

        public int CheckCount
        {
            get { return (int)GetValue(CheckCountProperty); }
            set { SetValue(CheckCountProperty, value); }
        }
    }
}
```

Note how we define the dependency properties. We use the same logic as in the previous example to make the control automatically generate a line 2Y chart after creating a *DataCollection* containing the *LineSeries2Y* objects. The *DataCollectionProperty* includes a callback method called *OnDataChanged*. Inside this callback method, we add an event handler to the *CollectionChanged* property when the *DataCollection* changes. Within the *CollectionChanged* handler, we set another private dependency property named *CheckCount* to the *DataCollection.Count*. If *CheckCount* > 0, we know that the *DataCollection* does contain *LineSeries2Y* objects, and we then set *FrameworkPropertyOptions* to

AffectsRender for the *CheckCount* property and WPF will re-render the chart control by calling the *OnRender* method when this property is changed.

Inside the *SetChart* method, we set the public properties of the *ChartStyle2Y* and *Legend* classes to the corresponding dependency properties of the chart control. This way, whenever the dependency properties in the *Line2YChart* class change, the properties in the *ChartStyle2Y* and *Legend* classes will change correspondingly.

You may notice from our chart control development that the implementation of dependency properties does not look very pretty and involves a great deal of duplicated code. In addition, the dependency property declarations can be quite error prone. You should consider using automatic code generation tools to help you create these dependency properties. In practice, I use T4 from Microsoft, which is part of Visual Studio, to generate dependency properties and CLR properties with the *INotifyPropertyChanged* interface as a partial class. This topic is beyond the scope of this book, but if you are interested, Microsoft (i.e., https://msdn.microsoft.com/en-us/library/dd820614.aspx) website provides a good overview.

Using Line 2Y Control

Using the line 2Y chart control, you can easily create line charts with two Y axes as presented in Chapter 4, but with much less effort. Add a new *UserControl* to the *Views* folder of the *Chapter07* project and name it *Line2YControlView*. Here is the XAML file for this view:

```
<UserControl x:Class="Chapter07.Views.Line2YControlView"
             xmlns="http://schemas.microsoft.com/winfx/2006/xaml/presentation"
             xmlns:x="http://schemas.microsoft.com/winfx/2006/xaml"
             xmlns:mc="http://schemas.openxmlformats.org/markup-compatibility/2006"
             xmlns:d="http://schemas.microsoft.com/expression/blend/2008"
             xmlns:local="clr-namespace:ChartControl;assembly=ChartControl"
             mc:Ignorable="d"
             d:DesignHeight="300" d:DesignWidth="500">
    <Grid>
        <Grid.ColumnDefinitions>
            <ColumnDefinition Width="*"/>
            <ColumnDefinition Width="150"/>
        </Grid.ColumnDefinitions>
        <Button x:Name="AddChart" Content="Add Chart" Width="100"
                Height="25" Grid.Column="1"/>
        <local:Line2YChart DataCollection="{Binding DataCollection}"
                Xmin="0" Xmax="30" XTick="5" Ymin="-20" Ymax="20" YTick="5"
                Y2min="100" Y2max="700" Y2Tick="100" XLabel="X" YLabel="Y"
                Y2Label="Y2" Title="Line 2Y Chart"
                GridlinePattern="Dot" GridlineColor="Green"
                Gridline2YColor="LightGray" Gridline2YPattern="Dash"
                IsLegend="True" LegendPosition="NorthWest"/>
    </Grid>
</UserControl>
```

Here, you simply create a line chart control exactly as you would create any other type of WPF element. You can specify various properties such as axis limits and chart styles in XAML and data bind the DataCollection property defined in the view model.

Add a new class to the *ViewModels* folder and name it *Line2YControlViewModel*. Here is the code for this class:

```csharp
using System;
using Caliburn.Micro;
using System.Collections.ObjectModel;
using System.ComponentModel.Composition;
using System.Windows;
using System.Windows.Media;
using ChartControl;

namespace Chapter07.ViewModels
{
    [Export(typeof(IScreen)), PartCreationPolicy(CreationPolicy.NonShared)]
    public class Line2YControlViewModel : Screen
    {
        private readonly IEventAggregator _events;
        [ImportingConstructor]
        public Line2YControlViewModel(IEventAggregator events)
        {
            this._events = events;
            DisplayName = "03. Line Y2 Chart";
            DataCollection = new BindableCollection<LineSeries2Y>();
        }

        public BindableCollection<LineSeries2Y> DataCollection { get; set; }

        public void AddChart()
        {
            DataCollection.Clear();

            //Add Y curve:
            var ds = new LineSeries2Y();
            ds.Symbols.BorderColor = Brushes.Blue;
            ds.Symbols.SymbolType = SymbolTypeEnum.OpenDiamond;
            ds.LineColor = Brushes.Blue;
            ds.LineThickness = 2;
            ds.SeriesName = "x*Cos(x)";
            ds.LinePattern = LinePatternEnum.Solid;
            for (int i = 0; i < 20; i++)
            {
                double x = 1.0 * i;
                double y = x * Math.Cos(x);
                ds.LinePoints.Add(new Point(x, y));
            }
            DataCollection.Add(ds);

            //Add Y2 curve:
            ds = new LineSeries2Y();
            ds.Is2YData = true;
            ds.Symbols.BorderColor = Brushes.Red;
            ds.Symbols.SymbolType = SymbolTypeEnum.Dot;
            ds.LineColor = Brushes.Red;
            ds.LineThickness = 2;
            ds.SeriesName = "100 + 20*x";
            ds.LinePattern = LinePatternEnum.DashDot;
            for (int i = 5; i < 30; i++)
            {
```

```
        double x = 1.0 * i;
        double y = 100.0 + 20 * x;
        ds.LinePoints.Add(new Point(x, y));
    }
    DataCollection.Add(ds);
  }
 }
}
```

Just like you did when you created line 2*Y* charts in Chapter 4, you first create *LineSeries2Y* objects and then add them to the chart control's *DataCollection*. The beauty of using the chart control is that you can use the standard MVVM pattern in the application, even though you created the chart control using dependency properties and a code-behind approach. Here, you just define the *DataCollection* property in the view model and bind it to the chart control. The *AddChart* method in the view model is also bound to the *Button* in the view by Caliburn.Micro's naming convention. This way, you have a perfect separation between the view and the view model, which meets the requirements of the MVVM pattern.

Running this example and clicking the *Add Chart* button generates the result shown in Figure 7-3. You can resize the chart to see how the chart gets updated automatically.

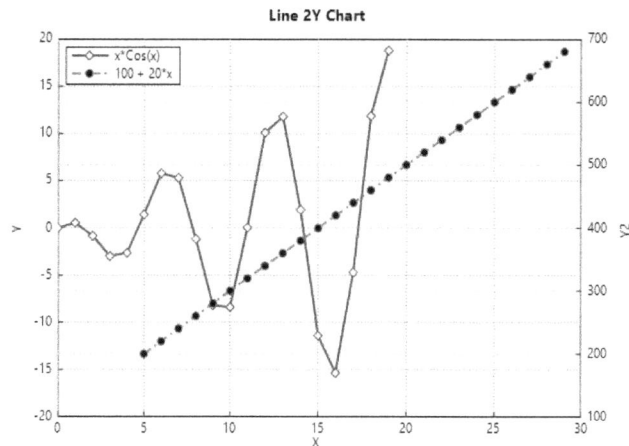

Figure 7-3. A line chart with two Y axes created using a chart control.

Stock Chart Control

In the preceding sections, I showed you how to create line chart controls and how to use them in WPF applications. Following the same procedure, we can also easily convert the stock charts presented in Chapter 6 into a user control.

Now go back to the *ChartControl* project. Add the three classes, *StockSeries*, *StockChartStyle*, and *TimeSeriesChartStyle*, from the *ChartModel* folder of the *Chapter06* project to the *ChartModel* folder of the current project, and change their namespaces to the *ChartControl*.

Add a new *UserControl* to the project and name it *StockChart*. Here is the XAML file for this view:

```
<UserControl x:Class="ChartControl.StockChart"
        xmlns="http://schemas.microsoft.com/winfx/2006/xaml/presentation"
```

```
            xmlns:x="http://schemas.microsoft.com/winfx/2006/xaml"
            xmlns:mc="http://schemas.openxmlformats.org/markup-compatibility/2006"
            xmlns:d="http://schemas.microsoft.com/expression/blend/2008"
            mc:Ignorable="d"
            d:DesignHeight="300" d:DesignWidth="300">
    <Grid>
        <Grid.ColumnDefinitions>
            <ColumnDefinition Width="Auto"/>
            <ColumnDefinition Name="column1" Width="*"/>
        </Grid.ColumnDefinitions>
        <Grid.RowDefinitions>
            <RowDefinition Height="Auto"/>
            <RowDefinition Name="row1" Height="*"/>
            <RowDefinition Height="Auto"/>
        </Grid.RowDefinitions>
        <TextBlock Margin="2" x:Name="tbTitle" Grid.Column="1" Grid.Row="0"
                RenderTransformOrigin="0.5,0.5" FontSize="14" FontWeight="Bold"
                HorizontalAlignment="Stretch" VerticalAlignment="Stretch"
                TextAlignment="Center" Text="Title"/>
        <TextBlock Margin="2" x:Name="tbXLabel" Grid.Column="1" Grid.Row="2"
                RenderTransformOrigin="0.5,0.5" TextAlignment="Center"
                Text="X Axis" FontWeight="Bold"/>
        <TextBlock Margin="2" Name="tbYLabel" Grid.Column="0" Grid.Row="1"
                FontWeight="Bold" RenderTransformOrigin="0.5,0.5"
                TextAlignment="Center" Text="Y Axis">
            <TextBlock.LayoutTransform>
                <RotateTransform Angle="-90"/>
            </TextBlock.LayoutTransform>
        </TextBlock>

        <Grid  Margin="0,0,0,0" x:Name ="chartGrid" Grid.Column="1" Grid.Row="1"
            ClipToBounds="False" Background="Transparent"
            SizeChanged="chartGrid_SizeChanged">
            <Canvas Margin="2" Name="textCanvas" Grid.Column="1" Grid.Row="1"
                    ClipToBounds="True" Width="{Binding ElementName=chartGrid,
                    Path=ActualWidth}" Height="{Binding ElementName=chartGrid,
                    Path=ActualHeight}">
                <Canvas Name="chartCanvas" ClipToBounds="True"/>
            </Canvas>
        </Grid>
    </Grid>
</UserControl>
```

This markup is basically similar to that used to create stock charts in Chapter 6, except that we add the event handler, *chartGrid_SizeChanged*, using the code-behind file instead of the MVVM *Message.Attach* method.

Defining Dependency Properties

Next, we need to design the public interface that the stock chart control exposes to the outside world. In other words, it is time to create the properties, methods, and events that the control consumer (the application that uses the control) will rely on to interact with the chart control.

You may want to expose to the outside world most of the properties of the *StockChartStyle* class from the stock chart example in Chapter 6, such as title and labels; at the same time, we will keep the classes from the original stock chart example project unchanged. In order to support WPF features such as data binding, styles, and animation, the control properties are always dependency properties.

Here is the code-behind file for the *StockChart* control:

```
using System;
using System.Collections.Generic;
using System.Linq;
using System.Windows;
using System.Windows.Controls;
using System.Windows.Media;
using Caliburn.Micro;
using System.Collections.Specialized;

namespace ChartControl
{
    /// <summary>
    /// Interaction logic for StockChart.xaml
    /// </summary>
    public partial class StockChart : UserControl
    {
        private StockChartStyle cs;

        public StockChart()
        {
            InitializeComponent();
            this.cs = new StockChartStyle();
            cs.TextCanvas = textCanvas;
            cs.ChartCanvas = chartCanvas;
        }

        protected override void OnRender(DrawingContext drawingContext)
        {
            SetChart();
        }

        private void chartGrid_SizeChanged(object sender, SizeChangedEventArgs e)
        {
            ResizeChart();
        }

        private void SetChart()
        {
            if (StockPrices == null)
                return;
            if (StockPrices.Count <= 0)
                return;

            cs.StockChartType = this.StockChartType;
            cs.Title = this.Title;
            cs.IsXGrid = this.IsXGrid;
            cs.IsYGrid = this.IsYGrid;
            cs.GridlineColor = this.GridlineColor;
```

```
    cs.GridlinePattern = this.GridlinePattern;
    ResizeChart();
}

private void    ResizeChart()
{
    chartCanvas.Children.Clear();
    textCanvas.Children.RemoveRange(1, textCanvas.Children.Count - 1);
    SetAxes();
    cs.DateList = new List<DateTime>();
    foreach (var p in StockPrices)
        cs.DateList.Add(p.Date);

    cs.AddTimeSeriesChartStyle(tbTitle, tbXLabel, tbYLabel);

    if (DataCollection.Count > 0)
        cs.SetStockChart(DataCollection);
}

private void SetAxes()
{
    cs.XLabel = "Date";
    cs.YLabel = "Stock Price";

    cs.Xmin = -1;
    cs.Xmax = StockPrices.Count;
    cs.XTick = (int)((cs.Xmax - cs.Xmin) / 5.01);

    double min = StockPrices.Min(x => x.PriceLow);
    double max = StockPrices.Max(x => x.PriceHigh);
    if (cs.StockChartType == StockChartTypeEnum.LineAdj)
    {
        min = StockPrices.Min(x => x.PriceAdj);
        max = StockPrices.Max(x => x.PriceAdj);
    }
    if (cs.StockChartType == StockChartTypeEnum.Volume)
    {
        min = StockPrices.Min(x => x.Volume);
        max = StockPrices.Max(x => x.Volume);
        cs.YLabel = "Volume";
    }
    double delta = (max - min) / 20.0;
    cs.Ymin = (int)(min - delta);
    cs.Ymax = (int)(max + delta);
    cs.YTick = (int)((max - min) / 5.01);
}

public static DependencyProperty StockChartTypeProperty =
            DependencyProperty.Register("StockChartType",
            typeof(StockChartTypeEnum),
            typeof(StockChart), new
            FrameworkPropertyMetadata(StockChartTypeEnum.Candlestick,
            FrameworkPropertyMetadataOptions.BindsTwoWayByDefault));

public StockChartTypeEnum StockChartType
```

```
    {
        get { return (StockChartTypeEnum)GetValue(StockChartTypeProperty); }
        set { SetValue(StockChartTypeProperty, value); }
    }

    public static DependencyProperty TitleProperty =
                DependencyProperty.Register("Title", typeof(string),
                typeof(StockChart),
                new FrameworkPropertyMetadata("My Title",
                FrameworkPropertyMetadataOptions.BindsTwoWayByDefault));

    public string Title
    {
        get { return (string)GetValue(TitleProperty); }
        set { SetValue(TitleProperty, value); }
    }

    public static DependencyProperty IsXGridProperty =
                DependencyProperty.Register("IsXGrid", typeof(bool),
                typeof(StockChart),
                new FrameworkPropertyMetadata(true,
                FrameworkPropertyMetadataOptions.BindsTwoWayByDefault));

    public bool IsXGrid
    {
        get { return (bool)GetValue(IsXGridProperty); }
        set { SetValue(IsXGridProperty, value); }
    }

    public static DependencyProperty IsYGridProperty =
                DependencyProperty.Register("IsYGrid", typeof(bool),
                typeof(StockChart),
                new FrameworkPropertyMetadata(true,
                FrameworkPropertyMetadataOptions.BindsTwoWayByDefault));

    public bool IsYGrid
    {
        get { return (bool)GetValue(IsYGridProperty); }
        set { SetValue(IsYGridProperty, value); }
    }

    public static DependencyProperty GridlineColorProperty =
                DependencyProperty.Register("GridlineColor", typeof(Brush),
                typeof(StockChart),
                new FrameworkPropertyMetadata(Brushes.Gray,
                FrameworkPropertyMetadataOptions.BindsTwoWayByDefault));

    public Brush GridlineColor
    {
        get { return (Brush)GetValue(GridlineColorProperty); }
        set { SetValue(GridlineColorProperty, value); }
    }

    public static DependencyProperty GridlinePatternProperty =
                DependencyProperty.Register("GridlinePattern",
```

```csharp
                    typeof(LinePatternEnum),
                    typeof(StockChart),
                    new FrameworkPropertyMetadata(LinePatternEnum.Solid,
                    FrameworkPropertyMetadataOptions.BindsTwoWayByDefault));

public LinePatternEnum GridlinePattern
{
    get { return (LinePatternEnum)GetValue(GridlinePatternProperty); }
    set { SetValue(GridlinePatternProperty, value); }
}

public static readonly DependencyProperty StockPricesProperty =
        DependencyProperty.Register("StockPrices",
        typeof(BindableCollection<StockPrice>), typeof(StockChart),
        new FrameworkPropertyMetadata(null,
        FrameworkPropertyMetadataOptions.BindsTwoWayByDefault));

public BindableCollection<StockPrice> StockPrices
{
    get { return
        (BindableCollection<StockPrice>)GetValue(StockPricesProperty); }
    set { SetValue(StockPricesProperty, value); }
}


public static readonly DependencyProperty DataCollectionProperty =
        DependencyProperty.Register("DataCollection",
        typeof(BindableCollection<StockSeries>), typeof(StockChart),
        new FrameworkPropertyMetadata(null,
        FrameworkPropertyMetadataOptions.BindsTwoWayByDefault,
        OnDataChanged));

public BindableCollection<StockSeries> DataCollection
{
    get { return
        (BindableCollection<StockSeries>)GetValue(DataCollectionProperty); }
    set { SetValue(DataCollectionProperty, value); }
}

private static void OnDataChanged(object sender,
    DependencyPropertyChangedEventArgs e)
{
    var sc = sender as StockChart;
    var dc = e.NewValue as BindableCollection<StockSeries>;
    if (dc != null)
        dc.CollectionChanged += sc.dc_CollectionChanged;
}

private void dc_CollectionChanged(object sender,
    NotifyCollectionChangedEventArgs e)
{
    if (DataCollection != null)
    {
        CheckCount = 0;
        if (DataCollection.Count > 0)
```

```
                        CheckCount = DataCollection.Count;
            }
        }

    private static DependencyProperty CheckCountProperty =
                DependencyProperty.Register("CheckCount", typeof(int),
                typeof(StockChart), new FrameworkPropertyMetadata(0,
                FrameworkPropertyMetadataOptions.AffectsRender));

    private int CheckCount
    {
        get { return (int)GetValue(CheckCountProperty); }
        set { SetValue(CheckCountProperty, value); }
    }
}

public class StockPrice
{
    public string Ticker { get; set; }
    public DateTime Date { get; set; }
    public double PriceOpen { get; set; }
    public double PriceHigh { get; set; }
    public double PriceLow { get; set; }
    public double PriceClose { get; set; }
    public double PriceAdj { get; set; }
    public double Volume { get; set; }
}
}
```

Note that this code-behind file includes a *StockPrice* class that was originally defined in the *Dal* (data access layer) class in the *Chapter06* project. In Chapter 6, the stock charts couple together with the *Dal* class that interacts directly with the database, which is fine for a single WPF application. However, we want to design a stock chart control that can be used for general applications with any data source rather than a single application with a specific database. To achieve this, we need to decouple the stock control from the *Dal* class, which is the reason we redefine the *StockPrice* entity class in the control's code-behind file. This way, the stock chart control we are designing can be used in a variety of .NET applications with stock data from any data source.

The rest of the code is similar to that used to create the line chart control. In particular, we check the *DataCollection*'s *CollectionChanged* event handler to process the stock chart. Note that inside the *SetChart* method, we set the public properties of the *StockChartStyle* class to the corresponding dependency properties of the chart control. The *SetChart* method also includes a *SetAxes* method that sets axis limits and ticks automatically according to the input stock data.

Here, we also add a *chartGrid_SizeChanged* event handler to the stock chart control. This handler ensures that the stock chart gets updated whenever the chart control is resized. Now you can build the control library by right clicking the *ChartControl* project and selecting Build.

Using the Stock Chart Control

Using the stock chart control, you can easily create the stock charts presented in Chapter 6 with much less effort. Add a new *UserControl* to the *Views* folder of the *Chapter07* project and name it *StockChartControlView*. Here is the XAML file for this view:

```xml
<UserControl x:Class="Chapter07.Views.StockChartControlView"
             xmlns="http://schemas.microsoft.com/winfx/2006/xaml/presentation"
             xmlns:x="http://schemas.microsoft.com/winfx/2006/xaml"
             xmlns:mc="http://schemas.openxmlformats.org/markup-compatibility/2006"
             xmlns:d="http://schemas.microsoft.com/expression/blend/2008"
             xmlns:local="clr-namespace:ChartControl;assembly=ChartControl"
             xmlns:cal="http://www.caliburnproject.org"
             mc:Ignorable="d"
             d:DesignHeight="400" d:DesignWidth="800">
    <Grid>
        <Grid.ColumnDefinitions>
            <ColumnDefinition Width="170"/>
            <ColumnDefinition Width="1*"/>
            <ColumnDefinition Width="2*"/>
        </Grid.ColumnDefinitions>
        <StackPanel Margin="5">
            <GroupBox Header="Get Stock Data" Margin="0 0 0 0">
                <StackPanel Margin="0 5 0 5">
                    <StackPanel Orientation="Horizontal">
                        <TextBlock Text="Ticker" Width="60"/>
                        <TextBox x:Name="Ticker" Width="80"/>
                    </StackPanel>
                    <StackPanel Orientation="Horizontal" Margin="0 5 0 0">
                        <TextBlock Text="Start Date" Width="60"/>
                        <TextBox x:Name="StartDate" Width="80"/>
                    </StackPanel>
                    <StackPanel Orientation="Horizontal" Margin="0 5 0 0">
                        <TextBlock Text="End Date" Width="60"/>
                        <TextBox x:Name="EndDate" Width="80"/>
                    </StackPanel>
                    <Button x:Name="GetStockData" Content="Get Stock Data"
                            Width="120" Margin="0 10 0 0"/>
                </StackPanel>
            </GroupBox>
            <TextBlock Text="Choose Stock Chart Type:" Margin="0 20 0 0"/>
            <ComboBox x:Name="StockChartType" Width="150" Margin="0 5 0 0"
                      HorizontalAlignment="Left" cal:Message.Attach="[Event
                      SelectionChanged]=[Action AddChart]"/>
        </StackPanel>

        <DataGrid x:Name="StockPrices" ColumnWidth="Auto" CanUserAddRows="False"
                  Grid.Column="1" FontSize="10"/>

        <local:StockChart Grid.Column="2" DataCollection="{Binding DataCollection}"
                          StockPrices="{Binding StockPrices}"
                          GridlinePattern="Dot" GridlineColor="Red"
                          StockChartType="{Binding SelectedStockChartType}"
                          Margin="10" Title="{Binding Title}"/>
    </Grid>
</UserControl>
```

The layout of this view is similar to that used in creating stock charts in Chapter 6. Here, you first get the stock data from database for a specified ticker and period; then you can choose the chart type from the *ComboBox* control. Note that I also attach this *ComboBox*'s *SelectionChanged* event to the *AddChart* method in the view model, so the program will update the chart whenever you select a different chart type.

Add a new class to the *ViewModels* folder and name it *StockChartControlViewModel*. Here is the code for this class:

```
using System;
using System.Linq;
using Caliburn.Micro;
using System.Collections.ObjectModel;
using System.ComponentModel.Composition;
using System.Collections.Generic;
using System.Windows;
using System.Windows.Media;
using System.Windows.Controls;
using Chapter07.Models.DataModel;
using Chapter06.Models.ChartModel;

namespace Chapter07.ViewModels
{
    [Export(typeof(IScreen)), PartCreationPolicy(CreationPolicy.NonShared)]
    public class StockChartControlViewModel : Screen
    {
        private readonly IEventAggregator _events;
        [ImportingConstructor]
        public StockChartControlViewModel(IEventAggregator events)
        {
            this._events = events;
            DisplayName = "03. Stock Chart";
            DataCollection = new BindableCollection<StockSeries>();
            StockPrices = new BindableCollection<ChartControl.StockPrice>();
            StartDate = Convert.ToDateTime("10/1/2014");
            EndDate = Convert.ToDateTime("1/1/2015");
            Ticker = "GS";
            model = new Dal();
        }

        private Dal model;
        public BindableCollection<StockSeries> DataCollection { get; set; }
        public BindableCollection<ChartControl.StockPrice> StockPrices { get; set; }

        private string title;
        public string Title
        {
            get { return title; }
            set
            {
                title = value;
                NotifyOfPropertyChange(() => Title);
            }
        }

        private string ticker;
        public string Ticker
        {
            get { return ticker; }
```

```
    set
    {
        ticker = value;
        NotifyOfPropertyChange(() => Ticker);
    }
}

private DateTime startDate;
public DateTime StartDate
{
    get { return startDate; }
    set
    {
        startDate = value;
        NotifyOfPropertyChange(() => StartDate);
    }
}

private DateTime endDate;
public DateTime EndDate
{
    get { return endDate; }
    set
    {
        endDate = value;
        NotifyOfPropertyChange(() => EndDate);
    }
}

private IEnumerable<StockChartTypeEnum> stockChartType;
public IEnumerable<StockChartTypeEnum> StockChartType
{
    get { return Enum.GetValues(typeof(StockChartTypeEnum)).
        Cast<StockChartTypeEnum>(); }
    set
    {
        stockChartType = value;
        NotifyOfPropertyChange(() => StockChartType);
    }
}

private StockChartTypeEnum selectedStockChartType =
    StockChartTypeEnum.LineAdj;
public StockChartTypeEnum SelectedStockChartType
{
    get { return selectedStockChartType; }
    set
    {
        selectedStockChartType = value;
        NotifyOfPropertyChange(() => SelectedStockChartType);
    }
}

public void GetStockData()
{
```

```
            model.DateStart = StartDate;
            model.DateEnd = EndDate;
            model.Ticker = Ticker;
            model.GetStockPrices();
            StockPrices.Clear();
            foreach (var p in model.StockPrices)
            {
                StockPrices.Add(new ChartControl.StockPrice
                {
                    Ticker = p.Ticker,
                    Date = p.Date,
                    PriceOpen = p.PriceOpen,
                    PriceHigh = p.PriceHigh,
                    PriceLow = p.PriceLow,
                    PriceClose = p.PriceClose,
                    PriceAdj = p.PriceAdj,
                    Volume = p.Volume
                });
            }

            AddChart();
        }

        public void AddChart()
        {
            Title = string.Format("{0}: {1}", Ticker, SelectedStockChartType);
            DataCollection.Clear();
            var ss = new StockSeries();
            ss.StockPrices = StockPrices;
            ss.LineColor = Brushes.DarkBlue;
            if (SelectedStockChartType == StockChartTypeEnum.Candlestick)
            {
                ss.FillColor1 = Brushes.DarkBlue;
                ss.FillColor2 = Brushes.White;
            }
            DataCollection.Add(ss);
        }
    }
}
```

You first need to get stock data from the entity data model using the *GetStockPrices* method implemented in the *Dal* class. Create the stock data entity model from the database following the procedure described in Chapter 6 and import the *Dal* class into the current project.

After getting stock data from the database, you need to feed the data to the stock chart control's *StockPrices* collection object, which is the interface between the data source and the chart control. Also, note that the *StockChartType* property of the chart control binds to the *SelectedStockChartType* (that is, the *SelectedItem*) of the *ComboBox*. This way, the chart control will update the chart when you choose a different chart type from the *ComboBox*.

Running this example generates the output shown in Figure 7-4.

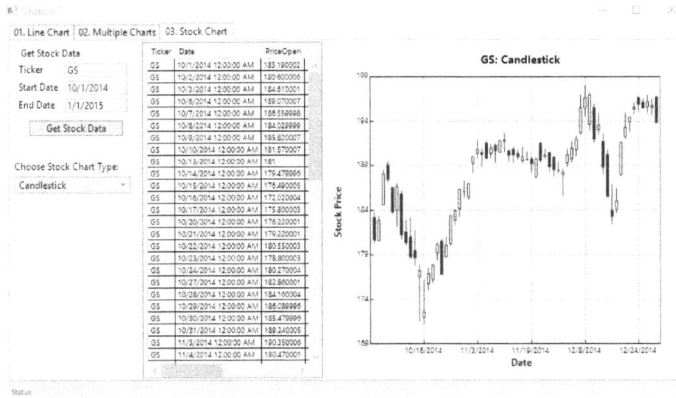

Figure 7-4. A stock chart created using a chart control.

Real-time Charts Using Chart Controls

In this section, I will show you how to dynamically update a chart created using the chart control to display real-time data. Real-time charts can be very useful in monitoring data obtained from sensors and test equipment, displaying stock market prices, and many other practical applications. When we use the chart control we developed in the revious sections, it is possible to continue adding data while the chart is being displayed.

The key steps for creating a real-time chart using the chart control are:

- Use asynchronous workflows to update a chart repeatedly. Here I will use the new .NET 4.5 features *async* and *await* to update the chart.

- Update the range of X- and Y-axes depending on the values being added to the chart.

- Use asynchronous workflows to generate values in the background.

Here, I will demonstrate real-time chart implementation using two examples. The first example creates a simple *Sine* line chart that will be updated in real-time, and the second example will mimic a real-time stock price chart by displaying daily stock data continuously.

Real-Time Line Charts

In this section I will show you how to create a real-time *Sine* line chart using the chart control. Add a new *UserControl* to the *Views* folder of the *Chapter07* project and name it *LineRealtimeView*. Here is the XAML file for this view:

```
<UserControl x:Class="Chapter07.Views.LineRealtimeView"
             xmlns="http://schemas.microsoft.com/winfx/2006/xaml/presentation"
             xmlns:x="http://schemas.microsoft.com/winfx/2006/xaml"
             xmlns:mc="http://schemas.openxmlformats.org/markup-compatibility/2006"
             xmlns:d="http://schemas.microsoft.com/expression/blend/2008"
             xmlns:local="clr-namespace:ChartControl;assembly=ChartControl"
             mc:Ignorable="d"
             d:DesignHeight="300" d:DesignWidth="400">
```

```
    <Grid>
        <Grid.ColumnDefinitions>
            <ColumnDefinition Width="*"/>
            <ColumnDefinition Width="150"/>
        </Grid.ColumnDefinitions>
        <StackPanel Grid.Column="1" Margin="0 20 0 0">
            <Button x:Name="StartChart" Content="Start Chart" Width="100"
                    Height="20"/>
            <Button x:Name="StopChart" Content="Stop chart" Width="100"
                    Height="20" Margin="0 10 0 0"/>
        </StackPanel>
        <local:LineChart DataCollection="{Binding DataCollection}"
                Xmin="{Binding Xmin}" Xmax="{Binding Xmax}" XTick="1"
                Ymin="-1.5" Ymax="1.5" YTick="0.5" XLabel="X" YLabel="Y"
                Title="My Line Chart" GridlinePattern="Dot"
                GridlineColor="Green"/>
    </Grid>
</UserControl>
```

Here, we add two buttons, *StartChart* and *StopChart*, that will be used to start or stop updating the chart in real time.

Add a new class to the *ViewModels* folder and name it *LineRealtimeViewModel*. Here is the code for this class:

```
using System;
using Caliburn.Micro;
using System.Collections.ObjectModel;
using System.ComponentModel.Composition;
using System.Windows;
using System.Windows.Media;
using ChartControl;
using System.Threading.Tasks;
using System.Threading;
using System.Windows.Threading;
using System.Windows.Documents;
using System.Collections.Generic;
using Chapter07.Models;

namespace Chapter07.ViewModels
{
    [Export(typeof(IScreen)), PartCreationPolicy(CreationPolicy.NonShared)]
    public class LineRealtimeViewModel : Screen
    {
        private readonly IEventAggregator _events;
        [ImportingConstructor]
        public LineRealtimeViewModel(IEventAggregator events)
        {
            this._events = events;
            DisplayName = "05. Line Realtime Chart";
            DataCollection = new BindableCollection<LineSeries>();
        }

        public BindableCollection<LineSeries> DataCollection{get;set;}

        private double xmin;
```

```
public double Xmin
{
    get { return xmin; }
    set
    {
        xmin = value;
        NotifyOfPropertyChange(() => Xmin);
    }
}

private double xmax;
public double Xmax
{
    get { return xmax; }
    set
    {
        xmax = value;
        NotifyOfPropertyChange(() => Xmax);
    }
}

private bool isStop = false;
public bool IsStop
{
    get { return isStop; }
    set
    {
        isStop = value;
        NotifyOfPropertyChange(() => IsStop);
    }
}

public async void StartChart()
{
    IsStop = false;
    LineSeries ds = new LineSeries();
    ds.LineColor = Brushes.Blue;
    ds.LineThickness = 2;
    ds.SeriesName = "Sine";
    ds.LinePattern = LinePatternEnum.Solid;
    ds.LinePoints.Clear();
    for (int i = 0; i < 50; i++)
    {
        double x = i / 5.0;
        double y = Math.Sin(x);
        ds.LinePoints.Add(new Point(x, y));
    }
    Xmin = 0;
    Xmax = ds.LinePoints[ds.LinePoints.Count - 1].X;

    await Task.Run(() =>
    {
        DataCollection.Clear();
        List<object> objList = new List<object>();
        objList.Add("Ready...");
```

```
                objList.Add(0);
                objList.Add(2000);
                objList.Add(0);

                for (int i = 50; i < 2000; i++)
                {
                    if (IsStop)
                        break;
                    Thread.Sleep(500);
                    DataCollection.Clear();
                    ds.LinePoints.RemoveAt(0);
                    double x = i / 5.0;
                    double y = Math.Sin(x);
                    ds.LinePoints.Add(new Point(x, y));
                    Xmin = ds.LinePoints[0].X;
                    Xmax = ds.LinePoints[ds.LinePoints.Count - 1].X;
                    DataCollection.Add(ds);

                    objList[0] = string.Format("Total Runs = 2000,
                                i={0}, x={1}, y={2:0.00}", i, x, y);
                    objList[3] = i;
                    _events.PublishOnUIThread(new ModelEvents(objList));
                }

                objList[0] = "Ready...";
                if (IsStop)
                    objList[0] = "Stop...";
                objList[1] = 0;
                objList[2] = 1;
                objList[3] = 0;
                _events.PublishOnUIThread(new ModelEvents(objList));
            });
        }

        public void StopChart()
        {
            IsStop = true;
        }
    }
}
```

Besides the *DataCollection* property, here we also add three other properties: *Xmin*, *Xmax*, and *IsStop*. The *Xmin* and *Xmax* properties need to be updated when the real-time data is being added to the chart. We do not need to update the *Y*-axis limits because we want to display a *Sine* function with a range of $[-1, 1]$, so we can set fixed limits for the *Y*-axis in XAML. The *IsStop* property is used to control the real-time updating status.

The magic happens in the *StartChart* method where we use the new *async* and *await* pair in .NET 4.5 to perform real-time updating. First, we create a new *LineSeries* object and set its initial point collection as the first 50 points of the *Sine* function. We also set the *X*-axis limits using the initial point collection. Next, within the *await* block, we mimics a real-time data source by removing an old data point from and adding a new data point to the *LineSeries* object's point collection every 500 *ms*, as specified by the *Thread.Sleep*(500) method. At the same time, we create an object list, *objList*, which is used by Caliburn.Micro to publish messages that report the progress of the real-time updating. This published message, subscribed to the *MainViewModel* is in turn used to update the status text and progress bar implemented in the *MainView*. The *StartChart* method also checks the *IsStop* property, and will exit the *for* loop when *IsStop* is true.

Running this example generates the results shown in Figure 7-5. You can see how the *Sine* line and X-axis limits get updated. The application also provides progress monitoring of the real-time updates through the status text and the program bar.

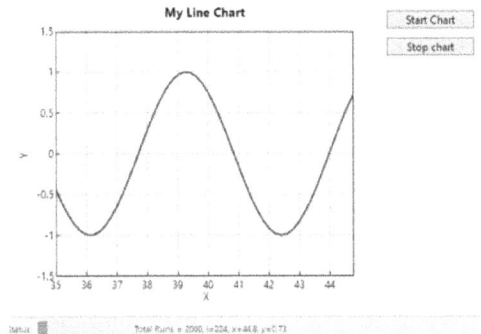

Figure 7-5. A real-time line chart created using a chart control.

Real-Time Stock Charts

Following the same procedure as that used in the previous section, we can easily create a real-time stock chart. Add a new *UserControl* to the *Views* folder and name it *StockRealtimeView*. Here is the markup for this view:

```
<UserControl x:Class="Chapter07.Views.StockRealtimeView"
             xmlns="http://schemas.microsoft.com/winfx/2006/xaml/presentation"
             xmlns:x="http://schemas.microsoft.com/winfx/2006/xaml"
             xmlns:mc="http://schemas.openxmlformats.org/markup-compatibility/2006"
             xmlns:d="http://schemas.microsoft.com/expression/blend/2008"
             xmlns:local="clr-namespace:ChartControl;assembly=ChartControl"
             xmlns:cal="http://www.caliburnproject.org"
             mc:Ignorable="d"
             d:DesignHeight="400" d:DesignWidth="800">
    <Grid>
        <Grid.ColumnDefinitions>
            <ColumnDefinition Width="170"/>
            <ColumnDefinition Width="1*"/>
            <ColumnDefinition Width="2*"/>
        </Grid.ColumnDefinitions>
        <StackPanel Margin="5">
            <GroupBox Header="Get Stock Data" Margin="0 0 0 0">
                <StackPanel Margin="0 5 0 5">
                    <StackPanel Orientation="Horizontal">
                        <TextBlock Text="Ticker" Width="60"/>
                        <TextBox x:Name="Ticker" Width="80"/>
                    </StackPanel>
                    <StackPanel Orientation="Horizontal" Margin="0 5 0 0">
                        <TextBlock Text="Start Date" Width="60"/>
                        <TextBox x:Name="StartDate" Width="80"/>
```

```xaml
                    </StackPanel>
                    <StackPanel Orientation="Horizontal" Margin="0 5 0 0">
                        <TextBlock Text="End Date" Width="60"/>
                        <TextBox x:Name="EndDate" Width="80"/>
                    </StackPanel>
                    <Button x:Name="GetStockData" Content="Get Stock Data"
                            Width="120" Margin="0 10 0 0"/>
                </StackPanel>
            </GroupBox>


            <GroupBox Header="Real Time Stock Chart" Margin="0 20 0 0">
                <StackPanel Margin="0 5 0 5">
                    <TextBlock Text="Choose Stock Chart Type:" Margin="0 0 0 0"/>
                    <ComboBox x:Name="StockChartType" Width="140"
                              Margin="0 5 0 0" HorizontalAlignment="Left"/>
                    <StackPanel Orientation="Horizontal" Margin="0 10 0 0">
                        <TextBlock Text="Chart Window:" Width="90"/>
                        <TextBox x:Name="ChartWindow" Width="50"/>
                    </StackPanel>
                    <Button x:Name="StartRealtime" Content="Start Real Time Chart"
                            Width="120" Margin="0 10 0 0"/>
                    <Button x:Name="StopRealtime" Content="Stop Real Time Chart"
                            Width="120" Margin="0 10 0 0"/>
                </StackPanel>
            </GroupBox>
        </StackPanel>

        <DataGrid x:Name="StockPricesAll" ColumnWidth="Auto"
                  CanUserAddRows="False" Grid.Column="1" FontSize="10"/>
        <local:StockChart Grid.Column="2" DataCollection="{Binding DataCollection}"
              StockPrices="{Binding StockPrices}"
              GridlinePattern="Dot" GridlineColor="Red"
              StockChartType="{Binding SelectedStockChartType}"
              Margin="10" Title="{Binding Title}"/>
    </Grid>
</UserControl>
```

This XAML file lets you retrieve stock data from the database by specifying the stock ticker, start date, and end date. Then, you can create a real-time stock chart by selecting the stock chart type and specifying the chart window, which is an integer number representing the number of days' worth of data you want to display on the chart.

Add a new class to the *ViewModels* folder and name it *StockRealtimeViewModel*. Here is the code for this class:

```csharp
using System;
using System.Linq;
using Caliburn.Micro;
using System.Collections.ObjectModel;
using System.ComponentModel.Composition;
using System.Collections.Generic;
using System.Windows;
using System.Windows.Media;
using System.Windows.Controls;
using Chapter07.Models.DataModel;
```

```
using Chapter07.Models;
using ChartControl;
using System.Threading.Tasks;
using System.Threading;

namespace Chapter07.ViewModels
{
    [Export(typeof(IScreen)), PartCreationPolicy(CreationPolicy.NonShared)]
    public class StockRealtimeViewModel : Screen
    {
        private readonly IEventAggregator _events;
        [ImportingConstructor]
        public StockRealtimeViewModel(IEventAggregator events)
        {
            this._events = events;
            DisplayName = "06. Realtime Stock Chart";
            DataCollection = new BindableCollection<StockSeries>();
            StockPricesAll = new BindableCollection<ChartControl.StockPrice>();
            StockPrices = new BindableCollection<ChartControl.StockPrice>();
            StartDate = Convert.ToDateTime("1/1/2010");
            EndDate = Convert.ToDateTime("1/1/2015");
            Ticker = "GS";
            model = new Dal();
        }

        private Dal model;
        public BindableCollection<StockSeries> DataCollection { get; set; }
        public BindableCollection<ChartControl.StockPrice>
                StockPricesAll { get; set; }
        public BindableCollection<ChartControl.StockPrice> StockPrices { get; set; }

        private string title;
        public string Title
        {
            get { return title; }
            set
            {
                title = value;
                NotifyOfPropertyChange(() => Title);
            }
        }

        private string ticker;
        public string Ticker
        {
            get { return ticker; }
            set
            {
                ticker = value;
                NotifyOfPropertyChange(() => Ticker);
            }
        }

        private DateTime startDate;
        public DateTime StartDate
```

```csharp
    {
        get { return startDate; }
        set
        {
            startDate = value;
            NotifyOfPropertyChange(() => StartDate);
        }
    }

    private int chartWindow = 30;
    public int ChartWindow
    {
        get { return chartWindow; }
        set
        {
            chartWindow = value;
            NotifyOfPropertyChange(() => ChartWindow);
        }
    }

    private DateTime endDate;
    public DateTime EndDate
    {
        get { return endDate; }
        set
        {
            endDate = value;
            NotifyOfPropertyChange(() => EndDate);
        }
    }

    private IEnumerable<StockChartTypeEnum> stockChartType;
    public IEnumerable<StockChartTypeEnum> StockChartType
    {
        get { return Enum.GetValues(typeof(StockChartTypeEnum)).
            Cast<StockChartTypeEnum>(); }
        set
        {
            stockChartType = value;
            NotifyOfPropertyChange(() => StockChartType);
        }
    }

    private StockChartTypeEnum selectedStockChartType =
            StockChartTypeEnum.Candlestick;
    public StockChartTypeEnum SelectedStockChartType
    {
        get { return selectedStockChartType; }
        set
        {
            selectedStockChartType = value;
            NotifyOfPropertyChange(() => SelectedStockChartType);
        }
    }
```

```csharp
private bool isStop = false;
public bool IsStop
{
    get { return isStop; }
    set
    {
        isStop = value;
        NotifyOfPropertyChange(() => IsStop);
    }
}

public void GetStockData()
{
    model.DateStart = StartDate;
    model.DateEnd = EndDate;
    model.Ticker = Ticker;
    model.GetStockPrices();
    StockPricesAll.Clear();
    foreach (var p in model.StockPrices)
    {
        StockPricesAll.Add(new ChartControl.StockPrice
        {
            Ticker = p.Ticker,
            Date = p.Date,
            PriceOpen = p.PriceOpen,
            PriceHigh = p.PriceHigh,
            PriceLow = p.PriceLow,
            PriceClose = p.PriceClose,
            PriceAdj = p.PriceAdj,
            Volume = p.Volume
        });
    }
}

public async void StartRealtime()
{
    IsStop = false;

    StockPrices.Clear();
    for (int i = 0; i < ChartWindow; i++)
    {
        StockPrices.Add(StockPricesAll[i]);
    }

    Title = string.Format("{0}: {1}", Ticker, SelectedStockChartType);
    List<object> objList = new List<object>();
    int totalRuns = StockPricesAll.Count - ChartWindow;
    objList.Add("Ready...");
    objList.Add(0);
    objList.Add(totalRuns);
    objList.Add(0);

    await Task.Run(() =>
    {
        for (int i = ChartWindow; i < StockPricesAll.Count; i++)
```

```
                    {
                        if (IsStop)
                            break;

                        Thread.Sleep(200);
                        StockPrices.RemoveAt(0);
                        StockPrices.Add(StockPricesAll[i]);

                        DataCollection.Clear();
                        var ss = new StockSeries();
                        ss.StockPrices = new
                            BindableCollection<ChartControl.StockPrice>();
                        ss.StockPrices = StockPrices;
                        ss.LineColor = Brushes.DarkBlue;
                        if (SelectedStockChartType == StockChartTypeEnum.Candlestick)
                        {
                            ss.FillColor1 = Brushes.DarkBlue;
                            ss.FillColor2 = Brushes.White;
                        }
                        DataCollection.Add(ss);

                        objList[0] = string.Format("Total runs = {0},
                            i = {1}", totalRuns, i - ChartWindow);
                        objList[3] = i - ChartWindow;
                        _events.PublishOnUIThread(new ModelEvents(objList));
                    }
                    objList[0] = "Ready...";
                    if (IsStop)
                        objList[0] = "Stop...";
                    objList[1] = 0;
                    objList[2] = 1;
                    objList[3] = 0;
                    _events.PublishOnUIThread(new ModelEvents(objList));

                });
            }

            public void StopRealtime()
            {
                IsStop = true;
            }
        }
    }
}
```

Here, we first retrieve the stock data for a specified ticker and period from database and display the data in a *DataGrid* control. Then, in the *StartRealtime* method, we initialize the *StockPrices* collection with data for the first number of days = *ChartWindow*. Inside the *for* loop, we simulate a real-time data source by removing an old data point from and adding a new data point to the *StockPrices collection* every 200 *ms*, as specified by the *Thread.Sleep*(200) method. At the same time, we create an object list, *objList*, which is used by Caliburn.Micro to publish messages that report the progress of the real-time updating. This published message, subscribed to by the *MainViewModel*, is in turn used to update the status text and the progress bar implemented in the *MainView*. The *StartRealtime* method also checks the *IsStop* property and will exit the *for* loop when *IsStop* is true. The *StartRealtime* method also uses the *async-await* feature to manage the real-time updating.

Running this example generates the results shown in Figure 7-6. You can see how the stock chart and X- and Y-axis limits get updated. The application also provides progress monitoring of the real-time updates through the status text and the program bar. You can create different real-time stock charts by selecting a different chart type or entering a different stock ticker.

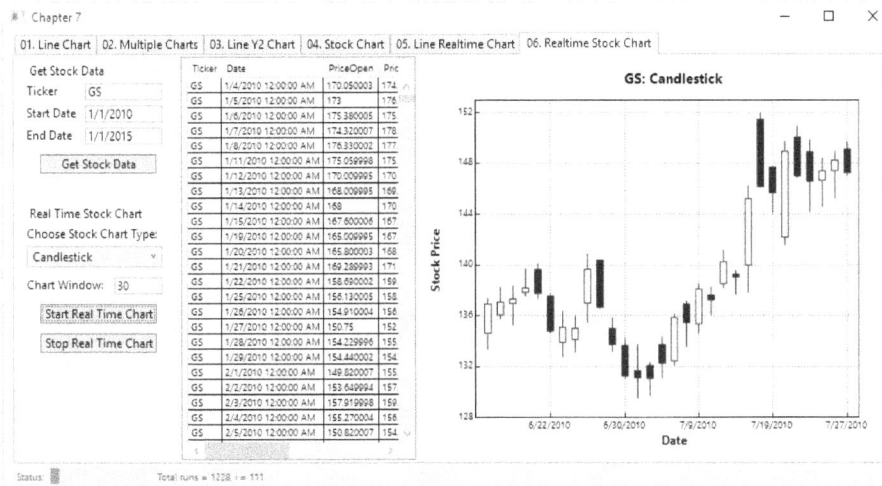

Figure 7-6. A real-time stock chart created using a chart control.

In this chapter, we converted the line charts and stock charts into a reusable chart control. Following the same procedure, you can also easily convert the 2D specialized charts implemented in Chapter 5 into a chart control. I will not repeat the conversion here and instead leave it to you as an exercise.

Chapter 8
3D Charts

In the previous chapters, we covered various 2D charts and 2D chart controls, including line charts, stock charts, and 2D specialized charts. In this chapter, I will show you how to create 3D charts. I will skip the mathematical basics behind 3D charts; you can refer to my previously published books, *Practical C# Charts and Graphics* and *Practical WPF Charts and Graphics*, for mathematical details.

I will start with a description of the 3D matrix in WPF and the coordinate system used for 3D charts, and show you how to create 3D coordinate axes, tick marks, axis labels, and gridlines. The 3D coordinate system used in 3D charts is the most fundamental part of creating 3D chart applications because it involves almost all of the matrix operations and transformations used to create 3D charts.

You will learn how to use a direct projection approach, without using the WPF 3D engine, to create sophisticated 3D charts with advanced features, such as *colormaps* and *colorbars*. I will show you how to create various 3D chart applications, including 3D line charts, 3D meshes, and surface charts, as well as a variety of specialized 3D charts, such as contour charts and 3D bar charts, among others. The example programs in this chapter provide basic solutions for 3D chart applications. Using this example code, with or without modifications, you can easily create your own professional and advanced 3D charts in your .NET applications.

3D Matrices in WPF

Matrix representations play an important role in creating 3D charts. A matrix is a multi-dimensional array. This section explains the basics of 3D matrices and transformations. General 3D transforms are quite complicated, but as is the case for 2D transformations, you can build more useful transforms with combinations of simple basic transforms, including translation, scaling, rotation, and projection. The following sections describe these fundamental transformations. Once you understand how to use these basic 3D transformations, you can always combine them to create more general 3D transformations.

3D Points and Vectors

WPF defines two 3D Point structures, *Point3D* and *Point4D*. The *Point3D* structure defines the *X*, *Y*, and *Z* coordinates of a point in 3D space. *Point4D* defines the *X*, *Y*, *Z*, and *W* coordinates of a point in a 3D homogeneous coordinate system, which is used to perform transformations with nonaffine 3D matrices. The *Vector3D* structure defines a displacement with components *X*, *Y*, and *Z* in 3D space.

You can represent a vector in 3D by a row array with three elements X, Y, and Z. For instance, you can create a 3D vector object using the following code snippet:

```
Vector3D v = new Vector3D(1, 2, 3);
```

Note that a *Vector3D* object and a *Point3D* object in WPF are two different objects. The following statement is invalid:

```
Vector3D v = new Point3D(1, 2, 3);
```

However, you can define a *Vector3D* object using *Point3D*, or vice versa. The following are valid statements:

```
Vector3D v1 = new Point3D(2, 3, 4) - new Point3D(1, 2, 3);
Vector3D v2 = (Vector3D)(new Point3D(1, 2, 3));
Point3D pt = (Point3D)(new Vector3D(1, 2, 3));
```

It is possible to cast a Point3D object to a Point4D object, as shown in the following statement:

```
var pt4 = (Point4D)(new Point3D(10, 15, 20));
```

The following code snippet is also valid:

```
var pt4 = (Point4D)(Point3D)(new Vector3D(10, 15, 20));
```

where the *Vector3D* object is first cast to a *Point3D* object, which is then cast to a *Point4D* object. In the preceding casting process, the Point4D object has the values: pt4 = (10, 15, 20, 1). The W component with a default value of 1, is automatically added.

You can perform standard operations on *Vector3D*, such as *Add*, *Subtract*, *Multiply*, *Divide*, *CrossProduct*, *AngleBetween*, and *Normalize*. For *Point3D* and *Point4D*, you can perform the following operations: *Add*, *Subtract*, *Multiply*, and *Offset*.

Matrix3D Structure

WPF defines a 3D matrix structure, *Matrix3D*, which is a 4 x 4 matrix in the 3D homogeneous coordinate system with the following row-vector syntax:

$$\begin{pmatrix} M_{11} & M_{12} & M_{13} & M_{14} \\ M_{21} & M_{22} & M_{23} & M_{24} \\ M_{31} & M_{32} & M_{33} & M_{34} \\ OffsetX & OffsetY & OffsetZ & M_{44} \end{pmatrix}$$

Unlike 2D matrices, here the last column is defined and accessible. The *Matrix3D* structure allows you to represent affine as well as nonaffine 3D transformations. Nonaffine transformations with nonzero M_{14}, M_{24}, or M_{34} values often represent perspective projection transformations.

All 16 of these elements are public properties of a *Matrix3D* structure. In particular, the elements of *OffsetX*, *OffsetY*, and *OffsetZ* represent translations in the X, Y, and Z directions, respectively. In addition to the element properties, there are other public properties associated with *Matrix3D* structures that are also useful in performing matrix operations:

- *Determinant* – Retrieves the determinant of the *Matrix3D* structure.
- *HasInverse* – Gets a value that indicates whether the *Matrix3D* is invertible.

- *Identity* – Changes a *Matrix3D* structure into an identity *Matrix3D*.

- *IsAffine* – Gets a value that indicates whether the *Matrix3D* structure is affine.

- *IsIdentity* – Determines whether the *Matrix3D* structure is an identity *Matrix3D*.

You can create a *Matrix3D* object in WPF by using overloaded constructors that take an array of double values as arguments. Please note that before using the *Matrix3D* structure in applications, you will need to add a reference to the *System.Windows.Media.Media3D* namespace. The following code snippet creates three *Matrix3D* objects that perform translation, scaling, and rotation transformations around the Z axis by specifying the corresponding matrix elements directly:

```
double dx = 3;
double dy = 2;
double dz = 1.5;
double sx = 0.5;
double sy = 1.5;
double sz = 2.5;
double theta = Math.PI / 4;
double sin = Math.Sin(theta);
double cos = Math.Cos(theta);
Matrix3D tm = new Matrix3D( 1,   0,   0, 0,
                            0,   1,   0, 0,
                            0,   0,   1, 0,
                           dx,  dy,  dz, 1);
Matrix3D sm = new Matrix3D(sx,   0,   0, 0,
                            0,  sy,   0, 0,
                            0,   0,  sz, 0,
                            0,   0,   0, 1);
Matrix3D rm = new Matrix3D(cos, sin, 0, 0,
                          -sin, cos, 0, 0,
                             0,   0, 1, 0,
                             0,   0, 0, 1);
```

The matrix *tm* is a translation matrix that translates an object by 3 units in the X direction, 2 units in the Y direction, and 1.5 units in the Z direction. The scaling matrix *sm* scales an object by a factor of 0.5 in the X direction, 1.5 in the Y direction, and 2.5 in the Z direction. Finally, the matrix *rm* is a rotation matrix that rotates an object about the Z axis by 45 degrees.

You can also perform standard matrix operations on the *Matrix3D* structure. For example, the *Invert* method is used to invert a *Matrix3D* object if it is invertible. This method takes no parameters. The *Multiply* method multiplies two matrices and returns the result in a new matrix.

Be careful when you apply *Matrix3D* to *Point3D*, *Point4D*, and *Vector3D* objects. For standard scaling and rotation, *Matrix3D* takes a form with both the last row and last column consisting of the elements (0, 0, 0, 1). In such cases, there will be no surprising results. For example:

```
Matrix3D m3 = new Matrix3D(   1, 0.5, 0, 0,
                           -0.5,   1, 0, 0,
                              0,   0, 1, 0,
                              0,   0, 0, 1);
Point3D pt3 = new Point3D(2, 3, 4);
Vector3D v3 = new Vector3D(2, 3, 4);
Point4D pt4 = new Point4D(2, 3, 4, 1);
Point3D pt3t = pt3 * m3;
Vector3D v3t = v3 * m3;
```

```
Point4D pt4t = pt4 * m3;
```

This generates the expected results of pt3t = (0.5, 4, 4), v3t = (0.5, 4, 4), and pt4t = (0.5, 4, 4, 1) after the transformation. However, if you add a translation in the X direction to *Matrix3D* by changing *m3* to the following:

```
Matrix3D m3 = new Matrix3D(    1, 0.5, 0, 0,
                            -0.5,   1, 0, 0,
                               0,   0, 1, 0,
                             100,   0, 0, 1);
```

then recalculating the transformation produces the output: pt3t = (100.5, 4, 4), v3t = (0.5, 4, 4), and pt4t = (100.5, 4, 4, 1). You can see that translating 100 units in the X direction has no effect on the *Vector3D* object. This is because the *Vector3D* object is defined in a real 3D space but not in a homogeneous coordinate system. The *Vector3D* object has no W component. When you transform a *Vector3D* object using *Matrix3D*, WPF simply uses the first 3 × 3 submatrix of the *Matrix3D*, and neglects the last column and the last row.

For a *Point3D* object, even though it is defined using three components, X, Y, and Z, the .NET framework implicitly adds a $W = 1$ component. That is why both pt3t and pt4t give the correct results.

Now let's change *m3* into a nonaffine matrix by adding a nonzero element of $M_{34} = 2$:

```
Matrix3D m3 = new Matrix3D(    1, 0.5, 0, 0,
                            -0.5,   1, 0, 0,
                               0,   0, 1, 2,
                             100,   0, 0, 1);
```

This corresponds to a transform matrix with a perspective projection. After applying this transformation, you will obtain the following "strange" results:

```
pt3t = (11.167, 0.444, 0.444)
v3t = (0.5, 4, 4)
pt4t = (100.5, 4, 4, 9)
```

What happened here? It is easy to understand the result of *v3t*, since a vector always neglects the last column and row of a *Matrix3D*. Thus, *v3t* will remain the same when you change the elements of the last row or last column. The result of *pt4t* is also expected because it is simply a direct multiplication of *pt4*m3* .

Let's take a close look at *pt3t*. This result is obtained in two steps. First, the *Matrix3D* and *Point3D* object are directly multiplied with an additional $W = 1$ component, which gives the result of *pt4t*. Then, *pt3t* is obtained by normalizing the X, Y, and Z components of *pt4t* with its W component:

```
pt3t  = (100.9/9, 4/9, 4/9) = (11.167, 0.444, 0.444)
```

In general, for an arbitrary *Point4D* = (x, y, z, w) in homogeneous coordinates, the plane at infinity is usually identified with a set of points with $w = 0$. When points are away from the plane at infinity, you can always use (x/w, y/w, z/w) to define the *Point3D*'s X, Y, Z components. WPF automatically performs this transform on *Point3D* objects and gives you the normalized results. The discussion presented here simply shows you the mathematical basis, used by WPF to perform transforms on *Point3D* objects.

3D Coordinate System

Here, I will show you how to create a 3D coordinate system using a direct projection method, without using the WPF 3D engine. Creating 3D coordinate axes on a 2D screen is understandably more involved than creating 2D coordinates. Here, I will use the azimuth and elevation view to control the orientation of the 3D charts and graphics objects displayed in the coordinate axes.

Azimuth and Elevation View

Specifying the viewpoint in terms of azimuth and elevation is conceptually simple. The 3D charts that will be represented in the following sections will use this azimuth and elevation view to display various 3D plots on a 2D computer screen. There are some limitations to this view setting, however. Azimuth and elevation view does not allow you to specify the actual position of the viewpoint – just its direction – and the Z-axis is always pointing up. In addition, it does not allow you to zoom in and out of the scene or perform arbitrary rotations and translations. Even with these limitations, this view is good enough for most 3D chart and graphics applications.

In this view setting, the conventional Cartesian coordinate system is used. The azimuth angle is a polar angle in the *X-Y* plane, with positive angles indicating a counterclockwise rotation of the viewpoint. Elevation is the angle above (positive angle) or below (negative angle) the *X-Y* plane, as shown in Figure 8-1.

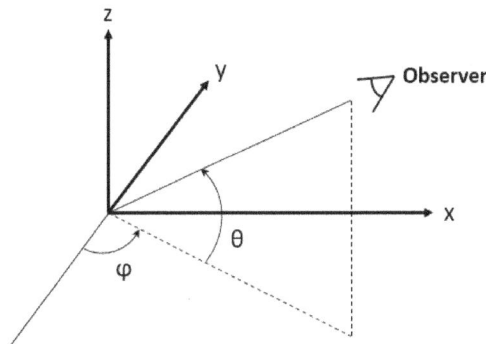

Figure 8-1. Azimuth and elevation view system.

We can construct the transformation matrix for this view system by considering two successive 2D rotations. First, we rotate the original coordinate system by an angle $-\varphi$ about the Z axis, then rotate the newly generated coordinate system by $\theta - \pi/2$ about the X axis. We can then obtain the combined effect of these two 2D rotations:

$$R_z(-\varphi)R_x\left(\theta - \frac{\pi}{2}\right) = \begin{pmatrix} \cos\varphi & -\sin\varphi & 0 & 0 \\ \sin\varphi & \cos\varphi & 0 & 0 \\ 0 & 0 & 1 & 0 \\ 0 & 0 & 0 & 1 \end{pmatrix} \begin{pmatrix} 1 & 0 & 0 & 0 \\ 0 & \sin\theta & -\cos\theta & 0 \\ 0 & \cos\theta & \sin\theta & 0 \\ 0 & 0 & 0 & 1 \end{pmatrix}$$

$$= \begin{pmatrix} \cos\varphi & -\sin\varphi\sin\theta & \sin\varphi\cos\theta & 0 \\ \sin\varphi & \cos\varphi\sin\theta & -\cos\varphi\cos\theta & 0 \\ 0 & \cos\theta & \sin\theta & 0 \\ 0 & 0 & 0 & 1 \end{pmatrix}$$

You can easily implement this azimuth and elevation view matrix in WPF. Open Visual Studio 2013, start a new WPF project, and name it *Chapter08*. Add Caliburn.Micro to *References*. Add new folders, *Models*, *ViewModels*, and *Views,* to the project. Add *AppBootstrapper.cs* to the *Models* folder, which is the same as that used in the example projects in previous chapters.

Add a *Window* to the *Views* folder and name it *MainView*. Add a class to the *ViewModels* folder and name it *MainViewModel*. The main view and view model are used to hold the tab items, which are similar to those used in the *Chapter07* project. You can open the *Chapter07* project in Visual Studio and check the code if you need a refresher. Also, do not forget to make corresponding changes to *App.xaml*.

Add a new folder to the *Models* folder and name it *ChartModel*. Add a new *ChartHelper* class to the project. Here is the code listing for this class:

```csharp
using System;
using System.Windows;
using System.Windows.Media;
using System.Windows.Media.Media3D;

namespace Chapter08.Models.ChartModel
{
    public static class ChartHelper
    {
        public static Matrix3D AzimuthElevation(double elevation, double azimuth)
        {
            // Make sure elevation is in the range of [-90, 90]:
            if (elevation > 90)
                elevation = 90;
            else if (elevation < -90)
                elevation = -90;

            // Make sure azimuth is in the range of [-180, 180]:
            if (azimuth > 180)
                azimuth = 180;
            else if (azimuth < -180)
                azimuth = -180;

            elevation = elevation * Math.PI / 180;
            azimuth = azimuth * Math.PI / 180;
            double sne = Math.Sin(elevation);
            double cne = Math.Cos(elevation);
            double sna = Math.Sin(azimuth);
            double cna = Math.Cos(azimuth);

            return new Matrix3D(cna, -sne * sna,  cne * sna, 0,
                                sna,  sne * cna, -cne * cna, 0,
                                  0,        cne,        sne, 0,
                                  0,          0,          0, 1);
        }
    }
}
```

This method takes elevation and azimuth angles as input parameters. In real-world 3D chart applications, we usually use parallel projection instead of perspective projection. This means that we can use the preceding azimuth and elevation view matrix to perform a 3D parallel projection on a 2D screen.

Creating a Cube

Here, I will show you how to create a simple 3D cube object using the azimuth and elevation view matrix presented in the previous section. Add a new *UserControl* to the *Views* folder and name it *CubeView*. Here is the XAML file for this view:

```xml
<UserControl x:Class="Chapter08.Views.CubeView"
             xmlns="http://schemas.microsoft.com/winfx/2006/xaml/presentation"
             xmlns:x="http://schemas.microsoft.com/winfx/2006/xaml"
             xmlns:mc="http://schemas.openxmlformats.org/markup-compatibility/2006"
             xmlns:d="http://schemas.microsoft.com/expression/blend/2008"
             xmlns:cal="http://www.caliburnproject.org"
             mc:Ignorable="d"
             d:DesignHeight="400" d:DesignWidth="400">

    <UserControl.Resources>
        <DataTemplate x:Key="cubeTemplate">
            <Polygon Points="{Binding PlgPoints}" Fill="{Binding PlgFill}"
            RenderTransform="{Binding PlgTransform}"/>
        </DataTemplate>
    </UserControl.Resources>

    <Grid Margin="20">
        <Grid.ColumnDefinitions>
            <ColumnDefinition Width="200"/>
            <ColumnDefinition Width="*"/>
        </Grid.ColumnDefinitions>
        <StackPanel Margin="5">
            <StackPanel Orientation="Horizontal">
                <TextBlock Text="Elevation:" Margin="0 0 10 0"/>
                <TextBlock Text="{Binding Elevation, StringFormat=N0}" Width="70" />
            </StackPanel>
            <Slider x:Name="Elevation" Minimum="-90" Maximum="90" Margin="0 5 0 0"
                    cal:Message.Attach="[Event ValueChanged]=[Action AddCube]"/>
            <StackPanel Orientation="Horizontal" Margin="0 10 0 0">
                <TextBlock Text="Azimuth" Margin="0 0 10 0"/>
                <TextBlock Text="{Binding Azimuth, StringFormat=N0}" Width="70"/>
            </StackPanel>
            <Slider x:Name="Azimuth" Minimum="-180" Maximum="180" Margin="0 5 0 0"
                    cal:Message.Attach="[Event ValueChanged]=[Action AddCube]"/>
        </StackPanel>
        <Grid x:Name="cubeGrid" Margin="10" Grid.Column="1"
              cal:Message.Attach="[Event Loaded]=[Action
              InitialLoad($this.ActualWidth, $this.ActualHeight)];
              [Event SizeChanged]=[Action InitialLoad($this.ActualWidth,
              $this.ActualHeight)]">
            <Canvas Width="{Binding ElementName=cubeGrid,
                    Path=ActualWidth}" Height="{Binding ElementName=cubeGrid,
                    Path=ActualHeight}" ClipToBounds="True"
                    Background="Transparent">
```

```
                    <ItemsControl ItemsSource="{Binding DataCollection}"
                                  ItemTemplate="{StaticResource cubeTemplate}">
                        <ItemsControl.ItemsPanel>
                            <ItemsPanelTemplate>
                                <Grid/>
                            </ItemsPanelTemplate>
                        </ItemsControl.ItemsPanel>
                    </ItemsControl>
                </Canvas>
            </Grid>
        </Grid>
</UserControl>
```

Note that here we use the same approach as we did for creating a line chart in Chapter 4; that is, binding a *BindableCollection* of *PolygonSeries* to a *Grid* control by using an *ItemsControl* and its *ItemsPanelTemplate* property. In order to update the view automatically when the collection changes, we first need to specify how the data items are represented in the view. To do this, we use a *DataTemplate* named *cubeTemplate* and add it to *UserControl*'s Resources. The *cubeTemplate* defines a *Polygon* object whose properties are bound directly to the corresponding properties of the data item (i.e., *PolygonSeries* in this example). This polygon object represents a face of the 3D cube that we are going to create. After defining the polygons using the data item in the *cubeTemplate*, we need to place the polygons on a panel. Here we use the *Grid*.

Also, note how the *ItemsControl*'s *ItemsSource* property is bound to the *PolygonSeries* collection. This is where we build the link between the business logic layer and the UI layer. The items in the *ItemsControl* should be represented using the *cubeTemplate* we defined earlier, which can be specified by the *ItemTemplate* property.

This way, regardless of the number of polygons you want to create in your view, you do not need to change your view. Just by making changes to the *PolygonSeries* collection in your view model, your application will automatically update. That is the beauty of the WPF MVVM framework.

We also bind the *Elevation* and *Azimuth* angles to two slider elements using Caliburn.Micro's naming convention, so that the cube will rotate when you move the sliders.

Add a new class to the *ViewModels* class and name it *CubeViewModel*. Here is the code for this class:

```
using System;
using Caliburn.Micro;
using System.ComponentModel.Composition;
using System.Windows;
using Chapter08.Models;
using System.Windows.Media;
using Chapter08.Models.ChartModel;
using System.Windows.Media.Media3D;
using System.Windows.Shapes;

namespace Chapter08.ViewModels
{
    [Export(typeof(IScreen)), PartCreationPolicy(CreationPolicy.NonShared)]
    public class CubeViewModel : Screen
    {
        private readonly IEventAggregator _events;
        [ImportingConstructor]
        public CubeViewModel(IEventAggregator events)
```

```
{
    this._events = events;
    DisplayName = "01. Cube";
    DataCollection = new BindableCollection<PolygonSeries>();
}

private Point center;
private Point3D[] vertices0;
private Point3D[] vertices;
private Face[] faces;
private bool isVisible;
public BindableCollection<PolygonSeries> DataCollection { get; set; }

private double elevation = 30;
public double Elevation
{
    get { return elevation; }
    set
    {
        elevation = value;
        NotifyOfPropertyChange(() => Elevation);
    }
}

private double azimuth = -30;
public double Azimuth
{
    get { return azimuth; }
    set
    {
        azimuth = value;
        NotifyOfPropertyChange(() => Azimuth);
    }
}

public void InitialLoad(double width, double height)
{
    center = new Point(width / 2, height / 2);
    center = new Point(width / 2, height / 2);
    double side = width / 4.0;
    if (height < width)
        side = height / 4.0;

    vertices0 = new Point3D[] { new Point3D(-side,-side,-side),
                                new Point3D( side,-side,-side),
                                new Point3D( side, side,-side),
                                new Point3D(-side, side,-side),
                                new Point3D(-side, side, side),
                                new Point3D( side, side, side),
                                new Point3D( side,-side, side),
                                new Point3D(-side,-side, side)};
    faces = new Face[] {new Face(0,1,2,3), new Face(4,5,6,7),
                        new Face(3,4,7,0), new Face(2,1,6,5),
                        new Face(5,4,3,2), new Face(0,7,6,1)};
    AddCube();
```

```
    }

public void AddCube()
{
    DataCollection.Clear();

    Matrix3D transformMatrix =
        ChartHelper.AzimuthElevation(Elevation, Azimuth);
    vertices = new Point3D[8];
    for (int i = 0; i < vertices0.Length; i++)
    {
        vertices[i] = Point3D.Multiply(vertices0[i], transformMatrix);
    }

    int ii = 0;
    foreach (Face face in this.faces)
    {
        ii++;
        Point3D va = vertices[face.VertexA];
        Point3D vb = vertices[face.VertexB];
        Point3D vc = vertices[face.VertexC];
        Point3D vd = vertices[face.VertexD];
        Vector3D normal = ChartHelper.NormalVector(va, vb, vc);
        Vector3D viewDirection = new Vector3D(0, 0, -1);
        double mixProduct = Vector3D.DotProduct(normal, viewDirection);
        isVisible = mixProduct > 0;
        if (isVisible)
        {
            byte red = 0;
            byte green = 0;
            byte blue = 0;
            if (ii == 1)
            {
                red = 255;
                green = 0;
                blue = 0;
            }
            else if (ii == 2)
            {
                red = 0;
                green = 255;
                blue = 0;
            }
            else if (ii == 3)
            {
                red = 0;
                green = 0;
                blue = 255;
            }
            else if (ii == 4)
            {
                red = 255;
                green = 0;
                blue = 255;
            }
```

```
            else if (ii == 5)
            {
                red = 255;
                green = 255;
                blue = 0;
            }
            else if (ii == 6)
            {
                red = 0;
                green = 255;
                blue = 255;
            }

            PolygonSeries ps = new PolygonSeries();
            PointCollection pc = new PointCollection();
            pc.Add(new Point(va.X, va.Y));
            pc.Add(new Point(vb.X, vb.Y));
            pc.Add(new Point(vc.X, vc.Y));
            pc.Add(new Point(vd.X, vd.Y));
            ps.PlgPoints = pc;
            ps.PlgFill =
                new SolidColorBrush(Color.FromArgb(255, red, green, blue));
            TranslateTransform tt = new TranslateTransform();
            tt.X = center.X;
            tt.Y = center.Y;
            ps.PlgTransform = tt;
            DataCollection.Add(ps);
            }
        }
    }
}

public class PolygonSeries
{
    public PointCollection PlgPoints { get; set; }
    public PolygonSeries()
    {
        PlgPoints = new PointCollection();
    }

    private Brush plgfill=Brushes.Gray;
    public Brush PlgFill
    {
        get { return plgfill; }
        set { plgfill = value; }
    }

    public TranslateTransform PlgTransform {get;set;}
}

public class Face
{
    public int VertexA, VertexB, VertexC, VertexD;
    public Face(int vertexA, int vertexB, int vertexC, int vertexD)
    {
```

```
            this.VertexA = vertexA;
            this.VertexB = vertexB;
            this.VertexC = vertexC;
            this.VertexD = vertexD;
        }
    }
}
```

Here, I add two classes, *PolygonSeries* and *Face*, to the view model. The *PolygonSeries* class creates a *PointCollection* object for a given *PolygonSeries*, and then defines the *Fill* and *TranslateTransform* properties for the polygon object. The *Face* class contains four vertex indices. . For a cube object, there are six faces, each with four vertices. The *Face* class allows you to easily create the faces of the cube.

Inside the *InitialLoad* method, we define a vertex point array and a face object array, which are used to create the cube object. The *AddCube* method first creates a transform matrix using the azimuth and elevation view defined in the *ChartHelper* class. We then perform the projection transformation on the vertex points. This way, we project the 3D point objects on a 2D screen.

In order to distinguish each face of the cube, we paint each face with a different color. Depending on the viewing direction, only some of the six faces will be visible at a time. We need to implement a technique that removes the back faces. Here, we use the sign of the dot product of the face's normal and the view direction to identify whether the face is a back or front face. If this dot product is less than or equal to zero, the surface is a back face, and we do not need to draw it on the screen.

Mathematically, we can represent a face in 3D using three points. We add a new method, *NormalVector*, to the *ChartHelper* class. This method takes three points, representing a face in 3D, as inputs, and returns a vector object that represents the normal of the face. Here is the code for this method:

```
public static Vector3D NormalVector(Point3D pt1, Point3D pt2, Point3D pt3)
{
    Vector3D v1 = new Vector3D();
    Vector3D v2 = new Vector3D();
    v1.X = pt2.X - pt1.X;
    v1.Y = pt2.Y - pt1.Y;
    v1.Z = pt2.Z - pt1.Z;
    v2.X = pt3.X - pt2.X;
    v2.Y = pt3.Y - pt2.Y;
    v2.Z = pt3.Z - pt1.Z;
    return Vector3D.CrossProduct(v1, v2);
}
```

Finally, we define the *PolygonSeries* and create a *PolygonSeries* collection, *DataCollection*, bound to the *ItemsSource* property of the *ItemsControl* in the view. The view will then draw a 2D polygon for each front face.

Running this example generates the output shown in Figure 8-2. You can play around by moving the slider bars to see how the cube rotates.

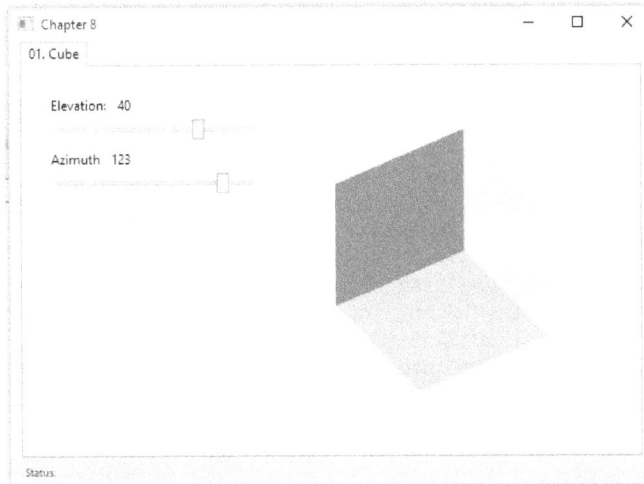

Figure 8-2. A cube created directly using azimuth and elevation view.

Chart Style in 3D

In previous sections, we presented the 3D matrix structure in WPF and the 3D coordinate system based on the azimuth and elevation view. In the current and following sections, I will show you how to create 3D charts using the azimuth and elevation view.

The chart style used in 3D charts is similar to that used in 2D. Add a new class to the *ChartModel* folder and name it *ChartStyle*. The following code snippet shows its member fields and corresponding public properties:

```
using System;
using System.Collections.Generic;
using System.Windows;
using System.Windows.Controls;
using System.Windows.Media;
using System.Windows.Media.Media3D;
using System.Windows.Shapes;

namespace Chart3DNoWPFEngine
{
    public class ChartStyle
    {
        private Canvas chartCanvas;
        private double xmin = -5;
        private double xmax = 5;
        private double ymin = -3;
        private double ymax = 3;
        private double zmin = -6;
        private double zmax = 6;
        private double xtick = 1;
        private double ytick = 1;
        private double ztick = 3;
        private FontFamily tickFont = new FontFamily("Arial Narrow");
```

```
private double tickFontSize =
    (double)new FontSizeConverter().ConvertFrom("8pt");
private Brush tickColor = Brushes.Black;
private string title = "My 3D Chart";
private FontFamily titleFont = new FontFamily("Arial Narrow");
private double titleFontSize =
    (double)new FontSizeConverter().ConvertFrom("14pt");
private Brush titleColor = Brushes.Black;
private string xLabel = "X Axis";
private string yLabel = "Y Axis";
private string zLabel = "Z Axis";
private FontFamily labelFont = new FontFamily("Arial Narrow");
private double labelFontSize =
    (double)new FontSizeConverter().ConvertFrom("10pt");
private Brush labelColor = Brushes.Black;
private double elevation = 30;
private double azimuth = -37.5;
private bool isXGrid = true;
private bool isYGrid = true;
private bool isZGrid = true;
private bool isColorBar = false;
private Line gridline = new Line();
private Brush gridlineColor = Brushes.LightGray;
private double gridlineThickness = 1;
private LineDashPatternEnum gridlinePattern = LineDashPatternEnum.Dash;
private Line axisLine = new Line();
private Brush axisColor = Brushes.Black;
private LineDashPatternEnum axisPattern = LineDashPatternEnum.Solid;
private double axisThickness = 1;

public Canvas ChartCanvas
{
    get { return chartCanvas; }
    set { chartCanvas = value; }
}

public bool IsColorBar
{
    get { return isColorBar; }
    set { isColorBar = value; }
}

public Brush AxisColor
{
    get { return axisColor; }
    set { axisColor = value; }
}

public LineDashPatternEnum AxisPattern
{
    get { return axisPattern; }
    set { axisPattern = value; }
}

public double AxisThickness
```

```
{
    get { return axisThickness; }
    set { axisThickness = value; }
}

public Brush GridlineColor
{
    get { return gridlineColor; }
    set { gridlineColor = value; }
}

public LineDashPatternEnum GridlinePattern
{
    get { return gridlinePattern; }
    set { gridlinePattern = value; }
}

public double GridlineThickness
{
    get { return gridlineThickness; }
    set { gridlineThickness = value; }
}

public FontFamily LabelFont
{
    get { return labelFont; }
    set { labelFont = value; }
}

public Brush LabelColor
{
    get { return labelColor; }
    set { labelColor = value; }
}

public double LabelFontSize
{
    get { return labelFontSize; }
    set { labelFontSize = value; }
}

public FontFamily TitleFont
{
    get { return titleFont; }
    set { titleFont = value; }
}

public Brush TitleColor
{
    get { return titleColor; }
    set { titleColor = value; }
}

public double TitleFontSize
{
```

```csharp
        get { return titleFontSize; }
        set { titleFontSize = value; }
    }

    public FontFamily TickFont
    {
        get { return tickFont; }
        set { tickFont = value; }
    }

    public Brush TickColor
    {
        get { return tickColor; }
        set { tickColor = value; }
    }

    public double TickFontSize
    {
        get { return tickFontSize; }
        set { tickFontSize = value; }
    }

    public bool IsXGrid
    {
        get { return isXGrid; }
        set { isXGrid = value; }
    }

    public bool IsYGrid
    {
        get { return isYGrid; }
        set { isYGrid = value; }
    }

    public bool IsZGrid
    {
        get { return isZGrid; }
        set { isZGrid = value; }
    }

    public string Title
    {
        get { return title; }
        set { title = value; }
    }

    public string XLabel
    {
        get { return xLabel; }
        set { xLabel = value; }
    }

    public string YLabel
    {
        get { return yLabel; }
```

```csharp
        set { yLabel = value; }
}

public string ZLabel
{
    get { return zLabel; }
    set { zLabel = value; }
}

public double Elevation
{
    get { return elevation; }
    set
    {
        elevation = value; }
}

public double Azimuth
{
    get { return azimuth; }
    set { azimuth = value; }
}

public double Xmax
{
    get { return xmax; }
    set { xmax = value; }
}

public double Xmin
{
    get { return xmin; }
    set { xmin = value; }
}

public double Ymax
{
    get { return ymax; }
    set { ymax = value; }
}

public double Ymin
{
    get { return ymin; }
    set { ymin = value; }
}

public double Zmax
{
    get { return zmax; }
    set { zmax = value; }
}

public double Zmin
{
```

```
            get { return zmin; }
            set { zmin = value; }
        }

        public double XTick
        {
            get { return xtick; }
            set { xtick = value; }
        }

        public double YTick
        {
            get { return ytick; }
            set { ytick = value; }
        }

        public double ZTick
        {
            get { return ztick; }
            set { ztick = value; }
        }
    }
public enum LineDashPatternEnum
{
        Solid = 1,
        Dash = 2,
        Dot = 3,
        DashDot = 4,
    }
    .....
}
```

You can specify and change the chart style for a 3D chart using the foregoing properties. If you need more features to control the appearance of your 3D charts, you can easily add your own member fields and corresponding properties to this class.

Another basic class needed in 3D charts is *DataSeries*, which will be discussed in the following example projects. Usually, you do not need to define the *DataCollection* object in 3D charts because most 3D charts display only one set of data.

3D Coordinate Axes

Correctly creating 3D coordinate axes is critical for 3D chart applications. First, we need to create the coordinates of the chart box, as shown in Figure 8-3. In 3D charts, all data are plotted within the chart box defined by [*xMin, xMax, yMin, yMax, zMin, zMax*] in the world coordinate system. We denote the coordinate axes by the bolded lines in the figure. The Z-axis is the vertical bold line, which can be independent of the elevation and azimuth angles. The *X*- and *Y*-axes, on the other hand, cannot be predefined. Which edge of the chart box represents the *X*- or *Y*-axis depends on both the elevation and azimuth angles.

In order to create such a coordinate system in WPF, we first need to create the eight-point coordinates of the chart box; then we select four of the points to define three coordinate axes. Add the following *ChartBoxCoordinates* method to the *ChartStyle* class:

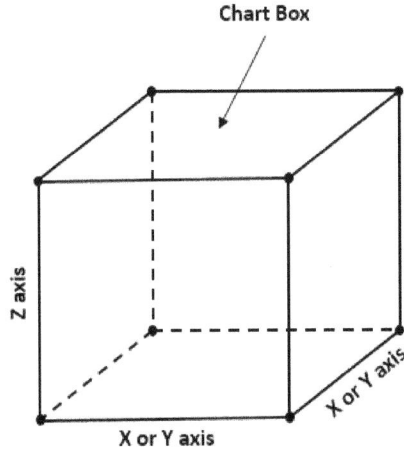

Figure 8-3. 3D chart box and coordinate axes.

```
private Point3D[] ChartBoxCoordinates()
{
    Point3D[] pta = new Point3D[8];
    pta[0] = new Point3D(Xmax, Ymin, Zmin);
    pta[1] = new Point3D(Xmin, Ymin, Zmin);
    pta[2] = new Point3D(Xmin, Ymax, Zmin);
    pta[3] = new Point3D(Xmin, Ymax, Zmax);
    pta[4] = new Point3D(Xmin, Ymin, Zmax);
    pta[5] = new Point3D(Xmax, Ymin, Zmax);
    pta[6] = new Point3D(Xmax, Ymax, Zmax);
    pta[7] = new Point3D(Xmax, Ymax, Zmin);
    Point3D[] pts = new Point3D[4];
    int[] npts = new int[] { 0, 1, 2, 3 };

    if (elevation >= 0)
    {
        if (azimuth >= -180 && azimuth < -90)
            npts = new int[] { 1, 2, 7, 6 };
        else if (azimuth >= -90 && azimuth < 0)
            npts = new int[] { 0, 1, 2, 3 };
        else if (azimuth >= 0 && azimuth < 90)
            npts = new int[] { 7, 0, 1, 4 };
        else if (azimuth >= 90 && azimuth <= 180)
            npts = new int[] { 2, 7, 0, 5 };
    }
    else if (elevation < 0)
    {
        if (azimuth >= -180 && azimuth < -90)
            npts = new int[] { 1, 0, 7, 6 };
        else if (azimuth >= -90 && azimuth < 0)
            npts = new int[] { 0, 7, 2, 3 };
        else if (azimuth >= 0 && azimuth < 90)
            npts = new int[] { 7, 2, 1, 4 };
        else if (azimuth >= 90 && azimuth <= 180)
            npts = new int[] { 2, 1, 0, 5 };
```

```
        }
        for (int i = 0; i < 4; i++)
            pts[i] = pta[npts[i]];
        return pts;
    }
```

In this method, we use a trial-and-error approach to select a different four-point array every time the azimuth and elevation angles change. Calling this method creates a point array of four points, which determines the *X*-, *Y*-, and *Z*-axes for arbitrary elevation and azimuth angles. Now we can create the coordinate axes by adding the following methods to the *ChartStyle* class:

```
public void AddLinePattern(Line line, Brush lineColor, double lineThickness,
    LineDashPatternEnum linePattern)
{
    line.Stroke = lineColor;
    line.StrokeThickness = lineThickness;
    switch (linePattern)
    {
        case LineDashPatternEnum.Dash:
            line.StrokeDashArray = new DoubleCollection(new double[2] { 4, 3 });
            break;
        case LineDashPatternEnum.Dot:
            line.StrokeDashArray = new DoubleCollection(new double[2] { 1, 2 });
            break;
        case LineDashPatternEnum.DashDot:
            line.StrokeDashArray =
                new DoubleCollection(new double[4] { 4, 2, 1, 2 });
            break;
    }
}

private void DrawLine(Point3D pt1, Point3D pt2, Brush lineColor,
    double lineThickness, LineDashPatternEnum linePattern)
{
    var line = new Line();
    AddLinePattern(line, lineColor, lineThickness, linePattern);
    line.X1 = pt1.X;
    line.Y1 = pt1.Y;
    line.X2 = pt2.X;
    line.Y2 = pt2.Y;
    ChartCanvas.Children.Add(line);
}

public Point3D Normalize3D(Matrix3D m, Point3D pt)
{
    Point3D result = new Point3D();

    // Normalize the point:
    double x1 = (pt.X - Xmin) / (Xmax - Xmin) - 0.5;
    double y1 = (pt.Y - Ymin) / (Ymax - Ymin) - 0.5;
    double z1 = (pt.Z - Zmin) / (Zmax - zmin) - 0.5;

    // Perform transformation on the point using matrix m:
    result.X = m.Transform(new Point3D(x1, y1, z1)).X;
    result.Y = m.Transform(new Point3D(x1, y1, z1)).Y;
```

```
    // Coordinate transformation from World to Device system:
    double xShift = 1.05;
    double xScale = 1;
    double yShift = 1.05;
    double yScale = 0.9;
    if (Title == "No Title")
    {
        yShift = 0.95;
        yScale = 1;
    }
    if (IsColorBar)
    {
        xShift = 0.95;
        xScale = 0.9;
    }
    result.X = (xShift + xScale * result.X) * ChartCanvas.Width / 2;
    result.Y = (yShift - yScale * result.Y) * ChartCanvas.Height / 2;
    return result;
}

private void AddAxes()
{
    Matrix3D m = ChartHelper.AzimuthElevation(Elevation, Azimuth);
    Point3D[] pts = ChartBoxCoordinates();
    for (int i = 0; i < pts.Length; i++)
    {
        pts[i] = Normalize3D(m, pts[i]);
    }
    DrawLine(pts[0], pts[1], AxisColor, AxisThickness, AxisPattern);
    DrawLine(pts[1], pts[2], AxisColor, AxisThickness, AxisPattern);
    DrawLine(pts[2], pts[3], AxisColor, AxisThickness, AxisPattern);
}
```

The *Normalize3D* method is very similar to the *NormalizePoint* method previously used in 2D. It takes the transform matrix and a *Point3D* object as inputs. In this method, we first normalize the X, Y, and Z data ranges into a unit cube so that the transformations that are performed on the point within this unit cube are independent from the real data ranges. Then we transform the normalized point using the transform matrix. Finally, we carry out the coordinate transformation from the world to device coordinate system. This method performs all of the transformations necessary for a point to be displayed on a 2D screen, which will greatly simplify the programming procedure for 3D chart applications.

You might notice that in this method, only the X and Y components of the point undergo the transformations, while the Z and W components retain their original values. You can see this from the code snippet:

```
    // Perform transformation on the point using matrix m:
    result.X = m.Transform(new Point3D(x1, y1, z1)).X;
    result.Y = m.Transform(new Point3D(x1, y1, z1)).Y;
```

The Z and W components need to retain their original information; otherwise, after the orthogonal transformations, the Z component might end up a combination of the original X, Y, and Z values, which would destroy the original Z coordinate information, meaning you could not use the Z component to compare the points' Z values. In 3D charts, we often do need the original Z coordinate information, such as when we apply color maps to a 3D chart.

In the *AddAxes* method, we first get the coordinates of the three coordinate axes by calling the *ChartBoxCoordinates* method. Then we perform the transformation and normalization on these four points using the elevation and azimuth matrix and the *Normalize3D* method. Finally, we use the *X* and *Y* components of the transformed points to draw the coordinate axes. Although the *AddAxes* method creates three coordinate axes, we still do not know which axis is the *X*- or *Y*-axis. The program will automatically tell you when you place labels on the coordinate axes. The *AddLinePattern* method is used to set the line style, while the *DrawLine* method is used to create a *Line* object on the *ChartCanvas*.

The following *AddTicks* method in the *ChartStyle* class creates tick marks on the coordinate axes:

```
private void AddTicks()
{
    Matrix3D m = ChartHelper.AzimuthElevation(Elevation, Azimuth);
    Point3D[] pta = new Point3D[2];
    Point3D[] pts = ChartBoxCoordinates();

    // Add x ticks:
    double offset = (Ymax - Ymin) / 30.0;
    double ticklength = offset;
    for (double x = Xmin; x <= Xmax; x = x + XTick)
    {
        if (Elevation >= 0)
        {
            if (Azimuth >= -90 && Azimuth < 90)
                ticklength = -offset;
        }
        else if (Elevation < 0)
        {
            if ((Azimuth >= -180 && Azimuth < -90) ||
                Azimuth >= 90 && Azimuth <= 180)
                ticklength = -(Ymax - Ymin) / 30;
        }
        pta[0] = new Point3D(x, pts[1].Y + ticklength, pts[1].Z);
        pta[1] = new Point3D(x, pts[1].Y, pts[1].Z);
        for (int i = 0; i < pta.Length; i++)
        {
            pta[i] = Normalize3D(m, pta[i]);
        }
        DrawLine(pta[0], pta[1], AxisColor, 1, LineDashPatternEnum.Solid);
    }

    // Add y ticks:
    offset = (Xmax - Xmin) / 30.0;
    ticklength = offset;
    for (double y = Ymin; y <= Ymax; y = y + YTick)
    {
        pts = ChartBoxCoordinates();
        if (Elevation >= 0)
        {
            if (Azimuth >= -180 && Azimuth < 0)
                ticklength = -offset;
        }
        else if (Elevation < 0)
        {
            if (Azimuth >= 0 && Azimuth < 180)
```

```
            ticklength = -offset;
    }
    pta[0] = new Point3D(pts[1].X + ticklength, y, pts[1].Z);
    pta[1] = new Point3D(pts[1].X, y, pts[1].Z);
    for (int i = 0; i < pta.Length; i++)
    {
        pta[i] = Normalize3D(m, pta[i]);
    }
    DrawLine(pta[0], pta[1], AxisColor, 1, LineDashPatternEnum.Solid);
}

// Add z ticks:
double xoffset = (Xmax - Xmin) / 45.0;
double yoffset = (Ymax - Ymin) / 20.0;
double xticklength = xoffset;
double yticklength = yoffset;
for (double z = Zmin; z <= Zmax; z = z + ZTick)
{
    if (Elevation >= 0)
    {
        if (Azimuth >= -180 && Azimuth < -90)
        {
            xticklength = 0;
            yticklength = yoffset;
        }
        else if (Azimuth >= -90 && Azimuth < 0)
        {
            xticklength = xoffset;
            yticklength = 0;
        }
        else if (Azimuth >= 0 && Azimuth < 90)
        {
            xticklength = 0;
            yticklength = -yoffset;
        }
        else if (Azimuth >= 90 && Azimuth <= 180)
        {
            xticklength = -xoffset;
            yticklength = 0;
        }
    }
    else if (Elevation < 0)
    {
        if (Azimuth >= -180 && Azimuth < -90)
        {
            yticklength = 0;
            xticklength = xoffset;
        }
        else if (Azimuth >= -90 && Azimuth < 0)
        {
            yticklength = -yoffset;
            xticklength = 0;
        }
        else if (Azimuth >= 0 && Azimuth < 90)
        {
```

```
                    yticklength = 0;
                    xticklength = -xoffset;
            }
            else if (Azimuth >= 90 && Azimuth <= 180)
            {
                    yticklength = yoffset;
                    xticklength = 0;
            }
        }

        pta[0] = new Point3D(pts[2].X, pts[2].Y, z);
        pta[1] = new Point3D(pts[2].X + yticklength, pts[2].Y + xticklength, z);
        for (int i = 0; i < pta.Length; i++)
        {
            pta[i] = Normalize3D(m, pta[i]);
        }
        DrawLine(pta[0], pta[1], AxisColor, 1, LineDashPatternEnum.Solid);
    }
}
```

In this method, we define the length of the ticks in terms of the axis limit instead of a fixed length in the device coordinate system. This keeps the ticks proportionally distributed when the chart is resized. In addition, note how we place the tick markers in their proper positions on the coordinate axes when the elevation and azimuth angles are changed.

Gridlines

As in 2D charts, gridlines in 3D charts can help you to get a better view of data ranges. In the case of 3D charts, we want to place gridlines on three faces located behind the data curves or surfaces. These three faces (or planes) must be properly selected according to the variation of the elevation and azimuth angles. The following *AddGridlines* method in the *ChartStyle* class creates gridlines on the proper faces:

```
private void AddGridlines()
{
    Matrix3D m = ChartHelper.AzimuthElevation(Elevation, Azimuth);
    Point3D[] pta = new Point3D[3];
    Point3D[] pts = ChartBoxCoordinates();

    // Draw x gridlines:
    if (IsXGrid)
    {
        for (double x = Xmin; x <= Xmax; x = x + XTick)
        {
            pts = ChartBoxCoordinates();
            pta[0] = new Point3D(x, pts[1].Y, pts[1].Z);
            if (Elevation >= 0)
            {
                if ((Azimuth >= -180 && Azimuth < -90) ||
                    (Azimuth >= 0 && Azimuth < 90))
                {
                    pta[1] = new Point3D(x, pts[0].Y, pts[1].Z);
                    pta[2] = new Point3D(x, pts[0].Y, pts[3].Z);
                }
                else
```

```
            {
                pta[1] = new Point3D(x, pts[2].Y, pts[1].Z);
                pta[2] = new Point3D(x, pts[2].Y, pts[3].Z);
            }
        }
        else if (Elevation < 0)
        {
            if ((Azimuth >= -180 && Azimuth < -90) ||
                (Azimuth >= 0 && Azimuth < 90))
            {
                pta[1] = new Point3D(x, pts[2].Y, pts[1].Z);
                pta[2] = new Point3D(x, pts[2].Y, pts[3].Z);
            }
            else
            {
                pta[1] = new Point3D(x, pts[0].Y, pts[1].Z);
                pta[2] = new Point3D(x, pts[0].Y, pts[3].Z);
            }
        }
        for (int i = 0; i < pta.Length; i++)
        {
            pta[i] = Normalize3D(m, pta[i]);
        }
        DrawLine(pta[0], pta[1], GridlineColor,
            GridlineThickness, GridlinePattern);
        DrawLine(pta[1], pta[2], GridlineColor,
            GridlineThickness, GridlinePattern);
    }

    // Draw y gridlines:
    if (IsYGrid)
    {
        for (double y = Ymin; y <= Ymax; y = y + YTick)
        {
            pts = ChartBoxCoordinates();
            pta[0] = new Point3D(pts[1].X, y, pts[1].Z);
            if (Elevation >= 0)
            {
                if ((Azimuth >= -180 && Azimuth < -90) ||
                    (Azimuth >= 0 && Azimuth < 90))
                {
                    pta[1] = new Point3D(pts[2].X, y, pts[1].Z);
                    pta[2] = new Point3D(pts[2].X, y, pts[3].Z);
                }
                else
                {
                    pta[1] = new Point3D(pts[0].X, y, pts[1].Z);
                    pta[2] = new Point3D(pts[0].X, y, pts[3].Z);
                }
            }
            if (elevation < 0)
            {
                if ((Azimuth >= -180 && Azimuth < -90) ||
                    (Azimuth >= 0 && Azimuth < 90))
                {
```

```
                    pta[1] = new Point3D(pts[0].X, y, pts[1].Z);
                    pta[2] = new Point3D(pts[0].X, y, pts[3].Z);

                }
                else
                {
                    pta[1] = new Point3D(pts[2].X, y, pts[1].Z);
                    pta[2] = new Point3D(pts[2].X, y, pts[3].Z);
                }
            }
            for (int i = 0; i < pta.Length; i++)
            {
                pta[i] = Normalize3D(m, pta[i]);
            }
            DrawLine(pta[0], pta[1], GridlineColor,
                GridlineThickness, GridlinePattern);
            DrawLine(pta[1], pta[2], GridlineColor,
                GridlineThickness, GridlinePattern);
        }
    }

    // Draw Z gridlines:
    if (IsZGrid)
    {
        for (double z = Zmin; z <= Zmax; z = z + ZTick)
        {
            pts = ChartBoxCoordinates();
            pta[0] = new Point3D(pts[2].X, pts[2].Y, z);
            if (Elevation >= 0)
            {
                if ((Azimuth >= -180 && Azimuth < -90) ||
                    (Azimuth >= 0 && Azimuth < 90))
                {
                    pta[1] = new Point3D(pts[2].X, pts[0].Y, z);
                    pta[2] = new Point3D(pts[0].X, pts[0].Y, z);
                }
                else
                {
                    pta[1] = new Point3D(pts[0].X, pts[2].Y, z);
                    pta[2] = new Point3D(pts[0].X, pts[1].Y, z);
                }
            }
            if (Elevation < 0)
            {
                if ((Azimuth >= -180 && Azimuth < -90) ||
                    (Azimuth >= 0 && Azimuth < 90))
                {
                    pta[1] = new Point3D(pts[0].X, pts[2].Y, z);
                    pta[2] = new Point3D(pts[0].X, pts[0].Y, z);
                }
                else
                {
                    pta[1] = new Point3D(pts[2].X, pts[0].Y, z);
                    pta[2] = new Point3D(pts[0].X, pts[0].Y, z);
                }
            }
```

```
            }
            for (int i = 0; i < pta.Length; i++)
            {
                pta[i] = Normalize3D(m, pta[i]);
            }
            DrawLine(pta[0], pta[1], GridlineColor,
                GridlineThickness, GridlinePattern);
            DrawLine(pta[1], pta[2], GridlineColor,
                GridlineThickness, GridlinePattern);
        }
    }
}
}
```

In this method, we create the X, Y, and Z gridlines on different faces, depending on values of the elevation and azimuth angles, ensuring that the gridlines are drawn on the right faces when the 3D chart is rotated.

Labels

3D labels include three components: the title, tick labels, and labels for the coordinate axes. Creating a title label in 3D is similar to doing so in 2D. However, the tick labels and axis labels in 3D charts are much more complicated than those in 2D charts. First, we need to position these labels properly by considering the variation of the elevation and azimuth angles. Then we need to rotate them to be parallel to the coordinate axes when the elevation and azimuth angles are changed. Finally, we want these labels to be properly spaced from the coordinate axes.

The following *AddLabels* method in the *ChartStyle* class creates labels in a 3D chart:

```
private void AddLabels()
{
    Matrix3D m = ChartHelper.AzimuthElevation(Elevation, Azimuth);
    Point3D pt = new Point3D();
    Point3D[] pts = ChartBoxCoordinates();
    TextBlock tb = new TextBlock();

    // Add x tick labels:
    double offset = (Ymax - Ymin) / 20;
    double labelSpace = offset;
    for (double x = Xmin; x <= Xmax; x = x + XTick)
    {
        if (Elevation >= 0)
        {
            if (Azimuth >= -90 && Azimuth < 90)
                labelSpace = -offset;
        }
        else if (Elevation < 0)
        {
            if ((Azimuth >= -180 && Azimuth < -90) ||
                Azimuth >= 90 && Azimuth <= 180)
                labelSpace = -offset;
        }
        pt = new Point3D(x, pts[1].Y + labelSpace, pts[1].Z);
        pt = Normalize3D(m, pt);
```

```csharp
        tb = new TextBlock();
        tb.Text = x.ToString();
        tb.Foreground = TickColor;
        tb.FontFamily = TickFont;
        tb.FontSize = TickFontSize;
        tb.TextAlignment = TextAlignment.Center;
        ChartCanvas.Children.Add(tb);
        Canvas.SetLeft(tb, pt.X);
        Canvas.SetTop(tb, pt.Y);
    }

    // Add y tick labels:
    offset = (Xmax - Xmin) / 20;
    labelSpace = offset;
    for (double y = Ymin; y <= Ymax; y = y + YTick)
    {
        pts = ChartBoxCoordinates();
        if (elevation >= 0)
        {
            if (azimuth >= -180 && azimuth < 0)
                labelSpace = -offset;
        }
        else if (elevation < 0)
        {
            if (azimuth >= 0 && azimuth < 180)
                labelSpace = -offset;
        }
        pt = new Point3D(pts[1].X + labelSpace, y, pts[1].Z);
        pt = Normalize3D(m, pt);
        tb = new TextBlock();
        tb.Text = y.ToString();
        tb.Foreground = TickColor;
        tb.FontFamily = TickFont;
        tb.FontSize = TickFontSize;
        tb.Measure(new Size(Double.PositiveInfinity,
            Double.PositiveInfinity));
        Size ytickSize = tb.DesiredSize;
        ChartCanvas.Children.Add(tb);
        Canvas.SetLeft(tb, pt.X - ytickSize.Width / 2);
        Canvas.SetTop(tb, pt.Y);
    }

    // Add z tick labels:
    double xoffset = (Xmax - Xmin) / 30.0;
    double yoffset = (Ymax - Ymin) / 15.0;
    double xlabelSpace = xoffset;
    double ylabelSpace = yoffset;
    tb = new TextBlock();
    tb.Text = "A";
    tb.Measure(new Size(Double.PositiveInfinity, Double.PositiveInfinity));
    Size size = tb.DesiredSize;

    for (double z = Zmin; z <= Zmax; z = z + ZTick)
    {
        pts = ChartBoxCoordinates();
```

```
if (Elevation >= 0)
{
    if (Azimuth >= -180 && Azimuth < -90)
    {
        xlabelSpace = 0;
        ylabelSpace = yoffset;
    }
    else if (Azimuth >= -90 && Azimuth < 0)
    {
        xlabelSpace = xoffset;
        ylabelSpace = 0;
    }
    else if (Azimuth >= 0 && Azimuth < 90)
    {
        xlabelSpace = 0;
        ylabelSpace = -yoffset;
    }
    else if (Azimuth >= 90 && Azimuth <= 180)
    {
        xlabelSpace = -xoffset;
        ylabelSpace = 0;
    }
}
else if (Elevation < 0)
{
    if (Azimuth >= -180 && Azimuth < -90)
    {
        ylabelSpace = 0;
        xlabelSpace = xoffset;
    }
    else if (Azimuth >= -90 && Azimuth < 0)
    {
        ylabelSpace = -yoffset;
        xlabelSpace = 0;
    }
    else if (Azimuth >= 0 && Azimuth < 90)
    {
        ylabelSpace = 0;
        xlabelSpace = -xoffset;
    }
    else if (Azimuth >= 90 && Azimuth <= 180)
    {
        ylabelSpace = yoffset;
        xlabelSpace = 0;
    }
}

pt = new Point3D(pts[2].X + ylabelSpace, pts[2].Y + xlabelSpace, z);
pt = Normalize3D(m, pt);
tb = new TextBlock();
tb.Text = z.ToString();
tb.Foreground = TickColor;
tb.FontFamily = TickFont;
tb.FontSize = TickFontSize;
tb.Measure(new Size(Double.PositiveInfinity,
```

```
            Double.PositiveInfinity));
        Size ztickSize = tb.DesiredSize;
        ChartCanvas.Children.Add(tb);
        Canvas.SetLeft(tb, pt.X - ztickSize.Width - 1);
        Canvas.SetTop(tb, pt.Y - ztickSize.Height / 2);
    }

    // Add Title:
    tb = new TextBlock();
    tb.Text = Title;
    tb.Foreground = TitleColor;
    tb.FontSize = TitleFontSize;
    tb.FontFamily = TitleFont;
    tb.Measure(new Size(Double.PositiveInfinity, Double.PositiveInfinity));
    Size titleSize = tb.DesiredSize;
    if (tb.Text != "No Title")
    {
        ChartCanvas.Children.Add(tb);
        Canvas.SetLeft(tb, ChartCanvas.Width / 2 - titleSize.Width / 2);
        Canvas.SetTop(tb, ChartCanvas.Height / 30);
    }

    // Add x axis label:
    offset = (Ymax - Ymin) / 3;
    labelSpace = offset;
    double offset1 = (Xmax - Xmin) / 10;
    double xc = offset1;
    if (Elevation >= 0)
    {
        if (Azimuth >= -90 && Azimuth < 90)
            labelSpace = -offset;
        if (Azimuth >= 0 && Azimuth <= 180)
            xc = -offset1;
    }
    else if (Elevation < 0)
    {
        if ((Azimuth >= -180 && Azimuth < -90) ||
            Azimuth >= 90 && Azimuth <= 180)
            labelSpace = -offset;
        if (Azimuth >= -180 && Azimuth <= 0)
            xc = -offset1;
    }
    Point3D[] pta = new Point3D[2];
    pta[0] = new Point3D(Xmin, pts[1].Y + labelSpace, pts[1].Z);
    pta[1] = new Point3D((Xmin + Xmax) / 2 - xc,
        pts[1].Y + labelSpace, pts[1].Z);
    pta[0] = Normalize3D(m, pta[0]);
    pta[1] = Normalize3D(m, pta[1]);
    double theta = Math.Atan((pta[1].Y - pta[0].Y) / (pta[1].X - pta[0].X));
    theta = theta * 180 / Math.PI;
    tb = new TextBlock();
    tb.Text = XLabel;
    tb.Foreground = LabelColor;
    tb.FontFamily = LabelFont;
    tb.FontSize = LabelFontSize;
```

```
tb.Measure(new Size(Double.PositiveInfinity, Double.PositiveInfinity));
Size xLabelSize = tb.DesiredSize;

TransformGroup tg = new TransformGroup();
RotateTransform rt = new RotateTransform(theta, 0.5, 0.5);
TranslateTransform tt = new TranslateTransform(
    pta[1].X + xLabelSize.Width / 2, pta[1].Y - xLabelSize.Height / 2);
tg.Children.Add(rt);
tg.Children.Add(tt);
tb.RenderTransform = tg;
ChartCanvas.Children.Add(tb);

// Add y axis label:
offset = (Xmax - Xmin) / 3;
offset1 = (Ymax - Ymin) / 5;
labelSpace = offset;
double yc = YTick;
if (Elevation >= 0)
{
    if (Azimuth >= -180 && Azimuth < 0)
        labelSpace = -offset;
    if (Azimuth >= -90 && Azimuth <= 90)
        yc = -offset1;
}
else if (Elevation < 0)
{
    yc = -offset1;
    if (Azimuth >= 0 && Azimuth < 180)
        labelSpace = -offset;
    if (Azimuth >= -90 && Azimuth <= 90)
        yc = offset1;
}
pta[0] = new Point3D(pts[1].X + labelSpace, Ymin, pts[1].Z);
pta[1] = new Point3D(pts[1].X + labelSpace,
    (Ymin + Ymax) / 2 + yc, pts[1].Z);
pta[0] = Normalize3D(m, pta[0]);
pta[1] = Normalize3D(m, pta[1]);

theta = (double)Math.Atan((pta[1].Y - pta[0].Y) /
    (pta[1].X - pta[0].X));
theta = theta * 180 / (double)Math.PI;
tb = new TextBlock();
tb.Text = YLabel;
tb.Foreground = LabelColor;
tb.FontFamily = LabelFont;
tb.FontSize = LabelFontSize;
tb.Measure(new Size(Double.PositiveInfinity, Double.PositiveInfinity));
Size yLabelSize = tb.DesiredSize;

tg = new TransformGroup();
tt = new TranslateTransform(pta[1].X - yLabelSize.Width / 2,
    pta[1].Y - yLabelSize.Height / 2);
rt = new RotateTransform(theta, 0.5, 0.5);
tg.Children.Add(rt);
tg.Children.Add(tt);
```

```
tb.RenderTransform = tg;
ChartCanvas.Children.Add(tb);

// Add z axis labels:
double zticklength = 10;
labelSpace = -1.3f * offset;
offset1 = (Zmax - Zmin) / 8;
double zc = -offset1;
for (double z = Zmin; z < Zmax; z = z + ZTick)
{
    tb = new TextBlock();
    tb.Text = z.ToString();
    tb.Measure(new Size(Double.PositiveInfinity,
        Double.PositiveInfinity));
    Size size1 = tb.DesiredSize;
    if (zticklength < size1.Width)
        zticklength = size1.Width;
}

double zlength = -zticklength;
if (Elevation >= 0)
{
    if (Azimuth >= -180 && Azimuth < -90)
    {
        zlength = -zticklength;
        labelSpace = -1.3f * offset;
        zc = -offset1;
    }
    else if (Azimuth >= -90 && Azimuth < 0)
    {
        zlength = zticklength;
        labelSpace = 2 * offset / 3;
        zc = offset1;
    }
    else if (Azimuth >= 0 && Azimuth < 90)
    {
        zlength = zticklength;
        labelSpace = 2 * offset / 3;
        zc = -offset1;
    }
    else if (Azimuth >= 90 && Azimuth <= 180)
    {
        zlength = -zticklength;
        labelSpace = -1.3f * offset;
        zc = offset1;
    }
}
else if (Elevation < 0)
{
    if (Azimuth >= -180 && Azimuth < -90)
    {
        zlength = -zticklength;
        labelSpace = -1.3f * offset;
        zc = offset1;
    }
}
```

```
        else if (Azimuth >= -90 && Azimuth < 0)
        {
            zlength = zticklength;
            labelSpace = 2 * offset / 3;
            zc = -offset1;
        }
        else if (Azimuth >= 0 && Azimuth < 90)
        {
            zlength = zticklength;
            labelSpace = 2 * offset / 3;
            zc = offset1;
        }
        else if (Azimuth >= 90 && Azimuth <= 180)
        {
            zlength = -zticklength;
            labelSpace = -1.3f * offset;
            zc = -offset1;
        }
    }
    pta[0] = new Point3D(pts[2].X - labelSpace, pts[2].Y,
        (Zmin + Zmax) / 2 + zc);

    pta[0] = Normalize3D(m, pta[0]);
    tb = new TextBlock();
    tb.Text = ZLabel;
    tb.Foreground = LabelColor;
    tb.FontFamily = LabelFont;
    tb.FontSize = LabelFontSize;
    tb.Measure(new Size(Double.PositiveInfinity, Double.PositiveInfinity));
    Size zLabelSize = tb.DesiredSize;

    tg = new TransformGroup();
    tt = new TranslateTransform(pta[0].X - zlength,
        pta[0].Y + zLabelSize.Width / 2);
    rt = new RotateTransform(270, 0.5, 0.5);
    tg.Children.Add(rt);
    tg.Children.Add(tt);
    tb.RenderTransform = tg;
    ChartCanvas.Children.Add(tb);
}
```

The *AddLabels* method may seem complicated because we need to adjust the positions of the labels according to the values of the elevation and azimuth angles.

Finally, in order to simplify the process of setting chart styles to our charts, we add a new public method, *SetChartStyle*, to the *ChartStyle* class:

```
public void SetChartStyle()
{
    AddTicks();
    AddGridlines();
    AddAxes();
    AddLabels();
}
```

Testing the Project

Now we can put together all of the code we implemented in the previous sections. Add a new *UserControl* to the *Views* folder and name it *Coordinate3DView*. Here is the markup for this view:

```
<UserControl x:Class="Chapter08.Views.Coordinate3DView"
             xmlns="http://schemas.microsoft.com/winfx/2006/xaml/presentation"
             xmlns:x="http://schemas.microsoft.com/winfx/2006/xaml"
             xmlns:mc="http://schemas.openxmlformats.org/markup-compatibility/2006"
             xmlns:d="http://schemas.microsoft.com/expression/blend/2008"
             xmlns:cal="http://www.caliburnproject.org"
             mc:Ignorable="d"
             d:DesignHeight="400" d:DesignWidth="520">
    <Grid>
        <Grid.ColumnDefinitions>
            <ColumnDefinition Width="200"/>
            <ColumnDefinition Width="*"/>
        </Grid.ColumnDefinitions>

        <StackPanel Margin="5">
            <StackPanel Orientation="Horizontal">
                <TextBlock Text="Elevation:" Margin="0 0 10 0"/>
                <TextBlock Text="{Binding Elevation, StringFormat=N0}" Width="70" />
            </StackPanel>
            <Slider x:Name="Elevation" Minimum="-90" Maximum="90" Margin="0 5 0 0"
                cal:Message.Attach="[Event ValueChanged]=[Action AddCoordinates]"/>
            <StackPanel Orientation="Horizontal" Margin="0 10 0 0">
                <TextBlock Text="Azimuth" Margin="0 0 10 0"/>
                <TextBlock Text="{Binding Azimuth, StringFormat=N0}" Width="70"/>
            </StackPanel>
            <Slider x:Name="Azimuth" Minimum="-180" Maximum="180" Margin="0 5 0 0"
                cal:Message.Attach="[Event ValueChanged]=[Action AddCoordinates]"/>
        </StackPanel>
        <Grid x:Name="chartGrid"  Margin="10" Grid.Row="0" Grid.Column="1"
              cal:Message.Attach="[Event Loaded]=[Action AddCoordinates];
              [Event SizeChanged]=[Action AddCoordinates]">
            <Border BorderBrush="Gray" BorderThickness="1">
                <Canvas x:Name="chartCanvas" Background="Transparent"
                    ClipToBounds="True" Width="{Binding ElementName=chartGrid,
                    Path=ActualWidth}" Height="{Binding ElementName=chartGrid,
                    Path=ActualHeight}"/>
            </Border>
        </Grid>
    </Grid>
</UserControl>
```

The layout of this view is very similar to that used in the previous *CubeView* example. We bind the evevation and azimuth angles to two slider objects so that we can rotate the 3D coordinate system by moving slider' bars. Add a new class to the *ViewModels* folder and name it *Coordinate3DViewModel*. Here is the code for this class:

```
using System;
using Caliburn.Micro;
using System.ComponentModel.Composition;
using System.Windows;
using Chapter08.Models;
```

```csharp
using System.Windows.Media;
using Chapter08.Models.ChartModel;
using System.Windows.Media.Media3D;
using System.Windows.Shapes;
using Chapter08.Views;

namespace Chapter08.ViewModels
{
    [Export(typeof(IScreen)), PartCreationPolicy(CreationPolicy.NonShared)]
    public class Coordinate3DViewModel : Screen
    {
         private readonly IEventAggregator _events;
        [ImportingConstructor]
        public Coordinate3DViewModel(IEventAggregator events)
        {
            this._events = events;
            DisplayName = "02. 3D Coordinates";
            cs = new ChartStyle();
        }

        private ChartStyle cs;

        private double elevation = 30;
        public double Elevation
        {
            get { return elevation; }
            set
            {
                elevation = value;
                NotifyOfPropertyChange(() => Elevation);
            }
        }

        private double azimuth = -30;
        public double Azimuth
        {
            get { return azimuth; }
            set
            {
                azimuth = value;
                NotifyOfPropertyChange(() => Azimuth);
            }
        }

        public void AddCoordinates()
        {
            var view = this.GetView() as Coordinate3DView;
            view.chartCanvas.Children.Clear();
            cs.ChartCanvas = view.chartCanvas;
            cs.GridlinePattern = LineDashPatternEnum.Solid;
            cs.Elevation = Elevation;
            cs.Azimuth = Azimuth;
            cs.SetChartStyle();
        }
    }
```

```
}
```

Here, we first define a *ChartStyle* object, *cs*, and the *Elevation* and *Azimuth* properties. We then implement an *AddCoordinates* method, in which we break the MVVM rule again (i.e., we use the view's element directly in our view model), just like we did when we created 2D charts in Chapter 4. As we discussed when we implemented 2D chart controls, you can create a 3D chart control to encapsulate the code; then, you can use this chart control to develop MVVM-compatible applications.

Running this example produces the output shown in Figure 8-4. You can examine how the coordinate axes, gridlines, and labels respond to the changes in the elevation and azimuth angles when you move the slider' bars.

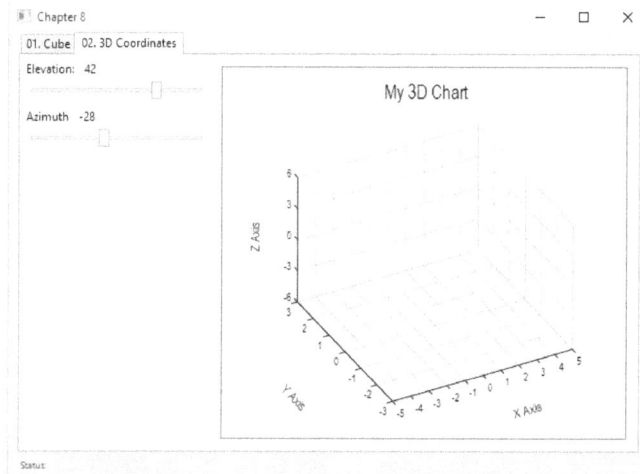

Figure 8-4. Coordinate system used in 3D charts.

3D Line Charts

In the previous section, we implemented the basic coordinate system for 3D charts in WPF without using the WPF 3D engine, a process that can seem quite involved. However, once you have finished this framework, you can use it without any modification for a wide variety of 3D chart applications. Here, I will show you how easy it is to create a 3D line chart based on this basic framework. The 3D line chart displays a 3D plot of a set of data points. It is similar to a 2D line chart, except it uses an additional *Z* component to provide data for the third dimension.

Implementation

Add a new class to the *ChartModel* class and name it *LineSeries3D*. This class is very similar to the *LineSeries* class we used extensively in creating 2D line charts, except that the *LinePoints* in this class must hold 3D points. Here is the code for this class:

```
using System;
using System.Collections.Generic;
using System.Windows;
using System.Windows.Media;
using System.Windows.Media.Media3D;
```

```
using System.Windows.Shapes;

namespace Chapter08.Models.ChartModel
{
    public class LineSeries3D
    {
        private Brush lineColor;
        private double lineThickness = 1;
        private LineDashPatternEnum linePattern;
        private List<Point3D> linePoints = new List<Point3D>();

        public LineSeries3D()
        {
            LinePoints = new List<Point3D>();
        }

        public List<Point3D> LinePoints
        {
            get { return linePoints; }
            set { linePoints = value; }
        }

        public Brush LineColor
        {
            get { return lineColor; }
            set { lineColor = value; }
        }

        public double LineThickness
        {
            get { return lineThickness; }
            set { lineThickness = value; }
        }

        public LineDashPatternEnum LinePattern
        {
            get { return linePattern; }
            set { linePattern = value; }
        }

        public void SetLinePattern(Polyline pLine, Brush color, double thickness)
        {
            pLine.Stroke = color;
            pLine.StrokeThickness = thickness;

            switch (LinePattern)
            {
                case LineDashPatternEnum.Dash:
                    pLine.StrokeDashArray =
                        new DoubleCollection(new double[2] { 4, 3 });
                    break;
                case LineDashPatternEnum.Dot:
                    pLine.StrokeDashArray =
                        new DoubleCollection(new double[2] { 1, 2 });
                    break;
```

```
                case LineDashPatternEnum.DashDot:
                    pLine.StrokeDashArray =
                        new DoubleCollection(new double[4] { 4, 2, 1, 2 });
                    break;
            }
        }


        public void AddLine3D(ChartStyle cs)
        {
            var pLine = new Polyline();
            Matrix3D m = ChartHelper.AzimuthElevation(cs.Elevation, cs.Azimuth);
            Point3D[] pts = new Point3D[LinePoints.Count];
            for (int i = 0; i < LinePoints.Count; i++)
            {
                pts[i] = cs.Normalize3D(m, LinePoints[i]);
                pLine.Points.Add(new Point(pts[i].X, pts[i].Y));
            }
            SetLinePattern(pLine, LineColor, LineThickness);
            cs.ChartCanvas.Children.Add(pLine);
        }
    }
}
```

You can see that this class is basically similar to that used in 2D chart applications. However, unlike 2D charts, here you do not need a *DataCollection* object, because typically you only want to draw one set of data points in a 3D chart. Drawing multiple sets of data points in a 3D chart usually becomes more confusing than doing so in 2D. If you do want to have this capability, you can easily add it to your applications using the *DataCollection* object the same way you did for 2D charts. To simplify our discussion, we will only consider 3D charts containing one set of data points.

We implement an *AddLine3D* method in the *LineSeries3D* class directly. Inside the *AddLine3D* method, we first perform the necessary transformations on the 3D data points using the *Normalize3D* method and the *Azimuth-Elevation* orthogonal projection matrix. Then, we draw the line chart using the *X* and *Y* components of the projected 3D data points.

Testing the Project

Now you can test the 3D line chart. Add a new *UserControl* to the *Views* folder and name it *Line3DView*. The XAML file used for this view is the same as that used in the previous *Coordinate3DView* example, except you will need to replace *AddCoordinates* with *AddChart*.

Add a new class to the *ViewModels* folder and name it *Line3DViewModel*. Here is the code for this class:

```
using System;
using Caliburn.Micro;
using System.ComponentModel.Composition;
using System.Windows;
using Chapter08.Models;
using System.Windows.Media;
using Chapter08.Models.ChartModel;
using System.Windows.Media.Media3D;
using System.Windows.Shapes;
using Chapter08.Views;
```

```csharp
namespace Chapter08.ViewModels
{
    [Export(typeof(IScreen)), PartCreationPolicy(CreationPolicy.NonShared)]
    public class Line3DViewModel : Screen
    {
        private readonly IEventAggregator _events;
        [ImportingConstructor]
        public Line3DViewModel(IEventAggregator events)
        {
            this._events = events;
            DisplayName = "03. 3D Line";
            cs = new ChartStyle();
        }

        private ChartStyle cs;

        private double elevation = 30;
        public double Elevation
        {
            get { return elevation; }
            set
            {
                elevation = value;
                NotifyOfPropertyChange(() => Elevation);
            }
        }

        private double azimuth = -30;
        public double Azimuth
        {
            get { return azimuth; }
            set
            {
                azimuth = value;
                NotifyOfPropertyChange(() => Azimuth);
            }
        }

        public void AddChart()
        {
            var view = this.GetView() as Line3DView;
            view.chartCanvas.Children.Clear();
            cs.ChartCanvas = view.chartCanvas;
            cs.GridlinePattern = LineDashPatternEnum.Solid;
            cs.Elevation = Elevation;
            cs.Azimuth = Azimuth;
            cs.Xmin = -1;
            cs.Xmax = 1;
            cs.Ymin = -1;
            cs.Ymax = 1;
            cs.Zmin = 0;
            cs.Zmax = 30;
            cs.XTick = 0.5;
            cs.YTick = 0.5;
```

```
cs.ZTick = 5;
cs.Title = "No Title";
cs.SetChartStyle();

var ds = new LineSeries3D();
ds.LineColor = Brushes.Red;
for (int i = 0; i < 300; i++)
{
    double t = 0.1 * i;
    double x = Math.Exp(-t / 30) * Math.Cos(t);
    double y = Math.Exp(-t / 30) * Math.Sin(t);
    double z = t;
    ds.LinePoints.Add(new Point3D(x, y, z));
}
ds.AddLine3D(cs);
        }
    }
}
```

Please note how we add the 3D data points to the *LinePoints* collection in the *AddChart* method.

This project generates the result shown in Figure 8-5. As with 2D line charts, here you can specify the line color, dash style, and thickness. You can also look at the line chart from different viewpoints by changing the elevation and azimuth angles using the sliders.

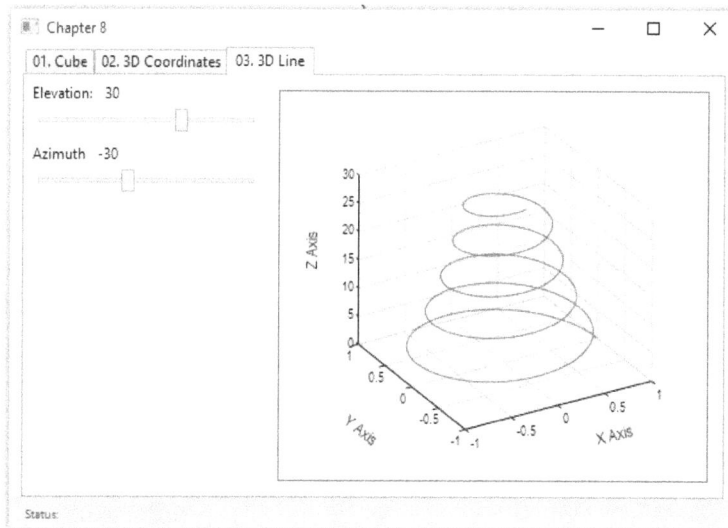

Figure 8-5. A 3D line chart.

3D Surface Charts

A 3D surface chart draws a Z function on a surface for each X and Y coordinate in a region of interest. In this section, we will discuss only simple types of surface charts. For each X and Y value, a simple surface can have at most one Z value. Complicated surfaces with multiple Z values for each pair of X and Y values were discussed in my previous published book *Practical WPF Charts and Graphics*.

We define a surface by the *Z*-coordinates of points above a rectangular grid in the *X-Y* plane. The surface chart is formed by joining adjacent points with straight lines. Surface charts are useful for visualizing 2D data arrays (i.e., matrices) that are too large to display in numerical form, and for graphing functions of two variables.

Here, I will show you how to create different types of surface charts. Mesh charts are a special case of surface charts that only draw the lines connecting the defining points, creating a wireframe surface. On the other hand, surface charts display both the connecting lines and the faces of the surface in color. I will implement these specific methods in WPF to create various surface-like charts, as listed below:

- *AddMesh* – Creates a mesh chart with or without hidden lines.
- *AddMeshZ* – Creates a mesh chart with a curtain (reference plane).
- *AddWaterfall* – Creates a chart similar to *MeshZ*, but without lines from the *Y* data.
- *AddSurface* – Creates a surface chart with or without a color map.

Implementation

The simplest way to store surface data is in a 2D array. For each point (*X*, *Y*) in the region defined for the surface, the (*X*, *Y*) entry in the array gives the *Z* coordinate of the corresponding point on the surface.

DataSeries Class

To make managing the surface easier, we can create a data structure specifically for surface charts in the *DataSeries* class. This class should contain variables to describe the data it holds, including the minimum *X* and *Y* data values, the spacing between the rows of data in the *X* and *Y* directions, and the number of data points in the *X* and *Y* directions. Add a new class to the *ChartModel* folder and name it *DataSeries3D*. The following is the code listing for this class:

```
using System;
using System.Collections.Generic;
using System.Windows;
using System.Windows.Media;
using System.Windows.Media.Media3D;
using System.Windows.Shapes;

namespace Chapter08.Models.ChartModel
{
    public class DataSeries3D : LineSeries3D
    {

        private double xLimitMin = -5;
        private double yLimitMin = 5;
        private double zLimitMin = -5;
        private double xSpacing = 1;
        private double ySpacing = 1;
        private double zSpacing = 1;
        private int xNumber = 10;
        private int yNumber = 10;
        private int zNumber = 10;

        public Point3D[,] PointArray { get; set; }
```

```csharp
public double XLimitMin
{
    get { return xLimitMin; }
    set { xLimitMin = value; }
}

public double YLimitMin
{
    get { return yLimitMin; }
    set { yLimitMin = value; }
}

public double ZLimitMin
{
    get { return zLimitMin; }
    set { zLimitMin = value; }
}

public double XSpacing
{
    get { return xSpacing; }
    set { xSpacing = value; }
}

public double YSpacing
{
    get { return ySpacing; }
    set { ySpacing = value; }
}

public double ZSpacing
{
    get { return zSpacing; }
    set { zSpacing = value; }
}

public int XNumber
{
    get { return xNumber; }
    set { xNumber = value; }
}

public int YNumber
{
    get { return yNumber; }
    set { yNumber = value; }
}

public int ZNumber
{
    get { return zNumber; }
    set { zNumber = value; }
}
```

```
public double ZDataMin()
{
    double zmin = 0;
    for (int i = 0; i < PointArray.GetLength(0); i++)
    {
        for (int j = 0; j < PointArray.GetLength(1); j++)
        {
            zmin = Math.Min(zmin, PointArray[i, j].Z);
        }
    }
    return zmin;
}

public double ZDataMax()
{
    double zmax = 0;
    for (int i = 0; i < PointArray.GetLength(0); i++)
    {
        for (int j = 0; j < PointArray.GetLength(1); j++)
        {
            zmax = Math.Max(zmax, PointArray[i, j].Z);
        }
    }
    return zmax;
}
    }
}
```

This class inherits from the LineSeries3D class and sets the data range for the *X*-, *Y*-, and *Z*-axes. It also contains a couple of public methods that compute the minimum and maximum of the data set.

Chart Functions

When we test our example 3D surface charts, we will use two 3D math functions, *Peak3D* and *Sinc3D*, which we put together in the *ChartHelper* class:

```
public static void Peak3D(ChartStyle cs, DataSeries3D ds)
{
    cs.Xmin = -3;
    cs.Xmax = 3;
    cs.Ymin = -3;
    cs.Ymax = 3;
    cs.Zmin = -8;
    cs.Zmax = 8;
    cs.XTick = 1;
    cs.YTick = 1;
    cs.ZTick = 4;

    ds.XLimitMin = cs.Xmin;
    ds.YLimitMin = cs.Ymin;
    ds.XSpacing = 0.2;
    ds.YSpacing = 0.2;
    ds.XNumber = Convert.ToInt16((cs.Xmax - cs.Xmin) / ds.XSpacing) + 1;
    ds.YNumber = Convert.ToInt16((cs.Ymax - cs.Ymin) / ds.YSpacing) + 1;
```

```
            Point3D[,] pts = new Point3D[ds.XNumber, ds.YNumber];
            for (int i = 0; i < ds.XNumber; i++)
            {
                for (int j = 0; j < ds.YNumber; j++)
                {
                    double x = ds.XLimitMin + i * ds.XSpacing;
                    double y = ds.YLimitMin + j * ds.YSpacing;
                    double z = 3 * Math.Pow((1 - x), 2) *
                        Math.Exp(-x * x - (y + 1) * (y + 1)) - 10 *
                        (0.2 * x - Math.Pow(x, 3) - Math.Pow(y, 5)) *
                        Math.Exp(-x * x - y * y) - 1 / 3 *
                        Math.Exp(-(x + 1) * (x + 1) - y * y);
                    pts[i, j] = new Point3D(x, y, z);
                }
            }
            ds.PointArray = pts;
        }

        public static void Sinc3D(ChartStyle cs, DataSeries3D ds)
        {
            cs.Xmin = -8;
            cs.Xmax = 8;
            cs.Ymin = -8;
            cs.Ymax = 8;
            cs.Zmin = -0.5f;
            cs.Zmax = 1;
            cs.XTick = 4;
            cs.YTick = 4;
            cs.ZTick = 0.5f;

            ds.XLimitMin = cs.Xmin;
            ds.YLimitMin = cs.Ymin;
            ds.XSpacing = 0.5;
            ds.YSpacing = 0.5;
            ds.XNumber = Convert.ToInt16((cs.Xmax - cs.Xmin) / ds.XSpacing) + 1;
            ds.YNumber = Convert.ToInt16((cs.Ymax - cs.Ymin) / ds.YSpacing) + 1;

            Point3D[,] pts = new Point3D[ds.XNumber, ds.YNumber];
            for (int i = 0; i < ds.XNumber; i++)
            {
                for (int j = 0; j < ds.YNumber; j++)
                {
                    double x = ds.XLimitMin + i * ds.XSpacing;
                    double y = ds.YLimitMin + j * ds.YSpacing;
                    double r = Math.Sqrt(x * x + y * y) + 0.000001;
                    double z = Math.Sin(r) / r;
                    pts[i, j] = new Point3D(x, y, z);
                }
            }
            ds.PointArray = pts;
        }
```

Both the *Peak3D* and *Sinc3D* methods generate data for testing mesh and surface charts.

Add3DChart Class

Now add the existing *ColormapBrush* class from Chapter 5 to the *ChartModel* folder, and change its namespace to *Chapter08.Models.ChartModel*. A detailed explanation on how to implement this class can be found in my previous published book, *Practical WPF Graphics Programming*. We will need this class when we create surface charts and colorbars. Add another new class to the *ChartModel* folder and name it *Add3DChart*. Here is the code listing for this class:

```
using System;
using System.Collections.Generic;
using System.Windows;
using System.Windows.Controls;
using System.Windows.Media;
using System.Windows.Media.Media3D;
using System.Windows.Shapes;

namespace Chapter08.Models.ChartModel
{
    public class Add3DChart
    {
        private SurfaceChartTypeEnum surfaceChartType = SurfaceChartTypeEnum.Mesh;
        private bool isColormap = true;
        private bool isHiddenLine = false;
        private bool isInterp = false;
        private int numberInterp = 2;
        private ColormapBrush colormap = new ColormapBrush();

        public ColormapBrush Colormap
        {
            get { return colormap; }
            set { colormap = value; }
        }

        public SurfaceChartTypeEnum SurfaceChartType
        {
            get { return surfaceChartType; }
            set { surfaceChartType = value; }
        }

        public bool IsColormap
        {
            get { return isColormap; }
            set { isColormap = value; }
        }

        public bool IsHiddenLine
        {
            get { return isHiddenLine; }
            set { isHiddenLine = value; }
        }

        public bool IsInterp
        {
            get { return isInterp; }
            set { isInterp = value; }
```

```
        }

    public int NumberInterp
    {
        get { return numberInterp; }
        set { numberInterp = value; }
    }


    public void Set3DChart(ChartStyle cs, DataSeries3D ds)
    {
        switch (SurfaceChartType)
        {
            case SurfaceChartTypeEnum.Mesh:
                AddMesh(cs, ds);
                break;
            case SurfaceChartTypeEnum.MeshZ:
                AddMeshZ(cs, ds);
                break;
            case SurfaceChartTypeEnum.Waterfall:
                AddWaterfall(cs, ds);
                break;
            case SurfaceChartTypeEnum.Surface:
                AddSurface(cs, ds);
                break;
        }
    }

    public void AddColorBar(ChartStyle cs, DataSeries3D ds, double zmin,
        double zmax)
    {
        TextBlock tb;
        tb = new TextBlock();
        tb.Text = "A";
        tb.FontFamily = cs.TickFont;
        tb.FontSize = cs.TickFontSize;
        tb.Measure(new Size(Double.PositiveInfinity, Double.PositiveInfinity));
        Size tickSize = tb.DesiredSize;

        double x = 6 * cs.ChartCanvas.Width / 7;
        double y = cs.ChartCanvas.Height / 10;
        double width = cs.ChartCanvas.Width / 25;
        double height = 8 * cs.ChartCanvas.Height / 10;
        Point3D[] pts = new Point3D[64];
        double dz = (zmax - zmin) / 63;

        // Create the color bar:
        Polygon plg;
        for (int i = 0; i < 64; i++)
        {
            pts[i] = new Point3D(x, y, zmin + i * dz);
        }
        for (int i = 0; i < 63; i++)
        {
            SolidColorBrush brush = GetBrush(pts[i].Z, zmin, zmax);
```

```
            double y1 = y + height - (pts[i].Z - zmin) * height / (zmax - zmin);
            double y2 = y + height - (pts[i + 1].Z - zmin) *
                height / (zmax - zmin);
            plg = new Polygon();
            plg.Points.Add(new Point(x, y2));
            plg.Points.Add(new Point(x + width, y2));
            plg.Points.Add(new Point(x + width, y1));
            plg.Points.Add(new Point(x, y1));
            plg.Fill = brush;
            plg.Stroke = brush;
            cs.ChartCanvas.Children.Add(plg);
        }
        Rectangle rect = new Rectangle();
        rect.Width = width + 2;
        rect.Height = height + 2;
        rect.Stroke = Brushes.Black;
        Canvas.SetLeft(rect, x - 1);
        Canvas.SetTop(rect, y - 1);
        cs.ChartCanvas.Children.Add(rect);

        // Add ticks and labels to the color bar:
        double tickLength = 0.15 * width;
        for (double z = zmin; z <= zmax; z = z + (zmax - zmin) / 6)
        {
            double yy = y + height - (z - zmin) * height / (zmax - zmin);
            AddTickLine(cs, new Point(x, yy), new Point(x + tickLength, yy));
            AddTickLine(cs, new Point(x + width, yy),
                new Point(x + width - tickLength, yy));
            tb = new TextBlock();
            tb.Text = (Math.Round(z, 2)).ToString();
            tb.FontFamily = cs.TickFont;
            tb.FontSize = cs.TickFontSize;
            cs.ChartCanvas.Children.Add(tb);
            Canvas.SetLeft(tb, x + width + 5);
            Canvas.SetTop(tb, yy - tickSize.Height / 2);
        }
    }

    private void AddTickLine(ChartStyle cs, Point pt1, Point pt2)
    {
        Line line = new Line();
        line.X1 = pt1.X;
        line.Y1 = pt1.Y;
        line.X2 = pt2.X;
        line.Y2 = pt2.Y;
        line.Stroke = Brushes.Black;
        cs.ChartCanvas.Children.Add(line);
    }

    private SolidColorBrush GetBrush(double z, double zmin, double zmax)
    {
        SolidColorBrush brush = new SolidColorBrush();
        Colormap.Ydivisions =
            (int)((zmax - zmin) / (Colormap.ColormapLength - 1));
        Colormap.Ymin = zmin;
```

```
            Colormap.Ymax = zmax;
            Colormap.Ydivisions = 64;
            int colorIndex = (int)(((Colormap.ColormapLength - 1) *
                (z - zmin) + zmax - z) / (zmax - zmin));
            if (colorIndex < 0)
                colorIndex = 0;
            if (colorIndex >= Colormap.ColormapLength)
                colorIndex = Colormap.ColormapLength - 1;
            brush = Colormap.ColormapBrushes()[colorIndex];
            return brush;
        }

        private void AddMesh(ChartStyle cs, DataSeries3D ds)
        {
            ......
        }

        private void AddMeshZ(ChartStyle cs, DataSeries3D ds)
        {
            ......
        }

        private void AddWaterfall(ChartStyle cs, DataSeries3D ds)
        {
            ......
        }

        private void AddSurface(ChartStyle cs, DataSeries3D ds)
        {
            ......
        }
    }

    public enum SurfaceChartTypeEnum
    {
        Surface = 1,
        Mesh = 2,
        MeshZ = 3,
        Waterfall = 4
    }
}
```

In this class, the field members and their corresponding public properties are used to control the appearance of various 3D charts. You can create a specific 3D chart by selecting the *SurfaceChartType* from the enumeration *SurfaceChartTypeEnum*. Here, you can see that four different chart types are available to select from in this enumeration. You can add more chart types to this enumeration and create their corresponding 3D charts the same way we do here.

The *ColormapBrush* property is used to create the colormap for a specified 3D chart type. The color map is associated with the *Z* value. The *AddColorBar* method creates a colorbar on the right side of a 3D chart. This colorbar, much like the legend in a 2D chart, indicates the data values for different colors in the colormap.

In the following few sections, I will present detailed procedures for creating various 3D charts.

Mesh Charts

To create mesh charts, we will add an *AddMesh* method to the *Add3DChart* class. The following is the code listing for this method:

```
private void AddMesh(ChartStyle cs, DataSeries3D ds)
{
    Matrix3D m = ChartHelper.AzimuthElevation(cs.Elevation, cs.Azimuth);
    Polygon plg = new Polygon();
    Point3D[,] pts = ds.PointArray;
    double[,] zValues = new double[pts.GetLength(0), pts.GetLength(1)];
    double zmin = ds.ZDataMin();
    double zmax = ds.ZDataMax();

    for (int i = 0; i < pts.GetLength(0); i++)
    {
        for (int j = 0; j < pts.GetLength(1); j++)
        {
            zValues[i, j] = pts[i, j].Z;
            pts[i, j] = cs.Normalize3D(m, pts[i, j]);
        }
    }

    // Draw mesh chart:
    for (int i = 0; i < pts.GetLength(0) - 1; i++)
    {
        int ii = i;
        if (cs.Elevation >= 0)
        {
            ii = i;
            if (cs.Azimuth >= -180 && cs.Azimuth < 0)
            {
                ii = pts.GetLength(0) - 2 - i;
            }
        }
        else
        {
            ii = pts.GetLength(0) - 2 - i;
            if (cs.Azimuth >= -180 && cs.Azimuth < 0)
            {
                ii = i;
            }
        }
        for (int j = 0; j < pts.GetLength(1) - 1; j++)
        {
            int jj = j;
            if (cs.Elevation < 0)
            {
                jj = pts.GetLength(1) - 2 - j;
            }
            plg = new Polygon();
            plg.Points.Add(new Point(pts[ii, jj].X, pts[ii, jj].Y));
            plg.Points.Add(new Point(pts[ii, jj + 1].X, pts[ii, jj + 1].Y));
            plg.Points.Add(new Point(pts[ii + 1, jj + 1].X,
                pts[ii + 1, jj + 1].Y));
```

```
                        plg.Points.Add(new Point(pts[ii + 1, jj].X, pts[ii + 1, jj].Y));

                        plg.Stroke = Brushes.Black;
                        plg.StrokeThickness = ds.LineThickness;
                        plg.Fill = Brushes.White;
                        if (IsHiddenLine)
                        {
                            plg.Fill = Brushes.Transparent;
                        }
                        if (IsColormap)
                        {
                            plg.Stroke = GetBrush(zValues[ii, jj], zmin, zmax);
                        }
                        cs.ChartCanvas.Children.Add(plg);
                    }
                }
                if (cs.IsColorBar && IsColormap)
                {
                    AddColorBar(cs, ds, zmin, zmax);
                }
            }
```

You can select the *Mesh* chart type using the following code snippet:

```
Add3DChart a3d = new Add3DChart();
A3d.SurfaceChartType = SurfaceChartTypeEnum.Mesh;
```

This lets you create a 3D mesh chart with or without hidden lines. You can also produce a mesh chart with a single color or with a complete scaled color map. We use the Z-order algorithm to remove hidden lines in a mesh plot. The Z-order algorithm draws polygons from back to front. A polygon drawn in this order can obscure only the polygon drawn before it. Filling the polygon with a white color (or the background color of the plot area) covers up any lines that should be obscured. Notice that when the elevation and azimuth angles change, we change the order of drawing the polygons, ensuring that the program always draws the polygons from back to front.

Here, I will show you how to create a mesh chart in a more general WPF application that includes various 3D charts. Add a new *UserControl* to the *Views* folder and name it *Chart3DView*. Here is the markup for this view:

```
<UserControl x:Class="Chapter08.Views.Chart3DView"
             xmlns="http://schemas.microsoft.com/winfx/2006/xaml/presentation"
             xmlns:x="http://schemas.microsoft.com/winfx/2006/xaml"
             xmlns:mc="http://schemas.openxmlformats.org/markup-compatibility/2006"
             xmlns:d="http://schemas.microsoft.com/expression/blend/2008"
             xmlns:cal="http://www.caliburnproject.org"
             mc:Ignorable="d"
             d:DesignHeight="400" d:DesignWidth="520">
    <Grid>
        <Grid.ColumnDefinitions>
            <ColumnDefinition Width="200"/>
            <ColumnDefinition Width="*"/>
        </Grid.ColumnDefinitions>

        <StackPanel Margin="5">
            <StackPanel Orientation="Horizontal">
                <TextBlock Text="Elevation:" Margin="0 0 10 0"/>
```

```
                <TextBlock Text="{Binding Elevation, StringFormat=N0}" Width="70" />
            </StackPanel>
            <Slider x:Name="Elevation" Minimum="-90" Maximum="90" Margin="0 5 0 0"
                    cal:Message.Attach="[Event ValueChanged]=[Action AddChart]"/>
            <StackPanel Orientation="Horizontal" Margin="0 10 0 0">
                <TextBlock Text="Azimuth" Margin="0 0 10 0"/>
                <TextBlock Text="{Binding Azimuth, StringFormat=N0}" Width="70"/>
            </StackPanel>
            <Slider x:Name="Azimuth" Minimum="-180" Maximum="180" Margin="0 5 0 0"
                    cal:Message.Attach="[Event ValueChanged]=[Action AddChart]"/>
            <TextBlock Text="Choose 3D Chart Type:" Margin="0 20 0 0"/>
            <ComboBox x:Name="SurfaceChartType" Width="150" Margin="0 5 0 0"
                    HorizontalAlignment="Left" cal:Message.Attach="[Event
                    SelectionChanged]=[Action AddChart]"/>
            <TextBlock Text="Chart Setting:" Margin="0 20 0 0"/>
            <ComboBox x:Name="ChartSetting" Width="150" Margin="0 5 0 0"
                    HorizontalAlignment="Left" cal:Message.Attach="[Event
                    SelectionChanged]=[Action AddChart]"/>
        </StackPanel>
        <Grid x:Name="chartGrid"  Margin="10" Grid.Row="0" Grid.Column="1"
            cal:Message.Attach="[Event Loaded]=[Action AddChart];[Event
            SizeChanged]=[Action AddChart]">
            <Border BorderBrush="Gray" BorderThickness="1">
                <Canvas x:Name="chartCanvas" Background="Transparent"
                        ClipToBounds="True" Width="{Binding ElementName=chartGrid,
                        Path=ActualWidth}" Height="{Binding ElementName=chartGrid,
                        Path=ActualHeight}" />
            </Border>
        </Grid>
    </Grid>
</UserControl>
```

In addition to two sliders, we also add two *ComboBox* objects that allow you to specify the chart type and set various parameters for the specified chart.

Add a new class to the *ViewModel* folder and name it *Chart3DViewModel*. Here is the code for this class:

```
using System;
using System.Linq;
using Caliburn.Micro;
using System.ComponentModel.Composition;
using System.Windows;
using Chapter08.Models;
using System.Windows.Media;
using Chapter08.Models.ChartModel;
using System.Windows.Media.Media3D;
using System.Windows.Shapes;
using Chapter08.Views;
using System.Collections.Generic;

namespace Chapter08.ViewModels
{
    [Export(typeof(IScreen)), PartCreationPolicy(CreationPolicy.NonShared)]
    public class Chart3DViewModel : Screen
    {
        private readonly IEventAggregator _events;
```

```
[ImportingConstructor]
public Chart3DViewModel(IEventAggregator events)
{
    this._events = events;
    DisplayName = "04. Mesh Chart";
    cs = new ChartStyle();
}

private ChartStyle cs;
private Add3DChart a3d;

private double elevation = 30;
public double Elevation
{
    get { return elevation; }
    set
    {
        elevation = value;
        NotifyOfPropertyChange(() => Elevation);
    }
}

private double azimuth = -37;
public double Azimuth
{
    get { return azimuth; }
    set
    {
        azimuth = value;
        NotifyOfPropertyChange(() => Azimuth);
    }
}

public BindableCollection<string> ChartSetting
{
    get { return new BindableCollection<string>
        { "MeshWithHiddenLines", "MeshNoHiddenLines",
          "MeshColormap", "SurfaceNoMesh", "SurfaceInterp" }; }
}

private string selectedChartSetting = "MeshWithHiddenLines";
public string SelectedChartSetting
{
    get { return selectedChartSetting; }
    set
    {
        selectedChartSetting = value;
        NotifyOfPropertyChange(() => SelectedChartSetting);
    }
}

private IEnumerable<SurfaceChartTypeEnum> surfaceChartType;
public IEnumerable<SurfaceChartTypeEnum> SurfaceChartType
{
    get { return Enum.GetValues(typeof(SurfaceChartTypeEnum)).
```

```
                Cast<SurfaceChartTypeEnum>(); }
    set
    {
        surfaceChartType = value;
        NotifyOfPropertyChange(() => SurfaceChartType);
    }
}

private SurfaceChartTypeEnum selectedSurfaceChartType =
    SurfaceChartTypeEnum.Mesh;
public SurfaceChartTypeEnum SelectedSurfaceChartType
{
    get { return selectedSurfaceChartType;}
    set
    {
        selectedSurfaceChartType = value;
        NotifyOfPropertyChange(() => SelectedSurfaceChartType);
    }
}

public void AddChart()
{
    DisplayName = "04. " + SelectedSurfaceChartType.ToString() + " Chart";
    var view = this.GetView() as Chart3DView;
    view.chartCanvas.Children.Clear();
    cs.ChartCanvas = view.chartCanvas;
    cs.GridlinePattern = LineDashPatternEnum.Solid;
    cs.Elevation = Elevation;
    cs.Azimuth = Azimuth;
    cs.Title = "No Title";
    cs.IsColorBar = true;
    if (SelectedSurfaceChartType == SurfaceChartTypeEnum.Mesh)
    {
        if (SelectedChartSetting == "MeshWithHiddenLines" ||
            SelectedChartSetting == "MeshNoHiddenLines")
            cs.IsColorBar = false;
    }
    cs.SetChartStyle();

    var ds = new DataSeries3D();
    ds.LineColor = Brushes.Black;

    if (SelectedSurfaceChartType == SurfaceChartTypeEnum.Mesh ||
        SelectedSurfaceChartType == SurfaceChartTypeEnum.Surface)
        ChartHelper.Peak3D(cs, ds);
    else
        ChartHelper.Sinc3D(cs, ds);

    a3d = new Add3DChart();
    a3d.SurfaceChartType = SelectedSurfaceChartType;

    if (SelectedSurfaceChartType == SurfaceChartTypeEnum.Mesh)
    {
        if (SelectedChartSetting == "MeshWithHiddenLines")
        {
```

```
                    a3d.IsColormap = false;
                    a3d.IsHiddenLine = true;
                }
                else if (SelectedChartSetting == "MeshNoHiddenLines")
                {
                    a3d.IsColormap = false;
                    a3d.IsHiddenLine = false;
                }
                else if (SelectedChartSetting == "MeshColormap")
                    a3d.IsColormap = true;
            }
            else if(SelectedSurfaceChartType == SurfaceChartTypeEnum.MeshZ)
            {
                a3d.IsColormap = true;
                a3d.Colormap.ColormapBrushType = ColormapBrushEnum.Cool;
            }
            else if (SelectedSurfaceChartType == SurfaceChartTypeEnum.Waterfall)
            {
                a3d.IsColormap = true;
                a3d.Colormap.ColormapBrushType = ColormapBrushEnum.Autumn;
            }
            else if (SelectedSurfaceChartType == SurfaceChartTypeEnum.Surface)
            {
                a3d.IsColormap = true;
                a3d.Colormap.ColormapBrushType = ColormapBrushEnum.Jet;

                if(SelectedChartSetting == "SurfaceNoMesh")
                {
                    ds.LineColor = Brushes.Transparent;
                }
                else if(SelectedChartSetting == "SurfaceInterp")
                {
                    ds.LineColor = Brushes.Transparent;
                    a3d.IsInterp = true;
                    a3d.NumberInterp = 3;
                }
            }
            a3d.Set3DChart(cs, ds);
        }
    }
}
```

Please note how we set the *ComboBox* object's *Items* and *SelectedItem* properties using Caliburn.Micro's naming convention. Inside the *AddChart* method, we specify the chart data using the predefined math functions in the *ChartHelper* class, *Peak3D* and *Sinc3D*, depending on the selected chart type.

Building and running this example, choosing *Mesh* from the chart type combobox, and choosing *MeshWithHiddenLines* from the chart setting combobox will create a mesh chart with the hidden lines visible, as shown in Figure 8-6.

Alternatively, selecting *MeshNoHiddenLines* from the chart setting combobox produces a mesh chart without hidden lines, as shown in Figure 8-7.

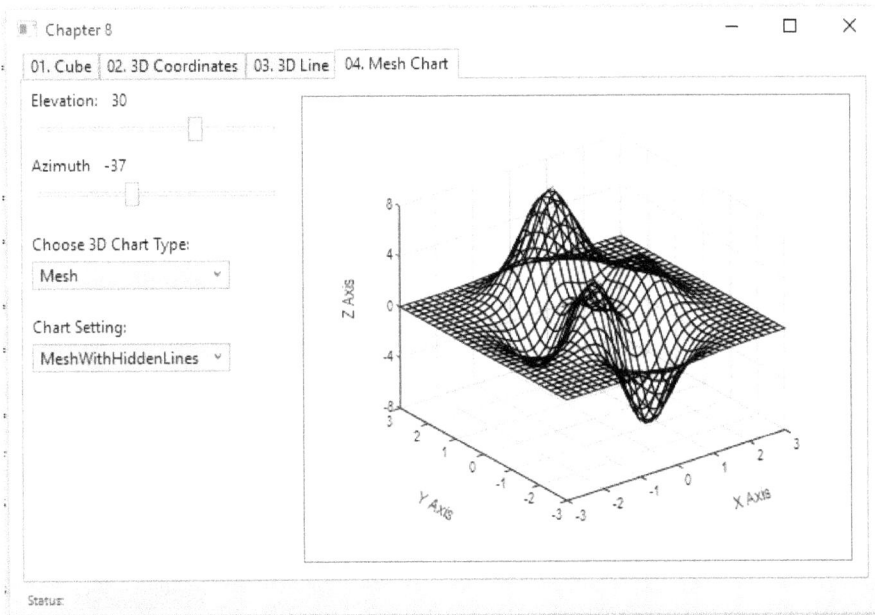

Figure 8-6. A mesh chart with hidden lines.

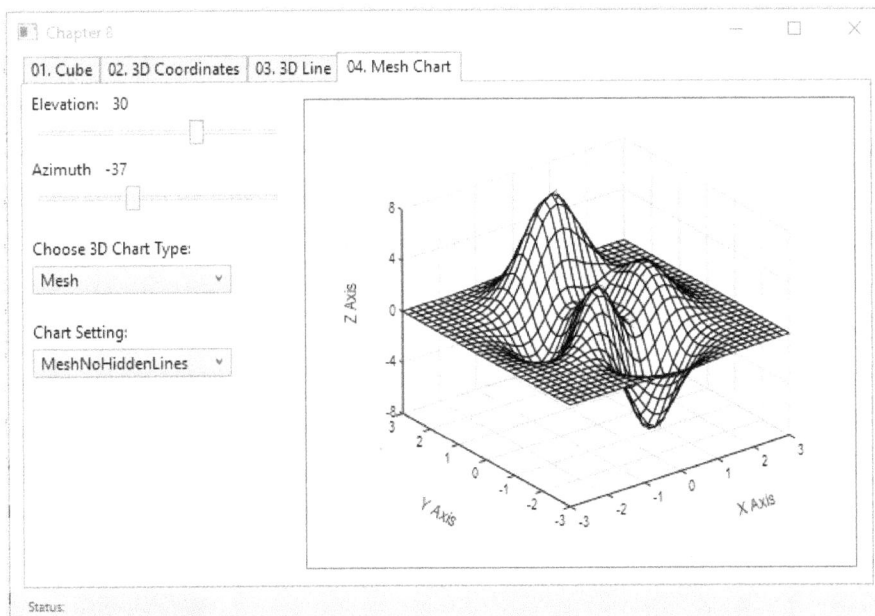

Figure 8-7. A mesh chart without hidden lines.

Furthermore, you can create a colomapped mesh chart with a colorbar by choosing *MeshColormap* from the chart setting combobox, as shown in Figure 8-8.

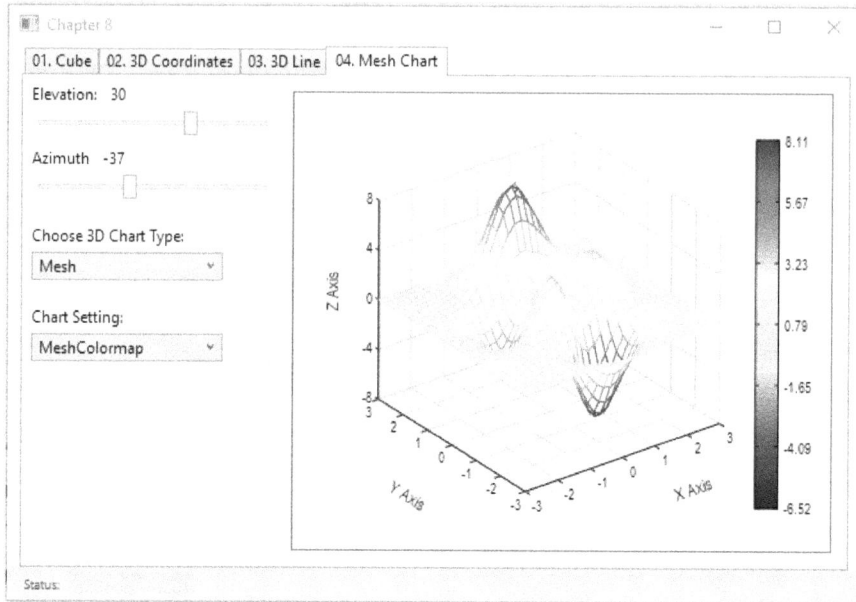

Figure 8-8. A mesh chart with a colormap and a colorbar.

Curtain Charts

The chart type *MeshZ* creates a curtain plot from a reference plane around the mesh chart. The curtain is drawn by dropping lines down from the edge of the surface to the plane parallel to the *X-Y* plane, at a height equal to the lowest point on the surface.

You can create a curtain chart using the following *AddMeshZ* method in the *Add3DChart* class:

```
private void AddMeshZ(ChartStyle cs, DataSeries3D ds)
{
    Matrix3D m = ChartHelper.AzimuthElevation(cs.Elevation, cs.Azimuth);
    Polygon plg = new Polygon();
    Point3D[,] pts = ds.PointArray;
    Point3D[,] pts1 = new Point3D[pts.GetLength(0), pts.GetLength(1)];
    double[,] zValues = new double[pts.GetLength(0), pts.GetLength(1)];
    double zmin = ds.ZDataMin();
    double zmax = ds.ZDataMax();

    for (int i = 0; i < pts.GetLength(0); i++)
    {
        for (int j = 0; j < pts.GetLength(1); j++)
        {
            zValues[i, j] = pts[i, j].Z;
            pts1[i, j] = new Point3D(pts[i, j].X, pts[i, j].Y, pts[i, j].Z);
            pts[i, j] = cs.Normalize3D(m, pts[i, j]);
        }
    }

    // Draw mesh using the z-order method:
    for (int i = 0; i < pts.GetLength(0) - 1; i++)
```

```
{
    int ii = i;
    if (cs.Elevation >= 0)
    {
        ii = i;
        if (cs.Azimuth >= -180 && cs.Azimuth < 0)
        {
            ii = pts.GetLength(0) - 2 - i;
        }
    }
    else
    {
        ii = pts.GetLength(0) - 2 - i;
        if (cs.Azimuth >= -180 && cs.Azimuth < 0)
        {
            ii = i;
        }
    }
    for (int j = 0; j < pts.GetLength(1) - 1; j++)
    {
        int jj = j;
        if (cs.Elevation < 0)
        {
            jj = pts.GetLength(1) - 2 - j;
        }
        plg = new Polygon();
        plg.Points.Add(new Point(pts[ii, jj].X, pts[ii, jj].Y));
        plg.Points.Add(new Point(pts[ii, jj + 1].X, pts[ii, jj + 1].Y));
        plg.Points.Add(new Point(pts[ii + 1, jj + 1].X,
            pts[ii + 1, jj + 1].Y));
        plg.Points.Add(new Point(pts[ii + 1, jj].X, pts[ii + 1, jj].Y));

        plg.Stroke = Brushes.Black;
        plg.StrokeThickness = ds.LineThickness;
        plg.Fill = Brushes.White;
        if (IsHiddenLine)
        {
            plg.Fill = Brushes.Transparent;
        }
        if (IsColormap)
        {
            plg.Stroke = GetBrush(zValues[ii, jj], zmin, zmax);
        }
        cs.ChartCanvas.Children.Add(plg);
    }
}

//Draw curtain lines:
Point3D[] pta = new Point3D[4];
for (int i = 0; i < pts1.GetLength(0); i++)
{
    int jj = pts1.GetLength(0) - 1;
    if (cs.Elevation >= 0)
    {
        if (cs.Azimuth >= -90 && cs.Azimuth <= 90)
```

```
                jj = 0;
        }
        else if (cs.Elevation < 0)
        {
            jj = 0;
            if (cs.Azimuth >= -90 && cs.Azimuth <= 90)
                jj = pts1.GetLength(0) - 1;
        }

        if (i < pts1.GetLength(0) - 1)
        {
            pta[0] = new Point3D(pts1[i, jj].X, pts1[i, jj].Y,
                pts1[i, jj].Z);
            pta[1] = new Point3D(pts1[i + 1, jj].X,
                pts1[i + 1, jj].Y, pts1[i + 1, jj].Z);
            pta[2] = new Point3D(pts1[i + 1, jj].X,
                pts1[i + 1, jj].Y, cs.Zmin);
            pta[3] = new Point3D(pts1[i, jj].X, pts1[i, jj].Y, cs.Zmin);
            for (int k = 0; k < 4; k++)
            {
                pta[k] = cs.Normalize3D(m, pta[k]);
            }
            plg = new Polygon();
            plg.Stroke = Brushes.Black;
            plg.StrokeThickness = ds.LineThickness;
            plg.Fill = Brushes.White;
            plg.Points.Add(new Point(pta[0].X, pta[0].Y));
            plg.Points.Add(new Point(pta[1].X, pta[1].Y));
            plg.Points.Add(new Point(pta[2].X, pta[2].Y));
            plg.Points.Add(new Point(pta[3].X, pta[3].Y));
            if (IsHiddenLine)
            {
                plg.Fill = Brushes.Transparent;
            }
            if (IsColormap)
            {
                plg.Stroke = GetBrush(pts1[i, jj].Z, zmin, zmax);
            }
            cs.ChartCanvas.Children.Add(plg);
        }
    }

    for (int j = 0; j < pts1.GetLength(1); j++)
    {
        int ii = 0;
        if (cs.Elevation >= 0)
        {
            if (cs.Azimuth >= 0 && cs.Azimuth <= 180)
            {
                ii = pts1.GetLength(1) - 1;
            }
        }
        else if (cs.Elevation < 0)
        {
            if (cs.Azimuth >= -180 && cs.Azimuth <= 0)
```

```
                    ii = pts1.GetLength(1) - 1;
            }
            if (j < pts1.GetLength(1) - 1)
            {
                pta[0] = new Point3D(pts1[ii, j].X, pts1[ii, j].Y,
                    pts1[ii, j].Z);
                pta[1] = new Point3D(pts1[ii, j + 1].X,
                    pts1[ii, j + 1].Y, pts1[ii, j + 1].Z);
                pta[2] = new Point3D(pts1[ii, j + 1].X,
                    pts1[ii, j + 1].Y, cs.Zmin);
                pta[3] = new Point3D(pts1[ii, j].X, pts1[ii, j].Y, cs.Zmin);
                for (int k = 0; k < 4; k++)
                    pta[k] = cs.Normalize3D(m, pta[k]);
                plg = new Polygon();
                plg.Stroke = Brushes.Black;
                plg.StrokeThickness = ds.LineThickness;
                plg.Fill = Brushes.White;
                plg.Points.Add(new Point(pta[0].X, pta[0].Y));
                plg.Points.Add(new Point(pta[1].X, pta[1].Y));
                plg.Points.Add(new Point(pta[2].X, pta[2].Y));
                plg.Points.Add(new Point(pta[3].X, pta[3].Y));
                if (IsHiddenLine)
                {
                    plg.Fill = Brushes.Transparent;
                }
                if (IsColormap)
                {
                    plg.Stroke = GetBrush(pts1[ii, j].Z, zmin, zmax);
                }
                cs.ChartCanvas.Children.Add(plg);
            }
        }
    }

    if (cs.IsColorBar && IsColormap)
    {
        AddColorBar(cs, ds, zmin, zmax);
    }
}
```

In this method, we first create a mesh plot, and then add the curtain to it. The curtain lines must be drawn on the appropriate surface when the elevation and azimuth angles change.

We can test the curtain chart by selecting *MeshZ* from the chart type combobox in the *Chart3DView* example. If you change the chart function to *Sinc3D* and the colormap brush to *Cool*, you will get the result shown in Figure 8-9.

Waterfall Charts

A waterfall chart draws a mesh plot similar to a curtain chart, but it does not generate vertical lines from the *X* component of the data. This produces a "waterfall" effect.

You can create a waterfall chart using the following *AddWaterfall* method in the *Add3DChart* class:

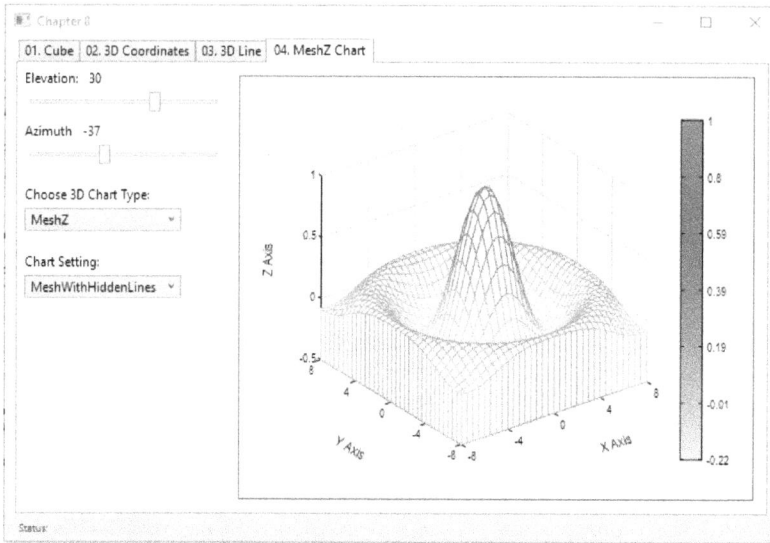

Figure 8-9. Curtain mesh chart.

```
private void AddWaterfall(ChartStyle cs, DataSeries3D ds)
{
    Matrix3D m = ChartHelper.AzimuthElevation(cs.Elevation, cs.Azimuth);
    Polygon plg = new Polygon();
    Point3D[,] pts = ds.PointArray;
    Point3D[] pt3 = new Point3D[pts.GetLength(0) + 2];
    double[] zValues = new double[pts.Length];
    Point[] pta = new Point[pts.GetLength(0) + 2];
    double zmin = ds.ZDataMin();
    double zmax = ds.ZDataMax();

    for (int j = 0; j < pts.GetLength(1); j++)
    {
        int jj = j;
        if (cs.Elevation >= 0)
        {
            if (cs.Azimuth >= -90 && cs.Azimuth < 90)
            {
                jj = pts.GetLength(1) - 1 - j;
            }
        }
        else if (cs.Elevation < 0)
        {
            jj = pts.GetLength(1) - 1 - j;
            if (cs.Azimuth >= -90 && cs.Azimuth < 90)
                jj = j;
        }
        for (int i = 0; i < pts.GetLength(0); i++)
        {
            pt3[i + 1] = pts[i, jj];

            if (i == 0)
            {
```

```
                pt3[0] = new Point3D(pt3[i + 1].X, pt3[i + 1].Y, cs.Zmin);
            }
            if (i == pts.GetLength(0) - 1)
            {
                pt3[pts.GetLength(0) + 1] = new Point3D(pt3[i + 1].X,
                    pt3[i + 1].Y, cs.Zmin);
            }
        }
        plg = new Polygon();
        for (int i = 0; i < pt3.Length; i++)
        {
            zValues[i] = pt3[i].Z;
            pt3[i] = cs.Normalize3D(m, pt3[i]);
            pta[i] = new Point(pt3[i].X, pt3[i].Y);
            plg.Points.Add(new Point(pt3[i].X, pt3[i].Y));
        }
        plg.Stroke = Brushes.Transparent;
        plg.StrokeThickness = ds.LineThickness;
        plg.Fill = Brushes.White;
        cs.ChartCanvas.Children.Add(plg);

        for (int i = 1; i < pt3.Length; i++)
        {
            Line line = new Line();
            line.Stroke = Brushes.Black;
            line.StrokeThickness = ds.LineThickness;
            if (IsColormap)
            {
                if (i < pt3.Length - 1)
                    line.Stroke = GetBrush(zValues[i], zmin, zmax);
                else
                    line.Stroke = GetBrush(zValues[i - 1], zmin, zmax);
            }
            line.X1 = pta[i - 1].X;
            line.Y1 = pta[i - 1].Y;
            line.X2 = pta[i].X;
            line.Y2 = pta[i].Y;
            cs.ChartCanvas.Children.Add(line);
        }
    }

    if (cs.IsColorBar && IsColormap)
    {
        AddColorBar(cs, ds, zmin, zmax);
    }
}
```

In this method, we first create the mesh plot, and then add vertical lines from the *Y* component of the data, producing the waterfall effect. The vertical lines must be drawn on the appropriate surface when the elevation and azimuth angles change.

We can test the waterfall chart by selecting *Waterfall* from the chart type combobox in the *Chart3DView* example. Changing the chart function to *Sinc3D* and the colormap brush to *Autumn* will result in the chart shown in Figure 8-10.

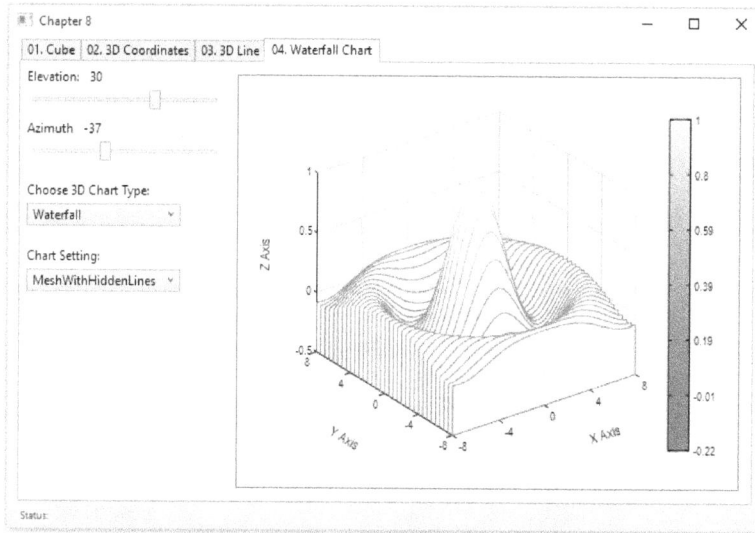

Figure 8-10. Waterfall chart.

Surface Charts

Surface charts are similar to mesh charts, in that both display data as a shaded surface. The difference between surface and mesh charts is that a surface chart creates colored quadrilaterals and black mesh lines, whereas a mesh plot creates only mesh lines, which can be black or colored.

We can create a surface chart using the following *AddSurface* method in the *Add3DChart* class:

```
private void AddSurface(ChartStyle cs, DataSeries3D ds)
{
    Matrix3D m = ChartHelper.AzimuthElevation(cs.Elevation, cs.Azimuth);
    Polygon plg = new Polygon();
    Point3D[,] pts = ds.PointArray;
    Point3D[,] pts1 = new Point3D[pts.GetLength(0), pts.GetLength(1)];
    //double[,] zValues = new double[pts.GetLength(0), pts.GetLength(1)];
    double zmin = ds.ZDataMin();
    double zmax = ds.ZDataMax();

    for (int i = 0; i < pts.GetLength(0); i++)
    {
        for (int j = 0; j < pts.GetLength(1); j++)
        {
            //zValues[i, j] = pts[i, j].Z;
            pts1[i, j] = pts[i, j];
            pts[i, j] = cs.Normalize3D(m, pts[i, j]);
        }
    }

    // Draw surface chart:
    if (!IsInterp)
    {
        for (int i = 0; i < pts.GetLength(0) - 1; i++)
        {
```

```
            int ii = i;
            if (cs.Elevation >= 0)
            {
                ii = i;
                if (cs.Azimuth >= -180 && cs.Azimuth < 0)
                {
                    ii = pts.GetLength(0) - 2 - i;
                }
            }
            else
            {
                ii = pts.GetLength(0) - 2 - i;
                if (cs.Azimuth >= -180 && cs.Azimuth < 0)
                {
                    ii = i;
                }
            }
            for (int j = 0; j < pts.GetLength(1) - 1; j++)
            {
                int jj = j;
                if (cs.Elevation < 0)
                {
                    jj = pts.GetLength(1) - 2 - j;
                }
                plg = new Polygon();
                plg.Points.Add(new Point(pts[ii, jj].X, pts[ii, jj].Y));
                plg.Points.Add(new Point(pts[ii, jj + 1].X,
                    pts[ii, jj + 1].Y));
                plg.Points.Add(new Point(pts[ii + 1, jj + 1].X,
                    pts[ii + 1, jj + 1].Y));
                plg.Points.Add(new Point(pts[ii + 1, jj].X,
                    pts[ii + 1, jj].Y));

                plg.StrokeThickness = ds.LineThickness;
                plg.Stroke = ds.LineColor;
                plg.Fill = GetBrush(pts1[ii, jj].Z, zmin, zmax);
                cs.ChartCanvas.Children.Add(plg);
            }
        }
        if (cs.IsColorBar && IsColormap)
        {
            AddColorBar(cs, ds, zmin, zmax);
        }
    }
    else if (IsInterp)
    {
        for (int i = 0; i < pts.GetLength(0) - 1; i++)
        {
            int ii = i;
            if (cs.Elevation >= 0)
            {
                ii = i;
                if (cs.Azimuth >= -180 && cs.Azimuth < 0)
                {
                    ii = pts.GetLength(0) - 2 - i;
```

```
                }
            }
            else
            {
                ii = pts.GetLength(0) - 2 - i;
                if (cs.Azimuth >= -180 && cs.Azimuth < 0)
                {
                    ii = i;
                }
            }
            for (int j = 0; j < pts.GetLength(1) - 1; j++)
            {
                int jj = j;
                if (cs.Elevation < 0)
                {
                    jj = pts.GetLength(1) - 2 - j;
                }

                Point3D[] points = new Point3D[4];
                points[0] = pts1[ii, j];
                points[1] = pts1[ii, j + 1];
                points[2] = pts1[ii + 1, j + 1];
                points[3] = pts1[ii + 1, j];
                Interp(cs, m, points, zmin, zmax);
                plg = new Polygon();
                plg.Stroke = ds.LineColor;
                plg.Points.Add(new Point(pts[ii, j].X, pts[ii, j].Y));
                plg.Points.Add(new Point(pts[ii, j + 1].X,
                    pts[ii, j + 1].Y));
                plg.Points.Add(new Point(pts[ii + 1, j + 1].X,
                    pts[ii + 1, j + 1].Y));
                plg.Points.Add(new Point(pts[ii + 1, j].X,
                    pts[ii + 1, j].Y));
                //cs.ChartCanvas.Children.Add(plg);
            }
        }
    }
    if (cs.IsColorBar && IsColormap)
    {
        AddColorBar(cs, ds, zmin, zmax);
    }
}
```

In this method, we draw surface charts using two different approaches: one is similar to that used to create mesh charts; the other applies interpolated shading to the surface plot by calling the following *Interp* method:

```
private void Interp(ChartStyle cs, Matrix3D m, Point3D[] pta,
    double zmin, double zmax)
{
    Polygon plg = new Polygon();
    Point[] points = new Point[4];
    int npoints = NumberInterp;
    Point3D[,] pts = new Point3D[npoints + 1, npoints + 1];
    Point3D[,] pts1 = new Point3D[npoints + 1, npoints + 1];
```

```
double x0 = pta[0].X;
double y0 = pta[0].Y;
double x1 = pta[2].X;
double y1 = pta[2].Y;
double dx = (x1 - x0) / npoints;
double dy = (y1 - y0) / npoints;
double c00 = pta[0].Z;
double c10 = pta[3].Z;
double c11 = pta[2].Z;
double c01 = pta[1].Z;
double x, y, c;

for (int i = 0; i <= npoints; i++)
{
    x = x0 + i * dx;
    for (int j = 0; j <= npoints; j++)
    {
        y = y0 + j * dy;
        c = (y1 - y) * ((x1 - x) * c00 + (x - x0) * c10) /
            (x1 - x0) / (y1 - y0) + (y - y0) * ((x1 - x) * c01 +
            (x - x0) * c11) / (x1 - x0) / (y1 - y0);
        pts[i, j] = new Point3D(x, y, c);
        pts1[i, j] = new Point3D(x, y, c);
        pts[i, j] = cs.Normalize3D(m, pts[i, j]);
    }
}

for (int i = 0; i < npoints; i++)
{
    for (int j = 0; j < npoints; j++)
    {
        plg = new Polygon();
        Brush brush = GetBrush(pts1[i, j].Z, zmin, zmax);
        plg.Fill = brush;
        plg.StrokeThickness = 0.1;
        plg.Stroke = brush;
        plg.Points.Add(new Point(pts[i, j].X, pts[i, j].Y));
        plg.Points.Add(new Point(pts[i + 1, j].X, pts[i + 1, j].Y));
        plg.Points.Add(new Point(pts[i + 1, j + 1].X,
            pts[i + 1, j + 1].Y));
        plg.Points.Add(new Point(pts[i, j + 1].X, pts[i, j + 1].Y));
        cs.ChartCanvas.Children.Add(plg);
    }
}
}
```

This interpolation method forces the color within each polygon of a surface chart to vary bilinearly, producing the effect of smooth color variation across the surface. You can control the fineness of the interpolated surface by changing the *NumberInterp* property.

We can test the surface chart by selecting *Surface* from the chart type combobox in the *Chart3DView* example. Using the *Sinc3D* math function and the *Jet* colormap brush will get the result shown in Figure 8-11.

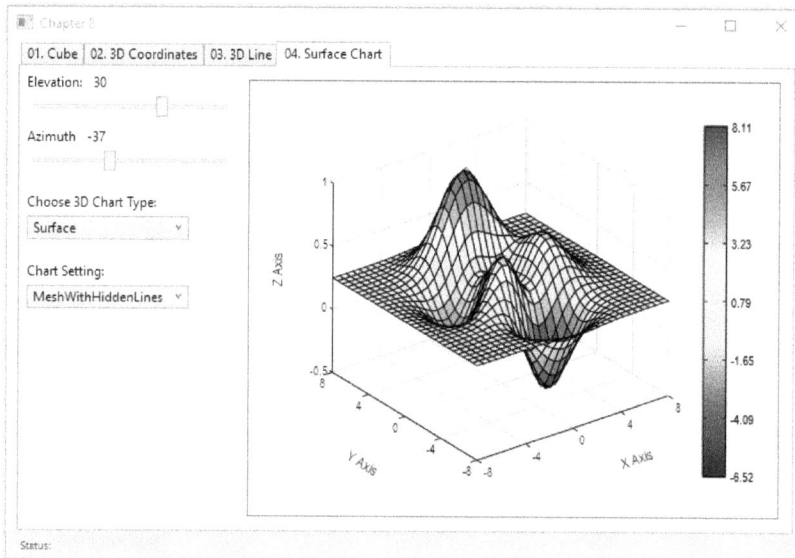

Figure 8-11. A standard surface chart.

You can also create a shaded surface chart without mesh lines by adding the following line of code:

```
ds.LineColor = Brushes.Transparent;
```

Choosing *SurfaceNoMesh* from the chart setting combobox produces the result shown in Figure 8-12.

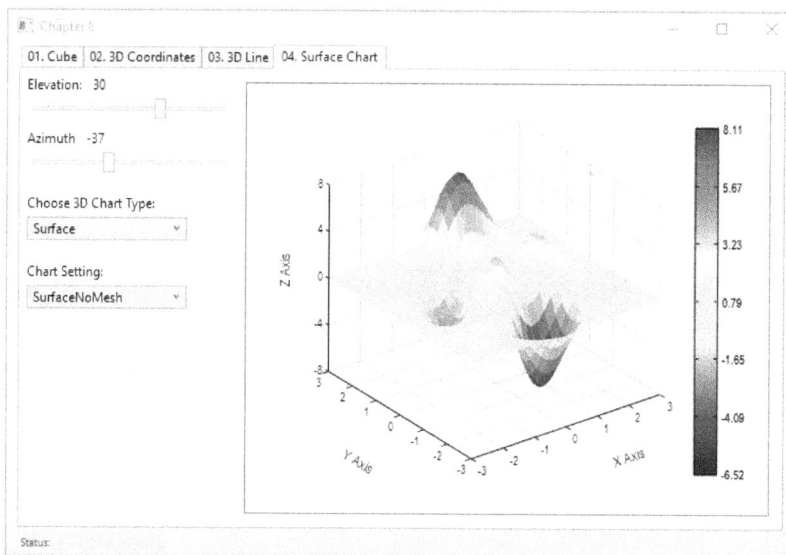

Figure 8-12. A surface chart without mesh lines.

As you can see from Figure 8-12, the colormap is still coarse, and a single color is clearly visible for each polygon on the surface. You can obtain a surface chart with a much smoother colormap by applying interpolated shading using the following code snippet:

```
ds.LineColor = Brushes.Transparent;
a3d.IsInterp = true;
a3d.NumberInterp = 3;
```

Selecting *SurfaceInterp* from the chart setting combobox generates the output shown in Figure 8-13.

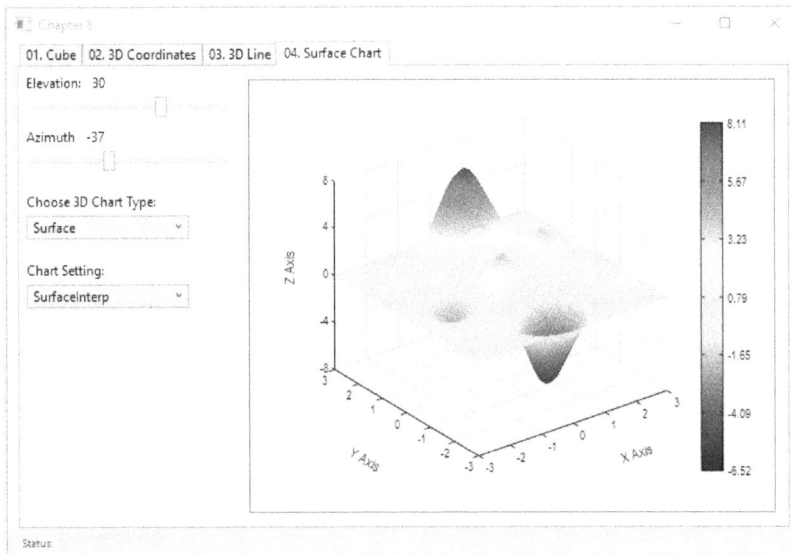

Figure 8-13. A surface chart with interpolated shading.

Specialized 3D Charts

In the previous sections, I showed you how to create simple 3D surface-like charts without using the WPF 3D engine. This approach allows you to create professional 3D chart applications in WPF with more advanced features, including colormaps and colorbars. Here, I will show you how to create a variety of specialized 3D charts, such as contour charts and 3D bar charts, among others, using the same framework discussed in the preceding sections. Based on these example projects, with or without modifications, you can easily create your own professional and sophisticated 3D charts in your .NET applications.

2D Chart Style

Some 3D specialized charts are actually projections of 3D charts on a 2D *X-Y* plane. For example, a contour chart helps visualize 3D surfaces on a 2D screen. In this case, we plot data values as a function of mesh grid points in the *X-Y* plane. Thus, these projected specialized 3D charts require a 2D-like chart style, similar to that used to create 2D charts in Chapter 4. However, this 2D-like chart style must also inherit some 3D features from the original 3D chart style used in creating surface charts, because the *X* and *Y* coordinates must be the projected coordinates in 3D space. Here, for your reference, I will list the source code of this 2D-like chart style.

Add a new class to the *ChartModel* folder and name it *ChartStyle2D*. This class inherits from the original 3D *ChartStyle* class:

```
using System;
using System.Windows.Controls;
using System.Windows;
using System.Windows.Media;
using System.Windows.Media.Media3D;
using System.Windows.Shapes;

namespace Chapter08.Models.ChartModel
{
    public class ChartStyle2D : ChartStyle
    {
        private double leftOffset = 20;
        private double bottomOffset = 40;
        private double rightOffset = 10;
        private Canvas chart2dCanvas = new Canvas();
        Border chart2dBorder;
        double colorbarWidth;
        Line gridline = new Line();

        public Canvas Chart2dCanvas
        {
            get { return chart2dCanvas; }
        }

        public ChartStyle2D()
        {
            chart2dBorder = new Border();
            chart2dBorder.BorderBrush = Brushes.Black;
            chart2dBorder.BorderThickness = new Thickness(1);
            chart2dBorder.Child = chart2dCanvas;
        }

        public void AddChartStyle2D()
        {
            colorbarWidth = ChartCanvas.Width / 7;
            ChartCanvas.Children.Clear();
            Chart2dCanvas.Children.Clear();
            ChartCanvas.Children.Add(chart2dBorder);
            Point pt = new Point();
            Line tick = new Line();
            double offset = 0;
            double dx, dy;
            TextBlock tb = new TextBlock();

            //  determine right offset:
            tb.Text = Xmax.ToString();
            tb.Measure(new Size(Double.PositiveInfinity, Double.PositiveInfinity));
            Size size = tb.DesiredSize;
            rightOffset = size.Width / 2 + 2;
```

```
// Determine left offset:
for (dy = Ymin; dy <= Ymax; dy += YTick)
{
    pt = NormalizePoint(new Point(Xmin, dy));
    tb = new TextBlock();
    tb.Text = dy.ToString();
    tb.TextAlignment = TextAlignment.Right;
    tb.Measure(new Size(Double.PositiveInfinity,
        Double.PositiveInfinity));
    size = tb.DesiredSize;
    if (offset < size.Width)
        offset = size.Width;
}
leftOffset = offset + 5 + 30;

Canvas.SetLeft(chart2dBorder, leftOffset);
Canvas.SetBottom(chart2dBorder, bottomOffset);
if (!IsColorBar)
    colorbarWidth = 0;
chart2dCanvas.Width = ChartCanvas.Width - leftOffset -
    rightOffset - colorbarWidth;
chart2dCanvas.Height = ChartCanvas.Height - bottomOffset -
    size.Height / 2;

// Create vertical gridlines:
if (IsYGrid == true)
{
    for (dx = Xmin + XTick; dx < Xmax; dx += XTick)
    {

        gridline = new Line();
        gridline.Stroke = GridlineColor;
        gridline.StrokeThickness = GridlineThickness;
        gridline.X1 = NormalizePoint(new Point(dx, Ymin)).X;
        gridline.Y1 = NormalizePoint(new Point(dx, Ymin)).Y;
        gridline.X2 = NormalizePoint(new Point(dx, Ymax)).X;
        gridline.Y2 = NormalizePoint(new Point(dx, Ymax)).Y;
        chart2dCanvas.Children.Add(gridline);
    }
}

// Create horizontal gridlines:
if (IsXGrid == true)
{
    for (dy = Ymin + YTick; dy < Ymax; dy += YTick)
    {
        gridline = new Line();
        gridline.Stroke = GridlineColor;
        gridline.StrokeThickness = GridlineThickness;
        gridline.X1 = NormalizePoint(new Point(Xmin, dy)).X;
        gridline.Y1 = NormalizePoint(new Point(Xmin, dy)).Y;
        gridline.X2 = NormalizePoint(new Point(Xmax, dy)).X;
        gridline.Y2 = NormalizePoint(new Point(Xmax, dy)).Y;
        chart2dCanvas.Children.Add(gridline);
    }
```

```
    }

    // Create x-axis tick marks:
    for (dx = Xmin; dx <= Xmax; dx += XTick)
    {
        pt = NormalizePoint(new Point(dx, Ymin));
        tick = new Line();
        tick.Stroke = Brushes.Black;
        tick.X1 = pt.X;
        tick.Y1 = pt.Y;
        tick.X2 = pt.X;
        tick.Y2 = pt.Y - 5;
        chart2dCanvas.Children.Add(tick);

        tb = new TextBlock();
        tb.Text = dx.ToString();
        tb.Measure(new Size(Double.PositiveInfinity,
            Double.PositiveInfinity));
        size = tb.DesiredSize;
        ChartCanvas.Children.Add(tb);
        Canvas.SetLeft(tb, leftOffset + pt.X - size.Width / 2);
        Canvas.SetTop(tb, pt.Y + 2 + size.Height / 2);
    }

    // Create y-axis tick marks:
    for (dy = Ymin; dy <= Ymax; dy += YTick)
    {
        pt = NormalizePoint(new Point(Xmin, dy));
        tick = new Line();
        tick.Stroke = Brushes.Black;
        tick.X1 = pt.X;
        tick.Y1 = pt.Y;
        tick.X2 = pt.X + 5;
        tick.Y2 = pt.Y;
        chart2dCanvas.Children.Add(tick);

        tb = new TextBlock();
        tb.Text = dy.ToString();
        tb.Measure(new Size(Double.PositiveInfinity,
            Double.PositiveInfinity));
        size = tb.DesiredSize;
        ChartCanvas.Children.Add(tb);
        Canvas.SetRight(tb, chart2dCanvas.Width + 10 + colorbarWidth);
        Canvas.SetTop(tb, pt.Y);
    }

    tb = new TextBlock();
    tb.Text = XLabel;
    tb.FontFamily = LabelFont;
    tb.FontSize = LabelFontSize;
    tb.Foreground = LabelColor;
    tb.Measure(new Size(Double.PositiveInfinity, Double.PositiveInfinity));
    size = tb.DesiredSize;
    ChartCanvas.Children.Add(tb);
    Canvas.SetBottom(tb, bottomOffset / 10);
```

```
        Canvas.SetLeft(tb, leftOffset + chart2dCanvas.Width / 2 -
            size.Width / 2);

        tb = new TextBlock();
        tb.Text = YLabel;
        tb.FontFamily = LabelFont;
        tb.FontSize = LabelFontSize;
        tb.Foreground = LabelColor;
        tb.RenderTransform = new RotateTransform(-90, 0.5, 0.5);

        tb.Measure(new Size(Double.PositiveInfinity, Double.PositiveInfinity));
        size = tb.DesiredSize;
        ChartCanvas.Children.Add(tb);
        Canvas.SetBottom(tb, chart2dCanvas.Height / 2 + size.Width / 3);
        Canvas.SetLeft(tb, leftOffset / 10);
    }

public Point NormalizePoint(Point pt)
{
        if (chart2dCanvas.Width.ToString() == "NaN")
            chart2dCanvas.Width = 270;
        if (chart2dCanvas.Height.ToString() == "NaN")
            chart2dCanvas.Height = 250;
        Point result = new Point();
        result.X = (pt.X - Xmin) * chart2dCanvas.Width / (Xmax - Xmin);
        result.Y = chart2dCanvas.Height -
            (pt.Y - Ymin) * chart2dCanvas.Height / (Ymax - Ymin);
        return result;
    }


public void AddColorBar2D(ChartStyle2D cs, DataSeries3D ds,
        Add3DChart a3d, double zmin, double zmax)
{
        TextBlock tb;
        tb = new TextBlock();
        tb.Text = "A";
        tb.FontFamily = cs.TickFont;
        tb.FontSize = cs.TickFontSize;
        tb.Measure(new Size(Double.PositiveInfinity, Double.PositiveInfinity));
        Size tickSize = tb.DesiredSize;

        double x = 8 * cs.ChartCanvas.Width / 9;
        double y = 7;
        double width = cs.ChartCanvas.Width / 25;
        double height = chart2dCanvas.Height;
        Point3D[] pts = new Point3D[64];
        double dz = (zmax - zmin) / 63;

        // Create the color bar:
        Polygon plg;
        for (int i = 0; i < 64; i++)
        {
            pts[i] = new Point3D(x, y, zmin + i * dz);
        }
```

```
                for (int i = 0; i < 63; i++)
                {
                    SolidColorBrush brush = a3d.GetBrush(pts[i].Z, zmin, zmax);
                    double y1 = y + height - (pts[i].Z - zmin) * height / (zmax - zmin);
                    double y2 = y + height - (pts[i + 1].Z - zmin) *
                        height / (zmax - zmin);
                    plg = new Polygon();
                    plg.Points.Add(new Point(x, y2));
                    plg.Points.Add(new Point(x + width, y2));
                    plg.Points.Add(new Point(x + width, y1));
                    plg.Points.Add(new Point(x, y1));
                    plg.Fill = brush;
                    plg.Stroke = brush;
                    cs.ChartCanvas.Children.Add(plg);
                }
                Rectangle rect = new Rectangle();
                rect.Width = width + 2;
                rect.Height = height + 2;
                rect.Stroke = Brushes.Black;
                Canvas.SetLeft(rect, x - 1);
                Canvas.SetTop(rect, y - 1);
                cs.ChartCanvas.Children.Add(rect);

                // Add ticks and labels to the color bar:
                double tickLength = 0.15 * width;
                for (double z = zmin; z <= zmax; z = z + (zmax - zmin) / 6)
                {
                    double yy = y + height - (z - zmin) * height / (zmax - zmin);
                    a3d.AddTickLine(cs, new Point(x, yy),
                        new Point(x + tickLength, yy));
                    a3d.AddTickLine(cs, new Point(x + width, yy),
                        new Point(x + width - tickLength, yy));
                    tb = new TextBlock();
                    tb.Text = (Math.Round(z, 2)).ToString();
                    tb.FontFamily = cs.TickFont;
                    tb.FontSize = cs.TickFontSize;
                    cs.ChartCanvas.Children.Add(tb);
                    Canvas.SetLeft(tb, x + width + 5);
                    Canvas.SetTop(tb, yy - tickSize.Height / 2);
                }
            }
        }
}
```

This class is basically similar to that used to create 2D charts in Chapter 4, except here we implement a colorbar on the right side.

AddS3DChart Class

In this section, we will implement the specialized 3D chart-related code in the *AddS3DChart* class. This class inherits from the *Add3DChart* class. Here is the code for this class:

```
using System;
using System.Collections.Generic;
using System.Windows;
```

```
using System.Windows.Controls;
using System.Windows.Media;
using System.Windows.Media.Media3D;
using System.Windows.Shapes;

namespace Chapter08.Models.ChartModel
{
    public class AddS3DChart : Add3DChart
    {
        private int numberContours = 10;
        private bool isBarSingleColor = true;
        private bool isLineColorMatch = false;
        private SChartTypeEnum sChartType = SChartTypeEnum.XYColor;
        private Polygon plg = new Polygon();

        public SChartTypeEnum SChartType
        {
            get { return sChartType; }
            set { sChartType = value; }
        }

        public int NumberContours
        {
            get { return numberContours; }
            set { numberContours = value; }
        }

        public bool IsBarSingleColor
        {
            get { return isBarSingleColor; }
            set { isBarSingleColor = value; }
        }

        public bool IsLineColorMatch
        {
            get { return isLineColorMatch; }
            set { isLineColorMatch = value; }
        }

        public void AddChart(ChartStyle2D cs, DataSeries3D ds)
        {
            switch (SChartType)
            {
                case SChartTypeEnum.XYColor:
                    cs.AddChartStyle2D();
                    if (cs.IsColorBar && IsColormap)
                    {
                        cs.AddColorBar2D(cs, ds, this, ds.ZDataMin(),
                            ds.ZDataMax());
                    }
                    AddXYColor(cs, ds);
                    break;

                case SChartTypeEnum.Contour:
                    cs.AddChartStyle2D();
```

```
                    if (cs.IsColorBar && IsColormap)
                    {
                        cs.AddColorBar2D(cs, ds, this, ds.ZDataMin(),
                            ds.ZDataMax());
                    }
                    AddContour(cs, ds);
                    break;

                case SChartTypeEnum.FillContour:
                    cs.AddChartStyle2D();
                    if (cs.IsColorBar && IsColormap)
                    {
                        cs.AddColorBar2D(cs, ds, this, ds.ZDataMin(),
                            ds.ZDataMax());
                    }
                    AddXYColor(cs, ds);
                    AddContour(cs, ds);
                    break;

                case SChartTypeEnum.MeshContour3D:
                    cs.SetChartStyle();
                    AddContour3D(cs, ds);
                    AddMesh(cs, ds);
                    break;

                case SChartTypeEnum.SurfaceContour3D:
                    cs.SetChartStyle();
                    AddContour3D(cs, ds);
                    AddSurface(cs, ds);
                    break;

                case SChartTypeEnum.SurfaceFillContour3D:
                    cs.SetChartStyle();
                    AddXYColor3D(cs, ds);
                    AddContour3D(cs, ds);
                    AddSurface(cs, ds);
                    break;
            }
        }

        private void AddXYColor(ChartStyle2D cs2d, DataSeries3D ds)
        {
            ......
        }

        private void AddContour(ChartStyle2D cs2d, DataSeries3D ds)
        {
            ......
        }

        private void AddXYColor3D(ChartStyle cs, DataSeries3D ds)
        {
            ......
        }
```

```
        private void AddContour3D(ChartStyle cs, DataSeries3D ds)
        {
            ......
        }

        public void AddBar3D(ChartStyle2D cs, Bar3DSeries bs)
        {
            ......
        }
    }

    public enum SChartTypeEnum
    {
        XYColor = 1,
        Contour = 2,
        FillContour = 3,
        MeshContour3D = 4,
        SurfaceContour3D = 5,
        SurfaceFillContour3D = 6,
        BarChart3D = 7
    }
}
```

In this class, the field members and their corresponding public properties are used to control the appearance of specialized 3D charts. You can create a specific 3D chart by selecting the *SChartType* from the enumeration *SChartTypeEnum*, which contains seven different chart types to select from. Some of these are a combination of a few different chart types. You can add more chart types to this enumeration and create their corresponding 3D charts in the same manner as we do here.

You may notice that several methods in the *AddS3DChart* class have only a signature. In the following few sections, I will present detailed implementations for these methods.

Color Charts on the *X-Y* Plane

The *X-Y* color chart can be considered as a projected surface chart on the *X-Y* plane. In fact, it is a rectangle mesh grid on the *X-Y* plane with colors determined by the data values at the grid points. Here, we create the *X-Y* color chart using each set of four adjacent points to define the polygon. Each polygon is shaded in a single color. As with surface charts, *X-Y* color charts can also have interpolated shading, in which each polygon is colored by bilinear interpolation of the colors at its four vertices using all elements of the data values. The minimum and maximum elements of the data values at grid points are assigned the first and last colors in the colormap. Colors for the remaining elements in the data values are determined by a linear mapping from value to colormap element.

Implementation

In this section, we will implement the *X-Y* color chart. Add a new private method, *AddXYColor*, to the *AddS3DChart* class:

```
        private void AddXYColor(ChartStyle2D cs2d, DataSeries3D ds)
        {
            Point3D[,] pts = ds.PointArray;
            double zmin = ds.ZDataMin();
            double zmax = ds.ZDataMax();
```

```
// Draw surface on the XY plane:
if (!IsInterp)
{
    for (int i = 0; i < pts.GetLength(0) - 1; i++)
    {
        for (int j = 0; j < pts.GetLength(1) - 1; j++)
        {
            plg = new Polygon();
            plg.Stroke = ds.LineColor;
            plg.StrokeThickness = ds.LineThickness;
            plg.Fill = GetBrush(pts[i, j].Z, zmin, zmax);
            if (IsLineColorMatch)
                plg.Stroke = GetBrush(pts[i, j].Z, zmin, zmax);
            plg.Points.Add(cs2d.NormalizePoint(new Point(pts[i, j].X,
                pts[i, j].Y)));
            plg.Points.Add(cs2d.NormalizePoint(new
                Point(pts[i, j + 1].X, pts[i, j + 1].Y)));
            plg.Points.Add(cs2d.NormalizePoint(new
                Point(pts[i + 1, j + 1].X, pts[i + 1, j + 1].Y)));
            plg.Points.Add(cs2d.NormalizePoint(new
                Point(pts[i + 1, j].X, pts[i + 1, j].Y)));
            cs2d.Chart2dCanvas.Children.Add(plg);
        }
    }
}
else if (IsInterp)
{
    for (int i = 0; i < pts.GetLength(0) - 1; i++)
    {
        for (int j = 0; j < pts.GetLength(1) - 1; j++)
        {
            Point3D[] points = new Point3D[4];
            points[0] = pts[i, j];
            points[1] = pts[i, j + 1];
            points[2] = pts[i + 1, j + 1];
            points[3] = pts[i + 1, j];

            Interp2D(cs2d, points, zmin, zmax);
            plg = new Polygon();
            plg.Stroke = ds.LineColor;
            if (IsLineColorMatch)
                plg.Stroke = GetBrush(pts[i, j].Z, zmin, zmax);
            plg.StrokeThickness = ds.LineThickness;
            plg.Fill = Brushes.Transparent;
            plg.Points.Add(cs2d.NormalizePoint(new
                Point(pts[i, j].X, pts[i, j].Y)));
            plg.Points.Add(cs2d.NormalizePoint(new
                Point(pts[i, j + 1].X, pts[i, j + 1].Y)));
            plg.Points.Add(cs2d.NormalizePoint(new
                Point(pts[i + 1, j + 1].X, pts[i + 1, j + 1].Y)));
            plg.Points.Add(cs2d.NormalizePoint(new
                Point(pts[i + 1, j].X, pts[i + 1, j].Y)));
            cs2d.Chart2dCanvas.Children.Add(plg);
```

```
                    }
                }
            }
    }
}

private void Interp2D(ChartStyle2D cs2d, Point3D[] pta, double zmin,
    double zmax)
{
    Polygon plg = new Polygon();
    Point[] points = new Point[4];
    int npoints = NumberInterp;
    Point3D[,] pts = new Point3D[npoints + 1, npoints + 1];
    double x0 = pta[0].X;
    double y0 = pta[0].Y;
    double x1 = pta[2].X;
    double y1 = pta[2].Y;
    double dx = (x1 - x0) / npoints;
    double dy = (y1 - y0) / npoints;
    double c00 = pta[0].Z;
    double c10 = pta[3].Z;
    double c11 = pta[2].Z;
    double c01 = pta[1].Z;
    double x, y, c;

    for (int i = 0; i <= npoints; i++)
    {
        x = x0 + i * dx;
        for (int j = 0; j <= npoints; j++)
        {
            y = y0 + j * dy;
            c = (y1 - y) * ((x1 - x) * c00 +
                (x - x0) * c10) / (x1 - x0) / (y1 - y0) +
                (y - y0) * ((x1 - x) * c01 +
                (x - x0) * c11) / (x1 - x0) / (y1 - y0);
            pts[i, j] = new Point3D(x, y, c);
        }
    }

    for (int i = 0; i < npoints; i++)
    {
        for (int j = 0; j < npoints; j++)
        {
            plg = new Polygon();
            Brush brush = GetBrush(pts[i, j].Z, zmin, zmax);
            plg.Fill = brush;
            plg.Stroke = brush;
            plg.Points.Add(cs2d.NormalizePoint(new
                Point(pts[i, j].X, pts[i, j].Y)));
            plg.Points.Add(cs2d.NormalizePoint(new
                Point(pts[i, j + 1].X, pts[i, j + 1].Y)));
            plg.Points.Add(cs2d.NormalizePoint(new
                Point(pts[i + 1, j + 1].X, pts[i + 1, j + 1].Y)));
            plg.Points.Add(cs2d.NormalizePoint(new
                Point(pts[i + 1, j].X, pts[i + 1, j].Y)));
            cs2d.Chart2dCanvas.Children.Add(plg);
```

```
                    }
                }
            }
```

In this method, we draw the *X-Y* color chart via two different approaches: one is the standard single-shaded approach; the other applies interpolated shading to the plot by calling the *Interp2D* method. This interpolation method forces the color within each polygon to vary bilinearly, producing the effect of a smooth color variation across the chart. You can control the fineness of the interpolated surface by changing the *NumberInterp* property.

Testing X-Y Color Charts

Here, I will show you how to create an *X-Y* color chart using the method implemented in the previous section. Add a new *UserControl* to the *Views* folder and name it *ChartS3DView*. Here is the markup for this view:

```
<UserControl x:Class="Chapter08.Views.ChartS3DView"
             xmlns="http://schemas.microsoft.com/winfx/2006/xaml/presentation"
             xmlns:x="http://schemas.microsoft.com/winfx/2006/xaml"
             xmlns:mc="http://schemas.openxmlformats.org/markup-compatibility/2006"
             xmlns:d="http://schemas.microsoft.com/expression/blend/2008"
             xmlns:cal="http://www.caliburnproject.org"
             mc:Ignorable="d"
             d:DesignHeight="400" d:DesignWidth="500">
    <Grid Margin="10">
        <Grid.ColumnDefinitions>
            <ColumnDefinition Width="200"/>
            <ColumnDefinition Width="*"/>
        </Grid.ColumnDefinitions>
        <StackPanel Margin="0 0 20 0">
            <TextBlock Text="Select Chart Type:"/>
            <ComboBox x:Name="SChartType" Width="150" Margin="0 5 0 0"
                      HorizontalAlignment="Left" cal:Message.Attach=
                      "[Event SelectionChanged]=[Action AddChart]"/>
            <GroupBox Header="X-Y Color" Margin="0 20 0 0">
                <StackPanel Margin="0 5 0 5">
                    <TextBlock Text="X-Y Color Chart Type:"/>
                    <ComboBox x:Name="XYColorType" Width="150" Margin="0 5 0 0"
                              HorizontalAlignment="Left"
                              cal:Message.Attach="[Event SelectionChanged]=
                    [Action AddChart]"/>
                </StackPanel>
            </GroupBox>
            <GroupBox Header="Contour" Margin="0 20 0 0">
                <StackPanel Margin="0 5 0 5">
                    <TextBlock Text="Contour Chart Type:"/>
                    <ComboBox x:Name="ContourType" Width="150" Margin="0 5 0 0"
                              HorizontalAlignment="Left" cal:Message.Attach=
                              "[Event SelectionChanged]=[Action AddChart]"/>
                </StackPanel>
            </GroupBox>
            <GroupBox Header="3D Bars" Margin="0 20 0 0">
                <StackPanel Margin="0 5 0 5">
                    <TextBlock Text="Bar Chart Type:"/>
```

```
                <ComboBox x:Name="Bar3DType" Width="150" Margin="0 5 0 0"
                          HorizontalAlignment="Left" cal:Message.Attach=
                          "[Event SelectionChanged]=[Action AddChart]"/>
            </StackPanel>
        </GroupBox>
    </StackPanel>
    <Grid x:Name="chartGrid" Margin="20" cal:Message.Attach=
          "[Event Loaded]=[Action AddChart];[Event SizeChanged]=
          [Action AddChart]" Grid.Column="1">
        <Canvas x:Name="chartCanvas" Background="Transparent"
                Width="{Binding ElementName=chartGrid,Path=ActualWidth}"
                Height="{Binding ElementName=chartGrid,Path=ActualHeight}"
                ClipToBounds="True"/>
    </Grid>
  </Grid>
</UserControl>
```

Here, we create a more general layout that we can use for testing not only the *X-Y* color chart but other specialized 3D charts as well.

Add a new class to the *ViewModels* folder and name it *ChartS3DViewModel*. Here is the code for this class:

```
using System;
using System.Linq;
using Caliburn.Micro;
using System.ComponentModel.Composition;
using System.Windows;
using Chapter08.Models;
using System.Windows.Media;
using Chapter08.Models.ChartModel;
using System.Windows.Media.Media3D;
using System.Windows.Shapes;
using Chapter08.Views;
using System.Collections.Generic;

namespace Chapter08.ViewModels
{
    [Export(typeof(IScreen)), PartCreationPolicy(CreationPolicy.NonShared)]
    public class ChartS3DViewModel : Screen
    {
        private readonly IEventAggregator _events;
        [ImportingConstructor]
        public ChartS3DViewModel(IEventAggregator events)
        {
            this._events = events;
            DisplayName = "05. Chart3D Specialized";
            cs = new ChartStyle2D();
        }

        private IEnumerable<SChartTypeEnum> sChartType;
        public IEnumerable<SChartTypeEnum> SChartType
        {
            get { return
                Enum.GetValues(typeof(SChartTypeEnum)).Cast<SChartTypeEnum>(); }
            set
```

```
            {
                sChartType = value;
                NotifyOfPropertyChange(() => SChartType);
            }
    }


    private SChartTypeEnum selectedSChartType = SChartTypeEnum.XYColor;
    public SChartTypeEnum SelectedSChartType
    {
        get { return selectedSChartType; }
        set
        {
            selectedSChartType = value;
            NotifyOfPropertyChange(() => SelectedSChartType);
        }
    }


    public BindableCollection<string> XYColorType
    {
        get { return new BindableCollection<string> { "BlackLines",
            "NoLinesNoInterp", "NoLinesWithInterp" }; }
    }


    private string selectedXYColorType = "BlackLines";
    public string SelectedXYColorType
    {
        get { return selectedXYColorType; }
        set
        {
            selectedXYColorType = value;
            NotifyOfPropertyChange(() => SelectedXYColorType);
        }
    }


    public BindableCollection<string> ContourType
    {
        get { return new BindableCollection<string> { "BlackLines",
            "LinesWithColormap" }; }
    }


    private string selectedContourType = "BlackLines";
    public string SelectedContourType
    {
        get { return selectedContourType; }
        set
        {
            selectedContourType = value;
            NotifyOfPropertyChange(() => SelectedContourType);
        }
    }


    public BindableCollection<string> Bar3DType
    {
        get { return new BindableCollection<string> { "SingleColor",
            "ColorMap", "ZeroZPlane" }; }
```

```
    }

    private string selectedBar3DType = "SingleColor";
    public string SelectedBar3DType
    {
        get { return selectedBar3DType; }
        set
        {
            selectedBar3DType = value;
            NotifyOfPropertyChange(() => SelectedBar3DType);
        }
    }

    private ChartStyle2D cs;
    private DataSeries3D ds;
    private AddS3DChart   s3d;
    private ChartS3DView view;

    private void SetInitialChart()
    {
        view = this.GetView() as ChartS3DView;
        view.chartCanvas.Children.Clear();
        cs.ChartCanvas = view.chartCanvas;
        cs.GridlinePattern = LineDashPatternEnum.Solid;
        cs.Elevation = 30;
        cs.Azimuth = -37;
        cs.Title = "No Title";
        cs.IsColorBar = true;

        ds = new DataSeries3D();
        ChartHelper.Peak3D(cs, ds);
        s3d = new AddS3DChart();
    }

    public void AddChart()
    {
        if (SelectedSChartType != SChartTypeEnum.BarChart3D)
            SetInitialChart();

        switch (SelectedSChartType)
        {
            case SChartTypeEnum.XYColor:
                AddXYColor();
                break;
            case SChartTypeEnum.Contour:
                AddContour();
                break;
            case SChartTypeEnum.FillContour:
                AddFilledContour();
                break;
            case SChartTypeEnum.MeshContour3D:
                AddMeshContour();
                break;
            case SChartTypeEnum.SurfaceContour3D:
                AddSurfaceContour();
```

```
                break;
          case SChartTypeEnum.SurfaceFillContour3D:
              AddSurfaceFilledContour();
              break;
          case SChartTypeEnum.BarChart3D:
              AddBar3D();
              break;
      }

      if (SelectedSChartType!= SChartTypeEnum.BarChart3D)
          s3d.AddChart(cs, ds);
  }

  private void AddXYColor()
  {
      s3d.SChartType = SChartTypeEnum.XYColor;
      DisplayName = "05. X-Y Color";

      if (SelectedXYColorType == "BlackLines")
      {
          ds.LineColor = Brushes.Black;
          s3d.IsInterp = false;
      }
      else if(SelectedXYColorType == "NoLinesNoInterp")
      {
          ds.LineColor = Brushes.Transparent;
          s3d.IsInterp = false;
      }
      else if (SelectedXYColorType == "NoLinesWithInterp")
      {
          ds.LineColor = Brushes.Transparent;
          s3d.IsInterp = true;
          s3d.NumberInterp = 5;
      }
  }

  private void AddContour()
  {
      s3d.SChartType = SChartTypeEnum.Contour;
      DisplayName = "05. Contour";
      s3d.NumberContours = 15;

      if (SelectedContourType == "BlackLines")
      {
          ds.LineColor = Brushes.Black;
          cs.IsColorBar = false;
      }
      else if(SelectedContourType == "LinesWithColormap")
      {
          cs.IsColorBar = true;
          s3d.IsLineColorMatch = true;
          s3d.Colormap.ColormapBrushType = ColormapBrushEnum.Jet;
      }
  }
```

```csharp
private void AddFilledContour()
{
    s3d.SChartType = SChartTypeEnum.FillContour;
    DisplayName = "05. Filled Contour";
    s3d.NumberContours = 15;
    cs.IsColorBar = true;
    s3d.IsLineColorMatch = true;
    s3d.Colormap.ColormapBrushType = ColormapBrushEnum.Jet;
    s3d.IsInterp = true;
    s3d.NumberInterp = 3;
}

private void AddMeshContour()
{
    s3d.SChartType = SChartTypeEnum.MeshContour3D;
    DisplayName = "05. Mesh Contour";
    s3d.NumberContours = 15;
    cs.IsColorBar = true;
    s3d.IsLineColorMatch = true;
    s3d.Colormap.ColormapBrushType = ColormapBrushEnum.Jet;
}

private void AddSurfaceContour()
{
    s3d.SChartType = SChartTypeEnum.SurfaceContour3D;
    DisplayName = "05. Surface Contour";
    s3d.NumberContours = 15;
    ds.LineColor = Brushes.Black;
    cs.IsColorBar = true;
    s3d.IsLineColorMatch = true;
    s3d.Colormap.ColormapBrushType = ColormapBrushEnum.Jet;
}

private void AddSurfaceFilledContour()
{
    s3d.SChartType = SChartTypeEnum.SurfaceFillContour3D;
    DisplayName = "05. Surface Filled Contour";
    s3d.NumberContours = 15;
    ds.LineColor = Brushes.Black;
    cs.IsColorBar = true;
    s3d.Colormap.ColormapBrushType = ColormapBrushEnum.Jet;
}

private void AddBar3D()
{
    view = this.GetView() as ChartS3DView;
    view.chartCanvas.Children.Clear();
    cs.ChartCanvas = view.chartCanvas;
    cs.GridlinePattern = LineDashPatternEnum.Solid;
    cs.Elevation = 30;
    cs.Azimuth = -37;
    cs.Title = "No Title";
    cs.IsColorBar = true;

    var ds3 = new Bar3DSeries();
```

```
ds3.LineColor = Brushes.Black;
ds3.XLength = 0.6;
ds3.YLength = 0.6;
ChartHelper.Peak3D(cs, ds3);

s3d = new AddS3DChart();
s3d.Colormap.ColormapBrushType = ColormapBrushEnum.Jet;
s3d.IsColormap = true;

if (SelectedBar3DType == "SingleColor")
{
    s3d.IsBarSingleColor = true;
    ds3.ZOrigin = cs.Zmin;
}
else if(SelectedBar3DType == "ColorMap")
{
    s3d.IsBarSingleColor = false;
    ds3.ZOrigin = cs.Zmin;
}
else if (SelectedBar3DType == "ZeroZPlane")
{
    s3d.IsBarSingleColor = true;
    ds3.ZOrigin = 0;
}

s3d.AddBar3D(cs, ds3);
        }
    }
}
```

You can use this view model to test various specialized 3D charts with different chart parameter settings. By running this project, selecting *XYColor* from the chart type combobox, and selecting *BlackLines* from the *X-Y* color chart type combobox, you will obtain the results shown in Figure 8-14.

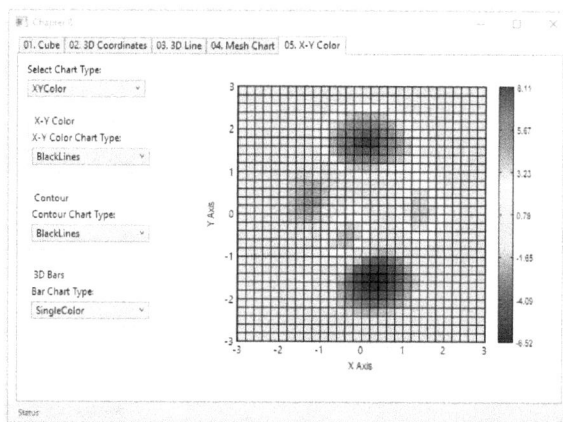

Figure 8-14. An X-Y color chart with black mesh lines.

You can remove the mesh lines from the *X-Y* color chart by changing the *LineColor* property from *Back* to *Transparent*:

```
ds.LineColor = Brushes.Transparent;
```

Selecting *NoLinesNoInterp* from the *X-Y* color chart type combobox generates the result shown in Figure 8-15.

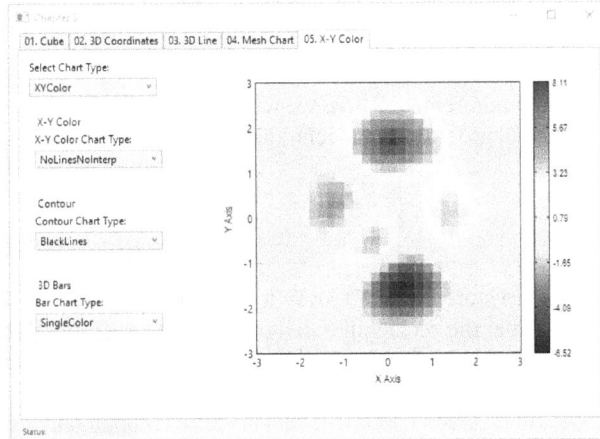

Figure 8-15. An X-Y color chart without mesh lines.

You can see from Figure 8-15 that each polygon on the *X-Y* color chart is shaded with a single color. You can obtain an *X-Y* color chart with a much smoother colormap by applying interpolated shading using the following modified code snippet:

```
s3d.IsInterp = true;
s3d.NumberInterp = 5;
```

Selecting *NoLinesWithInterp* from the *X-Y* color chart type combobox generates the result shown in Figure 8-16.

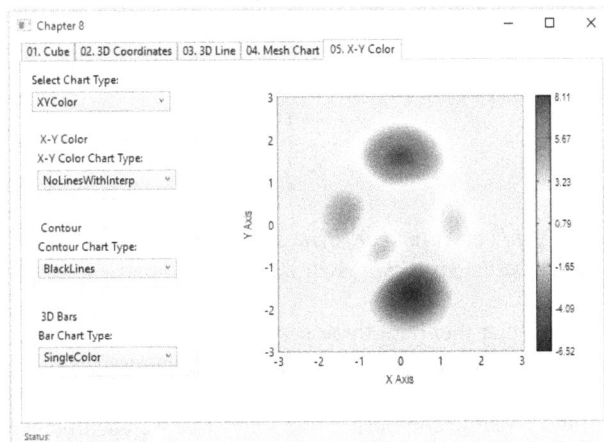

Figure 8-16. An X-Y color chart with an interpolated color shading.

Contour Charts

Contour charts help visualize of 3D surfaces on a 2D computer screen. In this case, we plot data values as a function of mesh grid points in the *X-Y* plane. In order to do contouring in a WPF application, you need to describe the data surface and the contour levels you want to draw. Given this information, the program will call an algorithm that calculates the line segments that make up a contour curve and then plot these line segments on your computer screen.

In order to satisfy the foregoing requirements, here we will use a relatively simple but reliable algorithm that does not require sophisticated programming techniques or a high level of mathematics to understand how it works.

Algorithm

Suppose that 3D surface data are stored in a 2D array to form a rectangular grid in the *X-Y* plane. We consider four grid points at a time: the rectangular cell (i, j), $(i + 1, j)$, $(i, j + 1)$, and $(i + 1, j + 1)$. This rectangular grid cell is further divided into two triangular grid cells, as shown in Figure 8-17. We can draw the contouring by systematically examining each triangular cell. Intersection points, if any, between each edge of the cell and a given contour-level curve are computed using bilinear interpolation. Line segments are plotted between intersection points of a contour-level curve, with each of the two edges belonging to the cell. Note that if any edges belonging to a triangular cell are intersected by a given-level curve, then exactly two edges are intersected.

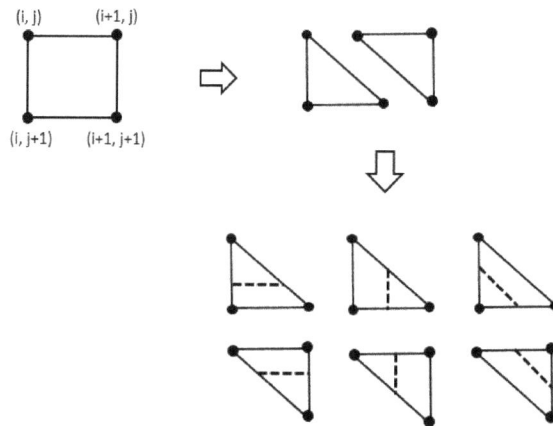

Figure 8-17. A rectangular grid cell is further divided into two triangular cells. Each triangular cell has three possible cases that draw different contour line segments.

You can see from Figure 8-17 that there are three cases for each triangular grid cell in which certain types of contouring line segments are drawn, depending on the contour level with respect to the data values at the grid points of a triangular cell. Thus, by examining all of the left and right triangular cells and adding together all of the possible contouring line segments, we can obtain a contour chart for any function or data set defined on a rectangular grid in the *X-Y* plane.

Implementation

Using the algorithm discussed in the previous section, we can easily create contour charts in .NET applications. Add two private methods, *AddContour* and *DrawLine*, to the *AddS3DChart* class:

```
private void AddContour(ChartStyle2D cs2d, DataSeries3D ds)
{
    Point[] pta = new Point[2];
    SolidColorBrush brush = Brushes.Black;
    Line line = new Line();
    Point3D[,] pts = ds.PointArray;
    double zmin = ds.ZDataMin();
    double zmax = ds.ZDataMax();
    double[] zlevels = new double[NumberContours];

    for (int i = 0; i < NumberContours; i++)
    {
        zlevels[i] = zmin + i * (zmax - zmin) / (NumberContours - 1);
    }

    int i0, i1, i2, j0, j1, j2;
    double zratio = 1;

    // Draw contour on the XY plane:
    for (int i = 0; i < pts.GetLength(0) - 1; i++)
    {
        for (int j = 0; j < pts.GetLength(1) - 1; j++)
        {
            if (IsColormap && SChartType != SChartTypeEnum.FillContour)
            {
                brush = GetBrush(pts[i, j].Z, zmin, zmax);
            }
            for (int k = 0; k < NumberContours; k++)
            {
                // Left triangle:
                i0 = i;
                j0 = j;
                i1 = i;
                j1 = j + 1;
                i2 = i + 1;
                j2 = j + 1;
                if ((zlevels[k] >= pts[i0, j0].Z &&
                    zlevels[k] < pts[i1, j1].Z ||
                    zlevels[k] < pts[i0, j0].Z &&
                    zlevels[k] >= pts[i1, j1].Z) &&
                    (zlevels[k] >= pts[i1, j1].Z &&
                    zlevels[k] < pts[i2, j2].Z ||
                    zlevels[k] < pts[i1, j1].Z &&
                    zlevels[k] >= pts[i2, j2].Z))
                {
                    zratio = (zlevels[k] - pts[i0, j0].Z) /
                        (pts[i1, j1].Z - pts[i0, j0].Z);
                    pta[0] = cs2d.NormalizePoint(new Point(pts[i0, j0].X,
                        (1 - zratio) * pts[i0, j0].Y + zratio *
                        pts[i1, j1].Y));
                    zratio = (zlevels[k] - pts[i1, j1].Z) /
```

```
                    (pts[i2, j2].Z - pts[i1, j1].Z);
                pta[1] = cs2d.NormalizePoint(new Point((1 - zratio) *
                    pts[i1, j1].X + zratio * pts[i2, j2].X,
                    pts[i1, j1].Y));
                DrawLine(cs2d, ds, brush, pta[0], pta[1]);
            }
            else if ((zlevels[k] >= pts[i0, j0].Z && zlevels[k]
                < pts[i2, j2].Z || zlevels[k] < pts[i0, j0].Z
                && zlevels[k] >= pts[i2, j2].Z) &&
                    (zlevels[k] >= pts[i1, j1].Z && zlevels[k] <
                pts[i2, j2].Z || zlevels[k] < pts[i1, j1].Z
                && zlevels[k] >= pts[i2, j2].Z))
            {
                zratio = (zlevels[k] - pts[i0, j0].Z) /
                    (pts[i2, j2].Z - pts[i0, j0].Z);
                pta[0] = cs2d.NormalizePoint(new Point((1 - zratio) *
                    pts[i0, j0].X + zratio * pts[i2, j2].X,
                    (1 - zratio) * pts[i0, j0].Y + zratio *
                    pts[i2, j2].Y));
                zratio = (zlevels[k] - pts[i1, j1].Z) / (
                    pts[i2, j2].Z - pts[i1, j1].Z);
                pta[1] = cs2d.NormalizePoint(new Point((1 - zratio) *
                    pts[i1, j1].X + zratio * pts[i2, j2].X,
                    pts[i1, j1].Y));
                DrawLine(cs2d, ds, brush, pta[0], pta[1]);
            }
            else if ((zlevels[k] >= pts[i0, j0].Z && zlevels[k]
             < pts[i1, j1].Z || zlevels[k] < pts[i0, j0].Z
             && zlevels[k] >= pts[i1, j1].Z) &&
                (zlevels[k] >= pts[i0, j0].Z && zlevels[k] <
             pts[i2, j2].Z || zlevels[k] < pts[i0, j0].Z &&
             zlevels[k] >= pts[i2, j2].Z))
            {
                zratio = (zlevels[k] - pts[i0, j0].Z) /
                    (pts[i1, j1].Z - pts[i0, j0].Z);
                pta[0] = cs2d.NormalizePoint(new Point(pts[i0, j0].X,
                    (1 - zratio) * pts[i0, j0].Y + zratio *
                    pts[i1, j1].Y));
                zratio = (zlevels[k] - pts[i0, j0].Z) /
                    (pts[i2, j2].Z - pts[i0, j0].Z);
                pta[1] = cs2d.NormalizePoint(new Point(pts[i0, j0].X *
                    (1 - zratio) + pts[i2, j2].X * zratio,
                    pts[i0, j0].Y * (1 - zratio) + pts[i2, j2].Y *
                    zratio));
                DrawLine(cs2d, ds, brush, pta[0], pta[1]);
            }

            // right triangle:
            i0 = i;
            j0 = j;
            i1 = i + 1;
            j1 = j;
            i2 = i + 1;
            j2 = j + 1;
            if ((zlevels[k] >= pts[i0, j0].Z && zlevels[k] <
```

```
            pts[i1, j1].Z || zlevels[k] < pts[i0, j0].Z
            && zlevels[k] >= pts[i1, j1].Z) &&
                (zlevels[k] >= pts[i1, j1].Z && zlevels[k]
            < pts[i2, j2].Z || zlevels[k] < pts[i1, j1].Z
            && zlevels[k] >= pts[i2, j2].Z))
        {
            zratio = (zlevels[k] - pts[i0, j0].Z) /
                (pts[i1, j1].Z - pts[i0, j0].Z);
            pta[0] = cs2d.NormalizePoint(new Point(pts[i0, j0].X *
                (1 - zratio) + pts[i1, j1].X * zratio,
                pts[i0, j0].Y));
            zratio = (zlevels[k] - pts[i1, j1].Z) /
                (pts[i2, j2].Z - pts[i1, j1].Z);
            pta[1] = cs2d.NormalizePoint(new Point(pts[i1, j1].X,
                pts[i1, j1].Y * (1 - zratio) + pts[i2, j2].Y *
                zratio));
            DrawLine(cs2d, ds, brush, pta[0], pta[1]);
        }
        else if ((zlevels[k] >= pts[i0, j0].Z && zlevels[k]
            < pts[i2, j2].Z || zlevels[k] < pts[i0, j0].Z
            && zlevels[k] >= pts[i2, j2].Z) &&
                (zlevels[k] >= pts[i1, j1].Z && zlevels[k] <
            pts[i2, j2].Z || zlevels[k] < pts[i1, j1].Z
            && zlevels[k] >= pts[i2, j2].Z))
        {
            zratio = (zlevels[k] - pts[i0, j0].Z) /
                (pts[i2, j2].Z - pts[i0, j0].Z);
            pta[0] = cs2d.NormalizePoint(new Point(pts[i0, j0].X *
                (1 - zratio) + pts[i2, j2].X * zratio,
                pts[i0, j0].Y *(1 - zratio) + pts[i2, j2].Y *
                zratio));
            zratio = (zlevels[k] - pts[i1, j1].Z) /
                (pts[i2, j2].Z - pts[i1, j1].Z);
            pta[1] = cs2d.NormalizePoint(new Point(pts[i1, j1].X,
                pts[i1, j1].Y * (1 - zratio) + pts[i2, j2].Y *
                zratio));
            DrawLine(cs2d, ds, brush, pta[0], pta[1]);
        }
        else if ((zlevels[k] >= pts[i0, j0].Z && zlevels[k]
            < pts[i1, j1].Z || zlevels[k] < pts[i0, j0].Z
            && zlevels[k] >= pts[i1, j1].Z) &&
                (zlevels[k] >= pts[i0, j0].Z && zlevels[k] <
            pts[i2, j2].Z || zlevels[k] < pts[i0, j0].Z
            && zlevels[k] >= pts[i2, j2].Z))
        {
            zratio = (zlevels[k] - pts[i0, j0].Z) /
                (pts[i1, j1].Z - pts[i0, j0].Z);
            pta[0] = cs2d.NormalizePoint(new Point(pts[i0, j0].X *
                (1 - zratio) + pts[i1, j1].X * zratio,
                pts[i0, j0].Y));
            zratio = (zlevels[k] - pts[i0, j0].Z) / (pts[i2, j2].Z -
                pts[i0, j0].Z);
            pta[1] = cs2d.NormalizePoint(new Point(pts[i0, j0].X *
                (1 - zratio) + pts[i2, j2].X * zratio, pts[i0, j0].Y
                * (1 - zratio) + pts[i2, j2].Y * zratio));
```

```
                        DrawLine(cs2d, ds, brush, pta[0], pta[1]);
                }
            }
        }
    }
}

private void DrawLine(ChartStyle2D cs2d, DataSeries3D ds,
    SolidColorBrush brush, Point pt0, Point pt1)
{
    Line line = new Line();
    if (IsLineColorMatch)
        line.Stroke = brush;
    else
        line.Stroke = ds.LineColor;
    line.StrokeThickness = ds.LineThickness;
    line.X1 = pt0.X;
    line.Y1 = pt0.Y;
    line.X2 = pt1.X;
    line.Y2 = pt1.Y;
    cs2d.Chart2dCanvas.Children.Add(line);
}
```

This method has several parameters that we use to control the appearance of the contour chart. The most important parameter is the *NumberContours* property, which determines how many contour lines will be drawn. You can also specify the *IsLineColorMatch* property to determine the color that will be used to draw the contour lines. If this property is set to false, a single color specified by the *LineColor* property is used to draw the contour. On the other hand, if this property is set to true, a colormapped color is used depending on the values of the contour levels.

Testing Contour Charts

We have already implemented the contour charts when we created the *ChartS3DView* example. By running the example, selecting *Contour* from the chart type combobox, and selecting *BlackLines* from the contour chart type combobox, you can obtain the result shown in Figure 8 -18.

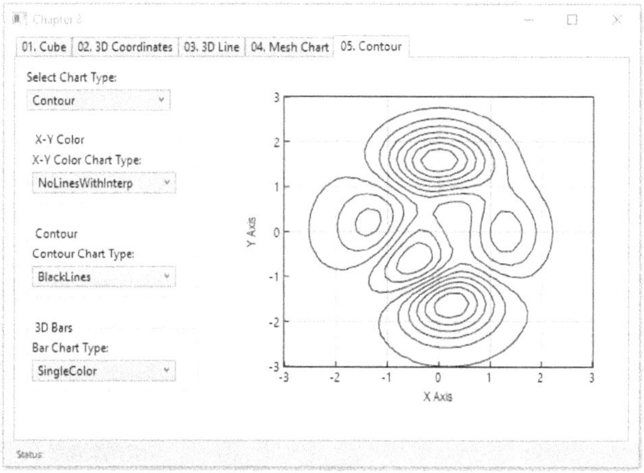

Figure 8-18. A contour chart.

You can also easily create a contour chart with colormapped contour lines by changing the following code snippet:

```
cs.IsColorBar = true;
s3d.IsLineColorMatch = true;
s3d.Colormap.ColormapBrushType = ColormapBrushEnum.Jet;
```

Selecting *LinesWithColormap* from the contour chart type combobox generates the colormapped contour chart shown in Figure 8-19.

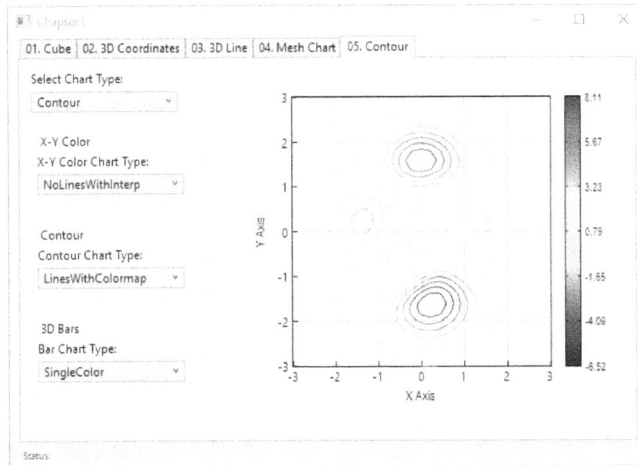

Figure 8 -19. A colormapped contour chart.

Combination Charts

Combination charts are a useful way to exploit the informative properties of various types of graphics charting methods. In this section, I will show you a few examples of common combination charts, including filled contour, mesh contour, surface contour, and surface-filled contour charts. By using a similar approach, you can create your own combination charts.

Notice that when we discussed *X-Y* color charts and contour charts in the previous sections, we drew these charts directly on the 2D computer screen. However, in order to combine a contour or *X-Y* color chart with a 3D surface chart, we must modify the original 2D *X-Y* color chart and contour chart to be consistent with the 3D coordinate system that the surface chart uses.

X-Y Color Charts in 3D

In creating our original 2D *X-Y* charts, we transform the world coordinates to device coordinates by using the *X* and *Y* components of the data points directly and neglecting the *Z* component. In order to add 3D features to our *X-Y* color charts, we must perform an orthogonal projection transformation on the *X* and *Y* components of the data points at a constant *Z* value (which is the projection plane where the *X-Y* color chart is drawn) using the elevation-azimuth transformation matrix defined in the *ChartHelper* class. The *AddXYColor3D* method in the *AddS3DChart* class is implemented as follows:

```
private void AddXYColor3D(ChartStyle cs, DataSeries3D ds)
{
```

```
Point3D[,] pts = ds.PointArray;
Point3D[,] pts1 = new Point3D[pts.GetLength(0), pts.GetLength(1)];
Matrix3D m = ChartHelper.AzimuthElevation(cs.Elevation, cs.Azimuth);
Polygon plg = new Polygon();

// Find the minumum and maximum z values:
double zmin = ds.ZDataMin();
double zmax = ds.ZDataMax();

// Perform transformation on points:
for (int i = 0; i < pts.GetLength(0); i++)
{
    for (int j = 0; j < pts.GetLength(1); j++)
    {
        // Make a deep copy the points array:
        pts1[i, j] = new Point3D(pts[i, j].X, pts[i, j].Y, cs.Zmin);
        pts1[i, j] = cs.Normalize3D(m, pts1[i, j]);
    }
}

// Draw surface on the XY plane:
for (int i = 0; i < pts.GetLength(0) - 1; i++)
{
    for (int j = 0; j < pts.GetLength(1) - 1; j++)
    {
        plg = new Polygon();
        plg.Points.Add(new Point(pts1[i, j].X, pts1[i, j].Y));
        plg.Points.Add(new Point(pts1[i, j + 1].X, pts1[i, j + 1].Y));
        plg.Points.Add(new Point(pts1[i + 1, j + 1].X,
            pts1[i + 1, j + 1].Y));
        plg.Points.Add(new Point(pts1[i + 1, j].X, pts1[i + 1, j].Y));
        plg.StrokeThickness = ds.LineThickness;
        plg.Fill = GetBrush(pts[i, j].Z, zmin, zmax);
        plg.Stroke = GetBrush(pts[i, j].Z, zmin, zmax);
        cs.ChartCanvas.Children.Add(plg);
    }
}
}
```

You can see that the transformation is indeed performed on the data points at a constant $Z = zmin$ using the elevation-azimuth transform matrix. This indicates that we will draw the X-Y color chart on the $Z = zmin$ plane.

Contour Charts in 3D

Similarly, in order to combine contour charts with 3D surface charts, we must create a contour chart consistent with the 3D coordinate system. The following listing is for the *AddContour3D* method in the *AddS3DChart* class:

```
private void AddContour3D(ChartStyle cs, DataSeries3D ds)
{
    Point3D[] pta = new Point3D[2];
    Point3D[,] pts = ds.PointArray;
    Matrix3D m = ChartHelper.AzimuthElevation(cs.Elevation, cs.Azimuth);
    SolidColorBrush brush = Brushes.Black;
```

```
// Find the minumum and maximum z values:
double zmin = ds.ZDataMin();
double zmax = ds.ZDataMax();
double[] zlevels = new Double[NumberContours];
for (int i = 0; i < NumberContours; i++)
{
    zlevels[i] = zmin + i * (zmax - zmin) / (NumberContours - 1);
}

int i0, i1, i2, j0, j1, j2;
double zratio = 1;

// Draw contour on the XY plane:
for (int i = 0; i < pts.GetLength(0) - 1; i++)
{
    for (int j = 0; j < pts.GetLength(1) - 1; j++)
    {
        if (IsColormap && SChartType != SChartTypeEnum.FillContour)
        {
            brush = GetBrush(pts[i, j].Z, zmin, zmax);
        }
        for (int k = 0; k < numberContours; k++)
        {
            // Left triangle:
            i0 = i;
            j0 = j;
            i1 = i;
            j1 = j + 1;
            i2 = i + 1;
            j2 = j + 1;
            if ((zlevels[k] >= pts[i0, j0].Z && zlevels[k] <
                pts[i1, j1].Z || zlevels[k] < pts[i0, j0].Z
                && zlevels[k] >= pts[i1, j1].Z) &&
                    (zlevels[k] >= pts[i1, j1].Z && zlevels[k]
                    < pts[i2, j2].Z || zlevels[k] < pts[i1, j1].Z
                    && zlevels[k] >= pts[i2, j2].Z))
            {
                zratio = (zlevels[k] - pts[i0, j0].Z) /
                    (pts[i1, j1].Z - pts[i0, j0].Z);
                pta[0] = new Point3D(pts[i0, j0].X, (1 - zratio) *
                    pts[i0, j0].Y + zratio * pts[i1, j1].Y, cs.Zmin);
                zratio = (zlevels[k] - pts[i1, j1].Z) /
                    (pts[i2, j2].Z - pts[i1, j1].Z);
                pta[1] = new Point3D((1 - zratio) * pts[i1, j1].X +
                    zratio * pts[i2, j2].X, pts[i1, j1].Y, cs.Zmin);
                pta[0] = cs.Normalize3D(m, pta[0]);
                pta[1] = cs.Normalize3D(m, pta[1]);
                DrawLine3D(cs, ds, brush, new Point(pta[0].X, pta[0].Y),
                    new Point(pta[1].X, pta[1].Y));
            }
            else if ((zlevels[k] >= pts[i0, j0].Z && zlevels[k]
                < pts[i2, j2].Z || zlevels[k] < pts[i0, j0].Z
                && zlevels[k] >= pts[i2, j2].Z) &&
                    (zlevels[k] >= pts[i1, j1].Z && zlevels[k]
```

```
                < pts[i2, j2].Z || zlevels[k] < pts[i1, j1].Z
                && zlevels[k] >= pts[i2, j2].Z))
        {
            zratio = (zlevels[k] - pts[i0, j0].Z) /
                (pts[i2, j2].Z - pts[i0, j0].Z);
            pta[0] = new Point3D((1 - zratio) * pts[i0, j0].X +
                zratio * pts[i2, j2].X, (1 - zratio) * pts[i0, j0].Y
                + zratio * pts[i2, j2].Y, cs.Zmin);
            zratio = (zlevels[k] - pts[i1, j1].Z) /
                (pts[i2, j2].Z - pts[i1, j1].Z);
            pta[1] = new Point3D((1 - zratio) * pts[i1, j1].X +
                zratio * pts[i2, j2].X, pts[i1, j1].Y, cs.Zmin);
            pta[0] = cs.Normalize3D(m, pta[0]);
            pta[1] = cs.Normalize3D(m, pta[1]);
            DrawLine3D(cs, ds, brush, new Point(pta[0].X, pta[0].Y),
                new Point(pta[1].X, pta[1].Y));
        }
        else if ((zlevels[k] >= pts[i0, j0].Z && zlevels[k]
            < pts[i1, j1].Z || zlevels[k] < pts[i0, j0].Z
            && zlevels[k] >= pts[i1, j1].Z) &&
                (zlevels[k] >= pts[i0, j0].Z && zlevels[k]
            < pts[i2, j2].Z || zlevels[k] < pts[i0, j0].Z
            && zlevels[k] >= pts[i2, j2].Z))
        {
            zratio = (zlevels[k] - pts[i0, j0].Z) /
                (pts[i1, j1].Z - pts[i0, j0].Z);
            pta[0] = new Point3D(pts[i0, j0].X, (1 - zratio) *
                pts[i0, j0].Y + zratio * pts[i1, j1].Y, cs.Zmin);
            zratio = (zlevels[k] - pts[i0, j0].Z) /
                (pts[i2, j2].Z - pts[i0, j0].Z);
            pta[1] = new Point3D(pts[i0, j0].X * (1 - zratio) +
                pts[i2, j2].X * zratio, pts[i0, j0].Y * (1 - zratio)
                + pts[i2, j2].Y * zratio, cs.Zmin);
            pta[0] = cs.Normalize3D(m, pta[0]);
            pta[1] = cs.Normalize3D(m, pta[1]);
            DrawLine3D(cs, ds, brush, new Point(pta[0].X, pta[0].Y),
                new Point(pta[1].X, pta[1].Y));
        }

        // right triangle:
        i0 = i;
        j0 = j;
        i1 = i + 1;
        j1 = j;
        i2 = i + 1;
        j2 = j + 1;
        if ((zlevels[k] >= pts[i0, j0].Z && zlevels[k] <
            pts[i1, j1].Z || zlevels[k] < pts[i0, j0].Z
            && zlevels[k] >= pts[i1, j1].Z) &&
                (zlevels[k] >= pts[i1, j1].Z && zlevels[k]
            < pts[i2, j2].Z || zlevels[k] < pts[i1, j1].Z
            && zlevels[k] >= pts[i2, j2].Z))
        {
            zratio = (zlevels[k] - pts[i0, j0].Z) /
                (pts[i1, j1].Z - pts[i0, j0].Z);
```

```
        pta[0] = new Point3D(pts[i0, j0].X * (1 - zratio) +
            pts[i1, j1].X * zratio, pts[i0, j0].Y, cs.Zmin);
        zratio = (zlevels[k] - pts[i1, j1].Z) /
            (pts[i2, j2].Z - pts[i1, j1].Z);
        pta[1] = new Point3D(pts[i1, j1].X, pts[i1, j1].Y *
            (1 - zratio) + pts[i2, j2].Y * zratio, cs.Zmin);
        pta[0] = cs.Normalize3D(m, pta[0]);
        pta[1] = cs.Normalize3D(m, pta[1]);
        DrawLine3D(cs, ds, brush, new Point(pta[0].X, pta[0].Y),
            new Point(pta[1].X, pta[1].Y));
    }
    else if ((zlevels[k] >= pts[i0, j0].Z && zlevels[k]
        < pts[i2, j2].Z || zlevels[k] < pts[i0, j0].Z
        && zlevels[k] >= pts[i2, j2].Z) &&
            (zlevels[k] >= pts[i1, j1].Z && zlevels[k] <
        pts[i2, j2].Z || zlevels[k] < pts[i1, j1].Z
        && zlevels[k] >= pts[i2, j2].Z))
    {
        zratio = (zlevels[k] - pts[i0, j0].Z) /
            (pts[i2, j2].Z - pts[i0, j0].Z);
        pta[0] = new Point3D(pts[i0, j0].X * (1 - zratio) +
            pts[i2, j2].X * zratio,
      pts[i0, j0].Y * (1 - zratio) + pts[i2, j2].Y * zratio,
            cs.Zmin);
        zratio = (zlevels[k] - pts[i1, j1].Z) /
            (pts[i2, j2].Z - pts[i1, j1].Z);
        pta[1] = new Point3D(pts[i1, j1].X, pts[i1, j1].Y *
            (1 - zratio) + pts[i2, j2].Y * zratio, cs.Zmin);
        pta[0] = cs.Normalize3D(m, pta[0]);
        pta[1] = cs.Normalize3D(m, pta[1]);
        DrawLine3D(cs, ds, brush, new Point(pta[0].X, pta[0].Y),
            new Point(pta[1].X, pta[1].Y));
    }
    else if ((zlevels[k] >= pts[i0, j0].Z && zlevels[k]
        < pts[i1, j1].Z || zlevels[k] < pts[i0, j0].Z
        && zlevels[k] >= pts[i1, j1].Z) &&
            (zlevels[k] >= pts[i0, j0].Z && zlevels[k] <
        pts[i2, j2].Z || zlevels[k] < pts[i0, j0].Z
        && zlevels[k] >= pts[i2, j2].Z))
    {
        zratio = (zlevels[k] - pts[i0, j0].Z) /
            (pts[i1, j1].Z - pts[i0, j0].Z);
        pta[0] = new Point3D(pts[i0, j0].X * (1 - zratio) +
            pts[i1, j1].X * zratio, pts[i0, j0].Y, cs.Zmin);
        zratio = (zlevels[k] - pts[i0, j0].Z) / (pts[i2, j2].Z -
            pts[i0, j0].Z);
        pta[1] = new Point3D(pts[i0, j0].X * (1 - zratio) +
            pts[i2, j2].X * zratio,
            pts[i0, j0].Y * (1 - zratio) + pts[i2, j2].Y *
            zratio, cs.Zmin);
        pta[0] = cs.Normalize3D(m, pta[0]);
        pta[1] = cs.Normalize3D(m, pta[1]);
        DrawLine3D(cs, ds, brush, new Point(pta[0].X, pta[0].Y),
            new Point(pta[1].X, pta[1].Y));
    }
```

```
            }
        }
    }
}

private void DrawLine3D(ChartStyle cs, DataSeries3D ds, SolidColorBrush
    brush, Point pt0, Point pt1)
{
    Line line = new Line();
    line.Stroke = ds.LineColor;
    if (IsLineColorMatch)
        line.Stroke = brush;
    line.StrokeThickness = ds.LineThickness;
    line.X1 = pt0.X;
    line.Y1 = pt0.Y;
    line.X2 = pt1.X;
    line.Y2 = pt1.Y;
    cs.ChartCanvas.Children.Add(line);
}
```

This method draws the contour chart on the $Z = zmin$ plane.

Filled Contour Charts

Here, I will show you how to create a simple filled contour chart by combining a contour chart with an *X-Y* color chart, as implemented previously in the *AddChart* method of the *AddS3DChart* class.

We have already implemented filled contour charts in the *ChartS3DView* example. By running the example and selecting *FillContour* from the chart type combobox, you can obtain the filled contour chart shown in Figure 8 -20.

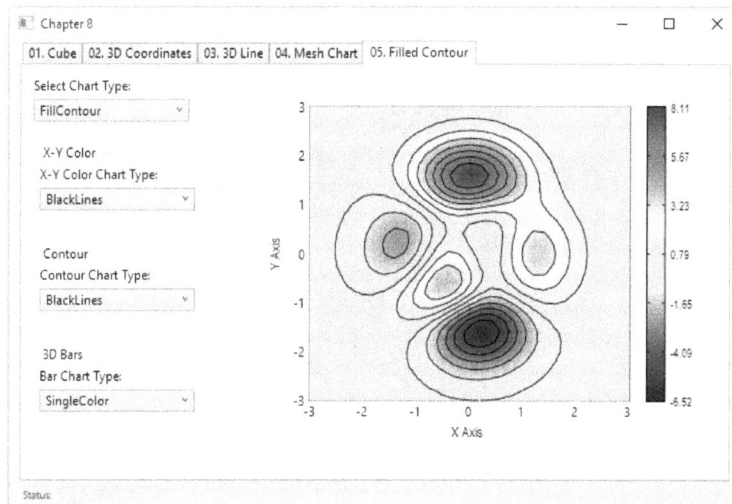

Figure 8-20. A filled contour chart.

Mesh Contour Charts

It is easy to create a mesh contour combination chart by using the *AddContour3D* and *AddMesh* methods successively.

We have already implemented mesh contour charts in the *ChartS3DView* example. By running the example and selecting *MeshContour3D* from the chart type combobox, you will obtain the mesh contour chart shown in Figure 8 -21.

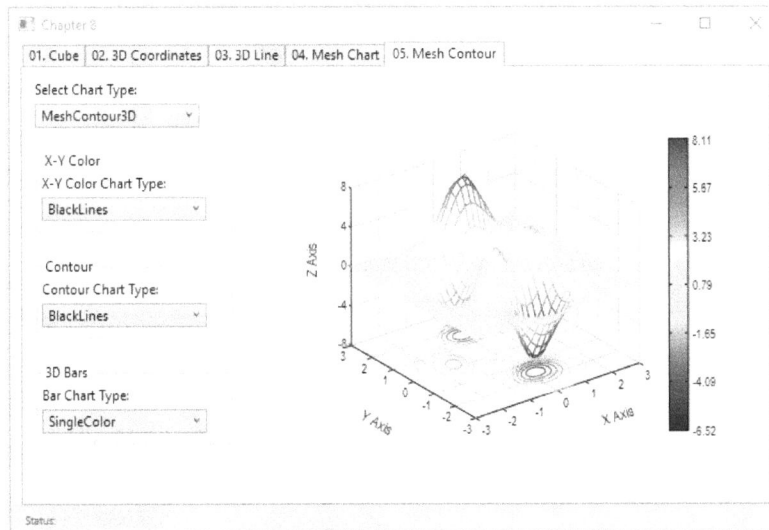

Figure 8-21. A mesh contour chart.

Surface Contour Charts

Similarly, you can easily create a surface contour chart by calling the *AddContour3D* and *AddSurface* methods successively.

We have already implemented surface contour charts in the *ChartS3DView* example. By running the example and selecting *SurfaceContour3D* from the chart type combobox, you will obtain the surface contour chart shown in Figure 8 -22.

Surface-Filled Contour Charts

Similarly, you can easily create a surface-filled contour chart by calling the *AddXYColor3D*, *AddContour3D* and *AddSurface* methods successively.

We have already implemented surface-filled contour charts in the *ChartS3DView* example. By running the example and selecting *SurfaceFillContour3D* from the chart type combobox, you will obtain the surface-filled contour chart shown in Figure 8 -23.

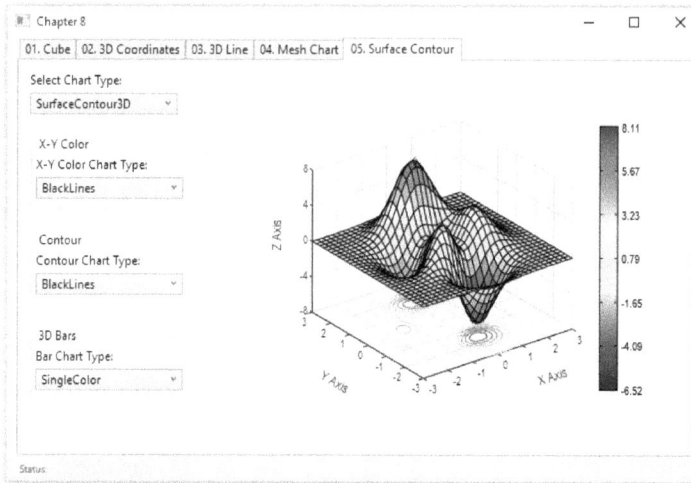

Figure 8-22. A surface contour chart.

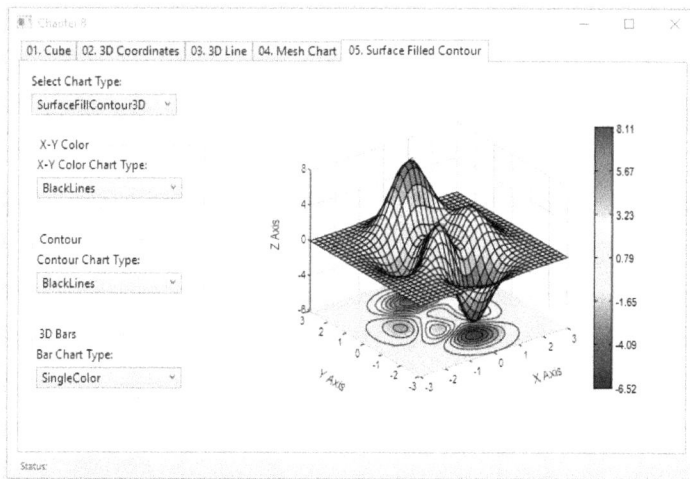

Figure 8-23 A surface-filled contour chart.

3D Bar Charts

Using the same data series as we did when we created mesh and surface charts, we can also create 3D bar charts. A 3D bar can be constructed in 3D space, as shown in Figure 8-24.

Suppose there is a data point (x, y, z) in 3D space. We can define a 3D bar around this point by specifying three parameters: *zorigin*, *xlength*, and *ylength*. The parameter *zorigin* defines the $Z = zorigin$ plane from which the 3D bar is filled; the two other parameters set the size of the 3D bar in the X and Y directions. These length parameters are measured as a percentage of the total amount of space available. Here, we set these parameters to be in the range [0.1, 0.5]. If you set *xlength* = *ylength* = 0.5, you will obtain the so-called histogram bar chart; namely, each bar fills the space up to its adjoining bars.

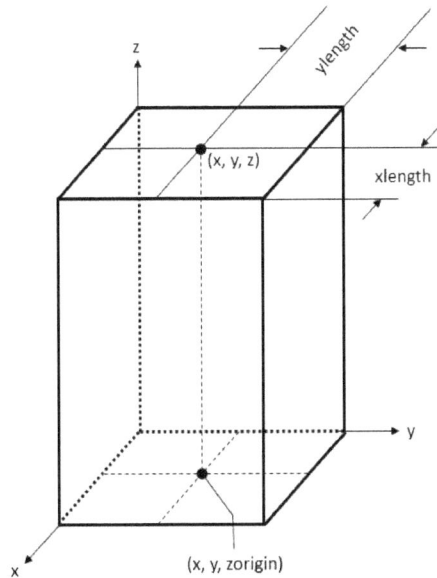

Figure 8-24. A 3D bar defined in 3D space.

Implementation

First we need to add a new class to the *ChartModel* folder and name it *Bar3DSeries*. Here is the code for this class:

```
using System;
using System.Collections.Generic;
using System.Windows;
using System.Windows.Controls;
using System.Windows.Media;
using System.Windows.Media.Media3D;
using System.Windows.Shapes;

namespace Chapter08.Models.ChartModel
{
    public class Bar3DSeries : DataSeries3D
    {
        private double xLength = 0.5;
        private double yLength = 0.5;
        private double zOrigin = 0;
        private bool isBarSingleColor = true;

        public bool IsBarSingleColor
        {
            get { return isBarSingleColor; }
            set { isBarSingleColor = value; }
        }

        public double ZOrigin
        {
            get { return zOrigin; }
```

```
        set { zOrigin = value; }
    }

    public double YLength
    {
        get { return yLength; }
        set { yLength = value; }
    }

    public double XLength
    {
        get { return xLength; }
        set { xLength = value; }
    }
  }
}
```

This class is very simple. We first define the field members and their corresponding public properties, which allow us to control the appearance and size of the 3D bars. The *bool* property *IsBarSingleColor* lets you specify whether the bars are drawn using a single color or a colormap. Next, we need to create an *AddBar3D* method in the *Draw3DChart* class:

```
public void AddBar3D(ChartStyle2D cs, Bar3DSeries bs)
{
    Matrix3D m = ChartHelper.AzimuthElevation(cs.Elevation, cs.Azimuth);
    Point[] pta = new Point[4];
    Point3D[,] pts = bs.PointArray;

    // Find the minumum and maximum z values:
    double zmin = bs.ZDataMin();
    double zmax = bs.ZDataMax();

    // Check parameters:
    double xlength = bs.XLength;
    if (xlength <= 0)
        xlength = 0.1 * bs.XSpacing;
    else if (xlength > 0.5)
        xlength = 0.5 * bs.XSpacing;
    else
        xlength = bs.XLength * bs.XSpacing;
    double ylength = bs.YLength;
    if (ylength <= 0)
        ylength = 0.1 * bs.YSpacing;
    else if (ylength > 0.5)
        ylength = 0.5 * bs.YSpacing;
    else
        ylength = bs.YLength * bs.YSpacing;
    double zorigin = bs.ZOrigin;

    // Draw 3D bars:
    for (int i = 0; i < pts.GetLength(0) - 1; i++)
    {
        for (int j = 0; j < pts.GetLength(1) - 1; j++)
        {
            int ii = i;
            int jj = j;
```

```
            if (cs.Azimuth >= -180 && cs.Azimuth < -90)
            {
                ii = pts.GetLength(0) - 2 - i;
                jj = j;
            }
            else if (cs.Azimuth >= -90 && cs.Azimuth < 0)
            {
                ii = pts.GetLength(0) - 2 - i;
                jj = pts.GetLength(1) - 2 - j;
            }
            else if (cs.Azimuth >= 0 && cs.Azimuth < 90)
            {
                ii = i;
                jj = pts.GetLength(1) - 2 - j;
            }
            else if (cs.Azimuth >= 90 && cs.Azimuth <= 180)
            {
                ii = i;
                jj = j;
            }
            DrawBar(cs, bs, m, pts[ii, jj], xlength, ylength, zorigin,
                zmax, zmin);
        }
    }
    if (cs.IsColorBar && IsColormap)
    {
        AddColorBar(cs, bs, zmin, zmax);
    }
}
```

In this method, we first examine whether the parameters provided by the user are in the right ranges. Then we examine the order of drawing the bars according to the variations of the elevation and azimuth angles, making sure that we always draw the bars in back-to-front order (the *Z*-order approach). As mentioned previously, when drawn in this order, a bar can obscure only the bars that have been drawn before it. When the program draws a bar, it fills it so that it covers up any bars that it should obscure. Finally, this method calls another method, *DrawBar*, which performs the actual bar-drawing task:

```
private void DrawBar(ChartStyle2D cs, Bar3DSeries bs, Matrix3D m,
    Point3D pt, double xlength, double ylength,
                    double zorign, double zmax, double zmin)
{
    SolidColorBrush lineBrush = (SolidColorBrush)bs.LineColor;
    SolidColorBrush fillBrush = GetBrush(pt.Z, zmin, zmax);
    Point3D[] pts = new Point3D[8];
    Point3D[] pts1 = new Point3D[8];
    Point3D[] pt3 = new Point3D[4];
    Point[] pta = new Point[4];

    pts[0] = new Point3D(pt.X - xlength, pt.Y - ylength, zorign);
    pts[1] = new Point3D(pt.X - xlength, pt.Y + ylength, zorign);
    pts[2] = new Point3D(pt.X + xlength, pt.Y + ylength, zorign);
    pts[3] = new Point3D(pt.X + xlength, pt.Y - ylength, zorign);
    pts[4] = new Point3D(pt.X + xlength, pt.Y - ylength, pt.Z);
    pts[5] = new Point3D(pt.X + xlength, pt.Y + ylength, pt.Z);
    pts[6] = new Point3D(pt.X - xlength, pt.Y + ylength, pt.Z);
```

```
    pts[7] = new Point3D(pt.X - xlength, pt.Y - ylength, pt.Z);

    for (int i = 0; i < pts.Length; i++)
    {
        pts1[i] = new Point3D(pts[i].X, pts[i].Y, pts[i].Z);
        pts[i] = cs.Normalize3D(m, pts[i]);
    }

    int[] nconfigs = new int[8];
    if (IsBarSingleColor)
    {
        pta[0] = new Point(pts[4].X, pts[4].Y);
        pta[1] = new Point(pts[5].X, pts[5].Y);
        pta[2] = new Point(pts[6].X, pts[6].Y);
        pta[3] = new Point(pts[7].X, pts[7].Y);
        DrawPolygon(cs, bs, pta, fillBrush, lineBrush);

        if (cs.Azimuth >= -180 && cs.Azimuth < -90)
        {
            nconfigs = new int[8] { 1, 2, 5, 6, 1, 0, 7, 6 };
        }
        else if (cs.Azimuth >= -90 && cs.Azimuth < 0)
        {
            nconfigs = new int[8] { 1, 0, 7, 6, 0, 3, 4, 7 };
        }
        else if (cs.Azimuth >= 0 && cs.Azimuth < 90)
        {
            nconfigs = new int[8] { 0, 3, 4, 7, 2, 3, 4, 5 };
        }
        else if (cs.Azimuth >= 90 && cs.Azimuth < 180)
        {
            nconfigs = new int[8] { 2, 3, 4, 5, 1, 2, 5, 6 };
        }
        pta[0] = new Point(pts[nconfigs[0]].X, pts[nconfigs[0]].Y);
        pta[1] = new Point(pts[nconfigs[1]].X, pts[nconfigs[1]].Y);
        pta[2] = new Point(pts[nconfigs[2]].X, pts[nconfigs[2]].Y);
        pta[3] = new Point(pts[nconfigs[3]].X, pts[nconfigs[3]].Y);
        DrawPolygon(cs, bs, pta, fillBrush, lineBrush);

        pta[0] = new Point(pts[nconfigs[4]].X, pts[nconfigs[4]].Y);
        pta[1] = new Point(pts[nconfigs[5]].X, pts[nconfigs[5]].Y);
        pta[2] = new Point(pts[nconfigs[6]].X, pts[nconfigs[6]].Y);
        pta[3] = new Point(pts[nconfigs[7]].X, pts[nconfigs[7]].Y);
        DrawPolygon(cs, bs, pta, fillBrush, lineBrush);
    }
    else if (!IsBarSingleColor && IsColormap)
    {
        pta[0] = new Point(pts[4].X, pts[4].Y);
        pta[1] = new Point(pts[5].X, pts[5].Y);
        pta[2] = new Point(pts[6].X, pts[6].Y);
        pta[3] = new Point(pts[7].X, pts[7].Y);
        DrawPolygon(cs, bs, pta, fillBrush, lineBrush);

        pta[0] = new Point(pts[0].X, pts[0].Y);
        pta[1] = new Point(pts[1].X, pts[1].Y);
```

```
pta[2] = new Point(pts[2].X, pts[2].Y);
pta[3] = new Point(pts[3].X, pts[3].Y);
fillBrush = GetBrush(pts1[0].Z, zmin, zmax);
DrawPolygon(cs, bs, pta, fillBrush, lineBrush);

double dz = (zmax - zmin) / 63;
if (pt.Z < zorign)
    dz = -dz;
int nz = (int)((pt.Z - zorign) / dz) + 1;
if (nz < 1)
    nz = 1;
double z = zorign;

if (cs.Azimuth >= -180 && cs.Azimuth < -90)
{
    nconfigs = new int[4] { 1, 2, 1, 0 };
}
else if (cs.Azimuth >= -90 && cs.Azimuth < 0)
{
    nconfigs = new int[4] { 1, 0, 0, 3 };
}
else if (cs.Azimuth >= 0 && cs.Azimuth < 90)
{
    nconfigs = new int[4] { 0, 3, 2, 3 };
}
else if (cs.Azimuth >= 90 && cs.Azimuth <= 180)
{
    nconfigs = new int[4] { 2, 3, 1, 2 };
}
for (int i = 0; i < nz; i++)
{
    z = zorign + i * dz;
    pt3[0] = new Point3D(pts1[nconfigs[0]].X,
        pts1[nconfigs[0]].Y, z);
    pt3[1] = new Point3D(pts1[nconfigs[1]].X,
        pts1[nconfigs[1]].Y, z);
    pt3[2] = new Point3D(pts1[nconfigs[1]].X,
        pts1[nconfigs[1]].Y, z + dz);
    pt3[3] = new Point3D(pts1[nconfigs[0]].X,
        pts1[nconfigs[0]].Y, z + dz);
    for (int j = 0; j < pt3.Length; j++)
    {
        pt3[j] = cs.Normalize3D(m, pt3[j]);
    }
    pta[0] = new Point(pt3[0].X, pt3[0].Y);
    pta[1] = new Point(pt3[1].X, pt3[1].Y);
    pta[2] = new Point(pt3[2].X, pt3[2].Y);
    pta[3] = new Point(pt3[3].X, pt3[3].Y);
    fillBrush = GetBrush(z, zmin, zmax);
    DrawPolygon(cs, bs, pta, fillBrush, fillBrush);
}
pt3[0] = new Point3D(pts1[nconfigs[0]].X,
    pts1[nconfigs[0]].Y, zorign);
pt3[1] = new Point3D(pts1[nconfigs[1]].X,
    pts1[nconfigs[1]].Y, zorign);
```

```
pt3[2] = new Point3D(pts1[nconfigs[1]].X,
    pts1[nconfigs[1]].Y, pt.Z);
pt3[3] = new Point3D(pts1[nconfigs[0]].X,
    pts1[nconfigs[0]].Y, pt.Z);
for (int j = 0; j < pt3.Length; j++)
{
    pt3[j] = cs.Normalize3D(m, pt3[j]);
}
pta[0] = new Point(pt3[0].X, pt3[0].Y);
pta[1] = new Point(pt3[1].X, pt3[1].Y);
pta[2] = new Point(pt3[2].X, pt3[2].Y);
pta[3] = new Point(pt3[3].X, pt3[3].Y);
fillBrush = Brushes.Transparent;
DrawPolygon(cs, bs, pta, fillBrush, lineBrush);

for (int i = 0; i < nz; i++)
{
    z = zorign + i * dz;
    pt3[0] = new Point3D(pts1[nconfigs[2]].X,
        pts1[nconfigs[2]].Y, z);
    pt3[1] = new Point3D(pts1[nconfigs[3]].X,
        pts1[nconfigs[3]].Y, z);
    pt3[2] = new Point3D(pts1[nconfigs[3]].X,
        pts1[nconfigs[3]].Y, z + dz);
    pt3[3] = new Point3D(pts1[nconfigs[2]].X,
        pts1[nconfigs[2]].Y, z + dz);

    for (int j = 0; j < pt3.Length; j++)
    {
        pt3[j] = cs.Normalize3D(m, pt3[j]);
    }
    pta[0] = new Point(pt3[0].X, pt3[0].Y);
    pta[1] = new Point(pt3[1].X, pt3[1].Y);
    pta[2] = new Point(pt3[2].X, pt3[2].Y);
    pta[3] = new Point(pt3[3].X, pt3[3].Y);
    fillBrush = GetBrush(z, zmin, zmax);
    DrawPolygon(cs, bs, pta, fillBrush, fillBrush);
}
pt3[0] = new Point3D(pts1[nconfigs[2]].X,
    pts1[nconfigs[2]].Y, zorign);
pt3[1] = new Point3D(pts1[nconfigs[3]].X,
    pts1[nconfigs[3]].Y, zorign);
pt3[2] = new Point3D(pts1[nconfigs[3]].X,
    pts1[nconfigs[3]].Y, pt.Z);
pt3[3] = new Point3D(pts1[nconfigs[2]].X,
    pts1[nconfigs[2]].Y, pt.Z);
for (int j = 0; j < pt3.Length; j++)
{
    pt3[j] = cs.Normalize3D(m, pt3[j]);
}
pta[0] = new Point(pt3[0].X, pt3[0].Y);
pta[1] = new Point(pt3[1].X, pt3[1].Y);
pta[2] = new Point(pt3[2].X, pt3[2].Y);
pta[3] = new Point(pt3[3].X, pt3[3].Y);
fillBrush = Brushes.Transparent;
```

```
            DrawPolygon(cs, bs, pta, fillBrush, lineBrush);
        }
    }

    private void DrawPolygon(ChartStyle2D cs, Bar3DSeries bs, Point[] pts,
        SolidColorBrush fillBrush, SolidColorBrush lineBrush)
    {
        Polygon plg = new Polygon();
        plg.Stroke = lineBrush;
        plg.StrokeThickness = bs.LineThickness;
        plg.Fill = fillBrush;
        for (int i = 0; i < pts.Length; i++)
        {
            plg.Points.Add(pts[i]);
        }
        cs.ChartCanvas.Children.Add(plg);
    }
}
```

In the *DrawBar* method, we first create the eight vertices of a 3D bar using a data point and the *xlength*, *ylength*, and *zorigin* parameters. We then perform an orthogonal projection transformation on these vertices using the azimuth-elevation matrix. Next, we consider two cases separately: drawing bars using a single color or using a colormap. For each case, we examine which faces should be drawn, depending on the elevation and azimuth angles. In the case of single-color shading, the color of a bar is determined by the Z value of the input point; in the case of a colormap, each bar is colormapped linearly from the *zorigin* to the Z value of its input point.

Testing 3D Bar Charts

Now, I will show you how to create 3D bar charts using the *ChartS3DView* example from the previous section, in which we have already implemented 3D bar charts. By running the example, selecting *BarChart3D* from the chart type combobox, and selecting *SingleColor* from the bar chart type combobox, you will obtain the 3D bar chart shown in Figure 8 -25.

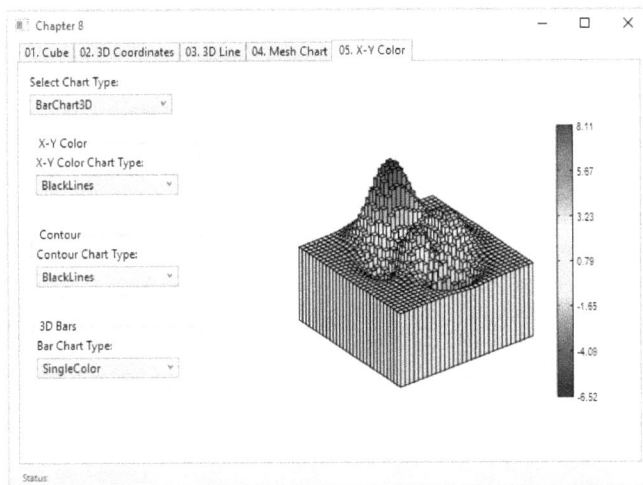

Figure 8-25. A single-colored 3D bar chart.

Here, we set *ZOrigin* = *cs.Zmin*. The bars are drawn in a single color bacause we set the parameter *IsBarSingleColor* to *true*.

If you set the property *IsBarSingleColor* to *false*, you will obtain a colormapped 3D bar chart. Choosing *ColorMap* from the bar chart type combobox produces the result shown in Figure 8-26.

You can also change the *ZOrigin* property. Choosing *ZeroZPlane* from the bar chart type combobox produces the result shown in Figure 8-27. Here, we set the *ZOrigin* = 0.

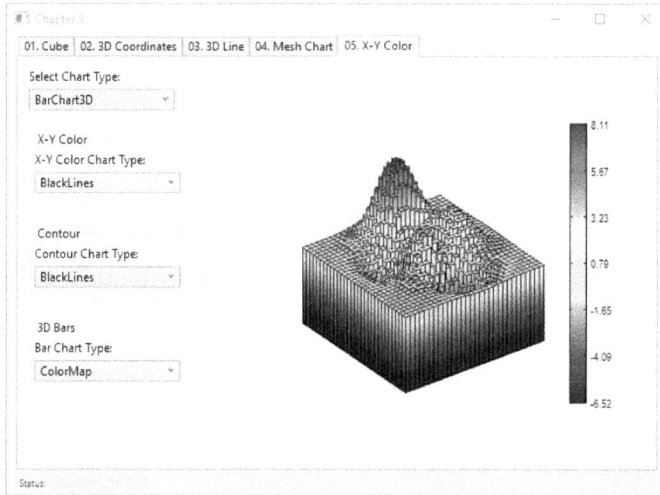

Figure 8-26. A colormapped 3D bar chart.

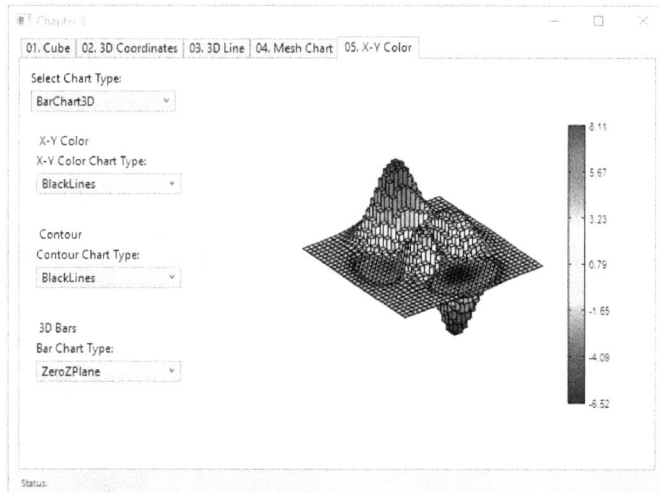

Figure 8-27. A single-colored 3D bar chart with Zorigin = 0.

Chapter 9
3D Chart Controls

In the previous chapter, we implemented the source code for all of the classes in our 3D chart applications directly. This approach works well, but, if you want to reuse the same code in multiple .NET applications, it becomes ineffective. In this chapter, I will show you how to convert various types of 3D charts into a powerful 3D chart control package and how to use this package in your WPF applications in a standard MVVM pattern.

For easy implementation, I will divide the different types of 3D charts into four modules, 3D line charts (*Line3D*), 3D surface-like charts (*Chart3D*), 3D specialized charts (*Chart3DS*), and 3D bar charts (*Bar3D*). Usually, each module in turn includes several chart types. For example, *Chart3D* includes *Mesh*, *Curtain*, *Waterfall*, and *Surface* charts. However, these different types of charts in the same module share the same 3D framework.

3D Line Charts

Creating a 3D chart control based on the 3D line charts developed in the previous chapter is easy. Open Visual Studio 2013, start a new WPF project, and name it *Chapter09*. Add Caliburn.Micro to *References*. Add the new folders, *Models*, *ViewModels*, and *Views,* to the project. Add *AppBootstrapper.cs* to the *Models* folder, which is the same file as that used in the example projects in previous chapters.

Add a *Window* to the *Views* folder and name it *MainView*. Add a class to the *ViewModels* folder and name it *MainViewModel*. The main view and view model are used to hold the tab items, which are similar to those used in the *Chapter08* project. You can open the Chapter08 project in Visual Studio and look over the code if you need a refresher. Also, do not forget to make corresponding changes to *App.xaml*.

Now, it is time to create a 3D chart user control. Right click the *Chapter09* solution and choose Add | New Project…to bring up the *Add New Project* dialog. Select a new *WPF User Control Library* from the templates and name it *Chart3DControl*. When you do this, Visual Studio 2013 creates an XAML markup file and a corresponding custom class to hold your initialization and event-handling code. This will generate a default user control named *UserControl1*. Rename it *Line3D* by right clicking *UserControl1*.xaml in the Solution Explorer and selecting Rename. You also need to change the name *UserControl1* to *Line3D* in both the XAML and the code-behind file for the control.

Add a new folder to the control and name it *ChartModel*. Add all existing classes from the *ChartModel* folder of the *Chapter08* project to the *ChartModel* folder of the current project, and change all of their namespaces from *Chapter08.Models.ChartModel* to *Chart3DControl*. In addition, you need to add Caliburn.Micro to the References of this project.

Here is the XAML file for this control:

```
<UserControl x:Class="Chart3DControl.Line3D"
             xmlns="http://schemas.microsoft.com/winfx/2006/xaml/presentation"
             xmlns:x="http://schemas.microsoft.com/winfx/2006/xaml"
             xmlns:mc="http://schemas.openxmlformats.org/markup-compatibility/2006"
             xmlns:d="http://schemas.microsoft.com/expression/blend/2008"
             mc:Ignorable="d"
             d:DesignHeight="300" d:DesignWidth="300">
    <Grid x:Name="chartGrid" Margin="20" SizeChanged="chartGrid_SizeChanged">
        <Canvas x:Name="chartCanvas" Background="Transparent"
        Width="{Binding ElementName=chartGrid,Path=ActualWidth}"
        Height="{Binding ElementName=chartGrid,Path=ActualHeight}"
        ClipToBounds="True"/>
    </Grid>
</UserControl>
```

This markup is very simple. You may notice that we are going to use the code-behind code to implement our chart control because we are not using the Caliburn.Micro's *Message.Attach* method for the event handlers, such as the *SizeChanged* events.

Here, I will show you how to create a 3D chart control based on dependency properties implemented in the code-behind file. Dependency properties provide a simple way to data bind when the source object is a WPF element and the source property is a dependency property, because dependency properties have built-in support for change notification. As a result, changing the value of the dependency property in the source object updates the bound property in the target object immediately. This is exactly what you want – and it happens without requiring you to build any additional infrastructure like an *INotifyPropertyChanged* interface.

Defining Dependency Properties

Next, you need to design the public interface that the 3D line chart control exposes to the outside world. In other words, it is time to create the properties, methods, and events that the control consumer (the application that uses the control) will rely on to interact with your 3D chart control.

You may want to expose to the outside world most of the properties in the *ChartStyle* class from the 3D line chart example in Chapter 8, such as axis limits, title, and labels; at the same time, we will keep the classes from the original 3D line chart example project unchanged. In order to support WPF features such as data binding, styles, and animation, the control properties are always dependency properties.

The first step in creating a dependency property is to define a static field for it, with the word *Property* added to the end of the property name. Add the following code to the code-behind file for the *Line3D* view:

```
using System;
using System.ComponentModel;
using System.Windows;
using System.Windows.Controls;
using System.Windows.Media;
using Caliburn.Micro;
using System.Windows.Media.Media3D;
```

```
using System.Collections.Specialized;

namespace Chart3DControl
{
    /// <summary>
    /// Interaction logic for UserControl1.xaml
    /// </summary>
    public partial class Line3D : UserControl
    {
        private ChartStyle cs;

        public Line3D()
        {
            InitializeComponent();
            this.cs = new ChartStyle();
            cs.ChartCanvas = chartCanvas;
        }

        private void chartGrid_SizeChanged(object sender, SizeChangedEventArgs e)
        {
            ResizeChart();
        }

        private void SetChart()
        {
            cs.Elevation = this.Elevation;
            cs.Azimuth = this.Azimuth;
            cs.Xmin = this.Xmin;
            cs.Xmax = this.Xmax;
            cs.Ymin = this.Ymin;
            cs.Ymax = this.Ymax;
            cs.Zmin = this.Zmin;
            cs.Zmax = this.Zmax;
            cs.XTick = this.XTick;
            cs.YTick = this.YTick;
            cs.ZTick = this.ZTick;
            cs.XLabel = this.XLabel;
            cs.YLabel = this.YLabel;
            cs.ZLabel = this.ZLabel;
            cs.Title = this.Title;
            cs.GridlineColor = this.GridlineColor;
            cs.GridlinePattern = this.GridlinePattern;
            cs.GridlineThickness = this.GridLineThickness;
            ResizeChart();
        }

        private void ResizeChart()
        {
            chartCanvas.Children.Clear();
            cs.SetChartStyle();

            if (DataCollection != null)
            {
                if (DataCollection.Count > 0)
                {
```

```
                          DataCollection[0].AddLine3D(cs);
              }
       }

}

public static DependencyProperty ElevationProperty =
    DependencyProperty.Register("Elevation", typeof(double),
    typeof(Line3D), new FrameworkPropertyMetadata(0.0,
    FrameworkPropertyMetadataOptions.BindsTwoWayByDefault));

public double Elevation
{
    get { return (double)GetValue(ElevationProperty); }
    set { SetValue(ElevationProperty, value); }
}

public static DependencyProperty AzimuthProperty =
    DependencyProperty.Register("Azimuth", typeof(double),
    typeof(Line3D), new FrameworkPropertyMetadata(0.0,
    FrameworkPropertyMetadataOptions.BindsTwoWayByDefault));

public double Azimuth
{
    get { return (double)GetValue(AzimuthProperty); }
    set { SetValue(AzimuthProperty, value); }
}

public static DependencyProperty XminProperty =
    DependencyProperty.Register("Xmin", typeof(double),
    typeof(Line3D), new FrameworkPropertyMetadata(0.0,
    FrameworkPropertyMetadataOptions.BindsTwoWayByDefault));

public double Xmin
{
    get { return (double)GetValue(XminProperty); }
    set { SetValue(XminProperty, value); }
}

public static DependencyProperty XmaxProperty =
    DependencyProperty.Register("Xmax", typeof(double),
    typeof(Line3D), new FrameworkPropertyMetadata(10.0,
    FrameworkPropertyMetadataOptions.BindsTwoWayByDefault));

public double Xmax
{
    get { return (double)GetValue(XmaxProperty); }
    set { SetValue(XmaxProperty, value); }
}

public static DependencyProperty YminProperty =
    DependencyProperty.Register("Ymin", typeof(double),
    typeof(Line3D), new FrameworkPropertyMetadata(0.0,
    FrameworkPropertyMetadataOptions.BindsTwoWayByDefault));
```

```
public double Ymin
{
    get { return (double)GetValue(YminProperty); }
    set { SetValue(YminProperty, value); }
}

public static DependencyProperty YmaxProperty =
    DependencyProperty.Register("Ymax", typeof(double),
    typeof(Line3D), new FrameworkPropertyMetadata(10.0,
    FrameworkPropertyMetadataOptions.BindsTwoWayByDefault));

public double Ymax
{
    get { return (double)GetValue(YmaxProperty); }
    set { SetValue(YmaxProperty, value); }
}

public static DependencyProperty ZminProperty =
    DependencyProperty.Register("Zmin", typeof(double),
    typeof(Line3D), new FrameworkPropertyMetadata(0.0,
    FrameworkPropertyMetadataOptions.BindsTwoWayByDefault));

public double Zmin
{
    get { return (double)GetValue(ZminProperty); }
    set { SetValue(ZminProperty, value); }
}

public static DependencyProperty ZmaxProperty =
    DependencyProperty.Register("Zmax", typeof(double),
    typeof(Line3D), new FrameworkPropertyMetadata(10.0,
    FrameworkPropertyMetadataOptions.BindsTwoWayByDefault));

public double Zmax
{
    get { return (double)GetValue(ZmaxProperty); }
    set { SetValue(ZmaxProperty, value); }
}

public static DependencyProperty XTickProperty =
    DependencyProperty.Register("XTick", typeof(double),
    typeof(Line3D), new FrameworkPropertyMetadata(2.0,
    FrameworkPropertyMetadataOptions.BindsTwoWayByDefault));

public double XTick
{
    get { return (double)GetValue(XTickProperty); }
    set { SetValue(XTickProperty, value); }
}

public static DependencyProperty YTickProperty =
    DependencyProperty.Register("YTick", typeof(double),
    typeof(Line3D), new FrameworkPropertyMetadata(2.0,
    FrameworkPropertyMetadataOptions.BindsTwoWayByDefault));
```

```
public double YTick
{
    get { return (double)GetValue(YTickProperty); }
    set { SetValue(YTickProperty, value); }
}

public static DependencyProperty ZTickProperty =
    DependencyProperty.Register("ZTick", typeof(double),
    typeof(Line3D), new FrameworkPropertyMetadata(2.0,
    FrameworkPropertyMetadataOptions.BindsTwoWayByDefault));

public double ZTick
{
    get { return (double)GetValue(ZTickProperty); }
    set { SetValue(ZTickProperty, value); }
}

public static DependencyProperty XLabelProperty =
    DependencyProperty.Register("XLabel", typeof(string),
    typeof(Line3D), new FrameworkPropertyMetadata("X Axis",
    FrameworkPropertyMetadataOptions.BindsTwoWayByDefault));

public string XLabel
{
    get { return (string)GetValue(XLabelProperty); }
    set { SetValue(XLabelProperty, value); }
}

public static DependencyProperty YLabelProperty =
    DependencyProperty.Register("YLabel", typeof(string),
    typeof(Line3D), new FrameworkPropertyMetadata("Y Axis",
    FrameworkPropertyMetadataOptions.BindsTwoWayByDefault));

public string YLabel
{
    get { return (string)GetValue(YLabelProperty); }
    set { SetValue(YLabelProperty, value); }
}

public static DependencyProperty ZLabelProperty =
    DependencyProperty.Register("ZLabel", typeof(string),
    typeof(Line3D), new FrameworkPropertyMetadata("Z Axis",
    FrameworkPropertyMetadataOptions.BindsTwoWayByDefault));

public string ZLabel
{
    get { return (string)GetValue(ZLabelProperty); }
    set { SetValue(ZLabelProperty, value); }
}

public static DependencyProperty TitleProperty =
    DependencyProperty.Register("Title", typeof(string),
    typeof(Line3D), new FrameworkPropertyMetadata("No Title",
    FrameworkPropertyMetadataOptions.BindsTwoWayByDefault));
```

```
public string Title
{
    get { return (string)GetValue(TitleProperty); }
    set { SetValue(TitleProperty, value); }
}

public static DependencyProperty GridlineColorProperty =
    DependencyProperty.Register("GridlineColor", typeof(Brush),
    typeof(Line3D), new FrameworkPropertyMetadata(Brushes.Gray,
    FrameworkPropertyMetadataOptions.BindsTwoWayByDefault));

public Brush GridlineColor
{
    get { return (Brush)GetValue(GridlineColorProperty); }
    set { SetValue(GridlineColorProperty, value); }
}

public static DependencyProperty GridLineThicknessProperty =
    DependencyProperty.Register("GridLineThickness", typeof(double),
    typeof(Line3D), new FrameworkPropertyMetadata(1.0,
    FrameworkPropertyMetadataOptions.BindsTwoWayByDefault));

public double GridLineThickness
{
    get { return (double)GetValue(GridLineThicknessProperty); }
    set { SetValue(GridLineThicknessProperty, value); }
}

public static DependencyProperty GridlinePatternProperty =
    DependencyProperty.Register("GridlinePattern",
    typeof(LineDashPatternEnum), typeof(Line3D),
    new FrameworkPropertyMetadata(LineDashPatternEnum.Solid,
    FrameworkPropertyMetadataOptions.BindsTwoWayByDefault));

public LineDashPatternEnum GridlinePattern
{
    get { return (LineDashPatternEnum)GetValue(GridlinePatternProperty); }
    set { SetValue(GridlinePatternProperty, value); }
}

private static DependencyProperty DataCollectionProperty =
    DependencyProperty.Register("DataCollection",
    typeof(BindableCollection<LineSeries3D>), typeof(Line3D),
    new FrameworkPropertyMetadata(null,
    FrameworkPropertyMetadataOptions.BindsTwoWayByDefault, OnDataChanged));

public BindableCollection<LineSeries3D> DataCollection
{
    get { return (BindableCollection<LineSeries3D>)
        GetValue(DataCollectionProperty); }
    set { SetValue(DataCollectionProperty, value); }
}

private static void OnDataChanged(object sender,
    DependencyPropertyChangedEventArgs e)
```

```
        {
            var lc = sender as Line3D;
            var dc = e.NewValue as BindableCollection<LineSeries3D>;
            if (dc != null)
                dc.CollectionChanged += lc.dc_CollectionChanged;
        }

        private void dc_CollectionChanged(object sender,
            NotifyCollectionChangedEventArgs e)
        {
            if (DataCollection != null)
            {
                CheckCount = 0;
                if (DataCollection.Count > 0)
                    CheckCount = DataCollection.Count;

            }
        }

        public static DependencyProperty CheckCountProperty =
            DependencyProperty.Register("CheckCount", typeof(int),
            typeof(Line3D), new FrameworkPropertyMetadata(0,
            FrameworkPropertyMetadataOptions.BindsTwoWayByDefault,
            new PropertyChangedCallback(OnStartChart)));

        public int CheckCount
        {
            get { return (int)GetValue(CheckCountProperty); }
            set { SetValue(CheckCountProperty, value); }
        }

        private static void OnStartChart(DependencyObject sender,
            DependencyPropertyChangedEventArgs e)
        {
            (sender as Line3D).SetChart();
        }
    }
}
```

Note how we define the dependency properties. Here, we use the *DepedencyObject* to register the dependency property into a property system to ensure that the object contains the property in it, and we can easily get or set the value of those properties. The property wrappers should not contain any logic, because properties may be set and retrieved directly using the *SetValue* and *GetValue* methods of the base *DependencyObject* class.

In some situations, you may want to execute certain logic and computation methods after setting the value for a dependency property. You can perform these tasks by implementing a callback method that fires when the property changes through either the property wrapper or a direct *SetValue* call.

For example, after creating the *DataCollection* containing all of the *LineSeries3D* objects, you may want the chart control to automatically create a corresponding 3D line chart for these *LineSeries* objects. The bolded code in the preceding code-behind file shows how to implement such a *PropertyChanged* callback method. The *DataCollectionProperty* includes a callback method called *OnDataChanged*. Inside this callback method, we add an event handler to the *CollectionChanged* property when the *DataCollection* changes. Within the *CollectionChanged* handler, we set another private dependency property called *CheckCount* to the *DataCollection.Count*. If *CheckCount* > 0, we know that the *DataCollection* contains *LineSeries3D* objects, and we then implement another callback method, *OnStartChart*, for the *CheckCount* property to create the line chart by calling the *SetChart* method.

Note that inside the *SetChart* method, we set public properties of the *ChartStyle* class to the corresponding dependency properties of the chart control. This way, whenever the dependency properties in the *Line3D* class change, the properties in the *ChartStyle* class will change correspondingly.

Here, we also add a *chartGrid_SizeChanged* event handler to the 3D line chart control. This handler ensures that the chart gets updated whenever the chart control is resized. Now, we can build the control library by right-clicking the *ChartControl* project and selecting Build.

Using 3D Line Chart Control

Now that the 3D line chart control is completed, we can use it in our *Chapter09* project. Open the *Chapter09* project in Visual Studio 2013. Add a new *UserControl* to the *Views* folder of the *Chapter09* project and name it *LineChartView*. In the new project, right click the References and select Add References… to bring up the "Add References" window. Click Solution and then Projects in the left pane of this window and highlight the *Chart3DControl*. Click OK to add the *Chart3DControl* to the current project. Doing this allows you to use the control in your WPF application just like a built-in element. Now, in the Solution Explorer, right-click the *Chapter09* project and select Set As StartUp Project. Here is the XAML file for the *LineChartView*:

```xml
<UserControl x:Class="Chapter09.Views.LineChartView"
             xmlns="http://schemas.microsoft.com/winfx/2006/xaml/presentation"
             xmlns:x="http://schemas.microsoft.com/winfx/2006/xaml"
             xmlns:mc="http://schemas.openxmlformats.org/markup-compatibility/2006"
             xmlns:d="http://schemas.microsoft.com/expression/blend/2008"
             xmlns:local="clr-namespace:Chart3DControl;assembly=Chart3DControl"
             mc:Ignorable="d"
             d:DesignHeight="300" d:DesignWidth="500">
    <Grid>
        <Grid.ColumnDefinitions>
            <ColumnDefinition Width="*"/>
            <ColumnDefinition Width="150"/>
        </Grid.ColumnDefinitions>
        <Button x:Name="AddChart" Content="Add Chart" Width="100" Height="25"
                Grid.Column="1"/>
        <local:Line3D DataCollection="{Binding DataCollection}" Xmin="-1" Xmax="1"
                XTick="0.5" Ymin="-1" Ymax="1" YTick="0.5" Zmin="0" Zmax="30"
                ZTick="5" XLabel="X" YLabel="Y" ZLabel="Z" Title="3D Line"
                GridlinePattern="Dot" GridlineColor="Green" GridLineThickness="1"
                Elevation="30" Azimuth="-30"/>
    </Grid>
</UserControl>
```

Here, we simply create a 3D line chart control exactly as we would create any other type of WPF element. Now, add a new class to the *ViewModels* folder and name it *LineChartViewModel*. Here is the code for this class:

```csharp
using System;
using Caliburn.Micro;
using System.Collections.ObjectModel;
using System.ComponentModel.Composition;
```

```
using System.Windows;
using System.Windows.Media;
using System.Windows.Media.Media3D;
using Chart3DControl;

namespace Chapter09.ViewModels
{
    [Export(typeof(IScreen)), PartCreationPolicy(CreationPolicy.NonShared)]
    public class LineChartViewModel : Screen
    {
        private readonly IEventAggregator _events;
        [ImportingConstructor]
        public LineChartViewModel(IEventAggregator events)
        {
            this._events = events;
            DisplayName = "01. Line Chart";
            DataCollection = new BindableCollection<LineSeries3D>();
        }

        public BindableCollection<LineSeries3D> DataCollection { get; set; }


        public void AddChart()
        {
            DataCollection.Clear();
            var ds = new LineSeries3D();
            ds.LineColor = Brushes.Red;
            for (int i = 0; i < 300; i++)
            {
                double t = 0.1 * i;
                double x = Math.Exp(-t / 30) * Math.Cos(t);
                double y = Math.Exp(-t / 30) * Math.Sin(t);
                double z = t;
                ds.LinePoints.Add(new Point3D(x, y, z));
            }
            DataCollection.Add(ds);
        }
    }
}
```

Just like we did when we created 3D line charts in Chapter 8, we first create a 3D line series (note that unlike a 2D chart, there should only be one *LineSeries3D* in a 3D chart) and then add it to the chart control's *DataCollection*. The beauty of using the chart control is that we can use the standard MVVM pattern in WPF applications, even though we create the chart control using dependency properties and a code-behind approach. Here, we simply define the *DataCollection* property in the view model and bind it to the chart control. The *AddChart* method in the view model is also bound to the *Button* in the view by Caliburn.Micro's naming convention. This way, we have a perfect separation between the view and the view model, which meets the requirements of the MVVM pattern perfectly!

Running this example and clicking the *Add Chart* button generates the result shown in Figure 9-1. You can resize the chart window to see how the chart is automatically updated.

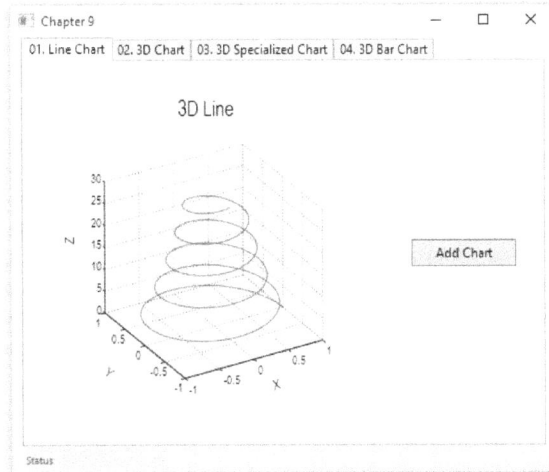

Figure 9-1. A 3D line chart created using a 3D chart control.

3D Surface-Like Charts

In Chapter 8, we created four types of surface-like charts: *Mesh*, *Curtain* (*MeshZ*), *Waterfall*, and *Surface* charts. In the preceding sections, I showed you how to create a 3D line chart control and how to use it in your WPF applications. Following the same procedure, we can also easily convert 3D surface-like charts into a 3D chart control.

Go back to the *Chart3DControl* project and add a new *UserControl* to the project named *Chart3D*. Here is the XAML file for this view:

```
<UserControl x:Class="Chart3DControl.Chart3D"
             xmlns="http://schemas.microsoft.com/winfx/2006/xaml/presentation"
             xmlns:x="http://schemas.microsoft.com/winfx/2006/xaml"
             xmlns:mc="http://schemas.openxmlformats.org/markup-compatibility/2006"
             xmlns:d="http://schemas.microsoft.com/expression/blend/2008"
             mc:Ignorable="d"
             d:DesignHeight="300" d:DesignWidth="300">
    <Grid x:Name="chartGrid" Margin="20" SizeChanged="chartGrid_SizeChanged">
        <Canvas x:Name="chartCanvas" Background="Transparent"
                Width="{Binding ElementName=chartGrid,Path=ActualWidth}"
                Height="{Binding ElementName=chartGrid,Path=ActualHeight}"
ClipToBounds="True"/>
    </Grid>
</UserControl>
```

This markup is similar to that used to create 3D line chart control in preceding example. Again we will use the code-behind approach and depedency proeprties to implement this control.

Defining Dependency Properties

The first step in creating a dependency property is to define a static field for it, with the word *Property* added to the end of the property name. The code-behind file for this control is very similar to that used in creating the 3D line chart control. However, I will still provide a complete code listing for this code-behind file for your reference:

```
using System;
using System.ComponentModel;
using System.Windows;
using System.Windows.Controls;
using System.Windows.Media;
using Caliburn.Micro;
using System.Windows.Media.Media3D;
using System.Collections.Specialized;

namespace Chart3DControl
{
    /// <summary>
    /// Interaction logic for Chart3D.xaml
    /// </summary>
    public partial class Chart3D : UserControl
    {
        private ChartStyle cs;
        private Add3DChart a3d;

        public Chart3D()
        {
            InitializeComponent();
            this.cs = new ChartStyle();
            this.a3d = new Add3DChart();
            cs.ChartCanvas = chartCanvas;
        }

        private void chartGrid_SizeChanged(object sender, SizeChangedEventArgs e)
        {
            ResizeChart();
        }

        private void SetChart()
        {
            cs.Elevation = this.Elevation;
            cs.Azimuth = this.Azimuth;
            cs.Xmin = this.Xmin;
            cs.Xmax = this.Xmax;
            cs.Ymin = this.Ymin;
            cs.Ymax = this.Ymax;
            cs.Zmin = this.Zmin;
            cs.Zmax = this.Zmax;
            cs.XTick = this.XTick;
            cs.YTick = this.YTick;
            cs.ZTick = this.ZTick;
            cs.XLabel = this.XLabel;
            cs.YLabel = this.YLabel;
            cs.ZLabel = this.ZLabel;
            cs.Title = this.Title;
            cs.GridlineColor = this.GridlineColor;
            cs.GridlinePattern = this.GridlinePattern;
            cs.GridlineThickness = this.GridLineThickness;
```

```
        cs.IsColorBar = this.IsColorbar;
        a3d.Colormap.ColormapBrushType = this.ColormapType;
        a3d.IsColormap = this.IsColormap;
        a3d.IsHiddenLine = this.IsHiddenLine;
        a3d.IsInterp = this.IsInterp;
        a3d.NumberInterp = this.NumberInterp;
        a3d.SurfaceChartType = this.Chart3DType;

        ResizeChart();
    }

    private void ResizeChart()
    {
        chartCanvas.Children.Clear();
        cs.SetChartStyle();

        if (DataCollection != null)
        {
            if (DataCollection.Count > 0)
            {
                a3d.Set3DChart(cs, DataCollection[0]);
            }
        }
    }

    public static DependencyProperty NumberInterpProperty =
        DependencyProperty.Register("NumberInterp", typeof(int),
        typeof(Chart3D), new FrameworkPropertyMetadata(2,
        FrameworkPropertyMetadataOptions.BindsTwoWayByDefault));

    public int NumberInterp
    {
        get { return (int)GetValue(NumberInterpProperty); }
        set { SetValue(NumberInterpProperty, value); }
    }

    public static DependencyProperty IsInterpProperty =
        DependencyProperty.Register("IsInterp", typeof(bool),
        typeof(Chart3D), new FrameworkPropertyMetadata(false,
        FrameworkPropertyMetadataOptions.BindsTwoWayByDefault));

    public bool IsInterp
    {
        get { return (bool)GetValue(IsInterpProperty); }
        set { SetValue(IsInterpProperty, value); }
    }

    public static DependencyProperty IsHiddenLineProperty =
        DependencyProperty.Register("IsHiddenLine", typeof(bool),
        typeof(Chart3D), new FrameworkPropertyMetadata(false,
        FrameworkPropertyMetadataOptions.BindsTwoWayByDefault));

    public bool IsHiddenLine
    {
        get { return (bool)GetValue(IsHiddenLineProperty); }
```

```
        set { SetValue(IsHiddenLineProperty, value); }
    }

    public static DependencyProperty IsColormapProperty =
        DependencyProperty.Register("IsColormap", typeof(bool),
        typeof(Chart3D), new FrameworkPropertyMetadata(true,
        FrameworkPropertyMetadataOptions.BindsTwoWayByDefault));

    public bool IsColormap
    {
        get { return (bool)GetValue(IsColormapProperty); }
        set { SetValue(IsColormapProperty, value); }
    }

    public static DependencyProperty IsColorbarProperty =
        DependencyProperty.Register("IsColorbar", typeof(bool),
        typeof(Chart3D), new FrameworkPropertyMetadata(true,
        FrameworkPropertyMetadataOptions.BindsTwoWayByDefault));

    public bool IsColorbar
    {
        get { return (bool)GetValue(IsColorbarProperty); }
        set { SetValue(IsColorbarProperty, value); }
    }

    public static DependencyProperty ColormapTypeProperty =
        DependencyProperty.Register("ColormapType", typeof(ColormapBrushEnum),
        typeof(Chart3D), new FrameworkPropertyMetadata(ColormapBrushEnum.Jet,
        FrameworkPropertyMetadataOptions.BindsTwoWayByDefault));

    public ColormapBrushEnum ColormapType
    {
        get { return (ColormapBrushEnum)GetValue(ColormapTypeProperty); }
        set { SetValue(ColormapTypeProperty, value); }
    }


    public static DependencyProperty Chart3DTypeProperty =
        DependencyProperty.Register("Chart3DType", typeof(SurfaceChartTypeEnum),
        typeof(Chart3D), new FrameworkPropertyMetadata(
        SurfaceChartTypeEnum.Surface,
        FrameworkPropertyMetadataOptions.BindsTwoWayByDefault));

    public SurfaceChartTypeEnum Chart3DType
    {
        get { return (SurfaceChartTypeEnum)GetValue(Chart3DTypeProperty); }
        set { SetValue(Chart3DTypeProperty, value); }
    }


    public static DependencyProperty ElevationProperty =
        DependencyProperty.Register("Elevation", typeof(double),
        typeof(Chart3D), new FrameworkPropertyMetadata(0.0,
        FrameworkPropertyMetadataOptions.BindsTwoWayByDefault));
```

```
public double Elevation
{
    get { return (double)GetValue(ElevationProperty); }
    set { SetValue(ElevationProperty, value); }
}

public static DependencyProperty AzimuthProperty =
    DependencyProperty.Register("Azimuth", typeof(double),
    typeof(Chart3D), new FrameworkPropertyMetadata(0.0,
    FrameworkPropertyMetadataOptions.BindsTwoWayByDefault));

public double Azimuth
{
    get { return (double)GetValue(AzimuthProperty); }
    set { SetValue(AzimuthProperty, value); }
}

public static DependencyProperty XminProperty =
    DependencyProperty.Register("Xmin", typeof(double),
    typeof(Chart3D), new FrameworkPropertyMetadata(0.0,
    FrameworkPropertyMetadataOptions.BindsTwoWayByDefault));

public double Xmin
{
    get { return (double)GetValue(XminProperty); }
    set { SetValue(XminProperty, value); }
}

public static DependencyProperty XmaxProperty =
    DependencyProperty.Register("Xmax", typeof(double),
    typeof(Chart3D), new FrameworkPropertyMetadata(10.0,
    FrameworkPropertyMetadataOptions.BindsTwoWayByDefault));

public double Xmax
{
    get { return (double)GetValue(XmaxProperty); }
    set { SetValue(XmaxProperty, value); }
}

public static DependencyProperty YminProperty =
    DependencyProperty.Register("Ymin", typeof(double),
    typeof(Chart3D), new FrameworkPropertyMetadata(0.0,
    FrameworkPropertyMetadataOptions.BindsTwoWayByDefault));

public double Ymin
{
    get { return (double)GetValue(YminProperty); }
    set { SetValue(YminProperty, value); }
}

public static DependencyProperty YmaxProperty =
    DependencyProperty.Register("Ymax", typeof(double),
    typeof(Chart3D), new FrameworkPropertyMetadata(10.0,
    FrameworkPropertyMetadataOptions.BindsTwoWayByDefault));
```

```
public double Ymax
{
    get { return (double)GetValue(YmaxProperty); }
    set { SetValue(YmaxProperty, value); }
}

public static DependencyProperty ZminProperty =
    DependencyProperty.Register("Zmin", typeof(double),
    typeof(Chart3D), new FrameworkPropertyMetadata(0.0,
    FrameworkPropertyMetadataOptions.BindsTwoWayByDefault));

public double Zmin
{
    get { return (double)GetValue(ZminProperty); }
    set { SetValue(ZminProperty, value); }
}

public static DependencyProperty ZmaxProperty =
    DependencyProperty.Register("Zmax", typeof(double),
    typeof(Chart3D), new FrameworkPropertyMetadata(10.0,
    FrameworkPropertyMetadataOptions.BindsTwoWayByDefault));

public double Zmax
{
    get { return (double)GetValue(ZmaxProperty); }
    set { SetValue(ZmaxProperty, value); }
}

public static DependencyProperty XTickProperty =
    DependencyProperty.Register("XTick", typeof(double),
    typeof(Chart3D), new FrameworkPropertyMetadata(2.0,
    FrameworkPropertyMetadataOptions.BindsTwoWayByDefault));

public double XTick
{
    get { return (double)GetValue(XTickProperty); }
    set { SetValue(XTickProperty, value); }
}

public static DependencyProperty YTickProperty =
    DependencyProperty.Register("YTick", typeof(double),
    typeof(Chart3D), new FrameworkPropertyMetadata(2.0,
    FrameworkPropertyMetadataOptions.BindsTwoWayByDefault));

public double YTick
{
    get { return (double)GetValue(YTickProperty); }
    set { SetValue(YTickProperty, value); }
}

public static DependencyProperty ZTickProperty =
    DependencyProperty.Register("ZTick", typeof(double),
    typeof(Chart3D), new FrameworkPropertyMetadata(2.0,
    FrameworkPropertyMetadataOptions.BindsTwoWayByDefault));
```

```
public double ZTick
{
    get { return (double)GetValue(ZTickProperty); }
    set { SetValue(ZTickProperty, value); }
}

public static DependencyProperty XLabelProperty =
    DependencyProperty.Register("XLabel", typeof(string),
    typeof(Chart3D), new FrameworkPropertyMetadata("X Axis",
    FrameworkPropertyMetadataOptions.BindsTwoWayByDefault));

public string XLabel
{
    get { return (string)GetValue(XLabelProperty); }
    set { SetValue(XLabelProperty, value); }
}

public static DependencyProperty YLabelProperty =
    DependencyProperty.Register("YLabel", typeof(string),
    typeof(Chart3D), new FrameworkPropertyMetadata("Y Axis",
    FrameworkPropertyMetadataOptions.BindsTwoWayByDefault));

public string YLabel
{
    get { return (string)GetValue(YLabelProperty); }
    set { SetValue(YLabelProperty, value); }
}

public static DependencyProperty ZLabelProperty =
    DependencyProperty.Register("ZLabel", typeof(string),
    typeof(Chart3D), new FrameworkPropertyMetadata("Z Axis",
    FrameworkPropertyMetadataOptions.BindsTwoWayByDefault));

public string ZLabel
{
    get { return (string)GetValue(ZLabelProperty); }
    set { SetValue(ZLabelProperty, value); }
}

public static DependencyProperty TitleProperty =
    DependencyProperty.Register("Title", typeof(string),
    typeof(Chart3D), new FrameworkPropertyMetadata("No Title",
    FrameworkPropertyMetadataOptions.BindsTwoWayByDefault));

public string Title
{
    get { return (string)GetValue(TitleProperty); }
    set { SetValue(TitleProperty, value); }
}

public static DependencyProperty GridlineColorProperty =
    DependencyProperty.Register("GridlineColor", typeof(Brush),
    typeof(Chart3D), new FrameworkPropertyMetadata(Brushes.Gray,
    FrameworkPropertyMetadataOptions.BindsTwoWayByDefault));
```

```
public Brush GridlineColor
{
    get { return (Brush)GetValue(GridlineColorProperty); }
    set { SetValue(GridlineColorProperty, value); }
}

public static DependencyProperty GridlinePatternProperty =


    DependencyProperty.Register("GridlinePattern",
    typeof(LineDashPatternEnum), typeof(Chart3D),
    new FrameworkPropertyMetadata(LineDashPatternEnum.Solid,
    FrameworkPropertyMetadataOptions.BindsTwoWayByDefault));

public static DependencyProperty GridLineThicknessProperty =
    DependencyProperty.Register("GridLineThickness", typeof(double),
    typeof(Chart3D), new FrameworkPropertyMetadata(1.0,
    FrameworkPropertyMetadataOptions.BindsTwoWayByDefault));

public double GridLineThickness
{
    get { return (double)GetValue(GridLineThicknessProperty); }
    set { SetValue(GridLineThicknessProperty, value); }
}

public LineDashPatternEnum GridlinePattern
{
    get { return (LineDashPatternEnum)GetValue(GridlinePatternProperty); }
    set { SetValue(GridlinePatternProperty, value); }
}


private static DependencyProperty DataCollectionProperty =
    DependencyProperty.Register("DataCollection",
    typeof(BindableCollection<DataSeries3D>), typeof(Chart3D),
    new FrameworkPropertyMetadata(null,
    FrameworkPropertyMetadataOptions.BindsTwoWayByDefault, OnDataChanged));

public BindableCollection<DataSeries3D> DataCollection
{
    get { return (BindableCollection<DataSeries3D>)
          GetValue(DataCollectionProperty); }
    set { SetValue(DataCollectionProperty, value); }
}

private static void OnDataChanged(object sender,
    DependencyPropertyChangedEventArgs e)
{
    var lc = sender as Chart3D;
    var dc = e.NewValue as BindableCollection<DataSeries3D>;
    if (dc != null)
        dc.CollectionChanged += lc.dc_CollectionChanged;
}
```

```
        private void dc_CollectionChanged(object sender,
            NotifyCollectionChangedEventArgs e)
        {
            if (DataCollection != null)
            {
                CheckCount = 0;
                if (DataCollection.Count > 0)
                    CheckCount = DataCollection.Count;
            }
        }

        public static DependencyProperty CheckCountProperty =
            DependencyProperty.Register("CheckCount", typeof(int),
            typeof(Chart3D), new FrameworkPropertyMetadata(0,
            FrameworkPropertyMetadataOptions.BindsTwoWayByDefault, OnStartChart));

        public int CheckCount
        {
            get { return (int)GetValue(CheckCountProperty); }
            set { SetValue(CheckCountProperty, value); }
        }

        private static void OnStartChart(DependencyObject sender,
            DependencyPropertyChangedEventArgs e)
        {
            (sender as Chart3D).SetChart();
        }
    }
}
```

Note how we define the dependency properties. We use the same logic to make the control automatically generate the 3D surface-like chart after creating the *DataCollection* containing the *DataSeries3D* object. The *DataCollectionProperty* includes a callback method called *OnDataChanged*. Inside this callback method, we add an event handler to the *CollectionChanged* property when the *DataCollection* changes. Within the *CollectionChanged* handler, we set another private dependency property called *CheckCount* to the *DataCollection.Count*. If *CheckCount* > 0, we know that the *DataCollection* contains a *DataSeries3D* object, and we then implement another callback method, *OnStartChart*, for the *CheckCount* property to create the 3D chart by calling the *SetChart* method.

Note that inside the *SetChart* method, we set the public properties of the *ChartStyle* and *Add3DChart* classes to the corresponding dependency properties of the chart control. This way, whenever the dependency properties in the *Chart3D* class change, the properties in the *ChartStyle* and *Add3DChart* classes will change correspondingly.

Here, we also add a *chart_Grid_SizeChanged* event handler to the 3D line chart control. This handler ensures that the chart gets updated whenever the chart control gets resized. Now, rebuild the control library by right-clicking the *ChartControl* project and selecting Build.

Using the 3D Surface-Like Chart Control

Here, I will show you how to use the 3D chart control to create a 3D surface-like chart. Open the *Chapter09* project in Visual Studio 2013. Add a new *UserControl* to the *Views* folder of the *Chapter09* project and name it *Chart3DView*. We have already added the *Chart3DControl* to the References when we made the 3D line chart example, so we do not need to add it to the project again. Here is the XAML file for the *Chart3DView*:

```xml
<UserControl x:Class="Chapter09.Views.Chart3DView"
             xmlns="http://schemas.microsoft.com/winfx/2006/xaml/presentation"
             xmlns:x="http://schemas.microsoft.com/winfx/2006/xaml"
             xmlns:mc="http://schemas.openxmlformats.org/markup-compatibility/2006"
             xmlns:d="http://schemas.microsoft.com/expression/blend/2008"
             xmlns:cal="http://www.caliburnproject.org"
             xmlns:local="clr-namespace:Chart3DControl;assembly=Chart3DControl"
             mc:Ignorable="d"
             d:DesignHeight="300" d:DesignWidth="500">
    <Grid Margin="10">
        <Grid.ColumnDefinitions>
            <ColumnDefinition Width="200"/>
            <ColumnDefinition Width="*"/>
        </Grid.ColumnDefinitions>
        <StackPanel>
            <TextBlock Text="Choose 3D Chart Type:" Margin="0 20 0 0"/>
            <ComboBox x:Name="Chart3DType" Width="150" Margin="0 5 0 0"
                    HorizontalAlignment="Left"/>
            <TextBlock Text="Choose Colormap Type:" Margin="0 20 0 0"/>
            <ComboBox x:Name="Colormap" Width="150" Margin="0 5 0 0"
                    HorizontalAlignment="Left"/>
            <CheckBox x:Name="IsColormap" Content="IsColormap?" Margin="0 20 0 0"/>
            <CheckBox x:Name="IsInterp" Content="IsInterp?" Margin="0 10 0 0"/>
            <Button x:Name="AddChart" Content="Start Chart" Width="100"
                    Margin="0 20 0 0" HorizontalAlignment="Left"/>
        </StackPanel>

        <local:Chart3D Grid.Column="1" DataCollection="{Binding DataCollection}"
                    Xmin="-3" Xmax="3" XTick="1" Ymin="-3" Ymax="3" YTick="1"
                    Zmin="-8" Zmax="8" ZTick="4" XLabel="X" YLabel="Y" ZLabel="Z"
                    GridlinePattern="Dot" GridlineColor="Green"
                    GridLineThickness="1" Elevation="30" Azimuth="-37"
                    IsColorbar="True" Chart3DType="{Binding SelectedChart3DType}"
                    ColormapType="{Binding SelectedColormap}" NumberInterp="3"
                    IsHiddenLine="False"
                    IsColormap="{Binding ElementName=IsColormap, Path=IsChecked}"
                    IsInterp="{Binding ElementName=IsInterp, Path=IsChecked}"/>
    </Grid>
</UserControl>
```

Note that here, not only can we specify properties directly in XAML for the *Chart3D* control, we can also data bind the control's *IsColormap* and *IsInterp* properties to the two checkboxes' *IsChecked* property, the same way we perform data binding for standard WPF elements.

Add a new class to the *ViewModels* and name it *Chart3DViewModel*. Here is the code for this class:

```
using System;
using System.Linq;
using Caliburn.Micro;
using System.ComponentModel.Composition;
using System.Windows;
using System.Windows.Media;
using System.Windows.Media.Media3D;
```

```csharp
using System.Windows.Shapes;
using System.Collections.Generic;
using Chart3DControl;
using Chapter09.Models;

namespace Chapter09.ViewModels
{
    [Export(typeof(IScreen)), PartCreationPolicy(CreationPolicy.NonShared)]
    public class Chart3DViewModel : Screen
    {
        private readonly IEventAggregator _events;
        [ImportingConstructor]
        public Chart3DViewModel(IEventAggregator events)
        {
            this._events = events;
            DisplayName = "02. 3D Chart";
            DataCollection = new BindableCollection<DataSeries3D>();
        }

        public BindableCollection<DataSeries3D> DataCollection { get; set; }

        private IEnumerable<SurfaceChartTypeEnum> chart3DType;
        public IEnumerable<SurfaceChartTypeEnum> Chart3DType
        {
            get { return Enum.GetValues(typeof(SurfaceChartTypeEnum)).
                Cast<SurfaceChartTypeEnum>(); }
            set
            {
                chart3DType = value;
                NotifyOfPropertyChange(() => Chart3DType);
            }
        }

        private SurfaceChartTypeEnum selectedChart3DType =
                SurfaceChartTypeEnum.Mesh;
        public SurfaceChartTypeEnum SelectedChart3DType
        {
            get { return selectedChart3DType; }
            set
            {
                selectedChart3DType = value;
                NotifyOfPropertyChange(() => SelectedChart3DType);
            }
        }

        private IEnumerable<ColormapBrushEnum> colormap;
        public IEnumerable<ColormapBrushEnum> Colormap
        {
            get { return Enum.GetValues(typeof(ColormapBrushEnum)).
                Cast<ColormapBrushEnum>(); }
            set
            {
                colormap = value;
                NotifyOfPropertyChange(() => Colormap);
            }
        }
```

```
        }

    private ColormapBrushEnum selectedColormap = ColormapBrushEnum.Jet;
    public ColormapBrushEnum SelectedColormap
    {
        get { return selectedColormap; }
        set
        {
            selectedColormap = value;
            NotifyOfPropertyChange(() => SelectedColormap);
        }
    }

    private bool isColormap = true;
    public bool IsColormap
    {
        get { return isColormap; }
        set
        {
            isColormap = value;
            NotifyOfPropertyChange(() => IsColormap);
        }
    }

    private bool isInterp = false;
    public bool IsInterp
    {
        get { return isInterp; }
        set
        {
            isInterp = value;
            NotifyOfPropertyChange(() => IsInterp);
        }
    }

    public void AddChart()
    {
        DataCollection.Clear();
        var ds = new DataSeries3D();
        ds.LineColor = Brushes.Black;
        ChartFunctions.Peak3D(ds);

        if(SelectedChart3DType == SurfaceChartTypeEnum.Surface)
        {
            if(IsInterp)
            {
                ds.LineColor = Brushes.Transparent;
            }
        }
        DataCollection.Add(ds);
    }
    }
}
```

Here, we first define several properties that we use to specify properties for the *Chart3D* control. The *AddChart* method is very simple, in which we create a *DataSeries3D* object and add it to the chart control's *DataCollection*. The beauty of using the chart control is that we can use the standard MVVM pattern in our applications, even though we create the chart control using the code-behind approach. Here, we just define the *DataCollection* property in the view model and bind it to the chart control.

We also add a static class, *ChartFunctions*, to the *Models* folder. This class includes the math functions, *Peak3D* and *Sinc3D*, which will be used to test the 3D chart control in this example. Here is the code for this class:

```
using Chart3DControl;
using System;
using System.Collections.Generic;
using System.Linq;
using System.Text;
using System.Threading.Tasks;
using System.Windows.Media.Media3D;

namespace Chapter09.Models
{
    public static class ChartFunctions
    {
        public static void Peak3D(DataSeries3D ds)
        {
            double xmin = -3;
            double xmax = 3;
            double ymin = -3;
            double ymax = 3;

            ds.XLimitMin = xmin;
            ds.YLimitMin = ymin;
            ds.XSpacing = 0.2;
            ds.YSpacing = 0.2;
            ds.XNumber = Convert.ToInt16((xmax - xmin) / ds.XSpacing) + 1;
            ds.YNumber = Convert.ToInt16((ymax - ymin) / ds.YSpacing) + 1;

            Point3D[,] pts = new Point3D[ds.XNumber, ds.YNumber];
            for (int i = 0; i < ds.XNumber; i++)
            {
                for (int j = 0; j < ds.YNumber; j++)
                {
                    double x = ds.XLimitMin + i * ds.XSpacing;
                    double y = ds.YLimitMin + j * ds.YSpacing;
                    double z = 3 * Math.Pow((1 - x), 2) *
                        Math.Exp(-x * x - (y + 1) * (y + 1)) - 10 *
                        (0.2 * x - Math.Pow(x, 3) - Math.Pow(y, 5)) *
                        Math.Exp(-x * x - y * y) - 1 / 3 *
                        Math.Exp(-(x + 1) * (x + 1) - y * y);
                    pts[i, j] = new Point3D(x, y, z);
                }
            }
            ds.PointArray = pts;
        }

        public static void Sinc3D(DataSeries3D ds)
```

```
    {
        double xmin = -8;
        double xmax = 8;
        double ymin = -8;
        double ymax = 8;

        ds.XLimitMin = xmin;
        ds.YLimitMin = ymin;
        ds.XSpacing = 0.5;
        ds.YSpacing = 0.5;
        ds.XNumber = Convert.ToInt16((xmax - xmin) / ds.XSpacing) + 1;
        ds.YNumber = Convert.ToInt16((ymax - ymin) / ds.YSpacing) + 1;

        Point3D[,] pts = new Point3D[ds.XNumber, ds.YNumber];
        for (int i = 0; i < ds.XNumber; i++)
        {
            for (int j = 0; j < ds.YNumber; j++)
            {
                double x = ds.XLimitMin + i * ds.XSpacing;
                double y = ds.YLimitMin + j * ds.YSpacing;
                double r = Math.Sqrt(x * x + y * y) + 0.000001;
                double z = Math.Sin(r) / r;
                pts[i, j] = new Point3D(x, y, z);
            }
        }
        ds.PointArray = pts;
    }
}
}
```

Running this example, unckecking the *IsColormap* checkbox, and clicking the *Add Chart* button generate the result shown in Figure 9-2.

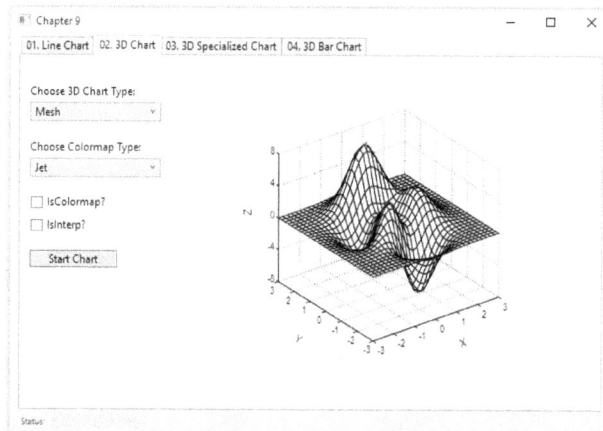

Figure 9-2. A black-line mesh chart created using a 3D chart control.

Checking the *IsColormap* checkbox produces the colormapped mesh chart shown in Figure 9-3.

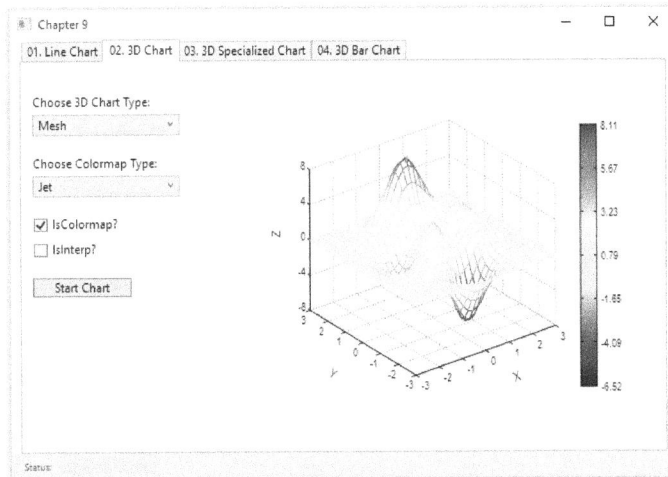

Figure 9-3. A colormapped mesh chart created using a 3D chart control.

Selecting *MeshZ* from the 3D chart type combobox produces the curtain chart shown in Figure 9-4.

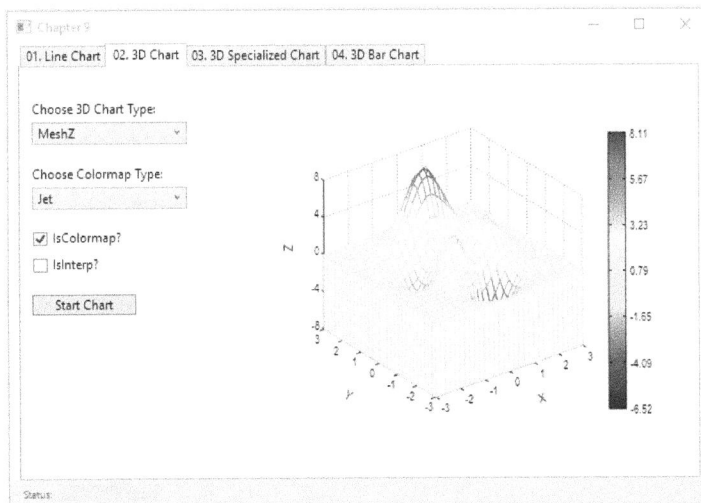

Figure 9-4. A curtain chart created using a 3D chart control.

Selecting *Waterfall* from the 3D chart type combobox generates the waterfall chart shown in Figure 9-5.

Selecting *Surface* from the 3D chart type combobox produces the surface chart shown in Figure 9-6.

Checking the *IsInterp* checkbox generates a surface chart with interpolated shading as shown in Figure 9-7.

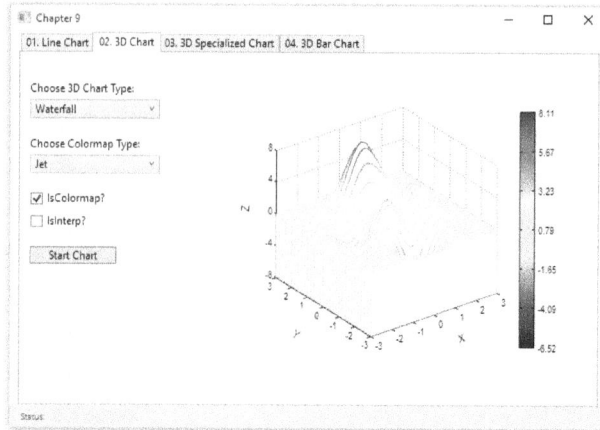

Figure 9-5. A waterfall chart created using a 3D chart control.

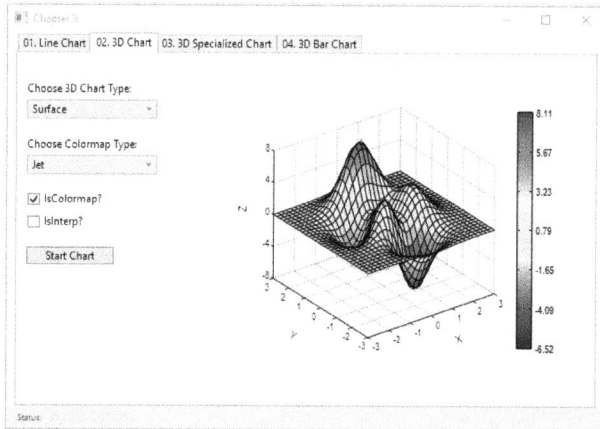

Figure 9-6. A surface chart created using a 3D chart control.

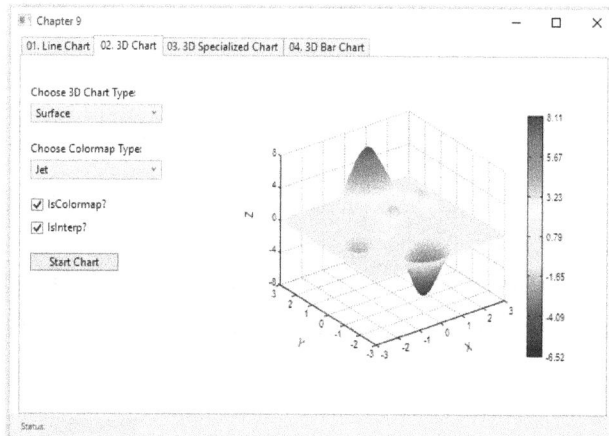

Figure 9-7. A surface chart with interpolated shading created using a 3D chart control.

From this example, you can see how easy it is to create various surface-like 3D charts using the 3D chart control. Furthermore, you can use this chart control to easily build MVVM-compatible applications with professional 3D charts.

3D Specialized Charts

In Chapter 8, we created six different types of 3D specialized charts, including *X-Y* color, contour, and 3D combination charts. In this section, I will show you how to convert these 3D specialized charts into a 3D chart control.

Go back to the *Chart3DControl* project. Add a new *UserControl* to the project and name it *Chart3DS*. Here is the XAML file for this view:

```xml
<UserControl x:Class="Chart3DControl.Chart3DS"
            xmlns="http://schemas.microsoft.com/winfx/2006/xaml/presentation"
            xmlns:x="http://schemas.microsoft.com/winfx/2006/xaml"
            xmlns:mc="http://schemas.openxmlformats.org/markup-compatibility/2006"
            xmlns:d="http://schemas.microsoft.com/expression/blend/2008"
            mc:Ignorable="d"
            d:DesignHeight="300" d:DesignWidth="300">
    <Grid x:Name="chartGrid" Margin="20" SizeChanged="chartGrid_SizeChanged">
        <Canvas x:Name="chartCanvas" Background="Transparent"
                Width="{Binding ElementName=chartGrid,Path=ActualWidth}"
                Height="{Binding ElementName=chartGrid,Path=ActualHeight}"
                ClipToBounds="True"/>
    </Grid>
</UserControl>
```

This markup is very simple. You may notice that we will be using the code-behind approach to implement this chart control because we do not use Caliburn.Micro's *Message.Attach* method for event handlers, such as the *SizeChanged* events.

Defining Dependency Properties

Next, we will design the public interface that the 3D specialized chart control exposes to the outside world. In other words, it is time to create the properties, methods, and events that the control consumer (the application that uses the control) will rely on to interact with your 3D chart control.

You may want to expose to the outside world most of the properties in the *ChartStyle2D* class, such as axis limits, title, and labels; at the same time, we will keep the classes from the original 3D specialized chart example project unchanged.

The code-behind file for this control is very similar to that used to create the 3D surface-like chart control. However, I will still provide a complete code listing for this code-behind file here for your reference:

```csharp
using System;
using System.ComponentModel;
using System.Windows;
using System.Windows.Controls;
using System.Windows.Media;
using Caliburn.Micro;
using System.Windows.Media.Media3D;
using System.Collections.Specialized;
```

```
namespace Chart3DControl
{
    /// <summary>
    /// Interaction logic for Chart3DS.xaml
    /// </summary>
    public partial class Chart3DS : UserControl
    {
        private ChartStyle2D cs;
        private AddS3DChart a3d;

        public Chart3DS()
        {
            InitializeComponent();
            this.cs = new ChartStyle2D();
            this.a3d = new AddS3DChart();
            cs.ChartCanvas = chartCanvas;
        }

        private void chartGrid_SizeChanged(object sender, SizeChangedEventArgs e)
        {
            ResizeChart();
        }

        private void SetChart()
        {
            cs.Elevation = this.Elevation;
            cs.Azimuth = this.Azimuth;
            cs.Xmin = this.Xmin;
            cs.Xmax = this.Xmax;
            cs.Ymin = this.Ymin;
            cs.Ymax = this.Ymax;
            cs.Zmin = this.Zmin;
            cs.Zmax = this.Zmax;
            cs.XTick = this.XTick;
            cs.YTick = this.YTick;
            cs.ZTick = this.ZTick;
            cs.XLabel = this.XLabel;
            cs.YLabel = this.YLabel;
            cs.ZLabel = this.ZLabel;
            cs.Title = this.Title;
            cs.GridlineColor = this.GridlineColor;
            cs.GridlinePattern = this.GridlinePattern;
            cs.GridlineThickness = this.GridLineThickness;
            cs.IsColorBar = this.IsColorbar;
            a3d.Colormap.ColormapBrushType = this.ColormapType;
            a3d.IsColormap = this.IsColormap;
            a3d.IsHiddenLine = this.IsHiddenLine;
            a3d.IsInterp = this.IsInterp;
            a3d.NumberInterp = this.NumberInterp;
            a3d.SChartType = this.Chart3DSType;
            a3d.NumberContours = this.NumberContours;
            a3d.IsLineColorMatch = this.IsLineColorMatch;

            ResizeChart();
```

```
    }

private void ResizeChart()
{
    chartCanvas.Children.Clear();
    cs.SetChartStyle();

    if (DataCollection != null)
    {
        if (DataCollection.Count > 0)
        {
            a3d.AddChart(cs, DataCollection[0]);
        }
    }
}

public static DependencyProperty NumberContoursProperty =
    DependencyProperty.Register("NumberContours", typeof(int),
    typeof(Chart3DS), new FrameworkPropertyMetadata(2,
    FrameworkPropertyMetadataOptions.BindsTwoWayByDefault));

public int NumberContours
{
    get { return (int)GetValue(NumberContoursProperty); }
    set { SetValue(NumberContoursProperty, value); }
}

public static DependencyProperty NumberInterpProperty =
    DependencyProperty.Register("NumberInterp", typeof(int),
    typeof(Chart3DS), new FrameworkPropertyMetadata(2,
    FrameworkPropertyMetadataOptions.BindsTwoWayByDefault));

public int NumberInterp
{
    get { return (int)GetValue(NumberInterpProperty); }
    set { SetValue(NumberInterpProperty, value); }
}

public static DependencyProperty IsLineColorMatchProperty =
    DependencyProperty.Register("IsLineColorMatch", typeof(bool),
    typeof(Chart3DS), new FrameworkPropertyMetadata(false,
    FrameworkPropertyMetadataOptions.BindsTwoWayByDefault));

public bool IsLineColorMatch
{
    get { return (bool)GetValue(IsLineColorMatchProperty); }
    set { SetValue(IsLineColorMatchProperty, value); }
}

public static DependencyProperty IsInterpProperty =
    DependencyProperty.Register("IsInterp", typeof(bool),
    typeof(Chart3DS), new FrameworkPropertyMetadata(false,
    FrameworkPropertyMetadataOptions.BindsTwoWayByDefault));

public bool IsInterp
```

```
    {
        get { return (bool)GetValue(IsInterpProperty); }
        set { SetValue(IsInterpProperty, value); }
    }

    public static DependencyProperty IsHiddenLineProperty =
        DependencyProperty.Register("IsHiddenLine", typeof(bool),
        typeof(Chart3DS), new FrameworkPropertyMetadata(false,
        FrameworkPropertyMetadataOptions.BindsTwoWayByDefault));

    public bool IsHiddenLine
    {
        get { return (bool)GetValue(IsHiddenLineProperty); }
        set { SetValue(IsHiddenLineProperty, value); }
    }

    public static DependencyProperty IsColormapProperty =
        DependencyProperty.Register("IsColormap", typeof(bool),
        typeof(Chart3DS), new FrameworkPropertyMetadata(true,
        FrameworkPropertyMetadataOptions.BindsTwoWayByDefault));

    public bool IsColormap
    {
        get { return (bool)GetValue(IsColormapProperty); }
        set { SetValue(IsColormapProperty, value); }
    }

    public static DependencyProperty IsColorbarProperty =
        DependencyProperty.Register("IsColorbar", typeof(bool),
        typeof(Chart3DS), new FrameworkPropertyMetadata(true,
        FrameworkPropertyMetadataOptions.BindsTwoWayByDefault));

    public bool IsColorbar
    {
        get { return (bool)GetValue(IsColorbarProperty); }
        set { SetValue(IsColorbarProperty, value); }
    }

    public static DependencyProperty ColormapTypeProperty =
        DependencyProperty.Register("ColormapType", typeof(ColormapBrushEnum),
        typeof(Chart3DS), new FrameworkPropertyMetadata(ColormapBrushEnum.Jet,
        FrameworkPropertyMetadataOptions.BindsTwoWayByDefault));

    public ColormapBrushEnum ColormapType
    {
        get { return (ColormapBrushEnum)GetValue(ColormapTypeProperty); }
        set { SetValue(ColormapTypeProperty, value); }
    }

    public static DependencyProperty Chart3DSTypeProperty =
        DependencyProperty.Register("Chart3DSType", typeof(SChartTypeEnum),
        typeof(Chart3DS), new FrameworkPropertyMetadata(SChartTypeEnum.XYColor,
        FrameworkPropertyMetadataOptions.BindsTwoWayByDefault));

    public SChartTypeEnum Chart3DSType
```

```csharp
{
    get { return (SChartTypeEnum)GetValue(Chart3DSTypeProperty); }
    set { SetValue(Chart3DSTypeProperty, value); }
}


public static DependencyProperty ElevationProperty =
    DependencyProperty.Register("Elevation", typeof(double),
    typeof(Chart3DS), new FrameworkPropertyMetadata(0.0,
    FrameworkPropertyMetadataOptions.BindsTwoWayByDefault));

public double Elevation
{
    get { return (double)GetValue(ElevationProperty); }
    set { SetValue(ElevationProperty, value); }
}

public static DependencyProperty AzimuthProperty =
    DependencyProperty.Register("Azimuth", typeof(double),
    typeof(Chart3DS), new FrameworkPropertyMetadata(0.0,
    FrameworkPropertyMetadataOptions.BindsTwoWayByDefault));

public double Azimuth
{
    get { return (double)GetValue(AzimuthProperty); }
    set { SetValue(AzimuthProperty, value); }
}

public static DependencyProperty XminProperty =
    DependencyProperty.Register("Xmin", typeof(double),
    typeof(Chart3DS), new FrameworkPropertyMetadata(0.0,
    FrameworkPropertyMetadataOptions.BindsTwoWayByDefault));

public double Xmin
{
    get { return (double)GetValue(XminProperty); }
    set { SetValue(XminProperty, value); }
}

public static DependencyProperty XmaxProperty =
    DependencyProperty.Register("Xmax", typeof(double),
    typeof(Chart3DS), new FrameworkPropertyMetadata(10.0,
    FrameworkPropertyMetadataOptions.BindsTwoWayByDefault));

public double Xmax
{
    get { return (double)GetValue(XmaxProperty); }
    set { SetValue(XmaxProperty, value); }
}

public static DependencyProperty YminProperty =
    DependencyProperty.Register("Ymin", typeof(double),
    typeof(Chart3DS), new FrameworkPropertyMetadata(0.0,
    FrameworkPropertyMetadataOptions.BindsTwoWayByDefault));
```

```csharp
public double Ymin
{
    get { return (double)GetValue(YminProperty); }
    set { SetValue(YminProperty, value); }
}

public static DependencyProperty YmaxProperty =
    DependencyProperty.Register("Ymax", typeof(double),
    typeof(Chart3DS), new FrameworkPropertyMetadata(10.0,
    FrameworkPropertyMetadataOptions.BindsTwoWayByDefault));

public double Ymax
{
    get { return (double)GetValue(YmaxProperty); }
    set { SetValue(YmaxProperty, value); }
}

public static DependencyProperty ZminProperty =
    DependencyProperty.Register("Zmin", typeof(double),
    typeof(Chart3DS), new FrameworkPropertyMetadata(0.0,
    FrameworkPropertyMetadataOptions.BindsTwoWayByDefault));

public double Zmin
{
    get { return (double)GetValue(ZminProperty); }
    set { SetValue(ZminProperty, value); }
}

public static DependencyProperty ZmaxProperty =
    DependencyProperty.Register("Zmax", typeof(double),
    typeof(Chart3DS), new FrameworkPropertyMetadata(10.0,
    FrameworkPropertyMetadataOptions.BindsTwoWayByDefault));

public double Zmax
{
    get { return (double)GetValue(ZmaxProperty); }
    set { SetValue(ZmaxProperty, value); }
}

public static DependencyProperty XTickProperty =
    DependencyProperty.Register("XTick", typeof(double),
    typeof(Chart3DS), new FrameworkPropertyMetadata(2.0,
    FrameworkPropertyMetadataOptions.BindsTwoWayByDefault));

public double XTick
{
    get { return (double)GetValue(XTickProperty); }
    set { SetValue(XTickProperty, value); }
}

public static DependencyProperty YTickProperty =
    DependencyProperty.Register("YTick", typeof(double),
    typeof(Chart3DS), new FrameworkPropertyMetadata(2.0,
    FrameworkPropertyMetadataOptions.BindsTwoWayByDefault));
```

```
public double YTick
{
    get { return (double)GetValue(YTickProperty); }
    set { SetValue(YTickProperty, value); }
}

public static DependencyProperty ZTickProperty =
    DependencyProperty.Register("ZTick", typeof(double),
    typeof(Chart3DS), new FrameworkPropertyMetadata(2.0,
    FrameworkPropertyMetadataOptions.BindsTwoWayByDefault));

public double ZTick
{
    get { return (double)GetValue(ZTickProperty); }
    set { SetValue(ZTickProperty, value); }
}

public static DependencyProperty XLabelProperty =
    DependencyProperty.Register("XLabel", typeof(string),
    typeof(Chart3DS), new FrameworkPropertyMetadata("X Axis",
    FrameworkPropertyMetadataOptions.BindsTwoWayByDefault));

public string XLabel
{
    get { return (string)GetValue(XLabelProperty); }
    set { SetValue(XLabelProperty, value); }
}

public static DependencyProperty YLabelProperty =
    DependencyProperty.Register("YLabel", typeof(string),
    typeof(Chart3DS), new FrameworkPropertyMetadata("Y Axis",
    FrameworkPropertyMetadataOptions.BindsTwoWayByDefault));

public string YLabel
{
    get { return (string)GetValue(YLabelProperty); }
    set { SetValue(YLabelProperty, value); }
}

public static DependencyProperty ZLabelProperty =
    DependencyProperty.Register("ZLabel", typeof(string),
    typeof(Chart3DS), new FrameworkPropertyMetadata("Z Axis",
    FrameworkPropertyMetadataOptions.BindsTwoWayByDefault));

public string ZLabel
{
    get { return (string)GetValue(ZLabelProperty); }
    set { SetValue(ZLabelProperty, value); }
}

public static DependencyProperty TitleProperty =
    DependencyProperty.Register("Title", typeof(string),
    typeof(Chart3DS), new FrameworkPropertyMetadata("No Title",
    FrameworkPropertyMetadataOptions.BindsTwoWayByDefault));
```

```
public string Title
{
    get { return (string)GetValue(TitleProperty); }
    set { SetValue(TitleProperty, value); }
}

public static DependencyProperty GridlineColorProperty =
    DependencyProperty.Register("GridlineColor", typeof(Brush),
    typeof(Chart3DS), new FrameworkPropertyMetadata(Brushes.Gray,
    FrameworkPropertyMetadataOptions.BindsTwoWayByDefault));

public Brush GridlineColor
{
    get { return (Brush)GetValue(GridlineColorProperty); }
    set { SetValue(GridlineColorProperty, value); }
}

public static DependencyProperty GridLineThicknessProperty =
    DependencyProperty.Register("GridLineThickness", typeof(double),
    typeof(Chart3DS), new FrameworkPropertyMetadata(1.0,
    FrameworkPropertyMetadataOptions.BindsTwoWayByDefault));

public double GridLineThickness
{
    get { return (double)GetValue(GridLineThicknessProperty); }
    set { SetValue(GridLineThicknessProperty, value); }
}

public static DependencyProperty GridlinePatternProperty =
    DependencyProperty.Register("GridlinePattern",
    typeof(LineDashPatternEnum), typeof(Chart3DS),
    new FrameworkPropertyMetadata(LineDashPatternEnum.Solid,
    FrameworkPropertyMetadataOptions.BindsTwoWayByDefault));

public LineDashPatternEnum GridlinePattern
{
    get { return (LineDashPatternEnum)GetValue(GridlinePatternProperty); }
    set { SetValue(GridlinePatternProperty, value); }
}


private static DependencyProperty DataCollectionProperty =
    DependencyProperty.Register("DataCollection",
    typeof(BindableCollection<DataSeries3D>), typeof(Chart3DS),
    new FrameworkPropertyMetadata(null,
    FrameworkPropertyMetadataOptions.BindsTwoWayByDefault, OnDataChanged));

public BindableCollection<DataSeries3D> DataCollection
{
    get { return (BindableCollection<DataSeries3D>)
        GetValue(DataCollectionProperty); }
    set { SetValue(DataCollectionProperty, value); }
}

private static void OnDataChanged(object sender,
```

```
            DependencyPropertyChangedEventArgs e)
    {
        var lc = sender as Chart3DS;
        var dc = e.NewValue as BindableCollection<DataSeries3D>;
        if (dc != null)
            dc.CollectionChanged += lc.dc_CollectionChanged;
    }

    private void dc_CollectionChanged(object sender,
        NotifyCollectionChangedEventArgs e)
    {
        if (DataCollection != null)
        {
            CheckCount = 0;
            if (DataCollection.Count > 0)
                CheckCount = DataCollection.Count;
        }
    }

    public static DependencyProperty CheckCountProperty =
        DependencyProperty.Register("CheckCount", typeof(int),
        typeof(Chart3DS), new FrameworkPropertyMetadata(0,
        FrameworkPropertyMetadataOptions.BindsTwoWayByDefault, OnStartChart));

    public int CheckCount
    {
        get { return (int)GetValue(CheckCountProperty); }
        set { SetValue(CheckCountProperty, value); }
    }

    private static void OnStartChart(DependencyObject sender,
        DependencyPropertyChangedEventArgs e)
    {
        (sender as Chart3DS).SetChart();
    }
    }
}
```

Note how we define the dependency properties. We use the same logic as that used in the line chart control to automatically generate the 3D specialized charts after creating the *DataCollection* that contains the *DataSeries3D* object.

Also note that inside the *SetChart* method, we set the public properties of the *ChartStyle2D* and *AddS3DChart* classes to the corresponding dependency properties of the chart control. This way, whenever the dependency properties in the *Chart3DS* class change, the properties in the *ChartStyle2D* and *AddS3DChart* classes will change correspondingly.

Using the 3D Specialized Chart Control

Here, I will show you how to use the 3D specialized chart control to create 3D specialized charts. Open the *Chapter09* project in Visual Studio 2013. Add a new *UserControl* to the *Views* folder of the *Chapter09* project and name it *Chart3DSView*. We have already added the *Chart3DControl* to the References when we made the 3D line chart example, so we do not need to add it again. Here is the XAML file for the *Chart3DSView*:

```
<UserControl x:Class="Chapter09.Views.Chart3DSView"
              xmlns="http://schemas.microsoft.com/winfx/2006/xaml/presentation"
              xmlns:x="http://schemas.microsoft.com/winfx/2006/xaml"
              xmlns:mc="http://schemas.openxmlformats.org/markup-compatibility/2006"
              xmlns:d="http://schemas.microsoft.com/expression/blend/2008"
              xmlns:local="clr-namespace:Chart3DControl;assembly=Chart3DControl"
              mc:Ignorable="d"
              d:DesignHeight="300" d:DesignWidth="500">
    <Grid Margin="10">
        <Grid.ColumnDefinitions>
            <ColumnDefinition Width="200"/>
            <ColumnDefinition Width="*"/>
        </Grid.ColumnDefinitions>
        <StackPanel>
            <TextBlock Text="3D Specialized Chart Type:" Margin="0 20 0 0"/>
            <ComboBox x:Name="Chart3DSType" Width="150" Margin="0 5 0 0"
                    HorizontalAlignment="Left"/>
            <TextBlock Text="Choose Colormap Type:" Margin="0 20 0 0"/>
            <ComboBox x:Name="Colormap" Width="150" Margin="0 5 0 0"
                    HorizontalAlignment="Left"/>
            <CheckBox x:Name="IsColormap" Content="IsColormap?" Margin="0 20 0 0"/>
            <CheckBox x:Name="IsInterp" Content="IsInterp?" Margin="0 10 0 0"/>
            <CheckBox x:Name="IsColorbar" Content="IsColorbar?" Margin="0 10 0 0"/>
            <CheckBox x:Name="IsLineColorMatch" Content="IsLineColorMatch?"
                    Margin="0 10 0 0"/>
            <GroupBox Header="X-Y Color" Margin="0 20 0 0">
                <StackPanel Margin="0 5 0 5">
                    <TextBlock Text="X-Y Color Chart Type:"/>
                    <ComboBox x:Name="XYColorType" Width="150" Margin="0 5 0 0"
                            HorizontalAlignment="Left"/>
                </StackPanel>
            </GroupBox>
            <GroupBox Header="Contour" Margin="0 20 0 0">
                <StackPanel Margin="0 5 0 5">
                    <TextBlock Text="Contour Chart Type:"/>
                    <ComboBox x:Name="ContourType" Width="150" Margin="0 5 0 0"
                            HorizontalAlignment="Left"/>
                </StackPanel>
            </GroupBox>
            <Button x:Name="AddChart" Content="Start Chart" Width="100"
                    Margin="0 20 0 0" HorizontalAlignment="Left"/>
        </StackPanel>

        <local:Chart3DS Grid.Column="1" DataCollection="{Binding DataCollection}"
                    Xmin="-3" Xmax="3" XTick="1" Ymin="-3" Ymax="3" YTick="1"
                    Zmin="-8" Zmax="8" ZTick="4" XLabel="X" YLabel="Y"
                    ZLabel="Z" GridlinePattern="Dot"  GridlineColor="Green"
                    GridLineThickness="1" Elevation="30" Azimuth="-37"
                    Chart3DSType="{Binding SelectedChart3DSType}"
                    ColormapType="{Binding SelectedColormap}"
                    NumberInterp="3" IsHiddenLine="False" NumberContours="15"
                    IsColormap="{Binding ElementName=IsColormap,
                    Path=IsChecked}"
                    IsInterp="{Binding ElementName=IsInterp, Path=IsChecked}"
                    IsColorbar="{Binding ElementName=IsColorbar,
```

```
                              Path=IsChecked}"
                              IsLineColorMatch="{Binding ElementName=IsLineColorMatch,
                              Path=IsChecked}"/>
    </Grid>
</UserControl>
```

Note here that not only can we specify properties directly in XAML for the *Chart3D* control, we can also data bind the control's properties to the checkboxes' *IsChecked* property, the same way we carry out data binding for standard WPF elements.

Add a new class to the *ViewModels* and name it *Chart3DSViewModel*. Here is the code for this class:

```
using System;
using System.Linq;
using Caliburn.Micro;
using System.ComponentModel.Composition;
using System.Windows;
using System.Windows.Media;
using System.Windows.Media.Media3D;
using System.Windows.Shapes;
using System.Collections.Generic;
using Chart3DControl;
using Chapter09.Models;

namespace Chapter09.ViewModels
{
    [Export(typeof(IScreen)), PartCreationPolicy(CreationPolicy.NonShared)]
    public class Chart3DSViewModel : Screen
    {
        private readonly IEventAggregator _events;
        [ImportingConstructor]
        public Chart3DSViewModel(IEventAggregator events)
        {
            this._events = events;
            DisplayName = "03. 3D Specialized Chart";
            DataCollection = new BindableCollection<DataSeries3D>();
        }

        private DataSeries3D ds;
        public BindableCollection<DataSeries3D> DataCollection { get; set; }


        private IEnumerable<SChartTypeEnum> chart3DSType;
        public IEnumerable<SChartTypeEnum> Chart3DSType
        {
            get { return Enum.GetValues(typeof(SChartTypeEnum)).
                Cast<SChartTypeEnum>(); }
            set
            {
                chart3DSType = value;
                NotifyOfPropertyChange(() => Chart3DSType);
            }
        }

        private SChartTypeEnum selectedChart3DSType = SChartTypeEnum.XYColor;
        public SChartTypeEnum SelectedChart3DSType
```

```
    {
        get { return selectedChart3DSType; }
        set
        {
            selectedChart3DSType = value;
            NotifyOfPropertyChange(() => SelectedChart3DSType);
        }
    }

    private IEnumerable<ColormapBrushEnum> colormap;
    public IEnumerable<ColormapBrushEnum> Colormap
    {
        get { return Enum.GetValues(typeof(ColormapBrushEnum)).
            Cast<ColormapBrushEnum>(); }
        set
        {
            colormap = value;
            NotifyOfPropertyChange(() => Colormap);
        }
    }

    private ColormapBrushEnum selectedColormap = ColormapBrushEnum.Jet;
    public ColormapBrushEnum SelectedColormap
    {
        get { return selectedColormap; }
        set
        {
            selectedColormap = value;
            NotifyOfPropertyChange(() => SelectedColormap);
        }
    }

    private bool isColormap = true;
    public bool IsColormap
    {
        get { return isColormap; }
        set
        {
            isColormap = value;
            NotifyOfPropertyChange(() => IsColormap);
        }
    }

    private bool isColorbar = true;
    public bool IsColorbar
    {
        get { return isColorbar; }
        set
        {
            isColorbar = value;
            NotifyOfPropertyChange(() => IsColorbar);
        }
    }

    private bool isInterp = false;
```

```csharp
public bool IsInterp
{
    get { return isInterp; }
    set
    {
        isInterp = value;
        NotifyOfPropertyChange(() => IsInterp);
    }
}

private bool isLineColorMatch = false;
public bool IsLineColorMatch
{
    get { return isLineColorMatch; }
    set
    {
        isLineColorMatch = value;
        NotifyOfPropertyChange(() => IsLineColorMatch);
    }
}

public BindableCollection<string> XYColorType
{
    get { return new BindableCollection<string>
            { "BlackLines", "NoLinesNoInterp", "NoLinesWithInterp" }; }
}

private string selectedXYColorType = "BlackLines";
public string SelectedXYColorType
{
    get { return selectedXYColorType; }
    set
    {
        selectedXYColorType = value;
        NotifyOfPropertyChange(() => SelectedXYColorType);
    }
}

public BindableCollection<string> ContourType
{
    get { return new BindableCollection<string>
        { "BlackLines", "LinesWithColormap" }; }
}

private string selectedContourType = "BlackLines";
public string SelectedContourType
{
    get { return selectedContourType; }
    set
    {
        selectedContourType = value;
        NotifyOfPropertyChange(() => SelectedContourType);
    }
}
```

```
public void AddChart()
{
    DataCollection.Clear();
    switch (SelectedChart3DSType)
    {
        case SChartTypeEnum.XYColor:
            AddXYColor();
            break;
        case SChartTypeEnum.Contour:
            AddContour();
            break;
        case SChartTypeEnum.FillContour:
            AddFilledContour();
            break;
        case SChartTypeEnum.MeshContour3D:
            AddMeshContour();
            break;
        case SChartTypeEnum.SurfaceContour3D:
            AddSurfaceContour();
            break;
        case SChartTypeEnum.SurfaceFillContour3D:
            AddSurfaceFillContour();
            break;
    }

    DataCollection.Add(ds);
}

private void AddXYColor()
{
    DisplayName = "03. X-Y Color";
    SelectedChart3DSType = SChartTypeEnum.XYColor;
    ds = new DataSeries3D();
    ChartFunctions.Peak3D(ds);

    if (SelectedXYColorType == "BlackLines")
    {
        ds.LineColor = Brushes.Black;
        IsInterp = false;
    }
    else if (SelectedXYColorType == "NoLinesNoInterp")
    {
        ds.LineColor = Brushes.Transparent;
        IsInterp = false;
    }
    else if (SelectedXYColorType == "NoLinesWithInterp")
    {
        ds.LineColor = Brushes.Transparent;
        IsInterp = true;
    }
}

private void AddContour()
{
    DisplayName = "03. Contour";
```

```
        SelectedChart3DSType = SChartTypeEnum.Contour;
        ds = new DataSeries3D();
        ChartFunctions.Peak3D(ds);

        if (SelectedContourType == "BlackLines")
        {
            ds.LineColor = Brushes.Black;
            IsColorbar = false;
        }
        else if (SelectedContourType == "LinesWithColormap")
        {
            IsColorbar = true;
            IsLineColorMatch = true;
            SelectedColormap = ColormapBrushEnum.Jet;
        }
    }

    private void AddFilledContour()
    {
        DisplayName = "03. Filled Contour";
        SelectedChart3DSType = SChartTypeEnum.FillContour;
        ds = new DataSeries3D();
        ChartFunctions.Peak3D(ds);

        IsColorbar = true;
        IsLineColorMatch = true;
        SelectedColormap = ColormapBrushEnum.Jet;
        IsInterp = true;
    }

    private void AddMeshContour()
    {
        DisplayName = "03. Mesh Contour";
        SelectedChart3DSType = SChartTypeEnum.MeshContour3D;
        ds = new DataSeries3D();
        ChartFunctions.Peak3D(ds);

        ds.LineColor = Brushes.Black;
        IsColorbar = true;
        IsLineColorMatch = true;
        SelectedColormap = ColormapBrushEnum.Jet;
    }

    private void AddSurfaceContour()
    {
        DisplayName = "03. Surface Contour";
        SelectedChart3DSType = SChartTypeEnum.SurfaceContour3D;
        ds = new DataSeries3D();
        ChartFunctions.Peak3D(ds);

        ds.LineColor = Brushes.Black;
        IsColorbar = true;
        IsLineColorMatch = true;
        SelectedColormap = ColormapBrushEnum.Jet;
    }
```

```
private void AddSurfaceFillContour()
{
    DisplayName = "03. Surface Contour";
    SelectedChart3DSType = SChartTypeEnum.SurfaceFillContour3D;
    ds = new DataSeries3D();
    ChartFunctions.Peak3D(ds);

    ds.LineColor = Brushes.Black;
    IsColorbar = true;
    isLineColorMatch = false;
    SelectedColormap = ColormapBrushEnum.Jet;
}
}
}
```

Here, we first define several properties that we use to specify properties for the *Chart3D* control. In the *AddChart* method, we create a *DataSeries3D* object and add it to the chart control's *DataCollection*. The beauty of using the chart control is that we can use the standard MVVM pattern in our applications, even though we create the chart control using the code-behind approach. Here, we simply define the *DataCollection* property in the view model and bind it to the chart control. The *AddChart* method then calls different methods for creating the specified 3D chart according to the selected chart type.

X-Y Color Charts

By running the example, selecting *XYColor* from the chart type combobox, and clicking the *Start Chart* button, you will obtain the *X-Y* color chart shown in Figure 9-8.

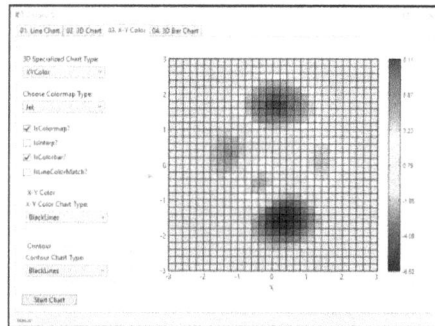

Figure 9-8. An X-Y color chart with mesh lines created using a 3D chart control.

You can remove the mesh lines from the *X-Y* color chart by selecting *NoLinesNoInterp* from the *X-Y* chart type combobox, as shown in Figure 9-10.

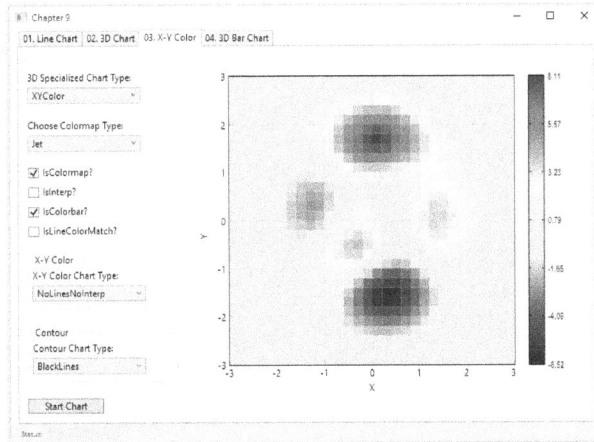

Figure 9-10. An X-Y color chart without mesh lines created using a 3D chart control.

You can see from Figure 9-10 that each polygon on the *X-Y* color chart is shaded in a single color. You can obtain an *X-Y* color chart with a much smoother colormap by applying interpolated shading if you select *NoLinesWithInterp* from the *X-Y* color chart type combobox, as shown in Figure 9-11.

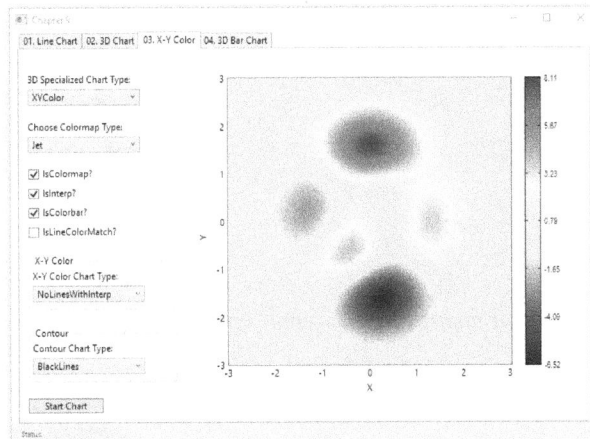

Figure 9-11. An X-Y color chart with interpolated shading created using a 3D chart control.

Contour Charts

You can use the same example as you did for *X-Y* color charts to create contour charts. Running the example, selecting *Contour* from the chart type combobox, unchecking all four checkboxes, and selecting *Blacklines* from the contour chart type combobox produces a contour chart with black lines, as shown in Figure 9-12.

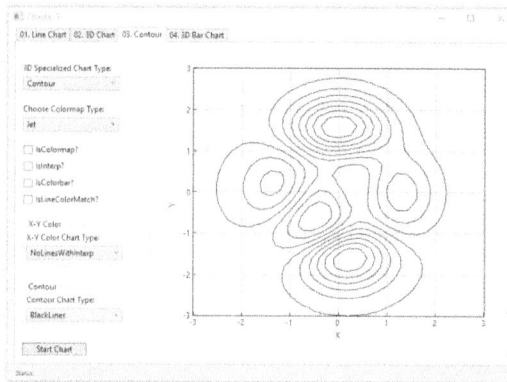

Figure 9-12. A contour chart created using a 3D chart control.

You can also easily create a contour chart with colormapped contour lines by selecting *LinesWithColormap* from the contour chart type combobox, as shown in Figure 9-13.

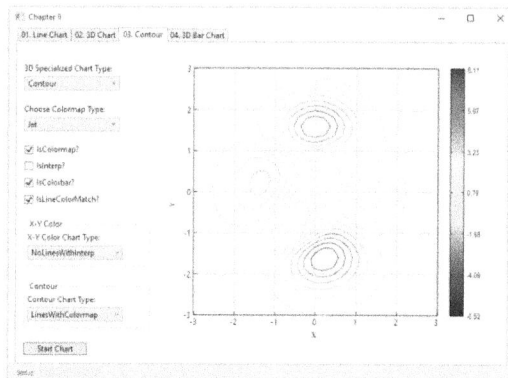

Figure 9-13. A colormapped contour chart created using a 3D chart control.

Selecting *FillContour* from the chart type produces the filled contour chart shown in Figure 9-14.

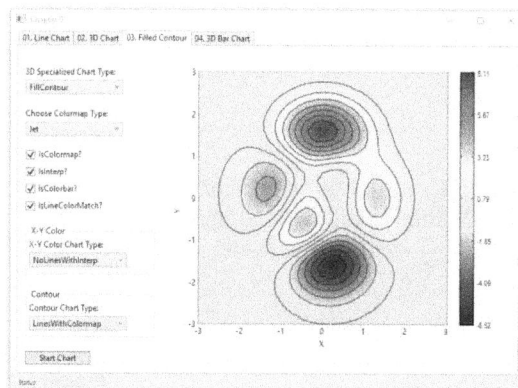

Figure 9-14. A filled contour chart created using a 3D chart control.

Combination Charts

Combination charts are a useful way to exploit the informative properties of various types of graphics charting methods. In this section, you will create some common combination charts, including mesh contour, surface contour, and surface-filled contour charts using the 3D chart control.

You can use the same example as you did for *X-Y* color charts to create 3D combination charts. Running the example, selecting *MeshContour3D* from the chart type combobox and checking all four checkboxes produces the mesh-contour combination chart shown in Figure 9-15.

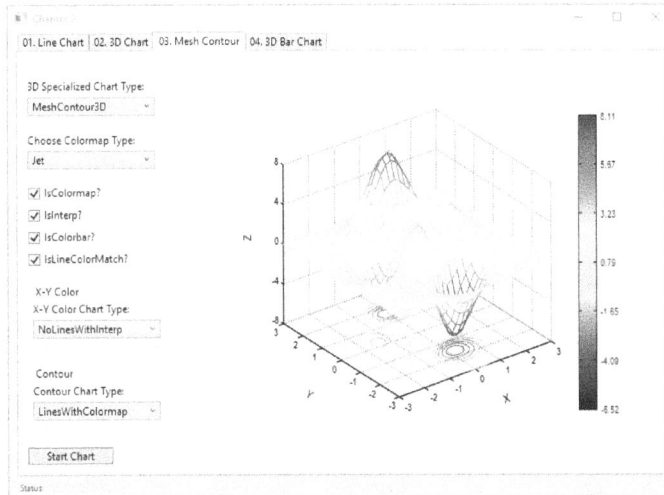

Figure 9-15. A mesh contour chart created using a 3D chart control.

Similarly, you can easily create a surface contour chart by choosing *SurfaceContour3D* from the chart type combobox and unckecking the *IsInterp* checkbox, as shown in Figure 9-16.

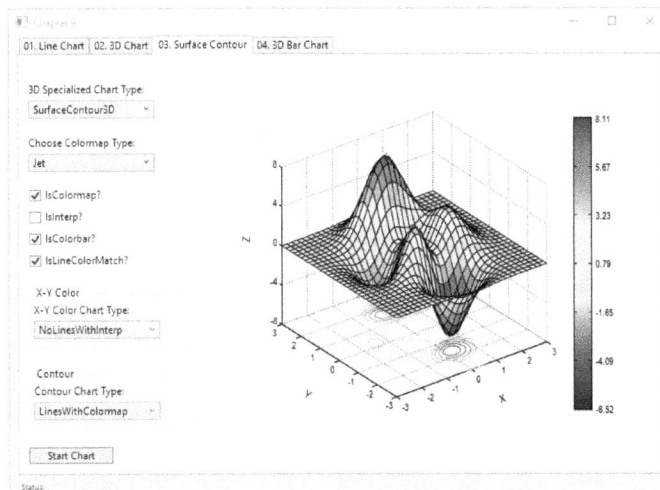

Figure 9-16. A surface contour chart created using a 3D chart control.

Finally, you can create a surface-filled contour chart by selecting *SurfaceFillContour3D* from the chart type combobox and unchecking both the *IsInterp* and *IsLineColorMatch* checkboxes, as shown in Figure 9-17.

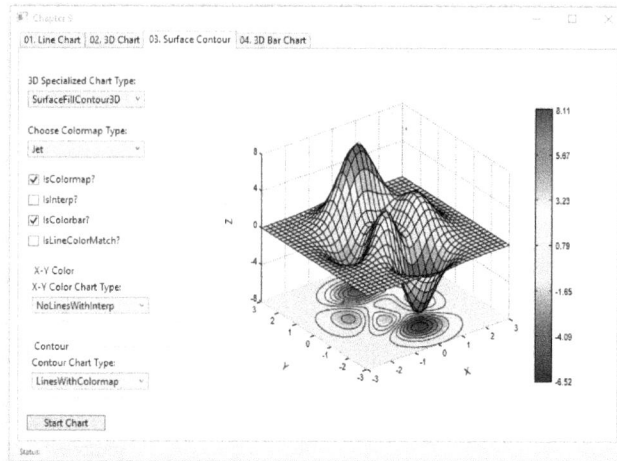

Figure 9-17. A surface-filled contour chart created using a 3D chart control.

3D Bar Charts

In Chapter 8, I presented detailed implementation for 3D bar charts. In this section, I will show you how to convert these 3D bar charts into a 3D bar chart control.

Go back to the *Chart3DControl* project. Add a new *UserControl* to the project and name it *Bar3D*. Here is the XAML file for this view:

```
<UserControl x:Class="Chart3DControl.Bar3D"
             xmlns="http://schemas.microsoft.com/winfx/2006/xaml/presentation"
             xmlns:x="http://schemas.microsoft.com/winfx/2006/xaml"
             xmlns:mc="http://schemas.openxmlformats.org/markup-compatibility/2006"
             xmlns:d="http://schemas.microsoft.com/expression/blend/2008"
             mc:Ignorable="d"
             d:DesignHeight="300" d:DesignWidth="300">
    <Grid x:Name="chartGrid" Margin="20" SizeChanged="chartGrid_SizeChanged">
        <Canvas x:Name="chartCanvas" Background="Transparent"
                Width="{Binding ElementName=chartGrid,Path=ActualWidth}"
                Height="{Binding ElementName=chartGrid,Path=ActualHeight}"
                ClipToBounds="True"/>
    </Grid>
</UserControl>
```

This XAML file is very simple. You may notice that we will be using the code-behind approach to implement this chart control because we do not use Caliburn.Micro's *Message.Attach* method for event handlers such as the *SizeChanged* events.

Defining Dependency Properties

Here, we want to expose to the outside world most of the properties in the *ChartStyle2D* class, such as axis limits, title, and labels; at the same time, we will keep the classes from the original 3D bar chart example project unchanged.

The code-behind file for this control is very similar to that used to create the 3D surface-like chart control. However, I will still provide a complete code listing for this code-behind file here for your reference:

```
using System;
using System.ComponentModel;
using System.Windows;
using System.Windows.Controls;
using System.Windows.Media;
using Caliburn.Micro;
using System.Windows.Media.Media3D;
using System.Collections.Specialized;

namespace Chart3DControl
{
    /// <summary>
    /// Interaction logic for Bar3D.xaml
    /// </summary>
    public partial class Bar3D : UserControl
    {
        private ChartStyle2D cs;
        private AddS3DChart a3d;

        public Bar3D()
        {
            InitializeComponent();
            this.cs = new ChartStyle2D();
            this.a3d = new AddS3DChart();
            cs.ChartCanvas = chartCanvas;
        }

        private void chartGrid_SizeChanged(object sender, SizeChangedEventArgs e)
        {
            ResizeChart();
        }

        private void SetChart()
        {
            cs.Elevation = this.Elevation;
            cs.Azimuth = this.Azimuth;
            cs.Xmin = this.Xmin;
            cs.Xmax = this.Xmax;
            cs.Ymin = this.Ymin;
            cs.Ymax = this.Ymax;
            cs.Zmin = this.Zmin;
            cs.Zmax = this.Zmax;
            cs.XTick = this.XTick;
            cs.YTick = this.YTick;
            cs.ZTick = this.ZTick;
            cs.XLabel = this.XLabel;
```

```
        cs.YLabel = this.YLabel;
        cs.ZLabel = this.ZLabel;
        cs.Title = this.Title;
        cs.GridlineColor = this.GridlineColor;
        cs.GridlinePattern = this.GridlinePattern;
        cs.GridlineThickness = this.GridLineThickness;
        cs.IsColorBar = this.IsColorbar;
        a3d.Colormap.ColormapBrushType = this.ColormapType;
        a3d.IsColormap = this.IsColormap;
        a3d.IsBarSingleColor = this.IsBarSingleColor;

        ResizeChart();
    }

    private void ResizeChart()
    {
        chartCanvas.Children.Clear();
        cs.SetChartStyle();

        if (DataCollection != null)
        {
            if (DataCollection.Count > 0)
            {
                a3d.AddBar3D(cs, DataCollection[0]);
            }
        }
    }

    public static DependencyProperty IsBarSingleColorProperty =
        DependencyProperty.Register("IsBarSingleColor", typeof(bool),
        typeof(Bar3D), new FrameworkPropertyMetadata(true,
        FrameworkPropertyMetadataOptions.BindsTwoWayByDefault));

    public bool IsBarSingleColor
    {
        get { return (bool)GetValue(IsBarSingleColorProperty); }
        set { SetValue(IsBarSingleColorProperty, value); }
    }

    public static DependencyProperty IsColormapProperty =
        DependencyProperty.Register("IsColormap", typeof(bool),
        typeof(Bar3D), new FrameworkPropertyMetadata(true,
        FrameworkPropertyMetadataOptions.BindsTwoWayByDefault));

    public bool IsColormap
    {
        get { return (bool)GetValue(IsColormapProperty); }
        set { SetValue(IsColormapProperty, value); }
    }

    public static DependencyProperty IsColorbarProperty =
        DependencyProperty.Register("IsColorbar", typeof(bool),
        typeof(Bar3D), new FrameworkPropertyMetadata(true,
        FrameworkPropertyMetadataOptions.BindsTwoWayByDefault));
```

```csharp
public bool IsColorbar
{
    get { return (bool)GetValue(IsColorbarProperty); }
    set { SetValue(IsColorbarProperty, value); }
}

public static DependencyProperty ColormapTypeProperty =
    DependencyProperty.Register("ColormapType", typeof(ColormapBrushEnum),
    typeof(Bar3D), new FrameworkPropertyMetadata(ColormapBrushEnum.Jet,
    FrameworkPropertyMetadataOptions.BindsTwoWayByDefault));

public ColormapBrushEnum ColormapType
{
    get { return (ColormapBrushEnum)GetValue(ColormapTypeProperty); }
    set { SetValue(ColormapTypeProperty, value); }
}


public static DependencyProperty ElevationProperty =
    DependencyProperty.Register("Elevation", typeof(double),
    typeof(Bar3D), new FrameworkPropertyMetadata(0.0,
    FrameworkPropertyMetadataOptions.BindsTwoWayByDefault));

public double Elevation
{
    get { return (double)GetValue(ElevationProperty); }
    set { SetValue(ElevationProperty, value); }
}

public static DependencyProperty AzimuthProperty =
    DependencyProperty.Register("Azimuth", typeof(double),
    typeof(Bar3D), new FrameworkPropertyMetadata(0.0,
    FrameworkPropertyMetadataOptions.BindsTwoWayByDefault));

public double Azimuth
{
    get { return (double)GetValue(AzimuthProperty); }
    set { SetValue(AzimuthProperty, value); }
}

public static DependencyProperty XminProperty =
    DependencyProperty.Register("Xmin", typeof(double),
    typeof(Bar3D), new FrameworkPropertyMetadata(0.0,
    FrameworkPropertyMetadataOptions.BindsTwoWayByDefault));

public double Xmin
{
    get { return (double)GetValue(XminProperty); }
    set { SetValue(XminProperty, value); }
}

public static DependencyProperty XmaxProperty =
    DependencyProperty.Register("Xmax", typeof(double),
    typeof(Bar3D), new FrameworkPropertyMetadata(10.0,
    FrameworkPropertyMetadataOptions.BindsTwoWayByDefault));
```

```csharp
public double Xmax
{
    get { return (double)GetValue(XmaxProperty); }
    set { SetValue(XmaxProperty, value); }
}

public static DependencyProperty YminProperty =
    DependencyProperty.Register("Ymin", typeof(double),
    typeof(Bar3D), new FrameworkPropertyMetadata(0.0,
    FrameworkPropertyMetadataOptions.BindsTwoWayByDefault));

public double Ymin
{
    get { return (double)GetValue(YminProperty); }
    set { SetValue(YminProperty, value); }
}

public static DependencyProperty YmaxProperty =
    DependencyProperty.Register("Ymax", typeof(double),
    typeof(Bar3D), new FrameworkPropertyMetadata(10.0,
    FrameworkPropertyMetadataOptions.BindsTwoWayByDefault));

public double Ymax
{
    get { return (double)GetValue(YmaxProperty); }
    set { SetValue(YmaxProperty, value); }
}

public static DependencyProperty ZminProperty =
    DependencyProperty.Register("Zmin", typeof(double),
    typeof(Bar3D), new FrameworkPropertyMetadata(0.0,
    FrameworkPropertyMetadataOptions.BindsTwoWayByDefault));

public double Zmin
{
    get { return (double)GetValue(ZminProperty); }
    set { SetValue(ZminProperty, value); }
}

public static DependencyProperty ZmaxProperty =
    DependencyProperty.Register("Zmax", typeof(double),
    typeof(Bar3D), new FrameworkPropertyMetadata(10.0,
    FrameworkPropertyMetadataOptions.BindsTwoWayByDefault));

public double Zmax
{
    get { return (double)GetValue(ZmaxProperty); }
    set { SetValue(ZmaxProperty, value); }
}

public static DependencyProperty XTickProperty =
    DependencyProperty.Register("XTick", typeof(double),
    typeof(Bar3D), new FrameworkPropertyMetadata(2.0,
    FrameworkPropertyMetadataOptions.BindsTwoWayByDefault));
```

```
public double XTick
{
    get { return (double)GetValue(XTickProperty); }
    set { SetValue(XTickProperty, value); }
}

public static DependencyProperty YTickProperty =
    DependencyProperty.Register("YTick", typeof(double),
    typeof(Bar3D), new FrameworkPropertyMetadata(2.0,
    FrameworkPropertyMetadataOptions.BindsTwoWayByDefault));

public double YTick
{
    get { return (double)GetValue(YTickProperty); }
    set { SetValue(YTickProperty, value); }
}

public static DependencyProperty ZTickProperty =
    DependencyProperty.Register("ZTick", typeof(double),
    typeof(Bar3D), new FrameworkPropertyMetadata(2.0,
    FrameworkPropertyMetadataOptions.BindsTwoWayByDefault));

public double ZTick
{
    get { return (double)GetValue(ZTickProperty); }
    set { SetValue(ZTickProperty, value); }
}

public static DependencyProperty XLabelProperty =
    DependencyProperty.Register("XLabel", typeof(string),
    typeof(Bar3D), new FrameworkPropertyMetadata("X Axis",
    FrameworkPropertyMetadataOptions.BindsTwoWayByDefault));

public string XLabel
{
    get { return (string)GetValue(XLabelProperty); }
    set { SetValue(XLabelProperty, value); }
}

public static DependencyProperty YLabelProperty =
    DependencyProperty.Register("YLabel", typeof(string),
    typeof(Bar3D), new FrameworkPropertyMetadata("Y Axis",
    FrameworkPropertyMetadataOptions.BindsTwoWayByDefault));

public string YLabel
{
    get { return (string)GetValue(YLabelProperty); }
    set { SetValue(YLabelProperty, value); }
}

public static DependencyProperty ZLabelProperty =
    DependencyProperty.Register("ZLabel", typeof(string),
    typeof(Bar3D), new FrameworkPropertyMetadata("Z Axis",
    FrameworkPropertyMetadataOptions.BindsTwoWayByDefault));
```

```
public string ZLabel
{
    get { return (string)GetValue(ZLabelProperty); }
    set { SetValue(ZLabelProperty, value); }
}

public static DependencyProperty TitleProperty =
    DependencyProperty.Register("Title", typeof(string),
    typeof(Bar3D), new FrameworkPropertyMetadata("No Title",
    FrameworkPropertyMetadataOptions.BindsTwoWayByDefault));

public string Title
{
    get { return (string)GetValue(TitleProperty); }
    set { SetValue(TitleProperty, value); }
}

public static DependencyProperty GridlineColorProperty =
    DependencyProperty.Register("GridlineColor", typeof(Brush),
    typeof(Bar3D), new FrameworkPropertyMetadata(Brushes.Gray,
    FrameworkPropertyMetadataOptions.BindsTwoWayByDefault));

public Brush GridlineColor
{
    get { return (Brush)GetValue(GridlineColorProperty); }
    set { SetValue(GridlineColorProperty, value); }
}

public static DependencyProperty GridLineThicknessProperty =
    DependencyProperty.Register("GridLineThickness", typeof(double),
    typeof(Bar3D), new FrameworkPropertyMetadata(1.0,
    FrameworkPropertyMetadataOptions.BindsTwoWayByDefault));

public double GridLineThickness
{
    get { return (double)GetValue(GridLineThicknessProperty); }
    set { SetValue(GridLineThicknessProperty, value); }
}

public static DependencyProperty GridlinePatternProperty =
    DependencyProperty.Register("GridlinePattern",
    typeof(LineDashPatternEnum), typeof(Bar3D),
    new FrameworkPropertyMetadata(LineDashPatternEnum.Solid,
    FrameworkPropertyMetadataOptions.BindsTwoWayByDefault));

public LineDashPatternEnum GridlinePattern
{
    get { return (LineDashPatternEnum)GetValue(GridlinePatternProperty); }
    set { SetValue(GridlinePatternProperty, value); }
}


private static DependencyProperty DataCollectionProperty =
    DependencyProperty.Register("DataCollection",
```

```
            typeof(BindableCollection<Bar3DSeries>), typeof(Bar3D),
            new FrameworkPropertyMetadata(null,
            FrameworkPropertyMetadataOptions.BindsTwoWayByDefault, OnDataChanged));

        public BindableCollection<Bar3DSeries> DataCollection
        {
            get { return (BindableCollection<Bar3DSeries>)
                GetValue(DataCollectionProperty); }
            set { SetValue(DataCollectionProperty, value); }
        }

        private static void OnDataChanged(object sender,
            DependencyPropertyChangedEventArgs e)
        {
            var lc = sender as Bar3D;
            var dc = e.NewValue as BindableCollection<Bar3DSeries>;
            if (dc != null)
                dc.CollectionChanged += lc.dc_CollectionChanged;
        }

        private void dc_CollectionChanged(object sender,
            NotifyCollectionChangedEventArgs e)
        {
            if (DataCollection != null)
            {
                CheckCount = 0;
                if (DataCollection.Count > 0)
                    CheckCount = DataCollection.Count;
            }
        }

        public static DependencyProperty CheckCountProperty =
            DependencyProperty.Register("CheckCount", typeof(int),
            typeof(Bar3D), new FrameworkPropertyMetadata(0,
            FrameworkPropertyMetadataOptions.BindsTwoWayByDefault, OnStartChart));

        public int CheckCount
        {
            get { return (int)GetValue(CheckCountProperty); }
            set { SetValue(CheckCountProperty, value); }
        }

        private static void OnStartChart(DependencyObject sender,
            DependencyPropertyChangedEventArgs e)
        {
            (sender as Bar3D).SetChart();
        }
    }
}
```

Note how we define the dependency properties. We use the same logic as we did for the line chart control to automatically generate the 3D bar chart after creating the *DataCollection* containing the *Bar3DSeries* object.

Also note that inside the *SetChart* method, we set the public properties of the *ChartStyle2D* and *AddS3DChart* classes to the corresponding dependency properties of the chart control. This way, whenever the dependency properties in the *Bar3D* class change, the properties in the *ChartStyle2D* and *AddS3DChart* class will change correspondingly.

Using 3D Bar Charts

Here, I will show you how to use the 3D bar chart control to create 3D bar charts. Open the *Chapter09* project in Visual Studio 2013. Add a new *UserControl* to the *Views* folder of the *Chapter09* project and name it *Bar3DView*. We have already added the *Chart3DControl* to the References when we made the the 3D line chart example, so we do not need to add it again. Here is the XAML file for the *Bar3DView*:

```
<UserControl x:Class="Chapter09.Views.Bar3DView"
            xmlns="http://schemas.microsoft.com/winfx/2006/xaml/presentation"
            xmlns:x="http://schemas.microsoft.com/winfx/2006/xaml"
            xmlns:mc="http://schemas.openxmlformats.org/markup-compatibility/2006"
            xmlns:d="http://schemas.microsoft.com/expression/blend/2008"
            xmlns:local="clr-namespace:Chart3DControl;assembly=Chart3DControl"
            mc:Ignorable="d"
            d:DesignHeight="300" d:DesignWidth="500">
    <Grid Margin="10">
        <Grid.ColumnDefinitions>
            <ColumnDefinition Width="200"/>
            <ColumnDefinition Width="*"/>
        </Grid.ColumnDefinitions>
        <StackPanel>
            <TextBlock Text="3D Bar Chart Type:" Margin="0 20 0 0"/>
            <ComboBox x:Name="Bar3DType" Width="150" Margin="0 5 0 0"
                    HorizontalAlignment="Left"/>
            <TextBlock Text="Choose Colormap Type:" Margin="0 20 0 0"/>
            <ComboBox x:Name="Colormap" Width="150" Margin="0 5 0 0"
                    HorizontalAlignment="Left"/>
            <CheckBox x:Name="IsColormap" Content="IsColormap?" Margin="0 20 0 0"/>
            <CheckBox x:Name="IsColorbar" Content="IsColorbar?" Margin="0 10 0 0"/>
            <Button x:Name="AddChart" Content="Start Chart" Width="100"
                    Margin="0 20 0 0" HorizontalAlignment="Left"/>
        </StackPanel>

        <local:Bar3D Grid.Column="1" DataCollection="{Binding DataCollection}"
                    Xmin="-3" Xmax="3" XTick="1" Ymin="-3" Ymax="3" YTick="1"
                    Zmin="-8" Zmax="8" ZTick="4" XLabel="X" YLabel="Y" ZLabel="Z"
                    GridlinePattern="Dot"  GridlineColor="Green"
                    GridLineThickness="1" Elevation="30" Azimuth="-37"
                    ColormapType="{Binding SelectedColormap}"
                    IsColormap="{Binding ElementName=IsColormap, Path=IsChecked}"
                    IsColorbar="{Binding ElementName=IsColorbar, Path=IsChecked}"
                    IsBarSingleColor="True"/>
    </Grid>
</UserControl>
```

Note here that not only can we specify properties directly in XAML for the *Chart3D* control, we can also we can data bind the control's properties to the checkboxes' *IsChecked* property, the same way we carry out data binding for standard WPF elements.

Add a new class to the *ViewModels* and name it *Bar3DViewModel*. Here is the code for this class:

```csharp
using System;
using System.Linq;
using Caliburn.Micro;
using System.ComponentModel.Composition;
using System.Windows;
using System.Windows.Media;
using System.Windows.Media.Media3D;
using System.Windows.Shapes;
using System.Collections.Generic;
using Chart3DControl;
using Chapter09.Models;
using System.Threading.Tasks;

namespace Chapter09.ViewModels
{
    [Export(typeof(IScreen)), PartCreationPolicy(CreationPolicy.NonShared)]
    public class Bar3DViewModel : Screen
    {
         private readonly IEventAggregator _events;
        [ImportingConstructor]
        public Bar3DViewModel(IEventAggregator events)
        {
            this._events = events;
            DisplayName = "04. 3D Bar Chart";
            DataCollection = new BindableCollection<Bar3DSeries>();
        }

        public BindableCollection<Bar3DSeries> DataCollection { get; set; }

        private IEnumerable<ColormapBrushEnum> colormap;
        public IEnumerable<ColormapBrushEnum> Colormap
        {
            get { return Enum.GetValues(typeof(ColormapBrushEnum)).
                Cast<ColormapBrushEnum>(); }
            set
            {
                colormap = value;
                NotifyOfPropertyChange(() => Colormap);
            }
        }

        private ColormapBrushEnum selectedColormap = ColormapBrushEnum.Jet;
        public ColormapBrushEnum SelectedColormap
        {
            get { return selectedColormap; }
            set
            {
                selectedColormap = value;
                NotifyOfPropertyChange(() => SelectedColormap);
            }
        }

        public BindableCollection<string> Bar3DType
        {
```

```csharp
            get { return new BindableCollection<string>
                { "MinZPlane", "ZeroZPlane" }; }
    }

    private string selectedBar3DType = "MinZPlane";
    public string SelectedBar3DType
    {
        get { return selectedBar3DType; }
        set
        {
            selectedBar3DType = value;
            NotifyOfPropertyChange(() => SelectedBar3DType);
        }
    }

    private bool isColormap = true;
    public bool IsColormap
    {
        get { return isColormap; }
        set
        {
            isColormap = value;
            NotifyOfPropertyChange(() => IsColormap);
        }
    }

    private bool isColorbar = true;
    public bool IsColorbar
    {
        get { return isColorbar; }
        set
        {
            isColorbar = value;
            NotifyOfPropertyChange(() => IsColorbar);
        }
    }

    public void AddChart()
    {
        DataCollection.Clear();
        var bs = new Bar3DSeries();
        bs.LineColor = Brushes.Black;
        bs.XLength = 0.5;
        bs.YLength = 0.5;
        ChartFunctions.Peak3D(bs);
        IsColormap = true;

        if (SelectedBar3DType == "MinZPlane")
            bs.ZOrigin = -8;
        else if (SelectedBar3DType == "ZeroZPlane")
            bs.ZOrigin = 0;

        DataCollection.Add(bs);
    }
}
```

}

Here, we first define several properties that we use to specify properties for the *Chart3D* control. In the *AddChart* method, we create a *Bar3DSeries* object and add it to the chart control's *DataCollection*. The beauty of using the chart control is that we can use the standard MVVM pattern in our applications, even though we create the chart control using the code-behind approach. We simply define the *DataCollection* property in the view model and bind it to the chart control. The *AddChart* method creates two bar charts, one with *ZOrigin = Zmin* and the other with *ZOrigin = 0*.

Running this example and selecting *MinZPlane* from the bar chart type combobox produces a 3D bar chart as shown in Figure 9-18.

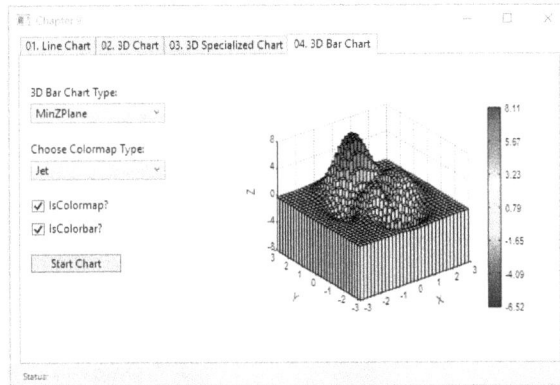

Figure 9-18. A 3D bar chart created using a 3D chart control.

Selecting *ZeroZPlane* from the bar chart type combobox and clicking the *Start Chart* button generate the output shown in Figure 9-19.

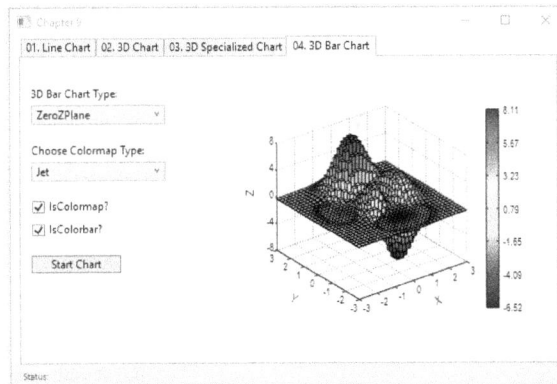

Figure 9-19. A 3D bar chart with ZOrigin = 0 created using a 3D chart control.

Index

www.ingramcontent.com/pod-product-compliance
Lightning Source LLC
Chambersburg PA
CBHW060956210326

41598CB00031B/4846